영단기 토익
다이렉트 700+

LC+RC 한 달 완성

영단기

영단기 토익 다이렉트 700+ LC+RC 한 달 완성

저자	유수연
기획 총괄	김도훈
기획 · 편집	정유상
마케팅 · 영업	양광열 김정현 양윤화 김보경 김보연
표지 디자인	황지예
내지 디자인	황지예
펴낸날	초판 1쇄 2019년 1월 2일
	초판 2쇄 2019년 5월 10일
펴낸이	김정택
펴낸곳	(주)에스티유니타스
등록번호	제2015-000186호
홈페이지	eng.conects.com
고객센터	카카오톡 플러스 친구 [영단기] / 영단기 1:1 게시판
주소	서울시 강남구 영동대로 417 오토웨이타워 3층
ISBN	979-11-6371-099-8 13740

잘못 만들어진 책은 구입처에서 바꿔 드립니다.
가격은 뒤표지에 있습니다.

이 책에 실린 모든 글과 사진, 일러스트를 포함한 디자인 및 편집 형태, 배포에 대한 권리는
(주)에스티유니타스에 있으므로 무단으로 전재하거나 복제, 배포할 수 없습니다. 파본은 교환해 드립니다.

토익 700+을 위한 첫발을 떼는 이들에게

취업과 이직을 준비하는 우리의 발목을 잡고 있는 어학 능력 시험, 그중에 가장 대표적인 것이 바로 토익입니다. 목표에 따라 원하는 점수는 다를 테지만 자신에게 주어진 시간이 한정되어 있다는 것은 모두가 느끼는 어려움일 것입니다.

하지만 분명한 건 토익은 여러분의 발목을 잡을 만큼 여러분의 인생에 있어서 중요하지 않다는 것입니다. 그저 단기간에 거쳐야 할 하나의 과정일 뿐입니다. 이 과정을 어떻게 거쳐갈 것인지가 더 중요합니다.

작은 일에서 한번이라도 성과를 내 본 사람이 다른 일에서도 성과를 낼 수 있습니다.
<영단기 토익 다이렉트 700+ LC+RC 한 달 완성>은 토익 강사로 18년간의 노하우를 고스란히 담아 여러분들이 효율적으로 700점 이상의 성과를 낼 수 있도록 꼭 필요한 부분만 정리한 책입니다. 이 책은 여러분이 단기간에 이 과정을 통과할 수 있게 도와주는 든든한 디딤돌이 될 것입니다. 빠르게 토익을 끝내고 여러분들이 하고자 하는 미래에 한발 더 가까이 다가서길 바랍니다.

이 책이 출판되기까지 애써주신 영단기 출판사, 온라인, 강남 학원 관계자분들께 감사드리며, 함께 고민해준 저희 연구소 직원들에게도 진심으로 감사하다는 말을 전합니다.
마지막으로 저를 비롯해 이 모든 분들의 노력과 정성이 여러분들에게 큰 힘이 될 수 있기를 희망합니다.

감사합니다.

저자 유수연 드림

목차

책의 구성 및 특징	004	TOEIC 파트별로 어떻게 나오나요?	008
토익 완성 플랜	006	꼭 알아 두어야 할 영어 기초	010
TOEIC 소개	007		

LC

PART 1

PART 1 기본 문제 풀이 전략	018
Chapter 1 사람 중심 사진	020
Chapter 2 사물 중심 사진	028

PART 2

PART 2 기본 문제 풀이 전략	038
Chapter 1 의문사 의문문 I	042
Chapter 2 의문사 의문문 II	050
Chapter 3 일반 의문문	058
Chapter 4 기타 질문과 답변	066

PART 3

PART 3 기본 문제 풀이 전략	076
Chapter 1 대화의 처음에 답이 나오는 문제	078
Chapter 2 질문의 특정 단어를 들어야 하는 문제	084
Chapter 3 화자의 의도와 시각 자료 연계 문제	090
Chapter 4 대화의 마지막에 답이 나오는 문제	098

PART 4

PART 4 기본 문제 풀이 전략	106
Chapter 1 전화 메시지 & 공공장소 안내 방송	108
Chapter 2 업무 회의 & 광고	114
Chapter 3 설명/연설 & 투어	120
Chapter 4 방송 & 인물 소개	126

RC

PART 5&6

PART 5&6 기본 문제 풀이 전략	134
Chapter 1 명사	136
Chapter 2 동사의 형태	144
Chapter 3 동사의 수 일치/태/시제	152
Chapter 4 대명사	162
Chapter 5 형용사	170
Chapter 6 부사	178
Chapter 7 분사	186
Chapter 8 to부정사/동명사	194
Chapter 9 접속사	200
Chapter 10 관계사	208
Chapter 11 비교/가정법/도치	216
Chapter 12 전치사	224
Chapter 13 PART 6	234

PART 7

PART 7 기본 문제 풀이 전략	248
Chapter 1 문제 유형	250
Chapter 2 지문 유형	272
Chapter 3 다중 지문 유형	292

+ ACTUAL TEST   304
(실전 모의고사)

*정답 및 해석(책속책)

책의 구성 및 특징

1. LC와 RC를 한 권에! 토익 700+ 한 달 완성 프로젝트!

<영단기 토익 다이렉트 700+ LC+RC 한 달 완성>은 토익 700+의 목표 점수를 쉽고 빠르게 달성할 수 있도록 토익 LC와 RC의 모든 파트를 한 권에 수록하였습니다. 군더더기 없이 핵심 내용만 수록하여 한 달 안에 토익 700+를 달성할 수 있습니다.

LC

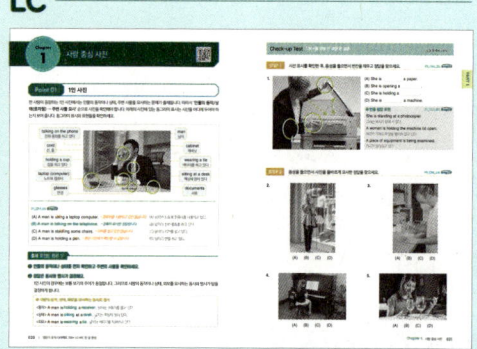

RC

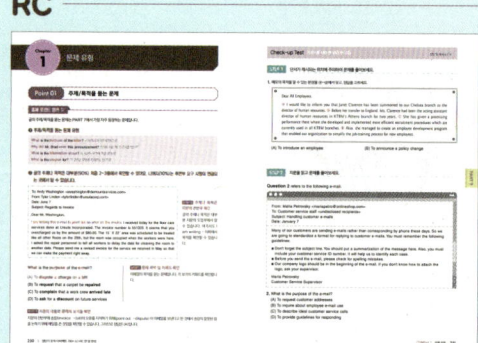

2. 토익 왕초보도 쉽게 공부할 수 있는 6단계 학습 구성

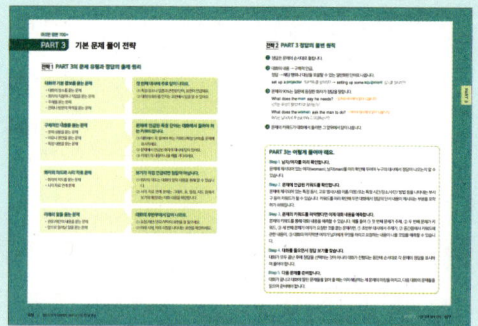

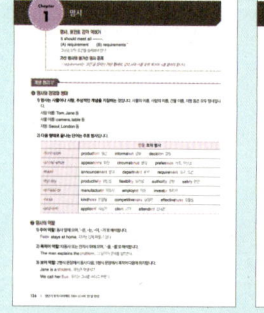

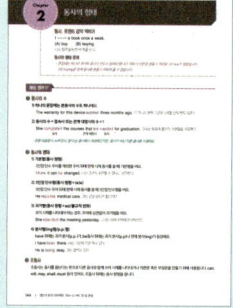

1) 파트별 기본 문제 풀이 전략
각 파트에 들어가기 앞서 문제에 쉽고 빠르게 적용할 수 있는 기본 문제 풀이 전략을 수록하였습니다.

2) 개념 정리(PART 5)
영어 초보자도 무리 없이 이해할 수 있도록 기본 개념을 쉽게 설명해 놓았습니다.

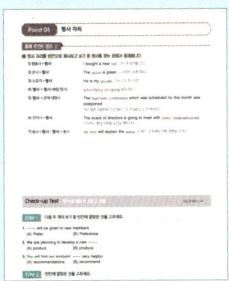

3) 출제 포인트 정리
각 유형에서 가장 핵심이 되는 출제 포인트를 정리했습니다.

4) 단계별 문제 풀이, Check-up Test!
STEP 1에서 유형의 출제 포인트를 연습하고, STEP 2에서 실전 문제로 확인할 수 있습니다.

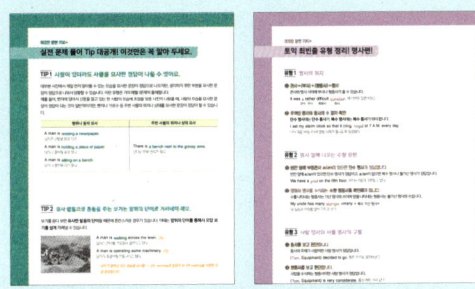
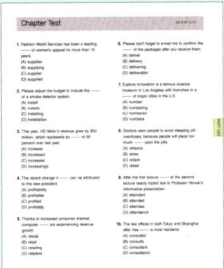

5) 실전 문제 풀이 Tip & 최빈출 유형
700+ 목표 달성을 위해 꼭 알아 두어야하는 실전 문제 Tip과 토익 최빈출 유형을 정리하여 수록하였습니다.

6) 실전 문제 풀이, Chapter Test!
실전과 똑같은 유형과 난이도의 실전 문제로 학습을 마무리할 수 있습니다.

3. mp3 & 누구보다 친절한 해설 PDF 무료 제공 [QR코드]

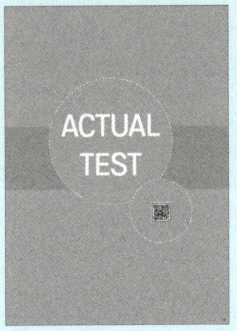

1) mp3
교재 내 QR 코드를 통해 mp3를 무료로 이용하실 수 있습니다. 또한 커넥츠 영단기 홈페이지(eng.conects.com)에서도 무료로 다운받으실 수 있습니다.

2) 누구보다 친절한 해설 PDF
정답 및 해석이 담긴 책속책 1 페이지에 있는 QR코드를 통해 누구보다 친절한 해설 PDF를 무료로 이용하실 수 있습니다.

토익 완성 플랜

토익 700+ 한 달 완성
하루에 LC와 RC 약 1개 Chapter씩 공부하여 토익 700+ 한 달(4주) 완성!

		1st Day	2nd Day	3rd Day	4th Day	5th Day
1st week	LC	PART 1 Chapter 1	PART 1 Chapter 2	PART 1 정리	PART 2 Chapter 1	PART 2 Chapter 2
	RC	PART 5&6 Chapter 1	PART 5&6 Chapter 2	PART 5&6 Chapter 3	PART 5&6 Chapter 4	PART 5&6 Chapter 5
2nd week	LC	PART 2 Chapter 3	PART 2 Chapter 4	PART 2 정리	PART 3 Chapter 1	PART 3 Chapter 2
	RC	PART 5&6 Chapter 6	PART 5&6 Chapter 7	PART 5&6 Chapter 8	PART 5&6 Chapter 9	PART 5&6 Chapter 1~8 정리
3rd week	LC	PART 3 Chapter 3	PART 3 Chapter 4	PART 3 정리	PART 4 Chapter 1	PART 4 Chapter 2
	RC	PART 5&6 Chapter 10	PART 5&6 Chapter 11	PART 5&6 Chapter 12	PART 5&6 Chapter 13	PART 5&6 Chapter 9~13 정리
4th week	LC	PART 4 Chapter 3	PART 4 Chapter 4	PART 4 정리	LC 총정리	ACTUAL TEST
	RC	PART 7 Chapter 1	PART 7 Chapter 2	PART 7 Chapter 3	PART 7 정리	ACTUAL TEST

TOEIC(Test of English for International Communication) 소개

TOEIC 시험

토익은 모국어가 영어가 아닌 사람이 일상적인 생활 또는 업무에서 의사소통이 가능한지를 평가하는 시험입니다. 현재 한국과 일본을 포함한 전 세계 약 150여개 국가의 기업과 기관에서 채용 및 평가, 승진, 영어 학습 프로그램 등에 활용되고 있습니다.

구성	PART	유형		문항 수	시간	점수
Listening	PART 1	사진 묘사		6	45분	495점
	PART 2	질의응답		25		
	PART 3	짧은 대화		39		
	PART 4	짧은 담화		30		
Reading	PART 5	단문 빈칸 채우기		30	75분	495점
	PART 6	장문 빈칸 채우기		16		
	PART 7	독해	단일 지문(10)	29		
			이중 지문(2)	10		
			삼중 지문(3)	15		
총 7개 PART				200문항	120분	990점

출제 범위 및 기준

출제 기관인 ETS에 따르면, TOEIC에서는 영어를 모국어로 사용하는 특정 국가에서만 쓰이는 표현이나 문법, 관용어들은 피합니다. 또한 특정 문화나 직업 분야에만 해당되거나 생소한 상황은 나오지 않습니다. LC의 경우 여러 나라 사람들의 이름과 다양한 영어 발음 및 액센트(미국, 영국, 캐나다, 호주, 뉴질랜드)가 출제됩니다.

출제 분야	세부 분야
General Business (일반 업무)	계약, 협상, 마케팅, 세일즈, 비즈니스 계획, 회의
Manufacturing (제조)	공장 관리, 조립 라인, 품질 관리
Finance, Budgeting (금융, 예산)	은행, 투자, 세금, 회계, 청구
Corporate Development (개발)	연구, 제품 개발
Office Work (사무실 업무)	임원 회의, 위원 회의, 편지, 메모, 전화, 팩스, E-mail, 사무 장비와 가구
Personnel (인사)	구인, 채용, 퇴직, 급여, 승진, 취업 지원과 자기소개
Housing, Corporate Property (주택, 기업 부동산)	건축, 설계서, 구입과 임대, 전기와 가스 서비스
Travel (여행)	기차, 비행기, 택시, 버스, 배, 유람선, 티켓, 일정, 역과 공항 안내, 자동차 렌트, 호텔, 예약, 연기와 취소

TOEIC 파트별로 어떻게 나오나요?

LC 파트

PART 1 사진 묘사 Photographs
총 6문항

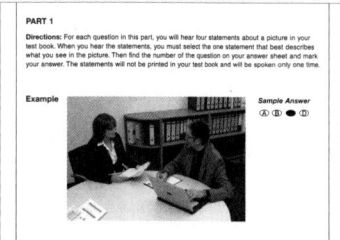

사진을 가장 잘 묘사한 문장을 고르는 파트로, 상황별 어휘 및 표현 구사력을 묻는 파트입니다.

문제지에는 각 문항마다 하나의 사진이 제시되어 있고, (A)~(D) 4개의 보기를 차례로 들려주면서 사진 속의 상황을 가장 잘 묘사한 것을 묻는 파트입니다.

Direction은 약 1분 20~30초 정도 나오며, 각 문제의 보기 (A)~(D)를 들려주고 난 후 5초 정도의 풀이 시간이 주어집니다.

PART 2 질의응답 Question-Response
총 25문항

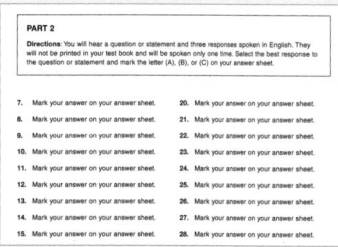

짧은 질문에 대한 적절한 답변을 찾는 파트로, 빠른 판단력으로 적절한 응답을 고르는 쌍방향 의사소통 능력을 테스트하는 파트입니다.

간단한 질문과 (A)~(C) 3개의 보기를 듣고 질문에 가장 적절한 답을 선택하는 파트입니다. 문제지에는 해당하는 문제와 관련된 정보는 없으며 보기의 번호들만 표기가 되어 있습니다.

약 2~30초간 Direction이 나오며, 한 문제가 끝나면 5초 정도의 문제 풀이 시간이 주어집니다.

PART 3 짧은 대화 Conversations
총 39문항, 13개의 짧은 대화

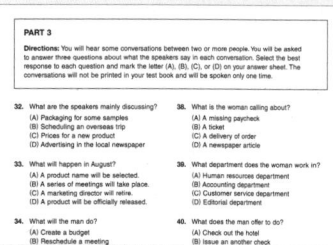

2~3인의 짧은 대화를 듣고 관련된 문제에 답을 고르는 파트로, 상황의 인지 및 정보 습득 능력을 평가하는 파트입니다.

문제지에 질문과 보기가 모두 쓰여 있고 대화를 들려줍니다. 하나의 대화당 3문제를 풀어야 합니다. 대화에 등장하는 내용과 관련된 질문이 등장하므로 질문을 미리 파악해 놓으면 어느 정도 대화의 내용을 예측할 수 있습니다. 일정표, 영수증, 그래프, 지도 등 시각 자료를 연계해 답을 찾는 문제도 출제됩니다.

Direction이 30초 정도 나오고 첫 번째 대화가 나옵니다. 대화가 끝나면 약 40초 동안 보기를 제외한 문제를 한 번씩 읽어 주면서 문제 풀이 시간이 주어집니다.

PART 4 짧은 담화 Short Talks
총 30문항, 10개 담화

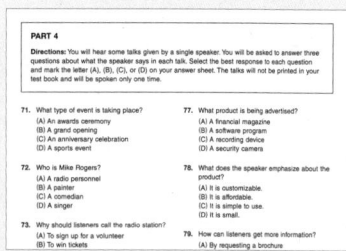

한 사람의 짧은 이야기를 듣고 답을 고르는 문제로, 내용에 대한 이해도와 정보 습득 능력을 평가하는 파트입니다.

문제지의 형태는 PART 3와 동일합니다. 다만 PART 3와는 달리 대화 대신 한 사람의 연설이나 담화, 설명 등이 나옵니다.

Direction이 30초 정도 나오고 첫 번째 담화가 나옵니다. 담화가 끝나면 약 40초 동안 보기를 제외한 문제를 한 번씩 읽어 주면서 문제풀이 시간이 주어집니다.

토익은 출제 의도를 알아야 단기간에 끝낼 수 있습니다.

RC 파트

PART 5 단문 빈칸 채우기 Incomplete Sentences 총 30문항

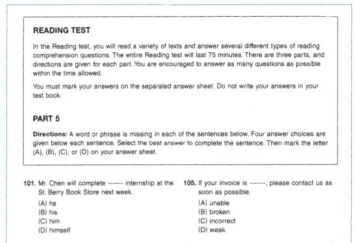

커뮤니케이션을 위해 가장 기본이 되는 하나의 영어 문장을 정확히 이해하고 쓸 수 있는지 품사의 배치나 기본적인 문법 및 어휘를 묻는 파트입니다.

문제지에는 빈칸이 포함된 하나의 문장과 보기 (A)~(D)가 제시됩니다. 제시된 보기 중에서 빈칸에 들어갈 단어를 선택해야 합니다. 주로 품사나 문법, 어휘 사용 능력을 묻습니다.

PART 6 장문 빈칸 채우기 Text Completion 총 16문항, 4지문

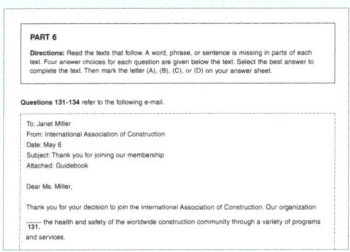

문서상에서 문맥을 이해하고 문장을 올바로 쓸 수 있는지를 묻는 파트입니다.

실제 사용되는 문서상에서 PART 5와 같이 문장에 빈칸을 만들어 놓고 그에 알맞은 단어나 문장을 넣는 파트입니다. 하나의 지문에 4개의 빈칸이 있으며, 그 중 한 문제는 알맞은 문장을 넣는 문제로 출제됩니다.
얼핏 PART 5와 유사해 보이지만, 해당 문장만으로 풀 수 있는 문제보단 지문의 앞뒤 내용을 확인해야 풀리는 문제가 더 많이 나옵니다.

PART 7 독해 Reading Comprehension 총 54문항, 15지문

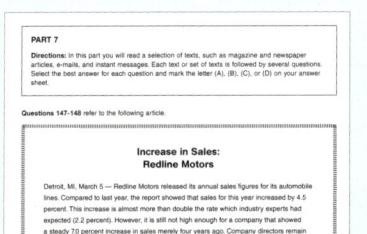

하나 혹은 다수의 문서(지문)를 읽고 관련된 문제들에 대해 가장 적절한 보기를 찾을 수 있는지 정보 검색 능력을 묻는 파트입니다.

1. 단일 지문 유형
문제지에는 일상 비즈니스 상황에서 등장할 만한 편지나 이메일, 공지, 기사 등의 지문과 함께 2~4문제가 함께 제시됩니다. 이런 식으로 총 10개의 지문이 등장합니다.
① 2문제 × 4개 지문 (8문제)
② 3문제 × 3개 지문 (9문제)
③ 4문제 × 3개 지문 (12문제)

2. 다중 지문 유형
상호 연관이 있는 두 개 이상의 지문이 등장하며, 이에 대해 5문제가 제시됩니다.
① 이중 지문 × 2개 (10문제)
② 삼중 지문 × 3개 (15문제)

꼭 알아 두어야 할 영어 기초

눈으로 풀어봐요!

A. 다음 문장에서 밑줄 친 단어의 품사를 적으세요. 　　　　　　　　　제한시간 30초

① <u>Last week</u> you canceled <u>your</u> subscription to *The New York Times*.
지난주에 당신은 <뉴욕 타임즈>의 구독을 취소하셨습니다.

② You <u>must</u> submit <u>an</u> application <u>with</u> details of your <u>academic</u> background.
당신은 자세한 학력을 포함한 지원서를 제출해야 합니다.

③ <u>This</u> week's safety inspection will be preformed <u>closely</u>.
이번 주의 안전 점검은 꼼꼼하게 진행될 것이다.

④ I would <u>appreciate</u> it <u>if</u> you send me an <u>issue</u> <u>by August 3</u>.
8월 3일까지 한 부를 보내 주시면 감사하겠습니다.

B. 다음 문장에서 주요 문장 성분(주어, 동사, 목적어, 보어)에 표시하세요. 　　제한시간 30초

① The accountant already revised the financial report before submitting it to the headquarters.
회계사가 재무 보고서를 본사에 제출하게 전에 이미 수정했다.

② If we receive your résumé by the end of this month, we will accept your application.
이달 말까지 당신의 이력서가 우리에게 도착한다면 당신의 지원을 받아들일 것입니다.

③ We recently added some exciting features to our new product.
우리는 최근 우리의 신제품에 흥미로운 기능들을 추가했습니다.

④ The recently purchased program made our website more simple.
최근에 구입한 프로그램은 우리의 웹사이트를 더욱 단순하게 만들어 주었습니다.

정답

A. ① Last week 부사(구), your 대명사
② must 조동사, an (부정)관사, with 전치사, academic 형용사
③ This 지시 형용사, closely 부사
④ appreciate 동사, if 접속사, issue 명사, August 3 부사(구)

B. ① The <u>accountant</u> already <u>revised</u> the <u>financial report</u> before submitting it to the headquarters.
　　　　주어　　　　　　　동사　　　　목적어

② If <u>we</u> <u>receive</u> your <u>résumé</u> by the end of this month, <u>we</u> <u>will accept</u> <u>your application</u>.
　　주어　동사　　　　목적어　　　　　　　　　　　　　주어　　동사　　　　목적어

③ <u>We</u> recently <u>added</u> some exciting <u>features</u> to our new product.
　주어　　　　　동사　　　　　　　　목적어

④ The recently purchased <u>program</u> <u>made</u> our <u>website</u> <u>more simple</u>.
　　　　　　　　　　　　주어　　　　동사　　　목적어　　목적격 보어

꼭 알아 두어야 할 영어 기초   애매했던 영어의 "품사", 제대로 알고 가자! (1)

보통 영어에서는 '감탄사'를 포함하여 8품사로 구분하지만 **토익에서는 관사와 분사까지 포함시켜** 정리하여 연습하는 것이 좋아요. **단어들은** 대개 하나의 품사로 고정되어 있지 않고 **여러 품사로 쓰일 수 있어요. 단어의 품사 구분은 문장 내에서의 쓰임을** 보고 판가름할 수 있어요.

명사	대명사	동사	형용사
부사	접속사	전치사	관사/분사

<u>The</u> <u>boy</u> <u>is</u> <u>one</u> <u>of</u> <u>my</u> <u>friends</u> <u>and</u> <u>he</u> <u>speaks</u> <u>English</u> <u>very</u> <u>fluently</u>.
관사 명사 동사 대명사 전치사 형용사 명사 접속사 대명사 동사 명사 부사 부사

그 소년은 나의 친구 중 한 명이고 그는 영어를 유창하게 해요.

- **명사** 사람·사물 등 모든 것의 이름
  <u>Tom</u> is a great <u>teacher</u>. 톰은 좋은 선생님입니다.
  The <u>bread</u> is delicious. 그 빵은 맛있습니다.

- **대명사** 앞에서 말한 명사를 대신해서 쓰이는 품사
  The boy is one of my friends and <u>he</u>(= the boy) is a student.
  그 소년은 내 친구 중 하나이고 그는 학생입니다.

- **동사** 동작, 행위, 움직임을 나타내는 품사
  We <u>did</u> a really good job. 우리들은 정말로 잘했습니다.
  I <u>love</u> you. 당신을 사랑해요.

- **형용사** 명사의 성질, 상태 등을 묘사하는 품사로 주로 명사 앞 혹은 be동사 뒤에 위치해요.
  This <u>book</u> is not mine. 이 책은 제 것이 아닙니다.
  Yoo teacher strongly believes that grade 990 <u>is</u> <u>possible</u>.
  유 선생님은 990점이 가능하다고 강력히 믿습니다.

꼭 알아 두어야 할 영어 기초   애매했던 영어의 "품사", 제대로 알고 가자! (2)

- **부사**   명사를 제외한 다양한 품사(형용사, 부사, 동사)나 문장 전체를 구체적으로 설명하는 품사로 동사 앞, 형용사 앞, 문장 맨 앞 혹은 끝 등 자유롭게 위치해요.
  This book is really easy for students. 이 책은 학생들에게 정말 쉽습니다.

- **접속사**   문장과 문장을 연결해 주는 연결어로 문장 하나당 동사 하나가 존재하기 때문에 접속사가 하나 추가될 때마다 동사도 하나 추가돼요.
  I like him. + He likes her. = I like him but he likes her.
  나는 그를 좋아합니다. + 그는 그녀를 좋아합니다. = 나는 그를 좋아하지만 그는 그녀를 좋아합니다.

- **전치사**   완전한 문장에 명사의 자리를 추가로 만들어 주는 품사로 명사 혹은 대명사 앞에 위치해서 시간, 장소, 방법 등을 나타냅니다.
  I met him + in the morning. 나는 그를 아침에 만났습니다. <시간>
  I met him + at the store. 나는 그를 가게에서 만났습니다. <장소>

- **관사**
  ① a/an(부정관사): 앞에서 언급되지 않았거나 불특정한 하나의 가산 명사를 가리킬 때 사용합니다.
  ② the(정관사): 이미 언급되었거나 특정 대상을 가리킬 때 사용합니다.
  a book 책 한 권   a boy 한 명의 소년   an idea 하나의 아이디어 <부정관사 a/an>
  The book is mine. 그 책은 저의 것입니다. <정관사 the>

- **분사**   동사가 형태를 바꾸어 품사가 형용사로 바뀐 것으로, 현재 분사(V-ing)와 과거 분사(p.p.)가 있어요.
  rising sun 떠오르는 태양 <현재 분사>
  a broken window 깨진 창문 <과거 분사>

꼭 알아 두어야 할 영어 기초

품사와 필수 문장 성분의 관계

각각의 품사는 문장에서 **주어, 서술어(동사), 목적어, 보어, 수식어 등의 역할**을 하는데 이를 **문장 성분**이라고 합니다.

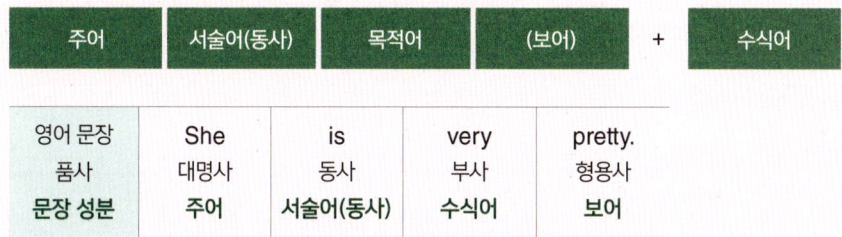

영어 문장	She	is	very	pretty.
품사	대명사	동사	부사	형용사
문장 성분	주어	서술어(동사)	수식어	보어

- **주어** 주로 문장 맨 앞에 위치하여 동작을 하는 사람 혹은 사물을 가리켜요.
  ⇨ **명사, 대명사, to 부정사, 명사절** 등이 올 수 있습니다.
  I want to go. 저는 가고 싶습니다. <대명사>
  To see is to believe. 보는 것이 믿는 것이다. <to 부정사>
  What they want is not my concern. 그들이 바라는 것은 제 관심사가 아닙니다. <명사절>

- **서술어(동사)** 주어 뒤에 위치하며, 하나의 문장에는 반드시 하나의 **동사**가 있어야 해요.
  You should do that again! 당신은 이것을 다시 해야 해요!

- **목적어** 동사 뒤에 위치합니다. (전치사 뒤에 나오는 명사도 전치사의 목적어라고 합니다.)
  ⇨ **명사, 대명사, 명사구(to 부정사, 동명사), 명사절** 등이 올 수 있습니다.
  He brought a dog. 그는 강아지를 데려왔습니다. <명사>
  I like reading a book. 저는 독서를 좋아합니다. <동명사>

- **보어** 부족한 의미를 보완하거나 구체적으로 설명해 주는 말로, 주격 보어, 목적격 보어가 있어요.
  ⇨ **형용사와 명사** 등이 올 수 있습니다.
  ① 주격 보어: It is clean. 그것은 깨끗합니다. <형용사>
  ② 목적격 보어: He made me a singer. 그는 저를 가수로 만들었습니다. <명사>

꼭 알아 두어야 할 영어 기초

구와 절이란?

- **구**

문장 성분들은 하나의 단어만으로 이루어지지만은 않습니다. 두 단어 이상이 만나서 하나의 역할을 하기도 하는데 우리는 이것을 "**구**"라고 합니다. 구는 **명사구, 동사구, 형용사구, 부사구** 등이 있으며 문장에서의 역할에 따라서 주어, 서술어, 목적어, 보어, 수식어의 역할을 하게 됩니다.

① **명사구** ⇨ 주어, 목적어, 보어의 역할
② **동사구** ⇨ 서술어의 역할
③ **형용사구, 부사구** ⇨ 수식어의 역할

Breakfast is not included <u>in the tour</u>. 조식은 투어에 포함되어 있지 않습니다.
　　　　　　　　　　　└▷ 전치사+명사 ⇨ 부사구

- **절**

"**절**"은 동사를 포함한 하나의 문장을 의미합니다. **명사절, 형용사절(관계사절), 부사절** 등이 있으며 주어, 목적어, 보어, 수식어의 역할을 합니다.

① **명사절** ⇨ 주어, 목적어, 보어의 역할
② **형용사절(관계사절), 부사절** ⇨ 수식어의 역할

Customers will receive an invoice <u>when they place a new order</u>.
고객들은 새로운 주문을 하면, 청구서를 받을 것입니다.　└▷ 시간 부사절 접속사+주어+동사 ~ ⇨ (시간) 부사절

꼭 알아 두어야 할 영어 기초

문제 풀이의 기본, 수식어구 제거

수식어는 주어, 서술어(동사), 목적어, 보어와는 달리 문장에 반드시 있어야 하는 주요 성분이 아니고 꾸며 주는 역할을 하는 보조적인 문장 성분이에요. 문장에 없어도 되는 성분이라서 **괄호로 묶어 보시면 문장의 구조를 좀 더 명확하게 볼 수 있어요.**

주로 형용사나 부사가 수식어에 해당하며, 두 단어 이상으로 구성되어 있기도 해요.

① 형용사/부사:
   Ms. Kim has almost completed her task. 김 씨는 그녀의 일을 거의 마쳤습니다.

② 전치사구(전치사+명사):
   I've met him at the meeting. 저는 회의에서 그를 만났습니다.

③ to부정사구(to부정사+목적어):
   To place an order I visited the store. 주문을 하기 위해 저는 그 상점에 방문했습니다.

④ 관계 대명사절(관계 대명사+주어+동사):
   Star Travel assists people who travel frequently. 스타 여행사는 자주 여행을 하는 사람들을 돕습니다.

The (great) artist (who is one of my friends) visited the convention hall (to deliver a speech).
　　형용사　　　관계 대명사절(형용사절)　　　　　　　　　　　　　　to부정사구

(제 친구 중 한 명인) (위대한) 예술가가 (연설을 하기 위해) 컨벤션 홀을 방문했습니다.

→ The artist visited the convention hall. 예술가가 컨벤션 홀을 방문했습니다.

문장의 구조가 훨씬 심플하게 보이죠?
문장에서 필요한 성분이나 품사를 찾을 땐 수식어구를 괄호로 묶고 문장 구조를 보는 게 진리네요.
그럼 문제에서 어떻게 적용하는지 한번 볼까요?

예제

George Burns received ------- from the head of the sales department.
(A) recommend
(B) recommendation
(C) recommendable
(D) recommended

George Burns / received / ------- (from the head) (of the sales department).
　주어　　　　동사　　　목적어　　수식어구　　　　　수식어구

처음 나오는 고유명사 George Burns가 주어이고 received가 동사이며, 빈칸 뒤의 'from+명사+of+명사'를 수식어구로 제거하면 빈칸은 목적어 자리임을 알 수 있어요. 목적어 자리에 올 수 있는 품사는 명사이므로 보기 중 명사인 (B) recommendation이 정답입니다.

PART 1

다이렉트

700+

Chapter 1. 사람 중심 사진

Chapter 2. 사물 중심 사진

이것만 알면 700+

PART 1 기본 문제 풀이 전략

전략 1 꼭 알아야 할 사진의 시선 처리 방법

❶ **인물의 동작과 상태**를 확인하세요.

❷ 사람들의 **상호 동작과 공통 행위**를 확인하세요.

❸ 여러 사람이 있더라도 **사람들 각각의 동작과 상태**도 확인해야 합니다.

❹ 사진 속 **사물들의 위치와 상태, 그리고 움직임**을 파악하세요.

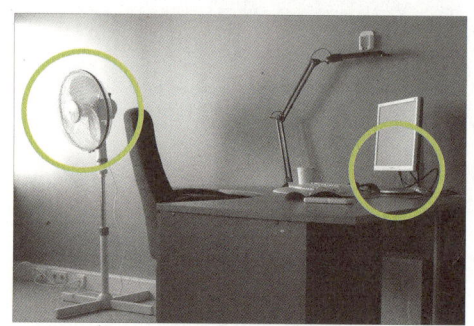

전략2 다 들으려고 하지 말고 오답 유형만 확인하고 소거합니다.

❶ **사진과 관계없는 동사와 명사**가 포함된 보기는 **오답**입니다.
❷ **수동태 진행형(being + p.p.)**은 대부분 **오답**입니다.
❸ **주관적인 의견**이 담긴 보기는 **오답**입니다. 포괄적이고 객관적인 사실만 묘사합니다.
❹ **유사 발음 혼동 보기**는 주변 단어를 통해 가려냅니다.

PART 1은 이렇게 풀어야 해요.

Step 1. 음성이 나오기 전에 **사진을 미리 보고** 시선을 떼지 않습니다.
Step 2. 음성을 들으면서 **빠르게 핵심어를 두 단어** 정도 받아씁니다.
Step 3. **사진과 관계없는 단어(동사, 명사)**가 들리면 바로 소거합니다.
Step 4. 하나씩 X표로 **오답을 소거**하면 결국 **남는 게 정답**입니다.

※ 이때 잘 들리지 않거나 모르는 표현이 나왔다 하더라도 당황하지 말고 ?나 △로 표시하고 넘겨야 합니다.

Chapter 1 사람 중심 사진

Point 01   1인 사진

한 사람이 등장하는 1인 사진에서는 인물의 동작이나 상태, 주변 사물을 묘사하는 문제가 출제됩니다. 따라서 '**인물의 동작/상태(옷차림) → 주변 사물 묘사**' 순으로 사진을 확인해야 합니다. 아래의 사진에 있는 동그라미 표시는 시선을 어디에 두어야 하는지 보여 줍니다. 동그라미 표시와 표현들을 확인하세요.

P1_Ch1_01. mp3

(A) A man is using a laptop computer. → 컴퓨터를 사용하고 있진 않습니다.   (A) 남자가 노트북 컴퓨터를 사용하고 있다.
(B) A man is talking on the telephone. → 정확히 묘사한 정답입니다.   (B) 남자가 전화 통화를 하고 있다.
(C) A man is stacking some chairs. → 의자를 쌓고 있진 않습니다.   (C) 남자가 의자를 쌓고 있다.
(D) A man is holding a pen. → 펜은 사진에서 확인할 수 없습니다.   (D) 남자가 펜을 쥐고 있다.

출제 포인트 정리

❶ 인물의 동작이나 상태를 먼저 확인하고 주변의 사물을 확인하세요.

❷ 정답은 동사와 명사가 결정해요.
    1인 사진의 경우에는 보통 보기의 주어가 동일합니다. 그러므로 사람의 동작이나 상태, 외모를 묘사하는 동사와 명사가 답을 결정하게 됩니다.

> ❖ 사람의 동작, 상태, 외모를 묘사하는 동사와 명사
>
> <동작> A man is holding a receiver. 남자는 수화기를 들고 있다.
> <상태> A man is sitting at a desk. 남자는 책상에 앉아 있다.
> <외모> A man is wearing a tie. 남자는 넥타이를 착용하고 있다.

Check-up Test 700+를 위해 한 걸음 한 걸음

정답 및 해석 p.002

STEP 1 시선 표시를 확인한 후, 음성을 들으면서 빈칸을 채우고 정답을 찾으세요.   P1_Ch1_02. mp3

1.
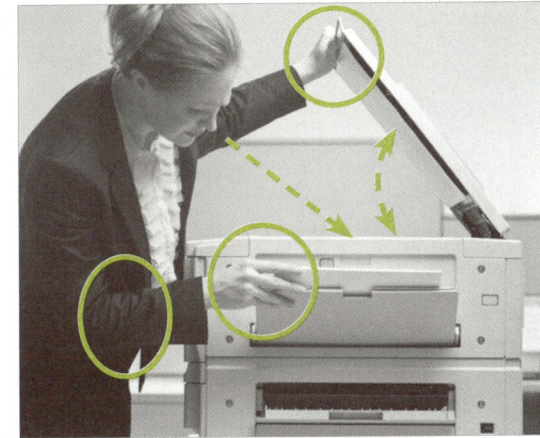

(A) She is _____ a paper.
(B) She is opening a _____.
(C) She is holding a _____.
(D) She is _____ a machine.

빈출 정답 표현   P1_Ch1_03. mp3
She is standing at a photocopier.
그녀는 복사기 앞에 서 있다.

A woman is holding the machine lid open.
여자가 기계의 뚜껑을 열어서 잡고 있다.

A piece of equipment is being examined.
기기가 점검되고 있다.

STEP 2 음성을 들으면서 사진을 올바르게 묘사한 정답을 찾으세요.   P1_Ch1_04. mp3

2.

(A) (B) (C) (D)

3.
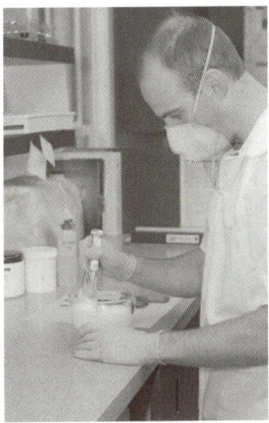
(A) (B) (C) (D)

4.

(A) (B) (C) (D)

5.

(A) (B) (C) (D)

Chapter 1. 사람 중심 사진   021

Point 02 2인 이상 사진

2인 이상 사진에서는 인물들의 공통된 동작과 개별 동작, 주변 사물을 묘사하는 문제가 출제됩니다. 따라서 사람들의 '**공통 동작 → 각 사람의 동작/상태(옷차림) → 주변 사물**' 순으로 사진을 파악해야 합니다. 아래의 사진에 있는 동그라미 표시는 시선을 어디에 두어야 하는지 보여 줍니다. 동그라미 표시와 표현들을 확인하세요.

P1_Ch1_05. mp3

(A) Some people are lined up for purchasing tickets. → 표를 구매하려 줄을 서 있지 않습니다.
  몇몇 사람들이 표를 구매하기 위해 줄을 서 있다.

(B) A vendor is selling some suitcases. → 여행 가방을 팔고 있지는 않습니다.
  행상인이 여행 가방을 팔고 있다.

(C) Some people are stopped to watch a performance. → 정확히 묘사한 정답입니다.
  몇몇 사람들이 공연을 보기 위해 멈춰 서 있다.

(D) A man is packing up his musical instruments. → 악기를 가방에 싸고 있진 않습니다.
  한 남자가 악기를 챙겨 넣고 있다.

출제 포인트 정리

❶ 공통 동작이나 상태를 먼저 확인하고 주요 인물들을 확인하세요.

❷ 사람이 있는 사진이라도 사물을 묘사한 정답이 나올 수 있어요.

사진 속에 사람이 등장하더라도 주변의 사물을 묘사하는 정답이 나올 수 있으므로 사물들의 위치나 상태도 꼼꼼히 확인해야 합니다.

❀ 사물의 상태를 묘사하는 경우

A street is paved with bricks. 거리가 벽돌로 포장되어 있다.

❀ 사람에 의해 특정 행위가 진행되고 있는 경우 – 수동태 진행형

A performance is being given on the street. 거리에서 공연이 이루어지고 있다.

Check-up Test 700+를 위해 한 걸음 한 걸음

정답 및 해석 p.002

STEP 1 시선 표시를 확인한 후, 음성을 들으면서 빈칸을 채우고 정답을 찾으세요. P1_Ch1_06. mp3

1.

(A) They are _____ along the shore.
(B) They are _____ their hands.
(C) A woman is _____ her sunglasses.
(D) A _____ is being _____ across a river.

❀ 빈출 정답 표현   P1_Ch1_07. mp3

They are standing near the water.
그들은 물가에 서 있다.

People are wearing sunglasses on their heads.
사람들이 선글라스를 머리에 쓰고 있다.

Some trees are growing along the shore.
나무들이 물가를 따라서 자라고 있다.

STEP 2 음성을 들으면서 사진을 올바르게 묘사한 정답을 찾으세요. P1_Ch1_08. mp3

2.

(A)   (B)   (C)   (D)

3.

(A)   (B)   (C)   (D)

4.

(A)   (B)   (C)   (D)

5.

(A)   (B)   (C)   (D)

Chapter 1. 사람 중심 사진   023

이것만 알면 700+

실전 문제 풀이 Tip 대공개! 이것만은 꼭 알아 두세요.

TIP 1 사람이 있더라도 사물을 묘사한 정답이 나올 수 있어요.

대부분 사진에서 제일 먼저 알아볼 수 있는 모습을 묘사한 문장이 정답으로 나오지만, 생각하지 못한 부분을 묘사한 문장이 정답으로 나와서 당황할 수 있습니다. 이런 유형은 거의 매월 1문제씩 출제됩니다.

예를 들어, 벤치에 앉아서 신문을 읽고 있는 한 사람의 모습에 초점을 맞춘 사진이 나왔을 때, 사람의 모습을 묘사한 문장이 정답이 되는 것이 일반적이지만, 벤치나 가로수 등 주변 사물의 위치나 상태를 묘사한 문장이 정답이 될 수 있습니다.

행위나 동작 묘사	주변 사물의 위치나 상태 묘사
A man is reading a newspaper. 남자가 신문을 읽고 있다. A man is holding a piece of paper. 남자가 종이를 들고 있다. A man is sitting on a bench. 남자가 벤치에 앉아 있다.	There is a bench next to the grassy area. 잔디밭 옆에 벤치가 있다.

TIP 2 유사 발음으로 혼동을 주는 보기는 앞뒤의 단어로 가려내야 해요.

보기를 듣다 보면 **유사한 발음의 단어**들 때문에 혼란스러운 경우가 있습니다. 이때는 **앞뒤의 단어를 통해서 오답 보기를 쉽게 가려**낼 수 있습니다.

A man is walking across the lawn. (X)
남자가 잔디를 가로질러 걸어가고 있다.

A man is operating some machinery. (O)
남자가 중장비를 작동시키고 있다.

→ 남자가 일하고 있는 모습을 묘사할 수 있는 working과 발음이 유사한 walking을 이용한 오답 함정입니다.

TIP 3 꼭 암기해야 할 PART 1 사람 관련 빈출 표현

P1_Ch1_09. mp3

- She is holding some merchandise.
  그녀는 물건을 손에 들고 있다.
- She is standing in front of some shelves.
  그녀는 선반 앞에 서 있다.
- She is wearing a muffler.
  그녀는 머플러를 착용하고 있다.
- She is examining an item.
  그녀는 상품을 살펴보고 있다.

- The women are working side by side.
  여자들이 나란히 일을 하고 있다.
- They are looking in the same direction.
  그들은 같은 방향을 바라보고 있다.
- One of the women is pointing at the screen.
  여자들 중 한 명이 화면을 가리키고 있다.
- There are some shelves above the monitor.
  모니터 위에 선반이 있다.

- They're working at a construction site.
  그들은 공사 현장에서 일하고 있다.
- One of the men is using a tool.
  남자들 중 한 명이 도구를 이용하고 있다.
- Both men are kneeling down.
  남자 두 명이 무릎을 꿇고 있다.
- Some construction work is being done.
  공사 작업이 진행되고 있다.

- They have taken their seats in the auditorium.
  그들은 강당의 좌석에 앉아 있다.
- Some people have gathered for a meeting.
  몇몇 사람들이 회의를 위해 모여 있다.
- People are seated in rows.
  사람들이 여러 줄로 앉아 있다.
- Some of the seats are unoccupied.
  몇몇 자리는 비어 있다.

Chapter Test P1_Ch1_10. mp3

1.

2.

3.

4.

5.

6.

Chapter 1. 사람 중심 사진   **027**

Chapter 2 사물 중심 사진

Point 01 실내 공간 사진

사람이 없는 사진인데 사람 명사가 들리면 오답입니다. 그렇기 때문에 사람이 등장하지 않는 실내 공간 사진은 '**사람 여부 확인 → 사물의 위치 및 상태**' 순으로 사진을 파악해야 합니다. 아래의 사진에 있는 동그라미 표시는 시선을 어디에 두어야 하는지 보여 줍니다. 동그라미 표시와 표현들을 확인하세요.

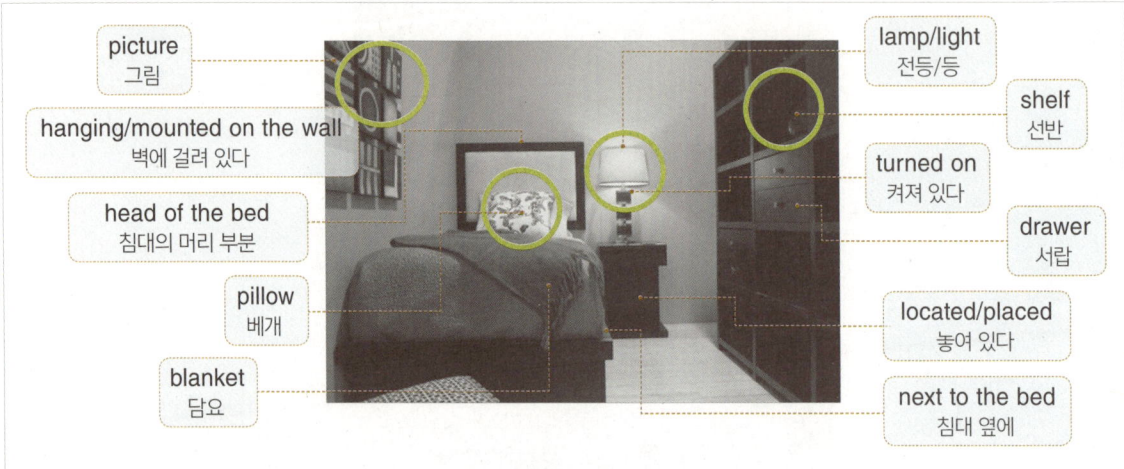

- picture 그림
- hanging/mounted on the wall 벽에 걸려 있다
- head of the bed 침대의 머리 부분
- pillow 베개
- blanket 담요
- lamp/light 전등/등
- shelf 선반
- turned on 켜져 있다
- drawer 서랍
- located/placed 놓여 있다
- next to the bed 침대 옆에

P1_Ch2_01. mp3

(A) A man is folding a blanket. → 담요는 있지만 개고 있는 사람은 없습니다.
(B) A lamp is hanging from a ceiling. → 전등은 탁자 위에 있습니다.
(C) A picture is mounted on the wall. → 정확히 묘사한 정답입니다.
(D) A pillow is located next to the cabinet. → 베개는 캐비닛 옆에 있지 않습니다.

(A) 남자가 담요를 개고 있다.
(B) 전등이 천장에 매달려 있다.
(C) 그림이 벽에 걸려 있다.
(D) 베개가 캐비닛 옆에 놓여 있다.

출제 포인트 정리

❶ 사람이 없는 사진에서 사람이 언급되면 무조건 오답이에요.

❷ 사물의 위치나 상태, 관계는 주로 전치사를 통해 알 수 있어요.
사물의 위치를 나타낼 때 가장 자주 쓰이는 전치사들은 반드시 암기해야 합니다.

❀ 사물의 위치와 방향을 나타내는 전치사

on ~ 위에(표면)	near/close to ~ 근처에	behind ~ 뒤에	to/toward ~ 쪽으로
at ~에(장소)	along ~을 따라	in front of ~ 앞에	across ~을 가로질러, 건너
over ~ 너머로	around ~ 사방에, 빙 둘러	above ~ 위에	through ~을 통해, ~을 지나
into ~ 안으로	opposite ~ 맞은편에	under ~ 아래에	against ~에 기대어
next to/beside/by ~ 옆에	between ~ 사이에, 중간에	inside ~ 안에	

Check-up Test 700+를 위해 한 걸음 한 걸음

정답 및 해석 p.003

STEP 1 시선 표시를 확인한 후, 음성을 들으면서 빈칸을 채우고 정답을 찾으세요.   P1_Ch2_02.

1.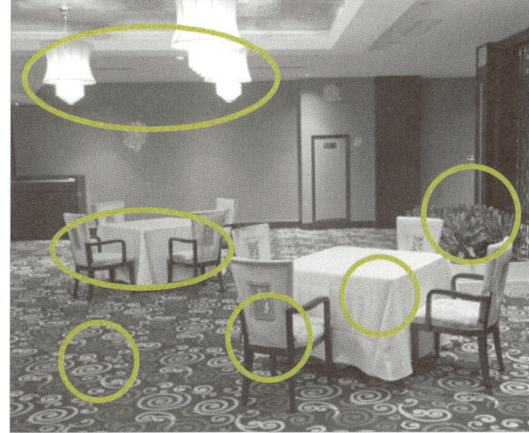

(A) A cafeteria is crowded with _____.
(B) A _____ has been hung above the _____.
(C) The tables are covered with _____.
(D) _____ have been placed on each _____.

❊ 빈출 정답 표현   P1_Ch2_03.

The chairs are unoccupied.
의자들이 비어 있다.

Lights are suspended from the ceiling.
전등이 천장에 걸려 있다.

A floor is covered with carpeting.
바닥이 카펫으로 덮여 있다.

STEP 2 음성을 들으면서 사진을 올바르게 묘사한 정답을 찾으세요.   P1_Ch2_04.

2.

(A) (B) (C) (D)

3.

(A) (B) (C) (D)

4.

(A) (B) (C) (D)

5.

(A) (B) (C) (D)

Chapter 2. 사물 중심 사진   **029**

Point 02 야외 배경 사진

야외 사진은 사물의 위치나 상태뿐 아니라 전반적인 분위기를 파악해야 합니다. **자연환경 또는 구조물(건물, 다리, 고속도로 등)들의 배치나 상태, 움직임**을 묘사하는 정답이 자주 출제되고 있습니다. 아래의 사진에 있는 동그라미 표시는 시선을 어디에 두어야 하는지 보여 줍니다. 동그라미 표시와 표현들을 확인하세요.

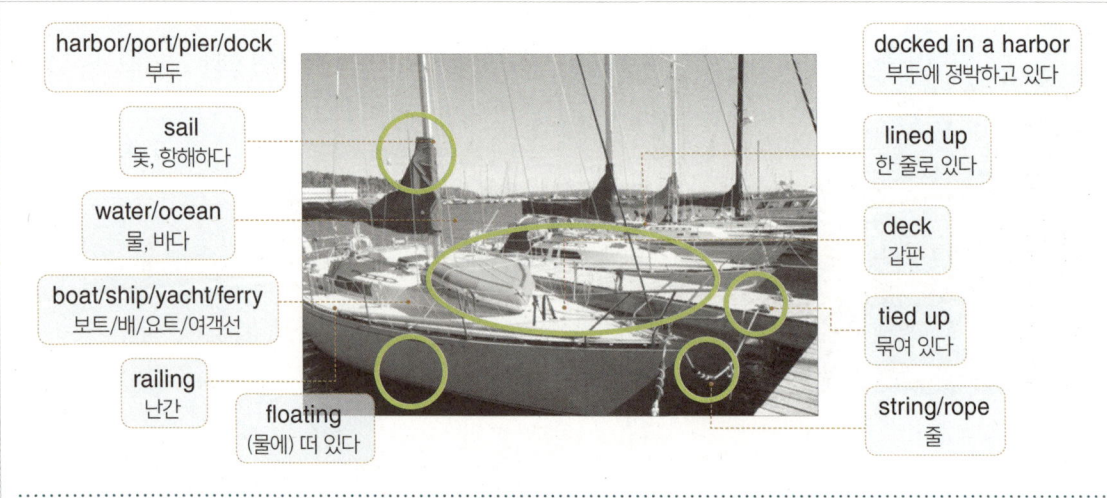

P1_Ch2_05. mp3

(A) Some people are swimming in the ocean. → *사람은 보이지 않습니다.*
(B) A sail is being raised on a boat. → *돛을 올리고 있는 사람은 없습니다.*
(C) Some boats are floating on the water. → *정확히 묘사한 정답입니다.*
(D) A ferry is sailing under the bridge. → *움직이는 배는 보이지 않습니다.*

(A) 몇몇 사람들이 바다에서 수영을 하고 있다.
(B) 돛이 배 위로 올라가고 있다.
(C) 몇몇 배들이 물 위에 떠 있다.
(D) 여객선이 다리 밑을 항해하고 있다.

출제 포인트 정리

❶ 사물들의 상태나 움직임뿐만 아니라 자연 현상들을 확인하세요.

❷ 구조물의 상태와 자연환경을 묘사하는 빈출 표현을 암기하세요.

익숙지 않은 구조물들의 상태나 배치, 자연환경을 묘사하는 표현은 반드시 알아 두어야 합니다.

> Some train tracks run alongside the buildings. 기찻길이 건물을 따라 나 있다.
> Buildings overlook a forest. 건물들이 숲을 내려다보고 있다.
> Waves are breaking along the shore. 파도가 해안을 따라 부서지고 있다.
> Water is flowing down the mountain. 물이 산 아래로 흘러가고 있다.
> A path leads to the building. 길이 건물로 이어져 있다.
> A path is shaded by some trees. 길에 나무들의 그림자가 드리워져 있다.
> Trees are casting shadows on the ground. 나무가 땅에 그림자를 드리우고 있다.
> A bridge spans a river. 다리가 강을 가로지르고 있다.
> A cafe window faces a street. 카페 창이 거리를 향해 있다.
> Cars are traveling in opposite directions. 차량들이 서로 반대 방향으로 운행하고 있다.

Check-up Test 700+를 위해 한 걸음 한 걸음

정답 및 해석 p.004

STEP 1 시선 표시를 확인한 후, 음성을 들으면서 빈칸을 채우고 정답을 찾으세요.   P1_Ch2_06. mp3

1.

(A) _____ _____ line the road.
(B) A _____ has been _____ for maintenance work.
(C) Some _____ are _____ the street.
(D) There are some _____ parked near the _____.

❖ 빈출 정답 표현   P1_Ch2_07. mp3

The road is under construction. 도로가 공사 중이다.
There are several cones along the road.
원뿔 모양의 물체가 도로를 따라 있다.
A part of the road has been closed for construction. 도로의 일부가 공사로 폐쇄되었다.

STEP 2 음성을 들으면서 사진을 올바르게 묘사한 정답을 찾으세요.   P1_Ch2_08. mp3

2.
(A) (B) (C) (D)

3.
(A) (B) (C) (D)

4.
(A) (B) (C) (D)

5.
(A) (B) (C) (D)

Chapter 2. 사물 중심 사진   031

이것만 알면 700+

실전 문제 풀이 Tip 대공개! 이것만은 꼭 알아 두세요.

TIP 1 사물이 놓여 있는 모습을 묘사하는 다양한 표현

일반적으로 **사물이 놓여 있는 모습**은 '**사물 주어 + be placed**'로 표현할 수 있습니다. 뿐만 아니라 situated, located, stored, displayed, put, set도 모두 사물이 놓여 있는 모습을 묘사하는 표현입니다.

또한 놓여 있는 상태를 좀 더 구체적으로 묘사하는 표현들은 다음과 같습니다.

spread out 흩어져 있다　　　　stacked 쌓여 있다　　　　be filled 채워져 있다
lined up 길게 줄 서 있다　　　arranged 정리되어 있다

TIP 2 PART 1에서 출제되는 수동태 진행형

❶ **사람이 없는 사진에서 수동태 진행형은 오답이에요.**
수동태 진행형은 '**사물 주어 + be being p.p.**'의 형태로 **사람이 사물을 가지고 동작을 진행하고 있는 것**을 의미합니다. 따라서 일반적으로 **사람이 없는 사진에서 보기에 being이 들렸다면 바로 정답에서 제외**해야 합니다.

❷ **수동태 진행형이 정답이 되는 예외가 있어요.**
　① 진열된 상태나 배경을 나타낼 때:
　　　display, decorate, exhibit, cast, occupy 등의 동사
　　　Some shadows are being cast on a balcony. 발코니에 그림자가 드리워져 있다.
　　　The goods are being displayed(= being put on display). 상품들이 진열되어 있다.

　② 기계에 의해 자동적으로 진행되는 동작을 나타낼 때:
　　　move, transport, spray 등의 동사
　　　Luggage is being moved on the conveyor belt. 수하물이 컨베이어 벨트 위에서 옮겨지고 있다.

TIP 3 꼭 암기해야 할 PART 1 사물 배경 빈출 표현

P1_Ch2_09. mp3

- A stone structure is over the water.
  돌로 된 구조물이 물 위에 있다.
- A bridge is being reflected into a river.
  다리가 강에 비치고 있다.
- The footbridge extends across the water.
  다리가 물을 가로질러 나 있다.
- A bridge crosses over the water.
  다리가 물을 가로질러 나 있다.

- Cars line both sides of the street.
  자동차들이 도로 양옆에 줄지어 있다.
- Trees are planted along the road.
  나무들이 길을 따라 심어져 있다.
- Vehicles are parked facing the same direction.
  차량들이 같은 방향으로 주차되어 있다.
- There is no car traffic on the road.
  도로에 운행되는 차량이 없다.

- The seats are arranged in a semicircle.
  좌석이 반원형으로 배열되어 있다.
- The auditorium is empty.
  객석이 비어 있다.
- Seats are facing a stage.
  좌석이 무대를 향하고 있다.
- None of the seats are occupied.
  좌석이 비어 있다.

- Tables and chairs are arranged in rows.
  테이블과 의자들이 여러 줄로 정렬되어 있다.
- A seating area has been set up outside.
  야외에 앉을 수 있는 곳이 세팅되어 있다.
- Tables are being shaded by umbrellas.
  테이블들에 우산으로 그늘이 져 있다.
- There are some bushes along the stone wall.
  돌담을 따라 덤불이 나 있다.

Chapter Test

1.

2.

3.

4.

5.

6.

PART 2

다이렉트

700+

Chapter 1. 의문사 의문문 I

Chapter 2. 의문사 의문문 II

Chapter 3. 일반 의문문

Chapter 4. 기타 질문과 답변

이것만 알면 700+

PART 2 기본 문제 풀이 전략

전략 1 꼭 암기해야 할 15가지 출제 유형

의문사 유형	1. Who 의문문 4. Why 의문문	2. Where 의문문 5. How 의문문	3. When 의문문 6. What/Which 의문문
비의문사 유형	7. 간접 의문문 10. 권유/제안/요청 의문문	8. 조동사 의문문 11. 부가/부정 의문문	9. 선택 의문문
평서문 유형	12. 평서문		
고난이도 답변 유형	13. I don't know형 답변 14. 반문 답변 15. 우회/간접 상황 답변		

※ p.039 <꼭 암기해야 할 15가지 출제 유형> 참고

전략 2 5가지 오답 유형

❶ 의문사 질문에 Yes/No 답변
❷ 다른 의문사(의도)에 대한 답변
❸ 질문과 일치하지 않는 주어, 대명사
❹ 유사 발음, 동일 어휘, 연상 어휘
❺ 시제 불일치

PART 2는 이렇게 풀어야 해요.

출제 유형과 오답 유형을 충분히 숙지한 후에 각 질문이 나올 때 문장 전체를 듣지 말고 앞의 2~3단어를 통해 질문의 의도만 파악해야 합니다.

Step 1. **'15가지 출제 유형'**과 **'5가지 오답 유형'**을 충분히 숙지합니다.
Step 2. **질문의 의도**를 알 수 있는 **앞부분** 위주로 2~3단어를 받아씁니다.
Step 3. 보기를 들으면서 5가지 **오답 유형에 걸리는 보기는 X 표시**를 합니다.
Step 4. 하나씩 X로 **오답을 소거하면 남는 보기**가 정답입니다.

※ 받아쓰기를 할 때는 모든 문장을 받아쓰는 것이 아니라, 질문의 의도를 파악할 수 있는 앞쪽 2~3단어만 적어야 합니다.

<꼭 암기해야 할 15가지 출제 유형>

1. Who 의문문
(1) 사람이나 단체 이름, 직업, 직책, 회사명 등으로 대답합니다.
(2) Yes/No로 대답할 수 없습니다.
(3) you/we/I로 대답할 수 있습니다.
(4) he/she/they로 대답할 수 없습니다.
(5) someone/no one 등의 부정 대명사가 빈출 답변입니다.

2. Where 의문문
(1) 보통 장소 부사구(전치사+장소 명사)를 동반하여 '장소, 지점, 방향, 위치'를 제시하는 보기가 답이 됩니다.
(2) Yes/No로 대답할 수 없습니다.
(3) 시간 관련 오답이 문제당 하나씩 나옵니다.
(4) 정보의 출처, 출신으로 대답합니다.
(5) 문제의 모든 보기가 전치사로 시작되는 경우를 주의합니다.

3. When 의문문
(1) 주로 '시간, 시점'을 의미하는 부사구 표현으로 정답이 제시됩니다.
(2) Yes/No로 대답할 수 없습니다.
(3) 장소 관련 오답이 문제당 하나씩 나옵니다.
(4) after, when, as soon as와 같은 시간 부사절 접속사가 포함된 표현이 자주 출제됩니다.
(5) 시제에 특히 유의해야 합니다.
(6) When 의문문과 How long 의문문의 답변을 구별해야 합니다.

4. Why 의문문
(1) 원인이나 이유를 설명하는 보기가 가장 일반적인 정답이고, 최근에는 문제점 혹은 busy, another work, cancel 등이 포함된 보기가 주로 답이 됩니다.
(2) Yes/No로 대답할 수 없습니다.
(3) to부정사나 because, because of 등의 목적/이유 구문이 빈출 정답 패턴입니다.
(4) How come ~?, What made ~?로 이유를 물을 수 있습니다.

5. How 의문문
(1) Yes/No로 대답할 수 없습니다.
(2) 'How do/조동사 ~'는 방법이나 수단으로 대답합니다.
(3) 'How be ~ go'는 상태 형용사나 부사로 대답합니다.
(4) 'How+형용사/부사'의 다양한 의문사 표현을 숙지합니다.
(5) How의 구어체 표현을 연습해 둡니다.
 - How come ~?, How about ~?, How does ~ look? 등

6. What/Which 의문문	(1) Yes/No로 대답할 수 없습니다. (2) What은 뒤의 명사가 답을 결정합니다. (3) Which 의문문의 빈출 정답 표현을 알아 둡니다. 　- the one + 수식어구/비교급 　- both, either, neither 　- anything, whichever (4) What의 구어체 의문을 연습해 둡니다. 　- What about ~?, What made ~?, What is he like? 등
7. 간접 의문문	Do you know, Can you tell me, I wonder 등으로 시작하는 의문문은 뒤에 오는 의문사를 들어야 답을 판단할 수 있습니다.
8. 조동사 의문문	(1) '~인지, ~하는지' 등의 사실 여부를 확인하는 질문입니다. (2) 기본적으로 'Yes/No + 부연 설명'의 형태로 답변합니다. (3) 조동사 의문문은 끝까지 들어야 '선택/부가/부정' 의문문인지 알 수 있습니다.
9. 선택 의문문	(1) 선택 의문문의 빈출 정답 표현을 알아 둡니다. 　- the one + 수식어구/비교급 　- both, either, neither 　- anything, whichever 　- or 앞뒤의 선택 사항 중 하나를 택한 표현 (2) '단어 or 단어', '구 or 구' 질문에는 Yes/No로 대답할 수 없습니다. (3) '문장 or 문장' 질문은 빈출 표현을 암기해 둡니다.
10. 권유/제안/ 요청 의문문	(1) 권유/제안/요청 의문문 빈출 질문 표현을 알아 둡니다. 　- Why don't you ~? 　- How about ~? 　- What about ~? 　- Do you want ~? 　- Should we ~? 　- Let's ~. (2) 제안/요청 의문문에 대한 답변 패턴을 알아 둡니다. 　- 동의, 찬성, 허락, 승인: That's good/great/interesting 등 　- 거절, 부정: I am sorry/afraid 등

11. 부가/부정 의문문	(1) 부가 의문문의 핵심은 평서문의 뒷부분입니다. (2) 질문이 긍정이든 부정이든 상관 없이 답변 내용이 긍정이면 무조건 Yes, 부정이면 무조건 No로 대답합니다.

12. 평서문	(1) 기본 답변 패턴은 동의 또는 맞장구입니다.
	(2) 일반 평서문
	   - 다음 행동을 제시하는 답변을 합니다.
	   - 추가로 관련 질문을 하는 답변을 합니다.
	   - 추가로 설명을 하는 답변을 합니다.
	(3) 권유형 평서문의 표현을 정리합니다.
	(4) 명령형 평서문의 표현을 정리합니다.

13. I don't know 형 답변	(1) '모른다' 유형의 다양한 표현을 정리합니다.
	   - I don't know.
	   - I wish I knew.
	   - I'll check.
	   - Ask your supervisor.
	   - It's not decided yet.
	   - It depends.
	(2) I don't know ~가 길어지면 주의해야 합니다.
	   - Q. Who is he?
	     A. I don't know where he was.
	   → 이러한 오답 패턴도 출제되니 주의합니다.

14. 반문 답변	질문에 대한 직접적인 대답을 하지 않고, 그 질문과 관련된 추가 정보 등을 묻는 다른 질문으로 답합니다.
15. 우회/간접 상황 답변	질문에 대해 직접적으로 답변하기보다는 간접적으로 상황을 알 수 있는 형태로 답변하거나 우회적으로 돌려서 답변합니다. 비의문사 의문문의 경우 Yes/No를 생략하고 답변을 합니다.

Chapter 1 의문사 의문문 I

Point 01 행위의 주체에 대한 답변을 찾는 Who 의문문

Who 의문문은 사람 이름이나 직위, 부서, 회사 이름으로 답해요. 'Mr./Ms. +사람 이름', 'it is +사람 이름', 혹은 'I think/I believe +사람 이름' 등 '사람 이름'이 포함된 표현들이 빈출 정답입니다. 직위, 부서명, 회사 이름 등 사람을 지칭하거나 사람이 소속된 곳을 나타내는 명사들도 답이 될 수 있어요.

Q. **Who attended** the annual sales meeting?   P2_Ch1_01. mp3
누가 연례 영업 회의에 참석했나요?

(A) **Yes**, in the morning. → 의문사 의문문에는 Yes/No로 답할 수 없어요.
네, 오전에요.

(B) **Thomas** did. → 참석한 사람의 이름을 구체적으로 언급하고 있으므로 정답이에요.
토마스가 (참석)했어요.

(C) **This week.** → 언제인지를 묻는 When 의문문에 대한 답변이므로 오답이에요.
이번 주입니다.

출제 포인트 정리

❶ 특정 사람이나 단체(이름, 직업, 직책, 회사명 등)로 대답해요.   P2_Ch1_02. mp3

Q. Who requested the change? 누가 변경을 요청했나요?
A. David did yesterday. 어제 데이비드가 했어요.

❷ you, we, I로 대답할 수 있어요.   P2_Ch1_03. mp3

Q. Who can open the storage room? 창고의 문은 누가 열 수 있나요?
A. I have the key. 제가 열쇠를 가지고 있어요.

❸ someone, no one 등의 부정 대명사로 답변하는 정답 보기가 자주 출제돼요.   P2_Ch1_04. mp3

Q. Who is the new marketing director? 누가 새로운 마케팅 이사인가요?
A. Someone from Tokyo. 도쿄에서 온 사람이랍니다.

❹ 난데없이 he, she, they로 대답할 수 없어요.   P2_Ch1_05. mp3

Q. Who can help me review the expense report? 누가 경비 보고서를 검토하는 것을 도와줄 수 있을까요?
A. She was just hired. 그녀는 이제 막 입사했어요.

Check-up Test 700+를 위해 한 걸음 한 걸음

정답 및 해석 p.005

STEP 1 문제를 풀며 질문의 의도와 정답/오답 유형을 파악하세요.   P2_Ch1_06. 🎧mp3

(1) 음성을 들으면서 질문의 의도를 파악하고 정답을 찾아보세요.

1. (A)   (B)   (C)   2. (A)   (B)   (C)

(2) 음성을 다시 들으면서 빈칸을 채우고 정답/오답 유형을 확인하세요.

1. _____ is the new _____?
   (A) It's _____ _____.
   (B) _____ open an _____.
   (C) _____ the _____.

오답 유형 check
- ❶ 의문사 질문에 Yes/No 답변
- ❷ 다른 의문사(의도)에 대한 답변
- ❸ 질문과 일치하지 않는 주어, 대명사
- ❹ 유사 발음, 동일 어휘, 연상 어휘
- ❺ 시제 불일치

2. _____ _____ The Best Sales Representative Of The Year Award?
   (A) _____, I know that.
   (B) _____ from the Southern regional _____.
   (C) _____ the end of the _____.

STEP 2 음성을 들으면서 올바른 답변을 찾으세요.   P2_Ch1_07. 🎧mp3

3. (A)   (B)   (C)
4. (A)   (B)   (C)
5. (A)   (B)   (C)
6. (A)   (B)   (C)
7. (A)   (B)   (C)
8. (A)   (B)   (C)

Point 02 장소에 대한 답변을 찾는 Where 의문문

Where 의문문은 장소나 출처로 답해요. 행위가 일어나는 장소나 목적지, 사물의 위치, 특정 정보나 사물의 출처 등을 묻는 질문이기 때문에 보통 장소 전치사구가 포함된 장소, 위치, 출처, 방향 등의 답변이 정답이 됩니다.

Q. **Where can I buy** some vegetables?   P2_Ch1_08. 🎧mp3
어디에서 채소를 살 수 있을까요?

(A) Try **the store on Kings Street**.
→ 물건을 어디서 살 수 있는지 묻는 질문에 구매할 수 있는 장소로 가게를 언급하고 있는 정답이에요.
킹스 거리에 있는 가게에 가 보세요.

(B) ~~Yes~~, I took them yesterday. → *의문사 의문문은 Yes/No로 답할 수 없어요.*
네, 어제 제가 가져갔어요.

(C) About **10 dollars**. → *금액 답변은 How much 의문문의 답변이므로 오답이에요.*
대략 10달러요.

출제 포인트 정리 ✧

❶ **장소 명사와 함께 장소, 위치, 방향, 지점으로 대답해요.**   P2_Ch1_09. 🎧mp3
   Q. **Where** will the conference be held this year? 올해 콘퍼런스는 어디서 열리나요?
   A. **In Vancouver**, as usual. 평소와 같이 밴쿠버에서요.

❷ **정보의 출처, 출신으로 대답해요.**   P2_Ch1_10. 🎧mp3
   Q. **Where** did you hear that news? 그 소식 어디서 들었어요?
   A. **One of my friends** told me. 제 친구 중 한 명이 얘기해 줬어요.

❸ **When(시점)과 관련된 오답이 문제당 하나씩 나와요.**   P2_Ch1_11. 🎧mp3
   Q. **Where** can I get my employee ID card? 어디서 제 사원증을 받을 수 있을까요?
   A. ~~Right before~~ the presentation. 발표 직전에요.

Check-up Test 700+를 위해 한 걸음 한 걸음

정답 및 해석 p.006

STEP 1 문제를 풀며 질문의 의도와 정답/오답 유형을 파악하세요.   P2_Ch1_12. mp3

(1) 음성을 들으면서 질문의 의도를 파악하고 정답을 찾아보세요.

1. (A)　(B)　(C)　　　　2. (A)　(B)　(C)

(2) 음성을 다시 들으면서 빈칸을 채우고 정답/오답 유형을 확인하세요.

1. _____ does Ms. Hurt _____ economics?
   (A) _____ a _____ in London.
   (B) _____ is not _____.
   (C) On _____ mostly.

2. _____ is Anthony _____ this week?
   (A) _____ _____, I think.
   (B) _____ the _____ _____.
   (C) _____, last _____.

오답 유형 check
- ❶ 의문사 질문에 Yes/No 답변
- ❷ 다른 의문사(의도)에 대한 답변
- ❸ 질문과 일치하지 않는 주어, 대명사
- ❹ 유사 발음, 동일 어휘, 연상 어휘
- ❺ 시제 불일치

STEP 2 음성을 들으면서 올바른 답변을 찾으세요.   P2_Ch1_13. mp3

3. (A)　(B)　(C)
4. (A)　(B)　(C)
5. (A)　(B)　(C)
6. (A)　(B)　(C)
7. (A)　(B)　(C)
8. (A)　(B)　(C)

Point 03   시간에 대한 답변을 찾는 When 의문문

When 의문문은 행위나 사건이 일어나는 **시점을 묻는 질문**이기 때문에 **시간 명사나 시간 부사로 답해요.** 따라서 시간이나 날짜, 요일 관련 표현들뿐만 아니라 시점을 나타내는 다양한 표현들을 미리 익혀 두는 것이 좋습니다.

Q. **When was** the computer repaired?   P2_Ch1_14. 🎧
　언제 컴퓨터가 고쳐졌나요?

(A) **No**, I was not. → *의문사 의문문은 Yes/No로 답할 수 없어요.*
　아니요, 저는 아니었어요.

(B) It was **last Tuesday**. → *언제였는지를 묻는 질문에 지난 화요일이라고 구체적인 과거 시점으로 답하고 있으므로 정답이에요.*
　지난 화요일이었어요.

(C) **Four** copies, please. → *수량을 묻는 How many 의문문에 대한 답변이므로 오답이에요.*
　4부 부탁해요.

출제 포인트 정리 ✦

❶ **'시간, 시점'을 의미하는 시간 명사 표현으로 답변해요.**   P2_Ch1_15. 🎧
　Q. When will the store be open? 그 가게는 언제 문을 열 예정인가요?
　A. Not until September. 9월에요.

❷ **after, when과 같은 시간 부사절 접속사로 답변해요.**   P2_Ch1_16. 🎧
　Q. When are we leaving for the hotel? 우린 언제 호텔로 출발하나요?
　A. As soon as a taxi arrives. 택시가 도착하자마요.

❸ **기간을 의미하는 How long 의문문의 답변을 주의하세요.**   P2_Ch1_17. 🎧
　Q. When was the last time to see Mr. Park? 박 씨를 마지막으로 본 건 언제인가요?
　A. ~~For~~ two days. (X) 이틀 동안이요.
　A. Two days ago. (O) 이틀 전에요.

Check-up Test 700+를 위해 한 걸음 한 걸음

정답 및 해석 p.007

STEP 1 문제를 풀며 질문의 의도와 정답/오답 유형을 파악하세요.   P2_Ch1_18. mp3

(1) 음성을 들으면서 질문의 의도를 파악하고 정답을 찾아보세요.

1. (A)　(B)　(C)　　　　　2. (A)　(B)　(C)

(2) 음성을 다시 들으면서 빈칸을 채우고 정답/오답 유형을 확인하세요.

1. _____ does the new secretary _____ work?
   (A) She needs _____ and _____.
   (B) _____ the _____ _____.
   (C) Actually, she _____ _____ _____.

<u>오답 유형 check</u>
- ❶ 의문사 질문에 Yes/No 답변
- ❷ 다른 의문사(의도)에 대한 답변
- ❸ 질문과 일치하지 않는 주어, 대명사
- ❹ 유사 발음, 동일 어휘, 연상 어휘
- ❺ 시제 불일치

2. _____ will the merger _____ _____?
   (A) _____ the _____.
   (B) _____ _____ _____.
   (C) _____ ___, you are right.

STEP 2 음성을 들으면서 올바른 답변을 찾으세요.   P2_Ch1_19. mp3

3. (A)　(B)　(C)
4. (A)　(B)　(C)
5. (A)　(B)　(C)
6. (A)　(B)　(C)
7. (A)　(B)　(C)
8. (A)　(B)　(C)

이것만 알면 700+

실전 문제 풀이 Tip 대공개! 이것만은 꼭 알아 두세요.

TIP 1 Who 의문문 빈출 답변 유형

❶ 사람 이름, 직책, 직위	David did it yesterday. 어제 데이비드가 했어요. Our manager is. 우리 매니저가요.
❷ 부서, 회사명	The personnel department. 인사부입니다. GE engineering company. GE 엔지니어링 회사입니다.
❸ 가족, 동료, 친구 등	My co-worker. 제 동료가요. His aunt. 그의 이모가요.
❹ 사람을 대신하는 대명사	I can help him. 제가 그 사람을 도울 수 있습니다. Everyone's planning on it. 모두가 그것을 계획하고 있습니다. No one, for now. 지금까진 아무도 없습니다. Someone from the maintenance department. 관리부 직원이요.

TIP 2 Where 의문문 빈출 답변 유형

❶ 장소 부사구	In Room 3. 3호실이요. At a university in Ohio. 오하이오에 있는 대학에서요. To a ski resort. 스키 리조트로요. On the third floor. 3층에요. Right here. 바로 여기에요. There's a car repair shop nearby. 근처에 자동차 정비소가 있어요.
❷ 출처, 대상	Check the website. 웹사이트를 확인하세요. Try the company directory. 회사 주소록을 살펴보세요. She gave it to me. 그녀가 제게 줬어요. From our dealer. 우리 판매상으로부터요. In the newspaper. 신문에서요.

TIP 3 When 의문문 빈출 답변 유형

❶ 시간 부사구	At 8 o'clock. 8시에요. On Wednesday afternoon. 수요일 오후에요. In two days. 이틀 후에요. By the end of the month. 월말까지요. Just now. 지금요. Next Sunday. 다음 주 일요일이요. About two weeks ago. 2주쯤 전에요. Yesterday evening. 어제 저녁에요.
❷ 시간 부사절	As soon as I can. 가능한 한 빨리요. Before getting off from work today. 오늘 퇴근 전에요. When Ms. Tylor confirms it. 타일러 씨가 확인하면요. By the time the meeting is over. 회의가 끝날 때쯤이요. Right after I e-mailed him. 그에게 이메일을 보낸 직후에요. Before it expires. (기간이) 만료되기 전에요. Not until the bank opens. 은행이 문을 열면요.

Chapter Test

1. Mark your answer. (A) (B) (C)
2. Mark your answer. (A) (B) (C)
3. Mark your answer. (A) (B) (C)
4. Mark your answer. (A) (B) (C)
5. Mark your answer. (A) (B) (C)
6. Mark your answer. (A) (B) (C)
7. Mark your answer. (A) (B) (C)
8. Mark your answer. (A) (B) (C)
9. Mark your answer. (A) (B) (C)
10. Mark your answer. (A) (B) (C)
11. Mark your answer. (A) (B) (C)
12. Mark your answer. (A) (B) (C)
13. Mark your answer. (A) (B) (C)
14. Mark your answer. (A) (B) (C)
15. Mark your answer. (A) (B) (C)

Chapter 2 의문사 의문문 II

Point 01 무엇에 대한 답변을 찾는 What/Which 의문문

What/Which 의문문은 시간에서 구체적인 행위까지 다양한 내용을 물을 수 있는 의문문으로, 뒤에 나오는 명사/동사에 따라 구체적인 대상이나 행위로 답하기 때문에, 뒤에 나오는 명사/동사를 잘 들어야 합니다.

> Q. **What color** did you **paint** the walls? P2_Ch2_01. mp3
> 무슨 색으로 벽을 칠했어요?
>
> (A) We didn't **call her**. → color와 발음이 유사한 call her를 이용한 오답이에요.
> 우리는 그녀에게 전화하지 않았어요.
>
> (B) It went very **well**. → wall과 발음이 유사한 well을 이용한 오답으로, How 의문문에 어울리는 답변이에요.
> 아주 잘 진행되었어요.
>
> (C) I chose **blue**. → 무슨 색으로 벽을 칠했냐는 질문에 선택한 색을 알리고 있으므로 정답이에요.
> 파란색을 골랐어요.

출제 포인트 정리

❶ 'What + 명사(time/date/price)'의 형태는 명사를 잘 들어야 해요. P2_Ch2_02. mp3
Q. What time does the bus to Seoul leave? 서울로 가는 버스는 언제 떠나나요?
A. In an hour. 한 시간 후에요.
→ What 뒤에 나온 명사의 의미에 맞게 대답해요.

❷ 대상을 묻는 What 의문문에는 주로 단답형으로 답변해요. P2_Ch2_03. mp3
Q. What should I include in my application? 제 지원서에 무엇을 포함시켜야 하나요?
A. A copy of your certificates. 당신의 자격증 사본이요.

❸ 행위를 묻는 질문에는 주로 문장으로 답변해요. P2_Ch2_04. mp3
Q. What happened to your tablet computer? 당신의 태블릿 컴퓨터에 무슨 일 있었어요?
A. It was broken. 고장 났어요.

❹ Which 의문문은 선택 의문문과 같이 the one ~으로 답변할 수 있어요. P2_Ch2_05. mp3
Q. Which restaurant have you visited? 어느 식당을 가 보셨나요?
A. The one across from the pharmacy. 약국 건너편에 있는 곳이요.

❺ 상대방의 의견은 What do you think ~?로 물어요. P2_Ch2_06. mp3
Q. What did you think of Mr. Park's report? 박 씨의 보고서에 대해 어떻게 생각했어요?
A. It seems good. 좋은 것 같아요.

Check-up Test 700+를 위해 한 걸음 한 걸음

정답 및 해석 p.009

STEP 1 문제를 풀며 질문의 의도와 정답/오답 유형을 파악하세요.   P2_Ch2_07.

(1) 음성을 들으면서 질문의 의도를 파악하고 정답을 찾아보세요.

1. (A)   (B)   (C)   2. (A)   (B)   (C)

(2) 음성을 다시 들으면서 빈칸을 채우고 정답/오답 유형을 확인하세요.

1. What _____ do you need?
   (A) I don't _____ it.
   (B) _____ you want.
   (C) Probably a _____.

2. _____ was the _____ of the meeting?
   (A) In _____ 114.
   (B) International _____.
   (C) Half _____ _____.

오답 유형 check

- ☐ ❶ 의문사 질문에 Yes/No 답변
- ☐ ❷ 다른 의문사(의도)에 대한 답변
- ☐ ❸ 질문과 일치하지 않는 주어, 대명사
- ☐ ❹ 유사 발음, 동일 어휘, 연상 어휘
- ☐ ❺ 시제 불일치

STEP 2 음성을 들으면서 올바른 답변을 찾으세요.   P2_Ch2_08.

3. (A)   (B)   (C)
4. (A)   (B)   (C)
5. (A)   (B)   (C)
6. (A)   (B)   (C)
7. (A)   (B)   (C)
8. (A)   (B)   (C)

Point 02 | 방법/의견에 대한 답변을 찾는 How 의문문

How 의문문은 기본적으로 **수단이나 방법, 의견** 등을 묻는 질문이에요. 하지만 **How** 뒤에 **형용사/부사**가 나올 때는 해당 형용사나 부사에 따라 답변을 해야 합니다. 따라서 **뒤에 나오는 형용사/부사**를 잘 들어야 해요.

Q. **How long** did your job interview **take**?　　　　　　　　　　　P2_Ch2_09. 🎵mp3
　면접이 얼마나 오래 걸렸나요?

(A) A **sales position**. → *job interview에서 연상할 수 있는 오답이에요.*
　판매직입니다.

(B) Take **a couple** of them. → *How many 의문문에 대한 답변이므로 오답이에요.*
　두어 개 가져가세요.

(C) **Only half an hour**. → *30분이라는 소요 시간으로 답변하고 있으므로 정답이에요.*
　30분밖에 안 걸렸어요.

출제 포인트 정리 ✦

❶ **How 의문문은 수단이나 방법을 제시하면 답이에요.**　P2_Ch2_10. 🎵mp3
　Q. **How** can I get to the nearest post office? 가장 가까운 우체국은 어떻게 가나요?
　A. Just **turn left** at the intersection. 교차로에서 좌측으로 가세요.

❷ **How 의문사는 뒤에 나오는 형용사나 부사가 답을 결정해요.**　P2_Ch2_11. 🎵mp3
　Q. **How far** are we from the airport? 우리는 공항에서 얼마나 멀리 있나요?
　A. About **two miles**. 약 2마일이요. *<거리>*
　→ 뒤에 나온 형용사나 부사에 따라 기간, 횟수, 거리, 가격, 양, 수로 대답해야 해요.

❸ **상대의 의견을 묻거나 제안을 할 때도 쓸 수 있어요.**　P2_Ch2_12. 🎵mp3
　① 상대의 의견을 물을 때는 'How did/do you like ~?'로 질문해요.
　　Q. **How did you like** the guest speaker this time? 이번에 초청 연사는 어땠나요?
　　A. His speech was **excellent**. 그의 연설은 매우 좋았어요.

　② 'How about ~?'은 상대의 의견을 묻거나 제안할 때 쓰는 표현이며, 반문 답변으로 종종 출제돼요.
　　Q. **How about** meeting in your office tomorrow? 내일 당신의 사무실에서 만나는 건 어때요?
　　A. **Sounds good**. 좋아요.

Check-up Test 700+를 위해 한 걸음 한 걸음

정답 및 해석 p.010

STEP 1 문제를 풀며 질문의 의도와 정답/오답 유형을 파악하세요.

P2_Ch2_13.

(1) 음성을 들으면서 질문의 의도를 파악하고 정답을 찾아보세요.

1. (A)　(B)　(C)　　　　2. (A)　(B)　(C)

(2) 음성을 다시 들으면서 빈칸을 채우고 정답/오답 유형을 확인하세요.

1. _____ _____ are the airplane tickets?
   (A) _____, we should go.
   (B) It's _____ _____ long.
   (C) They are over five hundred _____ each.

<u>오답 유형 check</u>
- ❶ 의문사 질문에 Yes/No 답변
- ❷ 다른 의문사(의도)에 대한 답변
- ❸ 질문과 일치하지 않는 주어, 대명사
- ❹ 유사 발음, 동일 어휘, 연상 어휘
- ❺ 시제 불일치

2. _____ did you _____ about an opening at our company?
   (A) We close every other _____.
   (B) _____ _____ the website.
   (C) Our new _____ is in the other _____.

STEP 2 음성을 들으면서 올바른 답변을 찾으세요.

P2_Ch2_14.

3. (A)　(B)　(C)
4. (A)　(B)　(C)
5. (A)　(B)　(C)
6. (A)　(B)　(C)
7. (A)　(B)　(C)
8. (A)　(B)　(C)

Point 03 이유/목적에 대한 답변을 찾는 Why 의문문

Why 의문문은 이유나 목적을 묻는 질문입니다. 따라서 주로 **이유로 답하고 변명(부정적)이나 문제점**으로 답하기도 해요.

Q. **Why** did you **call** customer service? P2_Ch2_15. 🎧mp3
왜 고객 서비스 센터에 전화했습니까?

(A) **Because** my refrigerator is broken.
　→ 전화를 한 이유에 대해서 이유의 접속사 because를 사용하여 직접적으로 설명하고 있으므로 정답이에요.
　냉장고가 고장 나서요.

(B) At **9:30**. → 시간을 묻는 When 의문문에 어울리는 답변이에요.
　9시 30분에요.

(C) **Peter** will do it. → 사람을 묻는 Who 의문문에 어울리는 답변이에요.
　피터가 할 것입니다.

출제 포인트 정리 ✨

❶ **이유나 원인을 설명하는 전치사나 접속사로 답변해요.** P2_Ch2_16. 🎧mp3

Q. Why did the director cancel the meeting? 이사님은 왜 회의를 취소하셨나요?
A. **Because** her train was delayed. 왜냐하면 그녀의 기차가 연착되었어요.

❷ **목적에 대한 답변을 할 때는 to부정사나 전치사 for를 자주 써요.** P2_Ch2_17. 🎧mp3

Q. Why did you come to work early today? 오늘 왜 이렇게 빨리 출근했어요?
A. **To avoid** the heavy traffic. 교통 체증을 피하려고요.

❸ **이유나 원인에 대해 변명이나 설명을 해요.** P2_Ch2_18. 🎧mp3

Q. Why isn't the marketing plan finished yet? 왜 아직 마케팅 계획이 끝나지 않았나요?
A. Mr. Kim was away last week. 지난주에 김 씨가 자리에 없었어요.

❹ **Why 의문문에서 꼭 알아 두어야 할 2가지!** P2_Ch2_19. 🎧mp3

① **Why don't you/we/I ~?는 상대에게 제안할 때 쓰는 표현이에요.**

　Q. **Why don't you** bring an umbrella with you? 우산을 챙기는 게 어때요?
　A. Thanks, I will. 고마워요. 그렇게 할게요.

② **What을 이용해서 이유나 원인을 묻기도 해요.**

　Q. **What is causing** all the noise? 왜 이렇게 소음이 나죠?
　A. There is some road construction. 도로 공사가 있어요.

Check-up Test 700+를 위해 한 걸음 한 걸음

정답 및 해석 p.010

STEP 1 문제를 풀며 질문의 의도와 정답/오답 유형을 파악하세요.

P2_Ch2_20. mp3

(1) 음성을 들으면서 질문의 의도를 파악하고 정답을 찾아보세요.

1. (A)   (B)   (C)   2. (A)   (B)   (C)

(2) 음성을 다시 들으면서 빈칸을 채우고 정답/오답 유형을 확인하세요.

1. _____ are you _____ to Perth?
   (A) _____ a new job.
   (B) _____, in _____ _____.
   (C) A long _____.

오답 유형 check
- ❶ 의문사 질문에 Yes/No 답변
- ❷ 다른 의문사(의도)에 대한 답변
- ❸ 질문과 일치하지 않는 주어, 대명사
- ❹ 유사 발음, 동일 어휘, 연상 어휘
- ❺ 시제 불일치

2. _____ did you _____ a new table?
   (A) I loaded _____ the _____.
   (B) The old one was _____.
   (C) Are there new __ _____?

STEP 2 음성을 들으면서 올바른 답변을 찾으세요.

P2_Ch2_21. mp3

3. (A)   (B)   (C)
4. (A)   (B)   (C)
5. (A)   (B)   (C)
6. (A)   (B)   (C)
7. (A)   (B)   (C)
8. (A)   (B)   (C)

Chapter 2. 의문사 의문문 II

이것만 알면 700+

실전 문제 풀이 Tip 대공개! 이것만은 꼭 알아 두세요.

TIP 1 다양한 형태의 What 의문문 구어체 표현

❶ **What about ~?** (권유, 제안의 질문)
What about eating out tonight? 오늘 밤에 외식 어때요?

❷ **What do you think ~? / What would/do you say ~?** (의견을 묻는 질문)
What do you think about the new research assistant? 새로 온 연구 보조원은 어떤가요?

❸ **What happened ~? / What's going on ~?** (일의 발생 또는 진행 상황을 묻는 질문)
What happened with the meeting? 회의는 어떻게 됐어요?

❹ **What + make/take/bring ~?** (일의 원인, 이유를 묻는 질문)
What made you come in so early today? 오늘 왜 이렇게 일찍 출근했어요?

❺ **What will/did you do with ~?** (일의 처리를 묻는 질문)
What will you do with the old computer? 예전 컴퓨터는 어떻게 할 거예요?

❻ **What ~ like?** (상태를 묻는 질문: 성격, 기호, 외모 등)
What is the new director like? 새로운 관리자는 어떤가요?
What does he look like? 그는 어떻게 생겼나요?

TIP 2 <How + 형용사/부사> 형태의 빈출 질문 유형

❶ **How many?** (숫자) → Three of each. 3개씩이요.
❷ **How much?** (금액) → Ten dollars each. 각 10달러요.
❸ **How often?** (빈도) → Once a month. 한 달에 한 번이요.
❹ **How long?** (소요 시간) → About six years, I guess. 6년 정도요.
❺ **How far?** (거리) → Only 3 minutes away on foot. 걸어서 3분밖에 안 걸려요.
❻ **How soon/late?** (시점) → Tomorrow afternoon. 내일 오후예요.

TIP 3 Why 의문문 빈출 답변 유형

❶ 이유/원인 (~ 때문에)	For an interview. 인터뷰 때문에요. Because of repair work. 수리 작업 때문에요. Due to the bad weather. 기상 악화 때문에요.
❷ 목적 (~하기 위해)	In order to meet the deadline. 마감 기한을 맞추기 위해서요. To clean up the room. 방을 청소하기 위해서요. So I can confirm the appointment. 약속을 확인하기 위해서입니다.
❸ 이유/변명	I was too busy. 너무 바빴어요. I forgot. 잊어버렸어요. I was going to ~. ~하려고 했어요. I thought ~. ~라고 생각했어요. I had to attend a meeting. 회의에 참석해야 했어요. He is stuck in traffic. 그는 차가 막혀 꼼짝도 못하고 있습니다.

Chapter Test

1. Mark your answer. (A) (B) (C)
2. Mark your answer. (A) (B) (C)
3. Mark your answer. (A) (B) (C)
4. Mark your answer. (A) (B) (C)
5. Mark your answer. (A) (B) (C)
6. Mark your answer. (A) (B) (C)
7. Mark your answer. (A) (B) (C)
8. Mark your answer. (A) (B) (C)
9. Mark your answer. (A) (B) (C)
10. Mark your answer. (A) (B) (C)
11. Mark your answer. (A) (B) (C)
12. Mark your answer. (A) (B) (C)
13. Mark your answer. (A) (B) (C)
14. Mark your answer. (A) (B) (C)
15. Mark your answer. (A) (B) (C)

Chapter 3 일반 의문문

Point 01 Yes/No로 답하는 일반 의문문

일반 의문문은 동사를 듣는 게 중요해요. 일반 의문문에는 **be동사 의문문, do/have/조동사 의문문**이 있으며, 사실을 확인하거나 상대의 의견을 묻는 질문입니다. 보통 **Yes/No로 대답하며, 부연 설명을 덧붙여요**. 또한, 대답의 내용이 Yes/No를 포함하고 있으면 Yes/No 없이도 대답할 수 있어요.

Q. Does the price include tax?   P2_Ch3_01. mp3
가격에 세금이 포함되어 있나요?

(A) **No, you have to pay extra.**
→ 포함되어 있지 않다는 의미의 No로 답하고, 뒤에 추가 금액을 내야 한다고 설명하고 있으므로 정답이에요.
아니요, 추가로 부담하셔야 합니다.

(B) I need a **taxi**. → tax와 유사한 발음인 taxi를 이용한 오답이에요.
저는 택시가 필요해요.

(C) It is too **expensive**. → price에서 연상할 수 있는 expensive를 이용한 오답이에요.
너무 비싸요.

출제 포인트 정리 ❖

❶ 질문의 동사에 대해 '네(Yes)/아니요(No)'라고 말하고 부연 설명을 해요.   P2_Ch3_02. mp3

Q. Are you going to be at the office this afternoon? 오늘 오후에 사무실에 계실 건가요?

A. No, I have a meeting with a client. 아니요, 저는 고객과 회의가 있어요.

→ 사무실에 있을 것인지 묻는 질문이므로 Yes(있을 것이다)/No(없을 것이다)로 대답해요.

❷ Yes/No를 생략하고 설명이나 이유/대안으로 답변해요.   P2_Ch3_03. mp3

Q. Do we have the printing paper in stock? 저희 출력 용지 재고가 있나요?

A. I can order it for you. 제가 주문해 드릴게요.

→ No(없다)라고 답변하진 않았지만 주문해 주겠다고 말하는 것은 No(없다)의 의미를 내포한 답변이에요.

❸ 중간에 의문사를 넣는 간접 의문문도 Yes/No 답변이 가능해요.   P2_Ch3_04. mp3

① 간접 의문문은 문장 중간에 나오는 의문사에 맞춰 대답해야 해요.

Q. Do you know why the marketing plan isn't finished yet? 왜 아직 마케팅 계획이 끝나지 않았는지 아시나요?

A. Mr. Kim was away last week. 지난주에 김 씨가 자리에 없었어요.

② 의문사가 있어도 간접 의문문은 Yes/No로 답변이 가능해요.

Q. Have you decided which design to buy? 어떤 디자인으로 구입할지 결정했어요?

A. Yes, that one seems very nice. 네, 저것이 매우 좋아 보입니다.

Check-up Test 700+를 위해 한 걸음 한 걸음

정답 및 해석 p.012

STEP 1 문제를 풀며 질문의 의도와 정답/오답 유형을 파악하세요. P2_Ch3_05. mp3

(1) 음성을 들으면서 질문의 의도를 파악하고 정답을 찾아보세요.

1. (A) (B) (C)   2. (A) (B) (C)

(2) 음성을 다시 들으면서 빈칸을 채우고 정답/오답 유형을 확인하세요.

1. Have you _____ writing your _____?
   (A) She _____ to him.
   (B) _____, I've been too _____.
   (C) That's good _____.

2. Is the new laser _____ _____ to use?
   (A) I need to _____ the manual _____.
   (B) Two _____ long.
   (C) From the new _____ _____.

오답 유형 check

- ❶ 의문사 질문에 Yes/No 답변
- ❷ 다른 의문사(의도)에 대한 답변
- ❸ 질문과 일치하지 않는 주어, 대명사
- ❹ 유사 발음, 동일 어휘, 연상 어휘
- ❺ 시제 불일치

STEP 2 음성을 들으면서 올바른 답변을 찾으세요. P2_Ch3_06. mp3

3. (A) (B) (C)
4. (A) (B) (C)
5. (A) (B) (C)
6. (A) (B) (C)
7. (A) (B) (C)
8. (A) (B) (C)

Point 02   선택의 응답을 요구하는 선택 의문문

선택 의문문은 **A or B**가 포함된 질문으로, 선택 사항 중에서 무엇을 선택할지 묻는 질문이에요. 따라서 **질문에 제시된 선택 사항 중 하나를 선택하여 답해요.** 또는 둘 다 선택하거나, 둘 다 선택하지 않거나, 제3의 선택을 할 수도 있어요.

> **Q. Can I expect** your e-mail **today or tomorrow**?   P2_Ch3_07. 🎧mp3🎧
> 이메일을 오늘 받을 수 있나요, 아니면 내일 받나요?
>
> (A) By **airmail**, please.
> → e-mail과 발음이 유사한 airmail을 이용한 오답으로 수단이나 방법을 묻는 How 의문문에 대한 답변이에요.
> 항공우편으로 부탁드려요.
>
> (B) By the end of **today**. → today와 tomorrow 중에 today를 선택한 답변이므로 정답이에요.
> 오늘 안으로요.
>
> (C) **Yes**, I can. → 선택 의문문은 Yes/No로 답변할 수 없으므로 오답이에요.
> 네, 제가 할 수 있어요.

출제 포인트 정리 ✦

❶ A or B의 선택 사항 중에 하나로 대답해요.   P2_Ch3_08. 🎧mp3🎧

     Q. Would you like some **coffee or tea**? 커피를 드시겠어요, 아니면 차를 드시겠어요?
     A. **Coffee** would be better. 커피가 더 좋아요.

❷ 'the one'을 이용해서 답변하는 경우가 많아요.   P2_Ch3_09. 🎧mp3🎧

     Q. Do you want to see the **monthly report** or the **yearly one**?
     월별 보고서를 보고 싶으신가요, 아니면 연도별 보고서를 보고 싶으신가요?
     A. **The one** for the whole fiscal year. 전체 회계 연도를 볼 수 있는 것이요.

❸ both/either/neither를 이용해 둘 다 좋거나 싫다고 답할 수 있어요.   P2_Ch3_10. 🎧mp3🎧

     Q. Should we take the **train or a taxi** to the airport?
     공항까지 기차를 타고 갈까요, 아니면 택시를 타고 갈까요?
     A. **Both** are fine with me. 저는 둘 다 괜찮아요.

❹ A나 B를 선택하는 게 아니라 제3의 답변인 C로 답할 수 있어요.   P2_Ch3_11. 🎧mp3🎧

     Q. Are you buying a laptop with a **bigger screen** or **a faster processor**?
     화면이 더 큰 노트북 컴퓨터를 구매할 건가요, 아니면 프로세서가 빠른 걸 구매할 건가요?
     A. I prefer a better sound quality. 음질이 더 좋은 걸 선호합니다.

❺ '문장 or 문장' 형태의 선택 의문문은 Yes/No 답변이 가능해요.   P2_Ch3_12. 🎧mp3🎧

     Q. Could you take a look at this design now, or are you too busy?
     지금 이 디자인을 봐 주실 수 있어요, 아니면 바쁘신가요?
     A. **No**, I'm available right now. 아니요, 지금 볼 수 있어요.

Check-up Test 700+를 위해 한 걸음 한 걸음

정답 및 해석 p.013

STEP 1 문제를 풀며 질문의 의도와 정답/오답 유형을 파악하세요.   P2_Ch3_13. mp3

(1) 음성을 들으면서 질문의 의도를 파악하고 정답을 찾아보세요.

1. (A)　(B)　(C)　　　　　2. (A)　(B)　(C)

(2) 음성을 다시 들으면서 빈칸을 채우고 정답/오답 유형을 확인하세요.

1. Is it better to buy a book _____ or _____ a _____?
   (A) It will be more _____.
   (B) _____, _____ didn't buy it.
   (C) Probably _____ a _____.

오답 유형 check
- ❶ 의문사 질문에 Yes/No 답변
- ❷ 다른 의문사(의도)에 대한 답변
- ❸ 질문과 일치하지 않는 주어, 대명사
- ❹ 유사 발음, 동일 어휘, 연상 어휘
- ❺ 시제 불일치

2. Would you like to eat _____ or _____ the _____?
   (A) It doesn't _____.
   (B) _____, that's not _____ _____.
   (C) _____ _____, thanks.

STEP 2 음성을 들으면서 올바른 답변을 찾으세요.   P2_Ch3_14. mp3

3. (A)　(B)　(C)
4. (A)　(B)　(C)
5. (A)　(B)　(C)
6. (A)　(B)　(C)
7. (A)　(B)　(C)
8. (A)　(B)　(C)

Chapter 3. 일반 의문문

Point 03　사실 확인을 요구하는 부가 의문문과 부정 의문문

부가 의문문은 평서문 뒤에 '그렇죠?, 안 그런가요?' 등의 질문을 붙여 사실을 확인하는 질문이고, **부정 의문문**은 일반 의문문에 부정어 not을 붙여 사실을 확인하는 질문입니다. 기본적으로 **긍정이면 Yes, 부정이면 No라고 답변하고**, 질문에 맞는 부연 설명을 덧붙여요. 또한, 대답의 내용이 Yes/No를 포함하고 있으면 Yes/No 없이도 대답할 수 있어요.

> **Q.** Don't you work the late shift?　　　　　　　　　　　P2_Ch3_15. mp3
> 　　당신은 야간 교대 근무를 하지 않나요?
>
> **(A)** You must go. → 늦게까지 근무(late shift)를 한다는 의미에서 연상할 수 있는 오답이에요.
> 　　당신이 가야 합니다.
>
> **(B)** Another shipment. → shift와 유사한 발음인 shipment를 이용한 오답이에요.
> 　　다른 선적입니다.
>
> **(C)** **No,** not any more. → 근무를 하지 않는다는 No 답변 뒤에 부연 설명을 하고 있으므로 정답이에요.
> 　　아니요, 더 이상은 하지 않습니다.

출제 포인트 정리 ✤

❶ **부정 의문문에서 처음 나오는 not(n't)은 신경 쓰지 마세요.**　P2_Ch3_16. mp3

　① **not(n't)과 상관없이 동사의 행위/상태에 따라 Yes/No로 답변해요.**

　　Q. Didn't you enjoy the discussion? 토론을 즐기지 않으셨나요?
　　A. Yes, it was very interesting. 네, 매우 재미있었습니다.
　　→ 토론을 즐겼는지(enjoy) 묻는 질문이므로 Yes(즐겼다)/No(즐기지 않았다)로 대답해요.

　② **Yes/No를 생략하고 답변할 수 있어요.**

　　Q. Hasn't the pamphlet already been finished? 팸플릿은 이미 끝내지 않았나요?
　　A. It will be ready soon. 곧 준비될 겁니다.
　　→ 곧(soon) 준비된다는 것은 No(끝내지 않았다)의 의미를 내포한 답변이에요.

❷ **부가 의문문은 문장 끝에 right?/isn't it?/do you? 등을 붙여요.**　P2_Ch3_17. mp3

　① **긍정이면 Yes, 부정이면 No라고 답변하고 부연 설명을 해요.**

　　Q. You've been to Australia before, haven't you? 호주에 가 본 적이 있으시죠, 그렇지 않나요?
　　A. Yes, it was great. 네, 멋졌습니다.

　② **Yes/No를 생략하고 답변할 수 있어요.**

　　Q. The Summer Jazz Festival was canceled, wasn't it? 여름 재즈 페스티벌은 취소되었죠, 그렇지 않나요?
　　A. It was, unfortunately. 취소되었어요, 아쉽게도요.

Check-up Test 700+를 위해 한 걸음 한 걸음

정답 및 해석 p.014

STEP 1 문제를 풀며 질문의 의도와 정답/오답 유형을 파악하세요.   P2_Ch3_18. mp3

(1) 음성을 들으면서 질문의 의도를 파악하고 정답을 찾아보세요.

1. (A)   (B)   (C)   2. (A)   (B)   (C)

(2) 음성을 다시 들으면서 빈칸을 채우고 정답/오답 유형을 확인하세요.

1. Isn't this the _____ _____?
   (A) _____, it is.
   (B) _____ was not _____.
   (C) I am _____ for a _____ company.

2. You don't _____ this _____, do you?
   (A) I have _____ _____.
   (B) That work ____ ____ to be done _____.
   (C) Maybe some new _____.

오답 유형 check
- ❶ 의문사 질문에 Yes/No 답변
- ❷ 다른 의문사(의도)에 대한 답변
- ❸ 질문과 일치하지 않는 주어, 대명사
- ❹ 유사 발음, 동일 어휘, 연상 어휘
- ❺ 시제 불일치

STEP 2 음성을 들으면서 올바른 답변을 찾으세요.   P2_Ch3_19. mp3

3. (A)   (B)   (C)
4. (A)   (B)   (C)
5. (A)   (B)   (C)
6. (A)   (B)   (C)
7. (A)   (B)   (C)
8. (A)   (B)   (C)

Chapter 3. 일반 의문문

이것만 알면 700+

실전 문제 풀이 Tip 대공개! 이것만은 꼭 알아 두세요.

TIP 1 일반 의문문은 조동사의 의미를 알아야 쉬워요.

❶ be/do	<사실 여부> 주로 사실, 행위, 상태의 여부를 묻는 질문이에요. Are there any rooms available for a meeting? 회의할 수 있는 방이 있나요?
❷ have/has	<경험/완료> 주로 경험이나 일의 완료 여부를 묻는 질문이에요. Have you read the reviews for that model? 그 모델에 대한 리뷰를 읽어 보셨어요? Have the sample products come in yet? 샘플 제품은 도착했어요?
❸ will	<의지/미래> 주어의 의지를 묻거나 미래의 행위나 상태를 묻는 질문이에요. Will you contact the client in New York? 뉴욕에 있는 고객에게 연락하시겠어요?
❹ should	<의견/확인> 상대의 의견을 묻거나 확인을 구할 때 자주 쓰여요. Should I open the window? 창문을 열까요?
❺ can/could	<요청/부탁> 상대에게 요청을 하거나 부탁할 때 주로 쓰여요. Could you help me finish this report? 제가 이 보고서를 끝내는 것을 도와주시겠어요? 주의 Do/Would you mind reviewing this presentation for me? 저를 위해 이 프레젠테이션을 검토해 주시겠어요?
❻ would	<권유/제안> 상대에게 권유를 하거나 제안할 때 자주 쓰여요. Would you like something to drink? 마실 것 좀 드릴까요? Would you like me to call you a taxi? 택시를 불러 드릴까요?

※ 요청/부탁, 권유/제안의 의문문은 Chapter 4에서 좀 더 자세히 다룰 예정입니다.

TIP 2 질문의 not과는 상관없이 긍정이면 Yes, 부정이면 No로 답변해야 해요.

부정 의문문을 우리말로 해석하면, '~ 안 했어요?'라는 의미입니다. 우리말에서는 '~ 안 했어요?'라고 부정의 의미를 넣어서 질문했을 때, '했다'는 말을 하려면 '아니요(No), 했어요(I did)'라고 말하는데 영어에서는 'No, I did.'라고 답변하지 않습니다.

영어의 부정 의문문에서 not은 '아니다'라는 부정의 의미가 아니라 자신의 의견을 강조하기 위한 것이며, 부정 의문문도 일반 의문문처럼 사실 여부를 확인하는 질문입니다. 따라서 영어에서 부정 의문문으로 물을 경우, 동사에 대한 답변이 긍정이면 'Yes, I did.', 부정이면 'No, I didn't.'로 답한다는 사실에 주의하세요.

Q. Didn't you bring an umbrella? 우산을 가져오지 않았나요?
A. Yes, it's in the car. 네, 차에 있어요.
→ 우산을 가져왔는지 아닌지 여부를 확인하는 부정 의문문에 Yes(긍정)로 답변하고, 차에 있다고 보충 설명을 덧붙였습니다.

Chapter Test P2_Ch3_20. mp3

1. Mark your answer. (A) (B) (C)
2. Mark your answer. (A) (B) (C)
3. Mark your answer. (A) (B) (C)
4. Mark your answer. (A) (B) (C)
5. Mark your answer. (A) (B) (C)
6. Mark your answer. (A) (B) (C)
7. Mark your answer. (A) (B) (C)
8. Mark your answer. (A) (B) (C)
9. Mark your answer. (A) (B) (C)
10. Mark your answer. (A) (B) (C)
11. Mark your answer. (A) (B) (C)
12. Mark your answer. (A) (B) (C)
13. Mark your answer. (A) (B) (C)
14. Mark your answer. (A) (B) (C)
15. Mark your answer. (A) (B) (C)

Chapter 4 기타 질문과 답변

Point 01 동의 및 거절의 응답을 요구하는 제안/요청문

권유/제안문과 요청/부탁문은 주로 일반 의문문으로 출제되지만 평서문의 형태로도 질문이 가능합니다. **권유/제안, 요청/부탁의 내용에 대해 수락이나 거절의 답변을 합니다.**

> Q. **Would you like to** join us for the party? P2_Ch4_01. mp3
> 우리와 파티에 함께 **가실래요**?
>
> (A) **That sounds good.** → 파티에 함께 가자는 상대방의 제안에 흔쾌히 가겠다고 답변하고 있으므로 정답이에요.
> 좋습니다.
>
> (B) Yes, it's ~~him~~. → Yes는 동의의 의미를 가지지만, 뒤에 나온 him은 질문에 언급되지 않았으므로 오답이에요.
> 네, 그 사람입니다.
>
> (C) You're ~~welcome~~. → 상대방이 감사의 인사를 했을 때 "괜찮아요.", "천만에요." 라고 말하는 답변이므로 오답이에요.
> 천만에요.

출제 포인트 정리

❶ **수락할 때는 Yes나 Sure, Thanks, Okay 등과 같은 표현을 써요.** P2_Ch4_02. mp3
   Q. Could you help me set up the tables and chairs? 테이블과 의자 설치하는 것을 도와주실 수 있으세요?
   A. Sure, I'd be happy to. 물론이죠, 기꺼이 해 드릴게요.

❷ **거절할 때는 No, Sorry 등과 함께 거절하는 이유를 언급해요.** P2_Ch4_03. mp3
   Q. Would you like me to bring some coffee? 커피를 가져다 드릴까요?
   A. No, thanks. I have mine. 아니요, 괜찮습니다. 제 것이 있습니다.

❸ **수락이나 거절로 답하는 것이 아니라 '이미 했다'고 답할 수 있어요.** P2_Ch4_04. mp3
   Q. Can you please turn off the heater when you leave? 나올 때 히터를 꺼 주시겠어요?
   A. It's already been turned off. 이미 꺼져 있어요.

❹ **평서문으로 제안이나 요청을 할 수 있어요.** P2_Ch4_05. mp3
   ① 상대에게 권유하거나 제안할 때는 **Let's ~나 I can do ~**라고 해요.
      Q. Let's meet at gate number 5. 5번 게이트에서 봅시다.
      A. OK, I'll see you there. 네, 거기서 뵐게요.

   ② 요청이나 부탁을 할 때는 주로 **Please ~나 I'd like to ~, I need ~**로 말해요.
      Q. Please show your identification as you enter the building. 건물에 들어올 때 신분증을 보여 주세요.
      A. Sorry, I left it in my car. 죄송해요, 제 차에 두고 왔어요.

Check-up Test 700+를 위해 한 걸음 한 걸음

정답 및 해석 p.016

STEP 1 문제를 풀며 질문의 의도와 정답/오답 유형을 파악하세요.   P2_Ch4_06. mp3

(1) 음성을 들으면서 질문의 의도를 파악하고 정답을 찾아보세요.

1. (A)　(B)　(C)　　　　2. (A)　(B)　(C)

(2) 음성을 다시 들으면서 빈칸을 채우고 정답/오답 유형을 확인하세요.

1. _____ you like me to _____ your luggage?
   (A) I really _____ it.
   (B) Is it your _____?
   (C) _____ _____. I can handle it.

오답 유형 check
- ① 의문사 질문에 Yes/No 답변
- ② 다른 의문사(의도)에 대한 답변
- ③ 질문과 일치하지 않는 주어, 대명사
- ④ 유사 발음, 동일 어휘, 연상 어휘
- ⑤ 시제 불일치

2. _____ I _____ your manual?
   (A) I think _____ can _____ me.
   (B) No, _____ __ _____ it by himself.
   (C) _____, _____ in my top drawer.

STEP 2 음성을 들으면서 올바른 답변을 찾으세요.   P2_Ch4_07.

3. (A)　(B)　(C)
4. (A)　(B)　(C)
5. (A)　(B)　(C)
6. (A)　(B)　(C)
7. (A)　(B)　(C)
8. (A)　(B)　(C)

Point 02 동의, 맞장구 및 부연 설명을 요구하는 평서문

평서문은 의문사 없이 어떤 사실을 말하는 문장이에요. 따라서 언급한 사실에 대해 **동의나 맞장구**하는 답변이 주로 정답으로 제시돼요. 또한, 다음 행동을 제시하거나 추가 질문 하는 답변도 가능해요.

> Q. Your apartment is conveniently located. P2_Ch4_08. mp3
> 당신의 아파트는 편리한 곳에 위치하고 있군요.
>
> (A) No, **she** needs to move. → 질문에 언급되지 않은 she가 등장했으므로 오답이에요.
>   아니에요, 그녀는 이사 가야 해요.
>
> (B) **At** the convenience **store**. → '전치사(at)+장소 명사'는 Where 의문문에 대한 답변이에요.
>   편의점에서요.
>
> (C) Yes, it only takes 5 minutes to get to work.
>   → 편리한 곳에 위치했다는 말에 동의하고 직장까지 얼마 걸리지 않는다고 부연 설명을 하고 있으므로 정답이에요.
>   네, 출근하는 데 5분밖에 걸리지 않아요.

출제 포인트 정리 ✨

❶ 평서문에서 자주 출제되는 5가지 내용과 4가지 답변이 있어요. P2_Ch4_09. mp3

평서문	답변
① 문제 상황 ② 감정/의견 ③ 권유/제안/요청/부탁 ④ 사실/상황 ⑤ 조언/지시	① 동의/맞장구 ② 대안 제시 ③ 다음 행동 제시 ④ 반문(관련 추가 질문)

① 문제 상황 ⇨ 대안 제시

  Q. The door to the meeting room is broken. 회의실 문이 고장 났어요.
  A. I'll call the maintenance department. 제가 관리부에 전화할게요.

② 감정/의견 ⇨ 동의/맞장구

  Q. I prefer buying my shirts in the store. 저는 그 가게에서 셔츠를 사는 것을 선호해요.
  A. Me, too. 저도요.

③ 권유/제안/요청/부탁 ⇨ 반문(관련 추가 질문)

  Q. I'd like to see last year's sales figures. 작년 매출 수치를 보고 싶습니다.
  A. Would you like me to print you a copy? 한 부 인쇄해 드릴까요?

④ 사실/상황 ⇨ 동의/맞장구

  Q. There is a special event at the community center. 주민 센터에서 특별한 행사가 있어요.
  A. Yes, I read an article about it. 네, 그것에 관한 기사를 읽었어요.

⑤ 조언/지시 ⇨ 동의/맞장구

  Q. We should tell Bill when we expect to arrive. 우리가 언제쯤 도착하는지 빌에게 알려야 합니다.
  A. Okay, I'll call him now. 좋습니다. 지금 그에게 전화하겠습니다.

Check-up Test 700+를 위해 한 걸음 한 걸음

정답 및 해석 p.017

STEP 1 문제를 풀며 질문의 의도와 정답/오답 유형을 파악하세요.

P2_Ch4_10. 🎧mp3

(1) 음성을 들으면서 질문의 의도를 파악하고 정답을 찾아보세요.

1. (A)　(B)　(C)　　　　2. (A)　(B)　(C)

(2) 음성을 다시 들으면서 빈칸을 채우고 정답/오답 유형을 확인하세요.

1. Our company is _____ for a _____ _____.
   (A) Maybe I'll _____.
   (B) A checking _____.
   (C) _____, _____ is not in my class.

   <u>오답 유형 check</u>
   □ ❶ 의문사 질문에 Yes/No 답변
   □ ❷ 다른 의문사(의도)에 대한 답변
   □ ❸ 질문과 일치하지 않는 주어, 대명사
   □ ❹ 유사 발음, 동일 어휘, 연상 어휘
   □ ❺ 시제 불일치

2. _____ show _____ _____ and boarding ticket.
   (A) _____ is not _____.
   (B) It's _____ the _____.
   (C) _____, _____ you are.

STEP 2 음성을 들으면서 올바른 답변을 찾으세요.

P2_Ch4_11. mp3

3. (A)　(B)　(C)
4. (A)　(B)　(C)
5. (A)　(B)　(C)
6. (A)　(B)　(C)
7. (A)　(B)　(C)
8. (A)　(B)　(C)

Chapter 4. 기타 질문과 답변   069

Point 03 | 직접적인 답변이 아닌 간접적인 회피성 답변

PART 2에서 기본적인 질문과 답변 형태만 나오는 것은 아니에요. 실제 상황에서 응용할 수 있는 여러 유형의 답변들이 있어요. 대표적으로 **상대방의 질문에 반문을 하거나, 직접적인 답변을 회피하고 우회적으로 답하거나, 모른다고 답변하는 경우**예요.

Q. **Can you help me** this afternoon?   P2_Ch4_12. 🎵mp3🎵
오늘 오후에 저 좀 도와주시겠어요?

(A) **She** was not there. → 질문에 she로 지칭할 만한 사람이 등장하지 않았으므로 오답이에요.
그녀는 거기에 없었어요.

(B) **Of course. What can I do?** → 상대방의 도움 요청에 구체적으로 무엇을 도와야 할지를 되묻는 답변이므로 정답이에요.
물론이죠. 무엇을 해 드릴까요?

(C) I found it **helpful**. → 질문의 help에서 연상 가능한 helpful을 이용한 오답이에요.
그게 유용하다는 것을 알게 됐어요.

출제 포인트 정리 ✤

❶ 모르겠다는 답변은 천하무적이에요.   P2_Ch4_13. 🎵mp3🎵

① 다른 사람에게 알아보라고 해요.
  Q. **Who** has Mr. Kim's mobile phone number? 누가 김 씨의 휴대폰 번호를 가지고 있나요?
  A. Ask his assistant. 그의 비서에게 물어보세요.

② 자신이 일정이나 리스트를 확인해 보겠다고 해요.
  Q. I'd like to discuss your marketing plans this week. 이번 주에 당신의 마케팅 계획을 논의하고 싶은데요.
  A. Let me check my schedule. 제 일정을 확인해 볼게요.

❷ 직접적으로 답변을 하지 않고 우회해서 답변을 해요.   P2_Ch4_14. 🎵mp3🎵

① 직접적인 답변을 하지 않아요.
  Q. **How long** does it take to drive to work? 운전해서 직장까지 얼마나 걸리나요?
  A. I usually walk. 저는 보통 걸어 다녀요.

② 일반 의문문에는 **Yes/No**를 생략한 채로 우회적으로 답변해요.
  Q. Haven't you contacted with the advertising agency? 광고 에이전시와 연락 안 해봤어요?
  A. I'm waiting for a response. 답변을 기다리고 있어요.

❸ 질문에 대해 추가적인 사항을 되묻는 반문 답변을 할 수 있어요.   P2_Ch4_15. 🎵mp3🎵

① 상대의 권유/제안도 반문 답변이 가능해요.
  Q. **Would you like to come** to the presentation? 발표에 오실 건가요?
  A. Who's presenting? 누가 발표하는데요?

② 평서문도 반문 답변이 가능해요.
  Q. **The company will reimburse you** for your travel expenses. 회사에서 출장 경비를 정산해 줄 겁니다.
  A. Is that a new policy? 새로운 정책인가요?

Check-up Test 700+를 위해 한 걸음 한 걸음

정답 및 해석 p.018

STEP 1 문제를 풀며 질문의 의도와 정답/오답 유형을 파악하세요.   P2_Ch4_16. mp3

(1) 음성을 들으면서 질문의 의도를 파악하고 정답을 찾아보세요.

1. (A)   (B)   (C)   2. (A)   (B)   (C)

(2) 음성을 다시 들으면서 빈칸을 채우고 정답/오답 유형을 확인하세요.

1. _____ is the annual _____ going to be _____?
   (A) At the end of _____ _____.
   (B) It hasn't been _____ yet.
   (C) _____, it was _____ _____.

오답 유형 check
- ❶ 의문사 질문에 Yes/No 답변
- ❷ 다른 의문사(의도)에 대한 답변
- ❸ 질문과 일치하지 않는 주어, 대명사
- ❹ 유사 발음, 동일 어휘, 연상 어휘
- ❺ 시제 불일치

2. _____ you _____ this chair to the store for me?
   (A) _____ you _____ it?
   (B) I _____ them in the cabinet.
   (C) _____ _____ from the date of _____.

STEP 2 음성을 들으면서 올바른 답변을 찾으세요.   P2_Ch4_17. mp3

3. (A)   (B)   (C)
4. (A)   (B)   (C)
5. (A)   (B)   (C)
6. (A)   (B)   (C)
7. (A)   (B)   (C)
8. (A)   (B)   (C)

이것만 알면 700+

실전 문제 풀이 Tip 대공개! 이것만은 꼭 알아 두세요.

TIP 1 권유/제안, 요청/부탁 빈출 질문 유형

❶ 권유/제안	Let's take a break for a while. 잠시 쉬죠. Why don't you buy this leather jacket? 이 가죽 재킷을 사는 건 어때요? Would you like to join our club? 우리 클럽에 가입하시겠어요? How about Friday night? 금요일 저녁은 어떠세요? Can I give you a hand? 제가 도와드릴까요?
❷ 요청/부탁	Could you do me a favor? 저를 도와주시겠습니까? Can you help me handle complaints from customers? 고객 불만을 처리하는 것 좀 도와주시겠어요? Would you mind waiting a little? 조금 기다려 주시겠습니까? May I use your computer? 당신의 컴퓨터를 사용해도 될까요? Do you mind showing us? 보여 주시겠습니까?

TIP 2 Would/Do you mind ~?는 승낙할 때 No로 대답합니다.

mind(꺼리다)라는 동사가 원래 부정의 의미를 가지고 있으므로, Would/Do you mind ~?로 양해/허락을 구하는 질문에 대해 승낙할 때는 No로 답변합니다. 이때의 No가 바로 '괜찮다'라는 의미로 허락을 의미합니다.

Would you mind if I join you? 제가 합석해도 괜찮을까요?
No, not at all. 네, 괜찮습니다.

그렇다면 Sure는 승낙일까요, 거절일까요? Sure는 Yes와 다르게 승낙을 의미합니다. Sure는 상대의 의도에 동의한다는 의미로 쓰기 때문에 Sure라고 하면 수락의 의미를 갖는다는 것도 알아 둡시다.

TIP 3 시험에 출제되는 천하무적 "모르겠다" 답변 유형

❶ 모른다	I don't know (yet). 모르겠어요. I have no idea. 모르겠어요.
❷ 아직 결정하지 않았다 (확실하지 않다)	I'm not sure. 확실치 않아요. We're still uncertain. 아직 확실하지 않아요. It hasn't been decided yet. 아직 결정되지 않았어요.
❸ 다른 이가 안다 (다른 이에게 물어보라)	Mr. Smith should know. 스미스 씨가 알 거예요. Ask Kevin. 케빈에게 물어보세요.
❹ 확인해 보겠다 (내가 알아보겠다)	Let me check. 확인해 볼게요. I'll let you know later. 나중에 알려 줄게요.
❺ 본 적이 없다 들은 바 없다 기억이 나지 않는다 아무도 모른다	I haven't seen it. 본 적 없어요. He hasn't told me. 그가 제게 말해 주지 않았어요. I don't remember. 기억이 나지 않아요. Nobody knows. 아무도 몰라요.

Chapter Test P2_Ch4_18. mp3

정답 및 해설 p.018

1. Mark your answer.   (A)   (B)   (C)
2. Mark your answer.   (A)   (B)   (C)
3. Mark your answer.   (A)   (B)   (C)
4. Mark your answer.   (A)   (B)   (C)
5. Mark your answer.   (A)   (B)   (C)
6. Mark your answer.   (A)   (B)   (C)
7. Mark your answer.   (A)   (B)   (C)
8. Mark your answer.   (A)   (B)   (C)
9. Mark your answer.   (A)   (B)   (C)
10. Mark your answer.   (A)   (B)   (C)
11. Mark your answer.   (A)   (B)   (C)
12. Mark your answer.   (A)   (B)   (C)
13. Mark your answer.   (A)   (B)   (C)
14. Mark your answer.   (A)   (B)   (C)
15. Mark your answer.   (A)   (B)   (C)

PART 3

다이렉트

700+

Chapter 1.
**대화의 처음에
답이 나오는 문제**

Chapter 2.
**질문의 특정 단어를
들어야 하는 문제**

Chapter 3.
**화자의 의도와
시각 자료 연계 문제**

Chapter 4.
**대화의 마지막에
답이 나오는 문제**

이것만 알면 700+

PART 3 기본 문제 풀이 전략

전략1 PART 3의 문제 유형과 정답의 출제 원리

대화의 기본 정보를 묻는 문제
- 대화의 장소를 묻는 문제
- 화자의 직장이나 직업을 묻는 문제
- 주제를 묻는 문제
- 전화나 방문의 목적을 묻는 문제

첫 번째 대사에 주로 답이 나와요.
① 특정 장소나 업종과 관련된 단어, 표현이 언급돼요.
② 대화의 화두를 던지는 표현에서 답을 알 수 있어요.

구체적인 내용을 묻는 문제
- 문제 상황을 묻는 문제
- 이유나 원인을 묻는 문제
- 특정 내용을 묻는 문제

문제에 언급된 특정 단어는 대화에서 들어야 하는 키워드입니다.
① 대화에서 꼭 들어야 하는 키워드(특정 단어)를 문제에 표시하세요.
② 문제에서 언급된 화자의 대사에 답이 있어요.
③ 키워드의 내용이 나올 때를 기다리세요.

화자의 의도와 시각 자료 문제
- 화자의 의도를 묻는 문제
- 시각 자료 연계 문제

보기가 직접 언급되면 정답이 아닙니다.
① 화자의 의도는 대화의 앞뒤 내용을 통해 알 수 있습니다.
② 시각 자료 연계 문제는 그래프, 표, 일정, 지도 등에서 보기와 매칭되는 대화 내용을 확인합니다.

미래의 일을 묻는 문제
- 권유/제안의 내용을 묻는 문제
- 앞으로 일어날 일을 묻는 문제

대화의 후반부에서 답이 나와요.
① 요청/제안/권유/부탁의 표현을 잘 들으세요.
② 미래 시제, 미래 시점을 나타내는 표현을 확인하세요.

전략 2 PART 3 정답의 불변 원칙

❶ 정답은 문제의 순서대로 들립니다.

❷ 대화의 내용 → 구체적 언급,
   정답 → 해당 행위나 대상을 포괄할 수 있는 일반화된 단어로 나옵니다.
   set up a projector 프로젝터를 설치하다 → **setting up some equipment** 장비를 설치하기

❸ 문제의 90%는 질문에 등장한 화자가 정답을 말합니다.
   What does the man say he needs? → 남자의 대사에서 답이 나옵니다.
   남자는 무엇이 필요하다고 말하는가?

   What does the woman ask the man to do? → 여자의 대사에서 답이 나옵니다.
   여자는 남자에게 무엇을 하라고 요청하는가?

❹ 문제의 키워드가 대화에서 들리면 그 앞뒤에서 답이 나옵니다.

PART 3는 이렇게 풀어야 해요.

Step 1. 남자/여자를 미리 확인합니다.
문제에 제시되어 있는 여자(woman), 남자(man)를 미리 확인해 두어야 누구의 대사에서 정답이 나오는지 알 수 있습니다.

Step 2. 문제에 언급된 키워드를 확인합니다.
문제에 제시되어 있는 특정 동사, 고유 명사(사람 이름/지명) 또는 특정 시간/장소/수단/ 방법 등을 나타내는 부사구 등이 키워드가 될 수 있습니다. 키워드를 미리 확인해 두면 대화에서 정답의 단서 내용이 제시되는 부분을 포착하기 쉬워집니다.

Step 3. 문제의 키워드를 파악했다면 이제 대화 내용을 예측합니다.
문제의 키워드를 통해 대화 내용을 예측할 수 있습니다. 예를 들어 ① 첫 번째 문제가 주제, ② 두 번째 문제가 키워드, ③ 세 번째 문제가 여자가 요청한 것을 묻는 문제라면, ① 초반부 대사에서 주제가, ② 중간쯤에서 키워드에 관한 내용이, ③ 대화의 마지막엔 여자가 남자에게 무엇을 하라고 요청하는 내용이 나올 것임을 예측할 수 있습니다.

Step 4. 대화를 들으면서 정답 보기를 찾습니다.
대화가 모두 끝난 후에 정답을 선택하는 것이 아니라 대화가 진행되는 동안에 순서대로 각 문제의 정답을 표시하며 풀어야 합니다.

Step 5. 다음 문제를 준비합니다.
대화가 끝나고 대화에 딸린 문제들을 읽어 줄 때는 이미 해당하는 세 문제의 마킹을 마치고, 다음 대화의 문제들을 읽으며 준비해야 합니다.

Chapter 1 대화의 처음에 답이 나오는 문제

Point 01 대화의 주제나 목적을 묻는 유형

대화의 주제나 전화/방문의 목적을 묻는 문제는 주로 첫 번째 문제로 출제되며, 보통 대화의 **첫 문장**을 들으면 해결할 수 있습니다.

― P3_Ch1_01. mp3 ―

What are the speakers **talking about**?
화자들은 무엇에 관하여 이야기하고 있는가?

(A) An **article** the **man** will **write** 남자가 쓸 기사
(B) A famous **actor** 유명 배우
(C) A furniture **store** 가구점
(D) Overseas **trips** 해외여행

→ 여자가 남자에게 신문에 낼 영화 리뷰(review)를 써 달라고 부탁하는 내용이므로 (A)가 정답이에요. (review → article)

W: Daniel, I'd like you to write a review of the new film *A Whole New World*. We'd like to feature it in the local arts section of Saturday's newspaper.
다니엘, 당신이 신작 영화 <완전히 새로운 세상>의 리뷰를 써 주면 좋겠어요. 토요일자 신문의 지역 문화 섹션에 특집으로 싣고 싶어요.

M: Wow, thanks a lot. I was planning to see it anyway, but most of the shows were sold out.
와, 정말 고마워요. 어쨌든 보러 가려고 했는데, 상영 회차 대부분이 매진되었더라고요.

출제 포인트 정리

❶ **calling**을 이용하여 전화의 목적을 말합니다.
   I'm calling about a billing problem. 청구서에 문제가 있어서 전화드립니다.

❷ 상대에게 질문이나 부탁을 합니다.
   Are you going to the director's presentation today? 오늘 그 임원이 하는 프레젠테이션에 갈 예정인가요?

❸ 자신이 원하는 것이 무엇인지 말합니다.
   I'd like you to write a review. 당신이 리뷰를 써 주면 좋겠습니다.

❹ 과거 상황과 관련된 배경을 설명하고 문제점이나 궁금한 사항에 대해 질문합니다.
   I bought a computer yesterday, **but it is not working** properly. 어제 컴퓨터를 샀는데, 제대로 작동이 되지 않아요.

❺ 특정 상황이나 사실을 언급합니다.
   I just read the e-mail about the training classes new employees are required to take.
   저는 방금 신입 사원들이 받아야 하는 교육에 대한 이메일을 읽었습니다.

❻ 주로 다음과 같은 질문을 사용하여 대화의 주제나 목적을 묻습니다.
   ① 대화의 주제를 묻는 문제 유형
      What are the speakers **mainly discussing**? 화자들은 주로 무엇에 대해 논의하고 있는가?
      What are the speakers **talking about**? 화자들은 무엇에 대해 이야기하고 있는가?

   ② 전화 목적이나 방문 목적을 묻는 문제 유형
      Why is the woman **calling**? 여자는 왜 전화를 하고 있는가?
      Why is the man **at the factory**? 남자는 왜 공장에 있는가?

Check-up Test 700+를 위해 한 걸음 한 걸음

정답 및 해석 p.020

STEP 1 문제의 키워드에 표시하고, 음성을 들으며 문제를 푼 뒤 빈칸을 채우세요.   P3_Ch1_02. mp3

1. What are the speakers mainly discussing?
 (A) Driving directions
 (B) A job description
 (C) Work assignments
 (D) A staff meeting

W: Daniel, would you like to _____ to _____ _____ _____ tomorrow morning? Since this is your first week here, it will be a good chance for you to meet our vehicle design staff.
M: That would be great. I've only met a couple of salespeople and I'd like to have a chance to know the others. Where will the meeting be held?

2. What is the purpose of the call?
 (A) To change an order
 (B) To confirm a reservation
 (C) To get a price estimate
 (D) To ask for a menu

W: Hi, _____ is Becky from _____ _____. I'm _____ to make a few _____ to the _____ for our office supplies this month. We need more cartridges and paper than we originally expected.
M: Certainly, so how many extra cartridges and paper do you need?

STEP 2 음성을 들으며 정답을 선택하세요.   P3_Ch1_03. mp3

3. What are the speakers discussing?
 (A) A local store
 (B) A festival schedule
 (C) An experienced accountant
 (D) A new restaurant

4. What is the purpose of the man's call?
 (A) To cancel a reservation
 (B) To request a refund
 (C) To inquire about tickets
 (D) To sign up for a class

5. Why is the man at the business?
 (A) To buy a gift
 (B) To send a package
 (C) To check on a repair
 (D) To get directions

6. What are the speakers mainly discussing?
 (A) A breakfast menu
 (B) A job interview
 (C) A newspaper article
 (D) A sales meeting

Point 02 대화의 장소나 화자의 직업을 묻는 유형

대화가 일어나는 **장소나 화자의 직업을 묻는** 문제는 처음 1~2문장에서 정답이 직접 언급되거나 대화에 등장한 장소·직업 관련 어휘를 통해서 확인할 수 있습니다.

▶ P3_Ch1_04. mp3

Where most likely are **the speakers**?
화자들은 어디에 있을 것 같은가?
(A) In a **warehouse** 창고에
(B) In a **paint store** 페인트 가게에
(C) In a **clothing shop** 옷 가게에
(D) In a **post office** 우체국에

↳ 이것들이(these) 페인트 샘플(samples of the paints)이라는 말을 통해 대화의 장소가 페인트 가게(paint store)라는 것을 알 수 있어요.

W: **Mr. Parker**, these are some of the color samples of **the paints** you could use on your walls. All colors are heat-resistant and therefore they are safe.
파커 씨, 이것이 당신 벽에 칠할 페인트 색상 샘플입니다. 모든 색상들이 내열성이어서 안전하답니다.

M: Well, they all look great, but I was wondering whether you have any darker colors. Could you show me some darker ones?
네, 다 좋아 보이는군요. 그런데 더 어두운 색상은 없는지 궁금했어요. 좀 더 어두운 페인트 색상을 보여 주시겠어요?

출제 포인트 정리

❶ 첫 대사로 나오는 자기소개나 인사말에서 직접적으로 화자의 직업이나 대화의 장소를 언급합니다.
   This is Janet from JR leasing office. 저는 JR 임대 사무실의 재닛입니다.
   Welcome to Collins Books. 콜린스 북스에 오신 것을 환영합니다.

❷ 특정 업무 관련 표현을 언급합니다.
   I'd like **two tickets** for Thursday night's **performance**.
   목요일 밤 공연 표 2매 주세요.

❸ here나 this를 통해서 대화의 장소를 알 수 있습니다.
   I'm glad to see you **here in Shane Auto Repairs**.
   여기 셰인 차량 정비소에서 뵙게 되어 반갑습니다.

   Our **firm** did all the **interior design work in this restaurant**.
   우리 회사가 이 레스토랑의 모든 인테리어 디자인 작업을 했습니다.

❹ 주로 다음과 같은 질문을 사용하여 대화의 장소나 화자의 직업을 묻습니다.
   ① 대화의 장소를 묻는 문제 유형
      Where are the **speakers**? 화자들은 어디에 있는가?
      Where is the **conversation** taking place? 대화는 어디에서 이루어지고 있는가?
   ② 화자들의 직업이나 업종을 묻는 문제 유형
      Who most likely is the **man**? 남자는 누구일 것 같은가?
      What business does the **woman work for**? 여자는 어떤 업체에서 근무하는가?

Check-up Test 700+를 위해 한 걸음 한 걸음

정답 및 해석 p.022

STEP 1 문제의 키워드에 표시하고, 음성을 들으며 문제를 푼 뒤 빈칸을 채우세요.   P3_Ch1_05. mp3

1. What type of business does the man work for?
   (A) A car rental agency
   (B) A landscaping company
   (C) An event-planning agency
   (D) A real estate firm

W: Hello, this is Mary Reed. I'm calling because _____ were _____ to _____ the _____ work last week, but your crew hasn't shown up for the last couple of days and there is still some work to finish. I was _____ if they are _____ today.
M: I'm sorry about that. Actually, the crew was overbooked yesterday and had to complete another job for a wedding being held today. They should be at your house this afternoon.

2. Where is the conversation taking place?
   (A) In a laboratory
   (B) In a library
   (C) In an electronics store
   (D) In a publishing office

W: Excuse me. I was trying to look for an article for some research I'm doing. But this computer isn't working properly.
W: Oh yes. Some of the computers _____ at Starkville _____ are a few years old. We are in the process of replacing them. What happened when you tried to use it?

STEP 2 음성을 들으며 정답을 선택하세요.   P3_Ch1_06. mp3

3. Where are the speakers?
   (A) At a photographer's studio
   (B) At a museum
   (C) At a real estate agency
   (D) At a concert hall

4. Who most likely is the man?
   (A) A bank teller
   (B) An apartment manager
   (C) An architect
   (D) A maintenance worker

5. Where most likely are the speakers?
   (A) At a school
   (B) At a bank
   (C) At a store
   (D) At a factory

6. Who most likely is the woman talking to?
   (A) A teacher
   (B) A hotel employee
   (C) A flight attendant
   (D) A client

Chapter 1. 대화의 처음에 답이 나오는 문제

이것만 알면 700+

실전 문제 풀이 Tip 대공개! 이것만은 꼭 알아 두세요.

TIP 1 알고 보면 주제를 묻는 문제

❶ **논의되고 있는 행사나 행위, 제품 등을 묻는 문제**

이런 유형의 문제들은 얼핏 키워드 문제 같지만 일종의 주제를 묻는 문제입니다. 그렇기 때문에 주로 첫 번째 문제로 등장하며 정답 역시 대화의 초반부에 등장합니다.

What kind of event is being held? 어떤 종류의 행사가 열리고 있는가?
What activity are the speakers mainly discussing? 화자들은 주로 어떤 활동에 대해서 이야기하고 있는가?

❷ **현재 진행/계획/준비 중인 일을 묻는 문제**

현재 진행/계획/준비 중인 일이 주로 대화의 주제가 되기 때문에 이러한 문제들도 일종의 주제를 묻는 문제입니다.

What project will the speakers be working on? 화자들은 어떤 프로젝트를 진행할 예정인가?
What are the speakers preparing for? 화자들이 무엇을 준비하고 있는가?
What is the woman trying to do? 여자는 무엇을 하려고 하는가?
What is the man planning to do? 남자는 무엇을 계획하고 있는가?

TIP 2 장소 문제 빈출 단서

❶ **대화의 초반에 buy, looking for 등의 표현이 들리면 store가 답이 돼요.**

I want to buy a new printer. 새 프린터를 사고 싶습니다.
Hello, can I help you find something? 안녕하세요. 뭐 찾으시는 거 있으세요?
Oh, yes. I'm looking for a new suitcase. 네. 새 여행용 가방을 찾고 있습니다.

❷ **인사말에서 장소를 알 수 있어요.**

Welcome to Noranda Pharmacy. Can I help you? 어서 오세요. 노란다 약국입니다. 도와드릴까요?
Good morning, thank you for calling the Hamilton City Hotel. How may I help you?
안녕하세요. 해밀턴 시티 호텔에 전화 주셔서 감사합니다. 어떻게 도와드릴까요?

❸ **특정 장소에서 쓸 수 있는 표현들이 들려요.**

① 자동차 정비소(car repair shop)에서 쓸 수 있는 표현

M: Hello. I'm calling about my car. My last name's Brown.
안녕하세요. 제 차 때문에 전화했어요. 제 이름은 브라운입니다.
W: Yes, Mr. Brown. We found a problem with your car battery.
네, 브라운 씨. 저희가 귀하의 차량 배터리에서 문제를 발견했어요.

② 은행(bank)에서 쓸 수 있는 표현

Hello, I'd like to deposit my paycheck into my savings account.
안녕하세요. 저는 제 급여를 제 예금 계좌로 입금하려고 합니다.

Chapter Test P3_Ch1_07 mp3

1. Where does the man most likely work?
   (A) At a museum
   (B) At a gas station
   (C) At a restaurant
   (D) At a theater

2. What does the woman ask about?
   (A) A map
   (B) A souvenir
   (C) Additional tickets
   (D) Available dates

3. What will the woman probably do next?
   (A) Contact her friends
   (B) Give her card number
   (C) Enjoy the concert
   (D) Pay cash

4. What are the speakers discussing?
   (A) An article in the paper
   (B) A fee for making an ad
   (C) An advertisement for an event
   (D) A renovation of a store

5. What problem does the man mention?
   (A) Work is being done too slowly.
   (B) An address was incorrect.
   (C) A wrong document was sent.
   (D) An item went to a different location.

6. What will the woman ask the agency to do?
   (A) Fax a new invoice
   (B) Call the newspaper
   (C) Come to the office
   (D) Complete a project earlier

7. Why is the man calling?
   (A) To cancel the order
   (B) To check on the status of an order
   (C) To add a birthday card
   (D) To change the address

8. What does the man imply when he says, "It's been almost a week"?
   (A) A package should have been delivered.
   (B) A fee needs to be paid soon.
   (C) A store is already opened.
   (D) A change is impossible.

9. What does the woman say about Monday?
   (A) The order was shipped out.
   (B) The new products have arrived.
   (C) There wasn't any postal service.
   (D) The computer system was down.

10. Where most likely does this conversation take place?
    (A) On a plane
    (B) At a bus stop
    (C) At a coffee shop
    (D) In a taxi

11. What is the woman concerned about?
    (A) Meeting new colleagues
    (B) Being late for work
    (C) Taking a wrong bus
    (D) Missing a bus

12. What does the man suggest that the woman do?
    (A) Buy a ticket first
    (B) Call the office
    (C) Use another mode of transportation
    (D) Make a reservation

Chapter 2 질문의 특정 단어를 들어야 하는 문제

Point 01   키워드를 이용하여 특정 정보를 묻는 유형

질문에서 언급된 사람이 여자인지 남자인지 그리고 어떤 내용을 묻는지 **키워드를 확인**해야 합니다. 질문에서 언급된 사람의 대사에서 키워드에 해당하는 내용을 확인할 수 있습니다.

P3_Ch2_01. 🎧 mp3

↳ 여자(woman)의 대사에서 자격증(certified) 관련 내용을 들어야 해요.

What does the **woman want** to become **certified** in?
여자는 어떤 자격증을 취득하길 원하는가?
(A) Computer **programming** 컴퓨터 프로그래밍
(B) **Teaching** safety regulations 안전 규칙 지도
(C) **Operating machinery** 기계 작동
(D) **Office** management 사무 관리

↳ 여자의 대사에서 남자가 지게차(forklifts) 자격증을 취득한 것 (got certified)을 확인한 후 본인도 그 자격증을 취득할까 생각 중이었다며 취득 방법을 묻고 있으므로 (C)가 정답이에요.
(forklifts → machinery)

W: Hey Adam, you just got certified to use the forklifts in the warehouse, right? I was thinking about doing that, too. What steps do I have to take?
이봐요, 애덤. 창고에서 지게차를 이용할 수 있는 자격증을 막 취득했지요, 그렇죠? 저도 그렇게 할까 생각 중이었어요. 어떤 단계를 거쳐야 하나요?

M: You have to take a written test on safety rules. So you have to take a class for it. I suggest you do it on the Internet.
안전 규칙에 관한 필기시험을 봐야 해요. 그러기 위해서 수업을 들어야 하고요. 인터넷으로 듣는 것을 권해요.

출제 포인트 정리 ✧

❶ **정답은 질문의 키워드에 해당하는 부분 앞뒤에서 나옵니다.**
① 질문의 특정 키워드에 표시하세요. 키워드와 관련된 내용이 대화에서 언급됩니다.

↳ 여자의 대사에서 답을 찾을 수 있어요.
Q. Why has the ⟨woman⟩ not reserved a hotel yet? 여자는 왜 아직 호텔을 예약하지 않았는가?
↳ 호텔 예약 관련 내용이 나올 것을 예상할 수 있어요.

② 질문에 등장한 해당 화자의 말에서 정답이 언급됩니다.

M: Nina, did you choose a hotel yet? 니나, 호텔 결정했어요?
W: Not yet. I'm still looking for a good deal, but everything in the city is so expensive.
아직 안 했어요. 아직 좋은 가격대를 찾고 있는데 시내에 있는 게 다 너무 비싸요.

A. She is looking for a good price. 그녀는 좋은 가격을 찾고 있다.

❷ **주로 다음과 같은 키워드를 사용하여 행위/대상이나 이유, 수단/방법 등을 묻습니다.**
What is the man **planning** for **next month**? 남자는 다음 달에 무엇을 할 계획인가?
Why is the man in **London**? 남자는 왜 런던에 있는가?
How did the women **learn** about the **business**? 여자들은 그 업체에 대해서 어떻게 알게 됐는가?
Where has the woman just **returned** from? 여자는 어디에서 막 돌아왔는가?

Check-up Test 700+를 위해 한 걸음 한 걸음

정답 및 해석 p.025

STEP 1 문제의 키워드에 표시하고, 음성을 들으며 문제를 푼 뒤 빈칸을 채우세요.   P3_Ch2_02.

1. How did the woman learn about the store?
   (A) She has been there before.
   (B) She read a review of it.
   (C) She knows the manager.
   (D) She has eaten there before.

> W: Have you been to the _____ _____ _____ downtown? I was there last weekend and it was full of people.
> W: Well, I haven't been there yet. But I _____ an online _____ about it. It gave a good rating and that's the main reason why I've decided to go there this Saturday.

2. Why has the shipment been delayed?
   (A) An order was not placed on time.
   (B) A machine broke down.
   (C) A form was incomplete.
   (D) A shipping document was lost.

> W: Did the latest _____ of children's jackets go out yet? I want to be sure that everything gets to the store on time.
> M: _____, we had a _____ _____ because one of our _____ on the production floor _____ _____ last night. But the store should have everything by the day after tomorrow.
> W: That's going to be too late. You'd better tell the delivery service to rush the shipment. That way the store will get the jackets by tomorrow.

STEP 2 음성을 들으며 정답을 선택하세요.   P3_Ch2_03.

3. What kind of business is the man calling?
   (A) A department store
   (B) A car rental agency
   (C) A restaurant
   (D) A consulting company

4. How can the man get a discount?
   (A) By presenting his employee ID
   (B) By filling out a form
   (C) By using a coupon
   (D) By bringing in new customers

5. What is the woman looking for?
   (A) A meeting agenda
   (B) A registration form
   (C) An engineering report
   (D) A telephone number

6. Why is Jim unavailable?
   (A) He is on vacation.
   (B) He is making a delivery.
   (C) He is working overseas.
   (D) He is with some clients.

Chapter 2. 질문의 특정 단어를 들어야 하는 문제   085

Point 02 　문제점/걱정이나 감정의 이유를 묻는 유형

문제점이나 걱정을 묻는 문제의 정답은 주로 대화의 전반부에 언급됩니다. concern, worry, problem 등이 키워드로 자주 등장하여 문제점이나 걱정의 이유를 묻거나 그 밖에 다른 여러 감정의 이유를 묻는 문제가 출제됩니다.

— P3_Ch2_04. mp3

What problem does the **woman** mention?
여자는 어떤 문제를 언급하는가?

(A) The **user manual** is **missing**.
사용자 설명서가 없다.
(B) The **wrong computer** model was sent.
다른 모델의 컴퓨터가 보내졌다.
(C) The computer is **not working properly**.
컴퓨터가 제대로 작동하지 않는다.
(D) The printer is **damaged**.
프린터가 망가졌다.

M: Hi, you have reached ABC Computer Technical Support. This is David. How can I help you today?
안녕하세요. ABC 컴퓨터 기술 지원부에 연결되셨습니다. 저는 데이비드입니다. 어떻게 도와드릴까요?

W: Hi, David. I purchased an ABC computer last week and I received it today. When I opened the box, I found there was no manual in it.
안녕하세요. 데이비드. 저는 지난주에 ABC 컴퓨터를 구입해서 오늘 받았습니다. 포장을 풀었을 때 설명서가 없다는 것을 알았습니다.

↳ 여자가 구입한 물건을 받아서 열어 보니 설명서가 없다(no manual)고 했으므로 (A)가 정답입니다. (no manual → manual is missing)

출제 포인트 정리

❶ 부정어를 이용하거나 문제점에 대해 직접 언급하는 경우

I'm having trouble with this spread sheet. 이 스프레드시트 때문에 애를 먹고 있습니다.
The photocopier is not working very well. 복사기가 잘 작동하지 않습니다.

❷ but, unfortunately와 함께 언급되는 경우

But unfortunately, we no longer have the frames you requested in stock.
하지만 안타깝게도 당신께서 요청하신 프레임은 더 이상 재고가 없습니다.

But when I went last year, the traffic was horrible.
하지만 제가 작년에 갔을 때는 교통 체증이 심했습니다.

❸ 주로 다음과 같은 질문을 사용하여 문제점/걱정 또는 기타 특정 감정의 이유를 묻습니다.

① 문제점/걱정을 묻는 문제 유형

What is the problem? 문제점이 무엇인가?
What is the man concerned/worried about? 남자는 무엇에 대해 걱정하고 있는가?
What problem does the man mention? 남자는 어떤 문제를 언급하는가?

② 기타 특정 감정의 이유를 묻는 문제 유형

Why is the woman disappointed? 여자는 왜 실망하는가?
Why does the woman apologize? 여자는 왜 사과하는가?
What is the man surprised about? 남자는 무엇에 대해 놀라워하는가?

Check-up Test 700+를 위해 한 걸음 한 걸음

정답 및 해석 p.026

STEP 1 문제의 키워드에 표시하고, 음성을 들으며 문제를 푼 뒤 빈칸을 채우세요.   P3_Ch2_05. mp3

1. What is the man concerned about?
   (A) Having his computer repaired
   (B) Finishing a report on time
   (C) Scheduling time off from work
   (D) Keeping his computer files secure

M: It is _____ for me to _____ the sales _____ by _____, and I have to prepare for the meeting on Tuesday morning. So I think I have to _____ _____ tonight to get it done.
W: Well, remember that our company is going to install the new security software tonight. The whole computer network will be shut down tomorrow.
M: Thanks for reminding me.

2. Why is the woman disappointed?
   (A) A theater is closed.
   (B) Performances have been canceled.
   (C) A friend is busy.
   (D) Tickets are unavailable.

M: Hey, Julie. You enjoy comedies, right? Have you seen the new play at the Collins Theater? The review in the newspaper said that it was really funny.
W: No, my friend and I tried to buy _____, _____ it's completely _____ _____. We're so _____. We were really looking forward to it.
M: Well. The article said more performances have been added since it has been so popular. Why don't you call the theater to see if you can get tickets now?

STEP 2 음성을 들으며 정답을 선택하세요.   P3_Ch2_06. mp3

3. Where most likely are the speakers?
   (A) At a dental office
   (B) At a department store
   (C) At a hotel
   (D) At a restaurant

4. Why does the woman apologize?
   (A) She has lost some paperwork.
   (B) She didn't bring an ID card.
   (C) She is late.
   (D) She canceled a subscription.

5. What are the speakers mainly discussing?
   (A) An advertising campaign
   (B) A fitness program
   (C) A college course
   (D) A project schedule

6. What is Christopher concerned about?
   (A) Updating some records
   (B) Locating a designer
   (C) Missing a due date
   (D) Exceeding a budget

이것만 알면 700+

실전 문제 풀이 Tip 대공개! 이것만은 꼭 알아 두세요.

TIP 1 과거의 내용은 전반부에, 미래의 내용은 후반부에 나옵니다.

❶ **과거 내용은 전반부에 나옵니다.**
과거의 사건이나 상황, 배경, 원인, 일정 등을 묻는 문제는 대화의 전반부에 단서가 있을 확률이 높습니다. recently, originally, yesterday 등의 어휘가 자주 사용되고, 주로 과거 시제나 현재 완료 시제로 등장합니다.

What event did the woman recently attend? 여자는 최근 어떤 행사에 참석했는가?
What has the company recently done? 회사는 최근에 무엇을 했는가?
What did the woman do this morning? 여자는 오늘 아침에 무엇을 했는가?
Why did Diana miss her appointment? 다이애나는 왜 약속을 지키지 못했는가?

❷ **미래 내용은 후반부에 나옵니다.**
앞으로 발생할 미래의 일정이나 할 일을 묻는 문제는 주로 대화의 후반부나 마지막에 단서가 언급됩니다. 대화에서 미래의 특정 시점을 언급한 부분 또는 대화가 끝나고 화자가 하겠다는 내용이나 상대의 요구나 요청, 제안의 내용이 답이 됩니다.

What will the man do next? 남자는 다음에 무슨 일을 할 것인가?
What does the woman say she will do tomorrow? 여자는 내일 무엇을 할 것이라고 말하는가?
What will take place in the afternoon? 오후에 무슨 일이 발생할 것인가?

TIP 2 3인 대화 유형

3인 대화 유형은 PART 3 전체 13개의 대화 중 2개 정도 출제됩니다. 기존 대화와 달리 화자가 '남1-남2-여' 또는 '남-여1-여2' 3인으로 구성되며 2인 대화보다 대화 전환(turn) 횟수가 더 많은 것이 특징입니다. 3명이라서 문제를 풀 때 혼란스러울 거 같지만 질문의 키워드 내용으로 대화를 예상하고 풀면 2인 대화와 크게 차이가 없습니다.

❶ **2인 대화 유형과 문제 유형은 다르지 않습니다.**

What problem are the speakers discussing? 화자들은 어떤 문제에 대해서 이야기하고 있는가?
Where do the speakers work? 화자들은 어디에서 일을 하는가?
What will the woman most likely do next? 여자는 다음에 무엇을 할 것 같은가?

❷ **성별이 같은 두 화자가 서로 동의하거나 공유하고 있는 의견 및 공통된 사항을 묻는 문제가 출제됩니다.**

Who most likely are the women? 여자들은 누구일 것 같은가?
How did the men learn about the business? 남자들은 그 업체에 대해 어떻게 알게 되었는가?

❸ **대화 속에 등장한 남자나 여자의 이름이 질문의 키워드인 문제가 출제됩니다.**
문제의 순서에 맞게 대화에서 해당 이름을 불러 주기 때문에 쉽게 풀 수 있습니다.

What will Mr. Brown most likely do next? 브라운 씨는 다음에 무엇을 할 것 같은가?

Chapter Test

1. Who is Karl Jacobs?
   (A) A receptionist
   (B) A reporter
   (C) An editor
   (D) A publisher

2. Why is the woman surprised?
   (A) An article has already released.
   (B) She missed an important meeting.
   (C) An interview has been canceled.
   (D) Mr. Jacobs arrived earlier than expected.

3. What is the man asked to do?
   (A) Find an available room
   (B) Transfer a call
   (C) Direct a visitor
   (D) Reserve a meeting room

4. What are the men concerned about?
   (A) Next week's meeting
   (B) A magazine layout
   (C) A special recipe
   (D) A group presentation

5. What do the men ask the woman to do?
   (A) Pick up an order
   (B) Revise an article
   (C) Call a supplier
   (D) Edit some pictures

6. What does the woman agree to do?
   (A) Read a proposal
   (B) Mail a package
   (C) Order dinner
   (D) Take some photos

7. What are the speakers mainly discussing?
   (A) A new budget
   (B) Some rental spaces
   (C) A new employee
   (D) A building renovation

8. Why does the man say, "We couldn't have done this without Frank Myer"?
   (A) To correct some misinformation
   (B) To praise a coworker
   (C) To suggest promoting a colleague
   (D) To ask for some help

9. What does a contract offer if a deadline is missed?
   (A) A full refund
   (B) A free delivery service
   (C) A reduction in rent
   (D) An extra discount

	Monday	Tuesday	Wednesday	Thursday
1st week			A seminar	
2nd week	Team Training			Client lunch
3rd week		Paris Fashion Week		
4th week		A board meeting		

10. Where will the speakers be on March 17th?
    (A) At a training center
    (B) At a fashion show
    (C) At a seminar
    (D) At a company dinner

11. Look at the graphic. In which week does the woman want an intern to start working?
    (A) 1st week
    (B) 2nd week
    (C) 3rd week
    (D) 4th week

12. What will the man probably do next?
    (A) Book a table at a restaurant
    (B) Send a fax to a hotel
    (C) Make a phone call
    (D) Prepare a presentation

Chapter 3 화자의 의도와 시각 자료 연계 문제

Point 01 화자의 의도를 묻는 유형

화자의 의도를 묻는 문제는 매회 3문제씩 출제됩니다. **앞뒤 문맥을 파악**하여 해당 발언의 의도/의미를 찾아야 합니다. 표면적인 의미를 묻는 것이 아니기 때문에 **주어진 표현과 동일한 단어가 있거나 같은 의미의 보기는 정답이 되지 않습니다**.

P3_Ch3_01. mp3

↪ 여자의 말에 앞서 남자가 어떤 내용을 말하는지 잘 들어야 해요.

Why does the woman say, "I will be out of town due to a business trip"?
여자는 왜 "저는 출장 때문에 여기에 없을 거예요"라고 말하는가?

(A) To **reassure** a coworker 동료를 확신시키기 위해
(B) To **reject** a **suggestion** 제안을 거절하기 위해
(C) To ask for **help** 도움을 요청하기 위해
(D) To **vist** another branch 다른 지점을 방문하기 위해

↪ 남자의 제안에 대해 but이라고 단서를 달면서 출장을 가야 한다고 말하였으므로 남자의 제안을 거절하는 것임을 알 수 있어요.

M: Owen, I have an extra ticket to the music festival in Luis theater. I was wondering if you want to go this Saturday. A great jazz band is playing there.
오웬, 제게 루이 극장에서 열리는 음악 페스티벌의 여분 티켓이 한 장 있어요. 이번 주 토요일에 갈 생각 있는지 궁금해서요. 멋진 재즈 밴드가 거기서 연주할 거예요.

W: I'd love to go, but I will be out of town due to a business trip.
정말 가고 싶은데, 저는 출장 때문에 여기에 없을 거예요.

M: That's too bad. Well, the tickets are good for this Saturday. 유감이네요. 이 티켓들은 이번 주 토요일에만 유효해요.

출제 포인트 정리

❶ 상대의 질문이나 부탁에서 답을 찾을 수 있어요.

Q. What does the woman mean when she says, "I need to pick up a client from the hotel"?
여자가 "저는 오후에 호텔에서 고객을 모시고 와야 해요"라고 말할 때 의미하는 것은 무엇인가?

> M: Are you going to the director's presentation today? 오늘 그 임원이 하는 프레젠테이션에 갈 예정인가요?
> W: I'm sorry. I need to pick up a client from the hotel. 죄송해요. 저는 오후에 호텔에서 고객을 모시고 와야 해요.

A. She cannot attend a presentation. 그녀는 프레젠테이션에 참석할 수 없다.

❷ 언급된 표현 뒤에 나오는 부연 설명을 통해 알 수 있어요.

Q. Why does the man say "your timing is good"? 남자는 왜 "타이밍이 좋으시네요"라고 말하는가?

> M: We try to help our customers find the best furniture for their needs. Plus your timing is good. This week everything is 20-30% off. 저희는 고객님들께서 요구에 맞는 최상의 가구를 찾을 수 있도록 도와드리려고 노력합니다. 게다가 타이밍이 좋으시네요. 이번 주에는 모든 상품을 20~30퍼센트 할인해요.

A. A store is offering a discount. 매장이 할인을 제공한다.

❸ 주로 다음과 같은 질문을 사용하여 화자의 의도를 묻습니다.

What does the man imply when he says, "I'll be out of the office tomorrow"?
남자가 "저는 내일 사무실에 없을 거예요"라고 말할 때 의미하는 것은 무엇인가?

Why does the woman say, "It's your first time to attend the conference"?
여자는 왜 "당신은 그 학회에 참석하는 게 처음이죠"라고 말하는가?

Check-up Test 700+를 위해 한 걸음 한 걸음

정답 및 해석 p.030

STEP 1 문제의 키워드에 표시하고, 음성을 들으며 문제를 푼 뒤 빈칸을 채우세요.

P3_Ch3_02. mp3

1. Why does the man say, "I'm leading the orientation for new employees on Tuesday"?
   (A) He is unhappy with an assignment.
   (B) He needs help for an orientation.
   (C) He is pleased with an opportunity.
   (D) He is unable to fulfill a request.

   W: Hi, Brad. One of our clients from New York will be here next week. _____ you _____ him up from _____ _____ on Tuesday morning?
   M: Oh, I'm leading the orientation for new employees on Tuesday.
   W: Hmm... I see. Maybe Jane's free?
   M: I think so. Do you want me to ask her?

2. Why does the woman say, "it's taking longer than I expected"?
   (A) To change a reservation
   (B) To apologize for a mistake
   (C) To ask for assistance
   (D) To decline an offer

   W: Last week I made a reservation for dinner tomorrow. But I am afraid I have to cancel it. I am in Tokyo on business and it's taking longer than I expected. _____ it be _____ for me to come another night _____?
   M: _____ _____. We still have tables available for dinner on Friday and Saturday. Which night would you prefer?
   W: Oh, Saturday would be perfect!

STEP 2 음성을 들으며 정답을 선택하세요.

P3_Ch3_03. mp3

3. Where does the conversation probably take place?
   (A) In a health clinic
   (B) In a research laboratory
   (C) In a university classroom
   (D) In a Human Resources office

4. What does the woman imply when she says, "Ms. Chan is on the phone right now"?
   (A) A phone cannot be used.
   (B) Ms. Chan has the information she needs.
   (C) The man needs to wait for a while.
   (D) She is not in charge of some work.

5. What is the purpose of the call?
   (A) To confirm a reservation
   (B) To postpone a schedule
   (C) To replace broken equipment
   (D) To complain about a messy room

6. What does the man mean when he says, "we have a board meeting at 10 o'clock"?
   (A) He wants to postpone a meeting.
   (B) He needs a task to be completed quickly.
   (C) He found his calendar is incorrect.
   (D) He would like more information.

Point 02 | 시각 자료와 연계하여 푸는 유형

주어진 **시각 자료**(표, 그래프, 일정, 약도, 전단, 기상 예보 등)와 대화 내용을 연계하여 정답을 찾는 문제로 매회 3문제씩 출제됩니다. 보기에 제시된 항목과 시각 자료에서 매칭되는 항목을 연결 키워드로 잡아야 합니다.

P3_Ch3_04. mp3

Chef Evelyn Dinner Specials	
Salad Buffet	10% off
All Pasta	15% off
Steak	20% off
Seafood	25% off

① 보기에 할인율이 나오므로 시각 자료에서 이와 매칭되는 메뉴를 연결 키워드로 잡아 대화에서 어떤 메뉴가 나오는지 잘 들어야 합니다.

Look at the graphic. Which discount will the speakers receive?
시각 자료를 보시오. 화자들은 얼마나 할인을 받을 것인가?
(A) 10%   (B) 15%
(C) 20%   (D) 25%

W: We are going to take Jane out to dinner tonight at Chef Evelyn's Restaurant.
우리 오늘 밤 제인을 에블린 셰프의 식당에 데려가서 저녁을 먹을 거예요.

M: That's a good idea. And actually, I just got a coupon for that restaurant. They're running some specials. See?
좋은 생각이네요. 사실 제게 그 식당의 쿠폰이 있어요. 특별 할인을 하는 게 있네요. 보이세요?

W: Hmm.... I know Jane likes seafood. We can order some seafood for everyone to share.
흠… 제가 알기로는 제인은 해산물을 좋아해요. 해산물을 주문해서 모두 같이 나눠 먹으면 되겠네요.

M: Sounds good. 좋네요.

② 해산물을 주문하겠다는 내용을 듣고 시각 자료를 확인하면 25%의 할인을 받을 것이라는 것을 알 수 있습니다.

출제 포인트 정리

❶ 해당 항목을 직접적으로 언급하는 유형

Phone Directory	
Department	Extension No.
Registration	104
Amenities	105
Dining	106
Maintenance	107

Let me give our **maintenance department** a call.
제가 관리부서에 전화할게요.
A. 107

❷ 수/양, 순위를 비교급, 최상급으로 언급하는 유형

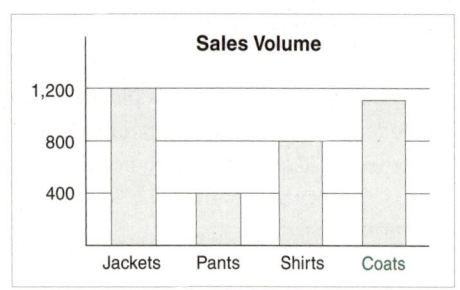

Please see **the second highest item** on the chart. Its sales have increased by 40%.
차트에서 두 번째 높은 항목을 봐주시기 바랍니다. 이 제품의 판매가 40% 증가했습니다.
A. Coats

❸ 장소나 위치를 나타내는 전치사를 통해 언급하는 유형 (지도)

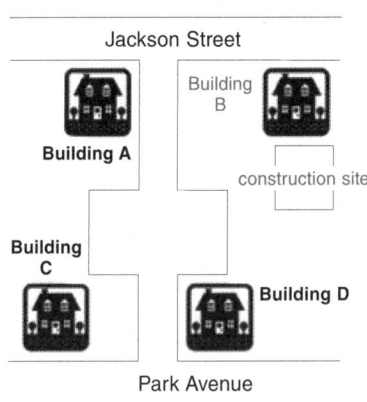

It is located next to the construction site.
공사장 옆에 위치해 있어요.
A. Building B

❹ 순서로 언급하는 유형

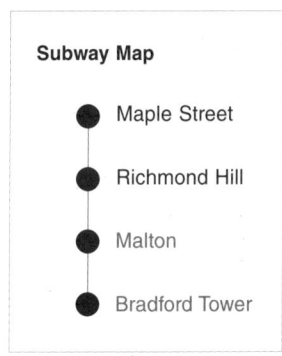

I don't remember the name but I'm sure it's the stop right after Malton.
이름은 기억나지 않는데, 말톤 바로 다음 역이에요.
A. Bradford Tower

❺ 주로 다음과 같은 질문을 사용하여 시각 자료와 연계된 내용을 묻습니다.

Look at the graphic. How much will the man pay for the stay?
시각 자료를 보시오. 남자는 숙박을 위해 얼마를 지불할 것인가?

Look at the graphic. Which flight ticket will the woman most likely book?
시각 자료를 보시오. 여자는 어떤 항공편 티켓을 예약할 것 같은가?

Check-up Test 700+를 위해 한 걸음 한 걸음

정답 및 해석 p.031

STEP 1 문제의 키워드에 표시하고, 음성을 들으며 문제를 푼 뒤 빈칸을 채우세요.   P3_Ch3_05. mp3

Shopping Mall Layout

Restaurant	C	Toys
A		
Jewelry shop		Clothing store
B		D

Entrance

1. Look at the graphic. Which store will the speakers most likely rent?
   (A) Store A
   (B) Store B
   (C) Store C
   (D) Store D

W: Simon, look at this shopping mall _____. Now we need to decide _____ _____ _____ our new beverage shop.
M: OK. Hmm... I think either of those corner stores near _____ _____ would be nice.
W: I agree with you, _____ the rent for those stores is much higher than the budget we have.
M: How about the store _____ the restaurant and the _____ _____? It would make sense to have a place where people can get some beverages next to the restaurant.
W: Sure. That makes sense.

Monthly Expenditure Report

Travel	$350
Full-time payroll	$3,000
Part-time payroll	$1,200
Training	$500

2. Look at the graphic. Which amount does the woman say may change?
   (A) $350
   (B) $3,000
   (C) $1,200
   (D) $500

M: I've just finished analyzing our monthly _____. Here is the report.
W: Hmm... It looks like our expenses have gone up this month. Maybe we should try to _____ some of _____ _____.
M: Well, you know? The holiday season is nearly over. So I think it would probably be possible.

STEP 2 음성을 들으며 정답을 선택하세요.   P3_Ch3_06. mp3

Destination	Departure time	Status
Wollongong	12:00 P.M.	30 minutes late
Bowral	12:20 P.M.	20 minutes late
Central Coast	1:30 P.M.	On time
Newcastle	2:00 P.M.	40 minutes late

3. Look at the graphic. What is the status of the man's train?
   (A) 30 minutes late
   (B) 20 minutes late
   (C) On time
   (D) 40 minutes late

4. Which industry do the speakers most likely work in?
   (A) Manufacturing
   (B) Tourism
   (C) Shipping
   (D) Financing

Daily Schedule - Kevin Tuesday	
9:00 A.M.	Appointment
10:00 A.M.	
11:00 A.M.	Presentation
12:00 P.M.	Lunch Break
1:00 P.M.	
2:00 P.M. - 6:00 P.M.	Factory

5. According to the woman, what will happen on Wednesday?
   (A) Some equipment will be installed.
   (B) A project will be ended.
   (C) She will have a training session.
   (D) She will go on a business trip.

6. Look at the graphic. What time will the speakers most likely meet?
   (A) 10:00 A.M.
   (B) 11:00 A.M.
   (C) 12:00 P.M.
   (D) 1:00 P.M.

이것만 알면 700+

실전 문제 풀이 Tip 대공개! 이것만은 꼭 알아 두세요.

TIP 1 가장 많이 출제되었던 화자의 의도 문제 정답 Top 5

❶ 상대에게 도움이나 해결책 제안

To make a suggestion 제안을 하기 위해
To propose an alternative 대안을 제시하기 위해
A colleague may be available for a job. 동료가 어떤 일을 할 수 있을 것이다.

❷ 걱정이나 놀람 등의 감정 표현

To express concern 걱정을 표현하기 위해
He is worried about missing a deadline. 마감일을 놓칠까 봐 걱정하고 있다.

❸ 지연이나 문제 상황 설명

To give an explanation 설명을 하기 위해
A coworker cannot attend a meeting. 동료가 회의에 참석을 할 수 없다.

❹ 도움이나 조언 요청

To request additional help 추가적인 도움을 요청하기 위해
To ask for help 도움을 요청하기 위해

❺ 제안이나 요청 거절

To decline a request 요청을 거절하기 위해
He does not have much time to talk. 그는 이야기할 시간이 많지 않다.
She cannot help the man. 그녀는 남자를 도와줄 수 없다.

TIP 2 두 개의 항목을 확인해야 하는 시각 자료 연계 문제를 주의하세요.

Seminar Fees

	Early (before Jan 11)	② Standard (After Jan 11)
① Professionals	$200	$250
Students	$100	$150

Q. Look at the graphic. How much will the firm most likely pay for the event?
시각 자료를 보시오. 회사는 행사를 위해 얼마를 지불할 것 같은가?

(A) $200   (B) $250
(C) $100   (D) $150

* ① company, attract, new customers → Professionals
② missed the early registration discount → Standard

M: I'd like to attend the marketing seminar on SNS in January and do you think the ① company would pay for it?
저는 1월에 SNS에 관한 마케팅 세미나에 참석하고 싶어요. 회사가 비용을 내줄까요?

W: That will be helpful for you. ① We're always looking for ways to attract new customers. How much will it be?
그거 도움이 될 거예요. 우린 항상 신규 고객을 모객하는 방법을 찾고 있어요. 얼마인가요?

M: I have the list here. Unfortunately, ② I missed the early registration discount.
여기 리스트가 있어요. 아쉽게도 조기 등록 할인은 놓쳤어요.

Chapter Test P3_Ch3_07. mp3

정답 및 해석 p.033

1. Why does the man say "It's not 3 o'clock"?
   (A) To refuse an invitation
   (B) To express surprise
   (C) To check the schedule
   (D) To ask for a deadline extension

2. What problem is the man having?
   (A) He cannot print some documents.
   (B) He did not receive a meeting agenda.
   (C) A client will be late.
   (D) There is no replacement part.

3. What does the woman offer to do?
   (A) Check a calendar
   (B) Revise a report
   (C) Provide some data
   (D) Contact a coworker

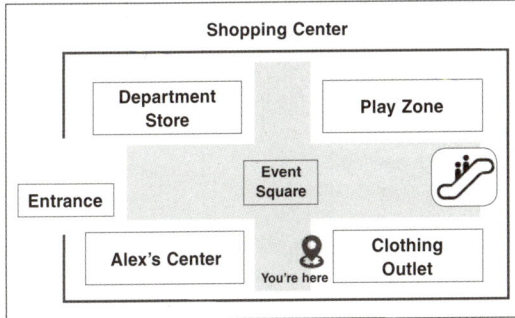

4. What does the woman want to do?
   (A) Have a job interview
   (B) Purchase some clothing
   (C) Return a product
   (D) Have an item repaired

5. Look at the graphic. Where will the woman most likely go next?
   (A) Department Store
   (B) Play Zone
   (C) Clothing Outlet
   (D) Alex's Center

6. What does the man say about the shopping center?
   (A) It has several events.
   (B) It will be closing soon.
   (C) Its escalators cannot be used.
   (D) Its parking is not free.

7. What do the speakers mainly discuss?
   (A) A renovation of a parking lot
   (B) A broken elevator
   (C) A deadline
   (D) A staff meeting

8. Which division does the woman most likely work in?
   (A) Personnel
   (B) Accounting
   (C) Sales
   (D) Maintenance

9. What does the man imply when he says, "I was there a few minutes ago"?
   (A) A meeting has already ended.
   (B) More explanation is needed.
   (C) A problem was not solved.
   (D) A new policy will be announced.

Standard Price
$10 per ticket

--- **Discounted Price** ---
$6 : on Friday
$5 : After 4 P.M.
$3 : for members or students

---

10. Where most likely are the speakers?
    (A) At a community center
    (B) At a park
    (C) At an outdoor theater
    (D) At an art center

11. Look at the graphic. Why did the man get a discount?
    (A) It is on Friday.
    (B) It is after 4 P.M.
    (C) He is a student.
    (D) He is a member.

12. What will the man most likely do next?
    (A) Take a guided tour
    (B) Read some brochures
    (C) Have some snacks
    (D) Go upstairs

Chapter 4 대화의 마지막에 답이 나오는 문제

Point 01 권유/제안, 요구/요청 사항을 묻는 유형

권유/제안, 요구/요청 사항을 묻는 문제는 주로 세 번째 문제로 등장하고 대화의 후반부에서 정답의 단서가 언급됩니다. 질문의 능/수동에 따라 **질문에 언급된 사람 혹은 상대방의 후반부 대사**를 집중해서 들어야 합니다.

P3_Ch4_01. 🎧mp3

> 대화의 후반부에서 남자가 요청하는 내용을 들어야 해요.

What does the **man request**?
남자가 요청하는 것은 무엇인가?

(A) **Contact** information 연락처
(B) A **revised schedule** 수정된 일정
(C) A website **address** 웹사이트 주소
(D) More **supplies** 더 많은 비품

> 남자의 마지막 대사에서 요청할 때 쓰는 표현인 Could you ~ 와 함께 바뀐 공사 일정을 보내 달라고 하고 있어요.
> (updated → revised)

W: I'm calling about your store at Pigeon Square. I'm sorry to inform you that the construction won't be completed by the end of this month.
피전 광장에 있는 당신의 매장에 관해서 전화드립니다. 이달 말까지 공사가 완공되지 않을 것임을 알려 드리게 되어 유감입니다.

M: Well, then what is the estimated date for completion?
음, 그럼 예상되는 완공일이 언제인가요?

W: We are still going to need two more extra days to finish the construction.
완공까지 이틀 정도 더 필요할 것입니다.

M: Alright. Could you send me the updated construction schedule at once so that I can readjust the grand opening to a new date?
알겠어요. 제가 개장일을 다른 날짜로 조정할 수 있게 지금 바로 바뀐 공사 일정을 보내 주시겠어요?

출제 포인트 정리

❶ '내가 ~할게요'라는 권유/제안의 표현을 잘 들어야 해요.
   Let me check the storeroom. 창고를 확인해 보겠습니다.
   I can get you a schedule. 일정표를 드리겠습니다.

❷ '~하세요, ~해 주세요'라는 요구/요청의 표현의 잘 들어야 해요.
   Could you leave me a number where I can reach you? 연락할 수 있는 번호를 남겨 주시겠어요?
   If you give me your address, I'll send you a brochure. 주소를 알려 주시면, 안내 책자를 보내 드리겠습니다.

❸ 주로 다음과 같은 질문을 사용하여 권유/제안, 요구/요청 사항을 묻습니다.
   ① 권유/제안 사항을 묻는 문제 유형
      What does the man offer to do? 남자는 무엇을 하겠다고 제안하는가?
      What does the woman suggest? 여자는 무엇을 제안하는가?
   ② 요구/요청 사항을 묻는 문제 유형
      What does the man request? 남자는 무엇을 요청하는가?
      What does the man ask the woman to do? 남자는 여자에게 무엇을 할 것을 요청하는가?

Check-up Test 700+를 위해 한 걸음 한 걸음

정답 및 해석 p.035

STEP 1 문제의 키워드에 표시하고, 음성을 들으며 문제를 푼 뒤 빈칸을 채우세요.

P3_Ch4_02. mp3

1. What does the woman ask the man to do?
   (A) Revise a budget proposal
   (B) Design a new logo
   (C) Manage a project
   (D) Interview a job candidate

> W: Steve, I don't know if you heard, but Ellen Kobayashi is leaving the company in two weeks. It's too bad because she's been doing such a great job with the advertising campaign for the new children's shampoo.
> M: Oh, I heard Ellen is leaving, but I did not know it was so soon. She's such an efficient coordinator. I'm sure she'll be missed.
> W: She certainly will be. In fact, we need someone to replace her right away. Since you are familiar with the product, I'd _____ you to _____ the _____ of the ad campaign.

2. What does the woman offer to do?
   (A) Pay in advance
   (B) Move back later
   (C) Mail the check
   (D) Find a new tenant

> W: Hi, this is Diana Roseland in apartment 208. I'm calling to let the management know that I will move out in three weeks.
> M: I'm not sure if you read the rental agreement, but all tenants must let us know at least four weeks in advance. So I'm afraid you must pay next month's rent.
> W: Is there any way you can deduct even a portion of it? I will _____ for _____ who could _____ into my _____ as soon as I move out.

STEP 2 음성을 들으며 정답을 선택하세요.

P3_Ch4_03. mp3

3. What is the conversation about?
   (A) Receiving an award
   (B) Applying for a position
   (C) Sending a package
   (D) Booking a hotel room

4. What type of company is the woman most likely working for?
   (A) A newspaper publisher
   (B) A property management firm
   (C) A hotel
   (D) A recording agency

5. What is the man asked to do?
   (A) Submit a document
   (B) Pay an application fee
   (C) Wait for a call
   (D) Call a hiring manager

6. What problem are the speakers discussing?
   (A) Contracting a manufacturer
   (B) Accessing some files
   (C) Finding some tools
   (D) Using a printer

7. What does the woman have to do today?
   (A) Prepare a contract
   (B) Practice a speech
   (C) Produce some booklets
   (D) Sort some mail

8. What does the man offer to give the woman?
   (A) A replacement part
   (B) A new password
   (C) A copy of a document
   (D) A software CD

Point 02 앞으로 일어날 일을 묻는 유형

다음에 할 일이나 특정 미래 시점에 발생할 일을 묻는 문제는 주로 세 번째 문제로 등장하며, 정답의 단서도 대화의 후반부에서 제시됩니다. 따라서 후반부 대사를 주의 깊게 들어야 합니다. 특히 **시간 부사 키워드**를 꼭 확인합니다.

P3_Ch4_04. mp3

> 남자의 마지막 대사에서 무엇을 하겠다고 하는지를 잘 들어야 해요.

What will the **man** probably **do next**?
남자는 다음에 무엇을 할 것인가?

(A) **Seat** some **customers**
고객을 자리에 앉히기
(B) **Change** into a **uniform**
유니폼으로 갈아입기
(C) **Call** a coworker
동료를 부르기
(D) Go to the **lobby**
로비로 가기

> 남자가 마지막 대사에서 이제 가서 유니폼으로 갈아입겠다고 했어요.

W: Oliver, three of our waiters called in sick today, so we are short-handed as of now. I will have someone else take over the cashier, and I want you to handle the customers in the main area along with Barbara and Kenneth.
올리버, 웨이터 세 명이 오늘 전화로 병가를 내서 지금 일손이 부족해요. 계산은 다른 사람에게 맡길 예정인데, 당신은 바바라와 케네스와 함께 홀에서 고객들을 응대해 주었으면 해요.

M: Sure, I can do that. But, will there be enough people for the rooms?
물론이죠, 제가 할게요. 그런데 내실에는 인원이 충분한가요?

W: I think it should be alright. However, if some problems occur either in the rooms or at the main area, notify me immediately. In the meantime, I'll be handling the second floor.
괜찮을 것 같아요. 그런데 만약 홀이나 내실에서 문제가 발생하면, 즉시 저에게 알려 주세요. 그동안 저는 2층을 맡겠습니다.

M: Okay, I'll go change into my uniform now.
알겠습니다. 이제 가서 유니폼으로 갈아입겠습니다.

출제 포인트 정리

❶ 해당 화자의 I will ~, Let me ~, I can ~ 을 잘 들어야 해요.

Let me talk to Chris in Accounting. → Contact a coworker
제가 회계부의 크리스에게 얘기할게요.   동료에게 연락하기

❷ 미래 의미의 시간 부사 키워드를 중심으로 정답이 언급돼요.

I'll send you a detailed invoice in the mail tomorrow. → Mail an invoice
제가 내일 자세한 송장을 우편으로 보내 드릴게요.   송장을 우편으로 보내기

❸ 주로 다음과 같은 질문을 사용하여 앞으로 일어날 일을 묻습니다.

① 바로 다음에 일어날 일을 묻는 문제 유형

What does the woman say she will do? 여자는 무엇을 할 것이라고 말하는가?
What will the man most likely do next? 남자는 다음에 무엇을 할 것 같은가?

② 특정 시점에 일어날 일을 묻는 키워드 문제 유형

What will happen next week? 다음 주에 무슨 일이 일어날 것인가?
What does the man have to do tomorrow? 남자는 내일 무엇을 해야 하는가?
What does the man say he will do on Monday? 남자는 월요일에 무엇을 할 것이라고 말하는가?

Check-up Test 700+를 위해 한 걸음 한 걸음

정답 및 해석 p.036

STEP 1 문제의 키워드에 표시하고, 음성을 들으며 문제를 푼 뒤 빈칸을 채우세요. P3_Ch4_05. mp3

1. What will the woman most likely do next?
   (A) Contact a colleague
   (B) Give the man a visitor's pass
   (C) Order a copy of a book
   (D) Check an inventory list

> M: Hi, I'd like to check out some rare books and articles which were published in the past.
> W: I'm sorry, sir. We don't allow old books and rare documents to leave the library. They're very fragile and the pages can tear easily. In fact, you should make a reservation and view those documents inside the library.
> M: Really? I didn't know that. Could I make an appointment then? I can only make it during the weekend.
> W: Let me _____ and _____ with _____ reference _____ if it's available during the weekend.

2. What will the woman do tomorrow afternoon?
   (A) Organize some documents
   (B) Shop for a new computer
   (C) Leave for a business trip
   (D) Stop by a store

> M: Hi, this is Anthony Mason from the technical department. You left a message saying that you were having trouble installing the software system on your laptop computer.
> W: Yes, thanks for calling me back. I spent two days installing it, but it's too difficult for me. I'm taking this laptop with me on a business trip next week, so I need to make sure it's working.
> M: Let's see. It could be a number of things. Why don't you bring your computer to _____ _____ _____ _____? I'll be here from 2 P.M. onwards.
> W: Sure, I will be _____ by 4 P.M. _____.

STEP 2 음성을 들으며 정답을 선택하세요. P3_Ch4_06. mp3

3. Who most likely is the woman?
   (A) A building manager
   (B) A real estate agent
   (C) An interior designer
   (D) A parking attendant

4. Why is the man disappointed?
   (A) A particular product is unavailable.
   (B) A deadline will not be met.
   (C) A location is too expensive.
   (D) Customer complaints have increased.

5. What will the speakers do on next Monday?
   (A) Visit a property
   (B) Modify a design
   (C) Inspect some packages
   (D) Negotiate a starting date

6. Why is the woman calling a magazine office?
   (A) To ask for subscribing a new magazine
   (B) To change delivery address
   (C) To cancel her subscription
   (D) To confirm an order

7. What does the man advise the woman of?
   (A) A method of shipment
   (B) The name of the city
   (C) An extra fee
   (D) Another magazine

8. What will the man most likely do next?
   (A) Change some customer information
   (B) Contact his supervisor
   (C) Visit a website
   (D) Make a reservation

이것만 알면 700+

실전 문제 풀이 Tip! 대공개! 이것만은 꼭 알아 두세요.

TIP 1 상대방의 말에서 답이 언급되는 유형

❶ **질문이 수동태**로 나오면, **상대방의 대사에서 답**을 찾아야 합니다.

What does the man ask the woman to do? 남자는 여자에게 무엇을 하라고 하는가?
→ 남자가 요청하는 것이므로 **남자의 대사에서 답**이 나옵니다.

What is the man asked to do? 남자는 무엇을 하도록 요청을 받는가?
→ 남자가 요청을 받는 것이니 **상대방인 여자의 대사에서 답**이 나옵니다.

❷ 상대방의 요청이나 부탁, 제안에 대해 **수락**하는 식으로 답이 언급될 수 있습니다. 이런 경우 단서가 질문에 언급된 사람의 대사에 있지 않고 앞선 **상대방의 대사**에 있으므로 주의해야 합니다.

Q. What does the man say he will do? 남자는 무엇을 할 것이라고 하는가?

> W: Can you tell me the tracking number of the shipment? 그 배송품의 추적 번호를 알려 주실 수 있나요?
> M: Sure. Hold on a second and I'll get that for you. 물론이죠. 잠깐만 기다리시면 바로 알려 드릴게요.

A. Provide a number 번호 제공

TIP 2 요청/제안 문제 기타 팁!

❶ **제안/요청 문제가 첫 번째 문제**로 나오는 경우

이런 경우 주로 첫 번째 대사에서 대화의 주제와 관련하여 무언가를 요청하는 내용으로 대화가 시작됩니다.

※ 제안/요청 문제와 유사한 질문 유형

What is the woman looking for? 여자는 무엇을 찾고 있는가?
What does the man want to do? 남자는 무엇을 하길 원하는가?

❷ 권유/제안, 요구/요청을 묻는 다양한 질문 유형

What does the man	recommend doing? 남자는 무엇을 하는 것을 추천하는가?
	suggest? 남자는 무엇을 제안하는가?
	advise the woman to do? 남자는 여자에게 무엇을 할 것을 조언하는가?
	remind the woman about? 남자는 여자에게 무엇에 대해 상기시키는가?
	inquire about? 남자는 무엇에 대해 묻는가?
	invite the woman to do? 남자는 여자에게 무엇을 하는 것을 권하는가?
	tell the woman to do? 남자는 여자에게 무엇을 하라고 말하는가?
	instruct the woman to do? 남자는 여자에게 무엇을 하라고 지시하는가?

Chapter Test P3_Ch4_07. mp3

정답 및 해설 p.038

1. Where most likely are the speakers?
   (A) At an employment fair
   (B) At an award ceremony
   (C) At a meeting with clients
   (D) At a job interview

2. What does the man mention about his company?
   (A) It offers annual bonuses.
   (B) It specializes in advertising.
   (C) It has a job opening.
   (D) It is moving to another city.

3. What does the woman say she will do?
   (A) Give some thought about applying for a position
   (B) Schedule an appointment
   (C) Prepare a presentation
   (D) Send the man a job description

4. What does the man say he just finished doing?
   (A) Setting up some equipment
   (B) Repairing a computer
   (C) Updating a website
   (D) Typing an agenda

5. What does the woman say she needs?
   (A) A list of staff members
   (B) Access to the Internet
   (C) An updated meeting agenda
   (D) An application for a position

6. What will the man most likely do next?
   (A) Submit an application
   (B) Review some documents
   (C) Visit an office
   (D) Bring a laptop computer

7. What is the woman interested in purchasing?
   (A) A scarf
   (B) A jacket
   (C) A sweater
   (D) A tie

8. What does the man mean when he says, "I am sorry"?
   (A) He is confused by prices.
   (B) He needs to leave soon.
   (C) An item is unavailable at a store.
   (D) Some merchandise is damaged.

9. What does the man suggest the woman do?
   (A) Go to another store
   (B) Purchase a different item
   (C) Visit the store's website
   (D) Come back next week

Additional Services
Hamilton Hotel

☐ Locker for your baggage	(24 hours)
☐ Rent a car	(24 hours)
☐ Business center	(9 A.M. - 10 P.M.)
☐ Laundry service	(9 A.M. - 9 P.M.)

10. What event will take place this weekend?
    (A) A music contest
    (B) A museum opening
    (C) A textile conference
    (D) A sports event

11. Look at the graphic. Which service does the man decide to add?
    (A) Locker for your baggage
    (B) Rent a car
    (C) Business center
    (D) Laundry service

12. What does the woman ask the man to do?
    (A) Pay with a credit card
    (B) Check a reservation number
    (C) Provide a form of identification
    (D) Show a ticket

PART 4

다이렉트

700+

Chapter 1.
**전화 메시지 &
공공장소 안내 방송**

Chapter 2.
업무 회의 & 광고

Chapter 3.
설명/연설 & 투어

Chapter 4.
방송 & 인물 소개

이것만 알면 700+

PART 4 기본 문제 풀이 전략

전략 1 PART 4의 문제 유형과 정답의 출제 원리

출제되는 문제의 유형은 PART 3와 동일하지만 두세 사람의 대화가 아니라 한 사람의 말(담화)을 듣고 답을 찾는 파트입니다.

담화의 기본 정보를 묻는 문제
- 담화의 장소를 묻는 문제
- 화자/청자의 직업과 업종을 묻는 문제
- 주제나 목적을 묻는 문제

주로 첫 번째 대사에서 답이 나와요.
① 장소와 직업은 담화에서 here, our, your 등과 함께 언급돼요.
② 담화의 주제나 목적 문제는 초반부를 집중해서 들어야 합니다.

구체적인 내용을 묻는 문제
- 문제 상황을 묻는 문제
- 이유나 원인을 묻는 문제
- 특정 내용을 묻는 문제

문제에 언급된 특정 단어는 담화에서 들어야 하는 키워드입니다.
① 담화에서 꼭 들어야 하는 키워드(특정 단어)를 문제에 표시하세요.
② 키워드를 중심으로 그 앞뒤에서 정답을 확인합니다.

화자의 의도와 시각 자료 문제
- 화자의 의도를 묻는 문제
- 시각 자료 연계 문제

보기가 직접 언급되면 정답이 아닙니다.
① 화자의 의도는 담화의 주변 내용을 통해 알 수 있습니다.
② 시각 자료 연계 문제는 그래프, 표, 일정, 지도 등에서 보기와 매칭되는 담화 내용을 확인합니다.

미래의 일을 묻는 문제
- 제안/요청의 내용을 묻는 문제
- 앞으로 일어날 일을 묻는 문제

담화의 후반부에서 답이 나와요.
① 요청/제안/권유/부탁의 표현을 확인합니다.
② 미래 시제, 미래 시점을 나타내는 표현을 확인하세요.

전략 2 시험에 나오는 8가지 담화의 유형

8가지 담화 유형의 특징만 알아도 문제의 유형과 정답의 위치를 쉽게 예상할 수 있습니다.

1. 전화 메시지	**전화로 음성 메시지**를 남기는 유형의 담화로 전화 메시지를 남기는 **순서나 표현**들이 정해져 있기 때문에 전화 영어 표현과 순서만 익혀도 쉽게 풀 수 있습니다.
2. 공공장소 안내 방송	많은 사람들이 이용하는 **공항, 기내, 기차역, 상점, 도서관 등에서 불특정 다수에게 안내**를 하거나 공지를 하는 담화 유형입니다. 주로 담화의 목적이나 주제를 묻기보다는 담화가 이루어지는 **장소와 문제 사항 또는 변경 사항 등에 대한 내용을 묻는 문제**가 많이 출제됩니다.

3. 회의 발췌	다양한 업종에서 이루어지는 **회의 내용을 발췌**한 담화입니다. 회사에서 하는 **직원회의**나 식당이나 공장에서 **업무를 시작하기 전에 진행하는 회의**가 주로 출제됩니다.
4. 광고	**호기심을 유발하거나 문제 해결을 위한 방법을 제시**한 후 광고되는 것의 특징을 설명하고 **구매 방법이나 문의 방법**에 대해 언급합니다.
5. 설명/연설	콘퍼런스, 세미나, 시상식장 등의 행사장에서 **진행자 또는 주최자가 행사의 시작을 알리거나 특정 내용에 대해 설명하거나 연설**을 하는 유형입니다.
6. 투어(관광/견학)	특정 장소를 다니면서 소개를 하는 내용입니다. 주로 **신입 사원들을 대상으로 회사나 공장을 돌아보면서 소개**하거나 관광지에서 **관광객을 대상으로 일정이나 관광지를 소개**합니다.
7. 방송(뉴스/날씨/교통)	**라디오 방송**의 뉴스나 프로그램입니다. 주로 **시설이나 건물 등의 건설 관련 내용 또는 기업 관련 뉴스**가 출제됩니다. 종종 날씨와 교통 방송도 출제됩니다.
8. 인물 소개	방송이나 행사장, 시상식 등에서 **초대 손님이나 연설자, 시상자, 직원 등을 소개**하는 내용입니다. 간략한 인사와 함께 **소개하는 사람의 직위나 직업, 업적, 이력 등을 언급**합니다. 그 후 소개되는 사람의 어떤 일을 할 것인지에 대해서 언급합니다.

PART 4는 이렇게 풀어야 해요.

Step 1. 문제를 미리 읽습니다.
- 문제의 유형을 파악합니다.
  기본적인 정보(상) → 구체적인 정보(중) → 요구/요청/제안/권유/당부(하)
- 문제의 키워드를 확인합니다. (고유 명사/특정 명사/특정 동사/시간/날짜/요일)
- (A)~(D)의 보기의 키워드를 미리 확인합니다. (동사 또는 명사)

Step 2. 문제의 키워드를 파악했다면 이제 담화의 이야기 전개를 예측합니다.
예를 들어 ① 첫 번째 문제가 화자의 신분, ② 두 번째 문제가 키워드, ③ 세 번째 문제가 요청한 것을 묻는 문제라면, ① 초반부에서 화자에 대한 내용, ② 중간쯤에서 키워드 관련 내용, ③ 마지막엔 화자가 청자에게 무엇을 하라고 요청하는 내용이 나올 것임을 예측할 수 있습니다.
※ *8가지 빈출 담화 유형에 익숙해지면 더욱 쉽게 예측할 수 있습니다.*

Step 3. 담화를 들으면서 보기에서 정답을 찾습니다.
담화가 모두 끝난 후에 정답을 선택하는 것이 아니라 담화가 진행되는 동안에 **정답은 순서대로 등장하기 때문에** 순서대로 각 문제의 정답을 표시하며 풀어야 합니다.

Step 4. 다음 문제를 준비합니다.
담화가 끝나고 담화에 딸린 문제들을 읽어 줄 때는 이미 해당하는 세 문제의 마킹을 마치고, 다음 담화의 문제들을 읽으며 준비해야 합니다.

Chapter 1 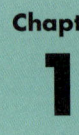 전화 메시지 & 공공장소 안내 방송

Point 01 전화 메시지

전화 메시지는 주로 '① 인사말/발신자/수신자 ▶ ② 목적 ▶ ③ 세부 내용 ▶ ④ 요청/당부 사항'의 순서로 전개됩니다. 전화 메시지의 목적은 **예약, 취소, 변경/지연, 확인, 항의, 제안, 소식 전달** 등이며, 종종 자동 응답기 메시지도 출제됩니다.

P4_Ch1_01. mp3

1. Where does the speaker probably work?
화자는 어디서 근무하는가? <직종>
A. At an appliance manufacturer 가전제품 제조회사에서
↳ *This is ~ 에서 화자가 가전제품 회사에서 근무함을 알 수 있습니다.*

2. What is the main purpose of the message?
메시지의 주된 목적은 무엇인가? <전화 목적>
A. To describe the responsibilities of a job
직무 내용을 설명하는 것
↳ *The manager is responsible for ~에서 담당 업무를 설명하고 있다는 것을 알 수 있습니다.*

3. According to the speaker, why should Mr. Johnson call him?
화자에 따르면, 왜 존슨 씨는 화자에게 전화해야 하는가? <제안/요청>
A. To express interest in a job
일자리에 대한 관심을 표명하기 위해
↳ *직책에 관심이 있으면 연락 달라고 했으므로, 존슨 씨는 일자리에 관심을 표하기 위해 화자에게 전화를 해야 함을 알 수 있습니다.*

Good morning. ■ **This is Adam Smith from Human Resources at Star Appliance, calling for Peter Johnson.** 안녕하세요. 저는 스타 가전제품의 인사부에서 근무하는 애덤 스미스이며, 피터 존슨 씨에게 전화드립니다.

Mr. Johnson, from your résumé, it looks like you are qualified for the managerial position in our marketing department. ■ **The manager is responsible for marketing new products in the sales and marketing division. Advertising and sales will be your biggest responsibility.** 존슨 씨, 당신의 이력서에 따르면 당신이 우리 마케팅 부서의 관리자 자리에 적임자로 보입니다. 매니저는 영업 및 마케팅 부서에서 신제품의 마케팅을 담당합니다. 광고와 영업이 가장 큰 업무가 될 것입니다.

You will find a complete job description on our website, www.starappliance.com. ■ **If you are interested in this position, please let me know. You can reach me at 506-4587.** Thank you. 저희 웹사이트 www.starappliance.com에서 전체 업무 내용을 확인하실 수 있습니다. 이 직책에 관심이 있으시면 알려 주세요. 506-4587로 연락주시면 됩니다. 감사합니다.

출제 포인트 정리

❶ **발신자와 수신자의 직업은 calling, you, your의 뒤를 잘 들어야 합니다.**
Hi, this is Janet Miller **calling from** Lopez Investment. 안녕하세요. 저는 로페즈 투자사에서 전화드리는 자넷 밀러입니다.
You have reached Dr. Lopez's office. 로페즈 선생님의 사무실로 전화하셨습니다.
This morning I heard about **your** restaurant on the radio. 오늘 아침에 라디오에서 당신의 식당에 대해서 들었어요.

❷ **전화의 목적이나 주제는 발신자의 소개가 끝나자마자 언급됩니다.**
This is Brandon **calling to** let you know that we have your car ready.
저는 브랜든이고 귀하의 차량이 준비되었음을 알려 드리기 위해 전화드립니다.
I'm calling about the schedule change. 일정 변경에 대해서 전화드립니다.

❸ **마지막에 항상 상대에게 요청이나 제안을 합니다.**
If you have any questions, **please** call us at 555-2580. 궁금한 게 있으시면 555-2580으로 전화 주세요.
You can also check our website. 또한 우리 웹사이트를 확인하시면 됩니다.

Check-up Test 700+를 위해 한 걸음 한 걸음

정답 및 해석 p.040

STEP 1 문제의 키워드에 표시하고, 음성을 들으며 문제를 푼 뒤 빈칸을 채우세요.   P4_Ch1_02. mp3

1. What's the purpose of the message?
   (A) To ask about a program
   (B) To introduce a service
   (C) To give a special offer
   (D) To answer an inquiry

2. What type of business is White Box?
   (A) An architectural firm
   (B) A clothing store
   (C) An Internet service provider
   (D) A website design company

3. What is the listener offered?
   (A) Free counseling
   (B) Free delivery
   (C) A discounted price
   (D) An exclusive design

Hello, Ms. Stephens. _____ is Alfredo Rodgers from White Box, _____ your call as you _____. Yes, _____ _____ can design _____ _____ for _____ new _____ store. If you could call me at 070-2589 and let me know a time that fits your schedule, I can arrange _____ _____ with one of our web designers _____ _____. That would be helpful for you in selecting the right design and features for your store's website.

STEP 2 음성을 들으며 정답을 선택하세요.   P4_Ch1_03. mp3

4. What is the problem with the laptop?
   (A) Some parts are missing.
   (B) The battery is not working.
   (C) The fan is not working.
   (D) It needs more memory.

5. According to the speaker, what will the listener have to do?
   (A) Call the manufacturer
   (B) Pay for a part
   (C) Buy some new equipment
   (D) Pick up the laptop

6. What does the speaker offer?
   (A) A new keyboard
   (B) Some coupons
   (C) Free installation
   (D) A discount

Point 02 공공장소 안내 방송

공공장소 안내 방송은 주로 '❶ 인사 및 공지 목적 ▶ ❷ 공지 내용 ▶ ❸ 당부 및 요청 ▶ ❹ 문의 및 연락처'의 순서로 전개됩니다. 공항(기내)이나 기차역 등 교통 시설에서 일정의 변경이나 취소를 알리는 안내 방송과 백화점이나 마트, 도서관 등에서 신규 코너 또는 (할인) 행사를 소개하거나 폐점을 알리는 안내 방송이 자주 등장합니다.

▶ P4_Ch1_04. mp3

1. Where is the announcement being made?
안내 방송은 어디에서 나오고 있는가? <장소>
A. At a supermarket 슈퍼마켓에서
↳ *Attention, ~ shoppers에서 안내 방송의 장소가 슈퍼마켓 같은 매장임을 알 수 있습니다.*

2. According to the speaker, how can listeners locate sale items?
화자에 따르면, 청자는 어떻게 할인 제품을 찾을 수 있는가? <키워드>
A. By looking for special labels 특별한 라벨을 찾아서
↳ *키워드인 sale items가 언급된 곳에서 할인 제품은 가격표에 노란 점이 찍혀 있다는 것을 알 수 있습니다.*

3. Why are listeners encouraged to visit the customer service desk?
왜 청자에게 고객 서비스 데스크를 방문하도록 권장하는가? <제안/요청>
A. To register for a shopper's card 고객 카드를 등록하기 위해
↳ *후반부에서 customer service desk를 잘 들어야 합니다. If you ~ 이하에서 카드가 없다면 고객 서비스 데스크를 방문해 신청하라고 했습니다.*

❶ Attention, Discount Mart shoppers, and thank you for shopping with us today. For this week only, we are offering 50% off on selected footwear. 디스카운트 마트 고객님, 주목해 주세요. 오늘 저희 매장을 이용해 주셔서 감사합니다. 오직 이번 주만 일부 신발 제품들에 대해 50% 할인을 제공하고 있습니다.

You can choose from running shoes, dress shoes, sandals, and much more! ❷ Sale items have a yellow dot on the price tag. The special offer applies to those items with yellow stickers only. 여러분은 운동화, 정장용 구두, 샌들, 그리고 다른 많은 제품들을 선택할 수 있습니다! 할인 제품들은 가격표에 노란 점이 찍혀 있습니다. 특별 할인은 노란 스티커가 붙어 있는 제품들에만 적용됩니다.

If you have our Discount Mart Shopper's Card, you will earn an extra 300 points for every item you purchase this week. ❸ If you don't have one, please visit our customer service desk at the back of the store to sign up for one today. 저희 디스카운트 마트 고객 카드를 가지고 계시다면, 이번 주에 구입한 모든 제품들에 대해서 추가로 300포인트를 얻을 수 있습니다. 만약 고객 카드가 없으시다면, 오늘 마트 뒤편에 있는 고객 서비스 데스크를 방문하여 신청하세요.

출제 포인트 정리

❶ 안내 방송의 장소와 화자/청자의 직업은 처음에 나오는 attention을 잘 들어야 합니다.

Attention all shoppers. 모든 쇼핑객들에게 알려드립니다.
Our store will be closing in 30 minutes. 저희 상점은 30분 후에 문을 닫을 예정입니다.

❷ 안내 방송의 목적은 주로 변경 사항이나 새로운 소식을 알리는 것입니다.

Before tonight's concert begins, we have some important reminders.
오늘 밤 공연이 시작되기 전에 몇 가지 중요한 사항을 다시 알려 드립니다.
I'm sorry to announce that the flight for New York has been delayed.
뉴욕행 비행기가 연기됨을 알려 드리게 되어 죄송합니다.

❸ 공지의 내용에 따라 청자들에게 혜택을 제안하거나 당부하는 내용이 이어집니다.

We kindly ask that you stay in your seats throughout the show.
공연이 진행되는 동안에 자리에 꼭 앉아 계시기 바랍니다.
Photographs are not allowed in the hall. 홀에서 사진은 찍으실 수 없습니다.
Remember to pick up your complimentary shopping bag before you leave.
가시기 전에 무료 쇼핑백을 가져가시기 바랍니다.

Check-up Test 700+를 위해 한 걸음 한 걸음

정답 및 해석 p.041

STEP 1 문제의 키워드에 표시하고, 음성을 들으며 문제를 푼 뒤 빈칸을 채우세요.   P4_Ch1_05. mp3

1. Where most likely would the announcement be heard?
   (A) At a train station
   (B) On a plane
   (C) At an airport
   (D) At a travel agency

2. According to the announcement, what has been changed?
   (A) The arrival time
   (B) The flight number
   (C) The departure gate
   (D) The departure time

3. What made the change necessary?
   (A) Mechanical problems
   (B) A baggage mix-up
   (C) The delay of a previous flight
   (D) Weather conditions

> Attention all passengers! East Wind Airlines' _____ 457 to Bangkok is now _____ for boarding at gate 12. All passengers should proceed to gate 12 with their _____ passes _____. This flight was supposed to _____ at 8 A.M. _____ it was _____ for 40 minutes _____ current _____ conditions. We apologize for the delay and changing departure time. Again, all passengers on flight 457 to Bangkok should now report to gate 12 for immediate boarding.

STEP 2 음성을 들으며 정답을 선택하세요.   P4_Ch1_06. mp3

4. What is the main purpose of the announcement?
   (A) To inform customers of a special sale
   (B) To explain the daily specials at a café
   (C) To give directions to a café
   (D) To announce the closing time of a museum

5. What does the speaker remind the listeners to do?
   (A) Purchase a souvenir
   (B) Collect their belongings
   (C) Order some snacks
   (D) Have their ticket ready

6. According to the speaker, what will happen next week?
   (A) A contest will be held.
   (B) A new exhibit will open.
   (C) An opening sale will end.
   (D) A renovation will begin.

이것만 알면 700+

실전 문제 풀이 Tip 대공개! 이것만은 꼭 알아 두세요.

TIP 1 전화 메시지 빈출 문제

유형	문제	정답
목적	Why is the speaker calling? 화자는 왜 전화하고 있는가?	전화의 목적과 화자의 직종은 맨 처음에 나옵니다.
직종	Who is the caller? 전화를 건 사람은 누구인가?	
제안/요청	What does the speaker say he can do? 화자는 무엇을 할 수 있다고 말하는가? What does the speaker ask the listener to do? 화자는 청자에게 무엇을 해 달라고 요청하는가?	내용을 설명하고 나면 후반부에 청자에게 제안이나 요청을 합니다.
화자 의도	Why does the speaker say, "I use Chef's Dream cookware"? 화자는 왜 "저는 셰프스 드림 조리 도구를 사용합니다"라고 말하는가?	화자의 의도는 주어진 표현의 앞뒤 내용에서 알 수 있습니다.
시각 자료	Look at the graphic. Which quantity needs to be changed? 시각 자료를 보시오. 어떤 수량이 변경되어야 하는가?	시각 자료에서 보기의 내용과 매칭되는 내용을 찾아야 합니다.

TIP 2 공공장소 안내 방송 빈출 문제

유형	문제	정답
장소	Where is this announcement being made? 이 안내 방송은 어디에서 나오는 것인가? Where most likely are the listeners? 청자들은 어디에 있을 것 같은가?	안내 방송이 나오는 장소는 담화의 시작 멘트에서 확인합니다.
문제점	What is the cause of the delay? 지연의 이유는 무엇인가? What problem does the speaker mention? 화자는 어떤 문제를 언급하고 있는가?	문제점이나 걱정 등 부정적인 내용이 언급됩니다.
내용	What can listeners find on the second floor? 청자들은 2층에서 무엇을 찾을 수 있는가? What is special about the new ID cards? 새로운 신분증의 특징은 무엇인가?	이유, 대상, 수단, 방법 등의 구체적인 내용을 묻는 문제는 문제의 키워드가 언급되는 부분에서 답을 찾을 수 있습니다.
시각 자료	Look at the graphic. What time will the ferry leave? 시각 자료를 보시오. 여객선은 몇 시에 출발할 것인가?	시각 자료로는 공공장소에서 볼 수 있는 티켓, 일정표, 광고, 지도 등이 제시됩니다.
제안/요청	What does the speaker recommend? 화자는 무엇을 권유하고 있는가? What are some listeners asked to do? 청자들은 무엇을 해야 하는가?	요청 사항이나 제안하는 내용은 후반부에 나옵니다.

Chapter Test

1. What is the purpose of the message?
   (A) To explain registration procedures
   (B) To provide directions
   (C) To announce office hours
   (D) To describe appointment policies

2. What will happen in February?
   (A) A construction project will start.
   (B) An address will change.
   (C) An additional service will be provided.
   (D) A department will be relocated.

3. Why should listeners press 0?
   (A) To repeat the recording
   (B) To leave a message
   (C) To speak to a representative
   (D) To hear an additional menu

   From **Perth** To **Sydney**
   Train Number: HJ 1052
   Depart 10:00 A.M.
   Arrive: 3:00 P.M.
   Platform: A10

4. According to the speaker, what has caused a problem?
   (A) A renovation
   (B) An electrical outage
   (C) Bad weather
   (D) An engine malfunction

5. Look at the graphic. According to the speaker, which piece of information will change?
   (A) Perth
   (B) HJ 1052
   (C) 3:00 P.M.
   (D) A10

6. What does the speaker say is being offered?
   (A) Local maps
   (B) Alternative transportation
   (C) Discount tickets
   (D) Meal vouchers

7. Where is the announcement being made?
   (A) At an airport
   (B) At a hardware store
   (C) At a supermarket
   (D) At a restaurant

8. Why does the speaker say, "It won't take much of your time"?
   (A) To correct a mistake
   (B) To promote a product
   (C) To request a change
   (D) To encourage participation

9. How can the listeners receive a coupon?
   (A) By purchasing items
   (B) By joining a membership
   (C) By visiting a website
   (D) By filling in a form

Order form	
Customer: Carla Fashion	
Product: Brochures	
500	Training Session
1,000	Conference
2,000	Customer Survey
20,000	Product Launching

10. Which department does the speaker most likely work in?
    (A) Accounting
    (B) Human resources
    (C) Marketing
    (D) Design

11. Look at the graphic. Which quantity needs to be revised?
    (A) 500
    (B) 1,000
    (C) 2,000
    (D) 20,000

12. What does the speaker say she will do this Friday?
    (A) Deliver a speech
    (B) Receive an invoice
    (C) Pick up an order
    (D) Check a website

Chapter 2 업무 회의 & 광고

Point 01 회의 발췌

업무 회의는 가장 많이 출제되는 유형으로, 주로 '❶ 환영/감사 인사 ▶ ❷ 회의 목적 ▶ ❸ 세부 사항 ▶ ❹ 당부 및 앞으로 벌어질 상황'의 순서로 전개됩니다. 기본적인 정보를 묻는 문제들의 출제 비중이 높으며, 회사나 식당 등에서 직원들을 대상으로 하는 매출 보고나 업무와 관련된 설명, 일정 전달 및 업무 할당 등의 내용이 주로 나옵니다.

P4_Ch2_01. mp3

1. Who most likely is the **speaker**?
화자는 누구일 것 같은가? <직종>
A. A **department head** 부서장
↳ As the director of research and development, I ~에서 화자는 부서 책임자라는 것을 알 수 있습니다.

2. According to the speaker, **how** is the NP-319 **different** from **earlier models**?
화자에 따르면 NP-319는 이전 모델들과 어떻게 다른가? <키워드>
A. It is **faster**. 더 빠르다.
↳ 키워드 NP-319를 언급한 뒤에, two times the processing speed than our previous versions라고 한 것으로 보아 이전 모델들보다 속도가 더 빠르다는 것을 알 수 있습니다.

3. What will **Jason Morris discuss**?
제이슨 모리스는 무엇에 대해 논의할 것인가? <미래>
A. The **advertising strategy** 광고 전략
↳ 키워드 Jason Morris를 언급한 뒤에, 어떻게 광고될 것인지에 대해 이야기해 줄 것이라고 했으므로 광고 전략에 대해 논의할 것임을 알 수 있습니다.

Good morning. I'm glad everyone came to the department meeting. Some topics that we will go over today are very important.
안녕하세요. 모두들 부서 회의에 와 주셔서 기쁩니다. 우리가 오늘 검토할 몇몇 주제들은 매우 중요합니다.

❶ As the director of research and development, I am thrilled to tell you that our new notepad ❷ NP-319 has passed all the required tests, and it will go on sale next month. I'm sure most of you know that ❷ the new model has two times the processing speed than our previous versions.
연구개발부의 책임자로서 저희의 새로운 노트패드 NP-319가 모든 필수적인 테스트들을 통과하고 다음 달부터 판매에 들어갈 것이라는 소식을 전하게 되어 매우 흥분됩니다. 여러분들 대부분 새로운 모델이 우리 이전 버전들보다 처리 속도가 두 배 더 빠르다는 것을 알고 계시리라 확신합니다.

❸ Jason Morris, our advertising director, is going to come out now and tell us about how the NP-319 will be advertised.
우리 광고 책임자이신 제이슨 모리스 씨가 지금 나오셔서 NP-319가 어떻게 광고될 것인지에 대해 우리에게 이야기해 주실 겁니다.

출제 포인트 정리

❶ **처음 인사말에서 특정 업종이나 직업과 관련된 내용이 등장합니다.**

Thanks for coming to today's board meeting. 오늘 이사회에 참석해 주셔서 감사합니다.
I'd like to start off our monthly sales meeting. 월례 영업 회의를 시작하겠습니다.

❷ **회의의 내용은 주로 정책, 매출 또는 업무상 지시 사항에 관한 것입니다.**

[인사] The next topic I want to discuss is staffing. 제가 다음으로 논의하고 싶은 주제는 인사입니다.
[의견] This meeting is to generate some ideas for increasing our TV sales.
이 회의는 저희 TV의 판매 증가를 위한 아이디어를 생각하기 위한 것입니다.
[정책] I'd like to discuss the company guidelines for travel. 출장 관련 회사 지침에 대해 얘기하고자 합니다.
[지시] I called this meeting to discuss how all cashiers at our store should interact with customers.
저희 가게의 모든 계산원들이 어떻게 고객에게 응대해야 하는지를 논의하기 위해 회의를 소집했습니다.

Check-up Test 700+를 위해 한 걸음 한 걸음

정답 및 해석 p.044

STEP 1 문제의 키워드에 표시하고, 음성을 들으며 문제를 푼 뒤 빈칸을 채우세요. P4_Ch2_02. mp3

1. According to the speaker, what benefits does International Trade Building offer?
   (A) It is closer to downtown.
   (B) The office is bigger.
   (C) The rent is cheaper.
   (D) It has a good view.

2. What are the employees asked to do?
   (A) Go down to the river
   (B) Get rid of personal documents
   (C) Disconnect all appliances
   (D) Sort through files

3. When will the move take place?
   (A) Wednesday
   (B) Thursday
   (C) Friday
   (D) Saturday

> I would like to inform everyone about the upcoming move to the _____ _____ _____. We've chosen that building because it has a _____ _____ of the Laurens River from our offices. We are using the same moving company that we used when we moved into this building five years ago. Those of you who were here at that time might remember the process. They are going to come and pack all the office furniture and electronic equipment. You need to pack your own stuff. It's a good time to organize all your documents. _____ _____ _____ all _____ in your departments and throw out materials you don't need. Make sure everything is done by Tuesday night. The _____ will be _____ everything on _____. Let me know if you have any questions.

STEP 2 음성을 들으며 정답을 선택하세요. P4_Ch2_03. mp3

4. According to the speaker, what was announced this morning?
   (A) The new management
   (B) A merger of two departments
   (C) The release of a new product
   (D) A special advertisement

5. Who are listeners told to contact?
   (A) Competitors
   (B) Programmers
   (C) Marketing staff
   (D) Existing customers

6. What are listeners asked to review?
   (A) A confidential report
   (B) A new price list
   (C) A name of a program
   (D) A product survey

Chapter 2. 업무 회의 & 광고

Point 02 광고

광고는 주로 '❶ 문제점 제기 및 광고 대상 소개 ▶ ❷ 특징/장점/혜택 ▶ ❸ 구매 제안 또는 지원/신청 방법 및 기간 제시'의 순서로 전개됩니다. 여행사, 식당, 세탁소, 스포츠 용품점, 가구점, 슈퍼마켓, 청소 대행업체, 음악사, 자동차 판매점 등의 다양한 광고가 등장해요.

P4_Ch2_04. mp3

1. **What event** is being **announced**?
   어떤 행사를 알리고 있는가? <광고 대상>
   A. **A food festival** 음식 축제
   ↳ 세계 음식 축제에 초대하고 있으므로 음식 축제에 대해 광고하고 있음을 알 수 있습니다.

2. **How** can people at the event **enter the contest**?
   행사에서 사람들은 어떻게 콘테스트에 참가할 수 있는가? <키워드>
   A. **By buying** an item 상품을 구매함으로써
   ↳ Everytime you make a purchase, you can enter a contest를 통해 구매할(buying) 때마다, 콘테스트에 참석할 수 있다는 것을 알 수 있습니다.

3. According to the advertisement, **what** can be **found online**?
   광고에 따르면, 온라인에서 무엇을 발견할 수 있는가? <키워드>
   A. **A directory of participating businesses**
   참가 업체들의 목록
   ↳ 웹사이트에 방문하면 a list of participating businesses(참가 업체들의 목록)를 확인할 수 있다는 것을 알 수 있습니다.

If you're looking for something fun to do with your family this weekend, ❶ come out to Victoria Park for the annual World Food Festival.
이번 주말에 가족과 함께 재미있게 할 수 있는 것을 찾으신다면, 연례 세계 음식 축제가 열리는 빅토리아 파크로 오세요.

At the festival, you can try different food from around the world prepared by local chefs. You will also be able to buy food items at a discounted price. ❷ Everytime you make a purchase, you can enter a contest to win meals at local restaurants.
축제에서는 현지 요리사들이 준비한 전 세계의 각기 다른 종류의 음식들을 맛보실 수 있습니다. 또한 음식들을 할인된 가격으로 살 수 있습니다. 음식을 구매하실 때마다, 지역 음식점에서 식사할 기회를 얻을 수 있는 콘테스트에 참여하실 수 있습니다.

❸ You can check a list of participating businesses when you visit our website at worldfoodfestival.com.
저희 웹사이트인 worldfoodfestival.com에 방문하시면, 참가 업체들의 목록을 확인하실 수 있습니다.

출제 포인트 정리

❶ 광고는 질문을 하거나 어려움에 대해 언급하면서 시작하는 경우가 많은데 이를 통해 광고의 대상을 알 수 있어요.

Are you looking for something special for your holiday?
휴가를 위해 특별한 것을 찾고 계시나요?

If you're experiencing difficulty in finding a proper moving company,
적당한 이사 회사를 찾으시는 데 어려움을 겪고 계신다면,

❷ 제품의 특징이나 장점은 special, benefit, advantage 등과 함께 언급되고 구매자에게 주어지는 혜택으로는 가격 할인이 자주 등장합니다.

The benefit to you as an employer is: you won't have to wait long.
고용인으로서 당신에게 주는 혜택은 길게 기다릴 필요가 없다는 것입니다.

You can purchase our brand-new items at discounted prices.
신제품들을 할인된 가격으로 구매하실 수 있습니다.

❸ 구매 방법 혹은 추가 정보나 혜택을 받을 수 있는 방법으로는 직접 방문, 전화, website 방문 등이 자주 언급됩니다.

For more information on our free service, call us today.
무료 서비스에 대한 추가 정보를 원하시면 오늘 저희에게 전화 주세요.

Visit us today at one of our stores and take advantage of our special offers.
오늘 저희 매장 중 한 곳을 방문하셔서 특별 할인의 혜택을 누리세요.

Check-up Test 700+를 위해 한 걸음 한 걸음

정답 및 해석 p.045

STEP 1 문제의 키워드에 표시하고, 음성을 들으며 문제를 푼 뒤 빈칸을 채우세요.   P4_Ch2_05. mp3

1. What merchandise is being advertised?
   (A) Garden flowers
   (B) Office equipment
   (C) Home decorations
   (D) Floor coverings

2. What change has taken place at the store?
   (A) A new item has arrived.
   (B) A showroom has been enlarged.
   (C) A manager has been replaced.
   (D) A wood floor area has been added.

3. When will the sale end?
   (A) On Thursday
   (B) On Friday
   (C) On Saturday
   (D) On Sunday

> Are you _____ about _____ your _____?
> Have you been looking for the right area rug that will match your home or office? Look no more! Rosedale Flooring has all the answers! We offer hundreds of products to meet all your needs, and we have a huge range of different colors to help you find the exact color you want in our _____ _____ _____.
> For a limited time only, we are offering 30% off on all products in the store. So come on out to our fabulous showroom in Rosedale Mall. You must hurry because the _____ _____ this _____.

STEP 2 음성을 들으며 정답을 선택하세요.   P4_Ch2_06. mp3

4. What type of business is being advertised?
   (A) A home cleaning service
   (B) A furniture supplier
   (C) An interior designer
   (D) A web design company

5. According to the advertisement, what can customers receive?
   (A) A full refund
   (B) A free delivery
   (C) A special discount
   (D) A gift

6. What can listeners do online?
   (A) Place an order
   (B) Check an order's status
   (C) Change an address
   (D) Customize a product

Chapter 2. 업무 회의 & 광고   117

이것만 알면 700+
실전 문제 풀이 Tip 대공개! 이것만은 꼭 알아 두세요.

TIP 1 회의 발췌 빈출 문제

유형	문제	정답
직종	Where does the speaker most likely work? 화자는 어디에서 일할 것 같은가? Who most likely are the listeners? 청자들은 누구일 것 같은가?	회의에 참석한 사람들의 직업이나 업종은 인사말에서 확인합니다.
주제/ 목적	What is the purpose of the meeting? 회의의 목적은 무엇인가? What is the speaker mainly talking about? 화자는 주로 무엇에 대해 이야기하고 있는가?	회의의 주제와 목적은 초반에 인사말이 끝난 후 바로 언급됩니다.
이유/ 변경	Why does the speaker thank the listeners? 화자는 왜 청자들에게 감사하는가? According to the speaker, what is being changed? 화자에 따르면, 무엇이 변경되고 있는가?	고마움 같은 감정의 이유 또는 업무상 변경 사항은 키워드를 통해 단서를 찾습니다.
제안/ 요청	What does the speaker suggest that the listeners do? 화자는 청자들에게 무엇을 하라고 제안하는가? What does the speaker ask the listeners to do? 화자는 청자들에게 무엇을 하라고 요청하는가?	회의 참석자에게 지시하거나 요청하는 내용은 마지막에 언급됩니다.

TIP 2 광고 빈출 문제

유형	문제	정답
광고 대상	What is being advertised? 무엇이 광고가 되고 있는가? What product does the company sell? 회사는 어떤 제품을 판매하는가?	광고하는 제품이나 서비스는 첫 문장에서 제시되는 문제 및 해결책을 통해 알 수 있습니다.
장점/ 혜택	What advantage does the company offer? 회사는 무슨 혜택을 제공하는가? What does the speaker say is special about Karl's Travel? 화자는 칼스 여행사에 대해 특별한 것이 무엇이라고 하는가?	제품이나 서비스를 소개한 후에는 특장점이나 혜택 등을 언급합니다.
제안/ 요청	Why should the listeners visit a website? 청자들은 왜 웹사이트를 방문해야 하는가? How can the listeners receive a free gift? 청자들은 어떻게 무료 선물을 받을 수 있는가?	구매를 유도하기 위해 광고의 마지막에는 (할인) 혜택을 받는 수단이나 방법을 제안하거나 권유합니다.

Chapter Test

1. What type of merchandise does Fairmont's sell?
   (A) Furniture
   (B) Cleaning tools
   (C) Kitchen supplies
   (D) Clothing

2. Why is the store selling items at a discounted price?
   (A) It is making room for new items.
   (B) It is going bankrupt.
   (C) It is closing for the summer.
   (D) It is celebrating a new location.

3. When does the promotion end?
   (A) On Thursday
   (B) On Friday
   (C) On Saturday
   (D) On Sunday

4. Who is being addressed?
   (A) Engineers
   (B) Salespeople
   (C) Clothing designers
   (D) Corporate executives

5. What will happen in March?
   (A) Prices will increase.
   (B) A catalog will be mailed.
   (C) A new store will open.
   (D) New products will become available.

6. What will the listeners do?
   (A) View sample items
   (B) Check client lists
   (C) Discuss packaging options
   (D) Set up a display

7. Who would be interested in this advertisement?
   (A) Restaurant owners
   (B) Office workers
   (C) Computer repair shops
   (D) Furniture stores

8. What does the speaker imply when he says, "It does much more than that"?
   (A) A company has made several donations.
   (B) A membership has more advantages.
   (C) An item has additional features.
   (D) A software is compatible with other equipment.

9. What will happen this weekend?
   (A) A sale will end.
   (B) An article will be released.
   (C) An advertising campaign will start.
   (D) A warranty will expire.

Dessert of the Day
- Olga Restaurant -

Monday	Chocolate Cake
Tuesday	Cheese Cake
Wednesday	Brownie Cookies
Thursday	Fresh Fruit Tart

10. Look at the graphic. Which dessert does the speaker say will be served two times this week?
    (A) Chocolate Cake
    (B) Cheese Cake
    (C) Brownie Cookies
    (D) Fresh Fruit Tart

11. Who is Katie Wilson?
    (A) A server
    (B) A consultant
    (C) A chef
    (D) A business owner

12. What does the speaker say is available in the staff room?
    (A) Order forms
    (B) A special menu
    (C) A training plan
    (D) New uniforms

Chapter 3 설명/연설 & 투어

Point 01 설명/연설

설명/연설은 주로 '❶ 환영, 감사의 인사 ▶ ❷ 목적/주제 ▶ ❸ 세부 사항 ▶ ❹ 당부 및 앞으로 벌어지는 상황 전달'의 순서로 전개됩니다. 오리엔테이션, 세미나, 워크숍 같은 **직원 교육 등의 행사에서의 설명/연설**이 주를 이루며, 종종 **제품이나 식당 메뉴 소개, 시상식장 같은 행사에서의 연설**이 출제되고 있습니다.

P4_Ch3_01. mp3

1. Who most likely are the **listeners**?
청자들은 누구일 것 같은가? <직종>
A. **Sales** representatives 영업 사원들
→ 환영 인사 후에 가장 촉망되는 영업 사원들을 선정했다고 언급하고 있으므로 청자들은 영업 사원들임을 알 수 있습니다.

2. What will the **workshop focus** on?
워크숍은 무엇에 초점을 맞출 것인가? <행사 주제>
A. **Interacting** with **clients** 고객들과 소통하기
→ 이번 워크숍에서 고객들과 함께 성공적으로 일하는 방법을 가르쳐 주겠다는 내용에서 '고객과 소통하기'가 워크숍의 주제라는 것을 알 수 있습니다.

3. How will the **survey** results be **used**?
설문 결과는 어떻게 사용될 것인가? <키워드>
A. To **assign** participants to **groups**
참가자들을 그룹에 배정하기 위해
→ 후반부에 설문 답변이 그룹을 나누는 데 도움이 될 것이라고 했으므로 그룹 배정에 사용될 것임을 알 수 있습니다.

Good morning ladies and gentlemen and welcome to the ABA leadership workshop. ❶ The personnel committee has chosen the most promising sales representatives from 120 of our international branch offices. 신사 숙녀 여러분, 안녕하세요. ABA 리더십 워크숍에 오신 것을 환영합니다. 인사 위원회는 우리 해외 지사에서 근무하는 120명 중 가장 촉망되는 영업 사원을 선정했습니다.

❷ During this workshop, we will teach you how to work successfully with your clients.
이번 워크숍 동안 우리는 여러분에게 고객들과 함께 성공적으로 일하는 방법을 가르쳐 드릴 예정입니다.

From now on, I am going to distribute a short survey about your previous professional experience for everyone to fill out. ❸ Your answers to each question will help us to divide you into groups for the afternoon sessions. 이제 제가 이전의 전문적인 경험에 대한 간단한 설문지를 나눠 드릴 테니 모두 작성해 주시기 바랍니다. 각 질문에 대한 여러분의 답변이 오후 시간을 위해 그룹을 나누는 데 도움이 될 것입니다.

출제 포인트 정리

❶ 처음 인사말이나 행사명에서 참석자들의 직종과 행사의 목적 및 장소를 확인할 수 있습니다.

Thank you for coming to our anniversary party. 저희 기념 파티에 와 주셔서 감사드립니다.
I am very excited to welcome all of you interns to our team. 우리 팀에 인턴으로 오신 여러분 모두를 환영합니다.
We hope you've been enjoying the conference on communication skills.
커뮤니케이션 스킬에 관한 콘퍼런스가 즐거우셨기를 바랍니다.

❷ 담화 이후에 할 일에는 will 등과 같은 미래 시제를 사용합니다.

During this new employee orientation, I'll give you some information about working here.
이 신입 사원 오리엔테이션에서 저는 여러분께 여기서 근무하는 것에 대한 정보를 드릴 것입니다.
We'll step outside and I'll show you how to properly operate the new equipment.
밖에 나가서 제가 여러분께 새로운 장비를 제대로 작동하는 방법을 보여 드릴 것입니다.
You might wonder why we're watching a video. 여러분들은 우리가 왜 영상을 볼 것인지 궁금하실 겁니다.

Check-up Test 700+를 위해 한 걸음 한 걸음

정답 및 해석 p.047

STEP 1 문제의 키워드에 표시하고, 음성을 들으며 문제를 푼 뒤 빈칸을 채우세요. P4_Ch3_02.

1. What will the workshop be about?
   (A) Assembling some equipment
   (B) Sketching a house
   (C) Renting some properties
   (D) Taking pictures of buildings

2. Where will listeners go?
   (A) To a historic residence
   (B) To a real estate agency
   (C) To an art gallery
   (D) To a local park

3. What will the speaker distribute?
   (A) Photo equipment
   (B) Writing tools
   (C) Equipment rental forms
   (D) A building map

_____ _____ for _____ to the architecture _____ _____ for beginners. You are going to learn all the basic techniques you need to know about photographing buildings. Today, _____ are _____ to _____ the Davenport _____, the one-hundred-year-old _____ that was used as a governor's mansion for many years. Once we get there, you'll quickly discover why it's a great place to learn photography. Before we get on the bus, let's check and see that everyone has the right gear. I would assume that most of you have brought your own equipment. If you haven't, we have some cameras, lenses, tripods, etc. that you can rent. I'm going to _____ _____ the _____ now. If you are going to _____ the _____, please _____ _____ out and bring it to the front.

STEP 2 음성을 들으며 정답을 선택하세요. P4_Ch3_03.

4. Who most likely are the listeners?
   (A) Facility visitors
   (B) Safety inspectors
   (C) New factory workers
   (D) Training officers

5. Why must listeners complete the program?
   (A) To have it posted
   (B) To receive a special code
   (C) To get a raise
   (D) To use some machinery

6. What will listeners receive at the end of the program?
   (A) A certificate of completion
   (B) A machine demonstration
   (C) A factory uniform
   (D) A tour of the corporate office

Chapter 3. 설명/연설 & 투어

Point 02 투어(관광/견학)

투어는 주로 '❶ 방문 인사 및 자기소개 ▶ ❷ 방문지 소개와 일정 ▶ ❸ 당부 및 주의 사항, 다음 일정'의 순서로 전개됩니다. 유적지나 국립 공원, 동물원 등의 관광지를 여행하는 상황, 버스 투어를 하며 주변에 보이는 건물이나 상황 및 이후 투어에 대해 설명하는 상황, 그리고 회사나 공장 등을 견학하는 신입 사원 오리엔테이션 상황이 자주 등장합니다.

▶ P4_Ch3_04. 🎵mp3🎵

1. Who most likely is the **speaker**?
화자는 누구겠는가? <직종>
A. A tour **guide** 투어 가이드
↳ 자신의 이름을 말하고 투어 가이드라고 자신을 소개하고 있습니다.

2. What is **prohibited** during the **tour**?
관광 중에 금지된 것은 무엇인가? <제안/요청>
A. Walking **off** the **path** 경로를 이탈하여 걷는 것
↳ 안전상의 이유로 광산 바닥을 걸어 다니는 것은 허용되지 않는다며 나무로 된 보도를 이탈하지 말라고 하였습니다.

3. What will the **speaker do next**?
화자는 다음에 무엇을 할 것인가? <다음 할 일>
A. Distribute **safety equipment** 안전 장비를 나누어 주기
↳ 후반부에 안전모를 건네줄 것이라고 했으므로 안전 장비를 나누어 줄 것임을 알 수 있습니다.

Good morning! Welcome to Wellington Gold Mine. I'm Carin Talbot. **❶** I'm the guide for your tour this morning.
안녕하세요! 웰링턴 금광에 오신 것을 환영합니다. 저는 케린 텔보트입니다. 저는 오늘 아침 여러분들의 관광 가이드입니다.

Once we go inside, you will see the area where people were working more than 90 years ago. You will also see some old mining tools, and I will explain how miners used them. For safety reasons, **❷** you are not allowed to walk on the mine floor. Please stay on the wooden walkway.
안으로 들어가시게 되면, 90년보다도 더 전에 사람들이 일을 했던 곳을 관람하시게 될 것입니다. 오래된 채굴 도구들도 보실 수 있으며, 광부들이 그것을 어떻게 사용하였는지에 대해서도 설명해 드릴 것입니다. 안전상의 이유로 광산의 바닥을 걸어 다니는 것은 허용되지 않습니다. 나무로 된 보도를 이탈하지 마시기 바랍니다.

❸ I will be passing you safety helmets now. Please check the light and see if it's working properly before you put it on.
이제 여러분에게 안전모를 건네 드릴 것입니다. 착용하시기 전에 안전모의 전등이 잘 작동되는지 확인하시기 바랍니다.

출제 포인트 정리

❶ 환영의 인사말에서 투어의 장소와 화자의 직업을 확인할 수 있습니다.

Good morning. My name is Kevin. I'll be your tour guide today.
안녕하세요, 제 이름은 케빈입니다. 저는 오늘 여러분의 여행 가이드입니다.

Welcome to Tyrone Motors. You'll see every step of the assembly process.
타이론 자동차 회사에 오신 걸 환영합니다. 여러분들은 조립 공정의 모든 단계를 보실 겁니다.

This is the last stop on our tour.
여기가 저희의 마지막 여행지입니다.

❷ 투어 중간이나 이후에는 해야 할 일들을 언급합니다.

I'll pass out booklets with information about the plants you'll be seeing.
저는 여러분들이 보시게 될 식물들에 대한 정보가 담긴 책자를 나눠 드릴 겁니다.

At that time, please turn off your mobile phones.
그때는 휴대폰을 끄시기 바랍니다.

Check-up Test 700+를 위해 한 걸음 한 걸음

정답 및 해석 p.048

STEP 1 문제의 키워드에 표시하고, 음성을 들으며 문제를 푼 뒤 빈칸을 채우세요.   P4_Ch3_05. mp3

1. Where most likely are the listeners?
   (A) At a photo studio
   (B) At a museum
   (C) At a hotel
   (D) At a paint factory

2. What does the speaker say about Lisa Thompson?
   (A) She is a sculptor.
   (B) She has won an award.
   (C) She is a business owner.
   (D) She is from another country.

3. According to the speaker, what should listeners do if they want to listen again?
   (A) Submit a request
   (B) Contact a manager after the tour
   (C) Visit a customer service center
   (D) Press a certain number on a device

_____ to the Madison Central Art _____, and thank you for purchasing this audio tour guide of the Lisa Thompson's _____ _____ Exhibit. This exhibit is the _____ _____ of Ms. Thompson's work ever assembled. You can see that each of the sculptures has a number beside it. To listen to the information about a particular piece, just press that number on the keypad of your audio device. If you'd like to _____ to these _____ _____ at any time, just _____ number 0.

STEP 2 음성을 들으며 정답을 선택하세요.   P4_Ch3_06. mp3

4. Who is the speaker?
   (A) A restaurant owner
   (B) A researcher
   (C) A museum donor
   (D) A tour guide

5. According to the speaker, what is the Royal History Research Center well known as?
   (A) A scenic location
   (B) A residence of a King of England
   (C) A collection of rare books
   (D) A seasonal menu

6. What does the speaker recommend doing in front of the building?
   (A) Visiting the gift shop
   (B) Taking some photos
   (C) Trying some food
   (D) Resting on a bench

이것만 알면 700+

실전 문제 풀이 Tip 대공개! 이것만은 꼭 알아 두세요.

TIP 1 설명/연설 빈출 문제

유형	문제	정답
주제	What is the speaker mainly discussing? 화자는 주로 무엇에 대해 이야기하고 있는가? What is the topic of the workshop? 워크숍의 주제는 무엇인가?	설명이나 연설의 주제와 화자/청자의 직업은 담화의 초반을 확인합니다.
직종	Who is the conference intended for? 이 콘퍼런스는 누구를 대상으로 하는가? Where does the speaker work? 화자는 어디에서 일하는가?	
내용	When was the company established? 회사는 언제 설립되었는가? What is special about the conference? 이 콘퍼런스의 무엇이 특별한가?	conference, training 등의 일정이나 장점 등 키워드를 확인합니다.
제안/요청	What are the listeners asked to do? 청자들은 무엇을 해야 하는가? What are listeners reminded to do? 청자들은 무엇을 하라는 얘기를 들었는가?	설명이 끝난 후에 할 일이나 벌어질 일은 담화의 후반부에서 언급합니다.
미래	What will most likely happen in ten minutes? 10분 후에는 어떤 일이 일어날 것인가? What will the speaker give the listeners? 화자는 청자들에게 무엇을 줄 것인가?	

TIP 2 투어(관광/견학) 빈출 문제

유형	문제	정답
직종	Who is the speaker? 화자는 누구인가? Who is the talk intended for? 담화의 대상(청자)은 누구인가?	담화의 초반에서 투어 장소와 화자/청자의 직업을 확인합니다. 화자 문제는 주로 '투어 가이드'와 '인사부 책임자'가 답으로 등장합니다.
장소	Where are the listeners? 청자들은 어디에 있는가? Where does the talk take place? 담화는 어디에서 이루어지는가?	
일정/내용	What does the speaker say about the gift shop? 화자가 선물 가게에 대해 말하는 것은 무엇인가? What is planned for five o'clock? 5시에는 무엇이 계획되어 있는가?	투어에서 등장하는 인물이나 건물, 시설 또는 일정을 확인합니다.
제안/요청	What does the speaker suggest the listeners do? 화자는 청자들에게 무엇을 하라고 제안하는가? What should the listeners avoid doing? 청자들은 무엇을 하는 것을 피해야 하는가?	청자들에게 한 당부의 내용이나 화자가 하겠다고 제안한 내용은 담화 후반부에서 확인합니다.

Chapter Test P4_Ch3_07

1. What does the factory produce?
   (A) Appliances
   (B) Candy
   (C) Automobiles
   (D) Shoes

2. What is special about the factory?
   (A) It is an award-winning facility.
   (B) It is the largest in the country.
   (C) It is one of the oldest of its kind.
   (D) It has just been renovated.

3. What will listeners get after the tour?
   (A) Free coupons
   (B) Product samples
   (C) An event's calendar
   (D) A questionnaire

4. Who is the speaker?
   (A) A radio host
   (B) A school principal
   (C) A conductor
   (D) A librarian

5. Where does the talk most likely take place?
   (A) At a university
   (B) At a library
   (C) At a concert hall
   (D) At a movie theater

6. What is the reason for the event?
   (A) To raise money
   (B) To show a film
   (C) To award a prize
   (D) To honor an artist

7. What problem does the speaker mention?
   (A) Some refreshments are not ready yet.
   (B) A room does not have enough seats.
   (C) Some speakers have not arrived.
   (D) A network system is not working properly.

8. What are listeners asked to present?
   (A) A receipt
   (B) An identification card
   (C) A completed application
   (D) A confirmation letter

9. Why does the speaker say, "we postponed the first keynote speech until 2 P.M."?
   (A) To reassure participants
   (B) To extend a deadline
   (C) To promote an event
   (D) To accept a suggestion

AT&A Telecom Service Plan			
Basic	**Standard**	**Smart**	**Premium**
$20 /month	$32 /month	$37 /month	$55 /month
Internet	Internet Custom TV	Internet Custom TV Phone	Internet Preferred TV Phone

10. Who most likely are the listeners?
    (A) Website developers
    (B) Maintenance staff
    (C) Call center representatives
    (D) Branch managers

11. Look at the graphic. What plan does the speaker say is the best?
    (A) Basic
    (B) Standard
    (C) Smart
    (D) Premium

12. What is offered to the listeners?
    (A) A bonus
    (B) A gift certificate
    (C) Free products
    (D) Additional vacation days

Chapter 4 — 방송 & 인물 소개

Point 01 방송(뉴스/날씨/교통)

방송은 주로 '❶ 인사말 및 프로그램 소개 ▶ ❷ 구체적인 내용 및 대안 ▶ ❸ 제안 및 다음 방송 안내'의 순서로 전개됩니다. 뉴스 방송의 주된 내용은 지역 뉴스(행사/도로 건설/건물 건립 등)나 기업 소식(확장/합병 등)입니다. 최근에는 팟캐스트의 내용도 종종 출제되고 있습니다.

P4_Ch4_01. mp3

1. Who most likely is the **speaker**?
화자는 누구일 것 같은가? <직종>
A. A **radio broadcaster** 라디오 진행자
↳ *You are listening ~ weather update*를 통해 청자들은 라디오 방송을 듣고 있고, 화자는 라디오를 진행하고 있음을 알 수 있습니다.

2. What does the speaker **suggest that listeners do**?
화자는 청자에게 무엇을 할 것을 제안하는가? <제안/요청>
A. **Drink a lot of water** 물을 많이 마시기
↳ 중간에 *Please ~* 이하에서 많은 물(= liquid)을 마실 것을 제안한다는 것을 알 수 있습니다.

3. According to the speaker, **what** can listeners **find** on the **website**? 화자에 따르면, 청자들은 웹사이트에서 무엇을 찾을 수 있는가? <키워드>
A. **Health information** 건강 정보
↳ 웹사이트는 주로 후반부에 언급됩니다. 마지막에 건강 유지 방법을 알고 싶다면 웹사이트를 방문하라고 했습니다.

Good afternoon! ❶ You are listening to WCTA 104.7. I'm Erika Fuller with your latest weather update. 안녕하세요! 여러분은 지금 WCTA 104.7을 듣고 계십니다. 저는 최신 일기 예보 소식을 전해 드리는 에리카 풀러입니다.

It's going to be another hot week this week. ❷ Please drink plenty of liquid to avoid becoming dehydrated. Doctors recommend 8 cups of water a day, but you should drink more if you are staying outside in this weather. 이번 주도 더운 날씨가 될 것으로 예상됩니다. 물을 많이 섭취하셔서, 탈수되지 않도록 하세요. 의사들은 하루에 8잔 정도의 물을 마실 것을 권하지만, 이러한 날씨에 외부에 있을 경우엔 좀 더 마셔야 합니다.

❸ If you would like to know how you can prepare yourself to stay healthy in this heat, please visit our website, www.wcta1047.com.
이러한 더위에 건강을 유지하도록 스스로 대비하는 방법을 알기 원하시면, 저희 웹사이트인 www.wcta1047.com을 방문하시기 바랍니다.

출제 포인트 정리

❶ 프로그램과 진행자에 대한 간단한 소개로 시작합니다.

This is Alan Carroll **with a special traffic update**. 저는 특별 교통 소식을 전하는 앨런 캐롤입니다.
Here is our London **correspondent** Natasha Anderson **reporting live from** London Bridge.
런던 브리지에서 생방송으로 전해 드리는 런던 특파원 나타샤 앤더슨입니다.
And now for today's local business news. 이제 오늘의 지역 비즈니스 소식입니다.

❷ 담화 후반에는 화자가 할 일이나 다음 방송 내용을 언급합니다.

Our next traffic report will be **in fifteen minutes**, so keep listening.
다음 교통 정보는 15분 후에 있을 예정이오니 계속 청취해 주시기 바랍니다.
After a commercial break, I'll be interviewing the CEO of K Group. 광고 후에 K그룹의 CEO를 인터뷰할 것입니다.

❸ 마지막에는 자세한 내용이나 추가 정보는 웹사이트에서 확인하라고 합니다.

For a full list, check out the city's **website**. 전체 목록은 시의 웹사이트를 확인하세요.
The **design is available** to the public on its **department website**. 디자인은 해당 부서의 웹사이트에서 누구나 보실 수 있습니다.

Check-up Test 700+를 위해 한 걸음 한 걸음

정답 및 해석 p.051

STEP 1 문제의 키워드에 표시하고, 음성을 들으며 문제를 푼 뒤 빈칸을 채우세요.   P4_Ch4_02. mp3

1. What is causing the traffic delay?
   (A) A rainstorm
   (B) A traffic accident
   (C) A stopped vehicle
   (D) A construction project

2. What are listeners advised to do?
   (A) Avoid the road construction
   (B) Use an alternative route
   (C) Drive more slowly
   (D) Stay home

3. How often will updates be given?
   (A) Every 10 minutes
   (B) Every 15 minutes
   (C) Every half hour
   (D) Every hour

_____ is Arnold Parker with the hourly _____ _____. The big news this morning is traffic throughout the Starkville area is slow _____ _____ the ongoing _____, which is expected to continue throughout the day. Due to the storms, some fallen trees are blocking access to the city highway to the Eastern Region. So you _____ consider _____ _____ _____ _____. The next _____ traffic _____ will be coming up at 10. For all the latest updates, please stay tuned.

STEP 2 음성을 들으며 정답을 선택하세요.   P4_Ch4_03. mp3

4. What is the broadcast mainly about?
   (A) A healthy diet
   (B) A company acquisition
   (C) An increased demand for organic food
   (D) The opening of a new local business

5. What will Kings Food Manufacturing do in the future?
   (A) Expand into the overseas market
   (B) Hire a business consultant
   (C) Reduce its marketing costs
   (D) Sell organic food

6. What did a spokesperson announce?
   (A) Employees will keep their jobs.
   (B) Salaries will increase.
   (C) The company will change its name.
   (D) A new advertisement will be aired.

Point 02 인물 소개

인물 소개는 주로 '❶ 인사말 및 목적 ▶ ❷ 인물 소개 및 경력/업적 ▶ ❸ 당부 및 앞으로 벌어질 상황'의 순서로 전개됩니다. 회사에서 **새로 부임한 사람이나 승진 또는 은퇴를 하는 직원을 소개**하는 내용, 시상식장에서 **수상자를 소개**하는 내용, 라디오나 특정 모임에서는 **초대 손님(저자, 가수, 기업인 등)을 소개**하는 내용이 자주 나옵니다.

▶ P4_Ch4_04. mp3

1. What is the **purpose** of the **talk**?
   담화의 목적은 무엇인가? <목적>
   A. To **introduce** an **award winner** 수상자를 소개하는 것
   ↳ Let me start 이하에서 올해의 수상자(award winner)인 스티브 코완 씨를 소개하고 있습니다.

2. According to the speaker, **what did Steve Cowan do**?
   화자에 따르면, 스티브 코완 씨는 무엇을 했는가? <키워드 – 업적>
   A. He **developed** a **new product**. 신제품을 개발했다.
   ↳ 새로운 식기세척기 개발에 중요한 역할을 담당했다고 했으므로 신제품을 개발했다는 내용이 정답입니다.

3. **What** will **Steve** do **next month**?
   스티브는 다음 달에 무엇을 할 것인가? <미래>
   A. **Take a trip** 출장 가기
   ↳ 후반부에 키워드 next month와 함께 홍보를 위해 영국에 간다고 했으므로 출장을 갈 것임을 알 수 있습니다.

Good evening, I'm Dan Brown. As the executive director, I'd like to thank everyone for coming to our employee awards banquet. ❶ Let me start right away by announcing this year's best product award winner, Steve Cowan.
안녕하십니까, 저는 댄 브라운입니다. 전무 이사로서, 직원 시상식에 참석해 주신 모든 분께 감사의 인사를 드리고 싶습니다. 올해의 최고 생산품 부문 수상자인 스티브 코완 씨를 발표하며 바로 시작하겠습니다.

❷ He was the key person in developing our new dishwasher. As you all know, this product is being very well received in the market right now.
그는 우리의 새로운 식기세척기 개발에 중요한 역할을 담당하였습니다. 모두 아시다시피, 이 제품은 현재 시장에서 매우 좋은 평가를 받고 있습니다.

❸ He is going to England next month to promote our product in that region. Let's give him a big hand as he walks on stage.
그는 다음 달에 영국에 가서 우리 제품을 그 지역에 홍보할 예정입니다. 그가 단상에 올라올 때 큰 박수로 환영합시다.

출제 포인트 정리

❶ 인물을 소개할 때, 직업이나 신분은 그 사람의 이름 앞뒤로 언급합니다.

Now I'd like to introduce our **new branch manager**, Samuel White.
이제 저는 우리의 새로운 지점장인 사무엘 화이트 씨를 소개하고자 합니다.

Joining me in the studio today is Craig Miller, who is a **corporate trainer for customer service** teams.
오늘 스튜디오에서 저와 함께하실 분은 크레이그 밀러 씨로 고객 서비스팀을 위한 기업 교육 강사입니다.

❷ 특정 인물을 소개하고 나면 그 사람의 경력이나 업적을 나열합니다.

She has spent the last six years analyzing customer's behavior.
그녀는 지난 6년간 고객의 행동을 분석해 왔습니다.

Ms. Morgan is famous for her research on air pollution. 모건 씨는 대기 오염에 대한 연구로 유명합니다.

❸ 마지막에는 인물의 연설 후에 질문을 유도하거나 의견을 요청하는 내용이 나옵니다.

She'll be joining us for a small reception immediately following her presentation.
그녀는 발표 직후에 우리와 함께 조촐한 환영회에 참석할 것입니다.

Afterwards, we'll be happy to answer any questions about the process.
그 후에 우리는 그 과정에 대한 어떤 질문에든 기꺼이 답변을 할 것입니다.

And then he'll stay for a while to sign copies of his new album.
그런 다음 그는 그의 앨범에 사인을 해 주기 위해 잠시 머무를 예정입니다.

Check-up Test 700+를 위해 한 걸음 한 걸음

정답 및 해석 p.052

STEP 1 문제의 키워드에 표시하고, 음성을 들으며 문제를 푼 뒤 빈칸을 채우세요.

P4_Ch4_05. mp3

1. What is Mr. Suzuki's profession?
   (A) A writer
   (B) A travel guide
   (C) A reporter
   (D) A chef

2. What will Mr. Suzuki do today?
   (A) Prepare some dishes
   (B) Give a demonstration
   (C) Judge a contest
   (D) Sign some books

3. According to the speaker, what has influenced Mr. Suzuki the most?
   (A) His travels around the world
   (B) His father's teachings
   (C) His studies in France
   (D) His special friends

I am so excited to have _____ Suzuki with us today. As you all know, he is one of the most popular chefs in the world, and _____ 's going to be the _____ of today's _____ _____. Ever since he was a little kid, he enjoyed cooking. His first teacher was his father, who was a sushi chef. He traveled through most Southeast Asian countries in his 20s. In a recent interview, he said that his _____ has _____ him _____ _____ in his cooking. When you take a look at the menu at his restaurant Little Tokyo, you can tell how much it has influenced him. Please welcome Chef Suzuki.

STEP 2 음성을 들으며 정답을 선택하세요.

P4_Ch4_06. mp3

4. What is the purpose of the talk?
   (A) To introduce a guest speaker
   (B) To give an award
   (C) To vote for a board member
   (D) To promote a new park

5. According to the speaker, what has Dr. Lim recently done?
   (A) Planted some trees
   (B) Graduated from school
   (C) Visited a park
   (D) Published a book

6. What will Dr. Lim speak about?
   (A) Teaching a course
   (B) Becoming a board member
   (C) Taking care of trees
   (D) Working two jobs

Chapter 4. 방송 & 인물 소개

이것만 알면 700+

실전 문제 풀이 Tip 대공개! 이것만은 꼭 알아 두세요.

TIP 1 방송(뉴스/날씨/교통) 빈출 문제

유형	문제	정답
방송 주제	What is the broadcast mainly about? 이 방송은 주로 무엇에 관한 것인가? What is the topic of this week's podcast? 이번 주 팟캐스트의 주제는 무엇인가?	방송의 주제는 프로그램 소개와 인사말 후에 언급됩니다. 뉴스의 주제로는 주로 대중교통 관련 내용이나 기업의 이전, 합병 등이 나옵니다.
내용	What benefit will the project provide to the public? 그 프로젝트는 대중들에게 어떤 혜택을 제공할 것인가? According to the speaker, what will Mr. Melder do? 화자에 따르면, 멜더 씨는 무엇을 할 것인가? Why is the organization raising money? 단체는 왜 기금을 모으고 있는가?	방송의 내용을 알 수 있는 키워드를 확인합니다. 특히 교통 방송이나 날씨 방송에서는 공사 중이니 다른 길로 돌아가라는 내용이 자주 나옵니다.
조언	What does the speaker recommend? 화자는 무엇을 권유하는가?	
미래	What are some listeners invited to do? 청자들에게 무엇을 하라고 하는가? What will the listeners hear next? 청자들은 다음에 무엇을 들을 것인가?	다음에 일어날 일은 담화의 마지막에 언급됩니다.

TIP 2 인물 소개 빈출 문제

유형	문제	정답
장소	Where does the introduction take place? 이 소개가 이루어지고 있는 곳은 어디인가? What type of event is taking place? 어떤 종류의 행사가 일어나고 있는가?	행사 주제와 장소, 참석자들의 직종은 환영 인사말을 확인합니다.
직종	Where do the listeners most likely work? 청자들은 어디에서 근무할 것 같은가?	
인물 관련	Who is Mr. Tanaka? 타나카 씨는 누구인가? What will Dr. Brown talk about? 브라운 박사는 무엇에 대해 이야기할 것인가? What does the speaker say Mr. Hamilton plans to do? 화자는 해밀턴 씨가 무엇을 할 계획이라고 말하는가?	소개하는 사람의 직위/직종을 언급하고 그 사람의 업적이나 할 일을 언급합니다.
제안/ 요청	What does the speaker request that listeners do? 화자는 청자들에게 무엇을 하라고 요청하는가? According to the speaker, what will participants be offered? 화자에 따르면, 참석자들에게 무엇이 제공될 것인가?	참석자들에게 제안하는 것은 담화의 마지막에 언급됩니다.

Chapter Test P4_Ch4_07. mp3

1. What is the talk mainly about?
   (A) The song of the week
   (B) A new CD release
   (C) A local band
   (D) A quiz show

2. What does the speaker say about the band's CD?
   (A) It was dedicated to the city.
   (B) It includes songs written by the lead singer.
   (C) It will be released soon.
   (D) It received great reviews.

3. What is the radio station offering to listeners?
   (A) Autographed CDs
   (B) Discount coupons
   (C) Backstage passes
   (D) Concert tickets

4. What is the purpose of the speech?
   (A) To propose a project
   (B) To give an award
   (C) To promote a tourist attraction
   (D) To present a budget

5. Who is Ms. Marshall?
   (A) A city official
   (B) An employee of an automobile company
   (C) An executive at an architectural firm
   (D) A museum curator

6. What does the speaker say about the Asian market?
   (A) The demand has increased.
   (B) It had deteriorated.
   (C) It has fluctuated.
   (D) It has too many restrictions.

7. What is the speaker reporting on?
   (A) A local business
   (B) A historical attraction
   (C) A food festival
   (D) A book signing

8. Why does the speaker say, "Jessica Baker traveled throughout Europe"?
   (A) To explain where some menus come from
   (B) To recommend tourist attractions
   (C) To express concerns about expenses
   (D) To promote a travel agency

9. What does the speaker recommend?
   (A) Visiting an ice cream shop
   (B) Trying some new flavors
   (C) Listening to the next news story
   (D) Taking a cooking lesson

Thursday	Friday	Saturday	Sunday
Rain	Cloudy	Partly Sunny	Sunny

10. What event is being discussed?
    (A) A music contest
    (B) A family event
    (C) A professional conference
    (D) A fundraiser

11. According to the speaker, what can the listeners do on a website?
    (A) Buy tickets for a performance
    (B) Find a list of businesses
    (C) Register for an activity
    (D) Make a donation

12. Look at the graphic. Which day is the event being held?
    (A) Thursday
    (B) Friday
    (C) Saturday
    (D) Sunday

PART 5&6

다이렉트

700+

Chapter 1. 명사

Chapter 2. 동사의 형태

Chapter 3. 동사의 수 일치/태/시제

Chapter 4. 대명사

Chapter 5. 형용사

Chapter 6. 부사

Chapter 7. 분사

Chapter 8. to부정사/동명사

Chapter 9. 접속사

Chapter 10. 관계사

Chapter 11. 비교/가정법/도치

Chapter 12. 전치사

Chapter 13. PART 6

이것만 알면 700+

PART 5&6 기본 문제 풀이 전략

전략 1 PART 5&6 어떻게 공부해야 할까요?

1. 문장 구조 분석을 통해 품사의 배열과 문법적인 근거를 찾는 습관을 가져야 합니다.
문제 풀이에서 가장 기본이 되는 것은 문장이 어떻게 구성되어 있는지 확인하는 것입니다.
문장은 마구잡이로 품사가 나열된 것이 아니라 특정한 규칙에 따라 품사들이 조화롭게 배열된 것입니다. 이것이 바로 문법입니다. 정확한 문장 구조 분석으로 문제 해결을 위한 문법적인 근거를 찾는 것이 가장 기본입니다.

2. 문제 해결을 위한 문법 사항을 정리합니다.
단순한 문법 공부로는 단기간에 원하는 점수를 받을 수 없습니다.
토익 시험에서 나오는 문법 사항을 체계적으로 정리해 두어야 합니다. 기출 유형 문제를 통해 토익 문법을 정리하되 빈출 유형이나 주의해야 할 사항들도 반드시 함께 정리합니다.

3. 문장 중에 답을 결정하는 단어를 찾아 객관적이고 논리적인 근거를 확보합니다.
막연하게 답이 될 것이란 생각으로 문제를 풀어서는 안 됩니다.
문장 안에 반드시 답을 결정하는 단어가 있습니다. 생각의 순서를 정리하여 답을 결정하는 객관적이고 논리적인 근거를 확보하는 것이 실수를 최대한 줄이고 정답률을 높일 수 있는 방법입니다.

4. 어휘는 언제, 누구와 출제되는지를 함께 암기합니다.
각 단어들이 어떻게 쓰이고 누구와 쓰이는지 반드시 알아야 합니다.
예를 들어, 동사를 암기할 때는 단순하게 의미만 암기하지 말고
① 자동사인지, 타동사인지
② 문장 안에서 어떤 패턴으로 활용되는지
③ 어떤 명사와 함께 쓰는지도 알아 두어야 합니다.
부사나 형용사의 경우에는 문장 내 위치나 함께 쓰이는 동사의 시제도 답을 결정하는 중요한 요소가 됩니다.

전략 2 꼭 알아야 하는 PART 5&6 전략

출제 유형	출제 유형별 전략
1. 품사 문제 보기가 모두 같은 어원에서 나온, 품사만 다른 단어들로 구성되어 있습니다.	문장 구조 분석을 통해 필요한 품사를 선택합니다. ① 문장 구조 분석을 통해 필요한 성분을 확인합니다. ② 품사의 배열을 확인합니다.
2. 문법 문제 품사 구분만으로 정답을 선택할 수 없는 문제들로, 관련 문법을 묻는 문제입니다.	적용해야 할 문법이 무엇인지를 확인해야 합니다. ① 문장 구조 분석을 통해 필요한 성분과 품사를 확인합니다. ② 문장에서 해당 문법에 대한 근거를 확보합니다. ※ PART 6 문법 문제 중에서 동사의 시제 문제의 경우 앞뒤 문맥을 통해 시간의 전후 관계를 파악해야 합니다.
3. 어휘 문제 보기가 동일한 품사의 서로 다른 단어들로 구성되어 있습니다.	문장에서 의미가 통한다고 정답이 되진 않습니다. 품사별로 답이 되는 근거를 찾을 수 있어야 합니다. ① 자동사 vs. 타동사를 확인합니다. ② 주어/목적어가 사람인지 사물인지 확인합니다. ③ 가산 명사 vs. 불가산 명사를 확인합니다. ④ 형용사는 어떤 종류의 명사를 수식하는지 확인합니다. ※ PART 6에서는 앞뒤 문맥을 통해 논리적으로 타당한 어휘를 선택해야 합니다.
4. PART 6 문장 삽입 문제 보기가 모두 문장으로 구성되어 있습니다.	문장 삽입 문제는 PART 6에서만 출제됩니다. 빈칸 앞뒤 문장을 확인하고 논리적으로 연결될 수 있는 문장을 선택해야 합니다.

PART 5&6은 이렇게 풀어야 해요.

Step 1. 보기를 통해 어떤 유형의 문제인지 확인하세요.

Step 2. 문장 구조 분석을 통해 주어/동사/목적어 등 필요한 문장 성분을 확인하세요.

Step 3. 해당 문장 성분이 취할 수 있는 품사와 품사의 배열 순서를 확인하세요.

Step 4. 관련 문법에 적용할 수 있는 근거를 확인하세요.

Step 5. 어휘 문제는 의미로만 풀어서는 안 되고 답의 근거를 확인하세요.

Chapter 1 명사

명사, 포인트 감각 익히기

It should meet all -------.
(A) requirement   (B) requirements
그것은 모든 요건을 충족해야 한다.

가산 명사와 불가산 명사 문제
→ requirement는 '요건'을 뜻하는 **가산 명사**로, 앞의 all과 수를 맞춰 복수의 -s를 붙여야 합니다.

개념 정리

❶ 명사의 정의와 형태

1) 명사는 사물이나 사람, 추상적인 개념을 지칭하는 것입니다. 사물의 이름, 사람의 이름, 건물 이름, 지명 등은 모두 명사입니다.

사람 이름: Tom, Jane 등
사물 이름: camera, table 등
지명: Seoul, London 등

2) 다음 형태로 끝나는 단어는 주로 명사입니다.

	빈출 토익 명사
-tion/-sion	produc**tion** 생산 informa**tion** 정보 deci**sion** 결정
-ance/-ence	appear**ance** 외관 circumst**ance** 환경 prefer**ence** 선호, 우선권
-ment	announce**ment** 발표 depart**ment** 부서 require**ment** 요구, 요건
-ity/-ety	productiv**ity** 생산성 flexibil**ity** 유연성 author**ity** 권한 saf**ety** 안전
-er/-ee/-or	manufactur**er** 제조사 employ**ee** 직원 invest**or** 투자자
-ness	kind**ness** 친절함 competitive**ness** 경쟁력 effective**ness** 효율성
-ant/-ent	applic**ant** 지원자 cli**ent** 고객 attend**ant** 안내원

❷ 명사의 역할

1) **주어 역할:** 동사 앞에 오며, '-은, -는, -이, -가'로 해석됩니다.
   Peter stays at home. 피터는 집에 머물고 있다.

2) **목적어 역할:** 타동사 또는 전치사 뒤에 오며, '-을, -를'로 해석됩니다.
   The man explains the problem. 그 남자가 문제를 설명한다.

3) **보어 역할:** 2형식 문장에서 동사 다음, 5형식 문장에서 목적어 다음에 위치합니다.
   Jane is a student. 제인은 학생이다.
   We call her Sue. 우리는 그녀를 수라고 부른다.

Check-up Test 700+를 위해 한 걸음 한 걸음

정답 및 해석 p.055

A. 다음 문장에서 명사를 모두 찾으세요.

① 마이크는 어제 그의 손님들을 만났다.

② 톰은 회계사이다.

③ 그 광고 회사는 영업 직원을 찾고 있다.

④ 우리 대표는 임원진들을 만날 예정이다.

⑤ 도움이 필요하면, 언제나 우리 사무실을 방문해 주세요.

B. 다음 중 명사를 모두 찾으세요.

① development ② location   ③ invited   ④ communication ⑤ attend
⑥ grown   ⑦ selection   ⑧ ability   ⑨ special   ⑩ qualified
⑪ although   ⑫ condition   ⑬ convene   ⑭ requirement   ⑮ accomplishment

C. 다음 문장에서 밑줄 친 단어가 어떤 역할을 하는지 쓰세요.

① <u>Mike</u> met his clients yesterday. 마이크는 어제 그의 손님들을 만났다.

② Tom is an <u>accountant</u>. 톰은 회계사이다.

③ The advertising agency is seeking <u>sales representatives</u>. 그 광고 회사는 영업 직원을 찾고 있다.

④ Our president is going to meet with <u>executives</u>. 우리 대표는 임원진들을 만날 예정이다.

⑤ If you need a help, visit our <u>office</u> anytime. 도움이 필요하면, 언제나 우리 사무실을 방문해 주세요.

Point 01 명사 자리

출제 포인트 정리

❶ 명사 자리를 빈칸으로 제시하고 보기 중 명사를 찾는 문제가 출제됩니다.

1) 형용사+**명사**		I bought a new hat. 나는 새 모자를 샀다.
2) 관사+**명사**		The apple is green. 그 사과는 초록색이다.
3) 소유격+**명사**		He is my cousin. 그는 나의 조카이다.
4) 명사+**명사** (복합 명사)		advertising company 광고 회사
5) 명사+관계 대명사		The business conference which was scheduled for this month was postponed. 이번 달로 예정되어 있던 비즈니스 콘퍼런스가 연기되었다.
6) 전치사+**명사**		The board of directors is going to meet with sales representatives. 이사진이 영업 사원들과 만날 예정이다.
7) 동사+**명사** / **명사**+동사		Mr. Kim will explain the issue. 김 씨가 그 문제에 대해 설명할 것이다.

Check-up Test 700+를 위해 한 걸음 한 걸음

정답 및 해석 p.055

STEP 1 다음 두 개의 보기 중 빈칸에 알맞은 것을 고르세요.

1. ------- will be given to new members.
   (A) Prefer (B) Preference

2. We are planning to develop a new -------.
   (A) product (B) produce

3. You will find our analysts' ------- very helpful.
   (A) recommendations (B) recommend

STEP 2 빈칸에 알맞은 것을 고르세요.

4. ------- of the online purchase will be sent to you by e-mail within 24 hours.
   (A) Confirms (B) Confirmation (C) Confirmed (D) Confirming

5. The consulting firm is offering a special -------.
   (A) promote (B) promotion (C) promoted (D) promoting

Point 02 가산 명사 = 셀 수 있는 명사

출제 포인트 정리

❶ 수를 셀 수 있는 명사를 가산 명사라고 합니다.

1) 가산 명사를 단수로 쓸 때는 **명사 앞에 관사 a/an**이나 **the**와 함께 써야 합니다.
   I have a book. 나는 책을 가지고 있다. (O)

2) 가산 명사를 복수로 쓸 때는 일반적으로 **명사 뒤에 -(e)s**를 붙입니다.
   I have books. 나는 책들을 가지고 있다. (O)

3) 가산 명사는 관사나 복수의 -(e)s 없이 단독으로 쓸 수 없습니다.
   I have book. (X)

빈출 사람 가산 명사

founder 설립자	**acquaintance** 지인	**advisor** 조언자	**analyst** 분석가
employee 직원	**distributor** 유통업자	**resident** 거주자	**representative** 대표자
attendee 참석자	**performer** 행위자	**recipient** 수취인	**guide** 가이드, 안내자
applicant 지원자	**writer** 작가	**president** 회장	**technician** 기술자
candidate 지원자	**producer** 생산자	**participant** 참가자	**supplier** 공급자

Check-up Test 700+를 위해 한 걸음 한 걸음

정답 및 해석 p.055

STEP 1 다음 두 개의 보기 중 빈칸에 알맞은 것을 고르세요.

1. My friend wrote ------- to me.
   (A) letter   (B) letters

2. ------- working in an assembly area must wear protective gear.
   (A) Employees   (B) Employee

3. Happy Foods, Inc. has become ------- in selling processed foods in China.
   (A) leader   (B) a leader

STEP 2 빈칸에 알맞은 것을 고르세요.

4. The package was redesigned after the manufacturer received ------- from distributors.
   (A) complain   (B) complained   (C) complaints   (D) complainer

5. Payment ------- are determined after a performance evaluation has been conducted by department managers at the end of each year.
   (A) increases   (B) increasing   (C) increased   (D) increase

Chapter 1. 명사

Point 03 불가산 명사 = 셀 수 없는 명사

출제 포인트 정리

❶ 수를 셀 수 없는 명사를 불가산 명사라고 합니다.

1) 불가산 명사는 앞에 부정관사(a/an)가 올 수 없고, 복수형으로 쓸 수 없습니다.
   an information (X)　　　　informations (X)

2) 불가산 명사는 수를 나타내는 형용사의 수식을 받을 수 없습니다.
   many, few + 불가산 명사 (X)

3) 불가산 명사는 한정사나 양을 나타내는 형용사의 수식을 받을 수 있습니다.
   this/that + 불가산 명사 (O)　　　much/a little + 불가산 명사 (O)

빈출 불가산 명사
information 정보　luggage 짐　advice 조언　news 소식　furniture 가구　equipment 장비
staff 직원　access 접근　research 연구　approval 승인　production 생산　merchandise 상품

불가산 명사로 혼동하기 쉬운 가산 명사
cost 경비　price 가격　expense 비용　instruction 설명　detail 상세한 설명　discount 할인
approach 방법　survey 조사　permit 허가　reason 이유　suggestion 제안　result 결과　plan 계획
alternative 대안　decision 결정

Check-up Test 700+를 위해 한 걸음 한 걸음
정답 및 해석 p.055

STEP 1 다음 두 개의 보기 중 빈칸에 알맞은 것을 고르세요.

1. Please give me ------- about that company.
   (A) information　　(B) informations

2. My father always gives me some good -------.
   (A) advices　　(B) advice

3. Final ------- from the general director is required for the new campaign.
   (A) approval　　(B) decision

STEP 2 빈칸에 알맞은 것을 고르세요.

4. The manager recommended purchasing some additional -------.
   (A) equipment　　(B) equipments　　(C) equips　　(D) equip

5. The marketing team conducted a ------- to find out how many hours children use the Internet every day.
   (A) research　　(B) progress　　(C) survey　　(D) broadcast

Point 04 명사 앞에 나오는 수량 표현

출제 포인트 정리

❶ 명사의 종류에 따라 앞에 나오는 수량 표현이 달라집니다.

우리말에서는 '많은', '적은'과 같은 표현을 수와 양을 구별하여 사용하진 않지만 영어는 **가산인지 불가산인지에 따라 수와 양의 표현을 다르게 사용**하므로 다음과 같은 **수량 표현**을 구분해서 알아 두어야 합니다.

each 각각의 every 모든 another 또 다른	+ 가산 단수 명사
a number of 많은 many 많은 both 둘 다의 a variety of 다양한 a few 몇 개의 few 거의 없는 several 몇몇의 various 다양한 숫자(two, three 등)	+ 가산 복수 명사
much 많은 an amount of 상당한 양의 a little 적은 little 거의 없는 less 더 적은 a great deal of 많은	+ 불가산 명사
all 모든 some 몇몇의 most 대부분의 other 다른 a lot of 많은	+ 가산 복수 명사, 불가산 명사
any 어느 no ~도 없는	+ 가산 단수/복수 명사, 불가산 명사

<u>Each</u> <u>item</u> is thoroughly inspected. 각각의 제품은 철저하게 점검된다.

At Ustart Inc., there are <u>many</u> <u>chances</u> of being promoted. 유스타트 사에서는 승진할 기회가 많다.

Thanks to various employee benefits, Max Corporation has <u>little</u> <u>turnover</u>.
다양한 직원 혜택으로 인해 맥스 사는 이직률이 낮다.

Use this coupon to purchase <u>any</u> <u>mobile app</u> for 10% off. 이 쿠폰을 이용해 모바일 앱을 10% 할인받아서 구매하세요.

Check-up Test 700+를 위해 한 걸음 한 걸음

정답 및 해석 p.055

STEP 1 다음 두 개의 보기 중 빈칸에 알맞은 것을 고르세요.

1. Many ------- are participating in the Job Fair.
   (A) graduates   (B) graduate

2. ------- employee was given their own personalized e-mail address by the company.
   (A) Every   (B) A few

3. He gave them ------- information through the phone.
   (A) much   (B) many

STEP 2 빈칸에 알맞은 것을 고르세요.

4. At the hotel lobby, a guest can ask a porter to bring ------- luggage to their room after they check in.
   (A) many   (B) the   (C) a   (D) each

5. ------- student willing to attend Professor Lee's lecture should sign up by the end of the week.
   (A) Both   (B) Any   (C) Few   (D) All

이것만 알면 700+

토익 최빈출 유형 정리! 명사편!

유형 1 명사의 위치

❶ **관사 + (부사) + (형용사) + 명사**
관사와 명사 사이에 부사나 형용사가 올 수 있습니다.
It was a rather difficult question. 꽤 어려운 질문이었다.
　　　관사 부사　형용사　　명사

❷ **주어인 명사와 동사의 수 일치 확인**
단수 명사에는 **단수 동사**가, **복수 명사**에는 **복수 동사**가 와야 합니다.
I set my alarm clock so that it (ring, rings) at 7 A.M. every day.
나는 매일 아침 7시에 알람 시계가 울리도록 설정했다.

유형 2 명사 앞에 나오는 수량 표현

❶ **빈칸 앞에 부정관사 a/an이 있으면 단수 명사가 정답입니다.**
빈칸 앞에 a/an이 있으면 단수 명사가 정답이고, a/an이 없으면 복수 명사나 불가산 명사가 정답입니다.
We have a pool on the fifth floor. 우리는 5층에 수영장이 있다.

❷ **앞에서 명사를 수식하는 수량 형용사를 확인해야 합니다.**
수를 나타내는 형용사는 가산 명사와 쓰이며 양을 나타내는 형용사는 불가산 명사와 쓰입니다.
My uncle has many stamps. <many + 복수 가산 명사>
내 삼촌은 우표를 많이 가지고 있다.

유형 3 사람 명사와 사물 명사의 구별

❶ **동사를 보고 판단합니다.**
동사의 주체가 사람이면 사람 명사가 정답입니다.
(Tom, Equipment) decided to go. 톰은 가기로 결정하였다.

❷ **형용사를 보고 판단합니다.**
사람을 수식하는 형용사이면 사람 명사가 정답입니다.
(Tom, Equipment) is very considerate. 톰은 매우 사려 깊다.

Chapter Test

1. Fashion World Services has been a leading ------- of women's apparel for more than 10 years.
   (A) supplies
   (B) supplying
   (C) supplier
   (D) supplied

2. Please adjust the budget to include the ------- of a smoke detector system.
   (A) install
   (B) installs
   (C) installing
   (D) installation

3. This year, HD Motor's revenue grew by $50 million, which represents an ------- of 50 percent over last year.
   (A) increase
   (B) increased
   (C) increases
   (D) increasingly

4. The recent change in ------- can be attributed to the new president.
   (A) profitability
   (B) profitable
   (C) profited
   (D) profitably

5. Thanks to increased consumer interest, computer ------- are experiencing revenue growth.
   (A) retails
   (B) retail
   (C) retailing
   (D) retailers

6. Please don't forget to e-mail me to confirm the ------- of the packages after you receive them.
   (A) deliver
   (B) delivery
   (C) delivering
   (D) deliverable

7. Explore Innovation is a famous science museum in Los Angeles with branches in a ------- of major cities in the U.S.
   (A) number
   (B) numbering
   (C) numbered
   (D) numbers

8. Doctors warn people to avoid sleeping pill overdoses, because people will place too much ------- upon the pills.
   (A) reliance
   (B) relies
   (C) reliant
   (D) relied

9. After the first lecture, ------- at the second lecture nearly tripled due to Professor Novak's informative presentation.
   (A) attendant
   (B) attended
   (C) attendee
   (D) attendance

10. The law offices in both Tokyo and Shanghai offer free ------- to local residents.
    (A) consulted
    (B) consults
    (C) consultant
    (D) consultation

Chapter 2 동사의 형태

동사, 포인트 감각 익히기

I ------- a book once a week.
(A) buy   (B) buying

나는 일주일에 한 번 책을 산다.

동사의 형태 문제

→ 문장에는 하나의 주어와 동사가 반드시 있어야 합니다. 따라서 빈칸은 본동사 자리로 (A) buy가 정답입니다.
  (B) buying은 현재 분사로 본동사 자리에 올 수 없습니다.

개념 정리

❶ 동사의 수

1) 하나의 문장에는 본동사의 수도 하나예요.

The warranty for this device expired three months ago. 이 기기의 보증 기간은 3개월 전에 만료되었다.

2) 동사의 수 = 접속사 또는 관계 대명사의 수+1

She completed the courses that are needed for graduation. 그녀는 졸업에 필요한 수업들을 수료했다.
    동사   관계 대명사   동사

→ 준동사(동명사, to부정사, 분사)는 동사에서 파생되었지만, 동사가 아닌 다른 품사로 사용돼요.

❷ 동사의 형태

1) 기본형(동사 원형)

3인칭 단수 주어를 제외한 주어 뒤에 현재 시제 동사를 쓸 때 기본형을 써요.

I think it can be changed. 나는 그것이 수정될 수 있다고 생각한다.

2) 3인칭 단수형(동사 원형+(e)s)

3인칭 단수 주어 뒤에 현재 시제 동사를 쓸 때 3인칭 단수형을 써요.

He requires medical care. 그는 건강 관리가 필요하다.

3) 과거형(동사 원형+ed/불규칙 변화)

과거 시제를 나타내야 하는 경우, 주어에 상관없이 과거형을 써요.

She attended the meeting yesterday. 그녀는 어제 회의에 참석하였다.

4) 분사형(ing형/p.p.형)

have 뒤에는 과거 분사(p.p.)가, be동사 뒤에는 과거 분사(p.p)나 현재 분사(ing)가 등장해요.

I have been there. 나는 그곳에 가본 적이 있다.

He is doing okay. 그는 잘하고 있다.

❸ 조동사

조동사는 동사를 돕는다는 뜻으로 다른 동사와 함께 쓰여 시제를 나타내거나 의문문 혹은 부정문을 만들기 위해 사용됩니다. can, will, may, shall, must 등이 있어요. 조동사 뒤에는 동사 원형을 씁니다.

Check-up Test 700+를 위해 한 걸음 한 걸음

정답 및 해설 p.056

A. 다음 문장에서 본동사를 모두 찾으세요.
① He arrived yesterday. 그는 어제 도착했다.
② We will decide how to conduct an online survey. 우리는 어떻게 온라인 설문 조사를 진행할지 결정할 것이다.
③ I hope that you can visit us next week. 다음 주에 저희를 방문하실 수 있길 바랍니다.
④ The board of directors appointed him as the new president. 이사회는 그를 새로운 대표로 임명했다.
⑤ Employees are required to behave responsibly, whether on duty or not.
직원들은 근무 중이든 아니든 책임감 있게 행동하도록 요구된다.

B. 다음 문장에서 밑줄 친 동사가 올바른 형태인지 확인하고 틀린 것은 바르게 고치세요.
① They can <u>do</u> anything even if it seems impossible. 그들은 심지어 불가능해 보이는 일도 할 수 있다.
② The vacation policy has <u>taking</u> effect since June 12th. 휴가 정책은 6월 12일부터 실행되고 있다.
③ She <u>answered</u> the questions that the teacher asked. 그녀는 선생님이 질문한 문제에 대답했다.
④ She <u>are</u> looking for something useful. 그녀는 유용한 무언가를 찾고 있다.
⑤ Mr. Holly will <u>submitting</u> an application. 홀리 씨는 신청서를 제출할 예정이다.

C. 다음 문장에서 어법상 틀린 부분을 찾아 바르게 고치세요.
① They appointing Jim as the new CFO. 그들은 짐을 새 CFO로 임명하였다.
② I don't know what I can doing. 내가 무엇을 할 수 있는지 모르겠다.
③ His academic achievements have been widely recognizing. 그의 학문적 업적은 크게 인정받고 있다.
④ She understood what I does. 그녀는 내가 하는 일을 이해했다.
⑤ We guarantee that EDM do not sold any defective products.
EDM 사에서는 결함이 있는 제품을 판매하지 않음을 보장합니다.

Point 01 자동사 vs. 타동사

출제 포인트 정리

❶ 자동사

1) 자동사는 목적어 없이 단독으로 문장을 완성합니다.
   I worked hard. 나는 열심히 일했다. → hard(열심히)는 부사입니다.

2) 전치사와 함께 쓰여 뒤에 목적어를 동반하여 타동사와 유사하게 사용됩니다.
   We arrived at our final destination. 우리는 마지막 목적지에 도착하였다.

3) 자동사는 수동태 불가: The sun (rises, is risen) in the east. 태양은 동쪽에서 뜬다.

빈출 자동사			
arrive 도착하다	respond/reply 대답하다	depart 출발하다	take place 발생하다
be ~이다	remain 여전히 ~이다	wait 기다리다	speak/talk 말하다
go 가다	participate 참가하다	agree 동의하다	work 일하다

❷ 타동사

1) 타동사는 항상 목적어와 함께 쓰입니다.
   We guarantee the quality of our products. 저희는 저희 제품의 품질을 보장합니다.

2) 타동사는 수동태 가능: The dishwasher was repaired by him. 식기세척기는 그에 의해 수리되었다.

	자동사	타동사
목적어 유무	X	O
수동태	X	O

Check-up Test 700+를 위해 한 걸음 한 걸음

정답 및 해석 p.056

STEP 1 다음 두 개의 보기 중 빈칸에 알맞은 것을 고르세요.

1. The international conference will ------- in Seoul over the weekend.
   (A) take place   (B) be taken place

2. When the clients ------- at the conference center, the president's welcoming speech had just finished.
   (A) arrived   (B) reached

3. People who register for morning classes can ------- in all of the activities sponsored by the City Arts Council.
   (A) attend   (B) participate

STEP 2 빈칸에 알맞은 것을 고르세요.

4. Our secretary, Christine Murray, ------- all incoming calls from 9 A.M. to 6 P.M.
   (A) answers   (B) responds   (C) replies   (D) talks

5. Sales of our digital camera have ------- drastically, so I believe it is about time to create a new product.
   (A) fallen   (B) refused   (C) performed   (D) acquired

Point 02 2형식 동사

출제 포인트 정리

❶ **2형식: 주어＋동사＋보어(명사/형용사)**

   1) 주어＋**2형식 동사**＋**형용사** → 형용사가 주어의 상태를 설명합니다.
      Mr. Kim is <u>diligent</u>. 김 씨는 부지런하다.

   2) 주어＋**2형식 동사**＋**명사** → 명사가 주어와 **동격**을 이루어야 합니다.
      Mr. Kim is <u>a hotel manager</u>. 김 씨는 호텔 매니저이다.

❷ **토익 시험에 나오는 빈출 2형식 동사 13개**

2형식 동사의 종류	빈출 동사	의미
be동사류 (상태 유지)	be, keep, remain, stay, last	~이다, ~한 상태이다
상태의 변화를 나타내는 동사	become (그 외 get, turn, grow)	~되다
의견/판단의 동사	seem, appear	~인 것 같다, ~처럼 보이다
지각 동사	sound, look, feel (그 외 taste, smell)	~한 맛/냄새/소리/느낌이다
판명/입증의 동사	prove, turn out	~인 것으로 판명 나다

→ *remain, seem, turn out, prove*는 to부정사를 목적 보어로 취할 수 있는 빈출 동사입니다.

Check-up Test 700+를 위해 한 걸음 한 걸음

정답 및 해석 p.056

STEP 1 다음 두 개의 보기 중 빈칸에 알맞은 것을 고르세요.

1. The technical expert claims that market trends become ------- with the use of data analysis.
   (A) predictable   (B) predictably

2. Maldives ------- the top vacation destination of tourists.
   (A) receives   (B) remains

3. Most interns seem ------- at first, but they become easily intimidated once they realize the work is beyond their abilities.
   (A) energetic   (B) energetically

STEP 2 빈칸에 알맞은 것을 고르세요.

4. Having worked at Juventus Bank for ten years, Alessandro Del Toro finally ------- the branch manager.
   (A) competed   (B) became   (C) continued   (D) thought

5. As Exxon has developed an integrated system, it has become increasingly ------- both locally and nationally.
   (A) visibility   (B) vision   (C) visible   (D) visions

Chapter 2. 동사의 형태 147

Point 03 4형식 동사와 5형식 동사

출제 포인트 정리

❶ 4형식 = 주어 + 동사 + 간접 목적어 + 직접 목적어

4형식 수여 동사는 '~을 …에게 주다'라는 의미를 갖고 있으며, **간접 목적어**에는 주로 **사람 명사**가, **직접 목적어**에는 **사물 명사**가 옵니다.

He bought me a ring. 그는 나에게 반지를 사주었다.

빈출 4형식 수여 동사			
give 주다	send 보내주다	buy 사 주다	+ 사람 목적어 + 사물 목적어
award 수여하다	tell 말해주다	present 증정하다	(~에게) (…을)
grant 수여하다	show 보여주다	offer 제공하다	

❷ 5형식 = 주어 + 동사 + 목적어 + 목적격 보어

목적격 보어 자리에는 동사에 따라 **명사, 형용사, 동사 원형, 과거 분사** 등이 올 수 있습니다.

A lot of phone calls made my day much more difficult. 많은 전화가 나의 하루를 훨씬 더 힘들게 만들었다.

빈출 5형식 동사		
(사역 동사) make, have, let 시키다		동사 원형(능동)/과거 분사(수동)
find 알다		형용사
keep, leave 유지시키다	+ 목적어 +	형용사
consider 간주하다		명사/형용사
appoint 임명하다, elect 선출하다		명사

Check-up Test 700+를 위해 한 걸음 한 걸음

정답 및 해석 p.056

STEP 1 다음 두 개의 보기 중 빈칸에 알맞은 것을 고르세요.

1. Valero Energy has decided to ------- its employees a special benefit package.
   (A) grant   (B) donate

2. The director considers it ------- to inspect all the assembly lines immediately.
   (A) necessary   (B) necessarily

3. The manager of the sales department found the last quarter sales statistics -------.
   (A) alarms   (B) alarming

STEP 2 빈칸에 알맞은 것을 고르세요.

4. We ------- receiving the awards a great accomplishment.
   (A) considered   (B) persuaded   (C) respected   (D) expected

5. Jossty Company has ------- Mr. Fitzpatrick a sales job.
   (A) asked   (B) hired   (C) relocated   (D) offered

Point 04 사람 목적어만 취하는 동사

출제 포인트 정리

❶ 특정 동사는 목적어로 사람 명사만을 취합니다.

다음의 동사들은 **사람 명사를 목적어**로 받고 그 뒤에 that절, to부정사, '전치사+명사'가 이어지는 형식을 취합니다. 이런 동사들의 목적어 자리에 사물 명사는 올 수 없습니다.

동사 (통보/알림)	목적어(~에게)	목적어(…을)	의미
tell inform	사람/회사/단체	about 명사 to부정사 that 주어+동사 ~	~에게 …에 대해 말하다 ~에게 …하라고 말하다 ~에게 …라고 말하다
notify		of+명사 that 주어+동사 ~	~에게 …을/…라고 통보하다
persuade convince			~에게 …을/…라고 설득시키다
remind			~에게 …을/…라고 상기시키다
assure			~에게 …을/…라고 확신시키다
advise			~에게 …을/…라고 충고하다

Mr. Yoon **assured** his employees that the takeover won't affect them.
윤 씨는 직원들에게 합병이 그들에게 어떠한 영향을 주지 않을 것이라고 보장했다.

Check-up Test 700+를 위해 한 걸음 한 걸음   정답 및 해석 p.057

STEP 1 다음 두 개의 보기 중 빈칸에 알맞은 것을 고르세요.

1. Clients ------- that the law offices of Peck will be closed on Friday for the holiday.
   (A) reminded   (B) are reminded

2. Please let Mr. Manuel's secretary know when you get there so she can ------- him of your arrival.
   (A) speak   (B) notify

3. Liberty Investment Club appreciates and welcomes your interest and ------- you to join others who are involved in real estate investment.
   (A) invites   (B) suggests

STEP 2 빈칸에 알맞은 것을 고르세요.

4. Ms. Douglas has ------- us on provisions of the federal Food, Drug and Cosmetic Act, which apply in our case.
   (A) designed   (B) proposed   (C) suggested   (D) advised

5. Make sure to ------- Mr. Noble that he needs to prepare a presentation.
   (A) accept   (B) notify   (C) deliver   (D) present

이것만 알면 700+
토익 최빈출 유형 정리! 동사의 형태편!

유형 1 빈출 '자동사 + 전치사'

전치사를 보고 알맞은 자동사를 고르거나 자동사를 보고 알맞은 전치사를 고르는 문제가 출제됩니다.

빈출 '자동사 + 전치사'		
refer to ~을 참조하다	focus on ~에 집중하다	benefit from ~로부터 이익을 얻다
deal with ~을 다루다	rely on ~을 의지하다	look into/through ~을 조사하다
refrain from ~을 삼가다	go through ~을 겪다	depend on ~에 달려 있다/의존하다
adhere to ~에 준수하다	comply with ~을 따르다	interfere with ~을 간섭하다
differ in ~이 다르다	consist of ~로 구성되다	compete with ~와 경쟁하다
object to ~에 반대하다		

The team (consisted, ~~composed~~) of 100 experts. 그 팀은 100명의 전문가로 구성되어 있다.

유형 2 유사 의미 자동사 vs. 타동사

유사한 의미의 동사들이 보기에 함께 등장하면 단순히 의미가 아닌, **목적어 유무에 따라 자/타동사를 구별**하여 풀어야 합니다.

자동사	타동사	의미	자동사	타동사	의미
merge with	acquire	인수하다	proceed	forward	보내다
emerge	reveal	나타나다	rise	raise	오르다
comply with	obey	준수하다	lead to	cause	초래하다
account for	explain	설명하다	agree to	approve	동의하다
expire	terminate	만료되다	remain	endure	유지하다
deal with	handle	처리하다	participate in	attend	참석하다

Dr. Greene will (handle, ~~deal~~) all inquiries about ongoing research.
그린 박사는 진행 중인 연구에 관한 모든 질문을 다룰 것이다.

유형 3 요구/허락/가능 동사 + 목적어 + to부정사

'요구/허락/가능'의 의미를 가진 특정 동사 뒤에는 '**목적어 + to부정사**'가 옵니다. 뒤의 구조를 보고 특정 동사를 찾는 문제나 특정 동사를 보고 뒤의 구조를 맞히는 문제가 출제됩니다.

빈출 '요구/허락/가능 동사 + 목적어 + to부정사'	
allow 목 to ~가 …하도록 허락하다	expect 목 to ~가 …할 거라 기대하다
cause 목 to ~가 …하도록 초래하다	instruct 목 to ~가 …하도록 지시하다
remind 목 to ~가 …하도록 상기시키다	convince 목 to ~가 …하도록 설득하다
enable 목 to ~가 …하는 것을 가능케 하다	advise 목 to ~가 …하도록 조언하다
encourage 목 to ~가 …하도록 고무시키다	invite 목 to ~가 …하도록 권유하다
ask/require 목 to ~가 …하도록 요청/요구하다	appoint 목 to ~가 …하도록 지명하다

Chapter Test

1. Anyone who was unable to ------- today's meeting should contact human resources.
   (A) arrive
   (B) achieve
   (C) attend
   (D) inform

2. HBOS is committed to ------- investors informed of all decisions and recent changes.
   (A) bringing
   (B) requiring
   (C) keeping
   (D) promoting

3. Our supervisor, Mr. Spiegel, ------- employees to take a 30-minute break after 4 P.M.
   (A) brings
   (B) allows
   (C) speaks
   (D) offers

4. Some people are against building a new chemical factory in their town, but many people are for it, because it ------- jobs.
   (A) results
   (B) creates
   (C) interests
   (D) appears

5. Thanks to the development of wireless technology, laptop users can ------- the Internet even when they are on the road.
   (A) access
   (B) access to
   (C) have access
   (D) have an access

6. Our company has ------- themselves plenty of patrons over the last few years.
   (A) won
   (B) had
   (C) took
   (D) went

7. Inventory control ------- within the responsibilities of the branch manager.
   (A) has
   (B) covers
   (C) marks
   (D) falls

8. The Asian dish at Holly's Café ------- with various vegetables.
   (A) to serve
   (B) will serve
   (C) is served
   (D) was serving

9. This morning's presentation has ------- the clients consider investing in pharmaceuticals.
   (A) become
   (B) made
   (C) brought
   (D) given

10. Engineers are expected to ------- the malfunction of the newly developed software completely and flawlessly.
    (A) arrive
    (B) address
    (C) satisfy
    (D) become

Chapter 3 동사의 수 일치/태/시제

동사의 수, 포인트 감각 익히기

The price of a home inspection ------- labor and maintenance costs.
(A) includes   (B) include
주택 점검비에는 인건비와 유지 비용이 포함되어 있다.

동사의 수 일치 문제
→ 빈칸은 본동사 자리인데 주어가 단수이므로 동사도 단수형이 되어야 합니다. 따라서 정답은 (A) includes입니다.

개념 정리

❶ 동사의 수 일치
동사는 주어와 수를 일치시켜야 해요.

<u>He</u> <u>knows</u> how to drive a car. 그는 운전하는 방법을 안다.

주어		동사의 수	현재 시제	현재 완료
복수	⇨	복수 동사	동사 원형	have p.p.(-ed)
단수	⇨	단수 동사	동사 원형+(-e)s	has p.p.(-ed)

❷ 동사의 형태

1) **능동태**: 주어가 어떤 일을 **스스로 한다**는 의미의 문장이에요.
   <u>He</u> <u>repaired</u> the dishwasher. 그는 식기세척기를 수리했다.

2) **수동태 (be+p.p.)**: 주어가 어떤 일을 **누군가에 의해 당한다**는 의미의 문장이에요.
   <u>The dishwasher</u> <u>was repaired</u> <u>by him</u>. 식기세척기는 그에 의해 수리되어졌다.

3) 능동태 문장을 수동태 문장으로 만들 수 있습니다.

① 능동태의 목적어 → 수동태의 주어로 이동
② 능동태의 동사 → 'be+p.p.' 형태로 변화
③ 능동태의 주어 → 'by+동작의 주체'로 변화 (생략 가능)

❸ 시제

1) **현재 시제**: 현재의 사실 혹은 상태, 주기적이고 일상적으로 반복되는 사실, 확실한 미래의 일
2) **과거 시제**: 과거에 발생했던 일이나 상태, 혹은 역사적인 사실
3) **미래 시제**: 아직 발생하지 않은 미래의 일

	현재	과거	미래
단순	is[are] / 동사 원형	was[were] / 동사 원형+(e)d / 불규칙	will+동사 원형
진행	is[are]+V-ing	was[were]+V-ing	will be+V-ing
완료	has[have]+p.p.	had+p.p.	will have+p.p.
완료 진행	has[have] been V-ing	had been V-ing	will have been V-ing

Check-up Test 700+를 위해 한 걸음 한 걸음

정답 및 해석 p.057

A. 다음 문장에서 동사를 모두 찾고 능동태인지 수동태인지 적으세요.

① She is doing her best. 그녀는 최선을 다하고 있다.
② This installation program will be launched next year. 이 설치 프로그램은 내년에 출시될 예정이다.
③ This printer that was donated from Mr. John is broken again. 존 씨가 기증한 프린터는 또 고장 났다.
④ Employees are supposed to attend the monthly meeting. 직원들은 월간 회의에 참석해야 한다.
⑤ Kim has been teaching English at the school since last year. 김 씨는 작년부터 학교에서 영어를 가르치고 있다.

B. 다음 밑줄 친 동사를 올바른 수동태로 바꾸세요.

① The door lock by me. 문이 나에 의해 닫혔다.
② The game saw by many people. 그 경기는 많은 사람들에 의해 시청되었다.
③ Visitors expect to wear a name tag. 방문객들은 명찰을 착용해야 한다.
④ Full-time employees give the freedom of flexible schedules. 정규직 직원들은 탄력 근무를 할 수 있는 자유를 받는다.
⑤ Mr. Carter elected president by people. 카터 씨는 사람들에 의해 대통령으로 선출되었다.

C. 다음 문장의 시제를 적으세요.

① I was working at 8 P.M. last night. 나는 어젯밤 저녁 8시에 근무를 하고 있었다.
② The movie has been playing for 4 weeks. 그 영화는 4주째 상영되고 있다.
③ My bus leaves promptly at 10:00 A.M. every day. 내가 타는 버스는 매일 오전 10시 정각에 떠난다.
④ A cup of tea was made for him by me. 내가 그를 위해 한 잔의 차를 준비하였다.
⑤ The first draft of the blueprint will be revised by the assistant architect.
설계도의 초안은 보조 건축기사에 의해 수정될 예정이다.

Point 01 동사의 수 일치

출제 포인트 정리

❶ 동사의 수 일치 문제는 아래의 3가지를 주의합니다.

1) 주어가 단수이면 동사도 단수, 주어가 복수이면 동사도 복수가 되어야 합니다.
   An apple is delicious. 사과가 맛있다.   Apples are delicious. 사과들이 맛있다.

2) 동명사구/to부정사구/명사절 뒤에는 단수 동사가 옵니다.
   Living alone is not easy. 자취는 쉽지 않다.

3) 주격 관계 대명사절의 동사의 수는 선행사가 결정합니다.
   I have an apple that was given to me by a friend. 나는 친구가 내게 준 사과를 갖고 있다.

❷ 주어가 '부분 대명사+of+명사'인 경우 of 뒤의 명사에 동사의 수를 일치시킵니다.

all, most, some, any, half 등 (부분 대명사)	+ of	가산 복수 명사 → 복수 동사 불가산 명사 → 단수 동사

All of the applicants are highly qualified. 모든 지원자들은 뛰어난 자격을 갖추었다.

> ◈ 수식어구 제거
>
> 동사 문제 풀이의 기본이자 첫 단계는 다음 7가지 수식어구를 걷어내고 주요 성분만 남기는 것입니다.
> **수식어구 종류:** ① 부사 ② 전치사+목적어 ③ to부정사+목적어 ④ 전치사+동명사+목적어
>   ⑤ 접속사+주어+동사 ⑥ 관계 대명사절 ⑦ 분사
>
> A professor of mathematics regularly hands out some materials that summarize everything.
>   전치사+목적어   부사   관계 대명사절
> → A professor hands out some materials. (단수 주어-단수 동사)
>   (수학) 교수는 (정기적으로) (모든 내용을 요약한) 자료들을 배부한다.

Check-up Test 700+를 위해 한 걸음 한 걸음

정답 및 해설 p.057

STEP 1 다음 두 개의 보기 중 빈칸에 알맞은 것을 고르세요.

1. Some of the information ------- missing.
   (A) is   (B) are

2. Anyone who ------- drilling equipment must wear safety glasses.
   (A) operate   (B) operates

3. ------- job-seekers is the best way to increase the employment rate in Quebec.
   (A) Help   (B) Helping

STEP 2 빈칸에 알맞은 것을 고르세요.

4. Mr. Mir ------- his company's new television advertisement and is very pleased with its quality.
   (A) see   (B) seen   (C) has seen   (D) seeing

5. The eligibility requirements for each course ------- from program to program.
   (A) varies   (B) various   (C) varying   (D) vary

Point 02 수동태

출제 포인트 정리

❶ 3형식 동사의 수동태

타동사 뒤에 목적어가 없으면 수동태가 되어야 합니다.

The house (was built, built) by us. 그 집은 우리에 의해 지어졌다.

❷ 4형식 동사의 수동태

목적어를 두 개 가지는 4형식 동사가 수동태가 되면 뒤에 목적어 한 개가 남습니다.

Carter was (given, provided) the task of finding the location for the Lorence Company's picnic.
카터 씨는 로렌스 회사의 야유회를 위한 장소를 찾는 임무를 부여받았다.

→ 수동태인데 빈칸 뒤에 목적어가 있으므로 2개의 목적어를 갖는 4형식 동사인 given이 정답입니다.

❸ 5형식 동사의 수동태

목적어와 목적격 보어를 가지는 5형식 동사가 수동태가 되면 뒤에 목적격 보어가 남습니다.

Visitors (are expected, expects) to wear a name tag at all times while at the factory.
방문객들은 공장에 있는 내내 이름표를 착용해야 한다.

→ '5형식 동사+목적어+to부정사'에서 목적어(visitors)가 주어 자리로 가서 'be+p.p.+to부정사'가 된 것이므로 수동태인 are expected가 정답입니다.

❹ '자동사+전치사'의 수동태

'자동사+전치사'의 형태로 숙어를 이루는 타동사구는 수동태가 가능합니다.

The passengers themselves should take care of any personal belongings. 승객들은 스스로 개인 소지품을 챙겨야 한다.
= Any personal belongings should be taken care of by the passengers themselves.

→ '자동사+전치사'가 하나의 타동사로 쓰이는 경우 수동태는 'be동사+과거 분사+전치사+(by+주어)'의 형태가 됩니다.

Check-up Test 700+를 위해 한 걸음 한 걸음

정답 및 해석 p.058

STEP 1 다음 두 개의 보기 중 빈칸에 알맞은 것을 고르세요.

1. The programs of this workshop should ------- by the organizer.
   (A) be checked   (B) check

2. Mr. Quinn is still ------- whether to expand our branch to California or to Michigan.
   (A) considering   (B) considered

3. Professor Grant from the research department ------- for giving lectures which inspire the students.
   (A) is known   (B) know

STEP 2 빈칸에 알맞은 것을 고르세요.

4. Regarding the acquisition, all the details will be ------- for in the report.
   (A) accounted   (B) explained   (C) told   (D) informed

5. One volunteer who will be working on Saturday ------- a letter yesterday about his responsibilities by the hospital.
   (A) was sending   (B) would send   (C) will be sent   (D) was sent

Point 03 빈출 수동태 표현

출제 포인트 정리

❶ 전치사 by가 아닌 다른 전치사를 취하는 수동태 표현들은 반드시 외워야 해요.

빈출 '수동태 동사+전치사'	
be related to ~와 관련되어 있다	be divided in(to) ~으로 나뉘다
be associated with ~과 관련되다	be assigned to ~에 배정되다
be equipped with ~을 갖추고 있다	be based on ~에 기반을 두다, 근거하다
be known for[as] ~로 유명하다	be convinced of ~을 확신하다
be disappointed in ~에 실망하다	be satisfied with ~에 만족하다
be acquainted with ~을 알고 있다	

York Monaco is known for developing smart appliances. 요크 모나코는 스마트기기 개발로 유명하다.

❷ '수동태 동사+to부정사'가 하나의 표현을 이루는 경우도 반드시 외워야 해요.

빈출 '수동태 동사+to부정사'	
be asked to부정사 ~하라고 요청받다	be allowed to부정사 ~하도록 허가받다
be required to부정사 ~하도록 요구받다	be entitled to부정사 ~할 자격이 있다
be encouraged to부정사 ~하라고 권고받다	be scheduled to부정사 ~할 예정이다
be supposed to부정사 ~하기로 되어 있다	be expected to부정사 ~할 것으로 기대되다

The representatives are required to notify their supervisor of their vacation time.
직원들은 상사에게 휴가 일정을 반드시 공지해야 한다.

Check-up Test 700+를 위해 한 걸음 한 걸음

정답 및 해석 p.058

STEP 1 다음 두 개의 보기 중 빈칸에 알맞은 것을 고르세요.

1. You are not allowed ------- electronic devices during the class.
   (A) use (B) to use

2. The number of sales is ------- to exceed more than 100 billion.
   (A) expect (B) expected

3. Applicants for positions in the factory ------- to possess at least a labor certification.
   (A) are required (B) has required

STEP 2 빈칸에 알맞은 것을 고르세요.

4. All employees are ------- to wear safety glasses when operating machinery.
   (A) ruled (B) protected (C) decided (D) required

5. KPMG ------- for creating advertisements that leave a strong impression on viewers.
   (A) is known (B) will know (C) to know (D) has known

Point 04 시제 결정 요소

출제 포인트 정리

❶ 시간 부사(구)

과거, 현재, 미래를 나타내는 **시간 부사(구)**를 통해 시제를 알 수 있어요.

Our restaurant receives fresh produce every day from local farms. <현재>
우리 식당은 지역 농장으로부터 매일 신선한 농산물을 받는다.
Last month, a number of products were launched. <과거> 지난달에 많은 상품들이 출시되었다.
We will take a vacation next month. <미래> 우리는 다음 달에 휴가를 보낼 것이다.

❷ 시간 접속사

시간 접속사를 통해 주절과 종속절(접속사가 이끄는 절)의 전후 순서와 시제를 알 수 있어요.

I will let you know after everything is confirmed. 모든 것이 확정된 이후에 알려 주겠다.
By the time I got the message, he had left home. 내가 메시지를 받았을 때쯤 그는 집을 떠났다.

> ❖ by the time의 문장 구조
>
> 과거 완료(had p.p.) + by the time + 과거
> 미래 완료(will have p.p.) + by the time + 현재
> He will have left by the time you come back. 네가 돌아 올 때쯤이면 그는 떠났을 것이다.

❸ 동사+접속사+동사

보통 **주절**과 **종속절**은 **시제가 동일**합니다.

We do not believe that she is honest. 우리는 그녀가 솔직하다고 생각하지 않는다.
When Mr. Kim worked here, he was recognized for his hard work and dedication.
김 씨가 이곳에서 근무했을 때, 그는 성실과 헌신으로 인정받았다.

Check-up Test 700+를 위해 한 걸음 한 걸음

정답 및 해석 p.058

STEP 1 다음 두 개의 보기 중 빈칸에 알맞은 것을 고르세요.

1. There is a notice that interns ------- at job fairs in Beijing next year.
   (A) were recruited   (B) will be recruited

2. By the time Mr. Harvey sends a new order, Best Office Supplies ------- a new price list.
   (A) had published   (B) will have published

3. Personnel records of employees ------- not allowed to be distributed without authorization.
   (A) are   (B) was

STEP 2 빈칸에 알맞은 것을 고르세요.

4. As soon as the technology department received approval, our team ------- the project.
   (A) has begun   (B) began   (C) were beginning   (D) begin

5. Our purchasing department ------- office supplies every Friday.
   (A) orders   (B) ordered   (C) ordering   (D) will order

Point 05 현재 시제

출제 포인트 정리

❶ 현재 시제가 정답이 되는 4가지

1) 일상적으로 반복되는 일을 나타내는 경우 – **빈도 부사**와 함께 자주 쓰입니다.
I teach business English every day. 나는 매일 비즈니스 영어를 가르친다.

빈출 현재 시제와 함께 자주 쓰이는 부사				
hourly 한 시간마다	daily 일일, 하루	monthly 달마다	annually 해마다	
regularly 정기적으로	always 항상	frequently 종종	usually 대개	generally 보통

2) 일반적인 사실이나 일정 기간 지속적으로 발생하는 일을 나타내는 경우
The Han River flows into the Yellow Sea. 한강은 황해로 흐른다.

3) 확정된 미래를 나타내는 경우
The plane leaves Seoul at 11:30. 그 비행기는 서울에서 11시 30분에 출발한다.

4) 시간이나 조건 부사절에서는 **현재 시제가 미래 시제를 대신**합니다.
She will call me when she (arrives, ~~will arrive~~) at the airport.
그녀는 공항에 도착할 때 저에게 연락을 할 것입니다.

Check-up Test 700+를 위해 한 걸음 한 걸음

정답 및 해석 p.058

STEP 1 다음 두 개의 보기 중 빈칸에 알맞은 것을 고르세요.

1. Once Mr. Nelson ------- to Hong Kong next month, he will take a tour of the factory and then negotiate the price.
   (A) goes (B) will go

2. Camion Vehicles Repair ------- extends its hours of operation for the summer season.
   (A) recently (B) always

3. During the next quarter, our stockholders ------- to see the net profit increase projected by the finance department.
   (A) hope (B) hoped

STEP 2 빈칸에 알맞은 것을 고르세요.

4. Sidewalks in most cities are ------- one meter wide.
   (A) widely (B) gradually (C) generally (D) formerly

5. The seminar information packets will be mailed to all attendees two days before the conference -------.
   (A) began (B) begins (C) beginning (D) begin

Point 06 과거 vs. 현재 완료

출제 포인트 정리

❶ 과거 시제

과거 시제(동사 원형＋ed/불규칙)는 과거에 발생한 사실을 나타냅니다.

I lost my wallet two weeks ago. 나는 이 주 전에 지갑을 잃어버렸다. (과거에 지갑을 잃어버렸고 현재 찾았는지는 확인 불가)

빈출 과거 시제와 함께 출제되는 시간 부사(구)
yesterday 어제   last year 작년에   two weeks ago 2주 전에

❷ 현재 완료 시제

현재 완료 시제(have[has]＋p.p.)는 과거의 특정 시점부터 현재까지 동작이나 상태의 지속을 나타냅니다.

I have lost my wallet lately. 나는 최근에 지갑을 잃어버렸다. (과거에 지갑을 잃어버려서 지금도 찾지 못했음)

빈출 현재 완료 시제와 함께 출제되는 시간 부사(구)
for the last ~ years 지난 ~년간   recently/lately 최근에
since last month 지난달부터   over the past/last＋시간 명사 지난 ~ 기간에 걸쳐

> ✤ since의 문장 구조
>
> Since ＋ 과거 시제/과거 시점, 주어 ＋ 현재 완료 시제 ~.
> This program has been implemented since 2016. 이 프로그램은 2016년부터 실시되고 있다.
> Since it was first launched, this program has been implemented. 처음 출시된 이후로, 이 프로그램은 실시되고 있다.

Check-up Test 700+를 위해 한 걸음 한 걸음

정답 및 해석 p.059

STEP 1   다음 두 개의 보기 중 빈칸에 알맞은 것을 고르세요.

1. In the past 30 years, more girls and women -------- in all types of sports than ever before.
   (A) participated   (B) have been participating

2. Ms. Park ------- employed by the same company in many different capacities over the last 20 years.
   (A) has been   (B) was

3. Mr. Parker, the director, has already ------- to boost the corporation's profits by 20 percent within a year.
   (A) promised   (B) promise

STEP 2   빈칸에 알맞은 것을 고르세요.

4. It has been three months since Ms. McDaniel ------- Lauren Sports.
   (A) join   (B) joins   (C) joined   (D) to join

5. Mr. Paul Newman, who ------- an important figure in the marketing industry for the past thirty years, will be the guest lecturer at Brunswick University.
   (A) will   (B) is   (C) was   (D) has been

이것만 알면 700+
토익 최빈출 유형 정리! 동사 태와 시제편!

유형 1 동사 문제 풀이 순서

❶ 구조 분석: 수식어구 제거하고 주어와 본동사 찾기
❷ 구조 분석을 토대로 빈칸이 동사 자리인지 확인하기
❸ 수 일치 확인: 주어가 단수인지, 복수인지 확인하기
❹ 보기에 제시된 동사가 자동사인지 타동사인지 확인하기
❺ 태 확인: 빈칸 뒤에 목적어의 유무 확인하기
❻ 시제 파악: 시간 부사나 접속사로 동사의 시제 파악하기

Mr. Cohen, (as chief financial officer for Hyunsung Co.), will assume responsibility (for budgeting and accounting) (from next year). 현성 사의 최고 재무 책임자로 있는 코헨 씨가 내년부터 예산과 회계 업무를 맡을 것이다.

유형 2 진행형 불가 동사

상태	remain 계속 ~이다 resemble 닮다 exist 존재하다 seem 보이다 appear 나타나다 be ~이다
소유	belong to ~에 속하다 possess 소유하다 own 소유하다 have 가지다
지각	taste 맛이 나다 feel 느낌이 나다 hear 들리다 smell 냄새가 나다 sound 소리가 나다 notice 의식하다
감정	love 사랑하다 like 좋아하다 hate 미워하다 want 원하다 desire 바라다 need 필요하다
인식	know 알다 believe 믿다 guess 추측하다 remember 기억하다

She (belongs, ~~is belonging~~) to a dance club. 그녀는 댄스 클럽에 속해 있다.

유형 3 <고난도> consider의 수동태

❶ 3형식 consider = consider + (동)명사
  → 수동태 = <목적어 + be considered>
❷ 5형식 consider = consider + 사람/사물 + (to부정사/as) + 형용사/명사
  → 수동태 = <목적어 + be considered + (to부정사/as) + 형용사/명사>

People will consider the new system seriously. (3형식)
→ The new system will be considered seriously. 그 새로운 시스템은 진지하게 고려될 것이다.

People consider the new system efficient. (5형식)
→ The new system is considered efficient. 그 새로운 시스템은 효율적이라고 생각된다.

Chapter Test

정답 및 해석 p.059

1. By now, the winners of the competition ------- by phone and by e-mail.
   (A) notified
   (B) will notify
   (C) are notifying
   (D) have been notified

2. Visitors ------- the city museum between the hours of 9 A.M. and 4 P.M.
   (A) tours
   (B) have toured
   (C) are toured
   (D) have been toured

3. Our clinic ------- local residents with exceptional dental care at an affordable price.
   (A) provide
   (B) provides
   (C) is provided
   (D) would have been provided

4. The librarian has requested that any overdue books or journals ------- by the end of the month.
   (A) be returned
   (B) to return
   (C) returns
   (D) returning

5. A competent manager ------- a working environment in which all staff members have the ability to work at their best.
   (A) create
   (B) creates
   (C) is created
   (D) creating

6. The difficulty that ------- with this approach was that most business owners were lacking a foundation in Internet marketing and web basics.
   (A) emerged
   (B) engaged
   (C) revealed
   (D) reacted

7. These handouts should not be ------- a replacement for a text book.
   (A) studied
   (B) granted
   (C) considered
   (D) allowed

8. In opposition to Mr. Salerno's suggestion, Ms. Simmons ------- to hire two secretaries instead of one.
   (A) like
   (B) was liking
   (C) would like
   (D) is liking

9. When Henderson Enterprises ------- its auto-mobile division, a number of senior managers were let go.
   (A) was restructured
   (B) restructures
   (C) was restructuring
   (D) to restructure

10. Dr. Jenning's seminar ------- in Room 101 today and tomorrow afternoon.
    (A) holds
    (B) has held
    (C) is holding
    (D) is being held

Chapter 4 대명사

대명사, 포인트 감각 익히기

As a salesman, ------- need to deal with more clients and build interpersonal relationships with them.

(A) you   (B) your

영업 사원으로서 당신은 더 많은 고객을 상대하고 그들과 대인 관계를 쌓아야 합니다.

대명사의 격 문제
→ 빈칸은 동사 need 앞 주어 자리이므로 주격 대명사인 (A) you가 정답입니다.

개념 정리

❶ 대명사의 종류

대명사는 앞에 나왔던 특정 명사의 반복을 피하기 위해 대신 쓰는 단어를 가리켜요.

1) 인칭 대명사: 사람 명사를 대신하는 품사로, 문장 내 역할에 따라 형태가 달라져요.
We have a meeting today. 우리는 오늘 회의가 있다.

2) 지시 대명사: 특정한 사람, 사물 등을 나타내는 품사입니다.
These(= These books) are very expensive. 이 책들은 매우 비싸다.
※ this(these), that(those)는 지시 형용사 혹은 지시 대명사로 사용이 가능해요.
This(지시 형용사) book 이 책   These(지시 대명사) are very expensive. 이 책들은 매우 비싸다.

3) 부정 대명사: 특정 대상을 가리키는 것이 아니라 어떤 종류인지만 알려 주는 대명사입니다.
My computer was broken so I have to buy one. 내 컴퓨터가 고장 나서 구매해야 한다.

❷ 한눈에 살펴보는 인칭 대명사

수	인칭/성		인칭 대명사			소유 대명사 (~의 것)	재귀 대명사 (~ 자신)
			주격 (~은; ~는)	소유격 (~의)	목적격 (~를)		
단수	1인칭		I	my	me	mine	myself
	2인칭		you	your	you	yours	yourself
	3인칭	남성	he	his	him	his	himself
		여성	she	her	her	hers	herself
		중성	it	its	it	-	itself
복수	1인칭		we	our	us	ours	ourselves
	2인칭		you	your	you	yours	yourselves
	3인칭		they	their	them	theirs	themselves

1) 주격 대명사: 문장의 주어 역할을 하며, 뒤에 동사가 나와요.
2) 소유격 대명사: 형용사 역할을 하며 뒤에 명사가 와야 해요.
3) 목적격 대명사: 타동사의 목적어나 전치사의 목적어 역할을 해요.
4) 소유 대명사: '소유격＋명사'로 바꾸어 쓸 수 있으며, 소유를 나타내요.

Check-up Test 700+를 위해 한 걸음 한 걸음

정답 및 해석 p.059

A. 다음 중 인칭 대명사를 모두 찾으세요.

① my ② all ③ him ④ some ⑤ themselves
⑥ few ⑦ theirs ⑧ most ⑨ hers ⑩ you
⑪ all ⑫ it ⑬ this ⑭ those ⑮ he

B. 다음 문장에서 밑줄 친 대명사의 격을 쓰세요.

① We hired a manager and he is here to see you.
우리는 관리자를 채용했고 그는 당신을 보러 여기 왔다.

② Supervisors were asked to manage their teams.
감독관들은 그들의 팀을 관리하는 것을 요청받았다.

③ The quality of our product is much better than yours.
우리 제품의 질이 당신 회사의 제품보다 훨씬 뛰어납니다.

④ Most companies have been reducing their labor costs and additional spending.
대부분의 회사들은 인건비와 추가 지출을 줄이고 있다.

⑤ Sanchez asked his manager to complete the project by himself.
산체스 씨는 그의 상사에게 그 프로젝트를 혼자서 끝내겠다고 요청했다.

C. 다음 문장에서 밑줄 친 대명사를 올바르게 바꾸세요.

① I know that her was in the room. 그녀가 그 방에 있었다는 것을 알고 있다.

② She was going to attend the conference hers. 그녀는 스스로 학회에 참석하려고 했다.

③ He decided to buy they. 그는 그것들을 구매하기로 결정했다.

④ Is this you pen? 이것은 당신의 펜인가요?

⑤ This problem is difficult for his. 이 문제는 그에게 어렵다.

Chapter 4. 대명사

Point 01　인칭 대명사의 격

출제 포인트 정리

❶ 주격 대명사
동사 앞 **주어 자리**에는 **주격 대명사**가 옵니다.
I bought a new car last week. 나는 지난주에 새 차를 샀다.
We are studying English. 우리들은 영어를 공부하고 있다.

❷ 목적격 대명사
동사나 전치사의 목적어 자리에는 **목적격 대명사**가 옵니다.
Dan will give it to you. 댄이 그것을 당신에게 줄 것이다.
Josh seems to be interested in me. 조시는 나에게 관심이 있는 것 같다.

❸ 소유격 대명사
명사 앞에는 **소유격 대명사**가 옵니다.
Your order will be shipped tomorrow. 귀하의 주문은 내일 발송될 것입니다.
The manager has approved her proposal. 관리자가 그녀의 제안서를 승인했다.

※ 소유격 대명사는 관사와 함께 사용할 수 없습니다.
　a your friend → your friend / a friend (O)

Check-up Test　700+를 위해 한 걸음 한 걸음
정답 및 해석 p.059

STEP 1　다음 두 개의 보기 중 빈칸에 알맞은 것을 고르세요.

1. We know ------- was not here.
   (A) he　　　　　　(B) him

2. Mr. Haas and his team were told to complete and bring ------- presentation materials to tomorrow's conference.
   (A) them　　　　　(B) their

3. Our supervisor was asked to manage ------- team.
   (A) she　　　　　　(B) her

STEP 2　빈칸에 알맞은 것을 고르세요.

4. The members of their group have all been selected, but Mr. Foreman may join -------.
   (A) they　　　(B) their　　　(C) them　　　(D) themselves

5. The vice president will visit our office tomorrow, so please have all ------- documents ready.
   (A) he　　　　(B) his　　　　(C) him　　　　(D) himself

Point 02 재귀 대명사

출제 포인트 정리

❶ 목적어 자리 재귀 대명사

재귀 대명사는 **주어와 목적어가 동일**할 때 목적어 자리에 옵니다. **목적어 자리**에 오는 재귀 대명사는 생략할 수 없습니다.

[재귀 대명사] 주어 = 목적어	[목적격 대명사] 주어 ≠ 목적어
She made herself famous. 그녀는 스스로를 유명하게 만들었다.	The book made her famous. 그 책은 그녀를 유명하게 만들었다.
She = herself (주어 = 목적어)	The book ≠ her (주어 ≠ 목적어)

❷ 강조의 재귀 대명사

주어 뒤, 완전한 문장의 끝에서 '직접, 스스로'라는 **부사어로 의미**를 강조하기 위해 재귀 대명사를 사용할 수 있습니다. 이때 재귀 대명사는 **생략이 가능합니다**.

John completed all assignments himself. 존은 스스로 모든 과제를 끝마쳤다.

빈출 재귀 대명사 관용 표현
by oneself 혼자서　　for oneself 혼자 힘으로　　of itself 저절로

The planning director completed the project by herself. 기획 담당자는 스스로 프로젝트를 마무리했다.

Check-up Test 700+를 위해 한 걸음 한 걸음

정답 및 해석 p.059

STEP 1 다음 두 개의 보기 중 빈칸에 알맞은 것을 고르세요.

1. Jane can't do all the work ------- in an office like this.
   (A) her　　　　　　(B) herself

2. Dr. Newton rarely schedules appointments ------- because he is too busy consulting other patients.
   (A) his　　　　　　(B) himself

3. Mr. Long had to finish his report by -------.
   (A) him　　　　　　(B) himself

STEP 2 빈칸에 알맞은 것을 고르세요.

4. Through her outstanding performance, Ms. Robin has shown ------- to be a valuable asset to our firm.
   (A) she　　　(B) her　　　(C) herself　　　(D) hers

5. Ms. Stella began the focus group interview by ------- but later was assisted by other marketers.
   (A) she　　　(B) her　　　(C) hers　　　(D) herself

Point 03 · one, another, other, the other 구분하기

출제 포인트 정리

❶ one vs. another vs. other vs. the other

1) **one, another, other, the other**는 부정 대명사라고 합니다.
2) one, another, other, the other는 형태에 따라 **형용사**로 쓰일 수 있으니, **각각의 품사와 동사의 수 일치**에 주의합니다.

	형용사	대명사	단수 동사	복수 동사
one (불특정한 사람, 사물)	O	O	O	X
another ('추가'의 의미)	O	O	O	X (예외 = another two weeks)
other (막연한 다수)	O	X	X	O
others (막연한 다수)	X	O	X	O
the other (나머지 하나)	O	O	O	X
the others (불특정한 다수 중 나머지 모두)	X	O	X	O
one another (둘 사이)	대명사로 목적어 자리에 위치하며 주어, 부사로는 사용 불가			
each other (세 명 이상)				

3) 형용사 one, another, the other + 단수 명사 + 단수 동사
   Another regular meeting is scheduled. 또 다른 정기 회의가 예정되어 있다.

4) 형용사 other + 복수 명사 + 복수 동사
   Other items were shipped yesterday. 다른 제품들은 어제 발송되었다.

Check-up Test 700+를 위해 한 걸음 한 걸음   정답 및 해석 p.060

STEP 1   다음 두 개의 보기 중 빈칸에 알맞은 것을 고르세요.

1. One of the leading online malls, Mona only offers coupons instead of ------- discounts to its online customers.
   (A) other   (B) another

2. Of the three options that are provided, two are not available to us, while ------- is acceptable and within our budget.
   (A) the other   (B) others

3. ------- products have not been as profitable as we expected.
   (A) Other   (B) Others

STEP 2   빈칸에 알맞은 것을 고르세요.

4. The manual for new users shows how to copy e-mails from one account to -------.
   (A) one   (B) another   (C) other   (D) one another

5. The NJ Transit is the most economic means of transportation for commuters, but ------- are also efficient as well.
   (A) other   (B) others   (C) the other   (D) another

Point 04 those와 one

출제 포인트 정리

❶ those
1) 지시 대명사 those + 복수 동사: Those are very expensive. 저것들은 매우 비싸다.
2) 지시 형용사 those + 복수 명사: Those books are very informative. 저 책들은 매우 유익하다.
3) 불특정 대상을 가리키는 부정 대명사 those (수식을 받을 수 있음)
   Only (those, them) with approval from the CEO could apply for the managerial position.
   회장의 승인을 받은 사람들만 관리직에 지원할 수 있었다.

❷ one
1) 수사 one: Do you want one apple or two? 사과 한 개 줄까? 아님 두 개 줄까?
2) 불특정 대상을 가리키는 부정 대명사 one: One must not neglect their duty. 누구나 자기 의무를 소홀히 해서는 안 된다.
3) one vs. it
   one은 앞서 언급된 명사와 같은 종류이지만 다른 개체일 때 사용하고, 대명사 it은 앞에서 언급된 특정 단수 명사, 바로 그 동일한 대상을 지칭할 때 사용합니다.
   I like my current job more than the old (one, it). 나는 현재의 일을 예전의 일보다 더 좋아한다.

> ✹ 관계사절의 선행사가 될 수 있는 대명사 [those, -one(someone, anyone)]
> They who have books are my friends. (X)
> → Those who have books are my friends. (O) 책들을 가지고 있는 사람들은 내 친구들이다.
> → Anyone who has a book is my friend. (O) 책을 가지고 있는 사람은 내 친구이다.

Check-up Test 700+를 위해 한 걸음 한 걸음

정답 및 해설 p.060

STEP 1 다음 두 개의 보기 중 빈칸에 알맞은 것을 고르세요.

1. ------- who are planning to go away for vacation need to take a look at the special offers.
   (A) Those   (B) Themselves

2. You are supposed to submit ------- reports by noon.
   (A) that   (B) those

3. This year's revenue figures from major rental agencies are similar to ------- of last year.
   (A) those   (B) that

STEP 2 빈칸에 알맞은 것을 고르세요.

4. Even though he was recently promoted to supervisor, Mr. Phillip's employees were more experienced than ------- of other teams.
   (A) it   (B) theirs   (C) them   (D) those

5. The testers say that ------- has more durability while the other features a more fascinating design.
   (A) whoever   (B) each   (C) one   (D) many

이것만 알면 700+
토익 최빈출 유형 정리! 대명사편!

유형 1 some vs. any vs. all vs. most

	품사	대신 받는 명사	쓰임
some	대명사, 형용사	가산 복수 명사, 불가산 명사	긍정문
any	대명사, 형용사	가산 단·복수 명사, 불가산 명사	부정·조건·의문문
all	대명사, 형용사, 부사	가산 복수 명사, 불가산 명사	all + (of) + (the) + 명사
most	대명사, 형용사, 부사	가산 복수 명사, 불가산 명사	most + (of) + 명사

You can choose any of these items. 이 물품들 중 아무거나 선택하셔도 돼요.

유형 2 every vs. each

	쓰임	의미	형태
every	한정사(형용사)	모든, ~마다	every + 단수 명사, every + 수사 + 복수 명사 (every + of + 복수 명사)
each	수량 형용사	각자의	each + 단수 명사
	대명사	각각, 각자	each of the/지시 형용사/소유격 + 복수 명사

(Each, ~~Every~~) of the marketers has a different approach to the issue.
마케터들은 각각 그 문제점에 다른 접근 방법을 가지고 있다.
→ every는 형용사이므로 명사 없이 단독으로 올 수 없습니다.

유형 3 소유 대명사 vs. 주격/목적격 대명사

소유 대명사와 주격/목적격 대명사를 구분하는 문제가 종종 출제됩니다.

Our price is higher than (~~you~~, yours). 우리 가격은 당신의 것보다 비싸다.
→ you를 쓰면 가격(our price)과 사람(you)을 비교하는 것이 됩니다. 가격과 사람은 비교 대상이 되지 않으므로 빈칸에는 yours(= your price)가 와야 합니다.

Chapter Test

1. All Airline companies request that, as a ticket holder, ------- present proof of identification.
   (A) yours
   (B) your
   (C) yourself
   (D) you

2. I am sure that Ms. Debra and I will accomplish our short-term goal, as her work style is similar to -------.
   (A) my
   (B) me
   (C) mine
   (D) myself

3. This year's sales figures from furniture businesses are similar to ------- of the preceding two years.
   (A) those
   (B) that
   (C) them
   (D) this

4. Kimberly's Food Market offered contract renewals to all its vendors, and ------- have already signed them.
   (A) each
   (B) much
   (C) most
   (D) everyone

5. This economic forecast predicted that most companies will be reducing ------- labour costs.
   (A) they
   (B) them
   (C) their
   (D) themselves

6. X-5 laser printers are sold out in our store, so if your store has -------, please send some of them immediately.
   (A) this
   (B) few
   (C) any
   (D) it

7. Before the departure, station staff must ensure that ------- of the tickets is collected from the passengers.
   (A) every
   (B) all
   (C) each
   (D) much

8. For the employee appreciation dinner, Ms. Finlay set up buffet tables for employees to help ------- to a variety of dishes.
   (A) they
   (B) themselves
   (C) theirs
   (D) their

9. The world renowned magazine *Watson Financial* released a list of start-up companies ------- considers to be the most promising.
   (A) it
   (B) its
   (C) its own
   (D) itself

10. Audience members are asked to not talk among ------- while discussions are going on.
    (A) their
    (B) them
    (C) theirs
    (D) themselves

Chapter 5 형용사

형용사, 포인트 감각 익히기

Before we release our new product, we need to conduct ------- research into the domestic market.
(A) additional   (B) additionally

신제품을 공개하기 전에 우리는 국내 시장에 대한 추가 조사를 실시해야 합니다.

형용사 자리 문제
→ 빈출 유형으로 '동사+-------+명사'의 빈칸에는 형용사가 답이 됩니다. 명사 research를 수식하는 형용사 (A)가 정답입니다.

개념 정리

❶ 형용사의 역할과 형태

1) 형용사는 명사의 모양, 성질, 크기, 개수 등을 구체적으로 설명하는 역할을 하며, 주로 수식하는 명사 앞에 위치해요.
This is a beautiful design. 이것은 아름다운 디자인이다.

2) 다음 형태로 끝나는 단어는 주로 형용사입니다.

형용사의 형태	빈출 형용사
-able/-ible	available 이용 가능한 edible 먹을 수 있는
-fic/-ive/-ory	terrific 멋진 competitive 경쟁을 하는 mandatory 강제적인
-ful/-y/-ous/-lent	hopeful 희망에 찬 hungry 배고픈 famous 유명한 excellent 우수한
-ular/-ilar	particular 특별한 similar 비슷한
-al/-ic	exceptional 우수한 economic 경제의
-ant/-tic	significant 중요한 relevant 관련 있는 enthusiastic 열정적인

※ '형용사+ly'는 부사지만, '명사+ly'는 형용사입니다.
   weekly meeting 주간 회의

❷ 형용사의 종류

형용사는 크게 5가지가 있어요.

형용사의 종류	뜻	빈출 형용사
성질 형용사	사람이나 사물의 특성을 나타내는 형용사	pretty, right, fat
수량 형용사	수나 양을 표현하는 형용사	some, any, no, little/few, many/much, each, every, half, all, both, double, twice
소유 형용사	소유격 대명사	my, your, her, his, our, its, their
지시 형용사	사람이나 사물을 지칭하는 형용사	this, that, these, those
의문 형용사	의문사 역할을 하면서 동시에 명사를 수식하는 형용사	which, what, whose

Check-up Test 700+를 위해 한 걸음 한 걸음

정답 및 해석 p.061

A. 다음 중 형용사를 모두 찾으세요.

① supplementary   ② critical   ③ although   ④ your   ⑤ since
⑥ half   ⑦ thrive   ⑧ innovative   ⑨ from   ⑩ inspect
⑪ drastically   ⑫ contract   ⑬ considerably   ⑭ of   ⑮ durable

B. 다음 문장에서 형용사를 찾으세요.

① We have technical problems. 우리는 기술적인 문제가 있다.
② He is a considerate man. 그는 사려 깊은 남자다.
③ This book is useful to me. 이 책은 나에게 유용하다.
④ The president was present at the meeting. 회장이 회의에 참석했다.
⑤ A variety of events make the game interesting. 다양한 행사들이 경기를 재미있게 한다.

C. 다음 괄호 안에서 알맞은 표현을 고르세요.

① its (strategic, strategically) growth 그것의 전략적 성장
② sound (financially, financial) conditions 건전한 재정 상태
③ (These, That) machines are not the ones that I requested. 이 기계들은 제가 요청한 물건이 아닙니다.
④ (Our, We) employees should follow all of the company policies from June 1st.
   우리의 직원들은 6월 1일부터 모든 회사 정책을 따라야 한다.
⑤ This position offers additional welfare benefits and a (competitive, competitiveness) salary.
   이 직책은 추가 복지 혜택과 높은 급여를 제공한다.

Point 01 형용사 자리

출제 포인트 정리

❶ 형용사는 명사를 수식하는 자리(명사 앞)와 2형식/5형식 동사 뒤 보어 자리에 위치합니다.

1) 관사/소유격 + **형용사** + 명사   an active step 적극적인 조치
2) 부사 + **형용사** + 명사   particularly small companies 특히 소규모 회사들
3) 타동사 + **형용사** + 명사   have technical problems 기술적인 문제들이 있다
4) 동명사/to부정사 + **형용사** + 명사   changing political conditions 정치적 상황을 변경하는 것
5) be동사/2형식 동사 + **형용사**   The children are creative. 아이들은 창의적이다.
   → 2형식 동사 보어 자리
6) 5형식 동사 + 목적어 + **형용사**   He makes me fat. 그가 나를 살찌게 한다.
   → 5형식 동사 목적격 보어 자리

※ 형용사 자리 문제에서 보기에 형용사와 분사(V-ing, p.p.)가 모두 있다면 형용사를 정답으로 고릅니다!

Check-up Test 700+를 위해 한 걸음 한 걸음

정답 및 해석 p.061

STEP 1 다음 두 개의 보기 중 빈칸에 알맞은 것을 고르세요.

1. After the ------- expense on advertising, the company paid its debt within five days.
   (A) initiation   (B) initial

2. As long as the employees remain -------, we should be able to achieve all of our monthly goals.
   (A) productive   (B) production

3. If you plan to become a successful architect, you must possess ------- knowledge in visual arts.
   (A) extensive   (B) extensively

STEP 2 빈칸에 알맞은 것을 고르세요.

4. When purchasing mail-order products, please make all checks ------- to Smith Industries Inc.
   (A) payable   (B) pays   (C) payment   (D) to pay

5. Personal information at Allianz is strictly ------- and can be released only with the employee's authorization.
   (A) confidentiality   (B) confiding   (C) confidence   (D) confidential

Point 02 형용사와 부사 구별하기

출제 포인트 정리

❶ 형용사 vs. 부사

1) **형용사**는 **명사를 수식**합니다.

   Confidential material is kept securely. 기밀 자료는 안전하게 보관된다.

2) **부사**는 **명사를 제외한 모든 품사를 수식**합니다. 심지어는 다른 부사나 문장 전체도 수식할 수 있습니다.

   관사/소유격 + **부사** + **형용사** + 명사   He revised his newly written books.
   그는 새롭게 쓰인 책들을 수정했다.

❷ 형용사 no vs. 부사 not

1) no는 형용사이므로 명사를 수식하고, not은 부사로 형용사를 수식합니다.

2) one 앞에 빈칸이 주어진 유형으로 출제될 수 있는데, 이때 one이 부정 대명사라면 빈칸에 형용사 no가 오고, one이 수사라면 빈칸에는 부사 not이 와야 합니다.

   No one is here. 아무도 여기에 없다.
   Not one of them is here. 그들 중 한 사람도 여기에 없다.

   ※ none은 대명사, never는 부사입니다.

Check-up Test 700+를 위해 한 걸음 한 걸음

정답 및 해석 p.061

STEP 1 다음 두 개의 보기 중 빈칸에 알맞은 것을 고르세요.

1. We need to purchase a ------- round black wooden table.
   (A) large   (B) largely

2. After three months of training, the new employees have become very ------- with company policies.
   (A) familiarly   (B) familiar

3. The president of Newcastle Inc. decided to get supplies from Browns Wholesales because their representative was the most ------- among them.
   (A) persuasive   (B) persuasively

STEP 2 빈칸에 알맞은 것을 고르세요.

4. There are ------- rooms available at Hotel Zeta, but there are still some rooms available at Hotel Omega.
   (A) no   (B) not   (C) none   (D) never

5. Morito Hotel has become an ------- popular venue for conferences since last year's renovations.
   (A) increasing   (B) increasingly   (C) increase   (D) increases

Point 03 수량 형용사

출제 포인트 정리

❶ 수량 형용사에 따라 뒤에 올 수 있는 명사의 종류가 다릅니다.

수량 형용사	가산 단수 명사	가산 복수 명사	불가산 명사
every / each / one / another	O	X	X
any	O	O	O
many / numerous / a number of / (a) few / fewer / both / multiple / several / various / a variety of / 수사(two, three, etc) each of / one of	X	O	X
much / a great deal of / (a) little / less	X	X	O
all / a lot of / lots of / plenty of / most / some / enough / other	X	O	O
the other	O	O	X
each of / one of	X	O	X

A few customers request a refund for defective products. 일부 고객들은 결함 제품 환불을 요청했다.

At the annual Electronics Expo, participants paid much attention to Hogo's products.
연례 전자 제품 박람회에서, 참가자들은 호고 제품에 크게 주목했다.

One of the new strategies is building relationship with others. 신규 전략 중 하나는 다른 기업과의 관계 구축이다.

Check-up Test 700+를 위해 한 걸음 한 걸음

정답 및 해석 p.061

STEP 1 다음 두 개의 보기 중 빈칸에 알맞은 것을 고르세요.

1. After the presentation, ------- staff members voted in favor of renovating the conference room.
   (A) many   (B) much

2. ------- information packet includes the introduction of our company as well as lists of our branches.
   (A) Every   (B) Few

3. ------- staff members are reminded to submit their account information to the secretary.
   (A) All   (B) Each

STEP 2 빈칸에 알맞은 것을 고르세요.

4. A recent consumers' report has shown that ------- customer feels confident about the economy.
   (A) other   (B) only   (C) even   (D) each

5. ------- Borrester Products employee should submit a weekly report by 3:00 P.M. on Friday.
   (A) Several   (B) All   (C) Any   (D) Few

Point 04   사람 수식 형용사 vs. 사물 수식 형용사

출제 포인트 정리

❶ 사람 수식 형용사 vs. 사물 수식 형용사
어원이 동일해도 사람을 수식하느냐 사물을 수식하느냐에 따라 답이 달라지는 유사 형용사 어휘 문제가 출제됩니다.

사람을 수식하는 형용사	사물을 수식하는 형용사
considerate 사려 깊은	considerable 상당한, 중요한
understanding 이해심이 많은	understandable 이해할 수 있는
argumentative 따지기 좋아하는	arguable 논쟁의 여지가 있는
respectable 존경받을 만한	respective 각각의
able 능력이 있는	possible 있을 수 있는

a (~~considerable~~, considerate) man 사려 깊은 사람

❷ 사람만 수식하는 형용사

anxious 갈망하는	keen/eager 열망하는	reluctant (to) (~하기를) 꺼려하는
willing (to) 기꺼이 ~하려하는	generous 관대한	polite 예의바른
confident 확신한	sure 확실한	

The manager is willing to do the work. 매니저는 기꺼이 그 일을 하려고 한다.

Check-up Test 700+를 위해 한 걸음 한 걸음
정답 및 해석 p.061

STEP 1   다음 두 개의 보기 중 빈칸에 알맞은 것을 고르세요.

1. The process of the development of the new product design shown in the presentation was clear and -------.
 (A) understanding   (B) understandable

2. PDSVA provides a secure storage service of ------- documents.
 (A) confident   (B) confidential

3. Our executive director was ------- to hear that Dr. Grey joined our company to co-develop a new source of energy.
 (A) convenient   (B) pleased

STEP 2   빈칸에 알맞은 것을 고르세요.

4. The taste may not be so great, but the ------- atmosphere of Tapas makes it one of the most popular restaurants in downtown.
 (A) pleasant   (B) tender   (C) confident   (D) fragile

5. I am ------- that he will attend the meeting.
 (A) complete   (B) confident   (C) obvious   (D) definite

이것만 알면 700+

토익 최빈출 유형 정리! 형용사편!

유형 1 빈출 이성/감정/판단 형용사

이성/감정/판단 형용사 뒤에 오는 that절엔 '(should)+동사 원형'이 옵니다.

| important 중요한 | imperative 반드시 해야 하는 | essential 필수적인 | necessary 필연적인 |

It is important that we (should) be kept informed of any new developments.
우리에게 새로운 진전 상황을 꼭 알려주는 게 중요하다.

유형 2 빈출 'be동사 + 형용사 + 전치사'

be accustomed to ~에 익숙하다	be mandatory for ~에게 의무적이다
be dependent on ~에 의존하다	be responsible for ~에 책임이 있다
be relevant to ~와 관련이 있다	be sufficient for ~에 충분하다
be eligible for ~의 자격이 있다	be suitable for ~에 적합하다
be enthusiastic about ~에 열광하다	be valid for ~에 유효하다, 타당하다

The team leader is responsible for boosting employees' morale.
팀장은 직원 사기 증진을 책임지고 있다.

유형 3 빈출 'be동사 + 형용사 + to부정사'

be able to부정사 ~할 수 있다	be eligible to부정사 ~할 자격이 있다
be ready to부정사 ~할 준비가 되다	be willing to부정사 기꺼이 ~하려 하다
be supposed to부정사 ~하기로 되어 있다	be entitled to부정사 ~할 자격이 있다
be pleased to부정사 ~해서 기분이 좋다	be qualified to부정사 ~할 자격이 있다
be likely to부정사 ~하기 쉽다	be eager to부정사 ~하기를 열망하다

According to the policy, staffs are entitled to receive 15 days of paid vacation.
정책에 따르면, 직원들은 15일의 유급 휴가를 받을 수 있다.

Chapter Test

1. Any server who has worked at ABC Restaurant for more than five years is ------- to apply for the manager position.
   (A) eligible
   (B) possible
   (C) measured
   (D) controlled

2. From next month, the speed limit on all ------- streets in London will be changed to 60 kilometers per hour.
   (A) residential
   (B) reside
   (C) residences
   (D) residentially

3. When attaching a contract to an e-mail, keep these documents -------.
   (A) secure
   (B) security
   (C) securely
   (D) securing

4. While Ms. Ferdinand was organizing a team, Mr. Baldwin was ------- for contacting the clients.
   (A) responsible
   (B) powerful
   (C) productive
   (D) possible

5. It is essential that no one ------- into the building after hours without proper identification.
   (A) admits
   (B) admitted
   (C) is admitting
   (D) be admitted

6. A practicing physician is required to renew a medical license ------- two years.
   (A) whenever
   (B) every
   (C) less
   (D) even

7. Mr. Lee will lead a series of workshops for ------- new employees.
   (A) few
   (B) every
   (C) all
   (D) either

8. At the current speed of production, Prime Tech will manufacture ------- products to meet the demand by this summer.
   (A) full
   (B) quick
   (C) enough
   (D) quickly

9. The most ------- part of the festival was the jazz concert.
   (A) impression
   (B) impressive
   (C) impresses
   (D) impressed

10. Visitors to Cambridge Museum are requested to be ------- and refrain from taking photos during their tour.
    (A) considered
    (B) consider
    (C) considerable
    (D) considerate

Chapter 6 부사

부사, 포인트 감각 익히기

The manager ------- solved the personal conflict between the two employees.
(A) effectively   (B) effective
매니저는 두 직원 사이의 개인적 갈등을 효과적으로 해결했다.

부사 자리 문제
→ 빈칸은 주어와 동사 사이에서 동사 solved를 수식하는 부사 자리이므로 (A) effectively가 정답입니다.

개념 정리

❶ 부사의 역할과 형태

1) 부사는 동사, 형용사, 부사, 문장을 꾸며 주는 역할을 하며, 문장의 필수 요소가 아니므로 **부사가 없더라도 완전한 문장**이 됩니다.

It was (too) expensive. 그것은 (너무) 비쌌다.

2) 주로 **형용사 뒤에 -ly를 붙이면 부사**가 됩니다.

형용사 + -ly → 부사
quick 빠른 + ly → quickly 빠르게
proper 적절한 + ly → properly 적절하게
probable 있음직한 + ly → probably 아마도
full 가득한 + ly → fully 가득하게
large 큰 + ly → largely 대체로
easy 쉬운 + ly → easily 쉽게

❷ 부사의 종류

시험에서는 **부사가 어떤 단어와 함께 쓰이고 어느 위치에 들어가는지를 따져 답을 선택**합니다.

종류	빈출 부사
시간 부사	already 이미, 벌써 now 지금 soon 곧 still 아직, 여전히 yesterday 어제 once 한때 ago 전에
빈도 부사	always 항상 usually 보통, 대개 sometimes 때때로, 가끔 often 종종
강조 부사	merely 단지 only 단지 just 단지, 막 exactly 정확하게 even 심지어 as well 또한 also 또한, 역시
정도 부사	very 매우 much 매우, 훨씬 enough 충분히 too 매우 quite 상당히, 꽤 completely 완전히 significantly 상당히
상태/방법 부사	hard 몹시, 심하게 well 잘 skillfully 능숙하게 easily 쉽게 quickly 빠르게 slowly 느리게 safely 안전하게
부정 부사	not ~이 아니다 never 결코 ~이 아니다 hardly, scarcely, rarely, seldom 거의 ~않다

Check-up Test 700+를 위해 한 걸음 한 걸음

정답 및 해석 p.062

A. 다음 중 부사를 모두 찾으세요.

① consistently ② allowance ③ urgent ④ between ⑤ frequently
⑥ valid ⑦ cover ⑧ considerably ⑨ height ⑩ intently
⑪ decline ⑫ friendly ⑬ formally ⑭ features ⑮ annually

B. 다음 문장에서 부사를 찾으세요.

① We will promptly answer your questions. 우리는 당신의 질문에 즉각 답변할 것입니다.
② He studied hard to get a good score. 그는 좋은 점수를 받기 위해 열심히 공부했다.
③ We will succeed only when our clients are satisfied. 우리는 고객이 만족할 때만 성공할 것입니다.
④ Fortunately, I had a chance to visit New York. 다행히도 뉴욕을 방문할 기회가 있었다.
⑤ According to recent studies, approximately seventy percent of the Asian population eats rice on a daily basis. 최근 연구에 따르면, 아시아 인구의 약 70%가 매일 밥을 먹는다.

C. 다음 문장에서 부사를 찾고, 그 종류를 적으세요.

① Oil prices increased sharply. 유가가 급격히 올랐다.
② I usually go jogging in the morning. 나는 보통 아침에 조깅하러 간다.
③ Only the Human Resources Department can access that building. 인사부만이 그 건물에 접근할 수 있다.
④ All employees should follow the revised policies carefully.
전 직원들은 수정된 회사 정책을 신중히 따라야 한다.
⑤ They have been conducting some online research lately to solve the problems.
그들은 문제를 해결하기 위해 최근에 온라인 연구를 실시하고 있다.

Chapter 6. 부사

Point 01 부사 자리

출제 포인트 정리

❶ 부사는 다양한 자리에 올 수 있습니다.

부사는 명사를 제외한 '동사, 형용사, 다른 부사, 문장 전체' 등을 수식할 수 있어서 다양한 자리에 올 수 있습니다. 따라서 시험에서 부사의 위치를 묻는 문제가 가장 많이 출제됩니다.

1) 주어+**부사**+동사	I usually go shopping alone. 나는 보통 혼자 쇼핑하러 간다.
2) 주어+동사+목적어+**부사**	He got the job, finally. 그는 마침내 그 일자리를 얻었다.
3) 관사+**부사**+형용사+명사	the newly developed program 새로 개발된 프로그램
4) be+**부사**+형용사/부사	She is very lovely. 그녀는 매우 사랑스럽다.
5) **부사**, 완전한 문장	Apparently, he is a professor. 분명히 그는 교수님이다.
6) 완전한 문장+**부사**	He is a professor, apparently. 분명히 그는 교수님이다.
7) be+**부사**+과거 분사	The system was finally created. 시스템이 마침내 개발되었다.
8) be+**부사**+현재 분사	The expenses are rapidly increasing. 비용이 급격히 증가하고 있다.
9) have+**부사**+과거 분사	I've never been there. 나는 그곳에 가본 적이 없다.
10) 자동사+**부사**+전치사	I live alone in Korea. 나는 한국에서 혼자 산다.
11) 조동사+**부사**+본동사	They might strongly argue that ~ 그들은 ~을 강하게 주장할 수도 있다.
12) to+**부사**+동사 원형	to easily solve the problem 쉽게 문제를 해결하기 위해
13) 전치사+**부사**+동명사	before finally arriving in USA 마침내 미국에 도착하기 전에

Check-up Test 700+를 위해 한 걸음 한 걸음

정답 및 해설 p.062

STEP 1 다음 두 개의 보기 중 빈칸에 알맞은 것을 고르세요.

1. Thanks to the new sorting software, all online applications were processed -------.
   (A) easy   (B) easily

2. Education officials say that the TOEIC test will be ------- monitored to prevent cheating.
   (A) close   (B) closely

3. Herbal spices have ------- played an essential role in Indian cuisine.
   (A) historically   (B) historical

STEP 2 빈칸에 알맞은 것을 고르세요.

4. Many customers at K-Mart are willing to pay a premium for food that is produced -------.
   (A) locality   (B) locals   (C) local   (D) locally

5. Mr. Park began his career as a shopkeeper at ABC Mart, but he has since become a ------- renowned businessman.
   (A) nation   (B) nationally   (C) national   (D) nationalizing

Point 02 특정 시제와 어울리는 부사

출제 포인트 정리

❶ 현재 시제와 어울리는 부사

> hourly 시간마다   annually 해마다   regularly 정기적으로   always 항상   frequently/often 종종, 자주
> sometimes 때때로   usually 대개, 보통

I usually eat lunch around 1 P.M. 나는 보통 오후 1시쯤 점심을 먹는다.

❷ 과거 시제와 어울리는 부사

> ago 전에   yesterday 어제   once 한때   before 이전에   originally 원래, 처음에는
> initially 처음에, 시초에   formerly 이전에   previously 이전에   already 이미

I went jogging yesterday morning. 나는 어제 아침 조깅하러 갔다.

❸ 미래 시제와 어울리는 부사

> soon/shortly 곧   immediately 즉시   tomorrow 내일   probably 아마도   next year 내년

I will go jogging tomorrow morning. 나는 내일 아침 조깅하러 갈 것이다.

❹ 현재 완료 시제와 어울리는 부사

> already 이미   yet 아직   ever 한 번이라도   since ~ 이래로   lately/recently 최근에

Initial projections have already been exceeded. 초기 전망치는 이미 초과했다.

Check-up Test 700+를 위해 한 걸음 한 걸음

정답 및 해석 p.062

STEP 1 다음 두 개의 보기 중 빈칸에 알맞은 것을 고르세요.

1. We have ------- moved to another area so please contact us at the new mailing address above.
   (A) currently   (B) recently

2. The design team has ------- started drawing a rough sketch of the car.
   (A) already   (B) ago

3. We ------- produced the model.
   (A) once   (B) ever

STEP 2 빈칸에 알맞은 것을 고르세요.

4. Paper and cartridges are ------- stored in the first cabinet next to the corner.
   (A) usually   (B) relatively   (C) slightly   (D) vaguely

5. Wilton Manufacturer will ------- be opening a large facility in Seoul.
   (A) soon   (B) such   (C) ever   (D) like

Point 03 빈출 부사 (1)

출제 포인트 정리

❶ 동작의 변화(증가/감소)를 수식하는 부사

의미	증가/감소 동사 수식 부사	* 증가/감소 동사
상당히, 매우	considerably, substantially, significantly, greatly	increase/rise 증가하다
뜻밖에, 놀랍게	unexpectedly, surprisingly	enlarge 확대하다
급격하게	sharply, dramatically	advance 증진되다
두드러지게	remarkably, noticeably	surge 상승하다
빠르게	quickly, rapidly	decrease/decline/reduce 감소하다
느리게	slowly	fall 떨어지다
꾸준히, 점진적으로	steadily, gradually	shrink 줄어들다
약간	slightly	

The business profits have been increasing steadily since Ms. Jennifer was appointed to vice president.
제니퍼 씨는 부대표로 임명된 이후로, 영업 이익이 꾸준히 늘어나고 있다.

❷ 숫자(수량 형용사/서수)를 수식하는 부사

의미	숫자 수식 부사	의미	숫자 수식 부사
거의	almost, nearly, about	최대한	up to
대략	approximately, roughly	~만큼	as many as, as much as
겨우	only, just, merely	~ 이상	over, more than
최소한, 적어도	at least, not less than	~ 이하	under, less than

The National Museum attracted nearly 5 million visitors. 국립 박물관에는 거의 5백만 명의 방문객들이 끌어모았다.

Check-up Test 700+를 위해 한 걸음 한 걸음

정답 및 해석 p.063

STEP 1 다음 두 개의 보기 중 빈칸에 알맞은 것을 고르세요.

1. According to the recently released report, the value of the nation's currency fell ------- during the recession.
   (A) sharp (B) sharply

2. ------- 30 percent of college freshmen nationwide must enroll in at least one remedial course.
   (A) Nearly (B) Justly

3. The airport is ------- twenty kilometers away from the hotel.
   (A) approximately (B) steadily

STEP 2 빈칸에 알맞은 것을 고르세요.

4. After ------- six months of renovations, Fourteenth Street Train Station will resume operation on Thursday.
   (A) again (B) rarely (C) almost (D) seldom

5. The numbers of volunteers grew ------- after the news showed the damages from the earthquake in Iceland.
   (A) accidentally (B) expressively (C) dramatically (D) eagerly

Point 04 빈출 부사 (2)

출제 포인트 정리

❶ still 아직도, 여전히

be동사/조동사 뒤, 일반 동사 앞에 쓰이며, 부정문에서는 **부정어 앞**에 위치합니다.
The contract is still valid. 그 계약은 아직 유효하다.
The shipment has still not arrived. 그 선적물은 아직 도착하지 않았다.

❷ yet 아직

1) **have yet to 동사 원형** 아직 ~하지 못했다 (부정의 의미를 갖지만 부정어와 함께 쓰지 않습니다.)
   The problem has yet to be adequately addressed. 그 문제는 아직 적절히 다루어지지 못했다.

2) **have not yet p.p.** 아직 ~하지 않았다
   The salary level has not yet been determined. 급여 수준은 아직 정해지지 않았다.

3) **be yet to 동사 원형** 아직 ~하지 못하다 (부정의 의미를 갖지만 부정어와 함께 쓰지 않습니다.)

❸ very 매우

동사를 수식하지 않으며, **형용사 또는 부사를 수식**합니다. 최상급을 수식할 때는 the very로 씁니다.
All employees should be very attentive to the needs of our customers.
모든 직원들은 고객들의 요구에 매우 귀를 기울여야 한다.

❹ highly 매우

very와 같이 동사를 수식하지 않고 **형용사와 부사를 수식**합니다. 특히 과거 분사를 수식하는 부사로 주로 출제됩니다.

highly recommended 적극적으로 추천받은   highly regarded 높이 평가되는
highly skilled 매우 숙련된   highly qualified 충분히 자격이 되는

Check-up Test 700+를 위해 한 걸음 한 걸음

정답 및 해석 p.063

STEP 1 다음 두 개의 보기 중 빈칸에 알맞은 것을 고르세요.

1. Kim's design for the community center was ------- regarded by all members of our department.
   (A) high   (B) highly

2. Our company has ------- to realize the importance of providing a good working environment for its employees.
   (A) yet   (B) ever

3. They decided it was worth some extra money to purchase the ------- best insurance policy on the market so as to secure their new patents.
   (A) very   (B) a lot

STEP 2 빈칸에 알맞은 것을 고르세요.

4. The board of directors has ------- not released the newly developed product for the next season.
   (A) yet   (B) almost   (C) once   (D) still

5. The new financial incentive plan for sales managers will prove to be ------- lucrative for some employees.
   (A) enough   (B) too much   (C) very   (D) well

이것만 알면 700+

토익 최빈출 유형 정리! 부사편!

유형 1 also(또한) vs. too(또한, 너무) vs. as well(~도 역시)

❶ **also**: '또한'의 의미이며, 위치는 자유롭지만 부정문에는 쓰이지 않습니다.
 – 부정문에서는 숙어로만 쓰이며 not (only) ~ but (also)의 형태를 취합니다.
 – 문장을 추가할 때 쓰이며 앞 문장에 주로 and가 있습니다.
 – 유의어인 as well, too, besides, altogether 등은 문장 끝에 위치합니다.
 This product is not only cheap but also long-lasting. 이 제품은 저렴할 뿐만 아니라 오래간다.

❷ **too**: '또한'이나 '너무'의 의미로 쓰입니다.
 – '또한'의 의미일 때는 문장 끝에 쓰입니다.
 – '너무'의 의미일 때는 형용사나 부사를 수식하는 강조 부사로 쓰이며, 'much/far/too + 형용사/부사', 'too many/much + (명사)'의 형태로 자주 출제됩니다.
 too much noise 너무 시끄러운 소음

❸ **as well**: 주로 문장 끝에 쓰입니다.
 As the company grew, the market share increased as well. 회사가 성장하면서 시장 점유율도 역시 증가했다.

유형 2 -ly 형태의 형용사 <명사 + -ly = 형용사>

lovely 사랑스러운	friendly 친근한	costly 비싼	timely 시기적절한	weekly 매주의
monthly 매달의	yearly 해마다, 연간의			
cf. <형용사 + -ly = 형용사>				
likely ~할 것 같은	lively 생기가 넘치는, 활발한			

Please include your purchase number in order to receive the timely response.
적시에 응답을 받기 위해서는, 구매 번호를 입력하여 주십시오.

유형 3 어원이 같은 일반 부사 vs. -ly형 부사

late	a. 늦은 ad. 늦게	lately	ad. 최근	high	a. 높은 ad. 높게	highly	ad. 매우
right	a. 옳은, 올바른 ad. 바로	rightly	ad. 올바르게	hard	a. 열심인, 힘든 ad. 열심히	hardly	ad. 거의 ~아니다
pretty	a. 매력적인 ad. 꽤, 비교적	prettily	ad. 곱게	clear	a. 명백한 ad. 명료하게	clearly	ad. 분명히
close	a. 가까운 ad. 가까이	closely	ad. 면밀히	*closely examine 철저히 조사하다			

The bus came one hour (late, lately). 그 버스는 한 시간 늦게 왔다.

Chapter Test

1. After postponing his studies for more than ten years, Mr. Ito ------- earned a degree in business.
   (A) thoroughly
   (B) distinctly
   (C) eventually
   (D) already

2. Our debit card is accepted at ------- all of the city's hotels and restaurants.
   (A) beyond
   (B) appropriately
   (C) indoors
   (D) almost

3. To find out more about an item on our website, ------- click the "Check on it" button.
   (A) mostly
   (B) simply
   (C) enough
   (D) quite

4. The downtown merchants have agreed to stay open ------- during the month of December.
   (A) late
   (B) lately
   (C) latest
   (D) lateness

5. Although Mr. Anderson has already signed the employment contract, he ------- needs to talk about the benefit package.
   (A) besides
   (B) also
   (C) either
   (D) yet

6. After suffering from stomach trouble last year, Mr. Lopez visits his physician ------- to get general health check-ups.
   (A) frequency
   (B) frequent
   (C) frequently
   (D) frequented

7. A recent study found that the online reporting system ------- reduces office supply ordering errors.
   (A) strictly
   (B) formerly
   (C) drastically
   (D) intensely

8. The refund will ------- be deposited into your account within two business days.
   (A) automatic
   (B) automaticity
   (C) automated
   (D) automatically

9. Although he studied architecture, Mr. Greene ------- works in carpentry.
   (A) rather
   (B) now
   (C) very
   (D) therefore

10. After the installation of the internal communication system, employees will ------- be able to access the files in their computers during their business trips.
    (A) now
    (B) yet
    (C) ever
    (D) once

Chapter 7 분사

분사, 포인트 감각 익히기
Our company will have a luncheon ------- its loyal employees.
(A) has honored　　(B) honoring
우리 회사는 충실한 직원들에게 명예를 주는 연회를 열 것이다.

분사 자리 문제
→ will have가 본동사이며 접속사나 관계사가 없기 때문에 문장 안에 동사가 하나여야 합니다. 따라서 빈칸은 동사가 아닌 분사 자리이므로 현재 분사인 (B)가 정답입니다.

개념 정리

❶ 분사의 역할과 종류
1) 분사는 '동사+ing' 형태의 현재 분사와 '동사+ed' 형태의 과거 분사가 있고, **명사를 꾸며 주는 형용사 역할**을 합니다.

2) 현재 분사와 과거 분사는 **형태와 의미**가 다릅니다.

종류	현재 분사	과거 분사
예	a working machine 작동하는 기계	a fixed machine 수리된 기계
형태	V-ing	V-ed
	work+-ing = working	fix+-ed = fixed
의미	능동, 진행	수동, 완료
	기계가 작동한다 [능동, 진행]	기계가 수리되었다 [수동, 완료]
역할	형용사	형용사

❷ 분사 구문
1) 분사 구문은 '(접속사)+분사'의 형태로 '접속사+주어+동사'로 되어 있는 부사절을 분사 형태의 부사구로 축약하여 만든 것입니다.

2) 분사 구문 만들기 3단계

최초 문장	After he(= Mike) checked all the details, Mike approved the proposal. 마이크는 모든 세부 사항들을 확인한 후 그 제안을 승인했다.
1단계: 접속사 생략	~~After~~ he(= Mike) checked all the details, Mike approved the proposal.
2단계: 부사절의 주어 생략 (주절의 주어와 동일한 경우에만)	~~He(= Mike)~~ checked all the details, Mike approved the proposal.
3단계: 부사절 동사 → 분사	~~checked~~ → Checking all the details, Mike approved the proposal.

※ 분사 구문에서 현재 분사(능동) 뒤에는 목적어가 오고, 과거 분사(수동) 뒤에는 목적어가 올 수 없습니다.

(~~Checked~~, Checking) all the details, Mike approved the proposal.

Check-up Test 700+를 위해 한 걸음 한 걸음

정답 및 해석 p.063

A. 다음 중 분사를 모두 찾으세요.

① selected ② major ③ emerging ④ considerable ⑤ qualified
⑥ secure ⑦ lasting ⑧ pleased ⑨ free ⑩ satisfied
⑪ separate ⑫ competitive ⑬ proposed ⑭ enclosed ⑮ surrounding

B. 다음 중 밑줄 친 동사를 알맞은 분사 형태로 바꾸세요.

① the <u>revise</u> book 수정된 책
② the <u>break</u> window 깨진 창문
③ an <u>experience</u> employee 숙련된 직원
④ the <u>rise</u> sun 떠오르는 태양
⑤ an <u>interest</u> movie 흥미로운 영화

C. 다음 문장에서 올바르지 않은 부분을 찾아 고치세요.

① A survey conducting by a polling firm 여론조사 회사에 의해 실시된 설문조사
② I found him stood on the road. 나는 그가 길에 서 있는 것을 발견했다.
③ A newly launched program is not activate. 새롭게 출시된 프로그램이 활성화되지 않는다.
④ There are many employees made our new products. 우리 신제품을 만드는 직원들이 많이 있다.
⑤ The Southern Island Inn offers free parking to all guests stay longer than two days.
서던 아일랜드 호텔은 이틀 이상 숙박하는 모든 고객들에게 무료 주차를 제공한다.

Point 01 분사 자리

출제 포인트 정리

❶ 분사는 문장에서 형용사 역할을 하며, 명사를 수식하는 자리와 주격/목적격 보어 자리에 올 수 있습니다.

1) 명사 앞 **형용사** 자리   a broken window 깨진 창문
2) 2형식 동사 뒤의 **보어** 자리   The girl is delighted. 그 소녀는 기쁘다.
3) 5형식 동사 뒤의 **목적격 보어** 자리   We will keep you informed. 당신께 연락을 드리겠습니다.
4) 명사+(주격 관계 대명사+be동사)+ **분사**   The boy (who is) reading a book 책을 읽고 있는 소년

❷ 분사 문제는 항상 풀이 순서를 정해 놓고 일관성 있게 풀어야 합니다.

1) 전체 문장의 접속사와 관계사의 수 확인
2) 필요한 동사의 수 확인 <접속사, 관계사의 수+1=동사의 수>
3) 빈칸이 동사인지 준동사(분사, 동명사, to부정사)인지 결정

Check-up Test 700+를 위해 한 걸음 한 걸음

정답 및 해석 p.064

STEP 1   다음 두 개의 보기 중 빈칸에 알맞은 것을 고르세요.

1. Kensington Inc. hired a local property management company to search potential sites for the ------- distribution center.
   (A) propose   (B) proposed

2. Every June, the vineyards in San Francisco become too ------- with tourists and wine experts.
   (A) crowded   (B) crowd

3. The clients found the sales pitch and presentation very -------.
   (A) convincing   (B) convince

STEP 2   빈칸에 알맞은 것을 고르세요.

4. The intern will deliver the ------- product to the supervisor by Friday.
   (A) finished   (B) finishing   (C) finish   (D) finishes

5. Policy makers intend to implement a number of new school programs ------- on the physical sciences.
   (A) focus   (B) focusing   (C) will focus   (D) have focused

Point 02 감정 동사의 분사

출제 포인트 정리

❶ 감정 동사의 사람 수식 vs. 사물 수식

감정 동사의 분사가 사물을 수식할 때는 현재 분사(V-ing)로, 사람을 수식할 때는 과거 분사(p.p.)로 씁니다.

The movie satisfied many people. 그 영화가 많은 사람들을 만족시켰다. <감정 동사>
→ Many people were satisfied. 많은 사람들이 만족했다. <과거 분사>
→ The movie was very satisfying. 그 영화는 매우 만족스러웠다. <현재 분사>

빈출 감정 동사	
interest 흥미를 갖게 하다	delight/please 기쁘게 하다
satisfy 만족시키다	thrill 황홀하게 만들다
excite 흥분시키다	tire 피로하게 만들다
disappoint 실망시키다	overwhelm 압도하다
amaze 놀라게 하다	fascinate 매료시키다
exhaust 지치게 하다	worry 걱정하게 하다

❷ 5형식 동사+목적어+감정 동사의 분사

'5형식 동사+목적어+감정 동사의 분사' 구조일 때, 목적어가 사물 명사이면 감정 동사의 현재 분사(V-ing)가, 사람 명사이면 과거 분사(p.p.)가 옵니다.

The clown made the show amusing. 그 광대는 공연을 재미있게 만들었다.
The show made the audience amused. 그 공연은 청중들을 재미있게 만들었다.

Check-up Test 700+를 위해 한 걸음 한 걸음

정답 및 해석 p.064

STEP 1 다음 두 개의 보기 중 빈칸에 알맞은 것을 고르세요.

1. The marketing team made an ------- recovery.
   (A) amazing   (B) amazed

2. The decrease in tourism could have ------- consequences for the local economy.
   (A) worrying   (B) worried

3. Those employees ------- in this training program must register in advance.
   (A) interesting   (B) interested

STEP 2 빈칸에 알맞은 것을 고르세요.

4. The movie was very popular but most critics were not ------- by it.
   (A) impressing   (B) impresses   (C) impress   (D) impressed

5. The board of directors has decided to implement a new service to keep customers -------.
   (A) satisfaction   (B) satisfy   (C) satisfyingly   (D) satisfied

Point 03 현재 분사 vs. 과거 분사

출제 포인트 정리

❶ 자동사는 현재 분사 형태로만 명사 수식이 가능합니다.

명사를 수식하는 경우, 자동사는 현재 분사만 가능합니다.

Employees (~~remained~~, remaining) in the office after 5 P.M. are advised to inform their supervisor.
오후 5시 이후 사무실에 남아 있는 직원들은 그들의 감독관에게 알려야 한다.

❷ 타동사의 경우, 능동/진행의 의미일 때는 현재 분사, 수동/완료의 의미일 때는 과거 분사를 씁니다.

1) 명사+**현재 분사**+명사

   빈칸 앞뒤에 모두 명사가 있으면 보기에서 현재 분사를 고릅니다.

   These are the instructions for customers using our equipment.
   이것은 우리의 장비를 이용하는 고객들을 위한 설명서이다.

2) 명사+**과거 분사**+전치사

   현재 분사 뒤에는 목적어가 올 수 있지만, 과거 분사 뒤에는 목적어가 올 수 없습니다.

   I read the article featured in the magazine. 나는 잡지에 나온 기사를 읽었다.

3) 관사/소유격+**분사**+명사

the + -------- + 명사	관사와 명사 사이에 빈칸이 있으면 빈칸은 과거 분사
the + -------- + 사람 명사	감정 동사의 분사라면 사람을 수식할 때는 과거 분사
the + -------- + 사물 명사	감정 동사의 분사라면 사물을 수식할 때는 현재 분사

   We need the revised books. 우리는 수정된 책들이 필요하다.

Check-up Test 700+를 위해 한 걸음 한 걸음

정답 및 해석 p.064

STEP 1 다음 두 개의 보기 중 빈칸에 알맞은 것을 고르세요.

1. Please place your payment in the ------- pre-paid envelope and return it by September 20.
   (A) enclosing   (B) enclosed

2. The idea ------- by one of our representatives to reduce unnecessary fees at the station has been well received.
   (A) suggesting   (B) suggested

3. Within only three seconds, you make a ------- impression on the other person.
   (A) lasting   (B) lasted

STEP 2 빈칸에 알맞은 것을 고르세요.

4. Because of his experience ------- workers on assembly lines, Mr. Lopez has been appointed to oversee the operation.
   (A) supervisor   (B) supervising   (C) supervise   (D) supervised

5. Central Trains apologizes for any inconvenience ------- by the ongoing renovations to the station.
   (A) causing   (B) caused   (C) cause   (D) causes

Point 04 분사 구문

출제 포인트 정리

❶ 부사절 접속사가 이끄는 문장을 분사 구문으로 만들 수 있습니다.

이때 부사절 접속사는 생략이 가능하고, 부사절 접속사가 생략되면 문두에 분사가 남습니다.

Because she missed her flight, Samantha went to the service desk for help.
→ (Because) Missing her flight, Samantha went to the service desk for help.
비행기를 놓쳐서, 사만다는 도움을 받기 위해 안내 창구로 갔다.

❷ 분사 구문에서 현재 분사와 과거 분사 구분하기

1) 분사 구문의 **현재 분사 뒤에는 목적어(명사)가** 옵니다.

After he reviews the project, the manager will implement it.
→ (After) Reviewing the project, the manager will implement it.
프로젝트를 검토한 후에, 매니저가 프로젝트를 시행할 것이다.

2) 분사 구문의 **과거 분사 뒤에는 목적어(명사)가 올 수 없습니다.**

After it is reviewed by the manager, the project will be implemented.
→ (After being) Reviewed by the manager, the project will be implemented.
그 프로젝트는 매니저에 의해 검토된 후에 시행될 것이다.

Check-up Test 700+를 위해 한 걸음 한 걸음

정답 및 해석 p.064

STEP 1 다음 두 개의 보기 중 빈칸에 알맞은 것을 고르세요.

1. As ------- in the meeting this morning, they will arrive at your office at noon on Friday, June 29th.
   (A) discussing   (B) discussed

2. ------- on the street, she met a friend of hers.
   (A) Walking   (B) Walked

3. ------- in the city's center, the tourist center promotes the understanding and continuity of contemporary cultures.
   (A) Located   (B) Locating

STEP 2 빈칸에 알맞은 것을 고르세요.

4. ------- to last quarter's disappointing earnings, the figures for this month indicate an encouraging trend.
   (A) Compared   (B) Comparing   (C) Comparative   (D) Comparisons

5. After ------- the brochures for the new year, be sure to send them to all the local distributors.
   (A) designed   (B) designs   (C) designing   (D) to design

이것만 알면 700+
토익 최빈출 유형 정리! 분사편!

유형 1 현재 분사 vs. 동명사

종류	현재 분사	동명사
어순	소유격/관사 + **V-ing**(현재 분사) + 명사	**V-ing**(동명사) + 소유격/관사 + 명사
예	an interesting book 재미있는 책	reading a book 책을 읽는 것
의미	그 행위를 하고 있는 명사 명사를 수식하는 형용사	명사를 목적어로 취하거나 단독으로 명사처럼 쓰이는 것

the process of (established, establishing) a new set of guidelines
새로운 가이드라인을 만드는 절차(과정)
→ 빈칸이 전치사 of와 관사 a 사이에 있으므로 동명사인 establishing이 정답입니다.

Various services on the Internet can be helpful in (located, locating) books which are difficult to find.
인터넷상의 다양한 서비스들이 찾기 어려운 책들을 찾는 데 도움이 될 수 있다.
→ 책을 돕는 것이 아니라 책을 찾는 행위를 돕는 것이므로 동명사 locating이 정답입니다.

유형 2 빈출 분사 형용사

talented 재능이 있는   qualified 자격이 있는   dedicated 헌신하는   renowned 유명한   skilled 능숙한
experienced 경험이 있는, 능숙한   existing 기존의   appealing 매력적인   promising 유망한
opposing 적대적인   outstanding 미지급된   demanding 힘든   detailed 상세한   challenging 어려운
leading 가장 중요한   noted 유명한   distinguished 저명한   attached 첨부된   rewarding 보람 있는
convincing 설득력 있는   designated 지명된

We are looking for experienced instructors to teach presentation skills.
우리는 발표 기술을 가르칠 경력 있는 강사를 찾고 있다.

유형 3 빈출 분사형 전치사

regarding ~에 관해서   concerning ~에 대해서   following ~ 다음에, 이후   including ~을 포함해서
excluding ~을 제외하고   barring ~이 없다면   considering ~을 고려하면   given ~을 고려하여
notwithstanding ~에도 불구하고   pending ~이 발생할 때까지   starting/beginning ~부터

Many economists including Samuel Jackson have published articles in the *Weekly Business*.
새뮤얼 잭슨을 포함한 많은 경제학자들이 <주간 비즈니스>에 기사를 내고 있다.

Chapter Test

1. ASC Publishing's upcoming children's book is being ------- by Eileen Suen.
   (A) illustrating
   (B) illustrated
   (C) illustration
   (D) illustrates

2. We are pleased to offer you a promotion to Director of European Operations ------- in France.
   (A) was based
   (B) based
   (C) basing
   (D) bases

3. The human resources department is confident that Mr. James is the most ------- candidate for the job.
   (A) qualified
   (B) qualifier
   (C) qualify
   (D) qualification

4. We are ------- to announce that a new director has joined the team here at Karl Industry.
   (A) pleased
   (B) pleasing
   (C) pleaser
   (D) please

5. When ------- your payment, be sure to include the bottom portion of your invoice.
   (A) mail
   (B) mails
   (C) mailing
   (D) mailed

6. Glory Consulting Firm helps ------- retailers by offering competitive business strategies for them.
   (A) emerged
   (B) emerging
   (C) emerge
   (D) emerges

7. The special offer is not valid on items ------- previous to publication of this advertisement.
   (A) purchase
   (B) purchaser
   (C) purchased
   (D) purchasing

8. The management of Anderson Enterprises is in the process of ------- a new set of guidelines for its international service.
   (A) established
   (B) establishing
   (C) establish
   (D) to establish

9. Kellogg Business School will hold an orientation session on May 1 for anyone ------- in registering for the next semester.
   (A) interested
   (B) interest
   (C) interesting
   (D) to interest

10. Daniel Mulder has been voted the most ------- member of our new sales group this year.
    (A) promise
    (B) promised
    (C) promises
    (D) promising

Chapter 8 to부정사/동명사

to부정사, 포인트 감각 익히기
All staff are required ------- to the policies.
(A) to adhere   (B) adhere
모든 직원들은 그 방침을 고수하도록 요구받았다.

to부정사 자리 문제
→ 문장에 본동사 is required가 있으므로 동사 adhere는 올 수 없습니다. 위 문장은 'require A to부정사(A가 ~하도록 요청하다)'의 수동태로 봐야 하므로 to부정사인 (A) to adhere가 정답입니다.

개념 정리

❶ to부정사

1) **to부정사**는 'to + 동사 원형'의 형태로 문장에서 **명사, 형용사, 부사 역할**을 합니다.

to부정사의 역할		
명사 역할	주어	To make a reservation by phone is necessary, before you leave. 떠나기 전에 전화로 예약을 하는 것이 필수적이다.
	목적어	We want to make a reservation in advance. 우리는 미리 예약을 하길 원한다.
	보어	My duty is to make a hotel reservation for the conference. 내 임무는 콘퍼런스를 위해 호텔 예약을 하는 것이다.
형용사 역할	명사 수식	We made a decision to reduce operating costs. 우리는 운영 자금을 줄이기로 결정을 내렸다.
부사 역할	문장 수식	To make a hotel reservation, please complete the online reservation form. 호텔을 예약하기 위해, 온라인 예약 신청서를 작성하시오.

2) to부정사의 **의미상 주어**는 '**for + 명사**'로 나타냅니다.

It's not easy for us to master a foreign language. 우리가 외국어를 숙달하는 것은 쉽지 않다.

❷ 동명사

1) 동명사는 '동사 원형 + -ing'의 형태로 문장에서 **명사 역할**을 합니다.

동명사의 역할		
명사 역할	주어	Playing the game is exciting. 그 경기를 하는 것은 흥미진진하다.
	목적어	He enjoys joining the party. 그는 파티에 참여하는 것을 즐긴다.
	보어	Ms. Peggy's responsibility is managing the store. 페기 씨의 임무는 상점을 관리하는 것이다.

2) 동명사의 **의미상 주어**는 동명사 앞에 '**소유격 대명사(명사's)**'로 나타냅니다.

Your notifying us of errors helps us revise our manuscripts.
당신이 우리에게 오류를 알려 주는 것이 원고를 수정하는 데 도움이 된다.

Check-up Test 700+를 위해 한 걸음 한 걸음

정답 및 해석 p.065

A. 다음 중 to부정사와 동명사를 모두 찾으세요.

① to begin   ② in order to   ③ maintaining   ④ requires   ⑤ employees
⑥ finance   ⑦ earning   ⑧ coincide with   ⑨ complimentary   ⑩ qualifications
⑪ dependent   ⑫ appointed   ⑬ approval   ⑭ comparison   ⑮ to experience

B. 다음 밑줄 친 준동사가 문장 내에서 어떤 역할을 하는지 쓰세요.

① The goal of this course is to enhance communication skills.
이 과정의 목표는 의사소통 기술을 향상시키는 것이다.

② To get the new identification card, all staff should visit the security office.
새로운 신분증을 받기 위해서, 모든 직원들은 보안 사무실을 방문해야 한다.

③ She is interested in designing clothes. 그녀는 옷을 디자인하는 데에 관심이 있다.

④ Every citizen has a right to vote. 모든 시민들은 투표권을 갖고 있다.

⑤ In an effort to reduce expenses, Barson Cosmetics halved its advertising budget.
비용을 줄이기 위한 노력의 일환으로, 바슨 화장품은 광고 예산을 절반으로 줄였다.

C. 다음 문장에서 올바르지 않은 부분을 찾아 고치세요.

① He seems be a teacher. 그는 선생님인 것 같다.

② He hopes been a movie director. 그는 영화감독이 되길 희망한다.

③ In order sell new products, our manager is encouraged to display them near the counter.
신제품을 팔기 위해, 우리 매니저는 카운터 근처에 그것들을 진열할 것을 권유받았다.

④ Mr. Brown is ready leave for a business trip on Tuesday.
브라운 씨는 화요일에 출장을 갈 준비가 되어 있다.

⑤ We are having trouble in find appropriate materials for remodeling.
우리는 리모델링을 위한 적절한 자재를 찾는 데 어려움을 겪고 있다.

Point 01 · to부정사 vs. 동명사

출제 포인트 정리

❶ to부정사를 목적어로 가지는 동사

주로 '계획, 제안, 예상, 노력, 결정, 요청, 희망' 등 앞으로의 일(미래)을 의미하는 동사들입니다.

We are expecting to complete this report ahead of schedule.
우리는 이 보고서를 예정보다 일찍 끝낼 것으로 예상하고 있다.

빈출 to부정사를 목적어로 취하는 동사	
hope 바라다 fail 실패하다 decide 결정하다 afford 여력이 되다 promise 약속하다 expect 예상하다 ask 요청하다 plan 계획하다 refuse 거절하다 intend 의도하다	+ to부정사

❷ 동명사를 목적어로 가지는 동사

대부분 '제안, 권유, 중단, 지속, 완료' 등의 의미를 갖는 동사들입니다.

TM Motors Co. considers merging with EM Cars. TM 자동차 회사는 EM 자동차 회사와 합병하는 것을 고려하고 있다.

빈출 동명사를 목적어로 취하는 동사	
finish 끝내다 avoid 피하다 mind 꺼리다 consider 고려하다 postpone 연기하다 keep 계속 ~하다 give up 포기하다 suggest 제안하다	+ 동명사

Check-up Test 700+를 위해 한 걸음 한 걸음

정답 및 해석 p.065

STEP 1 다음 두 개의 보기 중 빈칸에 알맞은 것을 고르세요.

1. We ------- to find out a solution to the technical problems.
   (A) failed   (B) considered

2. Even though the meeting is on Wednesday afternoon, we have yet to finish ------- the data gathered by our researchers.
   (A) calculating   (B) to calculate

3. The purpose of the workshop is ------- employees with information about effective time management practices.
   (A) to provide   (B) provided

STEP 2 빈칸에 알맞은 것을 고르세요.

4. A night manager's duties include ------- every customer record with request notes.
   (A) confirmation   (B) confirms   (C) confirming   (D) confirmed

5. Jason Manufacturing strives ------- communication between departments to affect business operations.
   (A) to enhance   (B) enhances   (C) is enhancing (D) enhanced

Point 02 · to부정사 vs. 전치사 to

출제 포인트 정리

❶ to부정사의 to와 전치사 to를 구별해야 합니다.

to부정사 [to + 동사 원형]	In order to get reimbursed, you must attach the orginal receipt. 환급을 받기 위해, 원본 영수증을 첨부해야 합니다.
전치사 to [to + 명사/동명사]	In addition to offering special discounts, we also provide free delivery service in September. 9월에 특별 할인을 제공할 뿐 아니라, 우리는 무료 배송 서비스도 제공한다.

❷ 빈출 '동사 + 전치사 to + 동명사/명사' 표현

be dedicated to 동명사/명사 ~하는 데 몰두하다, 헌신하다	be subject to 동명사/명사 ~하기 쉽다
be used/accustomed to 동명사/명사 ~하는 데 익숙하다	be opposed to 동명사/명사 ~하는 것에 반대하다
look forward to 동명사/명사 ~하기를 고대하다	

The meeting schedule can be subject to change. 회의 일정은 변경될 수 있다.

❸ 빈출 to부정사 표현

allow/permit 목적어 to부정사 ~가 …하도록 허가하다	in an effort/attempt to부정사 ~하기 위한 노력으로/시도로
ask/require 목적어 to부정사 ~가 …하도록 요청하다	in order to부정사 / so as to부정사 ~하기 위해서
be expected to부정사 ~하리라 예상되다	be able to부정사 ~할 수 있다

In an effort to expand production, employees should analyze sales report first.
생산량 증가를 위해, 직원들은 우선적으로 매출 보고서를 분석해야 한다.

Check-up Test 700+를 위해 한 걸음 한 걸음

정답 및 해석 p.065

STEP 1 다음 두 개의 보기 중 빈칸에 알맞은 것을 고르세요.

1. Our marketing team is looking forward to ------- the new software.
   (A) launch   (B) launching

2. ------- maintain a clean office, Mr. Cena advised all employees not to bring foods that are easy to spill.
   (A) In order to   (B) In regard to

3. We are dedicated to ------- our customers' expectations by offering affordable prices.
   (A) exceed   (B) exceeding

STEP 2 빈칸에 알맞은 것을 고르세요.

4. To a lot of editors, e-mail means being able to work from home as opposed to ------- to an office.
   (A) go   (B) going   (C) goes   (D) be going

5. All visitors must wear protective gear prior to ------- into the factory.
   (A) proceed   (B) proceeds   (C) proceeded   (D) proceeding

이것만 알면 700+

토익 최빈출 유형 정리! to부정사/동명사편!

유형 1 빈출 **to부정사 동반 명사**

ability 능력	decision 결정	**effort** 노력	plan 계획	way 방법
intention 의도	**purpose** 목적	attempt 시도	**goal** 목표	mission 임무

유형 2 빈출 **전치사 to 관용 표현**

타동사 + 목적어 + to	자동사 + to	기타
affix A to B A를 B에 붙이다	lead to ~을 초래하다	according to ~에 따르면
attribute A to B A를 B의 탓으로 하다	refer to ~을 참조하다	in addition to ~에 덧붙여
contribute A to B A를 B에 기부하다	react to ~에 반응하다	in response to ~에 대한 응답으로
compare A to B A를 B에 비유하다	reply/response to ~에 대답하다	in regard to ~에 관련하여

유형 3 명사 자리 문제에서 동명사가 정답이 되는 경우

❶ 뒤에 목적어를 수반한 경우: 타동사의 동명사는 뒤에 목적어를 동반합니다.

❷ 명사와 동명사의 뜻이 다른 경우

명사	-ing형 명사	명사	-ing형 명사
account 계좌	accounting 회계	purchase 구매	purchasing 구매 행위
fund 자금, 기금	funding 자금 지원	staff 직원	staffing 직원 배치
house 집	housing 주거, 숙소	seat 좌석	seating 좌석(집합적)
market 시장	marketing 마케팅	ticket 티켓	ticketing 발권
plan 계획	planning 계획 세우기	urge 충동	urging 요청, 간청
process 과정	processing 처리		

※ 대부분 명사는 가산 명사이고, 동명사는 행위에 해당하므로 불가산 명사입니다.

❸ 기존의 명사가 없고 -ing 형태의 명사만 있는 경우

beginning 시작	building 건물	opening 빈자리, 공석
belongings 소유물	painting 그림	surroundings 주변, 환경

유형 4 빈출 **동명사 관용 표현**

be good at -ing ~을 잘하다	have difficulty/trouble (in) -ing ~하는 데 어려움을 겪다
cannot help -ing ~하지 않을 수 없다	go -ing ~하러 가다
be worth -ing ~할 가치가 있다	spend A in -ing/on + 명사 ~하는 데 A를 소비하다
make a point of -ing 반드시 ~하다	feel like -ing ~하고 싶다

Chapter Test

1. For more information about our warranties or ------- your new product, please contact customer service.
   (A) to register
   (B) registered
   (C) registers
   (D) registration

2. Glenwick Organic Farm and Delmar Grocery Chain have entered a strategic partnership to ------- their market share.
   (A) increased
   (B) increasing
   (C) increases
   (D) increase

3. Unocity Shipping, Inc. is able to ------- good deals with its local suppliers.
   (A) negotiating
   (B) negotiates
   (C) negotiated
   (D) negotiate

4. To ------- an advertisement in *Weekly Economic Magazine*, e-mail your application and details to ads@weeklyeconomic.com.
   (A) placed
   (B) placing
   (C) placement
   (D) place

5. ------- the effects of technological innovation is far from easy, as they are not clear.
   (A) Researchers
   (B) Research
   (C) Researching
   (D) Researched

6. ------- us of your schedule in advance helps us better prepare for your needs during your business trip.
   (A) You notified
   (B) You notify
   (C) Your notifying
   (D) You are notifying

7. Mallorca Marketing Ltd. will arrange all the promotional events for the ------- of the flagship store.
   (A) opening
   (B) openness
   (C) openly
   (D) opens

8. It is necessary to create a handbook to assist graduating students who have difficulty in ------- a career path.
   (A) choose
   (B) chooses
   (C) choosing
   (D) chosen

9. The purpose of ------- history is to comprehend patterns in society, the economy and the government.
   (A) studied
   (B) studying
   (C) study
   (D) to study

10. The Nacy Department Store will be closing tomorrow to ------- its staff to take a special day off.
    (A) allow
    (B) prohibit
    (C) make
    (D) let

Chapter 9 접속사

접속사, 포인트 감각 익히기

Tesco will not disclose a customer's information ------- official permission is given.
(A) without   (B) unless
테스코는 공식적인 허가 없이는 고객의 정보를 공개하지 않을 것이다.

접속사 자리 문제

→ 문장에 동사가 두 개(disclose, is given) 있으므로 접속사가 필요합니다. 따라서 정답은 (B)입니다. (A)는 전치사로 명사를 동반합니다.

개념 정리

❶ 접속사 = 연결어

1) 접속사는 문장과 문장을 연결해 주는 '연결어'입니다.

2) 접속사의 수 +1 = 동사의 수: 문장과 문장을 연결시켜 주는 접속사가 있으면 동사의 개수가 늘어납니다.

I <u>know</u> that he <u>is</u> honest. 나는 그가 정직하다는 것을 안다.

3) 문장에서 중심이 되는 절을 '주절'이라고 하고 **접속사를 포함한 절을 '종속절'**이라고 합니다.

(종속절) Since she retired, (주절) we have been busy training her replacement.
그녀가 은퇴한 이후로, 우리는 그녀의 후임자를 교육시키느라 분주했다.

❷ 접속사의 종류

1) 등위 접속사: 같은 성분의 단어와 단어, 구와 구, 절과 절을 대등하게 연결하는 접속사
(and, or, but, yet, so(예외적으로 절과 절만 연결) 등)

He bought <u>a table</u> and <u>a chair</u>. 그는 테이블과 의자를 샀다.

2) 상관 접속사: 두 단어 이상이 짝을 이루는 접속사(등위 접속사의 일종으로 같은 성분을 대등하게 연결)
(both A and B, either A or B, not A but B, not only A but also B 등)

He was <u>not</u> <u>aggressive</u> but <u>decisive</u>. 그는 공격적인 것이 아니라 단호했던 것이었다.

3) 관계 대명사: 바로 앞의 명사를 꾸며 주는 형용사절을 이끄는 접속사
(which, who, whom 등)

There is <u>a restaurant</u> which serves Asian food. 아시아 음식을 파는 레스토랑이 있다.

4) 명사절 접속사: 문장의 주어, 목적어, 보어 역할을 하는 명사절을 이끄는 접속사
(what, that, if, whether, 의문사 등)

<u>That</u> he knows her is obvious. 그가 그녀를 안다는 것은 명백해요.

5) 부사절 접속사: '장소, 원인, 이유, 양보, 시간' 등의 부가적인 정보를 주절에 추가해 주는 접속사
(although, until, since, because, as, when 등)

I have lived here <u>since</u> I was a child. 나는 어릴 때부터 쭉 이곳에 살았다.

Check-up Test 700+를 위해 한 걸음 한 걸음

정답 및 해석 p.066

A. 다음 중 접속사 혹은 관계사를 찾으세요.

① however   ② although   ③ once   ④ thought   ⑤ build
⑥ what   ⑦ prevent   ⑧ at   ⑨ represent   ⑩ which
⑪ during   ⑫ so that   ⑬ according to   ⑭ since   ⑮ if

B. 다음 문장에서 접속사를 찾으세요.

① I worked a late shift. 나는 야간 조로 근무했었다.

② He is either smart or stupid. 그는 똑똑하거나 멍청하다.

③ She likes the book which was written by him. 그녀는 그가 쓴 책을 좋아한다.

④ I don't have much time because I have to make a presentation in an hour.
저는 한 시간 후에 발표를 해야 하기 때문에 시간이 없어요.

⑤ The product survey questionnaire has not been revised since the last advertisement was printed.
마지막 광고가 인쇄되고 난 이후에 제품 설문 조사지는 수정되지 않았다.

C. 다음 문장에서 접속사를 찾고 접속사의 종류를 적으세요.

① That she is competent is unbelievable. 그녀가 유능하다는 것은 믿을 수 없다.

② I know a manager who is very ambitious. 나는 매우 야망이 있는 매니저를 안다.

③ All employees must focus on the current market trend as well as the business news.
모든 직원들은 경제 소식뿐 아니라 현재 시장 트렌드에도 집중해야 한다.

④ Both the customer relations and advertising departments will be included in the training.
고객 관리부서와 광고부서 모두 연수에 포함될 것이다.

⑤ Since Maria Salgado has now been fired, Scott Parker will take over as our sales representative.
마리아 살가도 씨가 현재 해고되었기 때문에, 스콧 파커 씨가 우리 회사의 영업 사원 자리를 맡을 것이다.

Point 01 접속사 vs. 전치사 vs. 부사

출제 포인트 정리

❶ 접속사와 전치사, 부사를 구별하는 문제가 출제됩니다.

보기에 전치사, 접속사, 부사 등이 섞여 나오면 문장에서 동사의 개수를 확인합니다. 한 문장에 동사가 두 개라면 접속사가 답입니다.

Our hotel has a maximum occupancy of 300 guests, ------- the local hotel can accommodate only 100 guests. 우리 호텔은 최대 300명을 수용하는 반면 그 현지 호텔은 오직 100명만 수용할 수 있다.

(A) then *부사*   (B) despite *전치사*   (C) just *부사*   (D) whereas *부사절 접속사*

→ 빈칸 앞뒤로 완전한 문장이 있으므로 문장을 연결하는 부사절 접속사 (D)가 정답입니다.

❷ 전치사는 문장에서 명사를 추가할 때 사용하며, 부사는 문장 구조에 영향을 주지 않습니다.

❸ 동일한 의미의 접속사와 전치사

의미	접속사	전치사
<양보> ~에도 불구하고, 비록 ~일지라도	although, (even) though, while	despite, in spite of
<이유, 원인> ~ 때문에	because, since, as	because of, due to, owing to
<예외> ~을 제외하고	except that	aside from, except (for)
<시간> ~ 동안에	while	for, during

Check-up Test 700+를 위해 한 걸음 한 걸음

정답 및 해석 p.066

STEP 1 다음 두 개의 보기 중 빈칸에 알맞은 것을 고르세요.

1. There is still a high demand for automobiles ------- the gas price has been increasing steadily.
   (A) in spite of   (B) though

2. ------- the new movie directed by Gillian Moore was expected to be a hit at the box office, most critics gave it bad reviews.
   (A) Although   (B) Despite

3. According to the new regulations, all employees must wear their safety goggles and gloves ------- the press is in motion.
   (A) during   (B) while

STEP 2 빈칸에 알맞은 것을 고르세요.

4. Staff members must not leave the building ------- all the computers have been turned off.
   (A) prior   (B) with   (C) until   (D) even

5. Angela Andrews was hired as a new editor ------- she was the most qualified applicant.
   (A) for   (B) because   (C) just   (D) following

Point 02 부사절 접속사

출제 포인트 정리

❶ 부사절 접속사
2개의 완전한 문장을 연결합니다. (완전한 문장 + 접속사 + 완전한 문장)
Everyone likes her because she is kind. 그녀는 친절해서 모두가 그녀를 좋아한다.

❷ 양보 부사절 접속사
예상치 못한 결과나 기대와 반대되는 내용을 연결합니다.

양보	although, though, even though/if 비록 ~일지라도 whereas, while ~한 반면에

While I like the design, he likes the color of the product. 나는 그 디자인을 좋아하는 반면, 그는 그 제품의 색을 좋아한다.

❸ 시간/조건 부사절 접속사

시간	when ~할 때 before ~하기 전에 after ~한 후에 while ~ 동안에 once 일단 ~하면 as ~할 때 since ~ 이래로 as soon as ~하자마자 until/till ~할 때까지
조건	if(= provided/providing/supposing/given/assuming+(that)) 만약 ~라면 unless(= if ~ not) 만약 ~이 아니라면 only if ~해야만 (when) in case (that) ~한 경우에 as/so long as ~하는 한, ~의 조건으로

We will let you know before we (will leave, leave). 우리가 떠나기 전에 알려 드리겠습니다.
→ 시간/조건 부사절에서는 현재 시제가 미래의 의미를 대신합니다.

❹ 원인/목적의 부사절 접속사

이유/원인	because, since, as, now that ~이기 때문에
목적	so that, in order that ~하기 위해서, ~하도록

She works hard in order that she can get a promotion. 그녀는 승진하기 위해 열심히 일한다.

Check-up Test 700+를 위해 한 걸음 한 걸음

정답 및 해석 p.066

STEP 1 다음 두 개의 보기 중 빈칸에 알맞은 것을 고르세요.

1. ------- the conference is over, staff from the accounting department will submit their reports.
   (A) Who   (B) When

2. ------- the economy is recently showing an upward trend, experts expect that it will recover by the end of this year.
   (A) Because   (B) What

3. -------- the company grew, its market share increased as well.
   (A) As   (B) Which

STEP 2 빈칸에 알맞은 것을 고르세요.

4. ------- Mr. Hillman is not returning this week, he will send us an e-mail regarding the deal.
   (A) Although   (B) Therefore   (C) Whether   (D) Moreover

5. As long as Mr. Graham ------- our requests, we will be able to work less hours on Fridays and Saturdays.
   (A) approves   (B) will approve   (C) approve   (D) to approve

Point 03 명사절 접속사

출제 포인트 정리

❶ 명사절 접속사

명사절을 이끄는 접속사는 '명사절 접속사+문장'의 형태로 주어, 목적어, 보어 자리에 옵니다.

명사절 접속사	뒤따라오는 구조
that, if, whether, when, where, how, why, whose	+ 완전한 문장
what, who, whom	+ 불완전한 문장(주어 혹은 목적어가 없는 문장)
which, what	+ 선택 구문

Who did it is the question. 그것을 누가 했는지가 의문이다.
→ 접속사 Who 뒤에 주어가 없는 불완전한 문장이 왔습니다.

I don't know if she has that book. 그녀가 그 책을 가지고 있는지 모르겠다.
→ 접속사 if 뒤에 완전한 문장이 왔습니다.

❷ 명사절 접속사 how

1) how 뒤에 '방법(어떻게)'이 오면 'how+주어+동사+목적어(완전한 문장)'

These are the instructions about how we can use the merchandise.
이것은 우리가 이 제품을 어떻게 이용할 수 있는지에 대한 안내서이다.

2) how 뒤에 '상태(얼마나)'를 나타내는 **형용사/부사**가 오면 'how+형용사/부사+주어+동사'

I don't know how much it is. 나는 이게 얼마인지 모른다.

Check-up Test 700+를 위해 한 걸음 한 걸음

STEP 1 다음 두 개의 보기 중 빈칸에 알맞은 것을 고르세요.

1. The survey indicates ------- the public's demand has been rising over the past couple of months.
(A) what   (B) that

2. ------- Mr. Kim has worked here for almost ten years shows his dedication.
(A) When   (B) That

3. The employees at SSN are not sure ------- will be chosen as their new CEO.
(A) who   (B) whether

STEP 2 빈칸에 알맞은 것을 고르세요.

4. This lesson plan shows ------- you will be learning in Mass Media & Government 415.
(A) which   (B) where   (C) how   (D) what

5. We have not determined ------- the anniversary party will be held at the Milton Hotel or in Herry Park.
(A) regarding   (B) either   (C) nearby   (D) whether

Point 04 접속사 뒤 주어가 없다면?

출제 포인트 정리

❶ 접속사 뒤에 주어가 없을 경우

접속사 뒤에 주어가 없으면 빈칸 이하가 문장 내에서 하는 역할과 빈칸 뒤에 to부정사, 분사, 동사 중 어느 형태가 오는지 확인하세요.

등위 접속사 상관 접속사	중복되는 내용을 생략할 수 있기 때문에 뒤에 주어가 생략되어도 동사가 그대로 존재합니다. I will go there, and I will see you. → I will go there and see you. 내가 거기 가서 널 만날 것이다.
관계 대명사	관계 대명사 뒤에 동사 대신 분사를 씁니다. There is a boy who is reading a book. → There is a boy reading a book. 책을 읽고 있는 한 소년이 있다.
명사절 접속사	'의문사+to부정사' 형태가 됩니다. (if와 that은 제외) I don't know what I have to do. → I don't know what to do. 나는 뭘 해야 할지 모른다. ※ what to do: 목적어가 없는 불완전한 명사구 　how to fix it: 목적어가 있는 완전한 명사구
부사절 접속사	부사절 접속사 뒤의 주어가 생략되면 동사는 분사 형태가 됩니다. I was reading a book while I waited for a train. → I was reading a book while waiting for a train. 나는 열차를 기다리면서 책을 읽고 있었다.

Check-up Test 700+를 위해 한 걸음 한 걸음

정답 및 해석 p.067

STEP 1 다음 두 개의 보기 중 빈칸에 알맞은 것을 고르세요.

1. Please read the instructions carefully ------- consulting our support representative.
    (A) whether   (B) before

2. The contract will not be legitimate ------- signed by both the seller and the buyer.
    (A) without   (B) until

3. Kelly Furniture offers their customers a full refund ------- replaces it with another item, whichever is preferred.
    (A) neither   (B) or

STEP 2 빈칸에 알맞은 것을 고르세요.

4. The board of directors will decide today ------- to sign the contract.
    (A) whether   (B) after   (C) that   (D) about

5. ------- preparing to make a speech to the public, check to see if the audio system is working properly.
    (A) How   (B) When   (C) During   (D) Since

이것만 알면 700+
토익 최빈출 유형 정리! 접속사편!

유형1 빈출 상관 접속사

both A and B A, B 둘 다
either A or B A, B 둘 중 하나
not only A but (also) B = B as well as A A뿐만 아니라 B 역시
neither A nor B A, B 둘 다 아닌
not A but B = only B, not A A가 아닌 B

유형2 명사절 접속사 완벽 분석

명사절 접속사	의문사			뒤따라오는 구조		
	의문 대명사	의문 형용사	의문 부사	to부정사	불완전한 문장	완전한 문장
who	O	X	X	O	O	X
what	O	O	X	O	O	O (의문 형용사 포함)
which	O	O	X	O	O	O (의문 형용사 포함)
when	X	X	O	O	X	O
where	X	X	O	O	X	O
how	X	X	O	O	X	O
why	X	X	O	X	X	O
whether	–	–	–	O	X	O
that	–	–	–	X	X	O
if	–	–	–	X	X	O (문두 X)

의문 대명사: 의문사 역할 + 명사 역할
의문 형용사: 의문사 역할 + 형용사 역할

유형3 since의 품사별 뜻

since는 접속사, 전치사, 부사로 쓰이지만 접속사로 쓰일 때만 '~ 때문에'라는 의미를 가질 수 있습니다.

	접속사 since	전치사/부사 since
~ 이래로	O	O
~ 때문에	O	X

Chapter Test

정답 및 해석 p.067

1. ------- he is now retired, Mr. Khana is able to focus on his hobbies.
   (A) During
   (B) Therefore
   (C) When
   (D) Because

2. A company like Lular Manufacturing must know ------- products its competitors are trying to develop.
   (A) what
   (B) that
   (C) who
   (D) whose

3. Ms. Navarro will be out on Friday, ------- his assistant will attend a meeting on Friday instead.
   (A) like
   (B) until
   (C) that
   (D) so

4. ------- is convenient about the library is its automated check-out system.
   (A) Which
   (B) That
   (C) Why
   (D) What

5. Applying for membership can be done either by phone ------- on the Internet.
   (A) and
   (B) both
   (C) nor
   (D) or

6. Employees in the game developing industry often talk about ------- well it suits those who enjoy playing new games.
   (A) only
   (B) there
   (C) most
   (D) how

7. ------- Mr. Lopez is able to adjust his presentation, the departure date will be rescheduled for May 10.
   (A) Assuming
   (B) Excluding
   (C) Otherwise
   (D) Furthermore

8. The professor is considering changing his curriculum ------- students can write only one essay instead of two.
   (A) unless
   (B) so that
   (C) as though
   (D) either

9. ------- Elizabeth has been writing articles for five years, she has only been working as a journalist for a short time.
   (A) Although
   (B) Despite
   (C) However
   (D) But

10. ------- the souvenir shop is located next to the museum, it attracts many tourists.
    (A) Since
    (B) Due to
    (C) What
    (D) Besides

Chapter 10 관계사

관계사, 포인트 감각 익히기

We are looking for sales representatives ------- can handle complaints from customers.
(A) which   (B) who

우리는 고객들의 불만을 처리할 수 있는 판매 담당자를 찾고 있습니다.

관계사 격과 선행사 문제

→ 빈칸 앞에 명사가 있고 그 다음에 주어 혹은 목적어가 빠진 불완전한 문장이 등장하면 빈칸은 관계사 자리입니다. 선행사(sales representatives)가 사람 명사이므로 (B) who가 정답입니다.

개념 정리

❶ 관계 대명사의 역할과 형태

관계 대명사는 앞의 명사를 대신(대명사)하면서 동시에 뒤의 절을 연결(접속사)해 주는 대명사로 '**접속사＋대명사**'의 역할을 합니다. **접속사**의 역할을 하기 때문에 관계 대명사 뒤에 **동사가 추가**되고, **대명사**의 역할을 하기 때문에 **중복되는 명사 대신 관계 대명사를 사용**합니다.

The man who is cleaning the garden is my father.
정원을 청소하고 있는 사람은 나의 아버지이다.

The seminar that[which] I attended last Wednesday was very informative.
내가 지난 수요일에 참석했던 세미나는 매우 유익했다.

❷ 관계 대명사절 만드는 방법

1	I met the manager. The manager is in charge of room service. 나는 매니저를 만났다. 그 매니저는 룸서비스 담당이다. → 두 개의 문장이 있습니다.
2	I met the manager and the manager is in charge of room service. 나는 매니저를 만났고 그 매니저는 룸서비스 담당이다. → 두 문장을 접속사 and로 연결합니다.
3	I met the manager and he is in charge of room service. 나는 매니저를 만났고 그는 룸서비스 담당이다. → 반복되는 the manager 중 뒤의 것을 대명사 he로 바꿉니다.
4	I met the manager who is in charge of room service. 나는 룸서비스 담당인 매니저를 만났다. → 접속사 and와 중복된 대상을 받는 대명사 he를 관계 대명사 who로 바꿉니다.

※ 관계사는 접속사와 앞에서 이미 언급된 명사를 하나로 합친 것입니다. (and he = who) 따라서 관계사가 하나 있을 때마다 동사의 개수가 늘어납니다.

I met the manager who is in charge of room service.
　동사1　　　　　　　동사2

Check-up Test 700+를 위해 한 걸음 한 걸음

정답 및 해석 p.067

A. 다음 문장 중 관계 대명사를 모두 찾으세요.

① even if	② which	③ who	④ finalized	⑤ when
⑥ since	⑦ now that	⑧ undergo	⑨ so that	⑩ whom
⑪ elaborate	⑫ whose	⑬ regulation	⑭ that	⑮ on

B. 다음 문장에서 관계 대명사를 찾아 해당하는 격을 적으세요.

① I saw the boy who played basketball. 나는 농구를 하는 소년을 보았다.

② I gave the shirt which I bought yesterday to my friend. 나는 내가 어제 산 셔츠를 내 친구에게 주었다.

③ The new design that aimed at the Asian market was popular.
아시아 시장을 목표로 한 새로운 디자인이 인기가 있었다.

④ Mr. Simons joined the company whose brand value is worth $6.8 billion.
시몬스 씨는 브랜드 가치가 68억 달러인 회사에 입사했다.

⑤ The speaker whom we invited is giving a speech at the conference.
우리가 초대한 연사가 학회에서 연설을 하고 있다.

C. 다음 2개의 문장을 관계 대명사를 사용해 1개의 문장으로 만드세요.

① I know the man. The man is standing in the lobby.
나는 그 남자를 안다. 그 남자는 로비에 서 있다.

② This is a book for students. The students' first language is not Korean.
이것은 학생들을 위한 도서이다. 학생들의 모국어는 한국어가 아니다.

③ Edinburgh University Library has rare book collections. The rare book collections are internationally important.
에든버러 대학교 도서관은 희귀 도서를 소장하고 있다. 그 희귀 도서 소장본은 국제적으로 중요하다.

Point 01 관계사의 선택

출제 포인트 정리

❶ 관계 대명사를 선택할 때는 선행사와 격을 확인합니다.

1) **선행사**: 선행사가 사람인지 사물인지에 따라 관계사를 선택합니다.

   I will give you a book (which, ~~who~~) is written in easy English.
   제가 당신에게 쉬운 영어로 쓰인 책을 드리겠습니다.

2) **격**: 관계사 뒤의 문장 구조를 보고 주격, 목적격, 소유격 관계 대명사를 선택할 수 있습니다.

   선행사+**주격 관계 대명사**+~~주어~~+동사
   선행사+**목적격 관계 대명사**+주어+동사+목적어
   선행사+**소유격 관계 대명사**+완전한 문장

❷ 관계 대명사는 선행사와 격에 따라 형태가 달라져요.

선행사	주격	목적격	소유격
사람	who	who(m)	whose
사물	which	which	whose / of which
사람, 사물	that	that	X

He wants to marry a woman (who, ~~whom~~) truly loves him.
그는 그를 진정으로 사랑하는 여자와 결혼하고 싶어 한다.

Check-up Test 700+를 위해 한 걸음 한 걸음

정답 및 해석 p.067

STEP 1 다음 두 개의 보기 중 빈칸에 알맞은 것을 고르세요.

1. Sports drinks, ------- are often used to replenish energy levels, are a great help to athletes.
   (A) who   (B) which

2. Ms. Dockers is one of the three applicants ------- work experience includes more than ten years in the insurance field.
   (A) whose   (B) who

3. We will send an e-mail to remind them when the library books ------- they have borrowed should be returned.
   (A) that   (B) because

STEP 2 빈칸에 알맞은 것을 고르세요.

4. It is essential for people ------- work in customer service to have a basic understanding of operations management.
   (A) someone   (B) whose   (C) they   (D) who

5. A free concert ticket is available to anyone who ------- insurance online before July 1.
   (A) purchase   (B) to purchase (C) purchases   (D) purchasing

Point 02 목적격 관계 대명사

출제 포인트 정리

❶ 목적격 관계 대명사
관계사 절에 목적어가 없고, **관계 대명사가 목적어 역할**을 합니다.
I know the man that you met. 나는 네가 만났던 그 남자를 안다.

❷ 목적격 관계 대명사 생략
목적격 관계 대명사는 **생략이 가능**합니다.
The client (whom) we invited is in the meeting room.
우리가 초대한 고객이 회의실에 있다.

❸ 부정 대명사+of+목적격 관계 대명사
1) 사람 선행사+부분 대명사(one/all/some/both/most)+of+**whom**
   She has two daughters, all of whom became professors.
   그녀는 두 딸이 있는데, 두 딸 모두 교수가 되었다.

2) 사물 선행사+부분 대명사(one/all/some/both/most)+of+**which**
   Prinstar sells over $30 million worth of printer parts a year, half of which are sold in China.
   프린스타는 매년 프린터 부품을 3천만 달러 이상 판매하는데, 이것의 반은 중국에서 팔린다.

Check-up Test 700+를 위해 한 걸음 한 걸음   정답 및 해석 p.068

STEP 1 다음 두 개의 보기 중 빈칸에 알맞은 것을 고르세요.

1. The company has decided to recruit seven new employees next year, all of ------- are expected to be female.
   (A) them   (B) whom

2. Managers often have to decide between several courses of action, none of ------- are completely right or wrong.
   (A) whom   (B) which

3. I like the book ------- recently wrote.
   (A) he   (B) which

STEP 2 빈칸에 알맞은 것을 고르세요.

4. The school tries to hire employees from diverse backgrounds, but they now have only 10 teachers, most of ------- are men.
   (A) what   (B) which   (C) them   (D) whom

5. The Pest County Animal Health and Food Control Station has banned the marketing of a list of past-date-of-sale items, ------- of which had their original expiration dates removed.
   (A) many   (B) few   (C) little   (D) none

Point 03 관계 부사

출제 포인트 정리

❶ 선행사+관계 대명사+완전한 문장+전치사
  = 선행사+전치사+관계 대명사+완전한 문장
  = 선행사+관계 부사+완전한 문장

1	It is **the city**. + He lives in **the city**. 그곳은 도시이다. 그는 그 도시에서 산다.	두 개의 완전한 문장
2	It is the city which he lives in. 그곳은 그가 사는 도시이다.	관계 대명사+불완전한 문장(전치사의 목적어 X)
3	It is the city in which he lives. 그곳은 그가 사는 도시이다.	전치사+관계 대명사+완전한 문장
4	It is the city where he lives. 그곳은 그가 사는 도시이다.	관계 부사+완전한 문장

❷ 전치사+관계 대명사 = 관계 부사

'전치사+관계 대명사'는 관계 부사로 바꿀 수 있습니다.

선행사	전치사+관계 대명사	관계 부사
시간(time, day 등)	at/on/in+which	when
장소(place 등)	at/on/in+which	where
이유(the reason)	for+which	why
방법(they way)	in/by+which	how

※ 관계 부사 how는 선행사 the way와 함께 사용하지 못합니다.

Check-up Test 700+를 위해 한 걸음 한 걸음

정답 및 해석 p.068

STEP 1 다음 두 개의 보기 중 빈칸에 알맞은 것을 고르세요.

1. The handbook ------- I am referring now is about the policies of this company.
   (A) to which   (B) for which

2. The Motor Show, ------- annually demonstrates the newest concept cars, draws over ten thousand attendees.
   (A) where   (B) which

3. You'll be transported to our bungee platform on the historic Wakitaka Suspension Bridge, ------- you can take an exciting plunge 50 meters straight down toward the water below.
   (A) when   (B) where

STEP 2 빈칸에 알맞은 것을 고르세요.

4. The land ------- which our company wanted to construct a distribution center has been sold.
   (A) on   (B) from   (C) for   (D) to

5. The convention hall ------- the reception is being held is located near the airport.
   (A) upon   (B) where   (C) in that   (D) in it

Point 04 복합 관계사

출제 포인트 정리

❶ 복합 관계사 = 관계 대명사/관계 부사 + ever

복합 관계사	관계사 + ever	명사절	부사절	뒤에 오는 문장	복합 관계 형용사
복합 관계 대명사	whatever	~하는 것은 무엇이든	무엇을 ~한다 할지라도	불완전	어떤 ~라도 (뒤에 완전한 문장)
	whichever	~하는 것은 어느 것이든	어느 것을 ~한다 할지라도	불완전	어떤 ~라도 (뒤에 완전한 문장)
	whoever	~하는 사람 누구든	누가 ~할지라도	불완전	X
	whomever	~하는 사람은 누구에게나	누구를 ~한다 할지라도	불완전	X
복합 관계 부사	whenever	X	~때는 언제든지 언제 ~을 할지라도	완전	X
	wherever	X	~하는 어디든지 어디서 ~할지라도	완전	X
	however	X	아무리 ~할지라도	완전	X

You can buy whatever you want. <명사절> 네가 원하는 건 뭐든지 살 수 있다.
Whatever you want, you can take it. <부사절> 네가 원하는 게 무엇이든 넌 그걸 가질 수 있다.
Whatever method he takes, he can solve the problem easily. <복합 관계 형용사>
어떤 방법을 취할지라도, 그는 쉽게 문제를 풀 수 있을 것이다.

Check-up Test 700+를 위해 한 걸음 한 걸음

정답 및 해석 p.068

STEP 1 다음 두 개의 보기 중 빈칸에 알맞은 것을 고르세요.

1. ------- you go after work, you will see any of your colleagues downtown.
   (A) Whenever   (B) Wherever

2. Volunteers are allowed to take ------- promotional items remaining after the event.
   (A) whichever   (B) wherever

3. New employees ------- have worked at another company for more than 6 months may apply to have the probation period shortened or waived.
   (A) who   (B) whoever

STEP 2 빈칸에 알맞은 것을 고르세요.

4. For detailed information, applicants may inquire by either telephone or e-mail, ------- they prefer.
   (A) what   (B) which   (C) whoever   (D) whichever

5. Realty Online updates its website ------- new apartments are available for rental.
   (A) whenever   (B) therefore   (C) however   (D) furthermore

이것만 알면 700+

토익 최빈출 유형 정리! 관계사편!

유형 1 주격 관계 대명사 + be동사 생략

'주격 관계 대명사 + be동사'가 생략되면 명사와 분사(현재/과거)만 남게 됩니다.

선행사 + (주격 관계 대명사 + be동사) + **V-ing/p.p.**
        └→ 생략

Anyone (who is) interested in software security is welcome to attend the conference.
= Anyone interested in software security is welcome to attend the conference.
소프트웨어 보안에 관심이 있는 누구나 콘퍼런스에 참석하는 것을 환영한다.

유형 2 that의 6가지 역할

❶ 지시 형용사
지시 형용사 + 단수 명사
I need that report. 나는 저 보고서가 필요하다.

❷ 지시 대명사
지시 대명사 that은 단수 취급
That is not mine. 저것은 내 것이 아니다.

❸ 비교 구문에서 사용되는 that of
앞에 나온 명사 대체
Mr. John's work is much better than that of his friends. 존 씨가 한 일이 그의 친구들이 한 일보다 훨씬 낫다.

❹ 명사절 접속사
전체 문장의 주어 혹은 타동사의 목적어 자리에 위치 / that 뒤에 완전한 문장
I did not know that they attended the meeting. 나는 그들이 그 회의에 참석한 줄 몰랐다.

❺ 관계 대명사
절을 이끌어 앞의 명사 수식 / that 뒤에는 불완전한 문장
The new product that aimed at the Europe market was popular.
유럽 시장을 목표로 한 신제품이 인기가 있었다.

❻ 동격절
news, fact, agreement 등의 명사 다음의 동격절 that은 뒤에 완전한 절이 온다.
The company announced the plan that they will take over one of their competitors.
그 회사는 경쟁사들 중 한 곳을 인수할 것이라는 계획을 발표했다.

Chapter Test

1. All the supervisors are responsible for training new employees who should be familiar to each job well, ------- it is.
   (A) whenever
   (B) anyone
   (C) everything
   (D) whatever

2. Our financial expert identified some problems in the plan ------- should be addressed this week.
   (A) whichever
   (B) whose
   (C) that
   (D) who

3. We have received ten cartons, two of ------- were unexpectedly damaged in transit.
   (A) them
   (B) what
   (C) those
   (D) which

4. Drew Industry will be building one more factory in Detroit, ------- will enable the company to expedite the process of manufacturing.
   (A) there
   (B) which
   (C) what
   (D) then

5. The City Center Gallery is sponsoring local artists, ------- paintings will be on display from this summer.
   (A) which
   (B) their
   (C) whose
   (D) that

6. We will have to travel to the health center ------- the natives are being treated.
   (A) on
   (B) where
   (C) which
   (D) that

7. Please come to the post office by 3 P.M. and pick up the special delivery ------- you ordered.
   (A) then
   (B) what
   (C) when
   (D) that

8. In some industries, the employment base has relied on local schools, ------- host job fairs regularly.
   (A) where
   (B) and
   (C) but
   (D) which

9. The scientist ------- invented this year's most notable discovery was awarded the Nobel Prize.
   (A) who
   (B) some
   (C) he
   (D) also

10. The amount you ------- depends on which plan you choose.
    (A) save
    (B) saved
    (C) saving
    (D) to save

Chapter 10. 관계사

Chapter 11 비교/가정법/도치

비교, 포인트 감각 익히기

Buying new computers would be ------- than repairing them.
(A) cheaper   (B) cheapest
새 컴퓨터를 사는 것이 수리하는 것보다 쌀 것이다.

비교급 문제
→ 빈칸은 be동사의 보어 자리이므로 형용사가 올 자리이며, 빈칸 뒤의 비교급과 함께 쓰이는 than이 있으므로 (A) cheaper가 정답입니다.

개념 정리

❶ 원급 비교(as ~ as) / 비교급(more ~) / 최상급(the most ~)

1) 원급 비교, 비교급과 최상급으로 표현할 수 있는 품사는 **형용사**와 **부사**입니다.
2) 보통 둘 사이에서 '~보다 더 …한'이라는 의미를 나타낼 때 비교급을 씁니다.
3) 여러 대상 중에서 '**가장 ~한**'이라는 의미를 나타낼 때 최상급을 씁니다.

	원급	비교급(-er / more -)	최상급(-est / most -)
형용사	great 큰	greater 더 큰	the greatest 가장 큰
	easy 쉬운	easier 더 쉬운	the easiest 가장 쉬운
	precise 정확한	more precise 더 정확한	the most precise 가장 정확한
부사	widely 널리	more widely 더 널리	most widely 가장 널리
	densely 빽빽이	more densely 더 빽빽이	most densely 가장 빽빽이

❷ 가정법

가정이란 현재나 과거, 더 이전 과거인 대과거 중 어느 기준 시점에서 이미 일어났거나 미래에 일어날 일에 대한 사실 또는 상황에 반대되는 생각을 의미하며, 이를 표현한 것이 가정법입니다.

If we missed the train, we would have been late for the meeting.
만약 기차를 놓쳤다면, 우리는 회의에 늦었을 것이다.

❸ 도치

원칙적으로는 '주어+동사'의 어순을 취해야 하나 그 순서가 서로 뒤바뀌게 되는 경우를 '도치'라고 합니다.
도치 구문에서는 주로 강조하고자 하는 내용을 문장의 맨 앞으로 보냅니다.

I knew little that you would come so early.
→ Little did I know that you would come so early.
네가 그렇게 빨리 올 줄 꿈에도 생각 못했어.

Check-up Test 700+를 위해 한 걸음 한 걸음

정답 및 해설 p.069

A. 다음 형용사/부사를 비교급과 최상급 형태로 만드세요.

① sharp 날카로운   비교급 : _____   최상급 : _____

② firm 확고한   비교급 : _____   최상급 : _____

③ rapidly 급속히   비교급 : _____   최상급 : _____

④ profitable 수익성이 있는   비교급 : _____   최상급 : _____

⑤ energetically 정력적으로   비교급 : _____   최상급 : _____

B. 괄호에서 적절한 것을 고르세요.

① This machine is as (efficient / efficiently) as the old one.
이 기계는 예전 것만큼이나 효율적이다.

② This machine works as (efficient / efficiently) as the old one.
이 기계는 예전 것만큼이나 효율적으로 작동한다.

③ The computers in our department were purchased (more recent / more recently) than the fax machine.
우리 부서에 있는 컴퓨터들은 팩스보다 더 최근에 구매되었다.

④ The TV show earned (higher / the highest) ratings of any program in television history.
그 TV 프로그램은 텔레비전 역사상 그 어떤 프로그램보다도 가장 높은 시청률을 기록했다.

C. 괄호에서 적절한 것을 고르세요.

① Main Street Restaurant is one of the (more / most) popular restaurants in this area.
메인 스트리트 레스토랑은 이 지역에서 가장 인기 있는 식당 중 하나이다.

② Successful applicants will be contacted soon, (as / more) early as next week.
합격자들은 이르면 다음 주에 연락을 받을 것이다.

③ JJ Medicine provides (the better / the best) health care to people in this area.
JJ 의약은 이 지역 사람들에게 최상의 의료 서비스를 제공한다.

④ Our new wireless headphones allow our customers to enjoy (more / as) freedom to move around than before.
새 무선 헤드폰은 우리 고객들이 전보다 더 자유롭게 움직이는 걸 즐기도록 해 준다.

Point 01 비교급

출제 포인트 정리

❶ 비교급

1) 비교급은 형용사/부사 **앞에 more**나 **뒤에 -er**를 붙여서 만들며, 보통 둘 사이에서 '**~보다 더 …하다**'라는 의미로 쓰입니다.
2) 비교급의 품사는 **형용사 또는 부사**이며, 토익에서는 이 둘을 구분하는 품사 선택 문제가 자주 출제됩니다.

This campaign can help people use energy more effectively. *<완전한 문장 뒤 부사 자리>*
이 캠페인은 사람들이 에너지를 더 효율적으로 사용하도록 도와줄 것이다.

※ 완전한 문장 → 부사가 정답 / 불완전한 문장 → 형용사가 정답

❷ 비교급 강조 부사

much, even, still, far, a lot

Diamond is much stronger than steel. 다이아몬드는 강철보다 훨씬 더 강하다.

❸ 비교급 관용 표현

more than ~보다 더	less than ~보다 덜	no later than +날짜/시간 늦어도 ~까지
no more than(= only) 단지, 겨우	not less than(= at least) 적어도	
no longer 더 이상 아닌	more or less 다소, 어느 정도	
A rather than B B라기보다는 오히려 A	sooner than ~보다는 차라리	
비교급 than expected/anticipated 기대 이상으로	A senior to B A가 B보다 손위인	

The shipment should arrive no later than Monday. 그 물건은 늦어도 월요일까지 배달되어야 한다.

Check-up Test 700+를 위해 한 걸음 한 걸음

정답 및 해석 p.069

STEP 1 다음 두 개의 보기 중 빈칸에 알맞은 것을 고르세요.

1. Due to the increased demand, we have to find ways to deliver orders ------- than last year.
   (A) fast   (B) faster

2. Today's ever changing business environment requires us to learn new skills ------- than we had to in the past.
   (A) more quickly   (B) quicker

3. In case of an emergency, please vacate the building as ------- as possible.
   (A) rapid   (B) rapidly

STEP 2 빈칸에 알맞은 것을 고르세요.

4. The national museum attracts ------- 10,000 visitors each year.
   (A) very   (B) totally   (C) much   (D) more than

5. Advances in digital photography have made it ------- than ever to keep Cityscaping Imaging's laboratory stocked with up-to-date equipment.
   (A) harden   (B) harder   (C) hardly   (D) hard

Point 02 최상급

출제 포인트 정리

❶ 최상급
1) 최상급은 형용사나 부사 **앞에 the most를 쓰거나 뒤에 -est**를 붙여서 만들고, 셋 이상의 여러 대상 또는 정해진 범주에서 '(~ 중에서) 가장 …한'이라는 의미로 쓰입니다.
   He is the most reliable employee of the entire department. 그는 전체 부서에서 가장 믿음직한 직원이다.
2) 최상급 구문에서 **비교의 대상이나 범위**를 나타낼 때는 전치사 **of, in, on** 등을 씁니다.
   This park is the most beautiful place in the city. 이 공원은 도시에서 가장 아름다운 장소이다.
3) 최상급 앞에 소유격이 나오는 경우 the를 쓰지 않습니다.
   Steve is my best mentor. 스티브는 나의 최고의 멘토다.

❷ the+최상급+-ble류 형용사 (ex. possible, available)
   We ensure that the quality of our products is the finest of any available on the market.
   우리 상품이 시중에서 구매할 수 있는 것 중에 최고라고 믿습니다.

❸ the+최상급+ever(부사) (경험의 최상급)
   This result was the best ever. 이번 결과는 지금껏 최고였다.

❹ the+서수/single/very/next/only/by far+최상급
   the single most important problem 단 하나의 가장 중요한 문제점

Check-up Test 700+를 위해 한 걸음 한 걸음   정답 및 해석 p.069

STEP 1 다음 두 개의 보기 중 빈칸에 알맞은 것을 고르세요.

1. Southwear Industries makes the ------- hand-stitched leather wallets on the market.
   (A) finest   (B) finer

2. The ability to chat and send files through mobile phones will be regarded as the most ------- means of communication of the decade.
   (A) innovation   (B) innovative

3. Of the ten candidates that the manager interviewed, Mr. Jam is the -------- qualified.
   (A) most   (B) more

STEP 2 빈칸에 알맞은 것을 고르세요.

4. The packaging design for our new cosmetic products is the most ------- we have ever seen.
   (A) innovate   (B) innovative   (C) innovations   (D) innovatively

5. The Nbook XS is being advertised as the ------- laptop computer available in stores today.
   (A) faster   (B) fastest   (C) fast   (D) fastness

Point 03 가정법

출제 포인트 정리

❶ 가정법 과거: 현재의 반대를 가정합니다.
If + 주어 + **과거 동사**, 주어 + **would/should/could/might** + **동사 원형**
If I had a ticket, I could watch the movie. 나에게 표가 있다면, 영화를 볼 수 있을 것이다.

❷ 가정법 과거 완료: 과거의 반대를 가정합니다.
If + 주어 + **had p.p.**, 주어 + **would/should/could/might** + **have p.p.**
If I had worked a little longer, I could have finished the task.
내가 좀 더 오래 일했다면, 그 일을 끝낼 수 있었을 것이다.

❸ 가정법 미래: 실현될 가능성이 낮은 미래의 일을 가정합니다.
If + 주어 + **should** + **동사 원형**, ┌ 주어 + **will/may/can** + **동사 원형**
                                    └ **please** + **동사 원형**
If you should have any doubts, please trust your intuition. 만약 의심스럽다면, 직감을 믿으세요.

❹ 가정법 도치: if가 생략되면서 도치가 일어납니다.

If + 주어 + were/과거 동사		Were/과거 동사 + 주어
If + 주어 + had p.p.	➡	Had + 주어 + p.p.
If + 주어 + should + 동사 원형		Should + 주어 + 동사 원형

If the train should arrive on time, we will not be late.
= Should the train arrive on time, we will not be late. 기차가 제시간에만 온다면, 우리는 늦지 않을 것이다.

※ 가정법 문제는 의미를 묻는 것보다 시제를 묻는 문제가 많이 출제되므로 시제 법칙을 외워야 합니다.

Check-up Test 700+를 위해 한 걸음 한 걸음

정답 및 해석 p.069

STEP 1 다음 두 개의 보기 중 빈칸에 알맞은 것을 고르세요.

1. If we ------- the trouble to recycle more, we could decrease the number of landfills.
   (A) has taken   (B) took

2. If the accountant ------- cleared, the management would have granted him access to the confidential files.
   (A) has been   (B) had been

3. ------- I known your requests, I would have taken care of it.
   (A) If   (B) Had

STEP 2 빈칸에 알맞은 것을 고르세요.

4. If I had ------- the early train, I would not have been late for work.
   (A) catch   (B) caught   (C) catching   (D) catches

5. If the office manager ------- that the fax machine was not working properly, she could have called the repair company earlier.
   (A) is told   (B) told   (C) had been told   (D) will tell

Point 04 도치

출제 포인트 정리

❶ **부정어 도치**: 부정 부사어가 문장의 맨 앞으로 가면서 도치가 일어납니다.

> 부정어+조동사+주어+동사 ~
> ↳ seldom / hardly / scarcely / nor / neither / never / no sooner / not only 등

She could never forget about it. = Never could she forget about it. 그녀는 그것을 결코 잊을 수 없었다.

❷ **<only+시간 부사(구)/전치사구> 도치**

> Only+시간 부사(구)/전치사구+조동사+주어+동사 ~

The researchers only recently got a pay raise.
= Only recently did the researchers get a pay raise. 연구자들만 최근에 봉급 인상을 받았다.

❸ 편지나 문서에 함께 **동봉/첨부/포함하는 내용**이 있음을 알릴 때 자주 쓰이는 도치 표현이 있습니다.

> Enclosed/Attached/Included is ~

Enclosed is a list of those companies. 그 회사들의 목록을 동봉했습니다.

❹ **so 도치**: 부사인 so가 문두로 가면서 도치가 일어납니다.
So do I. 나도 그래.

Check-up Test 700+를 위해 한 걸음 한 걸음

정답 및 해석 p.070

STEP 1   다음 두 개의 보기 중 빈칸에 알맞은 것을 고르세요.

1. ------- find offensive messages directed at you posted on the board from other club members, you should report it to us immediately.
   (A) You   (B) Should you

2. ------- had we invested in Trytech Inc. than the stock market crashed.
   (A) No sooner   (B) As soon as

3. ------- you will find a copy of our standard confidentiality agreement.
   (A) Enclosing   (B) Enclosed

STEP 2   빈칸에 알맞은 것을 고르세요.

4. ------- have the government polices in China been positive for foreign companies.
   (A) Seldom   (B) Ever   (C) Although   (D) Even

5. Only recently have some marketers in the IT industry ------- the importance of artificial intelligence.
   (A) recognized   (B) recognizing   (C) recognition   (D) to recognize

Chapter 11. 비교/가정법/도치

이것만 알면 700+

토익 최빈출 유형 정리! 비교/가정법/도치편!

유형1 비교급 강조 부사

❶ 원급 강조 부사: very, so, too, just
This house is just as nice as that house. 이 집은 딱 저 집만큼 좋다.

❷ 비교급 강조 부사: much, even, still, far, by far, a lot
This vacation was much better than I expected. 이번 휴가는 예상했던 것보다 훨씬 더 좋았다.

❸ 최상급 강조 부사: much, quite, by far
Hao is by far the best Chinese restaurant we have ever tried in the city.
하우는 이 도시에서 우리가 가봤던 음식점들 중에서 가장 최고의 중국 음식점이다.

유형2 if를 대신하는 전치사와 접속사

providing (that), provided (that) ~한다면 as long as ~하는 한 unless (if ~ not) 만일 ~이 아니라면 but for ① ~했다면(과거) ~했을텐데 <가정법 과거 완료> ② except for ~를 제외하면	on condition that ~의 조건으로 in case ~하는 경우를 대비하여 given (that) ~을 고려[감안]하면 assuming (that) ~라고 가정하면 considering (that) ~을 고려[감안]하면 if not for 만약 ~이 없다면

유형3 시험에 출제되는 4가지 most

❶ 수량 형용사인 many/much의 최상급: the most+명사
He has the most money among us. 그가 우리 중 가장 많은 돈을 가지고 있다.

❷ 형용사와 부사의 최상급: the most+형용사/부사 (가장 ~한)
the most interesting 가장 흥미로운
※ most+부사 → 부사의 최상급 (동사구의 부사 최상급에는 the를 붙이지 않습니다.)
This question is asked most frequently. 이것이 가장 자주 하는 질문이다.

❸ 일반 형용사: most+복수 명사/불가산 명사
the 없이 most는 일반 형용사로 '대부분의'를 의미합니다.
most customers 대부분의 고객들

❹ 부정(부분) 대명사: most of the+명사
most of 뒤에는 특정 범위를 알려 주는 정관사(the)와 같은 한정사가 따라 나옵니다.
most of the customers 대부분의 고객들

Chapter Test

1. Tickets for this season sold out more quickly ------- we expected.
   (A) what
   (B) that
   (C) such
   (D) than

2. ------- all the documentation be ready, a construction permit should take only two weeks to process.
   (A) Whenever
   (B) Anywhere
   (C) As well as
   (D) Should

3. Success would not have been achieved ------- the feedback received from the customers.
   (A) if not for
   (B) as to
   (C) in that
   (D) so as

4. Finding short-term housing on his own was ------- than he had expected.
   (A) difficult
   (B) difficulty
   (C) more difficult
   (D) much difficulty

5. No one at AECOM Technology Corporation tried ------- than Judith Caldwell to improve employees' welfare and working conditions.
   (A) most enthusiastic
   (B) enthusiastic
   (C) more enthusiastically
   (D) enthusiastically

6. ------- all the PC games Magicsoft sells, Misty Island is the most popular game with teenagers.
   (A) By
   (B) Of
   (C) Out
   (D) Near

7. Last quarter, Anderson Consulting Exports set much higher sales goals for its staff than -------.
   (A) anticipated
   (B) anticipates
   (C) anticipating
   (D) anticipation

8. McGrady's Fast Food Restaurant introduced a self-service kiosk system to make orders even more ------- to customers.
   (A) access
   (B) accesses
   (C) accessible
   (D) accessibly

9. Since the interview for the sales position started promptly at 8 A.M., Ms. Jameson had to arrive at work ------- than usual.
   (A) early
   (B) earlier
   (C) earliest
   (D) earliness

10. Despite ------- than average ticket prices, every performance of our new play for the next six months is sold out.
    (A) larger
    (B) sooner
    (C) higher
    (D) earlier

Chapter 12 전치사

출제 포인트 정리

❶ At
① **시간/장소:** at two o'clock 2시에   at the bus stop 버스 정류장에서
② **속도:** at the speed of 60 miles an hour 시속 60마일의 속도로
③ **비율:** at the rate of 35% 35퍼센트의 비율로
④ **비용:** at the cost of $100 100달러의 비용으로   at no extra cost 추가 비용 없이
⑤ **가격:** at a reasonable price 합리적인 가격으로
⑥ **연락처:** at 080-123-3456 080-123-3456번으로

❷ In
① **시간:** in 10 minutes 10분 후에
    the + 최상급 + 기수 + in + 기간 명사   the first winner in the last five years 지난 5년 만에 최초의 우승자
② **장소**(특정 장소, 독립된 공간)**:** chairs in the room 방에 있는 의자
③ **업종/분야**(증가/감소/진보/경력 + in 분야)**:** an increase in sales 판매의 증가
④ **색상:** in blue 파란색인
⑤ **숙어:** be interested in ~에 관심 있다   be involved in ~에 연관되다   in advance of ~에 앞서   in detail 상세히
    in exchange for ~과 교환하여   in response to ~에 응답하여

❸ On/Upon
On
① **요일/날짜:** on Monday 월요일에   on July 4th 7월 4일에
② **장소:** on the tenth floor 10층에   on the computer 컴퓨터에 (있는)
③ **주제/대상**(= about/over/regarding 등)**:** a book on biology 생물학에 관한 책
④ **교통수단:** on the plane(= aboard the plane) 비행기에 탑승한
⑤ **여행/활동:** on vacation 휴가 중   on a tour 여행 중
⑥ **숙어:** depend on ~에 달려 있다/의존하다

Upon
① **~하자마자:** upon arrival 도착하자마자   on/upon request 요청을 받자마자

❹ For
① **기간:** for two years 2년 동안
② **목적/용도:** waiting for a train 기차를 기다리며   a desk for the office 사무실에서 쓸 책상
③ **가치/대가/교환:** I bought it for $100. 난 100달러로 그것을 샀다.
④ **to부정사의 의미상 주어:** It's easy for everyone to use this device. 이 장치는 모든 사람들이 사용하기에 쉽다.
⑤ **이유**(for V-ing = as a result of)**:** I'm sorry for interrupting you. 방해해서 죄송합니다.
⑥ **찬성:** vote for ~에 찬성 투표하다

⑦ 가정: but for(= if not) ~이 없다면
⑧ 숙어: be blamed for ~에 대해 비난받다   be awarded for ~ 때문에 상을 받다   be known for ~로 유명하다
　　　 be noted for ~로 알려져 있다
　　　 I was awarded for the design. 그 디자인 때문에 상을 받았다.

❺ By
① (시간) 완료(~까지): by the end of this year 올해 말까지
② 원인/방법(by V-ing: ~함으로써): We learn by writing. 우리는 쓰면서 배운다.
③ 주체(~에 의해서): published by the company 그 회사에서 출판된
④ 장소/위치(~ 옆에): by the door 문 옆에
⑤ 정도/비율(~만큼): by 10% 10퍼센트만큼
⑥ 수단/방법(~로): by land 육로로   by machine 기계로 만든

❻ Until
① 상태/지속(동사+until+시점):
　Visitors will stay until tomorrow morning. 방문객들은 내일 아침까지 머물 것이다.
※ 유사 의미 전치사인 by와 구분해야 합니다. until은 상태가 지속될 때 사용하고 by는 1회성 동작일 때 '완료 동사+by+시점'의 형태로 사용합니다.
　Please deliver all new models by the specific deadlines.
　정해진 기한까지 신규 모델을 모두 배송해주시기 바랍니다.

❼ Of
① 재료/구성 요소: consist of/be made of ~로 구성되어 있다
② 동격: the price of 500 won 가격 500원   the city of Seoul 서울이라는 도시
③ 소유/소속: the manager of the accounting department 회계부서의 매니저
④ 부분: a friend of mine 내 친구 중 하나   one of duties 임무 중 하나
⑤

research 조사/연구　　development 개발	of a product 제품의
sales 판매　　promotion 촉진/홍보	
distribution 배포　　withdrawal 철수	

⑥ 능력/특징/장점: workers of Daniel's ability 대니얼만큼의 능력을 가진 사람
⑦ 유래/기원/출처: a native of Oregon 오리건 주 출신의 사람
※ 주의: 'of+추상 명사=형용사'
　The matter is of great importance. 그 일은 매우 중요하다.

❽ With
① 공존: meet with a client 고객과 만나다
② 동반/동행/소지: take/bring/have+목적어+with+사람 …를 데려오다/가져오다
③ 조건/특성/소유/포함: a man with a cap 모자를 쓴 남자
④ 수단/재료: slice the potatoes with a knife 칼로 감자를 자르다
⑤ 숙어: keep up with ~을 따라잡다   provide/reward+사람+with 사물 ~에게 …를 제공/보상하다
　　　 comply with+법/규칙/기준 ~을 따르다   cooperate with+사람 ~와 협력하다
※ with -ing (X), without -ing (O)

❾ During
① 기간: during the day 하루 동안

② 사건/행위: during the movie 영화를 보는 동안에
※ during + 동명사(X) / during + 기간 명사(O) / during the last/past/next + 숫자 + 시간 명사
※ 접속사 while vs. 전치사 during
　　They slept (while, ~~during~~) in flight. 그들은 비행 동안 잠을 잤다.

❿ Before
① 시간: before the meeting 회의 전에　before the end of the week 주말 전에
　　　　two hours before the meeting 회의 두 시간 전에
※ 유사 빈출 전치사
　　prior to ~ 전에　ahead of ~에 앞서　in advance (of) 사전에/미리/~ 전에
　　at least two weeks in advance of the scheduled arrival 예정된 도착보다 적어도 2주 전에
※ ahead는 부사이지만 ahead of는 전치사입니다.

⓫ After / Following
After
① 기간(시간): after 10 minutes 10분 후에
② 숙어: shortly/soon/not long after + 명사 ~한 후 바로/즉시
　　　　one after another/one after the other 순차적으로
　　　　기간 + after/following + 명사(시점/사건/행위) ~한 후에

Following
① 전치사(~ 후에): Following the meeting with their direct boss, the employees handed in the report.
　　　　　　　　직속상관과의 회의가 있은 후에 직원들은 보고서를 제출했다.
② 형용사(다음의): in the following(= next) week 다음 주에
③ 명사(다음, 아래): The following is my address. 다음에 있는 것이 제 주소입니다.

⓬ Since
① 현재 완료 시제 + since + 과거 시점:
　　The fax machine has not been working since this morning. 팩스가 오늘 아침부터 계속 작동하지 않는다.
※ since는 전치사 외에도 접속사나 부사로 다양하게 출제되지만 전치사일 때에는 because of(~ 때문에)의 뜻이 될 수 없습니다.

⓭ Within
① 시간(기간): within 24 hours 24시간 내에
② 장소: within the airport 공항 내에　within the park 공원 내에
③ 거리: within walking distance 걸어서 갈 만한 거리에　within commuting distance 출퇴근할 만한 거리에
④ 조직/시스템: within the company 사내에
⑤ 한계/규칙: within regulation 규정 내에　within the budget 예산 안에서

⓮ Over
① 시간(= during): over the next five years 다음 5년 동안
② 주제/대상(= on/about): problem over the tax 세금에 대한 문제
③ 비교 대상: advantage over the other companies 다른 회사들보다 우위
④ 장소/위치/사물(~ 너머, 가로질러, 덮는): bridge over the river 강을 가로지르는 다리
※ 수사를 수식하는 부사 over를 주의하세요.
　　for over two years 2년 이상 동안

⑮ Behind(↔ ahead of)

① 위치/장소(~ 뒤에): behind me 내 뒤에서/뒤쪽에   behind the poll 기둥 뒤에

② 일정: behind schedule 일정보다 늦게 (↔ ahead of schedule 일정보다 이르게)

③ 업무/성취: lag/fall behind ~보다 뒤처지다

　　　　　　behind only The Pinetree in record sales 음반 판매에서 파인트리에게만 뒤처진

④ 담당/책임: the mastermind behind the new marketing strategies 새로운 마케팅 전략을 담당하는 사람

⑯ Because of

① 이유/원인(~ 때문에): because of a problem with the equipment 장비의 문제로 인해

※ 이유/원인을 의미하는 빈출 전치사

　　① due to ~ 때문에　② owing to ~ 때문에　③ on account of ~ 때문에

　　④ as a result of ~의 결과로서　⑤ thanks to ~ 덕분에

※ 이유/원인의 접속사: because, since, as

⑰ Despite

① 양보(~하더라도, ~에도 불구하고): despite the interruption 방해/장애에도 불구하고

※ 양보를 의미하는 빈출 전치사

　　① regardless of ~에 상관 없이　② in spite of ~에도 불구하고　③ notwithstanding ~에도 불구하고

※ 양보의 접속사: although, while, though

※ 양보의 (접속) 부사: nonetheless, nevertheless

⑱ About

① 전치사(주제/대상): favorable news reports about the company 회사에 대한 긍정적인 소식

② 형용사: be about to + 동사 원형 막 ~하려 하다

③ 부사(숫자 앞): in about 10 minutes 약 10분 후에

※ 주제/대상을 의미하는 빈출 전치사

　　① on / over / in[with] regard to / as to / as for

　　② concerning / regarding / pertaining to / related to

⑲ As

① 지위/자격/동격(~로서): work as a physician in a private practice 개인 병원의 내과 의사로 일하다

　　　　　　the original receipt as proof of purchase 구매를 증명하는 원본 영수증

⑳ From

① 시간/거리/범위/장소/동작의 시작이나 출발점:

　　fall from the sky 하늘에서 떨어지다　from June to October 6월부터 10월까지

　　about two blocks away from the bank 은행에서 약 2블록 떨어진

② 원래의 상태: Cheese is made from milk. 치즈는 우유로 만든다.

※ 상태의 변화 없이 단순한 구성 요소를 말할 때는 of를 씁니다.

　　The table is made of wood. 테이블은 나무로 만들어진다.

③ 근거/유래/출처/관점: from an educational point of view 교육적인 관점에서

　　　　　　draw a conclusion from the facts 사실에서 결론을 끌어내다　benefit from ~로부터의 혜택

　　　　　　remove/exempt/subtract from ~로부터 제거하다/면제되다/빼다

④ 차이/금지: different from ~과 다른
　　　　　　　restrain/prevent/prohibit/ban + 목적어 + from + V-ing ~가 …하는 것을 막다, 금지하다

㉑ To
① 방향/대상(~에(게)/으로): relocate our office to the downtown area 우리 사무실을 시내로 이전하다
　　　　　　　　　　　offer a discount to loyal customers 충 성도가 높은 고객들에게 할인을 제공하다
② 범위/도달점/결과(~까지): from 9 A.M. to 5 P.M. 오전 9시부터 오후 5시까지
　　　　　　　　　　　to a certain extent 어느 정도까지　change to blue 파란색으로 변하다
③ 일치/적합/필요: a solution to the problem 그 문제의 해결책　an answer to the question 그 질문에 대한 대답
　　　　　　　a key to the house 그 집의 열쇠

※ to부정사(to + <u>동사 원형</u>) vs. 전치사(to + <u>명사/동명사</u>)

㉒ Into
① 이동/변화/진보/방향(~(으)로): evolve into ~로 (진보)되다/진화하다　transfer A (in)to A를 B로 옮기다/보내다
　　　　　　　　　　　　　　convert A (in)to B A를 B로 바꾸다　expand A into B A를 B로 확장하다
　　　　　　　　　　　　　　integrate A into/with B A를 B로 합치다

※ onto: ~ (위)로

㉓ Through / Throughout
Through
① 장소(~을 통해): through the entrance 출입구를 통해
② 시간(~ 동안 내내): through the summer holiday 여름휴가 내내
③ 경험/절차(~을 통해): clear goods through customs 물품을 통관시키다
④ 방법/수단/매개(~을 통해, ~로)(= by means of):
　through network/experience/know-how/Internet 네트워크로/경험으로/노하우로/인터넷으로
※ by + 무관사 대표 명사
　by pen 펜으로
※ with + 구체적인 명사
　with this pen 이 펜으로

Throughout
① 장소(~의 도처에): search throughout the office 사무실을 모두 (샅샅이) 찾다
② 시간(~동안 내내): throughout my life 내 일생을 통해(내내)

㉔ Toward(s)
① 목표치/이동 방향/목적지: a step toward(s) current goals 현재 목표에 도달하기 위한 조치
② 태도/감정/트렌드: the trend toward(s) online banking services 온라인 은행 서비스로의 트렌드
③ 시간(= just before): toward(s) the end of this year 올해 말 전에(즈음에)

㉕ Up to
① **up to** + 수치(~까지): You can save up to 50%. 50%까지 절감하실 수 있습니다.

㉖ Among
among + (불특정 다수) 복수 명사: 셋 이상의 관계를 나타낼 때
① 위치(~ 사이에 (둘러싸여 있는)): He sat among the candidates. 그는 후보자들 사이에 앉았다.

② 소속/포함((여럿) 중의 (하나)): Our company ranked among the best firms. 우리 회사가 최고의 회사들 사이에 랭크됐다.
③ 배분/의견 공유(~ 사이에서 (셋 이상의 관계)): concern among economists 경제학자들 사이에서의 관심사
④ 관계(서로서로, 끼리끼리)(= with each other): Talk about it among yourselves. 여러분들끼리 논의해 보세요.

㉗ Across / Around / Opposite / Past / Near / Along / Alongside
장소나 이동과 관련하여 위치를 나타내는 빈출 전치사
① **across**(~의 건너편에): across the street 도로 건너에
② **around**(~의 주변에): around the corner 모퉁이 주변에
③ **opposite**(~의 반대편에)(= across from): The store is opposite the bank. 그 가게는 은행 맞은편에 있다.
④ **past**((장소, 시간 등을) 지나서 (더)): past the post office 우체국을 지나서
⑤ **near**(~ 가까이에)(= next to, beside, by): near the table 테이블 옆에
⑥ **along/alongside**(~을 따라서): walk along the river 강을 따라 걷다
※ along with: ~와 함께(동반, 첨부)

㉘ Except (for)
① 제외/예외(~를 제외하고는): 주로 all/every 뒤에 나옴
   I like all musical instruments except the guitar. 나는 기타를 제외하곤 모든 악기를 좋아한다.
② except vs. barring: barring은 미래/가정(= unless there is)을 나타냄
   The market will be stable barring some change. 어떤 변화만 없다면 시장은 안정될 것이다.
※ '제외/예외'를 의미하는 빈출 전치사
   excluding ~을 제외하고   aside/apart from ~ 외에

㉙ Besides
① 추가(~ 외에): besides drinks 음료 외에
※ 추가의 뜻을 의미하는 빈출 전치사
   in addition to ~에 더해서   A as well as B B뿐만 아니라 A도   plus(= and also) 그리고 또한
※ -s가 빠진 beside는 장소 전치사로 '~ 옆에(near, next to)'라는 의미입니다.

㉚ Instead of
① 대신(~을 대신하여): instead of coffee 커피 대신에
※ '~을 대신하여' 즉, 선택과 포기를 의미하는 유사 의미 빈출 전치사
   in place of ~ 대신에   rather than ~ 대신에(더 나은 것을 선택)   on behalf of ~을 대신하여(회사 등을 대표한다는 의미)
※ instead는 부사로 '대신에'의 의미로도 쓰입니다.

㉛ Without
① ~ 없이: without written permission/consent 서면 허가/동의 없이   without delay 지체 없이, 바로, 즉시
② ~하지 않고, ~ 없이: without having to pay 돈을 낼 필요 없이
③ (도움 등이) 없었다면: without your help 당신의 도움이 없었다면
④ 숙어: not/never ... without ~하지 않고 …하는 일은 없다, ~하면 반드시 …하다

㉜ Under
① 위치(~ 아래): under the table 테이블 아래에
② 수량(~ 이하): children under six 6살 미만의 아이들
③ 일/상황의 진행(~ 중인): under discussion/consideration/review 논의/고려/검토 중인
   under construction 공사 중인

④ 영향을 받고 있는 상태/조건/권한(~일 때, ~ 하에):
　　under control 통제하에, 지배하에　　under pressure 압박을 받고 있는　　under warranty 보증 기간 중인
　　under such conditions 그런 조건하에서　　under different circumstances 다른 상황일 때
　　under no circumstances 어떠한 경우라도　　under his leadership 그의 리더십 아래
　　under president Paula 폴라 사장 체제하에　　under the situation 상황상, 여건상
⑤ 법/규칙(~에 따라)(= according to): under the terms of agreement 합의서의 조항에 따라

㉝ Beneath
① 아래/바로 밑(= underneath): buried beneath Green Square 그린 스퀘어 바로 아래에 묻혀 있는

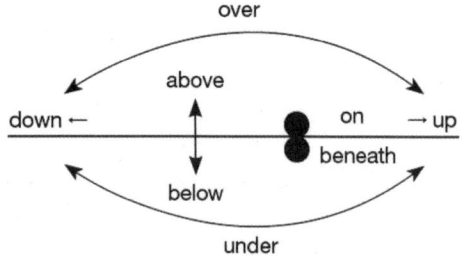

㉞ Beyond
① 시간((특정 시간이나 날짜) 이후에)(= after):
　　in the coming year and beyond 내년과 그리고 그 후에　　beyond 2017 2017년 너머(이후에)
② 위치/장소: beyond the entry gate 출입구 너머
③ 범위/기대치(수량/한계/레벨):
　　beyond our expectation 기대 이상으로　　beyond our capacity 수용력을 벗어나
　　beyond our experience 경험을 벗어나　　beyond our ability 능력 밖의
④ 불가능: beyond repair 수리가 불가능한　　beyond our control 통제 불가능한　　beyond our belief 믿기 힘든

㉟ Above / Below
① above(~ 이상) vs. below(~ 이하)

↑ above 이상 ↓ below 이하	+	expectation 기대 이상/이하 standard 기준치 이상/이하 average 평균 이상/이하 number/amount/level 수/양/수준 이상/이하

㊱ Out of
① 범위/능력/공간(~의 범위 밖의):
　　out of control 통제 불능의　　out of order 고장 난　　out of stock 재고가 없는　　out of date 낡은, 오래된
　　Keep out of the room. 그 방에 들어가지 마시오.

㊲ Like(↔ Unlike)
like
① 유사한 사물/사람(~인 것 같은/처럼):
　　It seems/looks/feels/sounds/tastes like + 명사 (~처럼) 같다/보이다/느끼다/들리다/맛이 나다
　　He is like his father. 그는 그의 아버지 같다(비슷하다).
② 구체적인 예(= for example, such as): office supplies like a stapler 스테이플러 같은 사무용품

unlike

① ~와 다른: unlike most other companies 대부분의 다른 회사들과는 다르게(달리)

㊳ Amid

① 상황(~이 한창인 가운데/동안)(= while):

amid concerns about the environment 환경에 대한 걱정이 있는 상황에서
amid indications of new economic growth 새로운 경제 성장의 조짐이 보이는 가운데

㊴ Against

① 반대/경쟁/대비:

decide advise lean vote compete	+against	~에 반대 결정하다 ~하지 않도록 조언하다 ~에 기대다 ~에 대해 반대표를 던지다 ~와 경쟁하다

※ 반의어 for는 '찬성/지지/동의'의 의미입니다.

㊵ Per

① per(~당) + 무관사 단위 명사: per person 1인당

※ every/another/per + 수사 + 단위 복수 명사 가능
every two weeks 2주마다

㊶ According to

① 출처: according to the president 사장(의 말)에 따르면
② 근거: according to the agreement 합의서에 따라

※ in accordance with + rule/system 법률/시스템에 따라

㊷ Worth

전치사

① 금전(~의 가치가 있는): be worth $1,000 1,000달러의 가치가 있다
② 시간/노력/일(~할 만한 가치가 있는): be worth the time/effort/work/visit 시간을 들일/노력할/일할/방문할 가치가 있다

명사(~만큼의)

① 숫자 + 단위 명사/금액 + worth of + 명사: hundred dollars' worth of 몇 백 달러 가치의
$100 worth of computer equipment 100달러짜리 컴퓨터 장비
② 숫자 + 시간 명사 + worth of + 명사: a week's worth of food 일주일 먹을 만큼의 식량

이것만 알면 700+

토익 최빈출 유형 정리! 전치사편!

유형 1 주의해야 하는 시간 전치사

❶ for vs. during

for + 수사 + 단위 시간 명사: 기간 내 동작/상황의 지속
The ticket is valid for only two weeks. 티켓은 2주간만 유효하다.

during + 특정 기간 명사: 특정 기간 내의 동작/상황의 발생
(단, '수사+명사'를 쓸 경우 반드시 정관사 the와 함께 씁니다.)
During my stay in London, I met Mr. Timothy. 런던에 머무르는 동안 난 티모시 씨를 만났다.

❷ by vs. until

일회성 동작 또는 완료의 동사 + **by** + 시점 명사:

arrive 도착하다 complete 완료하다 finish 끝내다 submit 제출하다 inform 알려 주다 return 반납하다 receive 받다	+	by	+	시점 명사

상태 지속 동사 + **until** + 시점 명사:

be 있다 remain 남아 있다 like 좋아하다 stay 머물다 work 일하다 continue 계속하다 sleep 자다 wait 기다리다	+	until	+	시점 명사

유형 2 분사 전치사

분사는 대부분 형용사로 쓰이지만, 일부는 전치사로 쓰이기도 합니다.

following ~ 후에
excluding ~을 제외하고
barring 어떤 일이 발생하지 않으면
based on ~을 근거/기초로
according to ~에 따르면
notwithstanding ~에도 불구하고   ※ 부사로도 쓰이는 것에 주의합니다.
pending ~이 발생할 때까지, ~을 기다리는 동안   ※ 형용사로는 '아직 결정되지 않은, 곧 발생할'이라는 의미입니다.
given ~을 고려[감안]하여   ※ given은 전치사, given that은 접속사
considering ~을 고려[감안]하여   ※ considering (that) 형태의 접속사로도 쓰입니다.
beginning/starting ~부터   ※ 뒤에 날짜나 요일이 옵니다.

including ~을 포함하여
regarding/concerning ~에 관하여
related to ~와 관련하여
compared with/to ~와 비교하여
pertaining to ~와 관계있는

Chapter Test

1. To receive a refund, merchandise should be returned ------- 30 days of purchase.
   (A) within
   (B) when
   (C) unless
   (D) always

2. You will not be given access to enter the laboratory ------- approval from your supervisor.
   (A) into
   (B) until
   (C) among
   (D) without

3. ------- its competitive benefits package, Anderson Legal Firm's employees show strong loyalty.
   (A) About
   (B) Within
   (C) On behalf of
   (D) Because of

4. Our bakery is open daily from 7:00 A.M. to 2:00 P.M. ------- on weekends.
   (A) except
   (B) until
   (C) nor
   (D) yet

5. The announcement of the best television advertisement award will be made ------- dinner time.
   (A) for
   (B) down
   (C) along
   (D) during

6. Most of our employees are eligible to receive a full pension ------- twenty-five years of employment.
   (A) after
   (B) toward
   (C) across
   (D) into

7. Because of its proximity ------- major tourist attractions, the Royal Hotel is often fully booked.
   (A) next to
   (B) near
   (C) to
   (D) by

8. In order to release the vehicle's parking brake, you should press lightly ------- the pedal with your foot.
   (A) up
   (B) on
   (C) of
   (D) in

9. The vice president greeted the board of directors ------- a luncheon yesterday in Ottawa.
   (A) at
   (B) had
   (C) such
   (D) where

10. Once you walk ------- the post office, you will see Jack & Jenny's Ice Cream at the end of the street.
    (A) between
    (B) down
    (C) during
    (D) past

Chapter 13 PART 6

PART 6, 포인트 감각 익히기
한 문장에서 여러 문장으로 바뀌었을 뿐 PART 6에서 등장하는 문제들은 대부분 PART 5의 문제와 동일한 형태입니다. 다른 점은 앞뒤 내용을 파악해서 정답을 찾아야 하는 문제가 출제된다는 것입니다.

1. 문제 풀이 기본 STEP

> **STEP 1** 빈칸이 있는 문장만 먼저 확인하세요.
> 빈칸이 포함된 하나의 문장만 먼저 구조를 분석합니다.
> 수식어구를 괄호로 묶고 나면 문장의 구조가 더 잘 보입니다.
> 특히, 알아 두어야 할 것은 <접속사/관계사 + 1 = 동사의 개수> 공식입니다.

> **STEP 2** 문장의 앞뒤 문맥을 확인하세요.
> 해당 문장만으로 정답 선택이 어려울 경우, 앞뒤 내용의 흐름과 동사의 시제를 확인합니다.

2. PART 6 유형별 문제 풀이 방법

문제 유형	이건 꼭 확인하세요
1. 품사를 묻는 문제 *문장 구조 분석이 필수입니다.*	① 문장 구조, 품사의 배열 ② 관련 문법
2. 동사의 형태를 묻는 문제 *본동사 → 수 → 태 → 시제 순으로 확인합니다.*	① 문장의 본동사 ② 주어와의 수 일치 ③ 목적어 유무와 태 ④ 문장 내의 시간 부사와 다른 동사들의 시제
3. 적절한 연결어를 찾는 문제 *빈칸 앞뒤의 문장 논리를 확인합니다.*	① 접속사/전치사/(접속) 부사 ② 지시 대명사/형용사
4. 어휘를 묻는 문제 *말이 된다고 해서 다 정답은 아닙니다.*	① 답을 결정하는 연결 단어 ② 동의어 ③ 포괄적인 단어
5. 빈칸에 알맞은 문장을 고르는 문제 *빈칸 앞뒤의 내용 흐름을 확인합니다.*	① 보기의 키워드 ② 답을 결정하는 연결 단어 ③ 지문의 내용이나 흐름과 상관없는 오답 보기

Check-up Test 700+를 위해 한 걸음 한 걸음

정답 및 해석 p.071

A. 밑줄 친 동사의 시제를 결정하는 근거가 되는 것을 찾으세요.

① February, 10

Dear OTNA Member:
Our next OTNA meeting will be held Wednesday, March 21st. The OTNA will host a presentation on Torrance History Celebrating 100 Years.

2월 10일

OTNA 회원님께:
우리의 다음 OTNA 회의가 3월 21일 수요일에 열립니다. OTNA는 100주년을 기념하는 토런스 역사에 관한 프레젠테이션을 주최할 것입니다.

② Each of our tour packages includes transportation, accommodation, meals, guided tours and more. And they also offer a great value to both independent and group travellers.

저희 여행 상품들은 각각 교통, 숙박, 식사, 가이드 관광 등을 포함합니다. 또한 개인과 단체 여행객 모두에게 탁월한 가치를 제공합니다.

B. 다음 괄호 안에서 알맞은 표현을 고르세요.

① Our record shows that you were a participant in one of our workshops presented by James Potter. We'd like to offer you the opportunity to (attend, lead) Mr. Potter's new workshop.

저희 기록은 당신이 제임스 포터 씨의 워크숍 중 하나의 참석자였음을 보여 줍니다. 저희는 당신에게 포터 씨의 새로운 워크숍에 참석할 수 있는 기회를 제공하고자 합니다.

② Does your floor need anything more?
Visit MJ Flooring Center & Design today for a complimentary interior design (activity, consultation). One of our highly trained staff members will meet with you to discuss what you need.

바닥에 더 필요한 것 없으세요?
무료 실내 디자인 상담을 위해 오늘 MJ 바닥 센터 앤 디자인을 방문하세요. 잘 교육받은 저희 직원이 고객님과 만나서 고객님께서 필요한 것에 대해 논의할 것입니다.

C. 다음 괄호 안에서 알맞은 표현을 고르세요.

① Please be aware that company vehicles are strictly for business use only. (However, Accordingly), they should not be used for personal use.

회사 차량은 철저히 오직 업무용으로만 사용됨을 알아두시기 바랍니다. 따라서 그것들을 개인적인 용도로 사용해서는 안 됩니다.

② The newly renovated gym should be operational by next month. While work is in progress, current members are asked to not use the front entrance. (Instead, For example), you should use the back entrance.

새로 수리된 체육관이 다음 달까지 운영될 것입니다. 작업이 이루어지는 동안에는 현재 회원님들께 정문을 이용하지 말아 주실 것을 요청드립니다. 대신, 후문을 이용하시는 것이 좋겠습니다.

Point 01 품사를 묻는 문제

출제 포인트 정리

❶ 품사를 묻는 문제
보기로 제시된 단어들의 어원이 모두 같고 품사가 다를 때는 의미를 파악해야 하는 문제가 아니라 **구조 및 품사를 묻는 문제**입니다. 해당 문장의 처음부터 끝까지 구조를 분석한 후에 문제 풀이를 시작해야 합니다.

❷ PART 6 구조 및 품사 문제 풀이 순서
① 보기의 뜻보다는 문장의 **구조를 분석하고 필요 품사**를 찾습니다.
② 문장 안에서 답에 영향을 주는 **문법적인 요소를 확인**합니다.

Check-up Test 700+를 위해 한 걸음 한 걸음

정답 및 해석 p.071

STEP 1 빈칸에 알맞은 것을 고르세요.

Questions 1-4 refer to the following letter.

Dear Mr. Anderson,

I have tried to contact you several times over the past two months requesting an explanation on why you have failed ------- your account with us. -------. Please see the attached file for more details about this amount.
          1.   2.

As you've ignored these requests, you are damaging the excellent credit record you had previously maintained with our company. -------, additional late fees are being incurred.
                                                3.

If you do not respond to this letter ------- the next five days, we will have no choice but to turn your account over for collection.
                                    4.

I am sorry that we must take such drastic action. However, you can preserve your credit rating if you make your payment today for the amount stated above.

1. (A) to settle
   (B) settling
   (C) settle
   (D) settled

2. (A) Thank you for opening an account with us.
   (B) However, it will be restored soon.
   (C) Please complete the form by next week.
   (D) The total amount due is now $ 7,000.

3. (A) In addition
   (B) For instance
   (C) Otherwise
   (D) Although

4. (A) while
   (B) since
   (C) within
   (D) once

Point 02 동사의 시제를 묻는 문제

출제 포인트 정리

❶ **동사 시제 문제의 답을 결정하는 단서를 찾아야 합니다.**
  ① 문장 안에 있는 **시간 부사나 시간 전치사**가 답을 결정합니다.
  ② **접속사**와 **다른 동사들의 시제**가 답을 결정합니다.
  ③ 전체 **지문의 시점**과 **앞뒤 문장의 동사의 시제**가 답을 결정합니다.

❷ **최다 빈출 시제**

① 현재	일반적인 사실, 주기적이고 일상적인 업무, 언제나 적용되는 규칙 등에 사용합니다.
② 미래 완료	문장에 미래 완료 시점이 반드시 제시되어야 합니다.
③ 미래 진행	확정된 미래 일정, 시간, 장소 등의 구체적인 정보가 동반되어야 합니다.
④ 현재 진행	현재 발생하고 있는 상황을 나타내거나 미래 진행을 대신합니다.

Check-up Test 700+를 위해 한 걸음 한 걸음   정답 및 해설 p.071

STEP 1 빈칸에 알맞은 것을 고르세요.

Questions 1-4 refer to the following e-mail.

TO: Alisha Olson
FROM: Donald Hernandez
DATE: December 15
SUBJECT: Desktop Publishing Program

You ------- an investigation into the possibility of switching suppliers for AG Inn's publicity materials from an outside company to an in-house desktop publishing software program on October 19th. -------.
                                                                                    2.
1.

I am pleased to report that all research has been completed as planned. A conclusion has been reached and I have ------- the resulting recommendation in the final section of the attached report, Desktop
                                 3.
Publishing Software: A Comparative Analysis.

Thank you for allowing me to work on this project. I have found it very ------- as well as informational. If
                                                                     4.
you have any questions or comments regarding this project, I would be happy to discuss them with you. I would also appreciate the opportunity to conduct research for you in other areas. You may reach me at (050) 555-1254, or e-mail me at dhernandez@kion.com.

1. (A) will request
   (B) request
   (C) requested
   (D) has requested

2. (A) It will take two days to replace computers.
   (B) Pursuant to this request, I submitted a proposal on October 27th.
   (C) We recently released a new software program.
   (D) They offer a variety of functions for advertising.

3. (A) taken
   (B) given
   (C) donated
   (D) assigned

4. (A) interest
   (B) interests
   (C) interested
   (D) interesting

Point 03   적절한 연결어를 찾는 문제

출제 포인트 정리

❶ PART 6에 출제되는 연결어

문장과 문장을 연결하는 **접속사**, 의미상 연결을 해주는 **접속 부사**, 그 외에 문장 안의 명사를 추가하는 **전치사** 문제가 출제됩니다. 또한 지문에서 한 번 언급된 것을 두 번 중복하여 언급하지 않기 위해서 쓰는 **지시 대명사, 지시 형용사, 수량 대명사, 인칭 대명사**도 최근 출제 비중이 높아지고 있습니다.

❷ 접속 부사 문제 풀이 방법

① 빈칸 앞이 **마침표**로 끝난 문장인지 **쉼표**로 연결되는 문장인지 확인해야 합니다.

주어+동사+목적어, **접속사**+주어+동사+목적어

주어+동사+목적어. **접속 부사**+주어+동사+목적어

- 접속 부사는 문법적으로는 두 문장을 연결할 수 없고 의미상으로만 연결합니다.
- 일반 부사도 문장을 수식하는 경우에는 접속 부사로 사용됩니다.

② 빈칸 앞뒤 문장의 **논리 관계**를 파악하고 알맞은 (접속) 부사를 찾습니다.

- 원인 ➪ 결과 / 포괄적 설명 ➪ 구체적인 예시 등 (p.241 빈출 접속 부사 참고)

Check-up Test 700+를 위해 한 걸음 한 걸음

정답 및 해석 p.071

STEP 1 빈칸에 알맞은 것을 고르세요.

Questions 1-4 refer to the following letter.

Dear Valued Customer,

Thank you for using our restaurant. For the last five years, we've tried to keep our menu prices the ------- as when we first opened. Unfortunately, we are forced to raise our prices by 4 percent ------- July 1 due to sharply rising prices for raw ingredients. We've made every effort to avoid this price increase. -------, we do not want to compromise on the quality of our food. Using the best ingredients available makes you happy whenever you visit our restaurant. -------. We appreciate your support and look forward to continuing to serve you.

Sincerely,

Brown Potter
Restaurant Manager

1. (A) actual
   (B) same
   (C) practical
   (D) exceptional

2. (A) effective
   (B) effectiveness
   (C) effectively
   (D) effects

3. (A) Similarly
   (B) Therefore
   (C) However
   (D) Accordingly

4. (A) Our restaurant is not profitable yet.
   (B) Our food is healthier than that of other restaurants.
   (C) We believe you will see that our food is still a great value.
   (D) We expect that nearby restaurants will raise their prices accordingly.

Point 04 어휘를 묻는 문제

출제 포인트 정리

❶ 어휘 문제는 해석상 말이 된다고 다 답이 되는 것은 아닙니다.

해당 문장만 보면 보기로 제시된 대부분의 단어들을 넣어도 말이 되는 것 같지만 그렇다고 답이 되는 것은 아닙니다. 반드시 빈칸 주변 문장에서 **객관적인 근거 단어를 확보**하여 답을 선택해야 합니다.

❷ 논리적으로 앞뒤의 내용을 연결할 수 있는 답을 찾아야 합니다.

① 해당 문장 앞뒤에서 연결되는 단어를 확보하여 답을 선택해야 합니다.
② 근거가 되는 단어들이 주로 구체적인 반면, 정답은 이들을 아우를 수 있는 포괄적인 단어인 경우가 대부분입니다.

Check-up Test 700+를 위해 한 걸음 한 걸음   정답 및 해석 p.071

STEP 1 빈칸에 알맞은 것을 고르세요.

Questions 1-4 refer to the following memo.

Attention all employees

The board of directors announced that they have decided to ------1.------ the company dress code.

Starting next month, employees will be required to wear new T-shirts imprinted with the company name and logo.

------2.------. You will be expected to wear it during your work shifts. ------3.------ shirts may be purchased for $12.00 each.

Please find an order form attached on which you are asked to indicate the size you require. Enclose payment if applicable. All orders should be submitted to Jessie Lopez in the purchasing office by no ------4.------ than Thursday, April 15.

---

1. (A) discuss
 (B) abolish
 (C) survey
 (D) revise

2. (A) I would appreciate it if you send me an idea.
 (B) Items will be on sale during the event.
 (C) All employees will receive one T-shirt free of charge.
 (D) A new company logo will be available on our website.

3. (A) Additional
 (B) Previous
 (C) Another
 (D) Striped

4. (A) lately
 (B) later
 (C) latest
 (D) late

Point 05 | 빈칸에 알맞은 문장을 고르는 문제

출제 포인트 정리

❶ 빈칸 앞뒤 문장에서 답을 결정하는 단어를 확인합니다.
① 보기에서 키워드를 먼저 정리합니다.
② 빈칸 앞뒤 문장에서 보기의 키워드와 연결되는 내용을 확인합니다.
③ **접속사, 접속 부사, 지시 대명사, 지시 형용사** 등 앞뒤의 내용을 이어주는 연결어를 확인합니다.

❷ 보기에서 하나씩 오답을 소거합니다.
① 보기에 문맥과 상관없는 단어가 나오면 오답입니다.
② 막연히 추가되어도 좋은 내용은 답이 아닙니다.
③ 보기의 내용이 본문과 관련 있더라도 빈칸의 위치에 어울리지 않는다면 답이 될 수 없습니다.

❸ 전체 지문을 파악해야 합니다.
① 반드시 전체 문서의 목적이나 상황, 시점들을 이해해야만 문제가 해결됩니다.
② 비즈니스 문서들은 글의 순서가 정해져 있고 **한 가지 정보를 한 번만 언급**하기 때문에 다른 부분에서 반복하여 언급되지 않습니다.

Check-up Test 700+를 위해 한 걸음 한 걸음

정답 및 해석 p.072

STEP 1 빈칸에 알맞은 것을 고르세요.

Questions 1-4 refer to the following letter.

August 7

Dear Mr. Brown,

I was pleased to meet you to ------- (1.) the opportunity as a sales representative position at your organization. I enjoyed hearing your vision during the interview. ------- (2.) believe my previous work as a sales clerk makes me a perfect candidate for the position. Also, I have extensive knowledge of the computer programs your company uses to analyze sales data. ------- (3.). Lastly, I believe I can be a valuable ------- (4.) to your company.

Thank you for having considered me for this job.

Sincerely,

Roger Moore

1. (A) discuss
   (B) discussed
   (C) having discussed
   (D) discusses

2. (A) You
   (B) They
   (C) I
   (D) We

3. (A) I'm looking forward to meeting you again.
   (B) Sales representative is an extremely valued position.
   (C) In particular, I have experience working with DataExcel 200.
   (D) I have attached recommendation letters from previous employers.

4. (A) software
   (B) experience
   (C) asset
   (D) profit

이것만 알면 700+
토익 최빈출 유형 정리! 빈출 접속 부사편!

however 그러나, 그렇지만	주제 전환 / 대조 At this time we cannot accept any larger items. However, this policy may change in the future. 지금은 커다란 물건을 받을 수 없습니다. 하지만 이 정책은 향후에 바뀔 수 있습니다.
otherwise 그렇지 않으면	(1) 접속 부사: 만약 그렇지 않다면 (2) 일반 부사: 다른 방법으로, 그밖에 달리 The bank will renew the contract unless notified otherwise. 달리 통보를 받지 않는다면 은행은 계약을 자동 연장할 것이다. They won although expected otherwise. 그들은 (이기지 못할 것이라고) 다르게 예상되었지만 이겼다. This is only a traditional area in an otherwise modern city. 이곳은 대부분 현대적인 도시에서 유일하게 전통적인 장소이다.
finally 마침내 / eventually 결국	after/although + 고난·역경·어려움의 내용, 주어 + finally/eventually + 동사
in addition 추가로 as well 또한, 역시 besides 게다가 furthermore 더욱이, 게다가 additionally/moreover 게다가 above all 무엇보다도	[추가] 앞 문장 일부 + 뒤 문장 일부
in fact 사실 for example/instance 예를 들어 in particular 특히 specifically 분명히, 명확하게	포괄적인 설명의 앞 문장 + in fact + 구체적인 실제 예 또는 구체적인 추가 설명
accordingly 부응해서, 맞춰	[앞 문장의 내용에 따라] Plan first and spend money accordingly. 계획을 먼저 세우고 그에 맞춰서 돈을 써라.
instead 대신 alternatively 그 대신에 rather 오히려	포기 + instead/alternatively/rather + 선택
since then 그때부터 afterward 나중에 thereafter 그 후에	[발생 순서] The first flight left at noon and the other left shortly thereafter. 첫 번째 비행기가 정오에 뜨고 다음에 바로 이어서 다른 비행기도 출발했다. I'd like water and afterward I'll have coffee. 나는 물을 먼저 마시고 그 다음에 커피를 마시겠다. ※ since then은 현재 완료 시제를 동반한다.
as a result 그 결과 therefore 그러므로 thus 이렇게 하여, 이와 같이 consequently 결과적으로	먼저 발생 + therefore + 나중 발생 상황 + as a result + 결과 내용
as always 언제나처럼 as usual 늘 그렇듯이	as always / as usual: 주기적이고 일상적인 경우 ※ in the case(그 경우에): 특정한 경우나 사람에게만 적용
nonetheless 그렇더라도 nevertheless 그렇기는 하지만	양보, 기대치의 반대 (= 접속사 although) (= 전치사 despite)
even so 그렇기는 하지만	사실 + even so + 사실의 반대/다름
however 그러나 (in the) meantime 그 동안에 meanwhile 그 동안에 by the way 그런데	전환 / 대조 / 대구
in short 요컨대	구체적(자세한 내용) + in short + 포괄적(요약)

Chapter Test

Questions 1-4 refer to the following notice.

As you may have realized, your membership will expire on August 19. Please fill in the attached form ------- your membership and continue to use the best equipment and machines Max Total Fitness provides to make your body healthy and beautiful.

To ensure that your service continues without any -------, we recommend that you register for our automatic billing program. ------- you are registered, you won't have to ever experience the inconvenience of renewing your membership again in the future.

-------. To celebrate our 5th anniversary, we will be offering a free one-month trial of our new yoga program "Jenna's Burning Yoga". If you enroll in this program, you will be able to receive a yoga mat absolutely free! For more information, please visit our website at www.maxfitness.com.

1. (A) renews
   (B) renewed
   (C) renew
   (D) to renew

2. (A) division
   (B) function
   (C) interruption
   (D) attraction

3. (A) While
   (B) Once
   (C) Because
   (D) Even though

4. (A) Thank you for joining our fitness center.
   (B) Also, we have good news for you.
   (C) Unfortunately, your machine will no longer be available.
   (D) Call today for a free consultation.

Questions 5-8 refer to the following e-mail.

Dear Ms. Kumar,

Thank you for ------- (5.) your expense report for the business trip you went on last month. However, I am afraid that I have to inform you about a few policies that you must follow when you write an expense report. First, if you sign your own expense report, it would be considered legally ineffective. ------- (6.), your manager should sign the report in order for the reimbursement to be processed. Also, if you wish to receive the ------- (7.) amount of the reimbursement, please make sure to include the receipts. They are used to prove the actual amount you've claimed during your business travels. ------- (8.).

Thank you.

Sincerely,
Jasmine Leonard

5. (A) reviewing
   (B) sending
   (C) asking
   (D) offering

6. (A) Instead
   (B) Likewise
   (C) Unless
   (D) Whereas

7. (A) full
   (B) fuller
   (C) fills
   (D) filling

8. (A) Any lost item can be claimed within a month.
   (B) Please resubmit the report after you make the necessary changes.
   (C) Again, I apologize for this mistake.
   (D) Please let me know if you need a new form.

Questions 9-12 refer to the following article.

April 1: The sales of jeans and skirts by 9 Jeans for All Humans have skyrocketed in parts of Europe. In response to this drastic ------- , 9 Jeans for All Humans will be opening factories and exclusive shops in Paris, London, and Rome by the end of this year. The Madrid branch currently ------- five shops. -------.
9.   10.
11.

"We never expected such success from our brand in the competitive fashion market of Europe. It still feels like a dream," said Michael Glass, founder and main designer of 9 Jeans for All Humans. "The creation of shops and factories ------- the hassle for customers who have been ordering outside their countries, causing them to pay extra for shipping fees."
                                                       12.

9. (A) cut
   (B) increase
   (C) reduction
   (D) completion

10. (A) operating
    (B) operated
    (C) operates
    (D) operation

11. (A) Finally, we offer various design training programs.
    (B) All our products are made from 100% cotton.
    (C) You can visit any of our shops to return your purchase.
    (D) It is also expected to add two more shops by the end of this month.

12. (A) will eliminate
    (B) has eliminated
    (C) eliminate
    (D) eliminated

Questions 13-16 refer to the following letter.

July 7

Mr. Derek Cohen
472 Bellville Way
Biloxi, MS 39530

Dear Mr. Cohen:

Thank you for using Silver Bank. You may have heard the recent news that Silver Bank and Hans Financial Co. have joined together to better serve you. As of July 1, the two financial companies -------. -------. There will be no immediate changes to your accounts. -------, you can expect a variety of products to become available to you. We encourage you to review the enclosed brochure highlighting some of our new -------. To learn more about any of these products, find our local branch nearest you or visit our website (www.HSbank.com).

Thank you for the opportunity to continue serving you.

Sincerely,

Max Butler
Managing Director

13. (A) will merge
    (B) can merge
    (C) being merged
    (D) have merged

14. (A) Because of the merger, we're closing our business.
    (B) We are now operating under the name Han-Silver Bank.
    (C) For this reason, I thank you for joining our bank.
    (D) The website is easy to use.

15. (A) In short
    (B) However
    (C) For instance
    (D) Therefore

16. (A) policies
    (B) staff
    (C) locations
    (D) offers

PART 7

다이렉트 700+

Chapter 1. 문제 유형

Chapter 2. 지문 유형

Chapter 3. 다중 지문 유형

PART 7 기본 문제 풀이 전략

이것만 알면 700+

전략 1 꼭 알아야 하는 독해 전략

1. 문서 유형별 작성 순서를 알아야 합니다.
업무용 문서는 유형에 따라 어느 정도 정해진 작성 순서와 방법이 있습니다. **문서 유형별 작성 순서를 이해**하고 있으면 **지문에서 문제와 보기의 키워드를 더 쉽고 빠르게 찾을 수 있습니다.**

2. 스키밍(skimming) & 스캐닝(scanning)을 이용해서 시간을 단축할 수 있습니다.
지문과 문제의 키워드 내용을 스키밍(skimming)과 스캐닝(scanning)을 이용해서 빠르게 검색하는 스킬이 필요합니다. 스키밍이란 전체 지문을 모두 읽고 이해하는 것이 아니라 20~30초 내로 지문을 빠르게 훑어보면서 주요 정보들을 확보하는 것입니다. 스캐닝은 문제의 키워드를 본문에서 빠르게 찾아내는 것을 의미합니다. 문서 유형별 작성 순서를 알고 스키밍과 스캐닝을 이용하면 효과가 배가 됩니다.

3. 오답을 소거해야 합니다.
정답을 찾는 것뿐만 아니라 오답을 소거하는 것도 중요합니다. 지문의 내용을 약간만 변형한 오답 보기가 등장하기 때문에, 보기의 키워드가 지문에 언급됐다고 바로 정답으로 선택하면 오답일 수 있습니다. 보기의 내용을 꼼꼼하게 확인하고 오답을 소거해야 오답을 선택하는 실수를 피할 수 있습니다.

4. 패러프레이징을 예상해야 합니다.
지문에서 구체적으로 언급된 내용이 정답에서는 포괄적인 표현으로 제시됩니다. 따라서 지문과 보기의 내용을 의미 중심으로 파악해야지 동일한 단어만 찾으면 안 됩니다.

5. 문제 유형별로 다른 전략으로 접근해야 합니다.
무조건 지문을 읽고 답을 찾으려 하지 말고 먼저 시험에 나오는 문제 유형별 풀이 전략을 학습하는 것이 효율적입니다. 따라서 시험에 출제되는 문제 유형별 스킬과 정확한 풀이 훈련이 중요합니다.

전략 2 PART 7 4대 원칙

원칙 ① 정답의 단서는 문제 순서대로 지문에 배치됩니다.

원칙 ② 문제를 먼저 분석한 후에 지문에서 단서를 찾습니다.

원칙 ③ 지문에서는 구체적으로 언급되고, 정답은 포괄적인 표현으로 제시됩니다.

원칙 ④ 보기의 오답들은 한 단어씩 오류를 숨기고 있습니다.

PART 7은 이렇게 풀어야 해요.

지문을 읽기 전에 먼저 문제 및 보기의 키워드를 확인하고, 스키밍(skimming)과 스캐닝(scanning)을 활용하여 지문을 파악합니다. 지문과 보기를 대조하여 최종적으로 정답을 선택합니다.

Step 1. 문제 및 보기 키워드 확인

Step 2. 지문 스키밍(skimming) & 스캐닝(scanning)

Step 3. 지문과 보기 대조 및 정답 선택

Chapter 1 문제 유형

Point 01 주제/목적을 묻는 문제

출제 포인트 정리

글의 주제/목적을 묻는 문제는 PART 7에서 가장 자주 등장하는 문제입니다.

❶ 주제/목적을 묻는 문제 유형

What is the purpose of the letter? 이 편지의 목적은 무엇인가?
Why did Mr. Brad write this announcement? 브래드 씨는 왜 이 공지를 썼는가?
What is the information about? 이 정보는 무엇에 관한 것인가?
What is the coupon for? 이 쿠폰은 무엇에 사용하는 것인가?

❷ 글의 주제나 목적은 대부분(90%) 처음 2~3줄에서 확인할 수 있어요. 나머지(10%)는 후반부 요구 사항이 언급되는 곳에서 알 수 있습니다.

To: Andy Washington <awashington@demountservices.com>
From: Tyler Linden <tylerlinden@ursulacorp.com>
Date: June 7
Subject: Regards to Invoice

Dear Mr. Washington,

I am writing this e-mail to point out an error on the invoice I received today for the floor care services done at Ursula Incorporated. The invoice number is 551328. It seems that you overcharged us by the amount of $80.00. The 15´ X 22´ area was scheduled to be treated like all other floors on the 29th, but the room was occupied when the workers were here. I asked the repair personnel to tell all workers to delay the date for cleaning the room to another date. Please send me a revised invoice for the service we received in May so that we can make the payment right away.

STEP 2 주제나 목적은 지문의 전반부 확인

글의 주제나 목적은 대부분 지문의 도입부에서 알 수 있습니다. 여기서도 I am writing ~ 이하에서 목적을 확인할 수 있습니다.

What is the purpose of the e-mail?

(A) To **dispute** a **charge** on a **bill**
(B) To **request** that a carpet be **repaired**
(C) To **complain** that a work crew **arrived late**
(D) To **ask** for a **discount** on future services

STEP 1 문제 파악 및 키워드 확인

이메일의 목적을 묻는 문제입니다. 각 보기의 키워드를 확인합니다.

STEP 3 지문의 내용과 문제의 보기들 확인

지문의 전반부에 송장(invoice → bill)의 오류를 지적하기 위해(point out → dispute) 이 이메일을 보낸다고 한 것에서 송장의 잘못된 점을 논하기 위해 메일을 쓴 것임을 확인할 수 있습니다. 그러므로 정답은 (A)입니다.

Check-up Test 700+를 위해 한 걸음 한 걸음

정답 및 해석 p.073

STEP 1 단서가 제시되는 위치에 주의하여 문제를 풀어보세요.

1. 메모의 목적을 알 수 있는 문장을 ⓐ~ⓓ에서 찾고, 정답을 고르세요.

> Dear All Employees,
>
> ⓐ I would like to inform you that Janet Clarence has been summoned to our Chelsea branch as the director of human resources. ⓑ Before her transfer to England, Ms. Clarence had been the acting assistant director of human resources in KTBM's Athens branch for two years. ⓒ She has given a promising performance there where she developed and implemented more efficient recruitment procedures which are currently used in all KTBM branches. ⓓ Also, she managed to create an employee development program that enabled our organization to simplify the job-training process for new employees.

(A) To introduce an employee (B) To announce a policy change

STEP 2 지문을 읽고 문제를 풀어보세요.

Question 2 refers to the following e-mail.

From: Maria Petrovsky <mariapetro@onlineshop.com>
To: Customer service staff <undisclosed recipients>
Subject: Handling customer e-mails
Date: January 7

Many of our customers are sending e-mails rather than corresponding by phone these days. So we are going to standardize a format for replying to customer e-mails. You must remember the following guidelines:

- Don't forget the subject line. You should put a summarization of the message here. Also, you must include your customer service ID number. It will help us to identify each case.
- Before you send the e-mail, please check for spelling mistakes.
- Our company logo should be in the beginning of the e-mail. If you don't know how to attach the logo, ask your supervisor.

Maria Petrovsky
Customer Service Supervisor

2. What is the purpose of the e-mail?
 (A) To request customer addresses
 (B) To inquire about employee e-mail use
 (C) To describe ideal customer service calls
 (D) To provide guidelines for responding

Point 02 발신자와 수신자에 관한 정보를 묻는 문제

출제 포인트 정리

문서의 발신자 혹은 수신자의 업무나 직업, 업종 등을 묻는 문제입니다. 특정 서식에서 등장하는 수신인 및 발신인에 대한 정보와 질문의 키워드로 등장한 사람 또는 회사의 이름을 지문에서 찾아 관련 업무나 업종을 확인해야 합니다.

❶ 발신자와 수신자에 관한 정보를 묻는 문제 유형

Who is this notice from? 누가 이 공지를 작성했는가?
For whom is the letter intended? 이 편지는 누구를 대상으로 쓰여졌는가?
What type of company produced this flyer? 어떤 종류의 회사가 이 전단을 제작했는가?
Who most likely is Mr. Kang? 강 씨는 누구일 것 같은가?

❷ 발신자(= I/We), 수신자(= You), 제3자를 확인합니다.

To: Dan Cole
From: Ingrid Stiller *(= I/We)*
Date: June 2
Subject: June 10 Installation

Dear Dr. Cole, *(= You)*

As we discussed during the meeting a few days ago, all medical centers need a reliable power source. I believe that our solar panel system could provide you with a superior energy source. In fact, you will realize that it is more cost-efficient and at the same time environmentally friendly. I would also like to mention that we are going to install the system during off hours, so you won't have to expect any inconvenience.

Yours sincerely,

Ingrid Stiller *(= I/We)*
Sales Director

STEP 2 이메일 발신자 및 서명 확인
이메일 상단의 From과, 맨 아래 서명을 확인합니다. 스틸러 씨가 이메일의 '발신자'임을 알 수 있습니다.

STEP 3 발신자와 관련된 정보 확인
이메일의 발신자와 관련된 정보는 I/We가 포함된 문장에서 찾습니다. I/We가 포함된 문장에서 발신자가 일하는 업체의 종류를 확인합니다.

For what type of business does **Ms. Stiller** most likely **work**?

(A) A **maintenance** service
(B) An **energy** company
(C) A **medical** staffing firm
(D) An **Internet** service provider

STEP 1 문제 파악 및 키워드 확인
스틸러 씨가 일하는 업체의 종류를 묻는 문제입니다.

STEP 4 지문의 내용과 문제의 보기들 확인
두 번째 줄 I believe that our solar panel system could provide you with a superior energy source(저희의 태양열 패널 시스템이 보다 우수한 에너지 공급원이 될 것이라고 생각합니다)에서 발신인이 에너지를 공급하는 회사에서 근무한다는 것을 확인할 수 있습니다. 따라서 (B)가 정답입니다.

Check-up Test 700+를 위해 한 걸음 한 걸음

정답 및 해석 p.073

STEP 1 단서가 제시되는 위치에 주의하여 문제를 풀어보세요.

1. A Happy Home이라는 업체가 어떤 일을 하는지 알 수 있는 문장을 ⓐ~ⓓ에서 찾고, 정답을 고르세요.

A Happy Home
Invites you
ⓐ To Spoil Your Family

- ⓑ Let us help you redesign your home, add space, and feel great!
- ⓒ Redecorate every room with the newest fashions.
- Our specialists help you coordinate your wallpaper, carpet, and furniture.
- Prices as low as $500 per room and 20% off for 3 or more rooms.
- ⓓ You don't want to leave your home? Don't worry, we'll come to you.
- All the work is done by A Happy Home; you don't have to lift a finger!

This Month's Special
Order a total home makeover and we'll give you a brand-new
Closet Organizer FREE!

3273 Tulsa Rd. Jacksonville, 10723, 806-786-9844

(A) A renovation agency (B) A real estate agency

STEP 2 지문을 읽고 문제를 풀어보세요.

Question 2 refers to the following notice.

Upon entry to Indonesia, each adult is allowed to bring in, tax-free, a maximum of one liter of alcoholic beverages and either 200 cigarettes, 50 cigars, or 100 grams of leaf tobacco. Cameras, video cameras, portable radios, cassette recorders, binoculars and sport equipment are admitted provided they are taken out of the country upon departure. They must be declared. Prohibited are firearms, Chinese printing and medicines, transceivers and cordless telephones. Films, pre-recorded video tapes, and laser disks must be screened by the Censor Board. There is no restriction on the movement of foreign currencies or travelers checks in and out of the country. However, the import and export of Indonesian hard currency exceeding Rp. 5 million is prohibited.

2. Who is this notice intended for?
    (A) Tourists
    (B) Government officials
    (C) Security personnel
    (D) Airport screeners

Point 03 구체적인 정보를 묻는 문제

출제 포인트 정리

언제, 어디서, 무엇을 등과 같은 구체적인 사항을 묻는 문제는 문제에 등장한 키워드를 지문에서 찾아서 보기와 비교해야 합니다.

❶ 구체적인 정보를 묻는 문제 유형

What event will be held on Thursday? 목요일에 어떤 행사가 열릴 것인가?
When was the seminar originally scheduled to be held? 세미나는 원래 언제 열릴 예정이었나?
For what has Garden Mart received awards? 가든 마트는 무엇 때문에 상 받았는가?

❷ 질문의 키워드를 파악하고 어디서 나올 만한 내용인지 확인하세요. 키워드와 동일한 어휘가 등장하기보다는 보통 패러프레이징되어 등장합니다.

February 24

Kolstad Norway
Customer Service Department

Dear Customer Service,

Last year on August 5, I bought a Kolstad refrigerator, the Z-501. As you are all aware, the product normally comes with a one-year limited warranty.

About two weeks ago, the refrigerator seemed to be making a strange noise, so I called in a technician on February 12 (invoice: 553NM9). The technician was able to find some flaws with the compressor and stated that parts needed to be replaced. The repair was promised to be completed in under five days, but it ended up taking ten days. As a result, approximately $200 worth of food has spoiled. On top of that, I received a bill yesterday requesting payment for the cost of the compressor and labor.

As far as I am concerned, the one-year limited warranty includes both parts and labor. Not only should the bill be canceled, but I believe that Kolstad must also be responsible for the food waste caused by late repairs. Please respond immediately upon receiving this mail.

Sincerely,
Miriam Pecker

STEP 2 키워드와 시간이 나오는 곳 확인
문제의 키워드와 보기의 시간이 나오는 곳을 확인합니다. 키워드는 유사한 의미의 다른 말로 패러프레이징되어 나올 수 있습니다.

When did Ms. Pecker request repairs on her refrigerator?

(A) On February 10
(B) **On February 12**
(C) On February 24
(D) On March 2

STEP 1 문제 파악
페커 씨가 냉장고 수리를 요청한 날을 묻는 문제입니다.

STEP 3 지문과 대조하여 정답 선택
이메일의 두 번째 단락 About two weeks ago, the refrigerator seemed ~에서 이상한 소리가 나서 2월 12일에 기술자를 불러 수리를 요청했다고 언급하였으므로 (B)가 정답입니다.

Check-up Test 700+를 위해 한 걸음 한 걸음

정답 및 해설 p.074

STEP 1 단서가 제시되는 위치에 주의하여 문제를 풀어보세요.

1. 업무 경력(work experience) 작성에 대한 강연을 진행하는 사람이 누구인지 알 수 있는 부분을 ⓐ~ⓓ에서 찾고, 정답을 고르세요.

Job fair
We wish that everyone can join SIT's (Seymore Institute of Technology) fifth annual job fair workshop!

This year's featured presentations and lectures are as follows:

10:15 A.M. ~ 11:30 A.M.	ⓐ Session 1: "Slowly Building Your Career from Day 1"	Lana Apples Codirector. SIT Career Development Team
11:30 A.M. ~ 12:30 P.M.	ⓑ Session 2: "For a Perfect Résumé and Cover Letter"	Jacob Grant Codirector. SIT Career Development Team
12:30 P.M. ~ 1:30 P.M.	ⓒ Session 3: "Tips for Successful Interviews"	Philip Nunez (guest lecturer) Professor of Business Communications, Waters School of Business
2:30 P.M. ~ 4:00 P.M.	ⓓ Session 4: "Where Are Your Sources?"	Sabrina Keys CEO, Truman&Bach Corp.

As with our previous workshops, this year's job fair is free.
A light meal will be served between Session 3 and Session 4.

(A) Lana Apples   (B) Jacob Grant   (C) Philip Nunez   (D) Sabrina Keys

STEP 2 지문을 읽고 문제를 풀어보세요.

Question 2 refers to the following notice.

Daily Tech
The Most Reliable Tech News Source

Dear Subscribers,

Today, we have an exciting announcement! Beginning next week, you will find "Eureka!", a brand new insert, in your newspaper every Monday. This new section will have unique and fun features and useful information previously found in other sections – puzzles, technology news, CEO interviews, and much more. Besides, you can see our popular technology column by Carlos Gutierrez and product reviews by Frederick Mann, whom you have selected as the Best Reviewer for 2 years in a row. You will also find our new advice column by the state's leading business consultant, Michael Alushin.

"Eureka!" will also appear on the Tech and Net website next week. Eureka! on the Web™ will also feature a new user-access area where you will be able to post comments, community announcements, and even photographs online. Check out http://www.dailytech.com/eureka next Monday, March 13.

2. Who just started writing a new column?
    (A) Carlos Gutierrez   (B) Frederick Mann   (C) Michael Alushin   (D) Paul Borelli

Point 04 미래 상황 또는 요청/당부/제안/방법을 묻는 문제

출제 포인트 정리

어떤 다음 행동을 제시했는지, 혹은 특정 행위를 위한 수단이나 방법이 무엇인지를 묻는 문제입니다.

❶ 미래 상황 또는 요청/당부/제안/방법을 묻는 문제 유형

What **does** Mr. Long **suggest that** Ms. Kim **do**? 롱 씨는 김 씨가 무엇을 하도록 제안하는가?
How **should an** application **be** submitted? 신청서는 어떻게 제출되어야 하는가?
What **does** Mr. Blake **tell** Ms. Coach **to do**? 블레이크 씨는 코치 씨에게 어떻게 하라고 말하는가?
According to the information, what **will happen on** December 11? 정보에 따르면, 12월 11일에 무슨 일이 일어날 것인가?

❷ 미래 상황 및 요구 관련 문제는 지문의 후반부에 정답이 있습니다.

❸ 미래 상황을 묻는 문제는 보통 구체적인 시간 부사어구를 동반합니다.

Best Sales Employee Awards Ceremony

Join us on this wonderful evening to honor an outstanding salesperson of Wingslide Motors. We are pleased to announce Megan Buchner as this year's Best Sales Employee. She recorded the highest in sales and her overall contribution and dedication to our company has been noteworthy.

Sunday, December 7
Hotel Baroque, 115 Antiga Road

Dinner will begin at 6:30 P.M.
Award ceremony will begin at 8:00 P.M.

To put your name on the list, please e-mail our marketing director Jenna Paxon at jenpaxon@wingslidemotors.com no later than November 17. After confirming your participation, Ms. Paxon will send you free tickets via mail.

STEP 2 지문의 후반부 확인

요청 사항은 대개 글의 후반부에 위치하므로 후반부에서 관련 표현을 찾습니다. 'Please + 동사 원형'은 상대방에게 부탁이나 요청을 할 때 쓰는 빈출 표현입니다.

What should recipients **do to attend** the event?

(A) Purchase **tickets** by December 7
(B) Visit the company's **website**
(C) **Contact** a **hotel** staff member
(D) **E-mail** a company **employee**

STEP 1 문제 파악 및 키워드 확인
초대장을 받은 사람이 요청받은 사항을 묻는 문제입니다.

STEP 3 지문의 내용과 문제의 보기들 확인
지문의 후반부에 list에 이름을 올리기(참석 신청) 위해서는 마케팅 부장에게 이메일을 보내라고 언급되어 있으므로 (D)가 정답입니다.
our marketing director → a company employee

Check-up Test 700+를 위해 한 걸음 한 걸음

정답 및 해석 p.075

STEP 1 단서가 제시되는 위치에 주의하여 문제를 풀어보세요.

1. 경매(auction)에서 생긴 수익금(money)은 어디에 쓰일 것인지(will be used) 알 수 있는 문장을 ⓐ~ⓓ에서 찾고, 정답을 고르세요.

> ⓐ Inaugurating a new tradition this year, the awards ceremony will be the main event at a gala to be held at the Dynasty Hotel on May 8. ⓑ The event includes a five-course meal, an auction, and the presentation of the awards. ⓒ Proceeds from the auction will be used to fund a new building and educational projects that will support our youth and our community. ⓓ If you have any question about this year's event, do not hesitate to contact me.
>
> Thank you for your cooperation.

(A) Local business initiatives
(B) Community enhancement programs

STEP 2 지문을 읽고 문제를 풀어보세요.

Question 2 refers to the following e-mail.

To	All Employees
From	Julian Amador
Subject	Farewell Banquet
Date	August 2

Dear Colleagues:

As you all know, Christopher Booth will be retiring from Km & G Inc. at the end of September. Christopher has been with Km & G for about 40 years. He started out in marketing in 1976, and 15 years later he moved to the sales department, where he worked for the next 20 years. His last 5 years as vice-president of the company have shown how much he will be missed.

We will be holding a formal farewell banquet at Figaro restaurant on October 15. Please contact me if you are able to attend. If you would like to contribute money towards a present for Christopher, please contact Don Johnson or Susan Boyles in the sales department.

Julian Amador

2. Who should staff members contact if they want to attend?
(A) Julian Amador
(B) Christopher Booth
(C) Don Johnson
(D) Susan Boyles

Point 05 Not-question 및 추론 문제

출제 포인트 정리

문제에 주로 (NOT) true, suggested, mentioned, indicated 등이 나오고, about이나 in 뒤에 키워드나 지문의 종류가 나옵니다. 먼저 보기의 내용을 한두 단어의 키워드로 정리한 뒤 지문의 내용을 각각의 보기와 비교해야 합니다.

❶ 추론 문제 유형

What is suggested about Red Star Hotel? 레드 스타 호텔에 대해 알 수 있는 것은 무엇인가?
What does the letter imply? 편지가 암시하는 것은 무엇인가?
What is indicated about the exhibition? 전시회에 대해서 나타내고 있는 것은 무엇인가?
What is NOT mentioned about Ms. Aoyama? 아오야마 씨에 대해 언급되지 않은 것은 무엇인가?

❷ Not-question 문제는 키워드를 확인한 후, 지문에서 보기의 내용을 찾아 언급된 내용을 오답으로 소거합니다.

HELP WANTED

Job Title: Front Desk Assistant
Working Hours: Full Time

Job description: This position is suitable for any individual who presents a kind, helpful, and (D) professional image. The main duties of a front desk assistant is to greet and register our guests, obtain payment information, and assign them to their rooms. One must also be responsible for (A) recording daily receipt logs and preparing checks and cash which need to be deposited at the bank. The ideal applicant is required to have completed basic courses in hospitality management. One must be (C) fluent in English and at least one Asian language. If you meet the conditions, please send your résumé and a cover letter to amandalogan@marshall.com. If you wish to speak directly to Ms. Logan about the position, please visit our office at 2200 Linden Drive at any time between 1 P.M. and 6 P.M., Monday to Friday. Our lines are usually busy handling customers, so do NOT call us, please.

STEP 2 지문에서 해당 내용을 찾아서 보기와 비교

지문에서 주로 '~을 해야 한다'고 표현되는 것이 자격 요건입니다. 자격 요건으로 언급된 것들을 찾아서 보기와 비교합니다.

What is NOT indicated as a requirement for the position?

(A) Knowing how to record **financial transactions**
(B) **Expertise** in **coordinating transportation**
(C) Ability to use **more than one language**
(D) Having a **businesslike appearance**

STEP 1 문제 파악 및 키워드 확인
자격 요건이 키워드이며, 자격 요건으로 언급되지 않은 것을 묻는 문제입니다. 보기의 키워드를 한두 단어로 정리합니다.

STEP 3 보기 중 지문에 언급된 내용을 소거하고 남은 답 선택
나머지는 조금씩 다르게 표현되어 언급되었지만, (B)의 transportation과 관련된 내용은 전혀 언급되지 않았으므로 (B)가 정답입니다.
(A) recording daily receipts logs → record financial transactions
(C) English and at least one Asian language → more than one language
(D) professional image → businesslike appearance

Check-up Test 700+를 위해 한 걸음 한 걸음

정답 및 해석 p.076

STEP 1 NOT에 주의하여 문제를 풀어보세요.

1. NCCA가 하는(support) 일(activity)이 아닌(NOT) 문장을 ⓐ~ⓓ에서 찾고 정답을 고르세요.

> August 12
>
> Dear family, friends, and colleagues:
>
> I am writing to inform you of a unique chance to help a worthwhile cause. I am participating in the 15th Annual Charity Run on Saturday, September 10th sponsored by the National Cross Country Association(NCCA). In preparation for the event, ⓐ I am jogging 17 kilometers three or four times a week. ⓑ The National Cross Country Association is a non-profit organization which helps runners develop safe and healthy exercise and dietary habits as well as train for endurance events. ⓒ We seek monetary and other donations to direct them to worthy causes all over the globe. ⓓ My local chapter is currently raising money to pay for vaccinations for children in impoverished regions.

(A) Training joggers   (B) Producing health videos

STEP 2 지문을 읽고 문제를 풀어보세요.

Question 2 refers to the following article.

> SHANGHAI, 19 May—Racing Cars, the sequel of a popular racing game by developer SEKA Games, was launched early this afternoon. Thousands of anticipated fans lined up in front of game stores early in the morning to purchase the game before it got sold out.
>
> The advertising strategy planned by SEKA Games itself turned out to be a success. It soon became a hot topic of discussion on the Internet, with fans eagerly awaiting its release. The new version of Racing Cars is not too different from the old version, but features updated versions of the vehicles as was requested by users. Many believed that Racing Cars would have trouble getting the spotlight, because most game brands rely on outside firms that focus on creating effective video game advertisements. In contrast, SEKA Games used its own marketing team who employed professional racers to appear on TV and online ads. Some of these celebrities also showed up at some of the stores to appeal to game players and racing fans.

2. What is suggested about SEKA Games?
  (A) Its headquarters is located in Shanghai.
  (B) It recently merged with another company.
  (C) Its products are more expensive than those of its competitors.
  (D) It pays attention to comments from its customers.

Point 06   동의어 문제

출제 포인트 정리

지문에 언급된 어휘와 의미가 가장 가까운 어휘를 고르는 문제입니다. 여러 보기의 의미를 모두 가지고 있는 다의어가 문제로 나오는 경우가 많으므로, 해당 문장이나 문맥 속에서 어떤 의미로 쓰였는지 파악해서 정답을 골라야 합니다.

❶ 동의어 문제 유형

> The word "located" in paragraph 3, line 4, is closest in meaning to:
> 세 번째 문단, 네 번째 줄의 단어 "located"와 의미가 가장 유사한 것은?
>
> In the letter, the word "astounded" in paragraph 1, line 3, is closest in meaning to:
> 편지에서 첫 번째 문단, 세 번째 줄의 단어 "astounded"와 의미가 가장 유사한 것은?

❷ 사전적 의미의 동의어가 아니라 본문에서의 문맥을 따져 대체할 수 있는 단어를 찾아야 합니다.

Dear Ms. Ginger,

I first want to thank you for giving me such a great tour of Classic Windsor Apartment Complex. The building itself was amazingly beautiful, the facilities seemed fairly new, and I especially liked its great location. I considered your recommendation of the room with the ocean view and extra storage space, but I decided to take the one with the balcony instead. I liked the fact that it had an outdoor, hardwood balcony that overlooks the park.

Given that my stay in Skippertown depends on the length of my overseas business, I have decided not to bring any of my furniture from Taipei since I don't think I will be staying here for a long period of time. It would be best if I could move in on the 14th of August. Once we arrange a time, I will stop by your office to complete the paperwork and sign up for a parking space. I will also have my deposit prepared as well.

John Madden

STEP 2 문장 내 의미 파악
질문에 명시된 위치에서 해당 단어가 나온 문장을 찾아서 그 단어가 문맥 속에서 어떤 의미로 쓰였는지 파악합니다.

In the e-mail, the word "overlooks" in paragraph 1, line 5, is closest in the meaning to:

(A) forgets about
(B) **provides a view of**
(C) gives an excuse for
(D) inspects the inside of

STEP 1 문제 파악: 단어 위치 확인
overlooks와 유사한 의미를 가진 단어를 찾는 문제입니다.

STEP 3 보기에서 유사한 의미로 쓰이는 단어 찾기
overlooks는 발코니에서 공원이 '내려다보인다'는 의미로 쓰인 것이므로, provides a view of가 대신 들어가도 같은 뜻이 됩니다. 따라서 (B)가 정답입니다.

Check-up Test 700+를 위해 한 걸음 한 걸음

정답 및 해설 p.076

STEP 1 주어진 단어의 의미에 주의하여 문제를 풀어보세요.

1. 다음의 밑줄 친 문장에서 case의 의미를 해석하고, 유사한 의미를 가진 단어를 고르세요.

Attention all passengers!

Thank you for riding with us today. In order to serve you better, the Central Park Station will undergo an upgrade. The construction will last from July 10 through August 12. During this period, some platforms may be closed. When this is the **case**, trains that normally stop at those platforms will stop elsewhere. Please listen to station announcements for your platforms or check the electronic schedule boards. Train arrival and departure times will remain the same.

Some self-ticketing machines and several exit gates will be closed as well. All stores and restaurants in the station will operate their regular hours. You can read about this renovation in the Metro Newsletter, which is available at the ticket office.

We apologize in advance for any inconvenience this construction will cause you.

Central Park Station Management

(A) situation (B) container

STEP 2 지문을 읽고 문제를 풀어보세요.

Question 2 refers to the following e-mail.

To: Isabella Gloria <bellegloria@elecmail.com>
From: Clark Liu <clarkliu@spectrum.com>
Date: May 23
Subject: Update

Dear Ms. Gloria,

I am with you on choosing brown and blue for your kitchen and bedrooms. However, I am a little worried about the choice you've made with your bathroom. Green is a typical color which most customers are not satisfied with long term. It would be better to reconsider and let me know again.

With the exception of #B51 Metallic Black, I could prepare all the other colors on your list. Magnifico has recently stopped producing that color. However, there is a similar color shade made by The Avant. The product number is #B106, so you might want to take a look at it. Also, to answer your question, the painting job should be able to start on June 5, and this will be more than enough time for the job to be completed before the 27th, leaving your apartment in good shape.

Best Regards,

Clark Liu, Color Counselor
Spectrum Interiors

2. In the e-mail, the word "shape" in paragraph 2, line 5, is closest in meaning to:
(A) pattern   (B) figure   (C) plan   (D) condition

Point 07   의도 파악 문제

출제 포인트 정리

의도 파악 문제는 주로 온라인 채팅 혹은 문자 메시지 지문에서 등장하며, 주어진 문장의 앞뒤 문맥을 통해 해당 표현이 어떤 의미인지 파악해야 합니다.

❶ 의도 파악 문제 유형

At 9:12 A.M., what does Mr. Adam mean when he writes, "None of your business"?
오전 9시 12분에 아담 씨가 "당신이 상관할 일이 아니에요"라고 썼을 때 의미하는 것은 무엇인가?

At 2:33 P.M., what most likely does Ms. Santos mean when she writes, "It's unbelievable"?
오후 2시 33분에 산토스 씨가 "믿을 수 없어요"라고 썼을 때 의미하는 것은 무엇일 것 같은가?

❷ 전체적인 상황을 포괄적으로 묘사하는 것이 정답입니다.

① 주어진 문장과 단순히 같은 의미의 답을 찾는 것이 아닙니다.
② 주어진 문장과 같은 의미인 보기는 오히려 오답입니다.
③ 지문에서 해당 문장의 앞뒤 문맥을 파악하고 포괄적인 답을 찾는 것이 관건입니다.

David Tucker [7:02 P.M.]:
Hi, Terry. I know you already left the office. But I have some questions I forgot to ask before my trip.

Terry Scott [7:04 P.M.]:
It's not a problem. How can I help you?

David Tucker [7:05 P.M.]:
I am here at Sydney Car Rentals, and they are asking about the insurance. Since it's my first trip for the company, I have no idea about our policy on this. Do I need to purchase insurance?

Terry Scott [7:08 P.M.]:
Absolutely, we need it before we rent a car.

STEP 2 문장 위치 파악
7:04 P.M. / Scott 질문에 명시된 위치를 파악해 지문에서 해당 문장을 찾습니다.

STEP 3 앞뒤 문맥에서 의미 파악
해당 문장의 앞뒤에서 내용이 연결될 수 있는 키워드를 찾고, 문맥 속에서 어떤 의미로 쓰였는지 파악합니다.

At 7:04 P.M., what does Mr. Scott mean when he writes, "It's not a problem"?

(A) He can get information easily on a company policy.
(B) He will go back to his office.
(C) He is willing to answer Mr. Tucker's questions.
(D) He advises Mr. Tucker not to buy insurance.

STEP 1 문제 파악
"It's not a problem."
"문제없어요." "문제되지 않아요"라는 말의 의미를 파악하는 문제입니다.

STEP 4 보기에서 전체적인 상황을 포괄적으로 묘사하는 정답 찾기
터커 씨가 출장을 가기 전에 확인해야 하는 사항을 물어보지 못했다고하자, 스콧 씨가 "It's not a problem(문제없어요)"이라는 말과 함께 무엇을 도와줄지(What can I help you?)를 묻고 있습니다. 즉, 스콧 씨는 터커 씨의 질문에 기꺼이 답해 주겠다는 의사를 보여주고 있는 것이므로 정답은 (C)입니다.

Check-up Test 700+를 위해 한 걸음 한 걸음

정답 및 해석 p.077

STEP 1 단서가 제시되는 위치에 주의하여 문제를 풀어보세요.

1. 다음의 메시지 대화에서 I know와 연결되는 키워드를 ⓐ~ⓓ에서 찾고, 다음 문제의 정답을 고르세요.

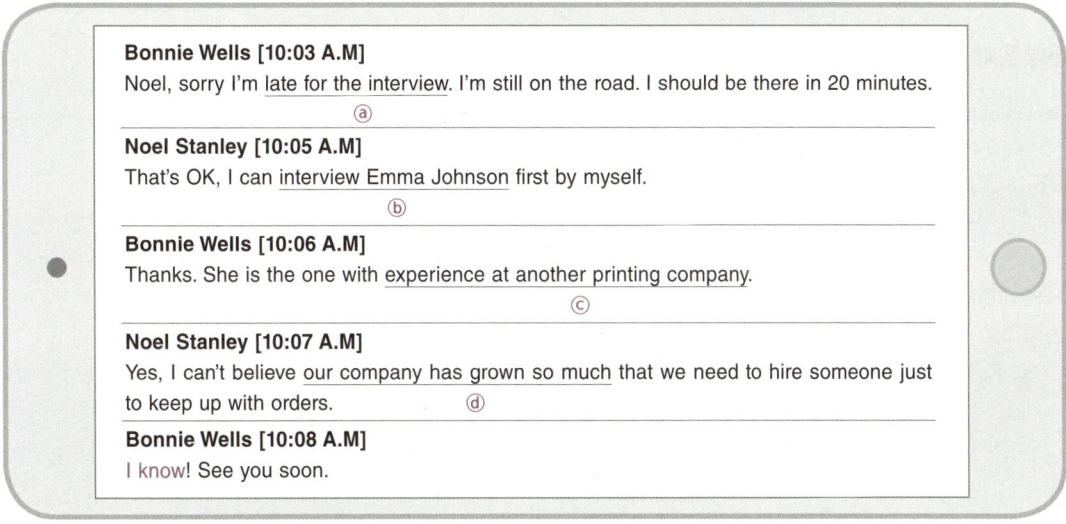

At 10:08 A.M., what does Ms. Wells mean when she writes, "I know"?

(A) She has met Mr. Stanley before.   (B) She is also surprised by the company's growth.

STEP 2 지문을 읽고 문제를 풀어보세요.

Question 2 refers to the following online chat discussion.

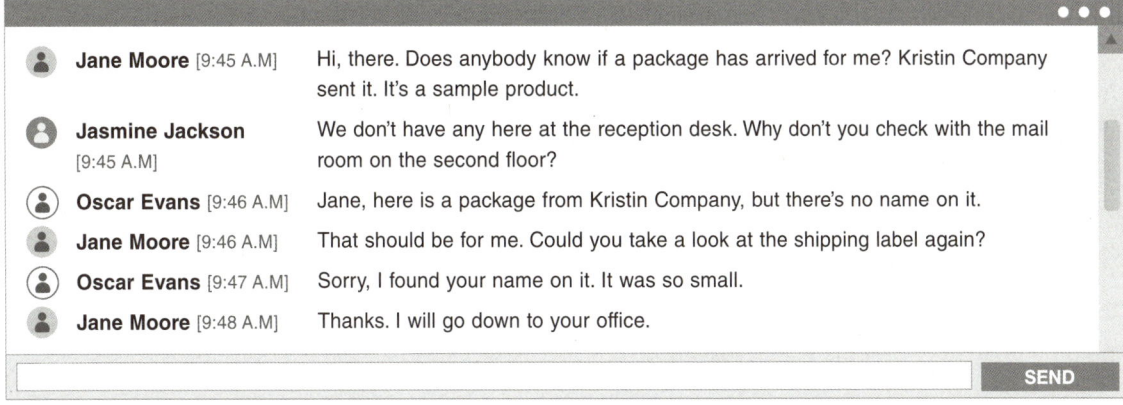

2. At 9:47 A.M., what does Mr. Evans most likely mean when he writes, "Sorry"?
   (A) He sent a package already.
   (B) He wants Ms. Moore to spell out her name.
   (C) He made a mistake reading a label.
   (D) He was late for a client meeting.

Point 08   문장 위치 찾기 문제

출제 포인트 정리

문장 위치 찾기 문제는 제시된 '문장(sentence)'이 들어가기에 가장 적절한 위치를 고르는 문제입니다. 문장이 들어가기 위해서는 해당 위치 앞뒤로 내용이 연결될 수 있는 연결어가 확보되는 것이 관건입니다.

❶ 문장 위치 찾기 문제 유형

In which of the positions marked [1], [2], [3], and [4] does the following sentence best belong?
"The lobby on the ground floor is going to be removed."
[1], [2], [3], [4]로 표시된 위치 중 다음 문장이 들어가기에 가장 적절한 곳은?
"1층에 있는 로비가 철거될 예정입니다."

❷ 앞뒤 내용을 연결해 주는 논리의 근거를 확보해야 합니다.

① 보기로 제시된 각 위치 앞뒤에서 해당 지시 형용사나 대명사가 지칭하는 것을 찾아서 연결해야 합니다.
② 접속사/전치사/부사/접속 부사 등과 같은 연결어들은 앞뒤 문맥의 연결 관계, 즉 추가, 역접, 대조, 인과, 순접 관계 등을 나타냅니다.
③ 주어진 문장의 키워드가 언급되어 있는 문단에 추가해야 합니다.

Pay Period and Time Sheet Policies

All checks will be posted by the 22nd of the next month for the pay period ending on the 15th of the current month. -[1]- For pay periods that end on the 23rd of the month, checks will be sent the next month on the 30th.

-[2]- In these cases, checks will be issued the day before. All full-time employees are required to register for direct deposit prior to the end of the pay period. -[3]-

Time Sheets
The following due dates have been set for all time sheets:
salaried monthly - last workday of each month
salaried biweekly - the 13th and 30th

Important!
Any employee who does not submit his/her time sheet by the deadline or who does not register for direct deposit will face a pay rollover. -[4]- There will be no exceptions to this policy.

STEP 2 단락별 내용 파악

STEP 3 보기 위치의 앞뒤 연결어 확인
[2] 뒤에 In these cases

In which of the positions marked [1], [2], [3], and [4] does the following sentence best belong?

"Exceptions will be made for pay periods that end on a holiday or over the long weekend."

(A) [1]   (B) [2]   (C) [3]   (D) [4]

STEP 1 문제 파악
"휴일 또는 긴 주말 동안에 만료되는 급여 산정 기간에 대해서는 예외가 있습니다."
pay period와 관련한 예외에 대한 내용이 언급될 위치를 찾아야 합니다.

STEP 4 보기 위치를 중심으로 단락별 키워드의 내용과 문맥 파악
첫 번째 단락은 pay period가 종료된 이후에 급여가 지급된다는 설명입니다. 두 번째 단락에서 In these cases(이런 경우에는)라는 특정 상황을 가정한 후 그 날짜보다 하루 전에 지급이 된다고 하고 있습니다. 따라서 these cases라고 지칭할 수 있는 상황이 앞에 제시되어야 하는데, 주어진 문장의 내용이 이 경우에 해당하는 것으로 볼 수 있습니다. 따라서 정답은 (B)가 됩니다.

Check-up Test 700+를 위해 한 걸음 한 걸음

정답 및 해설 p.078

STEP 1 단서가 제시되는 위치에 주의하여 문제를 풀어보세요.

1. 다음 문장에서 지문의 내용과 연결할 수 있는 단서를 ⓐ~ⓓ에서 찾고, 지문 속에 들어갈 위치를 고르세요.

"In addition, please let me know if you offer special packages for business travelers."
　　　ⓐ　　　　　　ⓑ　　　　　　　　　　ⓒ　　　　　　　　ⓓ

> To whom it may concern:
>
> In a few months, I will be traveling to China for an international textile industry conference, and I need a place to stay for several days in Shanghai. A couple of months ago a colleague of mine stayed at your hotel and highly recommended it to me. -[1]- Recently, when trying to access your website, I got a message saying that some of your facilities are being renovated. Fortunately, I came across this e-mail address in a travel magazine.
>
> I would like you to provide me with information about your room rates and availability. I plan to be in Shanghai from May 10 through May 13 and will require a single room during that period. -[2]-
>
> Thank you in advance for your information. I look forward to your response.
>
> Sincerely,
>
> Anita Olson

(A) [1]　　　　　(B) [2]

STEP 2 지문을 읽고 문제를 풀어보세요.

Question 2 refers to the following letter.

> Dear Ms. Coach,
>
> We have read the letter you sent us on the 11th. The production of Eco-100T has ended early this year. -[1]- However, we can still repair the appliance if you send it to us. Just make sure you put it in a package safely and securely since we are not responsible for unknown damages or lost packages. -[2]- After we receive your food processor, we will evaluate its condition and then one of our technicians will give you a call to discuss your repair options. If you wish to get it repaired, you will have to pay for the repair cost. -[3]- Once we receive your payment, we will then proceed with the repairs. In most cases, it usually takes us about two to three days to repair a defected machine, so you could receive your Eco-100T back within 10 days. -[4]- If you have any questions, please call our customer support or technical support representatives at 301) 225-2599.
>
> Sincerely,
>
> Nike Blake
> Service & Warranty Representative

2. In which of the positions marked [1], [2], [3], and [4] does the following sentence best belong?

"The cost is either payable by check or credit card."

(A) [1]　　　　(B) [2]　　　　(C) [3]　　　　(D) [4]

이것만 알면 700+

실전 문제 풀이 Tip 대공개! 이것만은 꼭 알아 두세요.

TIP 1 주제나 목적을 말하는 빈출 표현

I'm writing to ~. ~하기 위해서 글을 씁니다.
This letter/e-mail is to ~. ~하고자 이렇게 편지/이메일 드립니다.
in response to ~ ~에 대한 회신으로
Per your request, I'm sending ~. 귀하의 요청에 따라 ~을 보냅니다.
Thank you for ~. ~해 주셔서 감사합니다.
I've heard that ~. 저는 ~라는 얘기를 들었습니다.
I'm/My name is ~ and we're interested in ~. 저는 ~이고, ~에 대해 관심이 있습니다.
I'm pleased to let you know that ~. ~을 알려 드리게 되어 기쁩니다.

TIP 2 요청, 부탁, 당부, 제안 빈출 표현

Please let me know if you're interested in attending this event.
이 행사에 참석하는 데 관심이 있으면 알려 주세요.
You should/must/have to submit the application online. 온라인으로 신청서를 제출하셔야 합니다.
You are asked/requested/instructed/invited to arrive on time. 당신은 제시간에 도착해야 합니다.
Rearrange these files. 이 파일들을 다시 정리하세요.
Why don't you have your own garage? 당신만의 창고를 가지는 건 어떠세요?
We want/recommend/suggest/ask/require you to + 동사 원형 ~. 우리는 당신이 ~하실 것을 권합니다/요청합니다.

TIP 3 미래에 할 일이나 발생할 일을 나타내는 빈출 표현

Next is ~. 다음은 ~입니다.
We will/are going to ~. 우리는 ~할 것입니다.
Let's ~. ~을 합시다.
Contact the customer service manager by phone. 고객 서비스 직원에게 전화로 연락하세요.
Send an e-mail to ~. ~로 이메일을 보내주세요.
Furniture will be delivered on ~. 가구는 (언제) 배송될 예정입니다.
The renovation will take place between Monday and Friday.
보수 공사는 월요일에서 금요일까지 있을 것입니다.
be scheduled/planning/expected to ~. ~할 계획입니다.

TIP 4 빈출 패러프레이징

We have several interesting events coming up. 우리는 앞으로 재미있는 행사가 많이 있습니다.	→ It frequently hosts events. 행사를 자주 개최한다.
Thank you for your monetary contribution to Buketown Historical Society. 부크타운 역사학회에 보내 주신 기부금에 감사드립니다.	→ To acknowledge a donation 기부금을 받았음을 알리기 위해
We feel that your teaching experience will be a valuable addition to our school. 당신의 교습 경력이 우리 학교에 소중한 보탬이 될 것으로 생각합니다.	→ She has a lot of teaching experience. 그녀는 교습 경험이 많다.
I'm enclosing a brochure with photos of 50 of our most popular designs. 당사에서 가장 인기 있는 50가지 디자인의 사진이 실려 있는 소책자를 동봉합니다.	→ An illustrated booklet 그림이 있는 책자
Our online store will remain operational during this time. 우리의 온라인 매장은 이 기간 동안에 계속 운영될 것입니다.	→ It has products avaliable online. 온라인으로 판매하는 제품이 있다.
Please permit me to introduce myself and explain my qualifications. 저를 소개하고 제 자질에 대해 설명할 수 있도록 허락해 주십시오.	→ By requesting an interview with her 그녀와의 인터뷰를 요청함으로써

TIP 5 빈출 동의어

In order to expedite the check-in process when you arrive 도착했을 때, 체크인 수속을 빠르게 하기 위해서	→ speed up 속도를 높이다
According to the terms that follow 다음의 조건[조항]들에 따라서	→ conditions 조건
Our executive team worked tirelessly to secure an extension of the agreement. 우리 임원진은 계약 연장을 따내기 위해 줄기차게 일했습니다.	→ obtain 확보하다
Based on the reaction from people who attended this Friday's event 이번 금요일 행사에 참석했던 사람들로부터의 반응에 기초하여	→ response 반응
I would like to know if any changes in room assignment are warranted. 방 배정에 있어서 변경이 가능한지[보장되는지] 알고 싶습니다.	→ guaranteed 보장하다
Mr. Sato will assume responsibility for the company's marketing. 사토 씨는 회사의 마케팅 업무를 맡게 될 것입니다.	→ undertake 맡다
We maintain all of our equipment in ready-to-use condition. 우리는 장비를 모두 바로 사용할 수 있도록 유지합니다.	→ keep 유지하다

Chapter Test

Questions 1-3 refer to the following letter.

FR Kanon
8 Spring Gardens
London
SW1A 2BN

May 12

Allie Bowen
24 Sussex Place
London NW14SA

Dear Ms. Bowen,

Please find enclosed the MP3 Player you returned to us for repair under the terms of your warranty. We were unable to proceed with the repairs because of a violation of the terms of your warranty (attached).

Our technicians have found that the player has been disassembled by an unauthorized party to change its inner battery. Although the warranty covers incidental damage, wear and tear, and manufacturing defects, it does not cover "defects caused by modification or replacement of an item by any party other than a licensed manufacturer or authorized agent." A detailed report of these findings is also enclosed.

We recommend that you take your player to our local repair shop nearest you, where the repairs can be made at a flat cost of $25.

Thank you for your understanding and for choosing an MP3 player from FR Kanon.

Sincerely,

Evan Williams
Service Manager
Enclosures

---

1. What is the main purpose of the letter?
   (A) To give an estimate for a repair job
   (B) To thank a customer for a recent purchase
   (C) To explain why a request was not fulfilled
   (D) To request information about an MP3 player

2. What is NOT included with the letter?
   (A) A warranty
   (B) A findings report
   (C) An MP3 player
   (D) A refund

3. What is Ms. Bowen advised to do?
   (A) Visit a local repair shop
   (B) Purchase a new model
   (C) Register for an extended warranty
   (D) Call a FR Kanon representative

Questions 4-5 refer to the following online chat discussion.

	Marie Morgan (1:31 P.M.)	Hello, Mr. Nunez. How can I help you?
	Ralph Nunez (1:33 P.M.)	Hi, I've just received an e-mail confirming delivery of Alice's office supply order, but it has not arrived yet.
	Marie Morgan (1:34 P.M.)	I am sorry about that. Could you tell me your order number?
	Ralph Nunez (1:36 P.M.)	Let me see. It's NA-1009-5218.
	Marie Morgan (1:41 P.M.)	Thank you. I see that GoodPoint is a frequent customer. We appreciate your business. Our record shows that we sent that e-mail in error. Your order will be shipped this afternoon, so you should have it on Wednesday.
	Ralph Nunez (1:45 P.M.)	That explains it. I was surprised that the package would arrive this soon anyway. Thank you for your help.

4. What is suggested about GoodPoint?
   (A) It has changed its customer policies.
   (B) It is a delivery company.
   (C) It hired Mr. Morgan.
   (D) It has purchased from Alice before.

5. At 1:45 P.M., what does Mr. Nunez most likely mean when he writes, "That explains it"?
   (A) He missed an e-mail.
   (B) He can't remember the order number.
   (C) He found that an order had been changed.
   (D) He learned why he did not receive a package.

Questions 6-9 refer to the following advertisement.

You are invited to the grand opening of Cloverland Apartment this Friday, Saturday, and Sunday — September 23, 24, and 25 — to have a tour of one of the best residential complexes in town!

There will be guided tours of the complex on Friday from 5 P.M. to 7:30 P.M. and on Saturday and Sunday from 9 A.M. to 4 P.M. Plus, there will be a celebration for our Grand Opening on Saturday from 11 A.M. to 2 P.M. with refreshments, live bands, and door prizes.

So, come and have a good time as you walk around this beautiful apartment complex located on top of the hill overlooking Deep Creek Lake. There are several walking paths that take you to a lake where you can have a picnic, and there is a clubhouse right at the water's edge. The complex is so quiet that you will feel like you are out in the countryside, but you can go shopping, visit museums and enjoy city life in Montgomery's downtown within a few stops by train.

There are two, three, and four-bedroom apartments to choose from. All apartments contain spacious gourmet kitchens with top-of-the-line kitchen appliances. All floors are made of hardwood, and a storage room is optional. When you want to eat out, you can enjoy fine dining at Martin's, Cloverland's on-site restaurant. Martin's is open 24 hours a day, seven days a week.

You have an option of leasing these beautiful apartments for either one or two years. If you lease before September 30th, you will receive a $250 prize!

If you are interested in Cloverland, and want more information, please visit our website at www.cloverland.org.

6. What is being advertised?
   (A) The expansion of a city park
   (B) A tour of a gallery
   (C) A new apartment complex
   (D) A kitchen supply store

7. The word "right" in paragraph 3, line 3, is closest in meaning to
   (A) exactly
   (B) correctly
   (C) inside
   (D) without delay

8. What is NOT listed as a feature of Cloverland?
   (A) Places to walk
   (B) Large kitchens
   (C) A swimming pool
   (D) A restaurant

9. What is offered to individuals who sign an agreement before September 30?
   (A) A discounted meal at Martin's
   (B) An invitation to a picnic
   (C) A ticket to a museum
   (D) A cash reward

Questions 10-13 refer to the following e-mail.

From: Anna Lim
To: Ben Wallace
Subject: Petersburg Information
Date: June 16

Dear Mr. Wallace,

For everyone who will be attending Newman's Solar Energy Conference, we have made a list of places worthy of seeing in Petersburg. Below are some of the locations we recommend you to pay a visit. -[1]-

- Near the bronze statue in the center of Petersburg, there is small road where the some historical buildings still stand. -[2]- This pub has a two-hundred-year long tradition, serving some exotic flavored foods. They serve one of the best hot dogs and burgers in town, so keep that in mind as well.

- If the weather's good, you must check out Edwin Greens Park. All you have to do is take a short bus ride from the hotel. This large park accommodates exciting events such as festivals and carnivals during the evenings, so you wouldn't want to miss them while you are here in Petersburg. -[3]-

- Stop by Orange Beach and take a walk on the boardwalk. There are many shops that sell unique items along the boardwalk, so you may want to try going shopping.

If you want to find out more about Petersburg, our tourist information center is only a few steps away from Open Valley Hotel where you are staying, so please stop by when you are free. -[4]-

Thank you.

Anna Lim
Town Promotor

10. Why is the e-mail written?
    (A) To update a meeting agenda
    (B) To inform about local attractions
    (C) To provide directions to the conference venue
    (D) To announce that an event has been canceled

11. What is indicated about Edwin Greens Park?
    (A) It is a shopping center.
    (B) It is the site of a bus station.
    (C) It is closed on rainy days.
    (D) It is close to the hotel.

12. What should Mr. Wallace do for additional information about Petersburg?
    (A) Attend a reception
    (B) Contact his supervisor
    (C) Visit a tourist information office
    (D) Purchase a guided tour

13. In which of the positions marked [1], [2], [3], and [4] does the following sentence best belong?

    "Of these old buildings, there is an old pub called Brown Jugs."

    (A) [1]   (B) [2]   (C) [3]   (D) [4]

Chapter 2 지문 유형

Point 01 이메일 및 편지(E-mail & Letter)

출제 포인트 정리

토익에 등장하는 이메일/편지/팩스는 일상 업무에서 발생할 수 있는 사건들을 주제로 다루며, 회사와 특정 개인이나 고객, 또는 회사와 회사 간의 서신이 주를 이룹니다.

▶ **이메일 및 편지 유형에서 꼭 나오는 빈출 질문**

1) 메시지가 발송된 목적 혹은 주제를 묻는 질문
   Why was the letter written? 이 편지는 왜 작성되었는가?
2) 발신/수신인과 관련된 정보를 묻는 질문
   For what department does Nadine work? 내딘은 어떤 부서에서 근무하고 있는가?
3) 구체적인 정보(키워드)를 묻는 질문
   What is attached to the e-mail? 이 이메일에 첨부된 것은 무엇인가?
4) 요청, 제안, 수단, 방법을 묻는 질문
   What does Mr. Rawlings suggest that Ms. Larson do? 롤링스 씨는 라슨 씨에게 무엇을 하라고 제안하는가?

❶ 이메일과 편지의 전형적인 흐름을 반드시 알아 둡니다.
❷ 보낸 사람과 받는 사람의 정보를 확인합니다.
❸ 지문의 첫 단락 처음 1~2줄에서 주제와 목적을 확인합니다.
❹ 제안이나 요청, 당부의 내용은 지문의 후반부를 확인합니다.

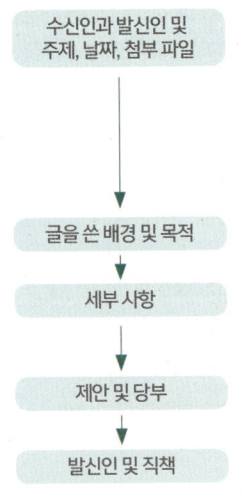

수신: 영업부 전 직원
발신: 니나 바스케즈 <ninavasquez@tnbcompany.com>
날짜: 4월 17일 수요일
제목: 직원 안내서
첨부: 중요 업데이트

직원들에게

T&B사 직원 안내서가 수정되었습니다. 수정된 정보는 직원 홈페이지에 게시되어 있습니다. 모든 정보를 확인하시려면, '직원 안내'를 클릭하세요. 또한 이 이메일에 해당 문서 파일을 첨부하였습니다. 시간을 내어 그 파일을 검토하시고, 최근에 변경된 사항들이 포함되어 있으니 강조 표시된 부분에 초점을 맞추실 것을 모든 직원들께 조언드립니다.

다음 주 금요일 회의에서, 저와 인사부의 라이츠 씨가 영업부에 영향을 줄 수 있는 모든 정책 변화에 대해 설명해 드릴 것입니다. 저희가 그 사항들을 상세히 설명한 후에, 여러분은 변화와 관련하여 질문을 하실 수 있으실 것입니다. 수정된 정책에 대해 더 알고 싶은 분은 직원 안내서를 가져가서, 본인의 상사와 이야기해 보실 것을 권합니다.

니나 바스케즈
판매부장

Check-up Test 700+를 위해 한 걸음 한 걸음

정답 및 해설 p.081

STEP 1 다음의 지문을 읽고 문제에 답하세요.

Questions 1-3 refer to the following e-mail.

To	All Employees of the Sales Department
From	Nina Vasquez <ninavasquez@tnbcompany.com>
Date	Wednesday, April 17
Subject	Employee Handbook
Attachment	Important Updates

Dear employees,

The T&B Company employee handbook has been revised. The updated information has been posted on the employee website. Click on "Staff Information" to view the entire information. Also, I have attached a file of the document in this e-mail. I advise all employees to spend some time reviewing the file and focusing on the highlighted areas, as they contain the recently made changes.

On next Friday's meeting, Ms. Lights from the human resources department and I will be addressing all changes to our policies that could affect the sales department. After we explain them in great detail, you may ask us any questions regarding the changes. If you wish to know more about the policy updates, we recommend that you take a copy of the handbook and consult your supervisors.

Thank you,

Nina Vasquez
Head Sales Manager, Sales Division

1. What is the purpose of the e-mail?
(A) To introduce a new human resources director
(B) To inform employees about updated regulations
(C) To ask employees to copy important documents
(D) To get some feedback about a redesigned website

2. According to the e-mail, what will happen next week?
(A) Information on the website will be updated.
(B) A new advertising campaign will be launched.
(C) A welcome reception will be held in the headquarters.
(D) Employees of the sales division will attend a meeting.

3. Why are recipients of the e-mail advised to contact their managers?
(A) To provide feedback on a presentation by Ms. Vasquez
(B) To set up a meeting with Ms. Lights
(C) To learn more about policy changes
(D) To obtain a copy of the handbook

Point 02 공지 및 메모(Notice & Memo)

출제 포인트 정리

특정 인물 또는 불특정 다수를 대상으로 정보를 알려 주기 위한 안내나 공지가 등장합니다. 사내 게시판이나 공공시설 또는 잡지, 신문에서 접할 수 있는 내용들이 주를 이룹니다.

▶ **공지나 메모 유형에서 꼭 나오는 빈출 질문**

1) 주제나 목적 또는 출처, 발신, 수신인을 묻는 질문

   What is the purpose of the event? 행사의 목적은 무엇인가?

   Where would the information most likely be found? 이 정보는 어디에서 볼 수 있을 것 같은가?

2) 공지 및 전달 사항과 관련한 구체적인 사실을 확인하는 문제

   What will happen on November 25? 11월 25일에는 무슨 일이 일어날 것인가?

   What problem does Frank mention? 프랭크는 무슨 문제를 언급하는가?

   What is suggested as a way to make equipment last longer? 장비의 수명을 연장할 수 있는 방법으로 제시되는 것은 무엇인가?

3) 추가적인 요청이나 당부 또는 제안 사항을 묻는 문제

   What are hotel employees instructed to do? 호텔 직원들은 무엇을 하라는 지시를 받는가?

   What are customers asked to do? 고객들은 무엇을 하라는 요청을 받는가?

❶ 공지나 메모는 제목에서 주제를 확인할 수 있습니다.
❷ 첫 단락에서 작성자와 공지를 받는 대상을 파악합니다.
❸ 단락별로 간략하게 어떤 내용인지 확인합니다.

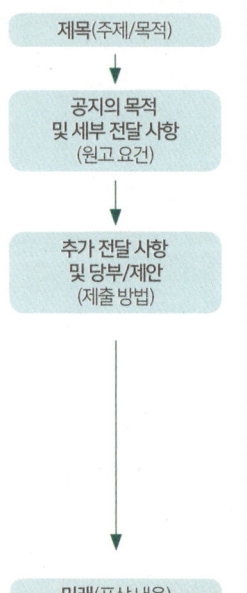

뮤직 인사이드
원고 제출 안내

<월간 뮤직 인사이드>에서 출간용 미청탁 원고를 받습니다. 저희의 스타일과 선호 사항에 부합할 수 있도록 여러분 모두 최신 호의 내용을 숙지할 것을 조언해 드립니다. 귀하의 원고는 이전에 다른 출판물에 사용된 적이 없으셔야 합니다. 원고는 모두 500에서 1,700자 사이로 작성되어야 하고, 행간은 한 줄씩 띄워 주셔야 합니다. 자필 원고는 심사 대상에서 제외된다는 점에 유의하여 주십시오.

원고는 전자 우편이나 보통 우편으로 보내실 수 있습니다. 선호하시는 연락 수단에 대한 정보를 포함하셨는지 반드시 확인해 주십시오. 어떠한 이유로든, 원고를 돌려받길 원하신다면, 원고를 보내실 때 우편 요금이 지불된 반송용 봉투를 동봉해 주셔야만 합니다. 저희는 보통 제출물에 대해 원고 수령 후 4주에서 6주 안에 응답을 드립니다. 아래 제시된 주소로 원고를 보내 주세요.

미국, 우편번호 47011
미시간 주 디트로이트 시
카렌턴 가 1557번지
월간 뮤직 인사이드
편집장 피터 라이언
이메일: peteryan@mgmonthly.com

원고가 채택된 분에게는 원고의 길이에 따라 400에서 1,000달러 사이의 원고료를 지불해 드릴 것입니다. 원고료는 원고가 채택된 후 5일 후에 당신의 계좌로 송금됩니다.

Check-up Test

STEP 1 다음의 지문을 읽고 문제에 답하세요.

Questions 1-3 refer to the following information.

The Music Inside
Submission Guidelines

Music Inside Monthly accepts unsolicited manuscripts for our publication. We advise all of you to become familiar with the contents from our latest issue in order to match our style and preference. Your manuscripts must not have been used in other publications before. They must all be between 500 and 1,700 words, and please make sure that they are double spaced. Please note that handwritten manuscripts will be exempt from consideration.

You can send in your manuscripts either by electronic or regular mail. Make sure you include information about your preferred means of contact. For any reason, should you need your manuscripts back, make sure you include a self-addressed pre-paid postage envelope when you submit your manuscripts. We usually respond to submissions within four to six weeks after receiving them. Please send your manuscripts to the address provided below:

Peter Ryan, Head Editor
Music Inside Monthly
1557 Carenton Road
Detroit MI, 47011
U.S.A
E-mail: peteryan@mgmonthly.com

Depending on the length of your manuscripts, accepted individuals will be paid between the amount of $400 and $1,000. Your payment will be transacted to your account five days after your manuscript is accepted.

1. What does the information suggest will help an author get a manuscript published?
  (A) Getting advance approval of an idea
  (B) Reading the most recent issue of the magazine
  (C) Writing on the suggested monthly theme
  (D) Writing a shorter article

2. What must be included with all submissions to *Music Inside Monthly*?
  (A) A cover letter listing previous publications
  (B) Details on how best to reach the author
  (C) A self-addressed, pre-paid postage envelope
  (D) Two copies of the manuscript

3. What is stated about manuscripts selected for publication?
  (A) They may have previously appeared in print.
  (B) They must be less than 1,500 words.
  (C) They are paid for based on length.
  (D) They will be published in the next issue.

Point 03 | 문자 메시지 및 온라인 채팅(Text Message & Online chatting)

출제 포인트 정리

토익에 등장하는 메시지 대화문에서는 여러 사람들이 함께 진행하고 있는 업무에 대한 내용이 자주 나옵니다. 문제 해결 혹은 일의 진행 상황 공유, 의견 취합 등의 내용이 주를 이룹니다.

▶ **문자 메시지와 온라인 채팅 유형에서 꼭 나오는 빈출 질문**

1) 메시지를 주고받는 목적 혹은 대화의 주제를 묻는 질문
   Why did Mr. Koh start the online chat discussion? 고 씨는 왜 온라인 채팅 대화를 시작했는가?
2) 대화 참여자와 관련된 정보를 묻는 질문
   Where most likely is Mr. Pascal? 파스칼 씨는 어디에 있을 것 같은가?
   Who most likely are the people writing on the message board? 전자 게시판에 글을 남기는 사람들은 누구일 것 같은가?
3) 구체적인 정보(키워드)를 묻는 질문
   What problem does Mr. Olinger mention? 올링거 씨는 어떤 문제를 언급하는가?
   What does Ms. Silva think about the new uniforms? 실바 씨는 새로운 유니폼에 대해서 어떻게 생각하는가?
4) 화자의 의도를 묻는 질문
   At 1:41 P.M., what does Ms. Kalla most likely mean when she writes, "Oh, no"?
   오후 1시 41분에, 칼라 씨가 "오, 안 돼요"라고 썼을 때 의미하는 것은 무엇인가?

❶ 처음 1~2번째 대화에서 주제를 확인할 수 있습니다.
❷ 등장인물들의 관계를 정리하세요.
❸ 화자의 의도 파악 문제는 앞뒤 내용을 파악하고 연결 키워드를 찾아야 합니다.
❹ 미래의 계획은 상대방 대사에서 권유/제안의 형태로 제시되기도 합니다.

해롤드 모리슨 [오전 10:00]
안녕하세요. 우리의 새로운 유니폼이 막 도착했어요. 여러분들의 유니폼을 가져가시면서, 어떻게 생각하시는지 말해 주세요.

조앤 누네즈 [오전 10:55]
와우, 스카프 대신 브로치가 있네요. 스카프는 쉽게 흘러내려서 승객들을 모실 때 방해가 되었거든요.

마리 케네디 [오전 11:13]
좋아요. 하지만 밝은 회색 블라우스는 거의 흰색처럼 보여요. 흰색은 쉽게 더러워지잖아요. 몇 년 전에 그것들 때문에 문제가 있었거든요. 기억하는 사람 있어요?

태미 로스 [오전 11:20]
저는 블라우스에 달린 멋진 칼라와 검은색 금속 단추가 마음에 드네요. 우리 회사 이미지하고 잘 맞아요.

조앤 누네즈 [오후 12:00]
저는 블라우스의 색이 좋다고 생각해요. 우리 현재 유니폼 색보다 더 나아요.

길버트 첸 [오후 12: 20]
저는 주머니가 달린 게 좋아요. 승객들을 모실 때 매우 유용할 거예요.

Check-up Test 700+를 위해 한 걸음 한 걸음

정답 및 해석 p.082

STEP 1 다음의 지문을 읽고 문제에 답하세요.

Questions 1-3 refer to the following electronic message board.

Harold Morrison [10:00 A.M.]
Hi, our new uniforms just arrived. When you take yours, tell me what you think.

Joan Nunez [10:55 A.M.]
Wow, we have a brooch instead of scarves. The scarves would easily slide down and get in the way when serving passengers.

Marie Kennedy [11:13 A.M.]
Good, but the light grey blouses look almost white. White gets dirty easily. We had a problem with those a couple of years ago. Does anyone remember that?

Tammy Ross [11:20 A.M.]
I like the fashionable collars and the black metal buttons on the blouses. They match our corporate image.

Joan Nunez [12:00 P.M.]
I think the color of the blouses is good. It's better than that of our current uniforms.

Gilbert Chen [12:20 P.M.]
I like that they come with pockets. They will be very useful when we are serving passengers.

---

1. Why did Mr. Morrison send the message?
   (A) To ask for some feedback
   (B) To report a problem
   (C) To announce an updated schedule
   (D) To confirm a policy change

2. At 11:13 A.M., what does Ms. Kennedy most likely mean when she writes, "Does anyone remember that?"
   (A) She prefers working in the air.
   (B) She likes the color white.
   (C) She agrees that a brooch is better.
   (D) She thinks the color will be a problem.

3. What does Mr. Chen think about the new uniforms?
   (A) He prefers their color.
   (B) He is happy that they have an addition.
   (C) He thinks they are too thin.
   (D) He likes that they are fashionable.

Point 04 광고(Advertisement)

출제 포인트 정리

광고는 상품이나 서비스 또는 회사를 홍보하는 광고와 직원이나 자원봉사자를 구하는 구인 광고가 출제되고 있습니다.

▶ 광고 유형에서 꼭 나오는 빈출 질문

1) 광고의 목적 또는 업종, 제품, 서비스 및 광고 대상을 묻는 질문

   What is the purpose of the advertisement? 이 광고의 목적은 무엇인가?
   What type of products does the company sell? 이 회사는 어떤 종류의 제품을 판매하는가?
   For whom is the advertisement intended? 이 광고의 대상은 누구인가?

2) 제품/서비스의 특징이나 장점, 할인 기간 또는 직책의 업무 내용, 자격 요건, 혜택 등 구체적인 정보를 묻는 질문

   What special service do they offer? 그들은 어떤 특별 서비스를 제공하는가?
   What is mentioned as a requirement for the position? 이 직책의 자격 요건으로 언급된 것은 무엇인가?
   What is NOT a stated duty of the floor manager? 현장 관리자의 업무로 언급된 것이 아닌 것은 무엇인가?

3) 회원 가입, 구매/지원 방법, 일정, 교통편 및 연락 정보를 묻는 질문

   How can customers receive a discount at Thomson's Food Market? 고객들은 톰슨 식품점에서 어떻게 할인을 받을 수 있는가?
   What can be found on the website? 웹사이트에서는 무엇을 볼 수 있는가?
   How can applicants apply for the position? 지원자들은 이 직책에 어떻게 지원할 수 있는가?
   By what date must an applicant submit an application? 지원자는 며칠까지 지원서를 제출해야 하는가?

❶ 상단의 제목이나 첫 번째 문장에서 업종이나 광고의 대상을 확인합니다.
❷ 단락별로 어떤 내용을 다루고 있는지 확인합니다.
❸ 광고가 사람들에게 무엇을 하라고 하는지 확인합니다.

광고 제목
(업체 이름 및 업종)
↓
회사/서비스 소개
↓
회사/서비스/제품의
특징과 장점
(자격 요건, 혜택, 업무 내용)
↓
연락 및 문의처

히스 로지
만족을 주는 품질

히스 로지는 분주한 뉴타운의 상업 지역 중심부에 위치해 있습니다. 10년 넘게 저희는 고객들에게 유동적인 회의 및 연회 장소, 세탁 서비스, 그리고 주요 공항 셔틀 서비스를 포함한 비할 데 없는 비즈니스 서비스를 제공해 왔습니다.

모든 고객들을 위해 저희는 다음과 같은 편의 시설을 완전 무료로 제공합니다.
- 와이파이 인터넷 연결
- 256개의 케이블 TV 채널
- 24시간 룸서비스 (아침 식사 포함)
- 구두 닦기 서비스
- 피트니스 시설 이용
- 신문이나 잡지 배달

히스 로지는 시내 및 주요 관광지와 단지 몇 블록 떨어진 곳에 있습니다. 뉴타운에서 즐겁게 지내실 수 있음을 보장합니다.

우편번호 61930
일리노이 주, 뉴타운 시
페전트 가 4890번지

연락 번호: (601) 0099-9911
www.heathlodge.com

Check-up Test 700+를 위해 한 걸음 한 걸음

정답 및 해석 p.082

STEP 1 다음의 지문을 읽고 문제에 답하세요.

Questions 1-2 refer to the following advertisement.

Heath Lodge
Quality to Satisfaction

Heath Lodge is located in the center of Newtown's busy business district. For more than ten years, we have been offering our guests incomparable business services which include flexible meeting and banquet space, laundry service, and shuttle service to major airports.

For all our guests, we offer the following amenities absolutely free.
- Wi-fi Internet connection
- Cable television with 256 channels
- 24-hour room service (breakfast included)
- Shoe polish service
- Use of the fitness facilities
- Newspaper or magazine delivery

Heath Lodge is only a few blocks away from downtown and major tourist attractions. We assure you a pleasant stay in Newtown!

4890 Peasant Road
Newtown IL, 61930

Contact Number: (601) 0099-9911
www.heathlodge.com

1. Where would the advertisement most likely be found?
(A) In a restaurant guide
(B) In a business magazine
(C) In a museum brochure
(D) In an art publication

2. What is NOT mentioned as a service which is free of charge?
(A) Internet access
(B) Newspaper delivery
(C) Airport transportation
(D) Television programing

Point 05 양식(Form)

출제 포인트 정리

각종 신청서(application)와 영수증(receipt) 또는 송장(invoice) 등이 자주 출제되는 양식입니다. 그밖에 여행 일정표(itinerary)를 포함한 각종 일정표(schedule)나 전화 메시지(message), 각종 리스트(list), 쿠폰(coupon, voucher), 명함(business card) 등도 자주 출제됩니다.

▶ **양식 유형에서 꼭 나오는 빈출 질문**

1) 목적(이유), 용도 또는 수신/발신인, 출처 등을 묻는 질문
   What service does Servelia Corporation provide? 서벨리아 주식회사는 어떤 서비스를 제공하는가?
   Why did Ms. Cohen complete the form? 코헨 씨는 왜 이 서류를 작성했는가?

2) 일정, 날짜, 금액, 수량 등의 구체적인 내용을 묻는 질문
   When does the Networking session end? 네트워킹 시간은 언제 끝나는가?
   How much will Mr. Lopez probably be charged? 로페즈 씨에게 얼마가 청구될 것인가?

3) 예외/부가 사항이나 수단/방법, 미래의 제안을 묻는 질문
   What restriction is placed on the coupon? 쿠폰에는 어떤 제한 사항이 있는가?
   What should Ms. Dunham do if she wants to attend the event? 던햄 씨가 그 행사에 참석하려면 어떻게 해야 하는가?

❶ 제목을 통해 어떤 용도의 서식인지 확인합니다.
❷ 작성된 부분의 내용을 꼼꼼히 확인합니다.
❸ 표나 서식 하단부에 있는 예외나 부가 설명을 확인합니다.

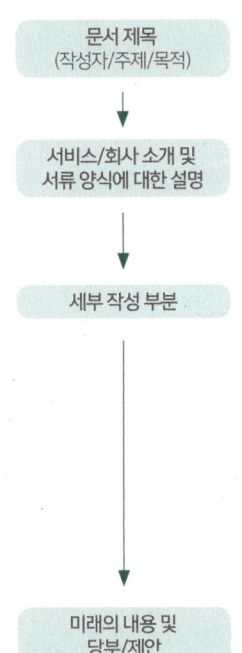

파이낸셜 타임즈
정기 구독 신청서

<파이낸셜 타임즈>는 세계 금융 시장에 대한 가장 풍부하고 새로운 정보를 제공해 드립니다. <파이낸셜 타임즈>는 수백만 명이 구독하는 명성이 높은 비즈니스 잡지이며, 귀하가 고객의 투자 자산에 대해 보다 정확한 판단을 할 수 있도록 도와드릴 것입니다.

매주, 수상 경력이 있는 이 잡지는 금융과 경제계의 전문가들이 작성한 기사와 칼럼을 특집으로 다룹니다. <파이낸셜 타임즈>는 항상 새로운 관련 소식들을 계속 알려 드릴 것입니다. 전화하셔서 <파이낸셜 타임즈>를 오늘 받으세요!

다음 중 하나를 선택하세요.
_____ <파이낸셜 타임즈> 2년 계약 (96회분)
        420.00달러 — 가판대 가격의 50% 할인
_____ <파이낸셜 타임즈> 1년 계약 (48회분)
        240.00달러 — 가판대 가격의 40% 할인
__✓__ <파이낸셜 타임즈> 6개월 (24회분)
        150.00달러 — 가판대 가격의 30% 할인

지불 방법:
(✓) 현금, (　) 수표, (　) 신용카드:

이 름: 그레고리 스틸
주 소: 우편번호 60603, 일리노이 주 시카고 시, 빌라 가 340번지

귀하의 첫 번째 잡지는 도착하는 데 3주에서 4주 정도 걸립니다.

Check-up Test

STEP 1 다음의 지문을 읽고 문제에 답하세요.

Questions 1-3 refer to the following form.

The Financial Times
Subscription Form

The Financial Times brings you the most ample, updated information about financial markets worldwide. *The Financial Times* is a highly regarded business magazine read by millions of people and it will help you to make more informed decisions about your client's investment portfolios.

Each week, this award-winning publication features articles and columns written by experts in the world of finance and economics. *The Financial Times* will always keep you informed with relevant updates. Please call and receive your *Financial Times* today!

Choose ONE of the following:

____ *The Financial Times* for TWO years (96 issues) for
$420.00 – a saving of 50% off the regular newsstand price

____ *The Financial Times* for ONE year (48 issues) for
$240.00 – a saving of 40% off the regular newsstand price

✓ *The Financial Times* for 6 months (24 issues) for
$150.00 – a saving of 30% off the regular newsstand price

Your Payment Method:
(✓) Cash, ( ) Check, ( ) Credit Card: _____

Name: Gregory Steel
Address: 340 Villa St. Chicago IL, 60603

Please allow three to four weeks for your first issue to arrive.

---

1. How often is *The Financial Times* published?
(A) Daily
(B) Weekly
(C) Monthly
(D) Annually

2. How much does a one-year subscription cost?
(A) $48.00
(B) $150.00
(C) $240.00
(D) $420.00

3. What is suggested about Gregory Steel?
(A) He is a financial advisor in Chicago.
(B) He has a subscription to *The Chicago Sun*.
(C) He has worked at Wolfgang & Brothers for three weeks.
(D) He writes a column in *The Financial Times*.

Point 06 기사(Article)

출제 포인트 정리

시각적으로 바로 파악할 수 있는 형식을 취하지는 않지만, 주제를 먼저 언급하는 전형적인 두괄식으로 주로 내용이 전개됩니다. 과거 사실로부터 미래 전망 등의 순으로 기승전결의 구조를 이룬다는 사실을 염두에 두고 문제를 풀어야 합니다.

▶ 기사 유형에서 꼭 나오는 빈출 질문

1) 기사의 주제나 배경을 묻는 질문

What does the article mainly discuss? 이 기사는 주로 무엇을 다루고 있는가?

In which section of a newspaper does the article most likely appear? 이 기사는 신문의 어떤 면에 나올 것 같은가?

2) 구체적인 사례나 일과 관련된 사실 여부를 확인하는 질문

Who is James Miller? 제임스 밀러는 누구인가?

According to the article, how long has Green Grocery been in business?
기사에 따르면, 그린 식품점은 얼마나 오래 사업을 하고 있는가?

What is suggested about PYL? PYL에 대해서 언급된 것은 무엇인가?

3) 미래 상황의 전망, 계획 또는 제안에 관한 질문

What does the article suggest will happen as a result of the project?
이 프로젝트의 결과로 일어날 것이라고 이 기사가 언급하고 있는 것은 무엇인가?

According to the article, how can people find out more about the product?
기사에 따르면, 사람들은 어떻게 해야 이 제품에 대해서 더 많이 알 수 있는가?

❶ 기사의 제목과 날짜를 확인합니다.
❷ 첫 단락 처음 1~2줄에서 기사의 주제나 대상을 확인할 수 있습니다.
❸ 문제에서 언급된 키워드는 단락별로 어느 위치에 있는지 확인해야 합니다.
❹ 미래의 전망이나 계획은 마지막 단락을 확인합니다.

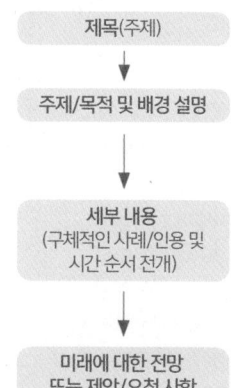

진정한 스페인을 맛보자

쇼핑객들이 '스페인'이라는 단어를 들으면 가장 먼저 떠올리는 것은 바르셀로나일 것입니다. 그러나 잠깐! 바르셀로나에서 멀지 않은 곳에서 당신은 스페인 최고의 쇼핑 지역을 찾을 수 있습니다. 바르셀로나 동쪽으로 차로 15분만 가면 아마도 가이드북에서 언급된 적 없는 도시인 타라고나에 도달할 수 있을 것입니다. 이 소도시에는 도자기, 보석, 모자, 그리고 목각 장식품과 같은 전통적인 지역 예술품들을 판매하는 상점이 30곳 이상 있습니다.

"타라고나는 전형적인 관광지는 아닙니다. 이곳의 상점들은 주로 지역 예술가들의 작품을 팔고 있죠"라고 에스파냐 보석점의 주인 후아나 게이츠는 말합니다. "여기에서 팔리는 물품들은 대부분 수작업으로 만든 것이어서 관광객들이 좋아하는 것 같습니다. 저는 이것이 타라고나를 스페인의 다른 도시와 구별되게 만드는 것이라고 생각합니다. 이것은 예술가들과 지역 업체 모두에게 정말 좋은 일입니다."

매년 5월, 타라고나 거리에서 5일간 비바 마나나 축제가 열린다는 것은 말할 것도 없습니다. 축제가 열리는 동안 예술가들은 거리를 따라 부스를 설치하여 공예품들을 파는데, 이국적인 스페인 음식과 음악이 곁들여집니다. 이 축제는 매년 인기를 더해가고 있어서 이 축제 기간에 타라고나에 방문하시려면 미리 계획을 짜두는 것이 현명합니다. 타라고나 지역 여관은 두 달 전에 미리 예약해야 합니다. 아니면 바르셀로나에는 호텔이 많이 있으니까 그곳으로 예약할 수 있습니다.

Check-up Test 700+를 위해 한 걸음 한 걸음

정답 및 해석 p.083

STEP 1 다음의 지문을 읽고 문제에 답하세요.

Questions 1-3 refer to the following article.

Enjoy Spain at Its Best

The first thing that pops up in the mind of shoppers when they hear the word "Spain" would be Barcelona. But wait! Not far from Barcelona, you can find some of the best shopping areas in Spain. A short, 15-minute drive to the east of Barcelona will get you to Taragona, a town which probably hasn't ever been mentioned in a guidebook. This small town has more than 30 shops that sell traditional local arts such as pottery, jewelry, hats, and wood carvings.

"Taragona is not your typical tourist attraction. The stores here feature work by local artists," says Joanna Gates, owner of Jewelry Espana. "Most of the items sold here are hand-made, and visitors seem to like that. This, I believe, is what distinguishes Taragona from other towns in Spain. It's really great for both the artists and for local businesses."

Not to mention that every May, the Viva Manana Festival is held for five days in the streets of Taragona. While the festival takes place, artists set up their booths along the streets to sell their goods accompanied by exotic Spanish food and music. This festival has been gaining popularity each year, so if you wish to visit Taragona during this time, it would be wise to plan ahead. For local inns in Taragona, you will want to reserve rooms two months earlier, or you could simply book a place in Barcelona since the city has numerous hotels to stay in.

1. What is the article mainly about?
 (A) The history of a town
 (B) Shopping opportunities in a town
 (C) The works of a local artist
 (D) Accommodations for tourists

2. According to the article, what is true about Taragona?
 (A) It is known for its charming inns and hotels.
 (B) It is accessible by train.
 (C) It is known for its scenic views.
 (D) It is near Barcelona.

3. What is NOT mentioned about the Viva Manana Festival?
 (A) It has been increasing in popularity.
 (B) It is free to the public.
 (C) It features musical entertainment.
 (D) It is held every year.

이것만 알면 700+

실전 문제 풀이 Tip 대공개! 이것만은 꼭 알아 두세요.

TIP 1 지문 유형별 빈출 내용

지문 유형	빈출 내용
이메일 및 편지 (E-mail & Letter)	❶ 요청 및 초대의 서신 [행사 참여 요청] 행사 참여, 연설 요청 [서류 검토 요청] 거래처에 서류상의 수정 사항 검토를 요청하는 팩스 [강연 초대] 특정 단체나 그룹에서 회원들을 강의나 모임에 초대하는 초대장 ❷ 고객에게 보내는 판매 홍보 서신 [판매 조건 제안] 대량 주문에 따른 가격 할인을 제안하는 편지 [홍보 서신] 독자들에게 새로 추가되는 부분에 대해 홍보하는 편지 ❸ 항의 및 환불, 사과의 서신 [부당 요금 항의] 고객이 잘못 청구된 요금에 대해 항의하거나 수정을 요청하는 편지 [환불 요청] 구매 제품의 하자로 인한 환불을 요청하는 고객의 편지 [업무 지연 사과] 배송 지연에 대해 사과하는 이메일
공지 및 메모 (Notice & Memo)	❶ 사내 안내 공지 [사내 공지] 복장 규정, 사무용품 절약, 장비 사용 등에 대한 회사 정책이나 수칙 공지 [사용법에 대한 정보] 장비나 기구의 올바른 사용법에 관한 공지 [자원봉사자 모집] 특정 행사에 지원을 나가거나 자원봉사에 참여할 사람들을 모집하는 공지 ❷ 관광 및 여행, 레저와 관련된 시설 이용 안내 [숙박 시설 이용 안내] 호텔 등의 숙박 업소 및 이용 가능한 시설 안내 [관광 및 여행 관련 공지] 박물관이나 미술관에서 일정이나 주의 사항 등을 알리는 공지 [안전 수칙 및 주의 사항] 수영장 등 공공시설의 이용자나 관리자들에게 안전 수칙 전달 ❸ 기타 공지 내용 [대회 및 행사] 영화 및 연극, 경연 등 공고 [교통수단] 버스나 열차, 항공기 승객들을 대상으로 하는 공지 [설문 조사] 제품이나 서비스 구매 후 고객들에게 설문 조사에 대한 공지
광고(Advertisement) - 일반 광고/구인 광고	❶ 구인 광고 [신입/경력직] 신입 직원이나 특정 업계의 근무 경력이 있는 경력 직원을 모집하는 광고 [파트타임 및 임시직] 연휴 기간 동안 일할 임시직 구인 광고 [신규 회원 모집] 헬스클럽이나 기타 여가 활동 관련 단체에서 신규 회원을 모집하는 광고 ❷ 일반 광고(제품, 서비스 및 업체 광고) [숙박 시설 개장 광고] 호텔(hotel), 인(inn) 등 숙박 시설 개장 광고 [제품 광고] 업무용 컴퓨터 소프트웨어나 사무실용 가구 등의 광고 [온라인 서비스 광고] 은행, 증권사 등의 온라인 서비스 광고 ❸ 할인 광고(제품, 서비스) [회원 혜택] 각종 상점의 회원 가입과 혜택 광고 [점포 이전] 점포 이전으로 특정 기간 동안 진행되는 할인 행사 광고

	[재고 정리] 신상품 입고로 인한 기존 상품 재고 정리 세일 광고 [기념일 할인] 특별한 날이나 판촉을 위해 일정 기간만 제공하는 할인 혜택 광고
기사(Article)	❶ 특정 업계나 기업에 관련된 기사 [업계 전망] 소비 및 이용 증가에 따른 업계 전망에 관한 기사 [업무 환경 및 조건] 재택근무에 관한 기사 [건물 인수] 한 회사가 특정 상업용 건물을 인수하는 내용의 기사 [외부 인물 영입] 신임 부사장을 영입한 회사에 대한 기사 ❷ 신제품(books, entertainment, products) 소개 [신제품 정보] 새로운 제품에 대한 정보를 주는 기사 [책 소개] 특정 작가의 출판물에 대한 출간 정보와 책 소개 ❸ 찬반론 관련 기사 [정책에 대한 찬반] 새로운 정책(교통 규제, 건설 등)에 관한 찬반 기사 [특정 정책이나 계획에 대한 입장] 농업, 상업 분야 등에서의 가용 자원을 감소시키는 시의 계획에 대한 업계의 입장을 반영한 기사 등 ❹ 공지 및 홍보성 기사 [공사 정보] 새 터널 공사 등을 알리는 기사 [홍보성 기사] 경연 및 행사를 알리는 기사 ❺ 성공 사례(person, company) 인터뷰 기사 [성공 사례 인터뷰 기사] 특정 업체의 성공을 인터뷰한 잡지 기사 [특정 사업 성장 기사] 어느 체인점의 성장에 관한 기사 [성공 사례 과정] 특정 기업의 설립 과정에 대한 설립자와의 인터뷰
양식(Form)	[application form] 입사 또는 입학, 가입, 지원, 신청서 등의 양식 [survey form] 제품 또는 서비스 구매 후 고객의 만족도를 조사하는 설문 양식 [schedule] 주로 항공편이나 워크숍 일정, 특정 행사 일정 등과 관련한 시간/요일/월별 등의 일정표 [bill, receipt] 전화 요금 등 각종 청구서나 구매 후의 영수증 [invoice] 상업 송장 및 주문서 [complaint form] 제품이나 서비스 구매 후 불만 사항을 기록하는 양식 [warranty] 제품이나 서비스에 대한 보증서 [contract] 장비나 건물 등의 임대 계약서나 특정 서비스 관련 계약서 [reimbursement form] 선 지출 또는 초과 지출한 출장 경비 등의 환급 신청서 [coupon] 구매 및 서비스 이용에 관한 할인 쿠폰이나 무료 쿠폰 [price list] 서비스나 제품 등의 가격 목록 [business card] 명함 [telephone message] 전화 메시지 메모 [sign] 표지판 [agenda] 회의 안건 목록
문자 메시지 및 온라인 채팅 (Text Message & Online Chatting)	[문제 상황] 업무상 발생한 어려움이나 문제점에 대한 논의 [업데이트] 변경 사항이나 신규 상황 관련 논의 [업무 요청] 프로젝트 진행 등 업무 과정에서 발행하는 필요 사항을 요청 [업무 확인] 계약서나 소포 등의 수신 확인 [의견 논의] 특정 이슈나 업무에 대한 논의

Chapter Test

Questions 1-3 refer to the following agenda.

Ryerson Art Gallery Executive Board
Summer Meeting Agenda, August 11th

Location: Ryerson Hotel, Conference Room A
Lunch: 12:00 P.M.-1:00 P.M. Ryerson Hotel's Sunset Dining Room

TIME	SPEAKER	TOPIC
1:00 - 1:30 P.M.	David London, Chief Financial Officer	Budget status
1:30 - 2:00 P.M.	Nate Mercado, Marketing Manager	Midyear attendance figures
2:00 - 2:30 P.M.	Nora Brown, Exhibitions Manager	Introducing upcoming exhibits
2:30 - 3:00 P.M.	Lacy Norton, Education Programs Manager	Proposals for expanding school outreach programs
3:00 - 3:15 P.M.	Ian Paisley, Museum President	Nominating candidates for next year's board chairperson position

1. What is stated about the meeting?
 (A) The new chairperson will oversee it.
 (B) A meal will be available to those who attend it.
 (C) It will be held in the gallery's conference room.
 (D) It will be open to all gallery employees.

2. Who will give a report on the number of visitors to the museum?
 (A) David London
 (B) Nate Mercado
 (C) Nora Brown
 (D) Ian Paisley

3. What is implied about the gallery?
 (A) Its income has exceeded expenses so far this year.
 (B) It is seeking more funding for new exhibits.
 (C) It provides educational programs for students.
 (D) Its president will resign in the near future.

Questions 4-6 refer to the following flyer.

The Asian Business Organization of Ann Arbor
invites you to a community event.

**Visions for Growth: Improving Asian American Businesses
in the Suburbs of Ann Arbor**

Panel Members:
Dr. Bakhanee Mandalou
Director of the Central Michigan Business Bureau

Ms. Diao Chan
President of the Asian Business Organization
Owner of Dynasty Incorporated
Founding Member of the Asian Business Organization of Ann Arbor

Dr. Makoto Tanaka
Professor of Business Psychology at Michigan State University, Ypsilanti, Michigan
Author of *Small Business of America Today*

This community event introduces to all Asians in the midwest region the basic principles of business strategies. It will be a great opportunity to learn about how to open your own business and help you find the right type of business that suits you. The panel members will willingly share this valuable information with you.

Date: Friday, November 2
Time: 5:30 P.M. to 8:30 P.M.
Cost: $25 ($10 for students who reside in Ann Arbor)
Location: Mosher Jordan Hall
1316 Geddes Ave.
Ann Arbor MI, 48104

Dinner will be complimentary to all who wish to attend this event. Call us at 734-657-8617 or visit www.abocommunity.com to register.

---

4. What event is being promoted?
   (A) A book signing
   (B) A product demonstration
   (C) A panel discussion
   (D) An academic lecture

5. Where will the event take place?
   (A) At the Asian Business Organization
   (B) At Mosher Jordan Hall
   (C) At the Central Michigan Business Bureau
   (D) At Michigan State University

6. What is stated about Dr. Tanaka?
   (A) He teaches business at a university in Michigan.
   (B) He plans to speak about Asian history.
   (C) He owns a small business in Michigan.
   (D) He is a member of the Asian Business Organization.

Questions 7-10 refer to the following advertisement.

World Job Search

For Employers

World Job Search (WJS) is an online-based recruitment website that exclusively focuses on filling senior executive positions. Our specially trained counselors seek out qualified and experienced candidates with high levels of education for our client companies. These counselors analyze more than 30,000 résumés to distinguish suitable matches among the list. Then, they conduct pre-interviews with these candidates to form a more detailed profile. Afterwards, employers receive a list of candidate profiles with an addition of recommendations on which candidates are regarded to be the best match to them.

For Job Seekers

World Job Search (WJS) provides job seekers with lists of prominent jobs and connects these offers from exceptional companies to them. As a paying member of WJS, you get to access our online search engine and are able to browse qualified job positions in more than 35 countries. We post job positions daily that offer yearly salaries of at least $100,000 or more. For members, we will also send you our exclusive business magazine, *World Business Times* monthly. This magazine contains some rare information that you can hardly find in other business magazines. Feel free to join us anytime at www.wjsjobs.com.

---

7. What is the goal of WJS?
(A) To help executive job seekers improve their résumés
(B) To connect highly skilled job seekers with top employers
(C) To help companies improve their productivity
(D) To train executives to work in new industries

8. According to the advertisement, what is NOT provided to client companies?
(A) A list of job seekers
(B) A specialist with whom to work
(C) Direct access to 30,000 résumés
(D) Suggestions on whom to consider for hiring

9. The word "regarded" in paragraph 1, line 7, is closest in meaning to
(A) looked
(B) considered
(C) related
(D) concerned

10. What is indicated about job seekers who use WJS?
(A) They speak several languages.
(B) They have taught university courses.
(C) They wish to earn up to $100,000 a year.
(D) They can get a paid membership.

Questions 11-13 refer to the following letter.

NS Office Depot

April 24th
Scott Taylor
Procurement Department
H&K Production Co.

Dear Mr. Taylor,

We have enclosed the items for H&K Production's order of office supplies for this month.

The order includes:
- 25 cases of printing paper with company logo
- 300 5x7 envelopes with company logo
- 25 three-ring binders with company logo

The quantity of the order was based on the contract you agreed to in March. You will continue to receive the same quantity of items shown above by the twenty-fifth day of every month until the end of the calendar year. If you would like to renew the agreement with us for the next year, please let us know in December.

Your next order will be delivered by May 25th. If you want to change the items or quantity of your orders, call our customer service at (425) 518-5723. Let us remind you that we offer special discount rates when you increase your order quantity. Once the order has been placed on the 14th day of the month, changes cannot be made, and refunds will not be issued.

Thank you for your business.

Sincerely,
Matthew A. Weir

---

11. What is the purpose of the letter?
    (A) To request payment for an order
    (B) To confirm the contents of a delivery
    (C) To change the terms of an agreement with a customer
    (D) To propose a new design for a company logo

12. What is indicated about H&K Production's April order?
    (A) It arrived late due to a printing problem.
    (B) Mr. Taylor received a discount for placing it in March.
    (C) It contains items that Mr. Taylor added to the order by telephone.
    (D) The quantity of items has not changed from the previous month.

13. According to the letter, what is offered by NS Office Depot?
    (A) A refund for any unused product that is returned
    (B) Delivery of Mr. Taylor's next order by the fourteenth day of the month
    (C) A discount on items that are ordered in larger quantities
    (D) Automatic renewal of Mr. Taylor's agreement with the company when the year ends

Questions 14-15 refer to the following article.

Rise of On-Time Flights

June 17—All airlines in America achieved the highest on-time records in May, according to the report presented last week by the Department of Air Transportation. The study on the nation's six largest airlines shows that the airlines had an on-time arrival rate of 90 percent in the previous month, up from 86 percent in April. The study has also shown that the highest arrival rate of the last year was only 83 percent in October and the average on-time rate for all of last year was 78 percent.

14. What is the article about?
    (A) A government policy
    (B) An airport contract
    (C) An airline study
    (D) A travel plan

15. What was the airlines' on-time arrival rate for May?
    (A) 78%
    (B) 83%
    (C) 86%
    (D) 90%

Questions 16-19 refer to the following article.

World Business Report

Kaiser Steel Corporation

Based in the center of Boston, Massachusetts, Kaiser Steel Corporation is one of the internationally well-known steel suppliers which has numerous clients worldwide. Their main source of production is sheet metal, which is used for railroad construction in all parts of the globe. Kaiser Steel owns 35% of Delinger&Brothers Corp., a steel manufacturer. Located in Mumbai, India, Delinger&Brothers focuses on Asian markets.

In an effort to develop the most durable steel products, Kaiser Steel is collaboratively developing a method to combine steel and titanium materials with Le Blanc Steels of Cannes, France. Project researchers from both industries are gathered in the newly built laboratories situated in Cannes.

Kaiser Steel is consisted of 5,000 employees and operates approximately 300 factories in twelve different countries. Its current president, Mr. Kevin Spikes, has been leading Kaiser Steel for more than fifteen years.

16. What is the purpose of the article?
    (A) To critique construction materials
    (B) To announce the appointment of a company president
    (C) To summarize a company's quarterly earnings
    (D) To describe a company's global activities

17. Where is Kaiser Steel Corporation's main office?
    (A) In Cannes
    (B) In Boston
    (C) In Mumbai
    (D) In Chicago

18. What is suggested about Delinger&Brother Corp.?
    (A) It is a new company.
    (B) It has about 5,000 employees.
    (C) It is a research center.
    (D) It is a regional supplier.

19. According to the article, what is the relationship between Le Blanc and Kaiser?
    (A) Le Blanc recycles Kaiser's sheet metal.
    (B) Le Blanc is owned by Kaiser.
    (C) Le Blanc and Kaiser are project partners.
    (D) Le Blanc and Kaiser are planning to merge.

Chapter 3 다중 지문 유형

Point 01 이중 지문(Double Passages) 연계 문제

출제 포인트 정리

이중 지문에서는 두 지문을 연계하여 풀어야 하는 연계 문제가 1~2문제 나오는데 주로 3~4번째 문제로 출제됩니다.

❶ 보기는 주로 지문에 언급된 고유 명사, 시간, 장소, 수량, 가격 등으로 되어 있습니다.
❷ 문제의 키워드가 언급된 지문에서는 정답의 단서를 직접적으로 제시하지 않습니다.
❸ 문제에서 언급된 키워드를 지문에서 찾은 후 그곳에서 다시 보기와 연결되는 키워드를 찾아야 합니다.

Questions 1 refers to the following menu and restaurant review.
→ 지문 1은 식당 메뉴이며, 지문 2는 그 식당에 대한 후기입니다.

지문 1

Golden Eagle Diner

Lunch Menu for
Monday - Thursday
11:00 A.M. - 4:00 P.M.

Sandwiches		**Side Dishes**	
Golden Eagle Original	$6.00	Sour pickles	$1.50
Andy's Style (cheddar cheese with onions)	$7.00	Coleslaw	$2.00
		Baby carrots	$2.00
The Classic BLT (sliced bacon with fresh lettuce and tomato)	$7.50	Green peas	$2.00
The Classic Italian (salami, cheddar cheese, and olives, with Italian sauce)	$8.50	**Desserts**	
		Today's pie	$4.50
		Ice cream sundae	$2.50
Turkey Delight (white turkey meat and vegetables with mustard)	$8.50	**Beverages**	
		Orange lemonade	$1.50
The Supreme Baldios (shrimp, crab meat, and tuna with tartar sauce)	$10.00	Iced tea	$2.00

The Classic Italian 항목의 salami에 표시: **1. 연결 키워드**

지문 2

Golden Eagle Diner, 240 Broad Ave. Palisades Park NJ — Of the many sandwich places in the city, Golden Eagle Diner is the newest in town. While they offer a high quality of food, they are considered to be one of the restaurants with reasonably priced menus, with $10.00 being their most expensive item on the list.

The side dishes aren't too special, but they actually seem to be better than those from other ordinary sandwich places. It is just that the sandwiches deserve most of the credit from Golden Eagle Diner. All sandwiches are made using freshly baked bread from the oven and the meat is cooked at a carefully measured temperature. Among its sandwiches, the salami sandwich is a must try. The salami is sliced thin and proves to be a perfect match with cheese and olives. In addition, the sweet and sour Italian sauce adds a delight to its already perfect taste.

To conclude, I suggest that everyone try Golden Eagle Diner the next time they go out for lunch. If you are planning on ordering some pie, just make sure you order at least two pieces.

---

1. What menu items does the reviewer mention as being particularly good?

(A) The Classic BLT
(B) The Classic Italian
(C) Turkey Delight
(D) The Supreme Baldios

STEP 1 문제와 키워드 위치 파악

보기는 지문 1에 언급된 고유 명사(메뉴명)입니다. 문제의 키워드(reviewer, good)는 지문 2에서 언급되고 있으므로 지문 2에서 연결 키워드를 확인해야 합니다.

STEP 2 지문 파악 순서: 지문 2 → 지문 1

연결 키워드는 보기의 키워드가 있는 지문(지문 1)이 아닌 문제의 키워드가 있는 지문(지문 2)에서 확인해야 합니다.

STEP 3 연결 키워드 파악

지문 2에서 키워드인 particularly good(Among its sandwiches ~)을 찾고 그 문장에서 보기와 연결할 수 있는 연결 키워드 salami를 확인합니다.

STEP 4 연결 키워드를 통한 정답 확인

지문 2에서 식당의 음식들에 대해 칭찬하면서 the salami sandwich is a must try라고 언급하고 있습니다. 하지만 구체적인 메뉴의 이름은 나타나 있지 않으므로 지문 1에서 살라미가 포함된 샌드위치 메뉴를 찾아야 합니다. 따라서 정답은 (B)가 됩니다.

Check-up Test 700+를 위해 한 걸음 한 걸음

정답 및 해석 p.086

STEP 1 다음의 지문을 읽고 문제에 답하세요.

Questions 1-5 refer to the following e-mails.

From: David Allen <davallen@marketingtoday.com>
To: Chen Xiao Hui <chenxh@marketingtoday.com>
Date: April 21
Subject: Schedule of marketing seminar

Hello Xiao Hui,

I've sent you an initial draft of the schedule for the marketing seminar in July. I'd appreciate it if you and other committee members would go over it. I'm very grateful to all in Hong Kong who are involved in preparing this seminar. I'm so thankful to you for offering to reserve the space at Royal Palace Hotel.

David

Day 1	10:30 A.M. 12:00 P.M. 2:00 P.M.	Keynote address and introductions in Diamond Hall, 3rd floor Lunch outside in the hotel's Skylark Terrace Restaurant Group meetings in seminar rooms 3-9, 3rd floor
Day 2	10:00 A.M. 12:15 P.M. 2:30 P.M.	Group meetings in seminar rooms 3-9, 3rd floor Lunch in the hotel's Stove Restaurant, 2nd floor Group meetings in seminar rooms 3-9, 3rd floor
Day 3	10:30 A.M. 12:00 P.M. 3:00 P.M.	Presentation rehearsals in Kinsey Hall C and D, 3rd floor Lunch outside in the hotel's Secret Garden Group presentations in Diamond Hall, 3rd floor

From	Chen Xiao Hui <chenxh@marketingtoday.com>
To	David Allen <davallen@marketingtoday.com>
Date	July 9
Subject	Weather during the seminar

Dear David,

We have a small problem. I went to the website of the National Weather Center, and checked the forecast for the days of the seminar. As you can see below, the weather might be a problem. It would be best if I tell the hotel to switch the lunch venues for the last two days. It's a good thing that the schedule won't go to the printer until July 13.

Have a nice day,
Xiao Hui

Weather Forecast for Hong Kong		
Tuesday, July 15 32℃ Sunny	Wednesday, July 16 31℃ Sunny, with a breeze	Thursday, July 17 27℃ Cloudy, 85% chance of shower

1. What is suggested about the seminar schedule in the first e-mail?
   (A) It was created by the committee in Hong Kong.
   (B) It is similar to the last year's seminar schedule.
   (C) It has been sent to the attendees.
   (D) It is still being developed.

2. What facility is NOT on the third floor of the hotel?
   (A) Kinsey Hall
   (B) The Diamond Hall
   (C) The Stove Restaurant
   (D) Seminar room 7

3. What is indicated about Ms. Chen?
   (A) She is helping to organize the seminar.
   (B) She will deliver the keynote address.
   (C) She spoke with a weather forecaster in Hong Kong.
   (D) She works at the Royal Palace Hotel.

4. Where does Mr. Chen suggest lunch should be served on Wednesday?
   (A) In the Diamond Hall
   (B) In the Secret Garden
   (C) In the Stove Restaurant
   (D) In the Skylark Terrace Restaurant

5. When is the conference scheduled to begin?
   (A) On July 9
   (B) On July 13
   (C) On July 15
   (D) On July 16

Point 02 삼중 지문(Triple Passages) 연계 문제

출제 포인트 정리

이중 지문과 마찬가지로 각기 다른 두 개의 지문을 연계하여 풀어야 하는 연계 문제가 약 1~2문제 정도 출제됩니다. 연계 문제를 풀 때 각각의 지문들이 어떻게 연결되어 있는지 확인하는 것이 기본입니다.

❶ 연계 문제는 주로 2-3번째 문제와 4-5번째 문제에서 출제됩니다.
❷ 세 지문 중에 어떤 지문과 어떤 지문을 봐야 할지를 파악하는 것이 중요합니다.
❸ 연결 키워드를 찾아 패러프레이징된 정답을 찾아야 합니다.

Questions 1-2 refer to the following advertisement and e-mails.
→ 지문 1은 집을 구해 달라는 메일, 지문 2는 임대 가능한 집의 목록, 지문 3은 지문 1에 대한 답신 메일입니다.

지문 1

To Jade Solomon <info@solomonestate.com>
From Lila Lupe <llupe@vivamail.com>
Date July 5
Subject Homes for rent

Dear Ms. Solomon,

A friend of mine suggested I contact you. My husband and I will be looking for a house to rent starting next month. We would like to have at least three bedrooms and a yard to enjoy gardening, which is our favorite hobby. We both work downtown, so we don't mind driving up there as long as the time doesn't exceed fifteen minutes. Lastly, we would like to live there for at least one year.

It will be great if we could start looking at rentals by next weekend. You may reach me anytime during regular business hours at 02-542-1213, but I will surely be available if you can call me in the evenings while I am at home (02-679-1213). I hope we can talk about this as soon as possible.

Sincerely,

Lila Lupe

지문 2

Homes for Rent in Ray City
Properties Represented by Jade Solomon

99 Carnegie Court ················· $270 per week
3 mid-sized bedrooms, 1 bath condominium in the center of downtown with beautiful shore view from this 7th floor unit. Easy access to parking area and bus stop within walking distance.

27 Steward Street ················· $340 per week
Single-level home with a veranda, 3 bedrooms, 2 bathrooms, 1 garage. Takes approximately 20 minutes to drive to downtown. Available for a maximum lease of one year.

790 Chamberlain Avenue ················· $370 per week
Large 5 bedrooms, 3 bathrooms, surrounded by peaceful environment in the suburbs.
Just 25 minutes by train to downtown. 1 spacious garage. Available for a maximum lease of two years.

33 Sandsville Parkway ················· $370 per week
Modern 4 bedrooms, 2 baths home with fence-surrounded yard and 1-car garage in suburban area close to the beach.
Just 10 minutes by car to reach downtown. Lease period can be negotiable.

SOLOMON & ASSOCIATES
2200 Montclair Driveway, Ray City 59016
567 321 2146
www.solomonestate.com
Your number ONE choice for choosing the right NEST!

지문 3

To Lila Lupe <llupe@vivamail.com>
From Jade Solomon <info@solomonestate.com>　→ 2. 문제 키워드
Date July 8
Re: Homes for rent

Dear Ms. Lupe,

Thanks for your e-mail inquiring homes for renting. I've been working with the residential properties in this neighborhood for over ten years. As you requested, I have looked over all the properties and found one that perfectly fits your requirements.

However, regarding the last requirement you mentioned, I need to discuss it first with the owner of the property. I will inform you about this issue as soon as possible.　→ 2. 연결 키워드　　→ 2. 문제 키워드

If you have any questions about the property, please call me at anytime on my mobile phone at 760-5424-1909. I hope we can talk about this as soon as possible.

Sincerely,

Jade Solomon

---

1. What property in the advertisement most likely meets Ms. Lupe's requirements?

(A) 99 Carnegie Court
(B) 27 Steward Street
(C) 790 Chamberlain Avenue
(D) 33 Sandsville Parkway

STEP 1 문제와 키워드 위치 파악

문제의 키워드는 지문 1에서 언급되고 있으며, 보기는 지문 2에 언급된 고유 명사(주소)로 구성되어 있습니다.

STEP 2 지문 파악 순서: 지문 1 → 지문 2

STEP 3 연결 키워드 파악

지문 1에서 Lupe가 원하는 요구 사항을 찾아 지문 2에서 이에 부합하는 집(property)을 찾아야 합니다.

STEP 4 연결 키워드를 통한 정답 확인

at least three bedrooms → 4 bedrooms
a yard → fence-surrounded yard
doesn't exceed fifteen minutes → 10 minutes by car
이와 같이 요구 사항에 부합하는 (D)가 정답입니다.

2. What does Ms. Solomon need to talk about with the property owner?

(A) The length of lease
(B) The rental price
(C) A renovation of the garage
(D) A possibility of installment

STEP 1 문제와 키워드 위치 파악

문제의 키워드인 Solomon이 작성한 이메일인 지문 3에서 키워드를 찾아야 합니다.

STEP 2 연결 키워드 파악

지문 3에서 문제의 키워드 need, owner가 언급된 앞 쪽에 the last requirement you mentioned가 있으므로 Lupe가 작성한 지문 1에서 마지막으로 요청한 사항을 확인합니다.

STEP 3 지문 파악 순서: 지문 3 → 지문 1

STEP 4 연결 키워드를 통한 정답 확인

지문 1에서 Lastly, we would like to live for at least one year를 통해 임대 기간(the length of lease)에 대해 집 주인과 이야기해야 함을 알 수 있으므로 정답은 (A)가 됩니다.

Chapter 3. 다중 지문 유형　297

Check-up Test

STEP 1 다음의 지문을 읽고 문제에 답하세요.

Questions 1-5 refer to the following schedule and e-mails.

[FIRST DRAFT COPY - July 7]

Cromwell Papers Inc.

07:30 A.M. - 08:30 A.M.	Breakfast and Opening Statement by Company President
08:30 A.M. - 10:30 A.M.	Workshop 1: Analysis of Current Trend in Paper Supplies
10:30 A.M. - 12:30 P.M.	Workshop 2: Overview of Cromwell Products
12:30 P.M. - 01:30 P.M.	Lunch
01:30 P.M. - 03:30 P.M.	Workshop 3: Learning the Basics of Writing Proposals
03:30 P.M. - 04:00 P.M.	Break
04:00 P.M. - 06:00 P.M.	Workshop 4: Giving Presentations

From Buela Cooper <buela@cromwellpp.com>
To Carleigh De Leon; Ryan McCarthy; Tania Ferreira; Jane S.Yamashiro
Date July 10
Subject workshop schedule

Dear all,

This e-mail is to notify you that there have been a few changes on the upcoming training program for the new sales staff. Firstly, Mr. Jameson will be in a meeting until 8:30 A.M., so I am afraid he won't be able to give the opening statement during breakfast. Rather than finding a replacement for Mr. Jameson, we decided to turn the breakfast into an orientation where new staff members could introduce themselves to each other.

In addition to the change mentioned above, we decided to switch the times for the last two workshops because Ms. Ramsey, the supervisor for the training program, has some conflicts with her schedule. I am sorry to say that I too won't be able to come to the training program.

Ryan, I would like to ask you to relay this information clearly to everyone as well as update and distribute the changed schedule. After, please call me for confirmation.

Buela Cooper

E-mail

From:	Ryan McCarthy <rmaccarthy@cromwellpp.com>
To:	Buela Cooper <buela@cromwellpp.com>
Date:	July 11
Re:	workshop schedule

Dear Ms. Cooper,

Thank you for letting me know these updates. It sounds like yesterday's meeting was very productive. I had hoped to be there, but my last-minute trip to Seattle couldn't be helped.

As you requested, I updated the changed schedule on our website but I could not e-mail your message to everyone since I don't have a list of new sales staff. So I tried to call you this morning a couple of times. Your assistant told me you are out of the office today. Please call me as soon as you get this e-mail.

Ryan McCarthy

---

1. What will the sales representatives do from 10:30 A.M. to 12:30 P.M.?
   (A) Meet the sales trainers
   (B) Introduce themselves to each other
   (C) Learn about the company's products
   (D) Tour the production facilities

2. Who is the president of Cromwell Papers?
   (A) Mr. Jameson
   (B) Mr. McCarthy
   (C) Ms. Cooper
   (D) Ms. Ramsey

3. In the first e-mail, the word "turn" in paragraph 1, line 4, is closest in meaning to
   (A) rotate
   (B) transform
   (C) bring
   (D) consider

4. According to the first e-mail, when will the participants learn about writing proposals?
   (A) From 7:30 A.M. to 8:30 A.M.
   (B) From 8:30 A.M. to 10:30 A.M.
   (C) From 1:30 P.M. to 3:30 P.M.
   (D) From 4:00 P.M. to 6:00 P.M.

5. What is suggested about Mr. McCarthy?
   (A) He missed the gathering on July 10th.
   (B) He is considering participating in the workshop.
   (C) He will lead one of the workshops.
   (D) He will call Ms. Cooper.

Chapter Test

Questions 1-5 refer to the following e-mail and survey.

From:	Ronald Stevens <ronstevens@elitehuntinghotels.com>
To:	Dan Inosanto <dinosanto@flipmail.com>
Date:	January 3
Subject:	Your stay at Elite Hunting Hotel

Confirmation Number: 20700650050532
VIP Membership Number: 100382MWL

Dear Mr. Inosanto,

Thank you for choosing to stay at Elite Hunting Hotel! The details of your hotel reservation are shown below. Please e-mail us at reservations@elitehuntinghotels.com if you need to make any necessary changes to your reservation. Please note that cancellations must be made at least one week in advance to avoid losing your deposit.

> Hotel location: 2005 Hoover St., Pheonix, NY 89014
> Room: 2 double beds, 12th floor
> Check-in: After 3:00 P.M., Saturday, January 17
> Check-out: By 11:00 A.M., Monday, January 19
> Number of people in room: 2
> Room rates for members: $199/night

Please contact our front desk at services@elitehuntinghotels.com for services such as ordering tickets, booking tours, or transportation services.

We hope you enjoyed your stay!
To better serve you in the future, we would appreciate it
if you could spend a moment in completing this survey.

1. How did you hear about Elite Hunting Hotels?
   TV _____   Magazine ✓   Travel agent _____   Internet _____   Other _____

2. What was the purpose of your trip? _____Vacation_____

3. Have you dined at Cozy Sky? If so, how would you rate our food?
   Outstanding _____   Good _____   Fair ✓   Unsatisfactory _____

4. How would you rate the quality of the housekeeping service?
   Outstanding ✓   Good _____   Fair _____   Unsatisfactory _____

5. Name and e-mail address (optional)   _Dan Inosanto dinosanto@flipmail.com_

If you are not a VIP member, join today! All our VIP members receive 15% off their room rates and are eligible for exclusive benefits only for VIP members. For more information, call us on 818-9909-1255 or visit our website at www.elitehuntinghotels.com

1. What is the purpose of the e-mail?
   (A) To promote a travel-rewards program
   (B) To offer a larger room to a hotel guest
   (C) To request participation in a survey
   (D) To confirm accommodation arrangements

2. On what date did Mr. Inosanto most likely arrive at Elite Hunting Hotel?
   (A) January 3
   (B) January 10
   (C) January 17
   (D) January 19

3. What is suggested about Mr. Inosanto?
   (A) He ordered theater tickets.
   (B) He paid a reduced room rate.
   (C) He used the services of a travel agency.
   (D) He changed his departure date.

4. What is indicated about Elite Hunting Hotel?
   (A) It has a restaurant.
   (B) It opened in January.
   (C) It primarily serves business travelers.
   (D) It advertises on the radio.

5. What does the survey indicate about Mr. Inosanto?
   (A) He received helpful information from the concierge.
   (B) He was very happy with the cleanliness of his room.
   (C) He appreciated having free Internet access.
   (D) He is a frequent visitor to New York.

Questions 6-10 refer to the following brochure, e-mail, and information.

Peppercity Gardens

Peppercity Gardens has been one of the most popular attractions for visitors from all over the world for more than twenty years. And this year, there are even more reasons to love this amazing place! This summer, Peppercity Gardens will offer several new events such as a tree-planting festival, a field trip to the arboretum, and a guided tour through Dawson Woods. On Saturdays, there will be a concert in the evening. As with last year, our rose tours will exhibit some of the most exotic roses. Starting in July, we will open classes for those who are interested in home gardening. Our group of experienced instructors will show you how to plant and grow flowers and edible vegetables.

Seasonal Hours (June 21 - October 8)
Monday - Tuesday: 8:00 A.M. - 7:00 P.M.
Wednesday - Friday: 8:00 A.M. - 10:00 P.M.
Saturday: 8:00 A.M. - 8:00 P.M.
Sunday: 8:00 A.M. - 6:00 P.M.

The Saturday concerts need a reservation.
Please visit our website at www.peppercitygardens.com

To: Isabelle Dakota
From: Edwin Wigan
Date: July 22
Subject: Peppercity Gardens Trip

I had such a wonderful time at Peppercity Gardens with my family last Saturday! Without any extra fee, our family enjoyed a perfect day at the garden. Thank you very much for showing me the brochure.

The weather was fantastic. Julia and the children took part in the tree-planting festival while I went on a rose tour. The flowers were gorgeous, and our guide was very knowledgeable. That was my favorite part of the day, without a doubt. Your recommendation was definitely worth following. I never imagined that such a nice place existed so close to my home. Since they offer a jazz concert at night, we stayed until the garden was closed. It's a pity that you couldn't join us. Next time, we will surely go together.

Thank you again for introducing the garden.

Sincerely,

Edwin Wigan

Peppercity Gardens

Ticket Price for Family

Ticket		Standard	Silver	Gold	Premium
Admission Fee		O	O	O	O
Activities	Tree planting	X	O	O	X
	Rose Garden (Guided tour)	X	X	O	O
	Field trip	X	X	X	O
	Home Gardening Class	X	X	X	O
	Music Concert	O	O	O	O

6. What is the purpose of the brochure?
   (A) To update a conference schedule
   (B) To request a donation to a charity
   (C) To provide information about a tourist attraction
   (D) To advertise a flower shop

7. What is indicated about the evening concerts?
   (A) Tickets are offered at a reduced price.
   (B) They start at the same time as the tree-planting festival.
   (C) They happen every day of the week.
   (D) They can be reserved online.

8. According to the e-mail, what did Mr. Wigan do at Peppercity Gardens?
   (A) He went to a company-sponsored event.
   (B) He attended a class.
   (C) He hiked in the woods.
   (D) He took a guided tour.

9. When did Mr. Wigan leave Peppercity Gardens?
   (A) At 6:00 P.M.
   (B) At 7:00 P.M.
   (C) At 8:00 P.M.
   (D) At 10:00 P.M.

10. Which ticket did Mr. Wigan most likely purchase?
    (A) A Standard ticket
    (B) A Silver ticket
    (C) A Gold ticket
    (D) A Premium ticket

ACTUAL TEST

PART 1

PART 2

PART 3

PART 4

PART 5

PART 6

PART 7

LISTENING TEST

In the Listening test, you will be asked to demonstrate how well you understand spoken English. The entire Listening test will last approximately 45 minutes. There are four parts, and directions are given for each part. You must mark your answers on the separate answer sheet. Do not write your answers in your test book.

PART 1

Directions: For each question in this part, you will hear four statements about a picture in your test book. When you hear the statements, you must select the one statement that best describes what you see in the picture. Then find the number of the question on your answer sheet and mark your answer. The statements will not be printed in your test book and will be spoken only one time.

Example

Sample Answer
 ●

Statement (C), "Binders are arranged on shelves," is the best description of the picture, so you should select answer (C) and mark it on your answer sheet.

1.

2.

GO ON TO THE NEXT PAGE

3.

4.

5.

6.

GO ON TO THE NEXT PAGE

PART 2

Directions: You will hear a question or statement and three responses spoken in English. They will not be printed in your test book and will be spoken only one time. Select the best response to the question or statement and mark the letter (A), (B), or (C) on your answer sheet.

7. Mark your answer on your answer sheet.
8. Mark your answer on your answer sheet.
9. Mark your answer on your answer sheet.
10. Mark your answer on your answer sheet.
11. Mark your answer on your answer sheet.
12. Mark your answer on your answer sheet.
13. Mark your answer on your answer sheet.
14. Mark your answer on your answer sheet.
15. Mark your answer on your answer sheet.
16. Mark your answer on your answer sheet.
17. Mark your answer on your answer sheet.
18. Mark your answer on your answer sheet.
19. Mark your answer on your answer sheet.
20. Mark your answer on your answer sheet.
21. Mark your answer on your answer sheet.
22. Mark your answer on your answer sheet.
23. Mark your answer on your answer sheet.
24. Mark your answer on your answer sheet.
25. Mark your answer on your answer sheet.
26. Mark your answer on your answer sheet.
27. Mark your answer on your answer sheet.
28. Mark your answer on your answer sheet.
29. Mark your answer on your answer sheet.
30. Mark your answer on your answer sheet.
31. Mark your answer on your answer sheet.

PART 3

Directions: You will hear some conversations between two or more people. You will be asked to answer three questions about what the speakers say in each conversation. Select the best response to each question and mark the letter (A), (B), (C), or (D) on your answer sheet. The conversations will not be printed in your test book and will be spoken only one time.

32. What are the speakers mainly discussing?
    (A) Packaging for some samples
    (B) Scheduling an overseas trip
    (C) Prices for a new product
    (D) Advertising in the local newspaper

33. What will happen in August?
    (A) A product name will be selected.
    (B) A series of meetings will take place.
    (C) A marketing director will retire.
    (D) A product will be officially released.

34. What will the man do?
    (A) Create a budget
    (B) Reschedule a meeting
    (C) Approve a design
    (D) Place an order

35. What event are the speakers planning to attend?
    (A) A music concert
    (B) A company picnic
    (C) An art exhibition
    (D) A publishing seminar

36. How did the woman learn about the event?
    (A) She read an article in a newspaper.
    (B) Her friend told her about the event.
    (C) She watched an advertisement on TV.
    (D) She got a brochure at work.

37. What does the woman suggest?
    (A) Asking for a help
    (B) Referring to a map
    (C) Parking in a car park
    (D) Walking around the gallery

38. What is the woman calling about?
    (A) A missing paycheck
    (B) A ticket
    (C) A delivery of order
    (D) A newspaper article

39. What department does the woman work in?
    (A) Human resources department
    (B) Accounting department
    (C) Customer service department
    (D) Editorial department

40. What does the man offer to do?
    (A) Check out the hotel
    (B) Issue an another check
    (C) Go to the post office
    (D) Make a reservation

41. Where does the conversation take place?
    (A) At a restaurant
    (B) At a furniture store
    (C) At a museum
    (D) At a jewelry shop

42. What does the woman suggest?
    (A) Taking a break
    (B) Going to another restaurant
    (C) Coming back later today
    (D) Making a reservation first

43. What does the woman say about her restaurant?
    (A) It opens at nine every day.
    (B) It closes at eleven o'clock.
    (C) It has many regular customers.
    (D) It has dinner specials.

GO ON TO THE NEXT PAGE

44. Who most likely is Julie?
    (A) A new employee
    (B) A reporter
    (C) A client
    (D) A receptionist

45. Why does the man say, "She's never done that before"?
    (A) To correct a misunderstanding
    (B) To offer some praise
    (C) To express concern
    (D) To request more help

46. What does the woman say she will do?
    (A) Revise a report
    (B) Schedule a meeting
    (C) Conduct an interview
    (D) Prepare a promotion

47. What did Jamie do recently?
    (A) She ordered some office equipment.
    (B) She attended a conference.
    (C) She created a product design.
    (D) She bought her laptop computer.

48. What does the man say about the product?
    (A) It was recently redesigned.
    (B) It is no longer available.
    (C) Its sales have been excellent.
    (D) Manufacturing costs have increased.

49. What did the distributor offer?
    (A) An upgraded model
    (B) Free shipping
    (C) The extension of a warranty
    (D) A discount on a future purchase

50. What business do the speakers most likely work for?
    (A) An art museum
    (B) An architectural office
    (C) A travel agency
    (D) A clothing company

51. Why does the man say, "My interview was canceled"?
    (A) To reject an invitation
    (B) To show his availability
    (C) To express concern about a schedule change
    (D) To discuss an unexpected problem

52. What does the woman tell the man to do?
    (A) Contact a local artist
    (B) Distribute some vouchers
    (C) Organize a fund-raising event
    (D) Have a meeting with his supervisor

53. What is the woman preparing to do?
    (A) Plan a business trip
    (B) Attend a reception
    (C) Give an interview
    (D) Conduct a training session

54. What will Richard bring to the woman?
    (A) Protective equipment
    (B) Safety guidebooks
    (C) A projector
    (D) Office supplies

55. What does the woman tell the men to do?
    (A) Make a proposal
    (B) Place an order
    (C) Give some feedback
    (D) Conduct research

56. Who most likely is the man?
    (A) A food caterer
    (B) An accountant
    (C) A banker
    (D) An international salesman

57. When will the seminar be held?
    (A) This Monday
    (B) Next Monday
    (C) This Thursday
    (D) Next Friday

58. What change does Joanna request?
    (A) A meeting room
    (B) Additional food items
    (C) A meeting agenda
    (D) A guest speaker

59. What are the speakers discussing?
    (A) The retirement of a president
    (B) The hiring of a new vice president
    (C) The company's upcoming event
    (D) The results of a community survey

60. What has James Miller done for the community?
    (A) He has revitalized the downtown area.
    (B) He has started a charitable program.
    (C) He has volunteered at local schools.
    (D) He has reduced government spending.

61. What does the man ask the woman to do?
    (A) Suggest ideas for future projects
    (B) Find a photograph of James Miller
    (C) Edit an article
    (D) Conduct an interview

Muraz Hotel	
Floor 5-7	Guest rooms
Floor 4	Fitness center
Floor 3	Business lounge
Floor 2	Conference halls
Floor 1	Restaurant

62. Who most likely is the man?
    (A) A guest speaker
    (B) A hotel clerk
    (C) A restaurant manager
    (D) An event organizer

63. What does the woman ask about?
    (A) Internet access
    (B) A repair store
    (C) A laundry service
    (D) Local attractions

64. Look at the graphic. Which floor will the woman go to next?
    (A) Floor 1
    (B) Floor 2
    (C) Floor 3
    (D) Floor 4

GO ON TO THE NEXT PAGE

Company	Minimum order	Cost per uniform
Geenie Printing	40	$5.8
Evan	30	$6.0
Mickey	10	$6.2
Jane's Prints	50	$5.6

65. Where do the speakers most likely work?
(A) At a design firm
(B) At a bakery
(C) At a restaurant
(D) At a clothing store

66. Look at the graphic. Which company will the speakers probably choose?
(A) Geenie Printing
(B) Evan
(C) Mickey
(D) Jane's Prints

67. What does the man say will happen on June 15?
(A) Some furniture will be delivered.
(B) A new business will open.
(C) An award ceremony will be held.
(D) A sale will end.

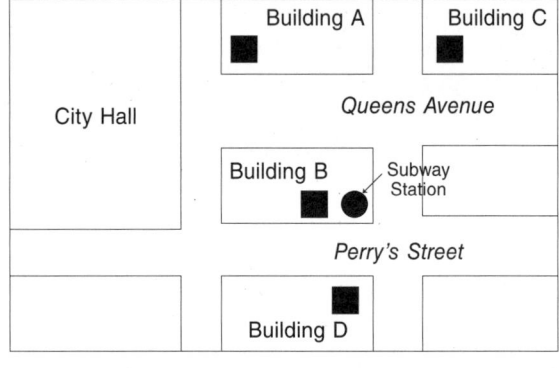

68. Who most likely is the man?
(A) A property manager
(B) A government officer
(C) A delivery person
(D) A postal worker

69. What problem does the man report?
(A) A delivery is misplaced.
(B) There is an accident on the road.
(C) Some information is missing.
(D) Some items have been damaged.

70. Look at the graphic. Where will the man go next?
(A) To building A
(B) To building B
(C) To building C
(D) To building D

PART 4

Directions: You will hear some talks given by a single speaker. You will be asked to answer three questions about what the speaker says in each talk. Select the best response to each question and mark the letter (A), (B), (C), or (D) on your answer sheet. The talks will not be printed in your test book and will be spoken only one time.

71. What type of event is taking place?
    (A) An awards ceremony
    (B) A grand opening
    (C) An anniversary celebration
    (D) A sports event

72. Who is Mike Rogers?
    (A) A radio personnel
    (B) A painter
    (C) A comedian
    (D) A singer

73. Why should listeners call the radio station?
    (A) To sign up for a volunteer
    (B) To win tickets
    (C) To buy a piece of art
    (D) To request a brochure

74. Where does the speaker most likely work?
    (A) At an accounting firm
    (B) At an advertising agency
    (C) At a restaurant
    (D) At a law office

75. What did the speaker do last week?
    (A) She hosted a dinner.
    (B) She attended a conference.
    (C) She made a reservation.
    (D) She went on holiday.

76. What does the speaker imply when she says, "I'm just across the street from you"?
    (A) An order will be delivered soon.
    (B) She wants to surprise the listener.
    (C) She is available to help.
    (D) She can easily visit the listener.

77. What product is being advertised?
    (A) A financial magazine
    (B) A software program
    (C) A recording device
    (D) A security camera

78. What does the speaker emphasize about the product?
    (A) It is customizable.
    (B) It is affordable.
    (C) It is simple to use.
    (D) It is small.

79. How can listeners get more information?
    (A) By requesting a brochure
    (B) By calling a toll-free number
    (C) By reading a magazine article
    (D) By sending an e-mail

80. What is the purpose of the call?
    (A) To introduce a product
    (B) To confirm a delivery date
    (C) To give some packing information
    (D) To change a time

81. According to the speaker, what will most likely happen on Wednesday?
    (A) An order will be delivered.
    (B) A project will be completed.
    (C) A machine will be repaired.
    (D) A product will be launched.

82. What is the listener asked to do?
    (A) Take some pictures of the product
    (B) Visit a store
    (C) Call to reschedule if needed
    (D) Pay the driver

GO ON TO THE NEXT PAGE

83. What is the purpose of the event?
    (A) To announce new changes
    (B) To promote a new product
    (C) To recognize employees
    (D) To dedicate a building

84. Where does the speaker most likely work?
    (A) At a city hall
    (B) At a marketing firm
    (C) At a chain restaurant
    (D) At a graphic design firm

85. What does the speaker mean when he says, "we didn't charge for that"?
    (A) He wanted to renew a contract.
    (B) He made a mistake on a invoice.
    (C) A sign has been given away.
    (D) A price has been reduced.

86. Where is the announcement taking place?
    (A) At a train station
    (B) At a factory
    (C) At an airport
    (D) At a theater

87. What does the speaker say is a problem?
    (A) Weather conditions are bad.
    (B) Seats were overbooked.
    (C) Some equipment is damaged.
    (D) There is a shortage of staff.

88. What does the speaker offer?
    (A) Sample products
    (B) A rental car
    (C) A discount coupon
    (D) Free membership

89. Who is Kevin Ford?
    (A) A painter
    (B) A writer
    (C) A politician
    (D) A businessman

90. According to the speaker, what will be shown during the tour?
    (A) A short historic movie
    (B) Rare books
    (C) Some pieces of furniture
    (D) Some sculptures

91. What will the listeners do next?
    (A) See a living room
    (B) Visit a park
    (C) Buy some books
    (D) Go for lunch

92. What is the speaker mainly talking about?
    (A) Changing old machines
    (B) Installing new equipment
    (C) Moving an office
    (D) Painting walls

93. Why does the speaker say, "We can save a lot of money"?
    (A) To ask for some help
    (B) To reject a suggestion
    (C) To correct a misunderstanding
    (D) To explain why a schedule is changed

94. What should listeners do on Thursday?
    (A) Pack all their belongings
    (B) Take the day off
    (C) Arrive an hour early
    (D) Unpack their boxes

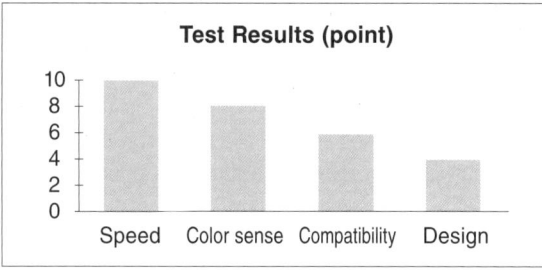
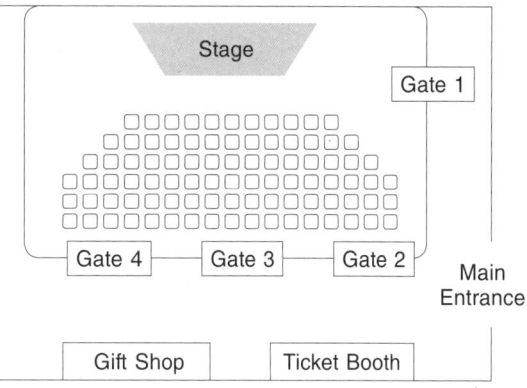

95. Where does the speaker say feedback came from?
    (A) A manager's meeting
    (B) An industry magazine
    (C) An advertising firm
    (D) A group of employees

96. Look at the graphic. Which feature will the listeners work on?
    (A) Speed
    (B) Color sense
    (C) Compatibility
    (D) Design

97. What are the listeners asked do by this weekend?
    (A) Consult with their supervisors
    (B) Make suggestions
    (C) Update a report
    (D) Find another vendor

98. According to the speaker, what is said about an event?
    (A) Local bands will perform.
    (B) Tickets are no longer available.
    (C) It will be broadcast live.
    (D) It will be the last of the series.

99. Look at the graphic. Which part of the concert hall was recently renovated?
    (A) Main entrance
    (B) Gate 1
    (C) Gate 2
    (D) Gate 4

100. What does the speaker remind the listeners to do?
    (A) Update a schedule
    (B) Put out some materials
    (C) Wear a uniform
    (D) Provide a direction

This is the end of the Listening test. Turn to Part 5 in your test book.

GO ON TO THE NEXT PAGE

ACTUAL TEST   317

READING TEST

In the Reading test, you will read a variety of texts and answer several different types of reading comprehension questions. The entire Reading test will last 75 minutes. There are three parts, and directions are given for each part. You are encouraged to answer as many questions as possible within the time allowed.

You must mark your answers on the separated answer sheet. Do not write your answers in your test book.

PART 5

Directions: A word or phrase is missing in each of the sentences below. Four answer choices are given below each sentence. Select the best answer to complete the sentence. Then mark the letter (A), (B), (C), or (D) on your answer sheet.

101. Mr. Chen will complete ------- internship at the St. Berry Book Store next week.
(A) he
(B) his
(C) him
(D) himself

102. Late applications for the training classes will not be -------.
(A) earned
(B) decided
(C) accepted
(D) solved

103. You should mail the ------- lease contract form along with relevant documents by June 1st.
(A) completely
(B) completion
(C) completed
(D) completing

104. The project made a valuable ------- to the development of the southern region.
(A) contribution
(B) contribute
(C) contributed
(D) contributing

105. If your invoice is -------, please contact us as soon as possible.
(A) unable
(B) broken
(C) incorrect
(D) weak

106. Ms. Lopez ------- with an architect last week about the urban renewal project.
(A) consults
(B) is consulting
(C) to consult
(D) consulted

107. Our annual banquet is usually held ------- a Friday night in December.
(A) at
(B) on
(C) up
(D) to

108. Mr. Brown has been named the construction site ------- while Mr. Allen is away on leave.
(A) supervisory
(B) supervision
(C) supervise
(D) supervisor

109. It is the user's ------- to save work-related files before the computer systems are upgraded.
(A) permission
(B) responsibility
(C) status
(D) reference

110. All sales representatives may wear ------- clothes, unless they have a meeting with clients.
(A) casual
(B) casualness
(C) casuals
(D) casually

111. ------- the manager is equally experienced in international and local markets, he has become an important asset to the company.
(A) During
(B) Therefore
(C) When
(D) Because

112. The supervisors of Asian Factory ------- to increase production of the newly launched computers by 50 percent.
(A) were told
(B) told
(C) tells
(D) telling

113. GT Company will promote its newest car, V-3000, ------- an extensive online marketing campaign.
(A) as
(B) of
(C) among
(D) through

114. The employee handbook describes the procedures for ------- ways of handling customer complaints.
(A) relative
(B) spacious
(C) various
(D) developing

115. Located one hour northwest of Seoul, our headquarters is ------- accessible by car or bus.
(A) easy
(B) easier
(C) easily
(D) ease

116. All financial experts are asked to submit their analysis reports on time ------- the short deadline.
(A) how much
(B) besides
(C) even though
(D) despite

117. Sera's Investment workers can get discounts at nearby stores by showing ------- of employment.
(A) print
(B) change
(C) goal
(D) proof

118. After ten years of service at Tom's restaurant chain, Lillian has ------- been given the Best Employee award.
(A) lastly
(B) especially
(C) finally
(D) exactly

119. Bank of Asia Corp. ------- appreciated your cooperation on the recent acquisition.
(A) deep
(B) deeply
(C) deepen
(D) depth

120. Jill Scott has ------- the next training seminar on the automated payroll system for October 10th.
(A) presented
(B) served
(C) invited
(D) scheduled

121. Mr. Yang had been promoted due to his ------- success.
(A) overwhelm
(B) overwhelming
(C) overwhelms
(D) overwhelmed

122. For business people ------- travel frequently, Star Travels offers special discounts.
(A) whichever
(B) which
(C) who
(D) whose

123. ------- available to work overtime on the weekends should e-mail the supervisor.
(A) Another
(B) Whoever
(C) Something
(D) Anyone

124. Due to the unexpected delay, we asked the research department to postpone the meeting until ------- in the week.
(A) that
(B) later
(C) past
(D) after

125. The questionnaire regarding the advertisement should be handed in today ------- they plan to present the results at tomorrow's meeting.
(A) whether or not
(B) in addition to
(C) in spite of
(D) regardless of

126. Although we arrived on time, it was so crowded that we had to wait ------- an hour to be seated.
(A) briefly
(B) nearly
(C) lately
(D) previously

127. If you have restarted your computer and it ------- to malfunction, contact our service representatives.
(A) had continued
(B) continuing
(C) will continue
(D) continues

128. Julie's Restaurant's menu features a ------- variety of fresh food items than Armelle's Kitchen's.
(A) wide
(B) wider
(C) widest
(D) widely

129. Our nation-wide retail ------- will provide our customers with high quality service.
(A) locations
(B) customers
(C) meetings
(D) expertise

130. While working at JBL Advertising, Mr. Park has ------- at communicating with its clients.
(A) organized
(B) excelled
(C) simplified
(D) instructed

PART 6

Directions: Read the texts that follow. A word, phrase, or sentence is missing in parts of each text. Four answer choices for each question are given below the text. Select the best answer to complete the text. Then mark the letter (A), (B), (C), or (D) on your answer sheet.

Questions 131-134 refer to the following e-mail.

To: Janet Miller
From: International Association of Construction
Date: May 6
Subject: Thank you for joining our membership
Attached: Guidebook

Dear Ms. Miller,

Thank you for your decision to join the International Association of Construction. Our organization ------- the health and safety of the worldwide construction community through a variety of programs and services.
                131.

Our ------- mission is to improve construction environments by advocating high safety standards in the
     132.
industry. We also provide professionally developed materials for new and experienced construction

workers. ------- .
         133.

Attached is a document detailing the benefits of ------- in our association. We look forward to helping
                                                  134.
you become a better, safer construction professional.

International Association of Construction

---

131. (A) would be supporting
(B) having supported
(C) supported
(D) supports

132. (A) frequent
(B) early
(C) primary
(D) previous

133. (A) However, it will complete its construction project on time.
(B) They feature up-to-date information on safety regulations and laws.
(C) In fact, we offer environmental education opportunities.
(D) Please send your résumés to be considered for the position.

134. (A) working
(B) diversity
(C) application
(D) membership

Questions 135-138 refer to the following article.

LONDON (August 10) — Chin Chen Apparel, a popular Chinese clothing manufacturer, will soon ------- its fashions in Europe. According to an interview with the EU Apparel News, the company's president, Robert Chen, reported that the first shipment of the company's latest sportswear and accessories will leave China in a few weeks. -------. Mr. Chen attributed Chin Chen's business move to a ------- demand for sportswear in Europe. "The recent trend is that more and more Europeans are wearing casual clothing and this is exactly ------- our company will provide."

135. (A) reduce
(B) design
(C) recall
(D) market

136. (A) Its sales were poor in European Market.
(B) It is even expected that new Chinese food will be launched next year.
(C) Another factor is the changes in consumer preferences.
(D) They will be available to European consumers as early as September.

137. (A) controlling
(B) rising
(C) questionable
(D) long-standing

138. (A) what
(B) which
(C) who
(D) when

Questions 139-142 refer to the following information.

4th Annual Fox Town Book Fair

The 4th Annual Fox Town Book Fair begins on Monday, March 20. ------- will last until Sunday, March 26. More than 100 famous authors and celebrities have been invited to participate. Readings, book signings, and panel discussions are scheduled, and ------- 3,000 attendees are expected.

The event will ------- Monday at 10 A.M. with a keynote discussion between best-selling novelist, Tamara Francis, and the president of Karl Culture Publishing Company, Melvin Dean, on the topic of recent trends in the publishing industry. -------. For details regarding the fair, including a complete list of events and author appearances, consult the Fox Town Book Fair website (www.foxtownbookfair.com).

139. (A) It
     (B) They
     (C) Most
     (D) Those

140. (A) approximating
     (B) approximated
     (C) approximates
     (D) approximately

141. (A) end
     (B) take
     (C) kick off
     (D) have

142. (A) Be sure to check any mistakes before submitting your article.
     (B) Both of the speakers are Fox Town natives.
     (C) Once the revised topics are made, please review it.
     (D) Unfortunately, its website is down for maintenance.

Questions 143-146 refer to the following letter.

Dear Evergreen Store shopper,

Thank you for your interest in joining Evergreen Store's Rewarding Loyalty program. Membership in this program ------- you to enjoy many exciting rewards. Your enrollment entitles you to early ------- about sales and special passes to private in-store events.
143. 144.

Enrolling in the program is easy. -------. Then, one of our customer service representatives in the store will be happy to process your application and issue a membership card to you.
145.

------- four weeks of the first purchase you make with your membership card, you will receive monthly statements detailing the points you have accumulated and the reward certificates you have earned. Membership is free of charge and can be canceled at any time. Visit an Evergreen Store today to start earning your rewards!
146.

Sincerely,

Ann Doyle
Director of Customer Service
Enclosure

143. (A) has allowed
(B) was allowing
(C) will allow
(D) allowed

144. (A) performance
(B) evaluation
(C) referral
(D) information

145. (A) You are now qualified for the program.
(B) Simply bring the enclosed application to our local store.
(C) It was started when we first opened.
(D) Thank you for shopping with us.

146. (A) Within
(B) Until
(C) Since
(D) Due to

PART 7

Directions: In this part you will read a selection of texts, such as magazine and newspaper articles, e-mails, and instant messages. Each text or set of texts is followed by several questions. Select the best answer for each question and mark the letter (A), (B), (C), or (D) on your answer sheet.

Questions 147-148 refer to the following article.

Increase in Sales: Redline Motors

Detroit, MI, March 5 — Redline Motors released its annual sales figures for its automobile lines. Compared to last year, the report showed that sales for this year increased by 4.5 percent. This increase is almost more than double the rate which industry experts had expected (2.2 percent). However, it is still not high enough for a company that showed a steady 7.0 percent increase in sales merely four years ago. Company directors remain positive; they showed their confidence by announcing that Redline Motors is in preparation to increase its production of automobiles during the next four years.

147. What is the purpose of the article?
(A) To advertise a new automobile
(B) To report on an increase in sales
(C) To describe a new trend in the market
(D) To announce that a factory will be built in Detroit

148. What is stated about the company directors?
(A) They are disappointed with the size of the increase.
(B) They are confident about the accuracy of the report.
(C) They want to make more automobiles over a four-year period.
(D) They plan to relocate the factory to another country.

Questions 149-150 refer to the following form.

Fiddler Corporation Security Center

On April 3, new security gates will be installed at the entrance of the parking lot. Those who park their cars in the parking lot must contact the security center to obtain access permits. Permits will allow entry to one parking area. If you wish to access additional areas, you need the approval of your manager.

To request a parking permit, please fill out the information below and send this form to the security center by April 1. If you have any troubles, contact Javier Lima at extension 30 for assistance.

Cut here and return the portion below

Employee Information

Name: *Christie Panama*   Employee Identification Number: *3462*

Department: *Technical Department*   Office: *207*   Parking Area: *2A*

Additional Access Needed? (Yes) No   Parking Area: *3C*

Vehicle Information

Approval Authorized By: *Louis Costa*   Date: *March 28*

Brand: *Wolkswagon*   Model: *Gulf*   Color: *Black*

License Plate: *LZC53U*

---

149. Why will Ms. Panama submit the form?

(A) To request an identification badge
(B) To sign up for a research seminar
(C) To correct her employee information
(D) To receive parking area access

150. What is indicated about Mr. Costa?

(A) He is Ms. Panama's manager.
(B) He occasionally drives to the office.
(C) He uses more than one parking area.
(D) He works in the security center.

Questions 151-152 refer to the following advertisement.

KH Headhunter.com

A large multinational corporation is seeking applicants interested in a top managerial position. The corporation is looking for a motivated, independent, highly effective individual with strong communication and team leadership skills.

The position requires dealing directly with the company's board of directors to report on and take charge of the public image for the company's high-end products and services.

The position involves directing product launches as well as developing and maintaining relationships with key clientele and important associates.

Applicants wishing to be considered should possess an MBA and have worked for at least ten years at a large IT company.

If you are interested, please send your résumé and a cover letter highlighting your experience to jklopez@khheadhunter.com.

151. Who will the successful candidate report to?
    (A) Company leaders
    (B) Key clientele
    (C) New consumers
    (D) Product managers

152. Which is NOT a requirement for applicants?
    (A) Good speaking skills
    (B) Advanced business education
    (C) Experience in the technology sector
    (D) Knowledge of the company's products

GO ON TO THE NEXT PAGE

Questions 153-154 refer to the following text message chain.

DUSTIN PARKER [11:15 A.M.]
I ordered ten meals for today's meeting but there are only eight here.

ANNE YANG [11:16 A.M.]
Really? I thought I checked all the orders. I'm sorry. I will call the restaurant right away and rush over there.

DUSTIN PARKER [11:28 A.M.]
The meeting will be over in about thirty minutes. How much longer will you be?

ANNE YANG [11:29 A.M.]
Maybe about twenty minutes. They didn't have the meals made. They're just about done though.

DUSTIN PARKER [11:30 A.M.]
Brian is presenting the marketing plan for our new refrigerator now. It's the last part of the presentation.

ANNE YANG [11:31 A.M.]
Okay, I should be there before his presentation ends.

DUSTIN PARKER [11:32 A.M.]
Sounds good. See you soon.

153. At 11:29 A.M., what does Ms. Yang mean when she writes, "They're just about done though"?

(A) The lunch time will be delayed.
(B) The meeting is almost finished.
(C) Most of the meals are gone.
(D) The order will be ready soon.

154. What is most likely true about Mr. Parker?

(A) He is leading a meeting.
(B) He works at an electronics company.
(C) He ordered some presents for clients.
(D) He forgot to bring his own lunch.

Questions 155-157 refer to the following information.

Holly Seinfield

Temporary Exhibit: The Lifework of Holly Seinfield
October 15 - December 7
First and Second Floor Gallery

The Bohemian Culture Museum is holding an exhibition this fall which includes the Lifework of Holly Seinfield, a well respected photographer and writer of the twentieth century. -[1]-. The exhibit will be featuring the background of Seinfield's life and illustrating the development of her career. Photographs and diaries which depict her childhood up to her present years will be on display. -[2]-. This upcoming exhibition has gathered some of her finest works from her old house in California and her present housing located in the center of Southern California. These collections of her writings and photographs will be placed on both the first and second floor of the gallery. -[3]-.

Advance registration for this wonderful exhibit is required. Tickets will be on sale starting September 2 and may only be purchased by visiting the Bohemian Culture Museum website at www.bohemianmuseum.com. -[4]-. All ticket buyers are allowed to view the exhibit only on the date and time printed on their tickets. For more information regarding the exhibit, call the Bohemian Culture Museum on (764) 188-1888.

155. What is the purpose of the information?
(A) To announce an upcoming event
(B) To publicize the opening of a new museum
(C) To advertise a recently published play
(D) To promote newly released films

156. What is stated about tickets?
(A) They will not be available before October 15.
(B) They can't be purchased online.
(C) They must be used on a specific date.
(D) They may be canceled at any time.

157. In which of the positions marked [1], [2], [3], and [4] does the following sentence best belong?

"In addition, a short documentary about Holly Seinfield will be shown on the basement floor."

(A) [1]
(B) [2]
(C) [3]
(D) [4]

Questions 158-160 refer to the following information.

Inner Sun Cinema
Employment Schedule Policy

Note: These policies are subject to change. Should any changes occur, all employees will be reminded beforehand.

Full-time Employees
Full-time employees must complete 40 hours in a week. The general schedule for a full-time worker is nine hours a day during the weekdays, but may be adjusted to work on the weekends. A full-time employee will receive overtime pay in a situation where one exceeds 40 hours of working time in a week. Full-time employees are eligible for a housing allowance of 5 percent of their salary. One hour-long lunch break is provided for all full-time employees.

Part-time Employees
Those who complete less than 40 hours are considered part-time employees. You may arrange your schedules with the managers. In normal cases, part-time employees should not go over the working hours that are stated in their contract. However, with the approval of the supervisors, part-time employees may receive overtime pay when they are assigned to work extra hours on a particular project. Part-time employees are eligible for a housing allowance of 3 percent of their salary. One hour-long lunch break is also provided for part-time employees.

Temporary Employees
A small number of temporary employees are often needed. These types of employees establish their schedules during contract negotiations. Unlike full-time or part-time workers, temporary employees are exempt from receiving housing allowance. In addition to this condition, they are not eligible for requesting overtime pay. As any other employees of Inner Sun Cinema, one hour-long lunch break is provided for all temporary employees as well.

158. Why is the information written?
(A) To announce that new workers have been hired
(B) To note the date of a rescheduled meeting
(C) To describe rules concerning hours and benefits
(D) To provide tips for conducting a housing search

159. What is indicated about part-time employees?
(A) They receive the same housing allowance that full-time workers do.
(B) Their schedules may include work from home.
(C) They are hired to work on special projects only.
(D) They may work overtime with a supervisor's permission.

160. What can temporary employees negotiate?
(A) The amount of their housing allowance
(B) The type of schedule they will receive
(C) The rate of overtime pay they will receive
(D) The length of their lunch break

Questions 161-163 refer to the following advertisement.

Opening Celebration

Scirocco Outlets

1503 Grand State Complex (Next to Jenna Jewelry & Accessories)
Tenafly, NJ, 07301

FREE polaroid camera with any purchase of $50 or more
(Grand State Complex only)

Specials:

20% off all underwear and socks
25% off shoes (sportwear only)
35% off any fashion accessories

Offer Valid from August 1 to August 30
Store Hours 9:00 A.M. to 9:00 P.M.

Sign up and receive our membership card that gives an additional
10% discount on any purchase for just $50 per year.
Apply for the card either at Grand State Complex or Pine Hill Plaza.
You may also receive the membership card online!

Visit our homepage (www.sciroccooutlets.com)
For this week only, you will receive 50% off of any necklaces
you buy only from our homepage!

---

161. What type of merchandise does Scirocco Outlets probably specialize in?

(A) Electronics
(B) Clothes
(C) Books
(D) Furniture

162. What is indicated about Scirocco Outlets?

(A) Its special offers will last for one week.
(B) It will stay open until 10:00 P.M. on August 1.
(C) Its salespeople are highly trained.
(D) It has more than one store location.

163. For which item will customers receive a discount when they purchase it online?

(A) A membership card
(B) A camera
(C) A necklace
(D) A shoe

Questions 164-167 refer to the following e-mail.

From: Rachel Carter, Park's Director <rcarter@kalamazoo.com>
To: Boris Becker <bbecker@kalamazoo.com>, Alex Kim <alexkim@kalamazoo.com>
Subject: Plans for June 16
Date: June 7

This week, four groups of hikers are scheduled to participate in an all-day hiking activity in Kalamazoo. You will be meeting with these groups when they arrive on Sunday morning and introduce them to the facilities near the mountain. Remember that two of the four groups will be staying overnight at the campsite, so you must give them a thorough explanation about the policies and regulations in relation to issues such as forest fires, food storage, and proper disposal of garbage. Lastly, before all groups leave from the visitor's center to start on the trail, make sure that all of them have checked out the updated information on our new website.

Thanks to our technical support team, the park's website is easy for everyone to navigate. If you haven't visited the site yet, please do so to familiarize yourself with the new layout, especially with the section which hikers might find useful. Some of these include links to local weather forecasts and our new travel plans and printing service. These features will help hikers create their own hiking maps based on their fitness level and the amount of time they want to spend hiking. These maps can then be printed and can act as a guide to hikers while they are on the trail. Please mention that while the printed maps are free of charge, donations are always happily accepted to maintain good care of the park facilities.

164. What is the purpose of the e-mail?

(A) To announce new hiking trails
(B) To provide directions to the visitor's center
(C) To show local weather forecasts
(D) To provide instructions to park employees

165. What will Boris Becker and Alex Kim most likely do on Sunday morning?

(A) Meet with the park's director
(B) Make reservations at the campsite
(C) Provide policy information to visitors
(D) Lead hikers through park trails

166. Where are all the hikers scheduled to meet?

(A) At the visitor's center
(B) At the food storage area
(C) At the technical support office
(D) At a campsite

167. According to the e-mail, what can hikers print for their own use?

(A) Meeting schedules
(B) Trail maps
(C) Park regulations
(D) Cabin reservations

Questions 168-171 refer to the following online chat session.

Alan Gomez [09:15 A.M.]
Good morning, everyone. I'd like to get together this Thursday. As you all know, our sales have decreased. We need to come up with some new plans.

Tracy Haynes [09:16 A.M.]
Yes, that's right.

Alan Gomez [09:17 A.M.]
The demand for office supplies is decreasing. So, I think expanding the Howard's catalog to include more products could be one solution.

Jonathon Graham [09:18 A.M.]
Cleaning products. All businesses need them for their offices.

Carla Romero [09:19 A.M.]
That's a good idea. I think we can also look into appliances like coffee makers and microwaves for use in break rooms.

Tracy Haynes [09:20 A.M.]
I agree. We could even sell office furniture.

Alan Gomez [09:22 A.M.]
Good ideas, all. At the Thursday meeting, I'd like each of you to present your own idea. And please include suppliers and costs in your presentation. I'll need that information for submitting a proposal to our directors.

Carla Romero [09:22 A.M.]
Sure thing.

Alan Gomez [09:24 A.M.]
Any questions? I'll e-mail you some guidelines this afternoon.

168. What type of product does Howard currently sell?
(A) Cleaning materials
(B) Office furniture
(C) Office supplies
(D) Kitchen appliances

169. At 09:15 A.M., what does Mr. Gomez mean when he writes, "We need to come up with some new plans"?
(A) The meeting needs to be held in a different place.
(B) The company needs to sell a wider range of items.
(C) The meeting needs to focus on more topics.
(D) The company needs to relocate its office.

170. What will Ms. Romero most likely do next?
(A) Purchase some appliances
(B) Send an e-mail to her coworkers
(C) Do some research
(D) Prepare a budget report

171. What will Mr. Gomez give the directors?
(A) Recent sales reports
(B) Information about costs
(C) A plan for updating the office space
(D) Recommendations for hiring new staff

Questions 172-175 refer to the following e-mail.

Date:	Thursday, December 20
To:	Jimmy Raynor <jimraynor@stcpractice.co.uk>
From:	Sam Duran <samduran@stcpractice.co.uk>
Subject:	My holiday

Hi, Jimmy,

I appreciate your decision to take over my responsibilities for a week until I return from my holiday next week. -[1]-.

First, as you know, there is a fax machine just outside our office. I would like to ask you to pick up all files from the fax machine every morning and afternoon. Please do not forget to hand them out promptly. Making and confirming appointments for the managing partners is one of my duties as well. Their schedules for next week have already been set up, but just in case, I left a copy of their schedule on your desk.

-[2]-. In case you haven't noticed, there is a case-review meeting in Room 101 on Wednesday, 10:30 A.M. Be sure to take notes during this meeting, type them up, and please e-mail them to everyone in the department before your lunch break. -[3]-.

Lastly, make sure you mail all the invoices to our clients by Friday afternoon. If you need any help, contact me or Sarah. -[4]-.

Thank you for helping!

Sincerely,

Sam Duran
Administrative Assistant

172. What is the purpose of the e-mail?
 (A) To provide a set of instructions
 (B) To describe the responsibilities of a new employee
 (C) To formally request time away from work
 (D) To finalize a meeting agenda

173. What is suggested about Mr. Raynor and Mr. Duran?
 (A) They were hired around the same time.
 (B) They work on different days.
 (C) They share an office space.
 (D) They have never met in person.

174. According to the e-mail, what is one task Mr. Duran usually performs every day?
 (A) Distributing faxes
 (B) Sending bills to clients
 (C) Taking notes at meetings
 (D) Scheduling holidays

175. In which of the positions marked [1], [2], [3], and [4] does the following sentence best belong?

 "Let me fill you in with some details of the duties which need to be taken care of."

 (A) [1]
 (B) [2]
 (C) [3]
 (D) [4]

Questions 176-180 refer to the following memo and e-mail.

DALTON TECHNOLOGY

From: Dino Hardy, Human Resources
To: Gale Medna, Administrative office
Date: February 6
Subject: New employee orientation

As you know it is time to prepare materials for our upcoming new employee orientation. You can obtain most of the supplies listed below from our regular supplier. However, please remember that Office Max has informed us that the planners with our logo printed on them are not available from them at this time.

All the materials should arrive no later than February 20 so that we can set up the seminar rooms before the orientation, which begins on February 23. Please contact me to confirm when the order has been placed and let me know the expected delivery date.

Thank you for your assistance.

List of materials
Writing Pads	200
10-packs of pens	220
Binder clips	222 boxes
Planners imprinted with the Dalton logo	290

E-mail

From: gmedna@daltontechnology.com
To: alopez@daltontechnology.com
Date: February 7, 13:20
Subject: Order for the upcoming orientation
Attachment: Orientation materials

Dear Ms. Lopez,

Dino Hardy is ordering the supplies he needs for the new employee orientation. Attached is a copy of his purchase order. I have already ordered the preapproved items from Office Max. At your earliest convenience, please authorize the purchase of the customized items he has requested. These will be ordered from Richter Office Supply Co. Once you have approved this transaction, I will ask Jennifer Cohen in the purchasing department to process that order as well. Mr. Hardy has told me that he needs all of the supplies no later than February 20.

Sincerely,

Gale Medna

176. Why was the memo written?
  (A) To provide the information of a new vendor
  (B) To request supplies for an event
  (C) To describe a series of events
  (D) To suggest changes for the design of a logo

177. In the memo, the word "available" in paragraph 1, line 4, is closest in meaning to
  (A) used
  (B) talked
  (C) purchased
  (D) reserved

178. What is the purpose of the e-mail?
  (A) To reserve a seminar room
  (B) To confirm a recent order
  (C) To recommend someone for a position
  (D) To request approval for a purchase

179. What will be purchased from Richter Office Supply Co.?
  (A) Note pads
  (B) Packs of pens
  (C) Binder clips
  (D) Planners

180. What is suggested about Jennifer Cohen?
  (A) She is responsible for organizing an event.
  (B) She has approved an order.
  (C) She has already contacted Office Max.
  (D) She works in the purchasing department.

Questions 181-185 refer to the following advertisement and list.

Enjoy "Star Travel" Tours

"Star Travel" tours provide you with a variety of local tasty food in the historic areas around Sydney, Canberra and Melbourne. One of our experienced guides gives information about the history and culture of each area where you visit, sampling specialities from each.

> Southern Town (Sydney)
>
> The tour is a progressive meal. At the first place you will stop for an appetizer. At the second location you will receive a sample-portion lunch and meet owner Gale Cohen, who is a Sydney-born award-winning chef. At the next restaurants, you will taste some of its finest food. And dessert will be served at the final location.
>
> When: 12:00 P.M. ~ 3:00 P.M. every Monday-Friday (not available Saturday and Sunday)
> Included: All food, a bottle of mineral water, and a brochure that includes a local map and details of all the restaurants and shops visited on the tour.
> Cost: $60 per person

For more information about our other tours,
please call 050-854-5289 or visit our website www.startravelworld.com.

Southern Town Restaurants
You will be visiting restaurants below in order listed.

1. Hugo's French
- Located at 145 Grande Street
- Specialize in southern French cuisine

2. Spathe
- Located at 107 East Street
- Restaurant combines European cuisine with live music during lunch hours
- Reservations required

3. Otaru Sushi
- Located at 1004 Queens Street
- Dishes displaying the best of Japan

4. Joey's Sweety
- Located at 356 King's Park Street
- Traditional and exotic sweets
- Closed Thursday

O'conail's Chocolate Cafe
- Located at 380 King's Park Street
- French-style chocolates made on site
- Alternate location for when Joey's Sweety is closed

181. What is suggested about 'Star Travel' tours in the advertisement?

(A) They offer a group discount.
(B) They are located in Sydney.
(C) They offer online reservations.
(D) They offer tours in different cities.

182. What is stated about guides?

(A) They are employed by restaurants.
(B) They provide information about history.
(C) They speak more than two languages.
(D) They were awarded by tourism department.

183. Where will tour participants meet Ms. Cohen?

(A) At Hugo's French
(B) At Spathe
(C) At Otaru Sushi
(D) At Joey's Sweety

184. What is NOT included on the Southern Town tour?

(A) Historical information
(B) A neighborhood map
(C) A discount coupon for future tours
(D) Musical entertainment

185. On what day will tour participants visit O'conail's Chocolate Cafe?

(A) Wednesday
(B) Thursday
(C) Friday
(D) Saturday

Questions 186-190 refer to the following advertisement and e-mails.

The Brownstone Hall in Kansas City offers a perfect atmosphere for any event. Whether it is a conference, a banquet, or an outdoor party, Brownstone is large enough to accommodate most groups. Through our restaurants, we can even offer catering services to guests. We have well-trained staff at your service to assist you for your ultimate satisfaction.

Reservations for Brownstone fill up very quickly, so if you are planning a big event, please call at least three weeks in advance. Send us an e-mail at rico@brownstone.com for reservations and give us the following information:

▶ Your name, organization, and contact information
▶ The type of event
▶ The date and time of your event
▶ The number of guests
▶ The preferred time to reach you

Remember, members of Brownstone Hall never have to pay the full amount!
If you wish to become a member, visit our website at www.brownstonehall.net. Reduced rates are also available for educational institutions and nonprofit groups.

To: Donald Rico <rico@brownstone.com>
From: Michael Hidalgo <MichHidalgo@colemanart.com>
Subject: Room Reservations
Date: August 15

Dear Mr. Rico,

Hi, my name is Michael Hidalgo, and I am the events administrator at the Coleman Art Center. We're planning on renting one of your facilities for our annual banquet on September 17 at 7 P.M.

Before making our reservation, I would like to be given a brief tour of some of the rooms that are available on that night. Also, I would like to know whether it is allowed to use an outside catering service for the banquet. The best time to reach me is between 5 P.M. to 8 P.M. on all business days. My number is 417-888-7878.

Thanks in advance.

Sincerely,

Michael Hidalgo

E-mail

To: Michael Hidalgo <MichHidalgo@colemanart.com>
From: Donald Rico <rico@brownstone.com>
Re: Room Reservations
Date: August 16

Dear Mr. Hidalgo

Thanks for your inquiring about renting our facilities and catering service for your event. Unfortunately, on the date you requested, there will be renovation work during that whole week. If you want, I can recommend another conference hall located outside the city. It would take 15 minutes from your art center. If you're interested in the place, please let me know so that I can contact them in advance. I'm sorry for the inconvenience this has caused.

Sincerely,

Donald Rico

---

186. What does the advertisement promote?
(A) A new restaurant
(B) A rental facility
(C) A business conference
(D) An art exhibit

187. What group is NOT offered a discount?
(A) Nonprofit organizations
(B) Members of the Brownstone Hall
(C) Relatives of Brownstone Hall employees
(D) Educational institutions

188. What type of event is Mr. Hidalgo planning?
(A) A company dinner
(B) A training session
(C) An award ceremony
(D) An annual conference

189. What will happen on September 17 at the Brownstone Hall?
(A) A banquet will be held.
(B) An art exhibit will be offered for free.
(C) A special offer will end.
(D) It will be under renovation.

190. What does Mr. Rico advise that Mr. Hidalgo do?
(A) Move a date
(B) Change a location
(C) Provide details about an event
(D) Rent more rooms

Questions 191-195 refer to the following e-mails and event schedule.

To: Edward Myers <edmyers@qwayne.com>
From: Janet Charles <jcharles@qwayne.com>
Date: February 17
Subject: Draft Schedule
Attachment: Draft Event Schedule

Hi Edward,

I have just completed making a draft of our schedule for March and April. So I attached it to this e-mail and I will put it in the event section on our website. But please note that we've not yet confirmed the location on April 28, which means the schedule might be changed. Please let me know if you have any questions or need to make any changes in the schedule.

Best regards,

Janet

Q-Wayne Enterprise Association
March-April Events
All events will be held in Park Resort Hotel.

March 14: 11:00 A.M. – 3:00 P.M. **Event:** Business Strategies Course **Location:** Main Hall 1F **Cost:** $50 at the door **Notes:** Advanced registration available ($40)	**April 16:** 11:30 A.M. – 12:45 P.M. **Event:** Networking Lunch (Buffet) **Location:** Seafood Gardens **Cost:** $20 in advance or $30 at the door **Notes:** Limited to 200 participants Advanced registration recommended
March 20: 9:00 A.M. – 3:00 P.M. **Event:** International Job Fair **Location:** Jordan Hall **Cost:** $30 **Notes:** Advanced registration only	**April 28:** 5:00 P.M. – 7:30 P.M. **Event:** Real Estate Investment Seminar **Location:** Main Hall 1F **Cost:** $40 **Notes:** Advanced registration not available

To: Janet Charles <jcharles@qwayne.com>
From: Edward Myers <edmyers@qwayne.com>
Date: March 3
Subject: Meeting updates

Janet,

As you are already aware, we hold an event committee meeting on the first day of every month. Our most recent meeting took place two days ago from 11:00 A.M. to 12:00 P.M.

Let me fill you in with some updates. We decided to extend the networking lunch, so it will now end at 1:00 P.M. The start time will remain the same. These changes are final, so please make the necessary changes on our website. By the way, if it's all right with you, would you mind working at the registration desk for the April 16 event?

Thanks.

Edward

191. Why did Ms. Charles write the e-mail?
(A) To get some feedback on an agenda
(B) To provide a draft schedule
(C) To inform a policy change
(D) To revise a report

192. Which event is subject to change?
(A) The business strategies course
(B) The international job fair
(C) The networking lunch
(D) The real estate investment seminar

193. What is suggested about the events provided by Q-wayne Enterprise Association?
(A) They require online reservation.
(B) They happen once a month.
(C) They will be held at the same hotel.
(D) They are only offered to association members.

194. According to the second e-mail, what is true about the networking event?
(A) Its location has been changed.
(B) Its time will be extended.
(C) It has been canceled.
(D) It needs more advertising.

195. What does Mr. Myers ask Ms. Charles to do?
(A) Work at the networking lunch
(B) Lead one of the events
(C) Share a survey result with guests speakers
(D) Recommend a guest speaker

Questions 196-200 refer to the following e-mails and schedule.

From: Vinny Fermat <vfermat@secadvisor.com>
To: Mary Vitter <maryvitter@secadvisor.com>
Subject: Holmes & Jarrett Company
Date: Tuesday, September 7, 4:15 P.M.

Hi Mary,

I just finished scheduling a meeting with representatives of Holmes & Jarrett Company(H&J) between 3:00 P.M. to 5:00 P.M. on Wednesday, September 15. We should take this opportunity seriously and properly introduce the strength of our security service to one of the leading construction companies in the nation. We will talk in the morning about how we are going to prepare for the first meeting with H&J.

I asked Antonio to check the appropriate train schedule to Metro City and reminded him to fax a copy to your office. One question. Are you going to be here in the Englewood office on September 15? If yes, I will ask Antonio to reserve two tickets to leave from Englewood to Metro City. If not, call Antonio to see whether there are tickets available leaving from Bronsun.

H&J will arrange a taxi to pick us up from the Metro City station at 2:30 P.M. They have also invited us to a dinner along with some H&J staff in a restaurant in Metro City called Havana Delight, from 6:00 to 8:00 P.M. The restaurant is about 15 minutes away from the station, so I assume we could take the train back to Englewood around at 8:15 P.M.

Vinny

RAIL CONNECT

Schedule Information, September-October
Scotchtown-Mayton Line

TRAIN NO.	1922(WD)	1023(WE)	7849(HD)	2007(EX)
Englewood	11:18 A.M.	11:21 A.M.	11:37 A.M.	1:41 P.M.
Bronsun	11:59 A.M.	12:02 P.M.	-	-
Crystal Lake	12:42 P.M.	12:45 P.M.	-	-
Horseville	1:23 P.M.	1:26 P.M.	12:53 P.M.	-
Metro City	2:15 P.M.	2:18 P.M.	-	-
San Marino	2:47 P.M.	2:50 P.M.	1:26 P.M.	3:18 P.M.

EX-Express service does not make any stops.
WE-Service operates only on the weekends.
WD-Service operates only on Mondays to Fridays.
HD-Holiday schedule; does not make all stops, effective on September 12 and October 3.

The railway's automated telephone service provides train information 24 hours a day: call 002-3355

Tickets
To purchase with a credit card:
Tickets can be purchased and printed by logging onto the website, www.railconnect.com/tickets, or from the ticket booth at the station entrance.
To purchase with cash:
Tickets can be purchased at either Lexington's newsstand near the waiting area, the ticket booth, or on board. Note that there is an extra charge of $5 if you purchase tickets on board.

From: Mary Vitter <maryvitter@secadvisor.com>
To: Vinny Fermat <vfermat@secadvisor.com>
RE: Holmes & Jarrett Company
Date: Wednesday, September 8, 11:00 A.M.

Hi, Vinny.

I just received your e-mail about the meeting with Holmes & Jarrett Company. However, I will be in Bronsun on September 15. As you suggested, I tried to call Antonio several times this morning to reserve a ticket but he did not answer. I have to attend a client meeting now, so could you please contact him to check the availability of the ticket for me and let me know whether he can get the tickets? Thanks for taking care of everything.

Your sincerely,

Mary

196. What type of business does Ms. Fermat work for?
(A) A travel agency
(B) A construction company
(C) A security firm
(D) A food restaurant chain

197. What is indicated about Holmes & Jarrett?
(A) Its office is located 30 minutes from the closest train station.
(B) It has been a partner of Security Advisors for many years.
(C) Its latest project is to construct a new building for Havana Delight.
(D) It is one of the leading construction companies.

198. What train will Ms. Fermat most likely take in order to attend the meeting?
(A) Train number 1922
(B) Train number 1023
(C) Train number 7849
(D) Train number 2007

199. According to the schedule, what is NOT mentioned as a way to purchase train tickets?
(A) Paying cash on board the train
(B) Using the railway's automated telephone system
(C) Going to Lexington's newsstand
(D) Visiting Rail Connect's website

200. What is suggested about Ms. Vitter?
(A) She will take a train with Ms. Fermat.
(B) She cannot attend a meeting in Metro City.
(C) She already reserved a ticket by herself.
(D) She will have a dinner with H&J staff on September 15.

Stop! This is the end of the test. If you finish before time is called, you may go back to Parts 5, 6, and 7 and check your work.

ACTUAL TEST

ANSWER SHEET

ACTUAL TEST
ANSWER SHEET

영단기 토익
다이렉트 700+

LC+RC 한 달 완성

누구보다
친절한
해설 PDF
무료 제공

정답 및 해석

영단기

PART 1

 사람 중심 사진

Point 01 1인 사진

Check-up Test
1. (D)　2. (D)　3. (C)　4. (D)　5. (B)

1.
(A) She is reading a paper.
(B) She is opening a box.
(C) She is holding a book.
(D) She is facing a machine.
(A) 그녀는 서류를 읽고 있다.
(B) 그녀는 상자를 열고 있다.
(C) 그녀는 책을 들고 있다.
(D) 그녀는 기계를 마주하고 있다.

2.
(A) She's talking to a customer.
(B) She's walking into the store.
(C) She's buying some clothes.
(D) She's looking at merchandise.
(A) 그녀는 손님과 이야기하고 있다.
(B) 그녀는 가게 안으로 걸어 들어가고 있다.
(C) 그녀는 옷을 몇 벌 사고 있다.
(D) 그녀는 상품을 보고 있다.

3.
(A) He's arranging supplies in a laboratory.
(B) He's hanging up his lab coat.
(C) He's wearing protective gloves.
(D) He's reaching into his pocket.
(A) 그는 실험실에서 비품을 정리하고 있다.
(B) 그는 실험실 가운을 걸고 있다.
(C) 그는 보호 장갑을 끼고 있다.
(D) 그는 주머니에 손을 넣고 있다.

4.
(A) A piano is being moved.
(B) A woman is standing on a stool.
(C) Some paper has been left on a music stand.
(D) A potted plant has been placed near the wall.
(A) 피아노를 옮기고 있는 중이다.
(B) 여자가 등받이 없는 의자 위에 서 있다.
(C) 보면대에 문서가 놓여 있다.
(D) 벽 근처에 화분이 놓여 있다.

5.
(A) A woman is washing a dish.
(B) A woman is studying a menu.
(C) A glass is being poured.
(D) The meal has been laid out on the table.
(A) 여자가 접시를 닦고 있다.
(B) 여자가 메뉴를 살펴보고 있다.
(C) 유리잔에 무언가를 따르고 있다.
(D) 음식이 테이블에 놓여 있다.

Point 02 2인 이상 사진

Check-up Test
1. (B)　2. (A)　3. (D)　4. (B)　5. (B)

1.
(A) They are walking along the shore.
(B) They are waving their hands.
(C) A woman is adjusting her sunglasses.
(D) A boat is being rowed across a river.
(A) 그들은 해안가를 따라 걷고 있다.
(B) 그들은 손을 흔들고 있다.
(C) 한 여자가 그녀의 선글라스를 조정하고 있다.
(D) 배의 노를 저어 강을 건너고 있다.

2.
(A) Some people are standing in front of a store.
(B) A customer is paying at a cash register.
(C) Some signs are posted on the wall.
(D) A woman is taking an item from a shelf.
(A) 사람들이 가게 앞에 서 있다.
(B) 손님이 계산대에서 돈을 지불하고 있다.
(C) 표지판이 벽에 게시되어 있다.
(D) 한 여자가 선반에서 물건을 꺼내고 있다.

3.
(A) Some people are waiting in line for food.
(B) A server is taking orders from customers.
(C) They are arranging some chairs.
(D) Some food is being cooked on a grill.
(A) 사람들이 줄을 서서 음식을 기다리고 있다.
(B) 종업원이 고객들에게 주문을 받고 있다.
(C) 그들은 의자를 정리하고 있다.
(D) 음식이 그릴 위에서 요리되고 있다.

4.
(A) They are focusing on the computer screen.
(B) Some people are attending a presentation.
(C) Office supplies are being distributed to people.
(D) One of the employees is opening the window.
(A) 그들은 컴퓨터 화면에 집중하고 있다.
(B) 사람들이 발표에 참석하고 있다.
(C) 사람들에게 사무용품이 배부되고 있다.
(D) 직원 중 한 사람이 창문을 열고 있다.

5.
(A) Some people are carrying a ladder.
(B) Some workers are constructing a roof.
(C) The fence is being torn down.
(D) Windows are being measured.
(A) 사람들이 사다리를 옮기고 있다.
(B) 작업자들이 지붕을 설치하고 있다.
(C) 울타리가 허물어지고 있다.
(D) 창문의 치수를 재고 있다.

Chapter Test
1. (C)　2. (D)　3. (D)　4. (B)　5. (C)　6. (C)

1.
(A) She is arranging a shelf.
(B) She is holding a box.
(C) She is pushing a cart.
(D) She is parking a car.
(A) 그녀는 선반을 정리하고 있다.
(B) 그녀는 상자를 들고 있다.
(C) 그녀는 카트를 밀고 있다.
(D) 그녀는 자동차를 주차하고 있다.

2.
(A) She's riding a bicycle.
(B) She's repairing a car.
(C) She's arranging some equipment.
(D) She's sitting in a vehicle.
(A) 그녀는 자전거를 타고 있다.
(B) 그녀는 자동차를 수리하고 있다.
(C) 그녀는 장비를 정리하고 있다.
(D) 그녀는 차량 안에 앉아 있다.

3.
(A) There is a reflection in a mirror.
(B) A necklace is displayed in the display case.
(C) They are examining some items with a magnifying glass.
(D) A salesperson is helping a customer select merchandise.
(A) 거울에 반사된 모습이 있다.
(B) 목걸이가 진열대에 진열되어 있다.
(C) 그들이 확대경으로 제품들을 살펴보고 있다.
(D) 판매원이 손님이 물건을 고르는 것을 돕고 있다.

4.
(A) They're buying a shopping cart.
(B) Some merchandise is being examined.
(C) Some shelves are being installed.
(D) A man is handing an item to a woman.
(A) 그들이 쇼핑 카트를 구매하고 있다.
(B) 제품을 보고 있다.
(C) 선반이 몇 개 설치되고 있다.
(D) 남자가 여자에게 물건을 건네고 있다.

5.
(A) They're having a talk.
(B) Computers have been arranged in a circle.
(C) Each person is seated in front of a workstation.
(D) Chairs are stacked in a room.
(A) 그들이 대화를 하고 있다.
(B) 컴퓨터가 원형으로 배열되어 있다.
(C) 사람들은 각자 작업 책상에 앉아 있다.
(D) 의자들이 방에 쌓여 있다.

6.
(A) A worker is spraying the ground.
(B) A man is squatting while holding some plants.
(C) Rows of potted plants are hanging in a greenhouse.
(D) The gardener is trimming the bushes.
(A) 작업자가 땅에 물을 뿌리고 있다.
(B) 남자가 화분들을 들고 쪼그려 앉아 있다.
(C) 화분에 심긴 식물들이 여러 줄로 온실에 매달려 있다.
(D) 정원사는 수풀을 다듬고 있다.

Chapter 2　사물 중심 사진

Point 01　실내 공간 사진

Check-up Test
1. (C)　2. (B)　3. (B)　4. (B)　5. (D)

1.
(A) A cafeteria is crowded with people.
(B) A picture has been hung above the window.
(C) The tables are covered with tablecloths.
(D) Vases have been placed on each table.
(A) 카페테리아가 사람들로 붐빈다.
(B) 그림이 창문 위에 걸려 있다.
(C) 테이블들이 테이블보로 덮여 있다.
(D) 꽃병이 각 테이블마다 놓여 있다.

2.
(A) Some curtains have been pulled closed.
(B) Some papers are spread out on a desk.
(C) The chair is occupied.
(D) Cabinets have been stocked with some supplies.
(A) 일부 커튼이 닫혀 있다.

(B) 종이들이 책상 위에 널려 있다.
(C) 의자에 사람이 앉아 있다.
(D) 캐비닛들이 물품으로 채워져 있다.

3.
(A) Food is being served on a tray.
(B) A dining area is set up for a meal.
(C) Some chairs are stacked at the corner.
(D) Some plates are piled in a sink.
(A) 음식이 쟁반으로 제공되고 있다.
(B) 식사를 위해 식사 공간이 마련되어 있다.
(C) 의자들이 구석에 쌓여 있다.
(D) 접시가 싱크대에 쌓여 있다.

4.
(A) A floor is being polished.
(B) Some artworks are being displayed.
(C) Tourists are gathering around an exhibition.
(D) Some cases have been emptied of their contents.
(A) 바닥을 닦고 있다.
(B) 예술품이 전시되고 있다.
(C) 관광객들이 전시품 주위로 모이고 있다.
(D) 일부 케이스가 내용물 없이 비어 있다.

5.
(A) A computer has been taken apart.
(B) A technician is working in a laboratory.
(C) A file drawer has been filled with documents.
(D) Some equipment has been placed on a counter.
(A) 컴퓨터가 분해되어 있다.
(B) 기술자가 실험실에서 일하고 있다.
(C) 파일 서랍이 문서로 가득 차 있다.
(D) 일부 장비가 상판 위에 놓여 있다.

Point 02 야외 배경 사진

Check-up Test
1. (B) 2. (B) 3. (C) 4. (A) 5. (A)

1.
(A) Street lamps line the road.
(B) A lane has been blocked for maintenance work.
(C) Some workers are repaving the street.
(D) There are some cars parked near the curb.
(A) 가로등들이 길을 따라 늘어서 있다.
(B) 정비 작업을 위해 도로가 막혀 있다.
(C) 작업자들이 거리를 재포장하고 있다.
(D) 연석 근처에 차들이 주차되어 있다.

2.
(A) A car has stopped at a service station.
(B) Vehicles are parked in multi-level structures.
(C) A man is entering the parking garage.
(D) Cars are driving across a bridge.
(A) 자동차가 주유소에 서 있다.
(B) 차량들이 여러 층의 구조물에 주차되어 있다.
(C) 남자가 주차장으로 들어가고 있다.
(D) 차들이 다리 위를 달리고 있다.

3.
(A) Some workers are repairing windows.
(B) Some potted plants are being watered.
(C) A balcony is attached to every apartment.
(D) A railing is being installed.
(A) 작업자들이 창문을 수리하고 있다.
(B) 화분에 물을 주고 있다.
(C) 발코니가 모든 아파트에 달려 있다.
(D) 난간을 설치하고 있다.

4.
(A) Some buildings are located near the shoreline.
(B) A ship is approaching a pier.
(C) Some people are paddling on the water.
(D) Some bushes are being planted along the street.
(A) 일부 빌딩들이 해안가에 있다.
(B) 배가 부두로 다가가고 있다.
(C) 사람들이 물 위에서 노를 젓고 있다.
(D) 길을 따라 관목들을 심고 있다.

5.
(A) Corridors are lined with arches.
(B) Trees are casting shadows on a building.
(C) There is a fence around the courtyard.
(D) A water fountain is spraying into the air.
(A) 복도가 아치형으로 이어져 있다.
(B) 나무들이 빌딩에 그림자를 드리우고 있다.
(C) 마당 주위에 울타리가 있다.
(D) 분수대에서 공중으로 물이 뿜어져 나오고 있다.

Chapter Test
1. (B) 2. (A) 3. (A) 4. (D) 5. (C) 6. (A)

1.
(A) All the cabinets have been opened.
(B) Some jars are arranged on shelves.
(C) Boxes are stacked on the floor.
(D) Drawers have been left open.
(A) 모든 캐비닛이 열려 있다.
(B) 병들이 선반에 정렬되어 있다.

(C) 상자들이 바닥에 쌓여 있다.
(D) 서랍들이 열려 있다.

2.
(A) The table is surrounded by chairs.
(B) Tables are stacked on top of each other.
(C) People are using some tools.
(D) There is a potted plant at the entrance of the building.
(A) 테이블이 의자로 둘러싸여 있다.
(B) 테이블들이 차곡차곡 쌓여 있다.
(C) 사람들이 연장을 사용하고 있다.
(D) 건물 입구에 화분이 하나 있다.

3.
(A) A car has stopped at a gas station.
(B) A car is entering a building.
(C) A woman is stepping onto a curb.
(D) Workers are watering the grass.
(A) 자동차가 주유소에 정차해 있다.
(B) 자동차가 건물에 들어가고 있다.
(C) 여자가 도로 경계석(연석)을 디디고 있다.
(D) 작업자들이 잔디에 물을 주고 있다.

4.
(A) The airplane is landing.
(B) The airplane is taking off at the airport.
(C) The runway is full of airplanes.
(D) The airplane is parked on the ground.
(A) 비행기가 착륙하고 있다.
(B) 비행기가 공항에서 이륙하고 있다.
(C) 활주로가 비행기로 가득 차 있다.
(D) 비행기가 땅에 세워져 있다.

5.
(A) A crowd has gathered in a circle.
(B) A building overlooks a river.
(C) A statue is mounted on a pedestal.
(D) The stairs lead to a forest.
(A) 군중이 둥글게 모여 있다.
(B) 빌딩이 강을 내려다보고 있다.
(C) 조각상이 받침대 위에 세워져 있다.
(D) 계단이 숲으로 연결되어 있다.

6.
(A) A lighthouse is situated near a shoreline.
(B) A ferry is approaching the island.
(C) A sailor is boarding a ship.
(D) Rocks are scattered along the water's edge.
(A) 등대가 해안선 가까이에 위치해 있다.
(B) 페리가 섬에 접근하고 있다.
(C) 선원이 배에 탑승하고 있다.
(D) 바위들이 물가를 따라 산발적으로 있다.

PART 2

Chapter 1 의문사 의문문 I

Point 01 행위의 주체에 대한 답변을 찾는 Who 의문문

Check-up Test

1. (A) 2. (B) 3. (A) 4. (A) 5. (C) 6. (B)
7. (C) 8. (A)

1. Who is the new accountant?
(A) It's David Long.
(B) To open an account.
(C) On the shelf.
누가 새로운 회계사인가요?
(A) 데이비드 롱이요.
(B) 계좌를 개설하기 위해서요.
(C) 선반 위에 있습니다.

2. Who won The Best Sales Representative Of The Year Award?
(A) Yes, I know that.
(B) Someone from the Southern regional office.
(C) At the end of the year.
누가 올해의 최고 영업 사원상을 수상했나요?
(A) 네, 알고 있어요.
(B) 남부 지사 사람입니다.
(C) 연말에요.

3. Who's the next guest speaker?
(A) The company vice president.
(B) Yes, it's loud.
(C) No, I spoke yesterday.
다음 초청 연사는 누구인가요?
(A) 회사 부사장님입니다.
(B) 네, 시끄럽습니다.
(C) 아니요, 저는 어제 말했습니다.

4. Who's designing the new company logo?
(A) McKinson company.
(B) At the warehouse.
(C) You have to log in.
누가 새로운 회사 로고를 디자인하나요?
(A) 맥킨슨 사입니다.
(B) 창고에요.
(C) 당신은 로그인해야 합니다.

5. Who was knocking at the door?
(A) I've locked it.
(B) Tonight at seven.
(C) Our new neighbor.

누가 문에서 노크를 하고 있었나요?
(A) 제가 그것을 잠갔어요.
(B) 오늘 밤 7시에요.
(C) 우리의 새 이웃이요.

6. Who is going to reinstall this program for me?
(A) Did you look under the table?
(B) Jane can help you.
(C) I have watched it already.

누가 저를 위해 이 프로그램을 재설치해 주실 건가요?
(A) 테이블 밑을 살펴보셨나요?
(B) 제인 씨가 당신을 도와줄 수 있어요.
(C) 저는 그것을 이미 봤어요.

7. Who's in charge of the marketing team?
(A) I've never been to that market.
(B) It's down the hall.
(C) Ms. Thompson, but she's not here.

마케팅팀은 누가 맡고 있나요?
(A) 저는 그 시장에 가 본 적이 없어요.
(B) 그것은 복도를 따라가면 있어요.
(C) 톰슨 씨요, 그런데 그녀는 여기 없어요.

8. Who do you think will be the next company president?
(A) No one is sure yet.
(B) This is my business.
(C) An electronics company.

누가 차기 사장이 될 것 같아요?
(A) 아직 아무도 몰라요.
(B) 제 일이에요.
(C) 전자 회사요.

> **Point 02** 장소에 대한 답변을 찾는 Where 의문문

Check-up Test
1. (A) 2. (B) 3. (B) 4. (B) 5. (C) 6. (C)
7. (C) 8. (B)

1. Where does Ms. Hurt teach economics?
(A) At a university in London.
(B) It is not efficient.
(C) On weekends mostly.

허트 씨는 어디에서 경제학을 가르치나요?
(A) 런던의 한 대학에서요.
(B) 효율적이지 못해요.
(C) 대부분 주말에요.

2. Where is Anthony going this week?
(A) By train, I think.
(B) To the shopping center.
(C) No, last week.

앤서니는 이번 주에 어딜 가나요?
(A) 기차로요. 제 생각에는요.
(B) 쇼핑센터에요.
(C) 아니요, 지난주요.

3. Where did you hear the news?
(A) No, that's not true.
(B) One of my colleagues told me.
(C) A new menu.

그 소식을 어디에서 들었어요?
(A) 아니요, 사실이 아닙니다.
(B) 동료 한 명이 말해 주었어요.
(C) 새로운 메뉴요.

4. Where does the bus to city center stop?
(A) Every hour on the hour.
(B) Just around the corner.
(C) No, it didn't.

시내로 가는 버스가 어디에서 서나요?
(A) 매시 정각에요.
(B) 바로 길모퉁이에서요.
(C) 아니요, 그렇지 않았어요.

5. Where are all the plates for the party?
(A) No, I'm not going.
(B) Did you cook?
(C) They are in the bottom drawer.

파티에 쓸 접시들은 다 어디에 있나요?
(A) 아니요, 저는 가지 않을 거예요.
(B) 당신이 요리하셨나요?
(C) 그것들은 맨 아래 서랍에 있어요.

6. Where's a good place to get some snacks?
(A) She eats it often.
(B) We are in second place.
(C) Across the street from the park.

간식을 살 만한 곳이 어디인가요?
(A) 그녀는 그것을 자주 먹어요.
(B) 우리는 2등이에요.
(C) 공원 건너편이요.

7. Where can I get paper for the copier?
(A) It'll take four.
(B) Not that I know of.
(C) Check the supply closet.

복사기 용지는 어디에 있나요?
(A) 4시간 걸릴 거예요.
(B) 제가 알기로는 아니에요.
(C) 물품 보관실을 확인해 보세요.

8. Where did Bill find the letter?
(A) In the middle of April.
(B) Margret gave it to him.

(C) It's fine with me.

빌은 그 편지를 어디서 찾았나요?
(A) 4월 중순에요.
(B) 마거릿이 그에게 줬어요.
(C) 전 괜찮아요.

Point 03 시간에 대한 답변을 찾는 When 의문문

Check-up Test

1. (C) 2. (B) 3. (C) 4. (C) 5. (A) 6. (A)
7. (C) 8. (A)

1. When does the new secretary begin work?
(A) She needs pens and notepads.
(B) At the front desk.
(C) Actually, she started this morning.

그 새로운 비서는 언제 일을 시작하나요?
(A) 그녀는 펜과 노트가 필요해요.
(B) 안내 데스크에요.
(C) 사실, 그녀는 오늘 아침에 시작했어요.

2. When will the merger take place?
(A) Between the companies.
(B) Sometime next week.
(C) Yes, you are right.

합병은 언제 되나요?
(A) 두 회사 간에요.
(B) 다음 주쯤에요.
(C) 네, 당신이 맞습니다.

3. When was the inspector supposed to arrive?
(A) The poster looks fine.
(B) Yes, she left already.
(C) At three o'clock.

검사관이 언제 도착하기로 했나요?
(A) 포스터는 좋아 보입니다.
(B) 네, 그녀는 벌써 떠났습니다.
(C) 3시 정각에요.

4. When will Ms. Kelly's paper be available?
(A) One please.
(B) The bookshop on High Street.
(C) She said this evening.

켈리 씨의 논문을 언제 볼 수 있을까요?
(A) 한 개 주세요.
(B) 하이 가에 있는 서점입니다.
(C) 그녀가 오늘 저녁이라고 했습니다.

5. When did you learn about your promotion?
(A) Just now.
(B) The division manager.
(C) By e-mail.

당신의 승진 사실을 언제 알았나요?
(A) 방금요.
(B) 부장요.
(C) 이메일로요.

6. When can we expect to receive the payment?
(A) In two days.
(B) Since last Monday.
(C) Certainly.

우리가 돈을 언제 받을 수 있을까요?
(A) 이틀 후에요.
(B) 지난주 월요일부터요.
(C) 물론이지요.

7. When did you buy your car?
(A) I'm afraid not.
(B) By myself.
(C) About a month ago.

당신은 언제 자동차를 구입했나요?
(A) 유감이지만 아니에요.
(B) 저 혼자서요.
(C) 약 한 달 전에요.

8. When's the new product demonstration?
(A) It does not start until 1 o'clock.
(B) At the stadium.
(C) For about five hours.

신제품 시연회는 언제 있나요?
(A) 1시에 시작해요.
(B) 경기장에서요.
(C) 거의 5시간 동안이요.

Chapter Test

1. (C)   2. (A)   3. (C)   4. (B)   5. (C)
6. (B)   7. (B)   8. (B)   9. (C)   10. (C)
11. (C) 12. (B) 13. (B) 14. (B) 15. (C)

1. When do you want to schedule an appointment?
(A) Yes, I was disappointed.
(B) That is too late.
(C) Sometime next month.

언제로 약속을 잡을까요?
(A) 네, 저는 실망했습니다.
(B) 그건 너무 늦습니다.
(C) 다음 달쯤에요.

2. Who already received their ID card?
(A) We got ours this morning.
(B) At the reception.

(C) That sounds good.

누가 벌써 신분증을 받았나요?
(A) 우리는 오늘 아침에 받았어요.
(B) 접수처에서요.
(C) 좋은 생각이에요.

3. Where can I leave my luggage?
(A) It's in the airport.
(B) I already have some.
(C) There's space by the door.

제 짐을 어디에 둘까요?
(A) 그건 공항에 있어요.
(B) 저는 이미 몇 개 가지고 있습니다.
(C) 문 옆에 공간이 있어요.

4. Who's responsible for organizing the conference?
(A) No, we only accept cash.
(B) Ms. Jenkins is.
(C) We have many responses.

누가 학회 준비를 담당하고 있나요?
(A) 아니요, 우리는 현금만 받습니다.
(B) 젠킨스 씨입니다.
(C) 우리는 많은 회신을 받았어요.

5. When can I expect to see a doctor?
(A) Yes, just a few more exams.
(B) She is a great nurse.
(C) He will be here in a minute.

의사 선생님을 언제 뵐 수 있을까요?
(A) 네, 몇 가지 검사만 더 하고요.
(B) 그녀는 훌륭한 간호사입니다.
(C) 그는 곧 여기 오실 겁니다.

6. Who locked the doors last night?
(A) He made a decision.
(B) I have no idea.
(C) This is the last one.

어젯밤에 누가 문을 잠갔나요?
(A) 그가 결정했어요.
(B) 저는 모르겠어요.
(C) 이게 마지막입니다.

7. Where did Victoria leave the reports?
(A) Yes, I found them.
(B) On your desk.
(C) From New York.

빅토리아가 보고서를 어디에 두었나요?
(A) 네, 제가 그것들을 찾았습니다.
(B) 당신 책상 위에요.
(C) 뉴욕에서요.

8. Who ordered a new computer for the lab?
(A) Yes, it is brand new.
(B) My supervisor did.
(C) Very expensive.

누가 연구실에 새 컴퓨터를 주문했나요?
(A) 네, 그건 신제품입니다.
(B) 제 상관이 (주문)했습니다.
(C) 매우 비쌉니다.

9. Where can I buy a new charger for my laptop?
(A) No, in my computer.
(B) Nothing will be changed.
(C) At the store downtown.

제 노트북의 새로운 충전기를 어디에서 살 수 있나요?
(A) 아니요, 제 컴퓨터 안에요.
(B) 아무것도 바뀌지 않을 것입니다.
(C) 시내에 있는 매장에서요.

10. When will the packages be delivered?
(A) No, at the post office.
(B) Free delivery.
(C) They were sent two days ago.

소포가 언제 배달될까요?
(A) 아니요, 우체국에요.
(B) 무료 배송입니다.
(C) 이틀 전에 발송했습니다.

11. Where is the annual management conference being held?
(A) Introductions to statistics.
(B) For the winter.
(C) In seminar room 301.

연례 경영 관리 학회는 어디에서 열리나요?
(A) 통계학 입문이요.
(B) 겨울을 위해서요.
(C) 301호 세미나실에서요.

12. When does everyone normally leave the office?
(A) Yes, they left here early.
(B) Around five.
(C) They left from the station.

다들 보통 언제 퇴근하나요?
(A) 네, 그들은 여기에서 일찍 나갔습니다.
(B) 5시쯤입니다.
(C) 그들은 역에서 떠났습니다.

13. Who prepared the sales report?
(A) In the news report.
(B) Jacob worked on it.
(C) I didn't know it was so expensive.

누가 영업 보고서를 준비했나요?
(A) 뉴스 보도에요.
(B) 제이콥이 작업했어요.
(C) 그게 그렇게 비싼 것인 줄 몰랐어요.

14. When will Amelia return from her business trip?
(A) While she was gone.
(B) She came back last weekend.
(C) By train.

아멜리아는 출장에서 언제 돌아오나요?
(A) 그녀가 없는 동안에요.
(B) 그녀는 지난 주말에 돌아왔습니다.
(C) 기차로요.

15. Where did Megan go for lunch?
(A) I haven't seen her.
(B) She said she did.
(C) To the cafeteria downstairs.

메건은 점심 먹으러 어디로 갔나요?
(A) 저는 그녀를 본 적이 없습니다.
(B) 그녀가 했다고 말했어요.
(C) 아래층 카페테리아로요.

Chapter 2 의문사 의문문 II

Point 01 무엇에 대한 답변을 찾는 What/Which 의문문

Check-up Test

1. (C) 2. (B) 3. (C) 4. (A) 5. (B) 6. (B)
7. (B) 8. (B)

1. What size do you need?
(A) I don't need it.
(B) Wherever you want.
(C) Probably a small.

어떤 사이즈가 필요하신가요?
(A) 저는 필요 없습니다.
(B) 어디든지 당신이 원하는 곳이요.
(C) 아마 작은 사이즈요.

2. What was the agenda of the meeting?
(A) In room 114.
(B) International trade.
(C) Half an hour.

회의의 의제가 무엇이었나요?
(A) 114호실에서요.
(B) 국제 무역입니다.
(C) 30분이요.

3. What will you be doing in Italy?
(A) I am afraid so.
(B) I'll arrive this weekend.
(C) I'm participating in a seminar.

이탈리아에서 무엇을 할 예정입니까?
(A) 유감스럽지만 그렇습니다.
(B) 저는 이번 주말에 도착할 예정입니다.
(C) 저는 세미나에 참석할 것입니다.

4. Which shirts do you want?
(A) The red ones.
(B) It's thirty dollars.
(C) No, I'll take one.

어떤 셔츠를 원하세요?
(A) 빨간색 셔츠요.
(B) 30달러입니다.
(C) 아니요, 하나 하겠습니다.

5. What form of payment do you prefer?
(A) My former address.
(B) I'll use a credit card.
(C) I'd prefer to.

어떤 지불 방식을 선호하시나요?
(A) 제 이전 주소요.
(B) 신용 카드를 사용할래요.
(C) 그게 더 좋아요.

6. Which building does Ms. Nelson work in?
(A) They're construction workers.
(B) The Tesco Building.
(C) It's in her office.

넬슨 씨는 어느 건물에서 일하나요?
(A) 그들은 건설 노동자들입니다.
(B) 테스코 빌딩입니다.
(C) 그건 그녀의 사무실에 있어요.

7. What will new employees work on?
(A) It isn't working.
(B) We have a new project for them.
(C) In an office.

신입 사원들은 어떤 일을 할 건가요?
(A) 그건 작동하지 않아요.
(B) 그들을 위한 새로운 프로젝트가 있어요.
(C) 사무실 안에요.

8. What do you think of the new floor plan?
(A) The architecture company.
(B) It's a good design.
(C) It needs to be mopped.

새로운 평면도에 대해서 어떻게 생각하세요?
(A) 건축 회사요.
(B) 디자인이 좋습니다.
(C) 걸레질을 해야 합니다.

Point 02 방법/의견에 대한 답변을 찾는 How 의문문

Check-up Test
1. (C) 2. (B) 3. (C) 4. (C) 5. (B) 6. (C)
7. (C) 8. (B)

1. How much are the airplane tickets?
(A) Yes, we should go.
(B) It's three hours long.
(C) They are over five hundred dollars each.
비행기 표가 얼마인가요?
(A) 네, 우리는 가야 합니다.
(B) 3시간 동안이요.
(C) 각각 500달러가 넘어요.

2. How did you learn about an opening at our company?
(A) We close every other Friday.
(B) By checking the website.
(C) Our new office is in the other building.
우리 회사에 공석이 있다는 것을 어떻게 알게 되셨나요?
(A) 우리는 격주로 금요일마다 문을 닫아요.
(B) 웹사이트를 확인했어요.
(C) 우리의 새로운 사무실은 다른 건물에 있어요.

3. How often should these cartridges be replaced?
(A) He often does.
(B) Yes, it is the place.
(C) Every couple of months.
이 카트리지는 얼마나 자주 교체해야 합니까?
(A) 그는 자주 그래요.
(B) 네, 이곳이 그 장소입니다.
(C) 두 달마다요.

4. How can I contact Dr. Wallace?
(A) I signed the contract.
(B) A different session.
(C) I'll give you her e-mail address.
월리스 박사님과 어떻게 연락할 수 있을까요?
(A) 제가 계약서에 서명했어요.
(B) 다른 세션이요.
(C) 이메일 주소를 알려 드릴게요.

5. How late is the library open?
(A) I haven't lately.
(B) Until 5 P.M.
(C) Five days a week.
그 도서관은 언제까지 문을 여나요?
(A) 최근에는 그런 적이 없어요.
(B) 오후 5시까지요.
(C) 일주일에 5일이요.

6. How's the newspaper article going?
(A) To the art museum.
(B) He's coming soon.
(C) I'm almost done with it.
신문 기사는 어떻게 진행되고 있나요?
(A) 미술관으로요.
(B) 그는 곧 와요.
(C) 거의 다 했어요.

7. How far is it to the hotel?
(A) It costs less this way.
(B) For one night, please.
(C) About five miles.
호텔까지 거리가 얼마나 되나요?
(A) 이렇게 하는 것이 비용이 덜 들어요.
(B) 1박으로 부탁합니다.
(C) 약 5마일 정도요.

8. How would you like your tea?
(A) Could you spell that?
(B) With milk, please.
(C) Yes, I would.
차를 어떻게 준비해 드릴까요?
(A) 철자를 알려 주시겠어요?
(B) 우유를 넣어서 부탁해요.
(C) 네, 그래요.

Point 03 이유/목적에 대한 답변을 찾는 Why 의문문

Check-up Test
1. (A) 2. (B) 3. (B) 4. (C) 5. (B) 6. (B)
7. (B) 8. (A)

1. Why are you moving to Perth?
(A) For a new job.
(B) Yes, in two weeks.
(C) A long movie.
왜 퍼스로 이사를 가나요?
(A) 새로운 일자리 때문에요.
(B) 네, 2주 후에요.
(C) 긴 영화요.

2. Why did you order a new table?
(A) I loaded all the boxes.
(B) The old one was broken.
(C) Are there new tables?
왜 새로운 테이블을 주문했나요?
(A) 제가 모든 상자를 실었어요.
(B) 전에 있던 것은 부서졌어요.
(C) 새로운 테이블이 있나요?

3. Why is the road closed to traffic?
(A) A heavy traffic jam.
(B) It needs to be repaired.
(C) Let's load the truck.
왜 그 도로는 차량 통행이 금지되었나요?
(A) 교통 체증이 심해요.
(B) 수리가 필요해요.
(C) 트럭에 실읍시다.

4. Why was the flight delayed?
(A) In October, I think.
(B) I really hope not.
(C) Due to bad weather.
왜 항공편이 지연되었나요?
(A) 제 생각에는 10월에요.
(B) 그러지 않기를 바라요.
(C) 기상 악화 때문에요.

5. Why did Ms. Morgan leave early today?
(A) About three hours ago.
(B) To meet a client.
(C) As soon as I can.
모건 씨는 오늘 왜 일찍 퇴근했죠?
(A) 약 3시간 전에요.
(B) 고객을 만나기 위해서요.
(C) 가능한 한 빨리요.

6. Why don't we look over the applications this afternoon?
(A) It was this morning.
(B) That's a good idea.
(C) Yes, on vacation.
오늘 오후에 지원서들을 검토하는 게 어때요?
(A) 오늘 아침이었어요.
(B) 좋은 생각이에요.
(C) 네, 휴가 중이에요.

7. Why didn't I see you at the banquet yesterday?
(A) No, it's by the entrance.
(B) I had to work late last night.
(C) It looks rather small.
어제 연회에서 제가 왜 당신을 보지 못했죠?
(A) 아뇨, 그것은 입구 옆에 있어요.
(B) 어젯밤 늦게까지 일해야 했거든요.
(C) 그것은 상당히 작아 보이네요.

8. Why did Jim decide to resign?
(A) In order to go back to school.
(B) In the contract.
(C) Until the end of the month.
짐은 왜 사임을 결정했나요?
(A) 학교로 돌아가기 위해서요.
(B) 계약서예요.
(C) 월말까지요.

Chapter Test

1. (A)	2. (B)	3. (A)	4. (A)	5. (A)
6. (C)	7. (A)	8. (C)	9. (C)	10. (A)
11. (B)	12. (C)	13. (A)	14. (B)	15. (A)

1. How long does it take to get to the hotel?
(A) About half an hour.
(B) By bus.
(C) I'll take two.
호텔에 도착하는 데 얼마나 걸리나요?
(A) 약 30분이요.
(B) 버스로요.
(C) 두 개 주세요.

2. What are you doing after the workshop?
(A) No, before work.
(B) I'm going back to the office.
(C) I thought it was today.
워크숍 후에 무엇을 하시나요?
(A) 아니요, 근무하기 전에요.
(B) 사무실로 다시 갈 거예요.
(C) 저는 오늘이라고 생각했어요.

3. Why did you change the table?
(A) To match the new chairs.
(B) Sometime before the end of next week.
(C) Olivia will do it.
왜 테이블을 바꿨나요?
(A) 새로운 의자들과 맞추기 위해서요.
(B) 다음 주 후반쯤에요.
(C) 올리비아가 할 거예요.

4. Which department do you work in?
(A) Accounting.
(B) She is working from home.
(C) Yes, that is the one.
당신은 어느 부서에서 일하세요?
(A) 회계부요.
(B) 그녀는 집에서 일하고 있어요.
(C) 네, 바로 저거예요.

5. How did you hear about the news?
(A) Through e-mail.
(B) Just a while ago.
(C) Yes, you can.
그 소식에 대해서 어떻게 들었어요?
(A) 이메일로요.
(B) 조금 전에요.
(C) 네, 가능합니다.

6. Why was the meeting rescheduled?
(A) In the office.

(B) It was going well.
(C) Dr. Rusell couldn't come.
회의 일정이 왜 변경되었나요?
(A) 사무실에요.
(B) 잘 진행되었어요.
(C) 러셀 박사가 올 수 없었거든요.

7. What was the meeting about?
(A) Work conditions.
(B) I think so.
(C) I met him once.
그 회의는 무엇에 대한 것이었나요?
(A) 근무 여건이요.
(B) 저도 그렇게 생각해요.
(C) 저는 그를 한 번 만났어요.

8. How do I open an account?
(A) If you have some free time.
(B) A lot of your monitors.
(C) Complete the blue slip.
계좌를 개설하려면 어떻게 해야 하나요?
(A) 시간이 되시면요.
(B) 당신이 가진 많은 모니터요.
(C) 파란색 종이를 작성하세요.

9. What are you going to do after your retirement?
(A) Just visit.
(B) It's over tomorrow.
(C) I'm starting my own business.
은퇴 후에 무엇을 할 계획이십니까?
(A) 그냥 들렀어요.
(B) 내일 끝납니다.
(C) 창업을 할 예정입니다.

10. Why is the post office closing?
(A) Because of a national holiday.
(B) Leave the door open.
(C) Everyone should leave.
우체국이 왜 문을 닫나요?
(A) 국경일이라서요.
(B) 문을 열어 두세요.
(C) 모두 나가야 해요.

11. What will the admission fee be?
(A) I heard so.
(B) Twenty dollars.
(C) On the corner of the main street.
입장료가 얼마일까요?
(A) 저도 그렇다고 들었습니다.
(B) 20달러요.
(C) 중심가 모퉁이에 있습니다.

12. How did Mr. Anderson like your presentation?
(A) No, he didn't say any.
(B) It was too late.
(C) He liked it a lot.
앤더슨 씨가 당신의 발표에 대해 어떻게 생각하셨나요?
(A) 아니요, 그는 아무 말도 하지 않았어요.
(B) 너무 늦었어요.
(C) 그는 아주 좋아했어요.

13. Why haven't we received a bill yet?
(A) The computer system is down.
(B) From a billing company.
(C) Yes, it's in the mail.
왜 아직 청구서를 받지 못했나요?
(A) 컴퓨터 시스템이 다운됐어요.
(B) 청구서 발부 회사로부터요.
(C) 네, 그것은 우편으로 오는 중이에요.

14. How many people responded to the e-mail?
(A) Yes, I will read it.
(B) Everyone except Austin.
(C) By tomorrow afternoon.
그 이메일에 몇 명이 응답했나요?
(A) 네, 제가 그걸 읽을게요.
(B) 오스틴을 제외한 모두가요.
(C) 내일 오후까지요.

15. Why don't you come over for dinner this week?
(A) Sorry, I am going out of town.
(B) To that new restaurant.
(C) It's been done for a while.
이번 주에 저녁 먹으러 오는 게 어때요?
(A) 죄송하지만 출장을 갈 거예요.
(B) 그 새로운 식당으로요.
(C) 한참 전에 끝났어요.

Chapter 3 일반 의문문

Point 01 Yes/No로 답하는 일반 의문문

Check-up Test

1. (B)   2. (A)   3. (B)   4. (B)   5. (B)   6. (C)
7. (A)   8. (A)

1. Have you finished writing your report?
(A) She reported to him.
(B) No, I've been too busy.
(C) That's good news.

보고서 작성을 완료했나요?
(A) 그녀가 그에게 보고했어요.
(B) 아니요, 저는 너무 바빴어요.
(C) 그거 좋은 소식이네요.

2. Is the new laser printer ready to use?
(A) I need to check the manual first.
(B) Two pages long.
(C) From the new office supplier.
새 레이저 프린터는 사용할 수 있게 준비됐나요?
(A) 매뉴얼을 먼저 확인해야 해요.
(B) 2페이지 분량이에요.
(C) 신규 사무용품 업체로부터요.

3. Is the grocery store open today?
(A) There are no farms near here.
(B) No, it is closed for renovations.
(C) Yes, it's on the shelf.
오늘 식료품점이 열였나요?
(A) 이 근처에는 농장이 없어요.
(B) 아니요, 보수 공사 때문에 문을 닫았어요.
(C) 네, 선반 위에 있어요.

4. Did the supplier sign the contract?
(A) A few signs.
(B) He hasn't received it yet.
(C) No, it is not connected.
공급업자가 계약서에 서명했나요?
(A) 몇 개의 간판이요.
(B) 그는 아직 그걸 받지 못했어요.
(C) 아니요, 그것은 연결되지 않았어요.

5. Do you know who sits at this desk?
(A) Upstairs and on the right.
(B) Our new senior.
(C) The disk is full already.
이 자리에 누가 앉는지 알아요?
(A) 위층 오른쪽에요.
(B) 새로 온 선배요.
(C) 이 디스크는 이미 꽉 찼어요.

6. Do you work in this building?
(A) Yes, it's working properly.
(B) A small company.
(C) No, I'm just visiting.
이 건물에서 일하시나요?
(A) 네, 제대로 작동되고 있어요.
(B) 작은 회사입니다.
(C) 아니요. 그냥 방문한 겁니다.

7. Were you able to sleep on the plane?
(A) Only for a few hours.
(B) I like it plain, thanks.
(C) We're flying to Denver.
비행기에서 잠을 잘 수 있었나요?
(A) 고작 몇 시간이요.
(B) 다른 거 없이 그냥 주세요. 고맙습니다.
(C) 우리는 비행기로 덴버에 갈 거예요.

8. Is Mr. Potter the new head of the marketing department?
(A) Yes, he started last Monday.
(B) We're ahead of schedule.
(C) No, in the staff meeting.
포터 씨가 마케팅 부서의 새로운 부서장인가요?
(A) 네, 지난 월요일부터 (그 일을) 시작했어요.
(B) 우리는 일정보다 빨라요.
(C) 아니요. 직원회의에서요.

Point 02 선택의 응답을 요구하는 선택 의문문

Check-up Test
1. (C) 2. (A) 3. (B) 4. (A) 5. (B) 6. (A)
7. (A) 8. (B)

1. Is it better to buy a book online or at a bookstore?
(A) It will be more expensive.
(B) No, he didn't buy it.
(C) Probably at a bookstore.
책을 온라인으로 구입하는 것이 나을까요, 아니면 서점에서 구입하는 것이 나을까요?
(A) 더 비쌀 거예요.
(B) 아니요, 그는 그것을 사지 않았어요.
(C) 아마도 서점에서요.

2. Would you like to eat inside or on the patio?
(A) It doesn't matter.
(B) No, that's not my choice.
(C) I will, thanks.
안쪽에서 드실 건가요, 아니면 파티오에서 드실 건가요?
(A) 상관없습니다.
(B) 아니요, 그건 제가 선택한 게 아니에요.
(C) 그럴게요, 감사합니다.

3. Do you want to send a gift or just a card?
(A) I received it.
(B) Let's send both.
(C) I came by car.
선물을 보내길 원하세요, 아니면 그냥 카드만 보내길 원하세요?
(A) 받았습니다.
(B) 둘 다 보내죠.
(C) 차로 왔어요.

4. Would you prefer wooden handle garden shears or plastic ones?
(A) The plastic ones look better.
(B) It was near the woods.
(C) A paper bag, please.
손잡이가 나무로 된 정원 가위를 원하세요, 아니면 플라스틱으로 된 것을 선호하세요?
(A) 플라스틱으로 된 것이 더 좋아 보이네요.
(B) 숲 근처에 있었어요.
(C) 종이봉투 하나 주세요.

5. Should I revise this memo before or after lunch?
(A) I'm not hungry, thanks.
(B) As soon as you can.
(C) Not very much.
제가 점심 식사 전에 회람을 수정할까요, 아니면 후에 할까요?
(A) 배고프지 않아요. 감사합니다.
(B) 가능한 한 빨리요.
(C) 그렇게 많지 않아요.

6. Would you rather stay until 5 or 6 o'clock today?
(A) The earlier time would be better.
(B) I can not find it.
(C) The presentation begins in one hour.
오늘 5시까지 있으시겠어요, 아니면 6시까지 있으시겠어요?
(A) 이른 시간이 더 낫죠.
(B) 찾을 수가 없어요.
(C) 발표는 한 시간 후에 시작합니다.

7. Are you busy with work right now or could you help me move my desk?
(A) I will be finished in a few minutes.
(B) The disk is next to the computer.
(C) I took a walk earlier today.
지금 일 때문에 바쁘신가요, 아니면 책상을 옮기는 것을 도와주실 수 있나요?
(A) 지금 하고 있는 일은 몇 분 후에 끝날 겁니다.
(B) 그 디스크는 컴퓨터 옆에 있습니다.
(C) 저는 오늘 일찍 산책했어요.

8. Should I leave the message with your secretary or mail it to you?
(A) After the meeting.
(B) You can leave it with anyone in my office.
(C) Another hour, I guess.
비서에게 메시지를 남길까요, 아니면 당신에게 메일을 보낼까요?
(A) 회의 후에요.
(B) 우리 사무실 사람 아무에게나 남기시면 됩니다.
(C) 제 생각으로는 한 시간 더요.

Point 03 | 사실 확인을 요구하는 부가 의문문과 부정 의문문

Check-up Test
1. (A)   2. (A)   3. (B)   4. (B)   5. (C)   6. (A)
7. (C)   8. (C)

1. Isn't this the latest edition?
(A) Yes, it is.
(B) He was not late.
(C) I am working for a publishing company.
이것이 최신판 아닌가요?
(A) 네, 맞습니다.
(B) 그는 늦지 않았어요.
(C) 저는 출판사에서 근무하고 있어요.

2. You don't need this manual, do you?
(A) I have one already.
(B) That work needs to be done soon.
(C) Maybe some new machines.
이 설명서 필요 없죠, 그렇죠?
(A) 이미 한 개 가지고 있어요.
(B) 그 작업은 곧 완료되어야 해요.
(C) 아마도 새로운 기계요.

3. Haven't we already visited the museum?
(A) He is a visitor.
(B) No, I've never been there.
(C) Sorry, it was a wrong number.
우리 그 박물관에 이미 가보지 않았나요?
(A) 그는 방문객이에요.
(B) 아니요, 저는 그곳에 가 본 적이 없어요.
(C) 죄송합니다. 번호가 잘못됐어요.

4. George left a package for me, didn't he?
(A) We have to pack them separately.
(B) I haven't seen one.
(C) By mail.
조지가 제게 소포를 남겼죠, 그렇지 않나요?
(A) 우리는 그것들을 각각 포장해야 해요.
(B) 저는 못 봤어요.
(C) 우편으로요.

5. Don't you travel to Paris frequently?
(A) He is not coming often.
(B) I met him at a conference in London.
(C) Not as often as I'd like.
당신은 파리로 자주 여행을 가지 않나요?
(A) 그는 자주 오지 않아요.
(B) 저는 런던에서 열린 학회에서 그를 만났어요.
(C) 제가 원하는 만큼 자주는 아니에요.

6. That man in the white shirt is Mr. Collins, isn't it?
(A) No, that's Mr. Cooper.
(B) In the accounting office.
(C) I prefer the black one.

저기 하얀 셔츠를 입은 사람이 콜린스 씨죠, 그렇지 않나요?
(A) 아니요, 그분은 쿠퍼 씨입니다.
(B) 회계 사무소에서요.
(C) 전 검은색을 더 좋아해요.

7. You'll be leaving for vacation on Friday, right?
(A) I left them at home.
(B) I had a wonderful time.
(C) That's what I'm planning.

금요일에 휴가 떠날 예정이죠, 맞죠?
(A) 그것들을 집에 두고 왔어요.
(B) 정말 좋은 시간이었어요.
(C) 바로 그게 제가 계획하고 있는 거예요.

8. Aren't we supposed to finish this project by tomorrow?
(A) The projector is next door.
(B) No, the store is usually not open.
(C) We have a few more days.

우리 이 프로젝트를 내일까지 끝내야 하지 않나요?
(A) 영사기는 옆방에 있어요.
(B) 아니요, 그 가게는 대개 문을 안 열어요.
(C) 우리 며칠 더 여유 있어요.

Chapter Test
1. (B) 2. (B) 3. (B) 4. (A) 5. (C)
6. (C) 7. (A) 8. (C) 9. (C) 10. (C)
11. (B) 12. (C) 13. (A) 14. (A) 15. (A)

1. Has the photocopier been repaired yet?
(A) Ten copies, please.
(B) No, the technician still has not arrived.
(C) She has not seen it.

복사기가 수리되었나요?
(A) 10부 부탁해요.
(B) 아니요, 기술자가 아직 도착하지 않았어요.
(C) 그녀는 그것을 보지 않았어요.

2. Would you like coffee or tea?
(A) Yes, please.
(B) Tea sounds good to me.
(C) Three copies.

커피를 드릴까요, 차를 드릴까요?
(A) 네, 부탁해요.
(B) 차가 좋을 것 같네요.
(C) 세 부요.

3. You went to the company picnic yesterday, didn't you?
(A) Yes, he did.
(B) No, I had to meet a client.
(C) Sorry, I will call you later.

당신은 어제 회사 야유회에 갔었죠, 그렇지 않나요?
(A) 네, 그가 했어요.
(B) 아니요, 저는 고객을 만나야 했어요.
(C) 죄송합니다, 제가 나중에 전화를 드리겠습니다.

4. Did they say why the bus is late?
(A) There is a mechanical problem.
(B) Yes, you can transfer to sales.
(C) It will be tomorrow.

왜 버스가 늦어지는지 그들이 말했습니까?
(A) 기계적인 문제가 있습니다.
(B) 네, 당신은 판매부서로 옮길 수 있습니다.
(C) 내일일 겁니다.

5. Do you want my home or my office phone number?
(A) Yes, it works fine.
(B) He stayed home.
(C) Could I have both?

집 전화번호를 알려 드릴까요, 아니면 사무실 전화번호를 알려 드릴까요?
(A) 네, 잘 작동하네요.
(B) 그는 집에 있었어요.
(C) 둘 다 받을 수 있을까요?

6. Aren't you going to join the celebration next week?
(A) He is not coming.
(B) It's a national holiday.
(C) Yes, I can't wait.

다음 주에 기념식에 갈 예정이지 않나요?
(A) 그는 오지 않아요.
(B) 국경일입니다.
(C) 네, 너무 기다려져요.

7. Have you heard the news about the merger?
(A) Yes, while I was in the meeting.
(B) On top of my desk.
(C) No, it's not new.

합병에 관한 소식 들으셨어요?
(A) 네, 회의 중에요.
(B) 제 책상 맨 위에요.
(C) 아니요, 그것은 새롭지 않아요.

8. Would you prefer a window or an aisle seat?
(A) I'll take three more.
(B) Yes, it is windy.
(C) Either one is fine.

창가 쪽 좌석과 통로 쪽 좌석 중에서 어느 것을 선호하세요?
(A) 세 개 더 가져갈게요.
(B) 네, 바람이 부네요.
(C) 어느 것이나 괜찮아요.

9. Doesn't this job require sales experience?
(A) That's a great experience.
(B) I'll schedule it.
(C) Yes, at least five years.
이 일자리는 판매 경력을 요구하지 않나요?
(A) 좋은 경험이에요.
(B) 제가 그 일정을 잡을게요.
(C) 네, 최소한 5년이요.

10. Will you be paying with a credit card?
(A) He paid attention.
(B) At the counter.
(C) No, with cash.
신용 카드로 지불하실 건가요?
(A) 그는 집중했어요.
(B) 창구에서요.
(C) 아니요, 현금으로요.

11. The mail hasn't arrived yet, has it?
(A) I have to buy stamps.
(B) I left it on your desk.
(C) He's speaking at 2.
우편물이 아직 도착하지 않았죠, 그죠?
(A) 저는 우표들을 구입해야 해요.
(B) 제가 당신 책상 위에 그것을 놓아두었어요.
(C) 그는 2시에 연설할 거예요.

12. Can I help you write a report or is there something else I can do?
(A) She did a good job.
(B) It is not mine, either.
(C) Thanks, but I can take care of it myself.
보고서 작성하는 것을 도와드릴까요, 아니면 제가 할 수 있는 다른 일이 있나요?
(A) 그녀가 잘 해냈어요.
(B) 제 것도 아닙니다.
(C) 고맙습니다만, 저 혼자 할 수 있습니다.

13. Are you sure the conference will take place at 5?
(A) I heard so.
(B) We had a good time.
(C) About the new policies.
학회가 5시에 열리는 것이 확실해요?
(A) 그렇게 들었어요.
(B) 우리는 즐거운 시간을 보냈어요.
(C) 새로운 정책에 관해서요.

14. Do you prefer the white jacket or the grey one?
(A) The white one seems more comfortable.
(B) More than one hundred dollars.
(C) Yes, they bought some.
흰색 재킷과 회색 재킷 중에 어느 것이 더 좋아요?
(A) 흰색이 더 편안해 보여요.
(B) 100달러가 넘어요.
(C) 네, 그들이 몇 개 샀어요.

15. We can leave early today, can't we?
(A) Yes, we can leave at noon.
(B) Leave it on the desk.
(C) No, he already left.
우리 오늘 일찍 출발할 수 있죠, 그렇지 않나요?
(A) 네, 정오에 출발할 수 있어요.
(B) 책상 위에 놓아두세요.
(C) 아니요, 그는 벌써 떠났어요.

 기타 질문과 답변

Point 01 동의 및 거절의 응답을 요구하는 제안/요청문

Check-up Test
1. (C) 2. (C) 3. (C) 4. (A) 5. (A) 6. (C)
7. (B) 8. (B)

1. Would you like me to carry your luggage?
(A) I really liked it.
(B) Is it your carrier?
(C) No thanks. I can handle it.
제가 짐을 옮겨 드릴까요?
(A) 저는 그것이 정말 마음에 들었어요.
(B) 그것이 당신의 캐리어인가요?
(C) 고맙습니다만 제가 할 수 있어요.

2. Can I borrow your manual?
(A) I think you can help me.
(B) No, he managed it by himself.
(C) Sure, look in my top drawer.
설명서를 빌릴 수 있을까요?
(A) 당신이 저를 도와주실 수 있을 것 같아요.
(B) 아니요, 그는 혼자서 해냈습니다.
(C) 물론이죠, 제 위쪽 서랍을 찾아보세요.

3. Could you please e-mail me your direct phone number?
(A) I read the report earlier.
(B) No, I didn't receive your call.
(C) Yes, I'll send it in a few minutes.
직통 전화번호 좀 메일로 보내 주실래요?
(A) 저는 그 보고서를 전에 읽었어요.
(B) 아니요, 전화 못 받았어요.
(C) 네, 몇 분 후에 보내 드릴게요.

4. Let's share a taxi to the airport.
(A) Oh, that sounds great.
(B) No, we didn't get it.
(C) She already saw the report.
공항까지 같이 택시를 타고 갑시다.
(A) 오, 좋은 생각이네요.
(B) 아니요, 우리는 못 받았어요.
(C) 그녀는 이미 그 보고서를 봤어요.

5. Why don't we meet after lunch to discuss the budget?
(A) I'll see if I'm available.
(B) She's a financial expert.
(C) Have you met him yet?
점심 식사 후에 만나서 예산에 대해 얘기하는 게 어때요?
(A) 시간이 되는지 확인해 볼게요.
(B) 그녀는 금융 전문가입니다.
(C) 그를 만나 봤나요?

6. Would you mind turning off your mobile phone?
(A) You are welcome.
(B) On the left.
(C) Sure, no problem.
휴대폰을 꺼 주시겠어요?
(A) 천만에요.
(B) 왼쪽으로요.
(C) 물론이죠. 문제없어요.

7. I'd like to open an account.
(A) Is it available this evening?
(B) Okay. Please fill out this form.
(C) He borrowed some money.
계좌를 개설하고 싶어요.
(A) 오늘 저녁에 가능한가요?
(B) 알겠습니다. 이 양식을 작성해 주세요.
(C) 그는 돈을 좀 빌렸어요.

8. Would you like a ride to work tomorrow?
(A) Yes, I can write it.
(B) I'd appreciate that.
(C) He stepped out for a walk.
내일 일하러 갈 때 태워 드릴까요?
(A) 네, 제가 쓸 수 있어요.
(B) 그렇게 해 주시면 감사하죠.
(C) 그는 산책하러 나갔어요.

1. Our company is looking for a new accountant.
(A) Maybe I'll apply.
(B) A checking account.
(C) No, he is not in my class.
우리 회사에서 새로운 회계사를 구하고 있어요.
(A) 제가 지원할까봐요.
(B) 당좌 예금 계좌요.
(C) 아니요, 그는 저희 반이 아니에요.

2. Please show your passport and boarding ticket.
(A) It is not mine.
(B) It's on the table.
(C) OK, here you are.
여권과 탑승권을 보여 주시기 바랍니다.
(A) 제 것이 아닙니다.
(B) 탁자 위에 있어요.
(C) 네, 여기 있어요.

3. I've never been to London.
(A) Neither have I.
(B) On holiday.
(C) When was that?
런던에 못 가봤어요.
(A) 저도요.
(B) 공휴일에요.
(C) 그게 언제였어요?

4. We'll need a saw to cut that wood.
(A) There's one in my toolbox.
(B) We saw him yesterday.
(C) Yes, I would.
저 나무를 자르기 위해 우리는 톱이 필요할 거예요.
(A) 제 공구 상자에 하나 있어요.
(B) 우리는 그를 어제 봤어요.
(C) 네, 그러겠습니다.

5. I need ten copies of this document by tomorrow.
(A) Where should I leave them for you?
(B) Who's the group leader?
(C) No, it wasn't very neat.
내일까지 이 문서 10부가 필요해요.
(A) 그것들을 어디에 둘까요?
(B) 인솔자가 누구인가요?
(C) 아니요, 그것은 아주 깔끔진 않았어요.

6. That copier isn't working anymore.
(A) A faster assembly line.
(B) Do you like working late?
(C) I thought it was fixed.
저 복사기는 더 이상 작동하지 않아요.
(A) 더 빠른 조립 라인이요.
(B) 늦게까지 일하는 것을 좋아하세요?
(C) 고친 줄 알았는데요.

> **Point 02** 동의, 맞장구 및 부연 설명을 요구하는 평서문

Check-up Test
1. (A) 2. (C) 3. (A) 4. (A) 5. (A) 6. (C)
7. (C) 8. (A)

7. My meeting is on the other side of town.
(A) Both sides of the paper.
(B) I don't see why not.
(C) You should take a train.

회의가 도시 반대편에서 있어요.
(A) 종이 양면 다요.
(B) 안 될 이유가 없어요.
(C) 기차를 타시는 게 좋겠네요.

8. Our supervisor wants to see the annual report as soon as possible.
(A) I sent it already.
(B) Not as far as I know.
(C) He sent it last night.

우리 상사가 연간 보고서를 가능한 한 빨리 보고 싶어 합니다.
(A) 제가 이미 보냈어요.
(B) 제가 아는 한 아니에요.
(C) 그가 어젯밤에 보냈어요.

> **Point 03** 직접적인 답변이 아닌 간접적인 회피성 답변
>
> **Check-up Test**
> 1. (B)　2. (A)　3. (B)　4. (B)　5. (A)　6. (A)
> 7. (A)　8. (C)

1. Where is the annual meeting going to be held?
(A) At the end of this month.
(B) It hasn't been decided yet.
(C) No, it was last year.

어디서 연례 회의가 열릴 예정인가요?
(A) 이번 달 말에요.
(B) 아직 결정되지 않았어요.
(C) 아니요, 그것은 작년이었어요.

2. Can you return this chair to the store for me?
(A) Don't you like it?
(B) I stored them in the cabinet.
(C) 10 days from the date of purchase.

저 대신 이 의자를 상점에 반품해 주시겠어요?
(A) 마음에 안 드세요?
(B) 제가 그것들을 캐비닛에 보관했어요.
(C) 구매한 날짜로부터 10일이요.

3. When is the annual sales meeting supposed to start?
(A) Our staff.
(B) I still haven't heard.
(C) Yes, it's open to the public.

연례 영업 회의를 언제 시작하기로 되어 있나요?
(A) 우리 직원이요.
(B) 아직 들은 바가 없어요.
(C) 네, 일반에 공개됩니다.

4. There are several mistakes in your report.
(A) More than ten.
(B) Where are they?
(C) Yes, the printer's fixed.

당신의 보고서에 몇 가지 오류가 있어요.
(A) 열 개가 넘어요.
(B) 어디에요?
(C) 네, 프린터는 수리되었어요.

5. When could I see a doctor next week?
(A) How about Thursday?
(B) He is a great doctor.
(C) Around the corner.

다음 주에 언제쯤 진료를 받을 수 있을까요?
(A) 목요일은 어떠신가요?
(B) 그는 훌륭한 의사입니다.
(C) 모퉁이를 돌아서요.

6. Haven't we received the package yet?
(A) Let me check.
(B) I packed it myself.
(C) How much is it?

소포를 아직 받지 못했나요?
(A) 확인해 볼게요.
(B) 제가 포장했어요.
(C) 얼마인가요?

7. Is Michael stopping by the warehouse today?
(A) He'll be here at 2.
(B) Stop at the corner.
(C) It departs tomorrow.

마이클이 오늘 창고에 들를 예정인가요?
(A) 그는 2시에 올 거예요.
(B) 모퉁이에서 멈춰 주세요.
(C) 그것은 내일 출발해요.

8. Did we meet our sales goals for this year?
(A) Because of the delay.
(B) We haven't been introduced.
(C) Ms. Walker might know.

우리가 올해의 매출 목표를 달성했나요?
(A) 지연 때문에요.
(B) 우린 소개받은 적이 없어요.
(C) 워커 씨가 알 거예요.

> **Chapter Test**
> 1. (B)　2. (B)　3. (A)　4. (B)　5. (A)
> 6. (A)　7. (B)　8. (B)　9. (B)　10. (C)
> 11. (C)　12. (A)　13. (B)　14. (C)　15. (C)

1. Would you like a copy of our magazine?
(A) The photocopier is not working.
(B) Yes, that'd be great.
(C) In the magazine.
저희 잡지 한 권 드릴까요?
(A) 복사기가 작동하지 않아요.
(B) 네, 좋아요.
(C) 잡지에서요.

2. This is the latest model that I recommend.
(A) A new car.
(B) How much does it cost?
(C) At our headquarters.
이것이 제가 추천하는 최신 모델입니다.
(A) 신형 차요.
(B) 가격이 얼마인가요?
(C) 저희 본사에서요.

3. Could you help me with the data entry?
(A) Sure, I will be there in a minute.
(B) No, she will be with you soon.
(C) Entry to the park is free.
데이터 입력을 도와주시겠어요?
(A) 물론이죠, 곧 갈게요.
(B) 아니요, 그녀가 곧 갈 거예요.
(C) 공원 입장은 무료입니다.

4. Who knows how to fix a broken fax machine?
(A) The light fixtures on the wall.
(B) We actually just ordered a new one.
(C) Three pages, please.
고장 난 팩스기를 고치는 방법을 누가 아나요?
(A) 벽에 조명들이요.
(B) 사실 새로운 기기를 주문했어요.
(C) 세 페이지 부탁해요.

5. Where is the nearest park?
(A) I'll check the map.
(B) I need a parking permit.
(C) They will close in an hour.
가장 가까운 공원이 어디인가요?
(A) 지도를 확인해 볼게요.
(B) 주차 허가증이 필요해요.
(C) 한 시간 후에 문을 닫을 거예요.

6. I've just finished all my paperwork.
(A) Could you help me then?
(B) He needs the paper.
(C) Sooner or later.
제 모든 서류 작업을 이제 막 끝냈어요.
(A) 그럼 저 좀 도와주시겠어요?
(B) 그는 그 종이가 필요해요.
(C) 조만간이요.

7. We should use a box instead of an envelope.
(A) Please send it to this address.
(B) Which is more expensive?
(C) It is not so far.
봉투 대신에 상자를 사용해야 합니다.
(A) 그것을 이 주소로 보내 주세요.
(B) 어떤 것이 더 비싼가요?
(C) 그렇게 멀지 않아요.

8. Why don't we write the report together?
(A) I don't have a ride.
(B) That might be more efficient.
(C) To the meeting.
보고서를 함께 작성하는 것이 어때요?
(A) 저를 태워 줄 사람이 없어요.
(B) 그게 더 효율적일 것 같아요.
(C) 회의에요.

9. Ms. Lante will present the new telephone designs at the meeting today.
(A) No, it's not too old.
(B) I'm looking forward to that.
(C) It's my new phone number.
란트 씨가 오늘 회의에서 새로운 전화기 디자인을 발표할 겁니다.
(A) 아니요, 그리 오래되지 않았습니다.
(B) 기대하고 있습니다.
(C) 제 새 전화번호입니다.

10. Why don't we take an express bus to the career fair?
(A) I don't have a teaching career.
(B) She bought it.
(C) It's too expensive.
취업 박람회에 고속버스를 타고 가는 게 어때요?
(A) 저는 교직 경력이 없어요.
(B) 그녀는 그것을 샀어요.
(C) 그것은 너무 비싸요.

11. We'd like to hire someone for a new branch in Japan.
(A) It's higher than we thought.
(B) He needs to go there.
(C) Ask the regional manager to recommend someone.
일본에 있는 새로운 지사에 사람을 고용하고 싶어요.
(A) 우리가 생각했던 것보다 높네요.
(B) 그는 그곳에 가야 해요.
(C) 지역 담당자에게 추천해 달라고 하세요.

12. None of us are familiar with the new filing system.
(A) Don't worry, you will get used to it.
(B) Sorry, I wasn't there.
(C) A new alarm system.
우리 중에는 새로운 문서 정리 시스템에 익숙한 사람이 아무도 없어요.
(A) 걱정하지 마세요, 곧 익숙해질 거예요.
(B) 죄송합니다, 저는 거기에 없었어요.

(C) 새로운 경보 시스템이요.

13. I have an appointment with a property manager this afternoon.
(A) Thanks for your offer.
(B) OK. I can meet the clients for you.
(C) A new building across the street.
저는 오늘 오후에 부동산 매니저와 약속이 있습니다.
(A) 제안해 주셔서 감사합니다.
(B) 괜찮아요. 제가 당신을 위해 고객을 만날 수 있어요.
(C) 길 건너편에 새로운 건물이요.

14. Could you help me find the book I am looking for?
(A) A magazine and a newspaper.
(B) I am looking forward to seeing you.
(C) Sure, but let me take care of this first.
책을 찾는 것을 도와주시겠어요?
(A) 잡지와 신문이요.
(B) 당신을 만나기를 기대하고 있습니다.
(C) 물론이죠. 하지만 이거 먼저 처리하고요.

15. Do you want to upgrade to the new computer or keep the one you have?
(A) Please download it.
(B) No, on your desk.
(C) It depends on the cost.
새로운 컴퓨터로 업그레이드하고 싶으세요, 아니면 그대로 쓰고 싶으세요?
(A) 그것을 다운로드해 주세요.
(B) 아니요, 당신 책상 위에요.
(C) 비용에 따라 다릅니다.

PART 3

 Chapter 1 대화의 처음에 답이 나오는 문제

Point 01 대화의 주제나 목적을 묻는 유형

Check-up Test
1. (D)　2. (A)　3. (A)　4. (C)　5. (C)　6. (B)

Question 1 refers to the following conversation.

W: Daniel, would you like to come to the staff meeting tomorrow morning? Since this is your first week here, it will be a good chance for you to meet our vehicle design staff.

M: That would be great. I've only met a couple of salespeople and I'd like to have a chance to know the others. Where will the meeting be held?

여: 다니엘, 내일 오전에 직원회의에 참석하시겠어요? 이번 주가 당신의 입사 첫 주이니, 차량 디자인팀 직원들을 만날 좋은 기회가 될 거예요.

남: 아주 좋을 것 같아요. 영업팀 직원 두세 명만 만나 봐서 다른 사람들도 만날 수 있는 기회가 있으면 좋겠어요. 회의는 어디에서 하죠?

1. 화자들은 무엇에 대해서 이야기하고 있는가?
(A) 운전 경로
(B) 직무 설명
(C) 업무 배정
(D) 직원회의

Question 2 refers to the following conversation.

W: Hi, this is Becky from Anderson Consulting. I'm calling to make a few changes to the order for our office supplies this month. We need more cartridges and paper than we originally expected.

M: Certainly, so how many extra cartridges and paper do you need?

여: 안녕하세요, 앤더슨 컨설팅 회사의 베키입니다. 이번 달 저희 사무용품 주문을 약간 변경하고자 전화드렸습니다. 원래 예상했던 것보다 카트리지와 용지가 더 필요해요.

남: 알겠습니다. 그럼 카트리지와 용지는 얼마나 더 필요하신가요?

2. 전화의 목적은 무엇인가?
(A) 주문을 변경하는 것
(B) 예약을 확인하는 것
(C) 가격 견적서를 얻는 것
(D) 메뉴를 물어보는 것

Question 3 refers to the following conversation.

W: Have you ever been to the Thomas Market? I love to shop there because everything is always so fresh.

M: Sure, I love to go there. They offer some great home-made desserts; cheesecakes, fruit tarts, crumbles and trifles.

W: Next time you go there, you should try their fresh home-baked bread which is one of the most popular items there.

여: 토마스 마켓에 가본 적 있어요? 모든 제품이 항상 신선해서 저는 거기에서 쇼핑하는 것을 좋아해요.

남: 물론이죠, 저도 거기 가는 것을 좋아해요. 그곳은 직접 만든 디저트를 제공하잖아요. 치즈 케이크, 과일 타르트, 크럼블과 트라이플요.

여: 다음에 가시면, 거기서 가장 인기 있는 제품 중 하나인 직접 갓 구운 빵을 드셔 보세요.

3. 화자들은 무엇에 대해 이야기하고 있는가?
(A) 지역 상점
(B) 축제 일정
(C) 경력 있는 회계사
(D) 새로운 음식점

Question 4 refers to the following conversation.

M: Hi, I'm calling to check if there are any tickets available for the concert in New York City on Friday, December 24th.

W: Yes, Row A is available at the box office on the day of the performance, priced at $25 each. Or you can make a reservation online in advance.

M: Could you please give me your website address? I would like to see more details on it.

남: 여보세요, 12월 24일 금요일에 뉴욕에서 열리는 콘서트의 티켓이 구매 가능한지 알아보려고 전화드렸습니다.

여: 네, 공연 당일 매표소에서 A열을 장당 25달러에 구매하실 수 있습니다. 아니면 사전에 온라인으로 예매가 가능합니다.

남: 웹사이트 주소 좀 알려 주시겠어요? 세부 사항을 더 알아보고 싶습니다.

4. 남자가 전화를 건 목적은 무엇인가?
(A) 예약을 취소하는 것
(B) 환불을 요청하는 것
(C) 티켓에 관해 문의하는 것
(D) 수업에 등록하는 것

Question 5 refers to the following conversation.

W: Welcome to Troy Electronics Store. How can I help you?

M: My name is Daniel Morrison. I dropped off my tablet yesterday. One of your technicians was going to replace the side button.

W: Let me check on that. Hey, Shane, did you help Mr. Morrison?

여: 트로이 전자 제품 매장에 오신 것을 환영합니다. 어떻게 도와드릴까요?

남: 제 이름은 대니얼 모리슨입니다. 저는 어제 태블릿 PC를 맡겼습니다. 여기 기술자 중 한 분이 측면 버튼을 교체해 주기로 했어요.

여: 제가 그 내용을 확인해 보겠습니다. 셰인 씨, 모리슨 씨를 도와주셨나요?

5. 남자는 왜 업체에 있는가?
(A) 선물을 구매하기 위해
(B) 소포를 발송하기 위해
(C) 수리를 확인하기 위해
(D) 길을 찾기 위해

Question 6 refers to the following conversation.

M: Helena, do you have time next Monday to interview someone with me for the editorial assistant position?

W: Let's see. Next Monday I have a breakfast meeting with the other department heads, and then a conference call with the publicity staff at 10 A.M. So why don't we schedule it for immediately after that?

M: Sure, that's fine. When will the conference call finish up?

W: We should be done by 10:30 A.M. Just send me an e-mail, and tell me when the applicant is coming.

남: 헬레나 씨, 다음 주 월요일에 저와 함께 편집 보조직에 지원한 사람의 면접을 하실 시간이 있나요?

여: 봅시다. 다음 주 월요일에 다른 부서장들과 조찬 회의가 있습니다. 그리고 그 다음 10시에 홍보 직원과 전화 회의가 있습니다. 그러니 그 직후로 일정을 잡는 게 어떤가요?

남: 네, 좋습니다. 전화 회의가 언제 끝나나요?

여: 10시 30분까지는 끝날 겁니다. 제게 이메일을 보내서 지원자가 언제 오는지 알려 주세요.

6. 화자들은 주로 무엇에 대해 이야기하고 있는가?
(A) 아침 식사 메뉴
(B) 취업 면접
(C) 신문 기사
(D) 영업 회의

Point 02 대화의 장소나 화자의 직업을 묻는 유형

Check-up Test

1. (B)   2. (B)   3. (B)   4. (B)   5. (C)   6. (B)

Question 1 refers to the following conversation.

W: Hello, this is Mary Reed. I'm calling because you were supposed to complete the landscaping work last week, but your crew hasn't shown up for the last couple of days and there is still some work to finish. I was wondering if they are coming today.

M: I'm sorry about that. Actually, the crew was overbooked yesterday and had to complete another job for a wedding being held today. They should be at your house this afternoon.

여: 여보세요, 저는 메리 리드입니다. 지난주에 조경 공사를 완료하기로 하셨는데, 작업하는 분들이 지난 이삼일 동안 오지 않았고 아직 마무리할 작업이 남아 있어서 전화드렸습니다. 그분들이 오늘 오시는지 궁금합니다.

남: 그 점은 죄송합니다. 사실은 작업팀이 어제 예약을 너무 많이 받았고 오늘 열리는 결혼식을 위해 다른 작업을 마무리해야 했습니다. 오늘 오후에는 고객님 댁에 갈 것입니다.

1. 남자는 어떤 종류의 업체에서 근무하는가?
(A) 렌터카 대리점
(B) 조경 회사
(C) 이벤트 기획사
(D) 부동산 회사

Question 2 refers to the following conversation.

M: Excuse me. I was trying to look for an article for some research I'm doing. But this computer isn't working properly.

W: Oh yes. Some of the computers here at Starkville Library are a few years old. We are in the process of replacing them. What happened when you tried to use it?

남: 실례합니다. 제가 진행 중인 연구를 위해 기사를 찾으려고 했는데 이 컴퓨터가 제대로 작동하지 않네요.

여: 아, 네. 이곳 스타크빌 도서관의 컴퓨터 중 일부는 몇 년 되었어요. 저희는 그것들을 교체하고 있는 중이에요. 사용하려고 하셨을 때 무슨 일이 있었나요?

2. 대화는 어디에서 이루어지고 있는가?
(A) 실험실에서
(B) 도서관에서
(C) 전자 제품 매장에서
(D) 출판사에서

Question 3 refers to the following conversation.

W: I've heard there will be a special exhibition on fashion photography in this museum. That's always been an interest of mine. When will the exhibition open?

M: Oh, we have already opened the exhibition. The problem is that, right now, it is fully booked, so we can't let anyone else in. I can give you a ticket for next week.

W: That's alright. I can wait until next week.

여: 이 미술관에서 패션 사진 특별전이 열릴 거라고 들었어요. 항상 관심이 있던 분야인데, 전시회는 언제 열리나요?

남: 아, 전시회는 이미 시작되었습니다. 문제는 지금 예약이 모두 차서 다른 손님을 입장시킬 수 없다는 것입니다. 다음 주 입장권은 드릴 수 있어요.

여: 좋아요. 다음 주까지 기다릴게요.

3. 화자들은 어디에 있는가?
(A) 사진 스튜디오에
(B) 미술관에
(C) 부동산 사무실에
(D) 콘서트홀에

Question 4 refers to the following conversation.

W: Good afternoon, this is Kimberly Adams from Riverview Apartment on Danes Road. My lease will expire next Friday, and I would like to know what I have to do before moving out.

M: Well, all you have to do is simply return the keys to our office. After you move out, we are going to inspect your apartment to see whether there is any damage. If there is none, we'll return the full security deposit.

W: Thanks a lot. I will stop by your office this afternoon.

여: 안녕하세요. 저는 데인스 가에 위치한 리버뷰 아파트에 사는 킴벌리 애덤스입니다. 제 임대 계약 기간이 다음 주 금요일에 만기되는데요, 이사 나가기 전에 제가 해야 할 일을 알고 싶네요.

남: 음, 저희 사무실에 열쇠를 반납하시기만 하면 됩니다. 이사를 가시고 나면 저희가 손상이 있는지 확인하기 위해 아파트를 점검할 것입니다. 손상이 없으면 보증금을 전액 돌려드립니다.

여: 감사합니다. 오늘 오후에 그쪽 사무실로 들르겠습니다.

4. 남자는 누구일 것 같은가?
(A) 은행원
(B) 아파트 관리자
(C) 건축가
(D) 유지 보수 직원

Question 5 refers to the following conversation.

M: Well, Sophia, this is the interior of my new grocery store. What do you think of the display?

W: Jacob! You did a great job! You know, I've always wanted to open my own business but I don't know where to start. How did you get started?

M: Well, I spent two years studying business administration at the Sherman Center. They provide sample business plans. But the best thing about studying there was that once a month I got a chance to talk one-on-one with a visiting business consultant.

남: 아, 소피아, 이게 제 새 식품점 인테리어예요. 디스플레이가 어때요?

여: 제이콥! 정말 잘했군요! 아시다시피 저는 항상 제 가게를 여는 것이 소원이었는데 어디서부터 시작해야 할지 모르겠어요. 어떻게 시작하셨나요?

남: 아, 저는 셔먼 센터에서 2년 동안 경영학을 공부했어요. 거기에서 샘플 사업 기획을 제공해 준답니다. 하지만 그곳에서 공부한 것 중 가장 좋았던 것은 한 달에 한 번 객원 비즈니스 상담가와 일대일로 이야기할 기회를 가진 것이었어요.

5. 화자들은 어디에 있을 것 같은가?
(A) 학교에
(B) 은행에
(C) 상점에
(D) 공장에

Question 6 refers to the following conversation.

W: Hello, this is Susan Miller. I'll be attending the International University Conference at your hotel next weekend and I'm calling to confirm my room reservation for Thursday and Friday nights.

M: Just a moment, Ms. Miller. Let me see. Yes, we have you booked for Thursday and Friday in a single room.

W: That's right. Oh, but I won't arrive at the hotel until nine or so because I'm flying in late on Thursday. So please make sure to hold the room for me.

여: 안녕하세요. 저는 수잔 밀러입니다. 저는 다음 주말 당신의 호텔에서 열리는 국제 대학 회의에 참석할 예정인데 목요일과 금요일 밤의 제 객실 예약을 확인하기 위해 전화했어요.

남: 잠시만요, 밀러 씨. 볼게요. 네, 목요일과 금요일 당신을 위해 예약된 싱글룸이 있네요.

여: 알겠습니다. 오, 그런데 목요일 늦게 비행기를 타기 때문에 9시가 되어야 호텔에 도착할 것 같아요. 그러니 방을 예약 상태로 그냥 두세요.

6. 여자와 이야기하고 있는 사람은 누구일 것 같은가?
(A) 교사
(B) 호텔 직원
(C) 비행기 승무원
(D) 고객

Chapter Test

1. (D)	2. (C)	3. (A)	4. (C)	5. (B)
6. (D)	7. (B)	8. (A)	9. (C)	10. (B)
11. (B)	12. (C)			

Questions 1-3 refer to the following conversation.

M: How can I help you?

W: Hello. **1** I bought tickets for Friday night's concert, but some of my friends also want to go. **2** So I need to buy some more tickets for them. Would that be possible?

M: I am very sorry, but it looks like all tickets are sold out for Friday night's concert. There are some seats available for Saturday though. Maybe you would want to exchange your tickets to Saturday and purchase some tickets for your friends?

W: I can do that? That would be great. Before I do that, **3** I should call my friends and see if Saturday is okay.

M: No problem.

남: 어떻게 도와드릴까요?

여: 안녕하세요. **1** 제가 금요일 밤 콘서트 티켓을 구매했는데요, 제 친구들 몇 명도 가고 싶어 해서요. **2** 그래서 친구들을 위해 티켓을 좀 더 구매해야 합니다. 가능할까요?

남: 정말 죄송합니다만 금요일 밤 콘서트의 티켓은 모두 매진된 것 같습니다. 그렇지만 토요일 공연은 좌석이 몇 개 남았습니다. 티켓을 토요일 공연 것으로 교환하고 친구들을 위한 티켓을 구입하는 건 어떠신가요?

여: 그렇게 할 수 있을까요? 그러는 게 좋을 것 같네요. 그러기 전에 **3** 친구들에게 전화해서 토요일이 괜찮은지 알아볼게요.

남: 문제없습니다.

1. 남자는 어디에서 일할 것 같은가?
(A) 박물관에서
(B) 주유소에서
(C) 식당에서
(D) 극장에서

2. 여자는 무엇에 대해 묻고 있는가?
(A) 지도
(B) 기념품
(C) 추가 티켓

(D) 이용 가능 날짜

3. 여자는 다음에 무엇을 할 것 같은가?
(A) 친구들에게 연락하기
(B) 카드 번호 알려 주기
(C) 콘서트 즐기기
(D) 현금으로 지불하기

Questions 4-6 refer to the following conversation.

W: Eric, did the advertising agency call? **4** I'm waiting for the advertisement for the opening of our second restaurant next week.

M: They just e-mailed us the ad, but they need to change a few things. **5** They mistakenly put in the address of our first restaurant. I called them and they said they will fix it by tomorrow morning.

W: We might have a problem. **6** I'm going to call them and ask them to get it done by today. We need to put it in this weekend's edition of the newspaper, and that means I have to send the ad to the newspaper by 6 o'clock today.

여: 에릭, 광고 대행사에서 전화 왔나요? 저는 다음 주에 있는 **4** 우리의 두 번째 레스토랑 개업을 위한 광고를 기다리고 있거든요.
남: 방금 이메일로 광고를 보내왔는데, 몇 가지 수정할 필요가 있더군요. **5** 그들이 실수로 첫 번째 레스토랑 주소를 넣었어요. 전화했더니, 내일 아침까지 그 부분을 수정하겠다고 했어요.
여: 곤란할 것 같은데요. **6** 제가 전화해서 오늘까지 끝내 달라고 부탁할게요. 이번 주말판 신문에 광고를 실어야 해서 제가 오늘 6시까지 광고를 신문사에 보내야 하거든요.

4. 화자들은 무엇에 대해 이야기하고 있는가?
(A) 신문의 기사
(B) 광고 제작 비용
(C) 행사를 위한 광고
(D) 상점 개조

5. 남자가 언급하고 있는 문제는 무엇인가?
(A) 작업이 너무 느리게 진행되고 있다.
(B) 주소가 틀렸다.
(C) 잘못된 문서가 전송되었다.
(D) 물건이 다른 장소로 갔다.

6. 여자가 업체에 요청한 것은 무엇인가?
(A) 새로운 송장을 팩스로 보내는 것
(B) 신문사에 전화하는 것
(C) 사무실로 오는 것
(D) 프로젝트를 좀 더 빨리 끝내는 것

Questions 7-9 refer to the following conversation.

M: Hello. **7** I'm calling because I purchased a product, but I haven't received it yet. I would like you to look into it, please. My order number is 57209.

W: I'm sorry about that. Let me look it up for you. It's a pair of gloves, right? **8** Our record shows that the package was sent out last Wednesday.

M: It's been almost a week. **8** Why is it not here yet? I bought the gloves for my friend's birthday. The birthday party is this Friday. I hope to give her the gift on that day.

W: As you know, **9** Monday was a holiday, so there was no postal service. I'm pretty sure the package will be delivered within a day or two.

남: 여보세요, **7** 제가 제품을 구입했는데, 아직 받지 못해서 전화드렸습니다. 그것에 대해 좀 알아봐 주셨으면 합니다. 제 주문 번호는 57209번입니다.
여: 정말 죄송합니다. 제가 알아봐 드릴게요. 장갑 한 켤레를 구입하셨네요, 그렇죠? **8** 저희 기록에 의하면 물건이 지난주 수요일에 발송됐다고 나와 있네요.
남: 거의 1주일 지났네요. **8** 왜 아직 도착하지 않은 거죠? 저는 제 친구의 생일 선물로 장갑을 샀습니다. 생일 파티는 이번 주 금요일이고요. 저는 그날 친구에게 선물을 줄 수 있었으면 좋겠어요.
여: 아시다시피 **9** 월요일은 휴일이라 우편 업무가 없었습니다. 틀림없이 그 물건이 하루나 이틀 내에 배송될 거예요.

7. 남자는 왜 전화하고 있는가?
(A) 주문을 취소하기 위해서
(B) 주문 상태를 확인하기 위해서
(C) 생일 카드를 추가하기 위해서
(D) 주소를 바꾸기 위해서

8. 남자가 "거의 1주일 지났네요"라고 말할 때 의미하는 것은 무엇인가?
(A) 소포가 배달되었어야 했다.
(B) 요금을 지불해야 한다.
(C) 상점은 이미 문을 열었다.
(D) 변경이 불가능하다.

9. 여자는 월요일에 대해서 말한 것은 무엇인가?
(A) 주문품이 발송되었다.
(B) 새로운 제품이 도착했다.
(C) 우편 업무가 없었다.
(D) 컴퓨터 시스템이 멈췄다.

Questions 10-12 refer to the following conversation.

W: Excuse me, **10** is this where the express bus to the airport stops?

M: That's right. This is the stop.

W: How often does the bus run?

M: It's scheduled to come every hour on the hour, but it's usually late.

W: Really? 11 I'm feeling nervous at the moment. Today is my first day at a new job at the Airport Baggage Terminal.

M: It should be here soon, but just in case, 12 you should take a taxi. There is a taxi stand across the street. You can catch one easily from there.

여: 실례합니다. 10 여기가 공항으로 가는 급행 버스가 서는 곳인가요?

남: 맞아요. 여기가 그 정류장이에요.

여: 얼마나 자주 버스가 다니나요?

남: 그 버스는 매시 정시에 오기로 되어 있는데 보통 늦어요.

여: 정말요? 11 저 지금 긴장되네요. 오늘이 공항 수하물 터미널에서 새로 일하는 첫날이거든요.

남: 버스가 금방 오긴 하겠지만, 만일을 대비해서 12 택시를 타는 게 좋겠네요. 길 건너편에 택시 승차장이 있어요. 거기서 택시를 쉽게 잡을 수 있을 거예요.

10. 대화는 어디에서 이루어지고 있는 것 같은가?
(A) 비행기 안에서
(B) 버스 정류장에서
(C) 커피숍에서
(D) 택시 안에서

11. 여자가 걱정하는 것은 무엇인가?
(A) 새로운 동료들을 만나는 것
(B) 직장에 지각하는 것
(C) 잘못된 버스를 타는 것
(D) 버스를 놓치는 것

12. 남자가 여자에게 제안하는 것은 무엇인가?
(A) 티켓을 먼저 사는 것
(B) 사무실에 전화하는 것
(C) 다른 종류의 교통수단을 이용하는 것
(D) 예약하는 것

Chapter 2 질문의 특정 단어를 들어야 하는 문제

Point 01 키워드를 이용하여 특정 정보를 묻는 유형

Check-up Test

1. (B)　2. (B)　3. (C)　4. (A)　5. (B)　6. (D)

Question 1 refers to the following conversation.

M: Have you been to the new grocery store downtown? I was there last weekend and it was full of people.

W: Well, I haven't been there yet. But I read an online review about it. It gave a good rating and that's the main reason why I've decided to go there this Saturday.

남: 시내에 새로 생긴 식료품점에 가봤어요? 지난 주말에 갔더니 사람들로 가득했어요.

여: 전 아직 안 가봤어요. 하지만 그곳에 관한 온라인 평을 읽었어요. 평이 좋았기 때문에 이번 주 토요일에 방문하기로 결정했답니다.

1. 여자는 상점에 대해 어떻게 알게 되었는가?
(A) 그곳에 가본 적이 있다.
(B) 그곳에 대한 평을 읽었다.
(C) 그곳의 매니저를 알고 있다.
(D) 전에 그곳에서 식사를 한 적이 있다.

Question 2 refers to the following conversation.

W: Did the latest shipment of children's jackets go out yet? I want to be sure that everything gets to the store on time.

M: Actually, we had a slight delay because one of our machines on the production floor broke down last night. But the store should have everything by the day after tomorrow.

W: That's going to be too late. You'd better tell the delivery service to rush the shipment. That way the store will get the jackets by tomorrow.

여: 아동용 재킷의 최신 상품이 발송됐나요? 모든 것이 제시간에 매장에 도착할 수 있도록 하고 싶어요.

남: 사실 어젯밤에 생산 라인의 기계 중 하나가 고장 나서 약간 지연이 있었어요. 하지만 모레까지는 상점이 모든 상품을 갖출 거예요.

여: 그러면 너무 늦을 거예요. 배송 회사에 배송을 서둘러 달라고 얘기하는 게 좋겠어요. 그러면 매장에서는 내일까지 재킷을 받을 수 있을 겁니다.

2. 배송이 왜 지연되었는가?
(A) 주문이 제시간에 이루어지지 않았다.
(B) 기계가 고장 났다.
(C) 서류를 제대로 작성하지 않았다.
(D) 발송 서류를 잃어버렸다.

Questions 3-4 refer to the following conversation.

M: Excuse me, I read some policies regarding **3** your restaurant. But could you explain in detail **4** how I can get a discount for BGB consulting employees?

W: Actually, to get a lower price, **4** just show your employee ID card when you pay.

M: But, I'm just starting my job today, so I won't have my ID card for another ten days.

W: I am sorry, but you will be charged the full price until you get an ID card.

남: 실례합니다, **3** 당신의 식당에 관한 정책을 읽었습니다. 그런데 제가 BGB 컨설팅 직원 **4** 할인을 받을 수 있는 방법을 자세히 설명해 주실 수 있을까요?

여: 네, 할인을 받으시려면, 계산할 때 **4** 사원증을 보여 주시면 됩니다.

남: 그런데, 제가 오늘 처음 근무를 시작해서 앞으로 10일 동안은 사원증이 없는데요.

여: 죄송합니다만 사원증을 받으실 때까지는 전액을 부담하셔야 합니다.

3. 남자는 어떤 종류의 업체에 전화하고 있는가?
(A) 백화점
(B) 렌터카 대리점
(C) 식당
(D) 컨설팅 회사

4. 남자는 어떻게 할인을 받을 수 있는가?
(A) 사원증을 제시해서
(B) 서류를 작성해서
(C) 쿠폰을 사용해서
(D) 신규 고객을 영입해서

Questions 5-6 refer to the following conversation.

W: Hi, Eddie. **5** Do you have a registration form for the environmental seminar? I want to register early.

M: Oh, I lent my entire packet of seminar materials to Jim because he's also planning to attend. Unfortunately, **6** he's at an all-day meeting with some clients today. So we have to wait until tomorrow to ask for them.

W: Umm... Do you know if we have any extra copies in the office?

M: No, I don't think we do. You could visit the seminar website. In fact, it'll probably be easier and faster to register online.

여: 안녕하세요, 에디. 환경 세미나의 **5** 신청서 있어요? 일찍 신청하고 싶어서요.

남: 아, 짐에게 세미나에 대한 자료를 모두 빌려줬어요. 왜냐하면 그도 세미나에 참석할 예정이거든요. 유감스럽게도 **6** 그는 오늘 하루 종일 고객과 회의가 있어요. 그걸 받으려면 내일까지 기다려야 해요.

여: 음… 사무실에 여유분이 있을까요?

남: 아니요. 없을 거예요. 세미나 웹사이트에 가보세요. 사실 온라인으로 등록하는 것이 아마도 더 쉽고 빠를 거예요.

5. 여자는 무엇을 찾고 있는가?
(A) 회의 안건
(B) 신청서
(C) 기술 보고서
(D) 전화번호

6. 왜 짐을 만날 수 없는가?
(A) 그는 휴가 중이다.
(B) 그는 배달을 하고 있다.
(C) 그는 해외에서 근무 중이다.
(D) 그는 고객들과 함께 있다.

Point 02 문제점/걱정이나 감정의 이유를 묻는 유형

Check-up Test
1. (B) 2. (D) 3. (A) 4. (C) 5. (B) 6. (D)

Question 1 refers to the following conversation.

M: It is impossible for me to finish the sales report by tomorrow, and I have to prepare for the meeting on Tuesday morning. So I think I have to stay late tonight to get it done.

W: Well, remember that our company is going to install the new security software tonight. The whole computer network will be shut down tomorrow.

M: Thanks for reminding me.

남: 제가 판매 보고서를 내일까지 끝내는 것은 불가능합니다. 화요일 오전 회의도 준비해야 해요. 끝내려면 오늘 밤 늦게까지 남아야 할 것 같아요.

여: 음, 우리 회사가 오늘 밤 새 보안 소프트웨어를 설치한다는 것을 기억하세요. 전체 컴퓨터 네트워크가 내일 차단될 거예요.

남: 알려 줘서 고마워요.

1. 남자는 무엇을 걱정하고 있는가?
(A) 컴퓨터를 수리하는 것
(B) 보고서를 제시간에 마치는 것
(C) 휴가 일정을 잡는 것
(D) 컴퓨터 파일을 안전하게 보관하는 것

Question 2 refers to the following conversation.

M: Hey, Julie. You enjoy comedies, right? Have you seen the new play at the Collins Theater? The review in the newspaper said that it was really funny.

W: No, my friend and I tried to buy tickets, but it's completely sold out. We're so disappointed. We were really looking forward to it.

M: Well, the article said more performances have been added since it has been so popular. Why don't you call the theater to see if you can get tickets now?

남: 안녕하세요, 줄리. 희극 좋아하죠? 콜린스 극장에서 공연하는 새 연극 봤어요? 신문에 나온 평에 따르면 정말 재미있대요.
여: 아뇨. 제 친구와 저는 티켓을 사려고 했는데 완전히 매진됐어요. 정말 실망스러웠어요. 정말 보고 싶었거든요.
남: 음, 기사에서는 그 연극이 인기가 너무 많아서 공연을 추가한다고 하더라고요. 이제 티켓을 살 수 있는지 극장에 전화해서 알아보지 그래요?

2. 여자는 왜 실망했는가?
(A) 극장이 문을 닫았다.
(B) 공연이 취소되었다.
(C) 친구가 바쁘다.
(D) 티켓을 구할 수 없다.

Questions 3-4 refer to the following conversation.

M: Hello, 3 welcome to North Hamilton Dental Clinic. How can I help you?

W: Hi, I'm Emma Miller. I have an appointment for a teeth cleaning.

M: Let me see. Oh, your appointment was at 3 o'clock.

W: I know, 4 I'm really sorry I'm late. Actually, it's my first time to visit your office, so I had trouble finding the building.

남: 안녕하세요, 3 노스 해밀턴 치과에 오신 것을 환영합니다. 어떻게 도와드릴까요?
여: 안녕하세요, 저는 엠마 밀러입니다. 저는 스케일링 예약을 했습니다.
남: 어디 봅시다. 오, 당신의 예약은 3시였네요.
여: 맞아요, 4 늦어서 정말 죄송합니다. 사실, 이번이 여기 병원을 처음 방문하는 것이어서 건물을 찾는 데 어려움을 겪었어요.

3. 화자들은 어디에 있을 것 같은가?
(A) 치과에
(B) 백화점에
(C) 호텔에
(D) 식당에

4. 여자는 왜 사과하는가?
(A) 일부 서류를 잃어버렸다.
(B) 신분증을 가져오지 않았다.
(C) 늦었다.
(D) 구독을 취소했다.

Questions 5-6 refer to the following conversation with three speakers.

W1: Hi, Michelle and I, 5 we are thinking about registering for a new fitness program at H&H Gym.

W2: They are offering a 10% discount for this month only. We're going to look around to check out their facilities. Would you like to go with us, Christopher?

M: That sounds great. But 6 I'm worried about going over my budget. Last week, I bought a new sofa on impulse.

W2: We can pay by installment. Or if you need more of a discount, I know one of the instructors there. So let me call him and see if he can give us an even better deal.

여1: 안녕하세요, 미셸 씨와 저는 H&H 체육관에서 하는 5 새로운 피트니스 프로그램에 등록할까 생각 중이에요.
여2: 그곳에서 이번 달에만 10% 할인을 해 준대요. 저희는 체육관의 시설을 확인하기 위해 둘러보러 갈 거예요. 저희와 함께 가실래요, 크리스토퍼 씨?
남: 좋은 생각이네요. 하지만 6 저는 예산을 초과할까 봐 걱정이에요. 지난주에 충동적으로 새로운 소파를 구매했거든요.
여2: 요금은 분납할 수 있어요. 할인을 더 받기를 원한다면, 제가 그곳의 강사 중 한 사람을 알아요. 그러니 그에게 전화해서 우리에게 할인을 더 해줄 수 있는지 알아볼게요.

5. 화자들은 주로 무엇에 대해 이야기하고 있는가?
(A) 광고 캠페인
(B) 피트니스 프로그램
(C) 대학 과정
(D) 프로젝트 일정

6. 크리스토퍼는 무엇에 관하여 걱정하고 있는가?
(A) 어떤 기록을 업데이트하는 것
(B) 디자이너를 찾는 것
(C) 마감일을 넘기는 것
(D) 예산을 초과하는 것

Chapter Test

1. (B)	2. (D)	3. (A)	4. (B)	5. (D)
6. (C)	7. (D)	8. (B)	9. (C)	10. (B)
11. (A)	12. (C)			

Questions 1-3 refer to the following conversation.

M: Hello, Ms. Williams, this is Howard from the reception desk. **1** Karl Jacobs is here. He says he's here for his 5 o'clock appointment.

W: Oh, **1** he's a reporter from *All Biz Magazine*. He's here to interview me for a story he's writing about our company. **2** I'm surprised he's here already though.

M: Should I ask him to wait or can you meet with him now?

W: I can see Mr. Jacobs now. **3** Could you check and see which meeting room is available?

M: Sure. Let me see. You can use room 204 on the second floor. Anything else I can do for you?

남: 안녕하세요, 윌리엄스 씨, 저는 접수 창구에 있는 하워드입니다. **1** 칼 제이콥스 씨가 와 계세요. 5시 약속 때문에 오셨다고 하세요.

여: 아, **1** 그분은 <올 비즈 매거진>의 기자세요. 우리 회사에 관해 쓰고 있는 이야기 때문에 저와 인터뷰를 하려고 오셨어요. **2** 하지만 벌써 오셨다니 놀랍네요.

남: 기다리시라고 할까요? 아니면 지금 만나시겠어요?

여: 제이콥스 씨를 지금 볼 수 있어요. **3** 어느 회의실이 비어 있는지 확인 좀 해 주시겠어요?

남: 물론이죠. 제가 좀 볼게요. 2층에 있는 204호를 사용하실 수 있어요. 또 필요한 것은 없으세요?

1. 칼 제이콥스는 누구인가?
(A) 접수 담당자
(B) 기자
(C) 편집자
(D) 출판인

2. 여자가 왜 놀랐는가?
(A) 기사가 벌써 발표되었다.
(B) 중요한 회의를 놓쳤다.
(C) 인터뷰가 취소되었다.
(D) 제이콥스 씨가 예상보다 일찍 도착했다.

3. 남자는 무엇하기를 요청받았는가?
(A) 빈 방을 찾는 것
(B) 전화를 돌려주는 것
(C) 방문객을 안내하는 것
(D) 회의실을 예약하는 것

Questions 4-6 refer to the following conversation with three speakers.

M1: Hi, Jane. **4** We've got a problem with the layout of next week's magazine.

M2: We should replace a couple of advertisements in the special local cuisine section we're publishing. Kevin and I will be working late today. However, **5** we really need your help with editing some photos.

W: Sure, I heard that the layout would have to be done over again. How can I help?

M2: Kevin will let you know exactly what we need. In the meantime, **6** I'm going to order some food for everyone staying late.

W: **6** Sounds good.

M2: What would you like for dinner?

남1: 안녕하세요, 제인. **4** 다음 주 잡지 레이아웃과 관련해서 문제가 있어요.

남2: 우리가 게재하는 특별 지역 요리 섹션에 있는 광고 두 개를 교체해야 해요. 케빈 씨와 저는 오늘 늦게까지 작업할 예정이에요. 그러나 **5** 사진을 편집하는 데 당신의 도움이 필요해요.

여: 물론이죠, 저는 레이아웃 작업을 다시 해야 한다고 들었어요. 어떻게 도와드릴까요?

남2: 케빈 씨가 정확히 우리에게 필요한 것을 알려 드릴 거예요. 그 동안, 저는 늦게까지 근무하는 사람들을 위해 **6** 음식을 주문할 거예요.

여: **6** 좋은 생각이에요.

남2: 저녁으로 무엇을 드실래요?

4. 남자들은 무엇을 걱정하는가?
(A) 다음 주 회의
(B) 잡지 레이아웃
(C) 특별 요리법
(D) 그룹 프레젠테이션

5. 남자들은 여자에게 무엇을 할 것을 요청하는가?
(A) 주문한 상품 수령하기
(B) 기사 수정하기
(C) 공급업자에게 전화하기
(D) 사진 편집하기

6. 여자는 무엇을 하는 것에 동의하는가?
(A) 제안서 읽기
(B) 소포 부치기
(C) 저녁 주문하기
(D) 사진 찍기

Questions 7-9 refer to the following conversation.

M: On my way here, **7** I dropped by the Mayfair Project. They were finishing up with the interior painting. I still can't believe we were able to convert an old manufacturing facility into a shopping mall within a year.

W: Yeah, I didn't think it was possible because we had to make several changes. **8** I thought it was going to take at least a few more months to change all the lights.

M: We couldn't have done this without Frank Myer, the project manager. **8** He knew exactly what needed to be done. It was amazing how he reorganized the schedule.

W: You're right. I'm so glad the project is going to finish on time anyway.

M: **9** The contract says all the store owners pay less rent for the first year if we don't finish the project by the deadline.

남: 여기로 오는 길에 **7** 메이페어 프로젝트에 잠시 들렀습니다. 실내 페인트칠이 거의 끝나가고 있더군요. 저는 아직도 우리가 오래된 생산 시설을 1년 안에 쇼핑몰로 바꿀 수 있었다는 게 믿어지지 않습니다.

여: 네, 여러 가지 바꾸어야 하는 것들이 있었기에 저 또한 그게 가능할 것이라고 생각하지 않았습니다. **8** 모든 전등을 교체하려면 적어도 몇 달은 더 걸릴 것이라고 생각했죠.

남: 프로젝트 관리자인 프랭크 마이어 없이는 불가능했을 거예요. **8** 그는 정확히 무엇을 해야 하는지를 알고 있었죠. 그가 어떻게 일정을 재조정했는지 정말 놀라웠어요.

여: 맞아요. 어쨌든 이 프로젝트가 일정에 맞게 끝나게 되어 기뻐요.

남: **9** 우리가 마감일까지 이 프로젝트를 끝내지 못한다면 모든 가게 주인들이 첫 1년 동안 임대료를 덜 지불한다고 계약서에 명시되어 있거든요.

7. 화자들은 주로 무엇에 대해 이야기하고 있는가?
(A) 새로운 예산안
(B) 임대 공간
(C) 신입 사원
(D) 건물 개조

8. 남자는 왜 "프랭크 마이어 없이는 불가능했을 거예요"라고 말하는가?
(A) 잘못된 정보를 정정하기 위해
(B) 동료를 칭찬하기 위해
(C) 동료의 승진을 제안하기 위해
(D) 도움을 요청하기 위해

9. 마감일을 지키지 못하면 무엇을 제공한다고 계약서에 되어 있는가?
(A) 전액 환불
(B) 무료 배송 서비스
(C) 임대료 인하
(D) 추가 할인

Questions 10-12 refer to the following conversation.

M: Irene, I'm coming from Personnel, and **11** I was told that David, the new intern, is going to start working on **10** March 17th. Isn't that during Fashion Week in Paris? Both of us will be out of the country attending the show.

W: That's right. **11** It would be better if he could come two weeks earlier. Do you think Personnel can change the start date?

M: I like that idea. That will give us time to train him before we leave. **12** I will call Personnel and see if they can do something about it.

남: 아이린, 인사과에서 오는 길인데, **11** 새로운 인턴 데이비드가 **10** 3월 17일에 일을 시작한다고 들었어요. **10** 그때는 파리 패션 위크 기간이지 않나요? 우리 둘 다 해외로 나가서 쇼에 참석할 거잖아요.

여: 그렇죠. **11** 그가 2주일 일찍 올 수 있다면 좋을 텐데요. 인사부에서 근무 시작 날짜를 바꿀 수 있을까요?

남: 좋은 생각이군요. 그럼 우리가 떠나기 전에 그를 교육할 시간이 생길 거예요. **12** 제가 인사과에 전화해서 그렇게 해 줄 수 있는지 알아볼게요.

	월요일	화요일	수요일	목요일
11 첫째 주			세미나	
둘째 주	팀 교육			고객과 점심 식사
셋째 주		파리 패션 위크		
넷째 주		이사회		

10. 화자들은 3월 17일에 어디에 있을 것인가?
(A) 교육 센터에
(B) 패션쇼에
(C) 세미나에
(D) 회사 저녁 회식에

11. 시각 자료를 보시오. 여자는 인턴이 몇 째 주에 일을 시작하기를 원하는가?
(A) 첫째 주
(B) 둘째 주
(C) 셋째 주
(D) 넷째 주

12. 남자가 다음에 할 일은 무엇이겠는가?
(A) 식당에 자리 예약하기
(B) 호텔로 팩스 보내기
(C) 전화하기
(D) 프레젠테이션 준비하기

Chapter 3 화자의 의도와 시각 자료 연계 문제

Point 01 화자의 의도를 묻는 유형

Check-up Test
1. (D) 2. (A) 3. (D) 4. (C) 5. (D) 6. (B)

Question 1 refers to the following conversation.

> W: Hi, Brad. One of our clients from New York will be here next week. Could you pick him up from the airport on Tuesday morning?
>
> M: Oh, I'm leading the orientation for new employees on Tuesday.
>
> W: Hmm... I see. Maybe Jane's free?
>
> M: I think so. Do you want me to ask her?
>
> 여: 안녕하세요, 브래드 씨. 뉴욕에 있는 우리 고객 중 한 분이 다음 주에 여기에 오실 거예요. 화요일 오전에 공항으로 그분 마중을 나갈 수 있나요?
> 남: 오, 저는 화요일에 신입 직원들을 위한 오리엔테이션을 진행할 예정입니다.
> 여: 음… 그렇군요. 제인 씨는 시간이 되겠죠?
> 남: 그럴 것 같아요. 제가 그녀에게 물어볼까요?

1. 남자는 왜 "저는 화요일에 신입 직원들을 위한 오리엔테이션을 진행할 예정입니다"라고 말하는가?
(A) 그는 업무에 불만이 있다.
(B) 그는 오리엔테이션에 도움이 필요하다.
(C) 그는 기회에 만족한다.
(D) 그는 요청을 들어줄 수 없다.

Question 2 refers to the following conversation.

> W: Last week I made a reservation for dinner tomorrow. But I am afraid I have to cancel it. I am in Tokyo on business and it's taking longer than I expected. Would it be possible for me to come another night instead?
>
> M: Of course. We still have tables available for dinner on Friday and Saturday. Which night would you prefer?
>
> W: Oh, Saturday would be perfect!
>
> 여: 지난주에 제가 내일 저녁 식사 예약을 했습니다. 그런데 유감스럽게도 그것을 취소해야 할 것 같습니다. 제가 사업상 도쿄에 와 있는데 예상보다 길어지고 있습니다. 대신 다른 날 밤에 방문해도 괜찮을까요?
> 남: 물론이죠. 금요일과 토요일 저녁에 자리가 아직 남아 있습니다. 어떤 날이 더 나으신가요?
> 여: 오, 토요일이 좋겠어요!

2. 여자는 왜 "예상보다 길어지고 있습니다"라고 말하는가?
(A) 예약을 변경하기 위해
(B) 실수에 대해 사과하기 위해
(C) 도움을 요청하기 위해
(D) 제의를 거절하기 위해

Questions 3-4 refer to the following conversation.

> M: Good morning. My name is Kevin Son. 4 I have an appointment with Ms. Chan 3 to discuss my employee benefits.
>
> W: Ms. Chan is on the phone right now. But 4 here is some information on health and other benefits to look at while you are waiting. Are you a new employee?
>
> M: Yes, I started working in the editorial department last week.
>
> W: Oh, then you must work for Lisa Jonson. She has been an editor here for a few months.
>
> 남: 안녕하세요. 제 이름은 케빈 손입니다. 3 제 복리 후생에 대해 논의하기 위해 4 챈 씨와 약속을 했습니다.
> 여: 챈 씨는 지금 통화 중입니다. 하지만 3 기다리는 동안 볼 수 있는 의료 혜택과 다른 복리 후생에 관한 정보가 여기 있습니다. 신입 직원이십니까?
> 남: 네. 지난주부터 편집부에서 근무하기 시작했습니다.
> 여: 아, 그러면 리사 존슨 씨 밑에서 근무하시겠네요. 그분은 몇 달 전부터 이곳에 편집장으로 계십니다.

3. 대화는 어디에서 이루어지겠는가?
(A) 진료소에서
(B) 연구소에서
(C) 대학 강의실에서
(D) 인사부 사무실에서

4. 여자가 "챈 씨는 지금 통화 중입니다"라고 말할 때 암시하는 것은 무엇인가?
(A) 전화를 사용할 수 없다.
(B) 챈 씨는 그녀가 필요한 정보를 가지고 있다.
(C) 남자는 잠시 동안 기다려야 한다.
(D) 그녀는 업무를 담당하고 있지 않다.

Questions 5-6 refer to the following conversation.

> M: Hi, Kim. Thank you for your work on reinstalling audio equipment in the auditorium yesterday. But 5 your staff didn't clean up properly.

W: Oh, **6** one of our technicians told me he'd be back this morning to take care of it.

M: Well, we have a board meeting at 10 o'clock.

W: Okay, so **6** I'll tell him to go to the auditorium right away.

M: Please tell him not to be late.

남: 안녕하세요, 킴 씨. 어제 강당에 오디오 장비를 다시 설치해 주셔서 감사드립니다. 그런데 **5** 당신의 직원이 제대로 청소하지 않았어요.

여: 오, **6** 우리 기술자 중 한 명이 그것을 처리하러 오늘 아침에 다시 간다고 했어요.

남: 음, 우리는 10시에 이사회 회의가 있어요.

여: 알겠습니다, 그러면 **6** 제가 그에게 지금 강당으로 가라고 말할게요.

남: 그에게 늦지 말아 달라고 말해 주세요.

5. 전화의 목적은 무엇인가?
(A) 예약을 확인하는 것
(B) 일정을 연기하는 것
(C) 고장 난 장비를 교체하는 것
(D) 지저분한 방에 대해서 불만을 제기하는 것

6. 남자가 "우리는 10시에 이사회 회의가 있어요"라고 말할 때 의미하는 것은 무엇인가?
(A) 그는 회의를 연기하길 원한다.
(B) 그는 일이 빨리 완료되기를 원한다.
(C) 그는 그의 일정표가 부정확한 것을 발견했다.
(D) 그는 더 많은 정보를 원한다.

Point 02 시각 자료와 연계하여 푸는 유형

1. (A)   2. (C)   3. (D)   4. (A)   5. (D)   6. (C)

Question 1 refers to the following conversation and layout.

W: Simon, look at this shopping mall layout. Now we need to decide where to open our new beverage shop.

M: OK. Hmm… I think either of those corner stores near the entrance would be nice.

W: I agree with you, but the rent for those stores is much higher than the budget we have.

M: How about the store between the restaurant and the jewelry shop? It would make sense to have a place where people can get some beverages next to the restaurant.

W: Sure. That makes sense.

여: 사이먼, 이 쇼핑몰 배치도를 보세요. 이제 우리는 새로운 음료 가게를 어디에 열지 결정해야 해요.

남: 알겠어요. 음… 입구 근처 코너에 있는 상점들 중 한 곳이 좋을 것 같아요.

여: 당신 의견에 동의해요, 그런데 그 상점들의 임대료는 우리가 가지고 있는 예산보다 훨씬 비싸요.

남: 식당과 보석 가게 사이에 있는 상점은 어때요? 식당 옆에서 음료를 구매할 수 있는 장소로 하는 게 맞을 수도 있겠네요.

여: 그래요. 당신이 옳은 것 같아요.

쇼핑몰 배치도

식당	C	장난감
A		
보석 가게		옷 가게
B		D

입구

1. 시각 자료를 보시오. 화자들은 어느 상점을 임대할 것 같은가?
(A) 상점 A
(B) 상점 B
(C) 상점 C
(D) 상점 D

Question 2 refers to the following conversation and list.

M: I've just finished analyzing our monthly expenditures. Here is the report.

W: Hmm… It looks like our expenses have gone up this month. Maybe we should try to reduce some of part-time payroll.

M: Well, you know? The holiday season is nearly over. So I think it would probably be possible.

남: 저는 방금 우리의 월간 지출 경비 분석을 끝냈습니다. 여기 보고서입니다.

여: 음… 이번 달에는 경비를 많이 사용한 것 같네요. 아마도 파트타임직 급여 지불 총액을 줄이도록 해봐야 할 것 같습니다.

남: 음, 그거 아세요? 휴가 시즌이 거의 끝나갑니다. 그러니 그러는 것이 아마 가능할 거라고 생각합니다.

월간 지출 경비 보고서

출장	350달러
상근직 급여 지불 총액	3,000달러
파트타임직 급여 지불 총액	1,200달러
교육	500달러

2. 시각 자료를 보시오. 여자는 어떤 금액이 달라질 수 있다고 말하는가?

(A) 350달러
(B) 3,000달러
(C) 1,200달러
(D) 500달러

Questions 3-4 refer to the following conversation and departure board.

M: Elena. It's me, Doug. I'm calling because I'm going to be late. **3** My train was supposed to leave for Newcastle at 2 o'clock, but it's been delayed.

W: Oh, no! We have an important meeting with some investors this afternoon. You're supposed to be presenting **4** the new packaging materials our company is making this year.

M: Take it easy. The delay's less than an hour, so I still might get there in time.

W: Maybe, but I'll reschedule for tomorrow morning. They are from one of the biggest investment companies, and we could bring in a lot of money if they agree with our proposal.

남: 엘레나. 저예요, 더그. 늦을 것 같아서 전화드려요. **3** 기차가 2시에 뉴캐슬로 출발하기로 되어 있었는데 지연되었어요.

여: 오, 안 돼요! 우리는 오늘 오후에 투자자들과 중요한 회의가 있어요. 당신은 **4** 우리 회사가 올해 제작하고 있는 새로운 포장 재료를 발표하기로 되어 있잖아요.

남: 걱정 마세요. 지연 시간은 1시간 미만이니 제가 제시간에 도착할 수 있을 거예요.

여: 그렇겠지요, 그렇지만 제가 내일 오전으로 일정을 변경할게요. 그들은 가장 큰 투자 회사 중 한 곳에서 오고, 만약 그들이 우리 제안에 동의하면 우리는 많은 돈을 벌 수 있어요.

도착지	출발 시간	상황
울런공	오후 12:00	30분 지연
버릴	오후 12:20	20분 지연
센트럴 코스트	오후 1:30	정시
3 뉴캐슬	오후 2:00	**40분 지연**

3. 시각 자료를 보시오. 남자의 기차의 상황은 어떠한가?
(A) 30분 지연
(B) 20분 지연
(C) 정시에
(D) 40분 지연

4. 화자들은 어느 업종에 종사하고 있겠는가?
(A) 제조업
(B) 관광업
(C) 운송업
(D) 금융업

Questions 5-6 refer to the following conversation and flow chart.

M: Hi, Kathryn. Do you have time to meet next week? I'd like to discuss the training software we're developing.

W: Sure, Kevin. But **5** I'll go on a business trip on Wednesday with my boss to meet some potential clients in Boston.

M: OK, how about Tuesday? I'll be in our factory all afternoon, but I'll be available in the morning.

W: Good, I have time all morning.

M: Actually, **6** I have a presentation, so why don't we meet right after that?

W: **6** OK, we can have some snacks then.

남: 안녕하세요, 캐스린. 다음 주에 만날 시간 있으세요? 우리가 개발하고 있는 교육 소프트웨어에 대해서 논의하고 싶어서요.

여: 물론이죠, 케빈. 그런데 제가 보스턴에서 잠재 고객들을 만나기 위해 상사와 함께 **5** 수요일에 출장을 갈 예정이에요.

남: 알겠습니다, 화요일 어떠세요? 저는 오후에는 내내 공장에 있을 테지만 그날 아침에는 시간이 될 거예요.

여: 좋습니다, 저는 오전 내내 시간이 돼요.

남: 사실, **6** 제가 발표가 있으니 그 직후에 만나는 게 어떠세요?

여: **6** 알겠습니다. 우리는 그때 간단히 식사를 할 수 있겠네요.

일과표 – 케빈 화요일	
오전 9시	약속
오전 10시	
오전 11시	**6** 발표
6 오후 12시	점심시간
오후 1시	
오후 2시 – 오후 6시	공장

5. 여자의 말에 따르면, 수요일에 무슨 일이 있을 것인가?
(A) 일부 장비가 설치될 것이다.
(B) 프로젝트가 끝날 것이다.
(C) 그녀는 교육이 있을 것이다.
(D) 그녀는 출장을 갈 것이다.

6. 시각 자료를 보시오. 화자들은 몇 시에 만날 것 같은가?
(A) 오전 10시
(B) 오전 11시
(C) 오후 12시
(D) 오후 1시

Chapter Test

1. (B) 2. (A) 3. (D) 4. (D) 5. (A)
6. (B) 7. (B) 8. (D) 9. (C) 10. (D)
11. (A) 12. (D)

Questions 1-3 refer to the following conversation.

W: Justin, do you have the last year's sales report ready yet? **1** We have a meeting with Kevin in an hour.

M: It's not 3 o'clock?

W: Well, actually, he called me early in the morning. He had to change our meeting because he has an urgent matter this afternoon.

M: Oh, no. I don't have the report ready yet. **2** I've been having problems with the printer all morning, so someone from technical support is looking at it now.

W: Hmm… well, **3** I'll call Kevin and ask if we can meet after lunch.

여: 저스틴 씨, 작년 매출 보고서가 준비되었나요? **1** 우리는 1시간 후에 케빈 씨와 회의가 있습니다.

남: 3시 아닌가요?

여: 음, 사실, 그가 아침 일찍 저에게 전화했어요. 그가 오늘 오후에 급한 일이 있어서 우리의 회의를 변경해야 했어요.

남: 오, 안 돼요. 아직 보고서가 준비되지 않았어요. **2** 오전 내내 프린터에 문제가 있어서, 지금 기술지원팀에서 프린터를 살펴보고 있어요.

여: 음… 네, **3** 케빈 씨에게 전화해서 점심 이후에 만날 수 있는지 물어볼게요.

1. 남자는 왜 "3시 아닌가요"라고 말하는가?
(A) 초대를 거절하기 위해
(B) 놀라움을 표현하기 위해
(C) 일정을 확인하기 위해
(D) 마감일 연장을 요청하기 위해

2. 남자가 가지고 있는 문제는 무엇인가?
(A) 그는 문서를 인쇄할 수 없다.
(B) 그는 회의 안건을 받지 않았다.
(C) 고객이 늦을 것이다.
(D) 교체 부품이 없다.

3. 여자는 무엇을 하겠다고 제안하는가?
(A) 일정 확인하기
(B) 보고서 수정하기
(C) 자료 제공하기
(D) 동료에게 연락하기

Questions 4-6 refer to the following conversation and map.

W: Excuse me. Sorry to interrupt you. Do you work here at this shopping center?

M: Yes, I work at this beauty shop. Do you need a help?

W: Well, I'm looking for Karlson Sound. **4** I need to have these headphones repaired.

M: Okay, here is the center's directory. **5** We're here next to Clothing Outlet. Just go straight past the event square. Karlson Sound will be right across from Play Zone.

W: Okay, thank you.

M: Also, **6** this shopping center will close at 9, so you'd better hurry up.

W: Thank you for the reminder.

여: 실례합니다. 방해해서 죄송해요. 이 쇼핑센터에서 일하시나요?
남: 네, 여기 미용실에서 일합니다. 도움이 필요하신가요?
여: 음, 저는 칼슨 사운드를 찾고 있습니다. **4** 이 헤드폰을 고쳐야 하거든요.
남: 그러시군요, 여기 센터 안내 책자가 있습니다. **5** 우리는 여기 의류 아울렛 옆에 있어요. 이벤트 광장을 지나서 그냥 직진하시면 됩니다. 칼슨 사운드는 플레이 존 바로 맞은편에 있을 거예요.
여: 알겠습니다, 감사합니다.
남: 또한, **6** 이 쇼핑센터는 9시에 문을 닫을 것이니 서두르시는 게 좋을 것 같습니다.
여: 알려 주셔서 감사합니다.

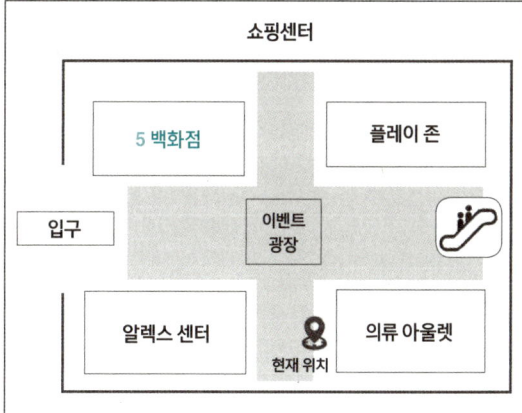

4. 여자는 무엇을 하려고 하는가?
(A) 면접 보기
(B) 옷 구입하기
(C) 상품 반품하기
(D) 상품 수리하기

5. 시각 자료를 보시오. 여자는 어디로 갈 것 같은가?
(A) 백화점

(B) 플레이 존
(C) 의류 아울렛
(D) 알렉스 센터

6. 남자는 쇼핑센터에 대해 무엇이라고 말하는가?
(A) 몇몇 행사가 있다.
(B) 곧 문을 닫을 예정이다.
(C) 에스컬레이터를 이용할 수 없다.
(D) 주차는 무료가 아니다.

Questions 7-9 refer to the following conversation.

> M: Hey, Shannon. **7** I found that there's something wrong with the elevator next to the back entrance connected with the parking lots. Whenever closing its door, it makes some noise and doesn't work properly.
> W: Really? **9** It should have already been fixed. Last week, Jane from Accounting told me about it, so **8** I had one of our maintenance crew workers check it immediately.
> M: I was there a few minutes ago. **9** Anyway, please go and check it right away.

> 남: 저기, 섀넌. 주차장과 연결된 후문 옆에 있는 **7** 엘리베이터에 문제가 있는 것을 발견했어요. 문이 닫힐 때마다 소리가 나고 제대로 작동하지 않아요.
> 여: 정말요? **9** 그건 이미 고쳐졌을 거예요. 지난주에 회계부의 제인이 그것에 대해 저에게 말해서 **8** 우리 정비사 중 한 명에게 즉시 확인하라고 했어요.
> 남: **제가 거기에 몇 분 전에 있었는데요**. **9** 어쨌든 지금 바로 가서 확인해 주세요.

7. 화자들은 주로 무엇에 관하여 이야기하는가?
(A) 주차장 보수 공사
(B) 고장 난 엘리베이터
(C) 마감일
(D) 직원회의

8. 여자는 어느 부서에서 일할 것 같은가?
(A) 인사부
(B) 회계부
(C) 영업부
(D) 유지 관리부

9. 남자가 "제가 거기에 몇 분 전에 있었는데요"라고 말할 때 암시하는 것은 무엇인가?
(A) 회의는 이미 끝났다.
(B) 설명이 더 필요하다.
(C) 문제가 해결되지 않았다.
(D) 새로운 정책이 발표될 것이다.

Questions 10-12 refer to the following conversation and sign.

> W: Good afternoon, Sir. **10** Welcome to the River Valley Art Center. How can I help you?
> M: I'll take one standard ticket, please. I'm visiting this area on vacation. I wanted to see your art collection before hiking.
> W: Great. **11** That will be six dollars.
> M: Hmm... I thought it would be more. Oh, I see.
> W: If you're interested, we will have a small talk with local artists about their works and this town's history. It will begin in about half an hour.
> M: Sounds good. I'm really interested in the history. How can I attend it?
> W: **12** It will be on the second floor. So, you can take the elevator to the upstairs meeting room.

> 여: 안녕하세요, 선생님. **10** 리버 밸리 아트 센터에 오신 것을 환영합니다. 어떻게 도와드릴까요?
> 남: 일반 티켓 하나 주세요. 휴가차 이곳을 방문하고 있습니다. 하이킹 전에 이곳의 미술품을 보고 싶었어요.
> 여: 좋아요. **11** 6달러가 되겠습니다.
> 남: 음… 더 비쌀 줄 알았는데요. 오, 알겠습니다.
> 여: 관심이 있으시다면 우리는 지역 예술가들과 그들의 작품 및 이 도시의 역사에 대해서 이야기하는 시간이 있습니다. 약 30분 후에 시작할 거예요.
> 남: 좋네요. 저는 역사에 대해서 정말 관심이 있어요. 어떻게 참석할 수 있죠?
> 여: **12** 그것은 2층에서 있을 겁니다. 그러니 엘리베이터를 타고 위층에 있는 회의실로 가시면 됩니다.

일반 가격
티켓당 10달러
--- 할인 가격 ---
11 6달러 : 금요일
5달러 : 오후 4시 이후
3달러 : 회원 또는 학생

10. 화자들은 어디에 있는 것 같은가?
(A) 지역 문화 센터에
(B) 공원에
(C) 야외 극장에
(D) 아트 센터에

11. 시각 자료를 보시오. 남자는 왜 할인을 받았는가?
(A) 금요일이다.
(B) 오후 4시 이후이다.
(C) 그는 학생이다.
(D) 그는 회원이다.

12. 남자는 다음에 무엇을 할 것 같은가?
(A) 가이드 투어 하기
(B) 책자 읽기
(C) 간식 먹기
(D) 위층으로 가기

Chapter 4 대화의 마지막에 답이 나오는 문제

Point 01 권유/제안, 요구/요청 사항을 묻는 유형

Check-up Test
1. (C) 2. (D) 3. (B) 4. (C) 5. (A) 6. (B)
7. (A) 8. (C)

Question 1 refers to the following conservation.

W: Steve, I don't know if you heard, but Ellen Kobayashi is leaving the company in two weeks. It's too bad because she's been doing such a great job with the advertising campaign for the new children's shampoo.

M: Oh, I heard Ellen is leaving, but I did not know it was so soon. She's such an efficient coordinator. I'm sure she'll be missed.

W: She certainly will be. In fact, we need someone to replace her right away. Since you are familiar with the product, I'd like you to take over the coordination of the ad campaign.

여: 스티브, 들었는지 모르겠는데, 엘렌 고바야시가 2주 후에 회사를 그만둔대요. 새로운 어린이용 샴푸의 광고 캠페인을 훌륭하게 하고 있기 때문에 참 유감이에요.

남: 아, 엘렌 씨가 그만둘 거란 얘기는 들었는데 이렇게 빠를 줄은 몰랐어요. 그녀는 정말 일 잘하는 코디네이터였어요. 분명히 그녀가 그리울 거예요.

여: 정말 그녀가 그리울 거예요. 사실 우리는 즉시 그녀를 대체할 사람이 필요해요. 당신이 그 제품을 잘 알고 있으니까 당신이 그 광고의 코디네이션을 맡아 주면 좋겠어요.

1. 여자는 남자에게 무엇을 하라고 요청하는가?
(A) 예산 제안서 수정
(B) 새로운 로고 디자인
(C) 프로젝트 관리
(D) 지원자 면접

Question 2 refers to the following conversation.

W: Hi, this is Diana Roseland in apartment 208. I'm calling to let the management know that I will move out in three weeks.

M: I'm not sure if you read the rental agreement, but all tenants must let us know at least four weeks in advance. So I'm afraid you must pay next month's rent.

W: Is there any way you can deduct even a portion of it? I will look for someone who could move into my place as soon as I move out.

여: 안녕하세요, 아파트 208호에 사는 다이애나 로즈랜드입니다. 제가 3주 후에 이사한다고 관리실에 알리기 위해 전화했습니다.

남: 임대 계약서를 읽어 보셨는지 모르겠지만, 모든 세입자는 적어도 4주 전에 미리 저희에게 알려 주셔야 합니다. 그래서 유감스럽지만 다음 달 집세를 지불하셔야 합니다.

여: 그렇다면 조금이라도 감해 주실 수 있는 방법이 있을까요? 제가 이사를 나가자마자 제 아파트로 이사할 수 있는 사람을 찾아볼게요.

2. 여자는 무엇을 하겠다고 제안하는가?
(A) 미리 결제하는 것
(B) 나중에 다시 이사 오는 것
(C) 수표를 우편으로 보내는 것
(D) 새로운 세입자를 찾는 것

Questions 3-5 refer to the following conversation.

M: Hello, can you put me through to Human Resources? My name is Shindy Smith, and 3 I'm calling to ask whether they have received my résumé and application for the night manager position.

W: Hi, actually I can check for your records here. Do you want me to look over it?

M: Yes, please. 4 I sent them to Choice Hotel's corporate headquarters two days ago and I was wondering if you need any more documents.

W: We have everything we need except 5 a letter of recommendation. You need to submit it before the end of this month.

남: 여보세요, 저를 인사부로 연결해 주실 수 있나요? 제 이름은 신디 스미스이고, 3 제 야간 관리직 지원서와 이력서를 받았는지 알아보려고 전화드렸습니다.

여: 안녕하세요, 제가 이곳에서 당신의 기록을 확인해 드릴 수 있습니다. 확인해 드릴까요?

남: 네. 저는 이틀 전에 4 초이스 호텔 기업 본사로 그것들을 보냈고, 또 다른 서류가 필요한지 궁금합니다.

여: 5 추천서를 제외하고는 필요한 모든 서류가 구비되었네요. 5 그것을 이달 말까지 제출하셔야 합니다.

3. 무엇에 관한 대화인가?
(A) 상을 받는 것
(B) 일자리에 지원하는 것
(C) 소포를 보내는 것
(D) 호텔 방을 예약하는 것

4. 여자는 어떤 종류의 회사에서 근무하고 있겠는가?
(A) 신문사
(B) 부동산 관리 사무소
(C) 호텔
(D) 녹음 대행사

5. 남자는 무엇을 하도록 요청받는가?
(A) 서류를 제출하는 것
(B) 신청료를 지불하는 것
(C) 전화를 기다리는 것
(D) 채용 담당자에게 전화하는 것

6. 화자들은 어떤 문제에 대해 이야기하고 있는가?
(A) 제조업체와 계약하는 것
(B) 파일에 접근하는 것
(C) 도구를 찾는 것
(D) 프린터를 사용하는 것

7. 여자는 오늘 무엇을 해야 하는가?
(A) 계약서 준비
(B) 연설 연습
(C) 소책자 제작
(D) 우편물 분류

8. 남자는 여자에게 무엇을 주겠다고 제안하는가?
(A) 대체 부품
(B) 새로운 암호
(C) 서류 복사본
(D) 소프트웨어 CD

Questions 6-8 refer to the following conversation.

W: Hi, Jonathan. **6** Can you access the file on the corporate network? Since this morning, I have not been able to log in at all. My computer keeps on giving me error messages.

M: Everyone has been experiencing the same problem. I just called technical support and they told me that this issue with the network is affecting the whole company and probably won't be resolved until tomorrow afternoon.

W: I am in trouble now. **7** My supervisor expects me to draft a new contract for the subcontractors by the end of the day and in order to do that, I need to include our standard terms and conditions stored on the company server. Do you have any idea how I can get them?

M: Well, **8** I've got a printed contract with Toshiba Manufacturing. You can simply retype the terms from that document.

여: 안녕하세요, 조나단. **6** 회사 네트워크에 있는 파일에 접근할 수 있나요? 오늘 오전부터 전혀 로그인이 되지 않아요. 제 컴퓨터에 계속 에러 메시지가 떠요.

남: 모두들 같은 문제를 겪고 있어요. 방금 기술 지원 부서에 전화했는데, 네트워크와 관련된 이 문제는 전체 회사에 영향을 미치고 있고 아마도 내일 오후나 되어야 해결할 수 있을 것 같다고 말했어요.

여: 저는 지금 곤경에 처했어요. **7** 제 상사는 제가 오늘까지 하청업자와의 새로운 계약서 초안을 작성하는 것으로 예상하고 있고 그러기 위해서는 회사 컴퓨터 서버에 저장된 표준 계약 조항을 포함시켜야 해요. 그것들을 구할 수 있는 방법이 있을까요?

남: 음, 제가 도시바 제조사와의 **8** 계약서 출력본을 가지고 있어요. 그 서류에 있는 조항을 단순히 다시 타이핑하면 될 거예요.

Point 02 앞으로 일어날 일을 묻는 유형

Check-up Test
1. (A) 2. (D) 3. (B) 4. (C) 5. (A) 6. (B)
7. (C) 8. (A)

Question 1 refers to the following conversation.

M: Hi, I'd like to check out some rare books and articles which were published in the past.

W: I'm sorry, sir. We don't allow old books and rare documents to leave the library. They're very fragile and the pages can tear easily. In fact, you should make a reservation and view those documents inside the library.

M: Really? I didn't know that. Could I make an appointment then? I can only make it during the weekend.

W: Let me go and check with our reference librarian if it's available during the weekend.

남: 안녕하세요, 과거에 발행된 희귀한 도서나 기사를 대출하고 싶습니다.

여: 죄송합니다, 회원님. 고서나 희귀 문서는 도서관 밖으로 반출할 수 없습니다. 그것들은 매우 취약하고 페이지가 떨어지기 쉽습니다. 실은, 예약을 하고 도서관 내부에서 그 문서들을 보실 수 있습니다.

남: 정말요? 그건 몰랐습니다. 그럼 예약을 할 수 있을까요? 제가 주말에만 올 수 있거든요.

여: 주말 동안에 이용할 수 있는지 저희 사서에게 가서 확인해 보겠습니다.

1. 여자가 다음에 할 일은 무엇일 것 같은가?
(A) 동료에게 연락하기

(B) 남자에게 방문객 출입증 주기
(C) 책 한 권 주문하기
(D) 재고 목록 확인하기

Question 2 refers to the following conversation.

> M: Hi, this is Anthony Mason from the technical department. You left a message saying that you were having trouble installing the software system on your laptop computer.
> W: Yes, thanks for calling me back. I spent two days installing it, but it's too difficult for me. I'm taking this laptop with me on a business trip next week, so I need to make sure it's working.
> M: Let's see. It could be a number of things. Why don't you bring your computer to our store tomorrow afternoon? I'll be here from 2 P.M. onwards.
> W: Sure, I will be there by 4 P.M. tomorrow.

> 남: 안녕하세요, 저는 기술부의 앤서니 메이슨입니다. 노트북에 소프트웨어 시스템을 설치하는 데 문제가 있다는 메시지를 남기셨네요.
> 여: 네, 전화 주셔서 감사합니다. 그것을 설치하려고 이틀이나 보냈는데, 저에게는 너무 어려워요. 제가 이 노트북을 다음 주 출장에 가져가야 해서, 이것이 제대로 작동하도록 해야 해요.
> 남: 어디 봅시다. 많은 요인이 있을 수 있어요. 내일 오후에 저희 매장에 컴퓨터를 가져오시겠어요? 저는 오후 2시 이후에 계속 여기에 있을 거예요.
> 여: 네, 내일 오후 4시까지 그곳으로 갈게요.

2. 여자는 내일 오후에 무엇을 할 예정인가?
(A) 서류 준비하기
(B) 새 컴퓨터 사기
(C) 출장 가기
(D) 가게에 들르기

Questions 3-5 refer to the following conversation.

> W: Hi, Jeremy. 3 I'm calling about the property you're looking for. Unfortunately, 4 most of the locations you liked in the city center are over your budget, but I think I found a place you may like in Southern Region.
> M: Hmm.... 4 That's not really what I wanted. I told you that I wanted to open my store in the city center.
> W: Well, you know, it's quite reasonably priced and it has its own parking area in front of the store.
> M: Actually, it would be nice to have some parking spots for my customers. 5 Can we meet on next Monday to look at the property?
> W: 5 Sure, I'm available on next Monday.

> 여: 안녕하세요, 제레미 씨. 3 찾고 계신 부동산 때문에 전화드렸습니다. 안타깝게도, 4 당신이 마음에 들어 했던 도심부에 있는 장소의 대부분은 당신의 예산을 초과합니다만 남부 지역에 당신이 좋아할 만한 장소를 제가 찾은 것 같습니다.
> 남: 음… 4 그건 제가 정말 원했던 건 아닙니다. 제 가게를 도심부에 개점하고 싶다고 말씀드렸습니다.
> 여: 음, 있잖아요, 그곳은 정말 합리적인 가격이고 가게 앞에 전용 주차장이 있습니다.
> 남: 실은, 고객들을 위해 주차 공간이 있으면 좋을 것 같네요. 5 다음 주 월요일에 만나서 건물을 볼 수 있을까요?
> 여: 5 물론이죠, 저는 다음 주 월요일에 시간이 됩니다.

3. 여자는 누구일 것 같은가?
(A) 건물 관리인
(B) 부동산 중개인
(C) 인테리어 디자이너
(D) 주차 요원

4. 남자는 왜 실망하는가?
(A) 특정 제품을 구매할 수 없다.
(B) 마감 기한을 지키지 못할 것이다.
(C) 장소가 너무 비싸다.
(D) 고객 불만이 증가했다.

5. 화자들은 다음 주 월요일에 무엇을 할 것인가?
(A) 건물 방문하기
(B) 디자인 수정하기
(C) 소포 (파손 여부) 검사하기
(D) 시작일 협상하기

Questions 6-8 refer to the following conversation.

> W: Hello. My name is Jennifer Cohen. 6 I'm calling about my magazine delivery. I'm planning to move out of the city, so 6 I'd like to change my delivery address.
> M: Okay, I can do that for you. 7 Do you know that there is an additional charge for delivery outside of the city?
> W: Oh, no, I didn't. Then, it could be delivered to my office? It's in the city. Is that okay?
> M: That won't be a problem. Could you let me know that address? 8 I'll go ahead and make the change in our records right away.

> 여: 안녕하세요. 제 이름은 제니퍼 코헨입니다. 6 제 잡지 배송에 관련해서 전화드렸어요. 저는 다른 도시로 이사를 계획 중이라 6 배송지 주소를 변경했으면 해요.

남: 알겠습니다. 그렇게 해 드릴 수 있어요. **7 다른 도시로 배송할 때 추가 비용이 드는 것은 알고 계시죠?**

여: 오, 아니요, 그건 몰랐어요. 그렇다면 사무실에서 받을 수 있을까요? 제 사무실은 시내에 있어요. 괜찮죠?

남: 문제 될 것 없습니다. 주소를 알려 주시겠어요? **8 제가 바로 저희 기록을 바꿔 드릴게요.**

6. 여자는 왜 잡지사에 전화하는가?
(A) 새 잡지의 구독을 요청하기 위해
(B) 배송지 주소를 변경하기 위해
(C) 구독을 취소하기 위해
(D) 주문을 확인하기 위해

7. 남자는 여자에게 무엇에 대해 조언하는가?
(A) 배송 방법
(B) 도시의 이름
(C) 추가 요금
(D) 다른 잡지

8. 남자는 다음에 무엇을 할 것 같은가?
(A) 고객 정보 변경
(B) 상사에게 연락
(C) 웹사이트 방문
(D) 예약

여: 감사합니다! 만나서 반가워요. 당신 회사도 오늘 밤 상을 받지 않았나요?

남: 네, 굉장했어요. 그런데 **2 저희 회사가 현재 수석 그래픽 디자이너 자리가 공석이에요.** 만약 관심 있으시다면 더 말씀을 드리고 싶은데요.

여: 음, 이직은 아직 생각해보지 않아서요. 하지만 꽤 흥미롭게 들리네요. **3 명함 하나 주시겠어요?** 생각을 좀 해볼게요.

1. 화자들은 어디에 있을 것 같은가?
(A) 채용 박람회에
(B) 시상식에
(C) 고객과의 회의 자리에
(D) 구직 면접에

2. 남자는 자신의 회사에 대해 뭐라고 언급하는가?
(A) 연례 보너스를 준다.
(B) 광고가 전문이다.
(C) 공석이 있다.
(D) 다른 도시로 옮길 것이다.

3. 여자는 무엇을 할 것이라고 말하는가?
(A) 일자리에 지원하는 것에 대해 생각해 보는 것
(B) 약속 일정을 잡는 것
(C) 발표를 준비하는 것
(D) 남자에게 직무 기술서를 보내는 것

Chapter Test

1. (B)	2. (C)	3. (A)	4. (A)	5. (B)
6. (C)	7. (B)	8. (C)	9. (A)	10. (C)
11. (A)	12. (C)			

Questions 1-3 refer to the following conversation.

M: Ms. Kelly? Hello, I'm James at Jay Graphic Design. **1 Congratulations on your award this evening!** The best design award is quite an achievement.

W: Thank you! It's nice to meet you. And your company also received some awards tonight, right?

M: Yes, that was exciting. By the way, **2 my company has an opening for a senior graphic designer right now.** If you're interested, I'd like to tell you more about it.

W: Well, I haven't thought about changing jobs. But it certainly sounds interesting. **3 Why don't you give me your card and I'll consider it.**

남: 켈리 씨죠? 안녕하세요, 저는 제이 그래픽 디자인의 제임스입니다. **1 오늘 저녁 수상을 축하드려요!** 최우수 디자인상은 굉장한 성취죠.

Questions 4-6 refer to the following conversation.

M: Okay, Nancy. The seminar room is prepared for the monthly staff meeting. **4 I just set up the laptop computer and projector** so it should be ready for your presentation.

W: Thanks. Oh, **5 is this computer connected to the Internet?** I'm going to show everyone the updates on our website.

M: Hmm. You may need a password for connecting to the Internet. **6 I can go and get it from our administration office downstairs.**

남: 좋아요, 낸시. 세미나 룸에 월간 직원회의 준비가 되어 있어요. **4 제가 방금 노트북 컴퓨터와 프로젝터를 설치했으니** 당신의 프레젠테이션을 위한 준비가 다 됐을 거예요.

여: 고마워요. 아, **5 이 컴퓨터는 인터넷에 연결되어 있죠?** 모두에게 웹사이트가 업데이트된 것을 보여줄 예정이에요.

남: 흠. 인터넷을 연결하려면 패스워드가 필요할 거예요. **6 제가 아래층 행정실에 가서 받아올게요.**

4. 남자는 이제 막 무엇을 끝냈다고 말하는가?
(A) 장비를 설치하는 것
(B) 컴퓨터를 수리하는 것
(C) 웹사이트를 업데이트하는 것
(D) 의제를 타이핑하는 것

5. 여자는 무엇이 필요하다고 말하는가?
(A) 직원들의 명단
(B) 인터넷 접속
(C) 최신 회의 안건
(D) 구직 지원서

6. 남자는 다음에 무엇을 할 것 같은가?
(A) 신청서 제출하기
(B) 서류 검토하기
(C) 사무실 방문하기
(D) 노트북 컴퓨터 가져오기

8. 남자가 "죄송합니다"라고 말할 때 의미하는 것은 무엇인가?
(A) 그는 가격 때문에 혼란스럽다.
(B) 그는 곧 떠나야 한다.
(C) 상품을 상점에서 구입할 수 없다.
(D) 일부 상품이 손상되었다.

9. 남자는 여자에게 무엇을 하라고 제안하는가?
(A) 다른 매장에 가는 것
(B) 다른 물건을 구입하는 것
(C) 매장의 웹사이트를 방문하는 것
(D) 다음 주에 다시 오는 것

Questions 7-9 refer to the following conversation.

W: Excuse me, 7 I need this jacket in a bigger size. 8 I'm looking for a medium but I've only found small.

M: I'm sorry, 8 but that's all we have in stock. Next week, we're receiving our winter merchandise. So they're no longer available.

W: Oh, that's too bad. I really like that color. I have never seen anything like it in other stores nearby.

M: Well, 9 I recommend that you try looking online. You might be able to find what you want on our website.

W: Hmm… Can I use this computer to make an online order?

M: Sure, if you have a membership ID. And our website's now offering big discounts on fall items until the end of this month.

W: That's good to know. I will try it.

여: 실례합니다, 7 이 재킷 더 큰 사이즈가 필요해요. 8 미디엄 사이즈를 찾고 있는데 스몰 사이즈만 있네요.

남: **죄송합니다만** 8 재고가 그게 전부입니다. 다음 주에 겨울 상품이 들어오거든요. 그래서 그것들은 더 이상 구매하실 수 없습니다.

여: 아, 실망이네요. 저 색상이 정말로 마음에 드는데요. 근처의 다른 매장에서 그런 것을 보지 못했거든요.

남: 그럼, 9 온라인으로 찾아보시는 것을 권해 드립니다. 저희 웹사이트에서 고객님이 원하시는 것을 찾을 수도 있어요.

여: 음… 온라인 주문을 위해 이 컴퓨터를 사용하면 되나요?

남: 네, 회원 아이디가 있으시면요. 그리고 지금 저희 웹사이트에서는 이달 말까지 가을 상품에 대해 큰 폭의 할인을 제공하고 있어요.

여: 좋은 정보네요. 시도해 봐야겠어요.

7. 여자는 무엇을 사는 데 관심이 있는가?
(A) 스카프
(B) 재킷
(C) 스웨터
(D) 넥타이

Questions 10-12 refer to the following conversation and list.

M: Hi, I'd like to check in. My name is Martin Watts. I booked a room last Monday 10 for attending the International Textile Conference this weekend.

W: Oh, sure. The hotel's full of conference participants. OK, your room's ready. Would you like to add any of these services? You can choose any of them with a small additional cost.

M: Well, I have a car, so I don't need to rent a car. Let's see. 11 I'll add this first one. Is it really available at all hours?

W: Yes, and it's right behind the reception desk. OK, I'll put that on your bill. Now, 12 I just need a photo ID. Do you have your passport or driver's license with you?

남: 안녕하세요, 체크인을 하고 싶은데요. 제 이름은 마틴 와츠입니다. 10 이번 주말 국제 섬유 학회에 참가하기 위해 지난 월요일에 방을 예약했습니다.

여: 오, 알겠습니다. 호텔은 학회 참가자로 가득 찼습니다. 네, 방이 준비되었습니다. 이 서비스 중에서 추가하고 싶으신 게 있습니까? 약간의 추가 요금만 지불하시면 이 중 아무거나 선택하실 수 있습니다.

남: 음, 저는 차가 있으니 차를 빌릴 필요는 없습니다. 어디 한번 봅시다. 11 첫 번째 것을 추가하겠습니다. 정말로 하루 종일 이용할 수 있나요?

여: 네, 그리고 그건 접수처 바로 뒤에 있습니다. 알겠습니다, 제가 당신의 청구서에 표시해 두겠습니다. 이제, 12 사진이 부착된 신분증만 필요합니다. 여권이나 운전면허증 가지고 계신가요?

추가 서비스
해밀턴 호텔

☐ 11 수하물 보관함 (24시간)
☐ 차량 대여 (24시간)
☐ 비즈니스 센터 (오전 9시 – 오후 10시)
☐ 세탁 서비스 (오전 9시 – 오후 9시)

10. 이번 주말에 어떤 행사가 열릴 것인가?
(A) 음악 경연 대회
(B) 박물관 개장
(C) 섬유 학회
(D) 스포츠 경기

11. 시각 자료를 보시오. 남자는 어떤 서비스를 추가하기로 결정하는가?
(A) 수하물 보관함
(B) 차량 대여
(C) 비즈니스 센터
(D) 세탁 서비스

12. 여자는 남자에게 무엇을 하라고 요청하는가?
(A) 신용카드로 결제하기
(B) 예약 번호 확인하기
(C) 신분증 제공하기
(D) 티켓 보여주기

PART 4

Chapter 1 전화 메시지 & 공공장소 안내 방송

Point 01 전화 메시지

Check-up Test
1. (D)   2. (A)   3. (A)   4. (B)   5. (B)   6. (D)

Questions 1-3 refer to the following telephone message.

M: Hello, Ms. Stephens. This is Alfredo Rodgers from White Box, 1 returning your call as you requested. Yes, 2 my company can design a website for your new clothing store. If you could call me at 070-2589 and let me know a time that fits your schedule, 3 I can arrange a consultation with one of our web designers for free. That would be helpful for you in selecting the right design and features for your store's website.

남: 스티븐스 씨, 안녕하세요. 저는 화이트 박스의 알프레도 로저스인데요. 1 귀하께서 요청하신 대로 회신 전화드립니다. 네, 2 저희 회사는 귀하의 새로운 의류점의 웹사이트를 디자인할 수 있습니다. 070-2589번으로 전화해서 편한 시간을 알려 주시면 3 저희 웹 디자이너 중 한 명과의 무료 상담을 주선해 드릴 수 있습니다. 그렇게 하면 귀하가 상점의 웹사이트에 맞는 디자인과 기능들을 선택하는 데 도움이 될 것입니다.

1. 메시지의 목적은 무엇인가?
(A) 프로그램에 대해 묻는 것
(B) 서비스를 소개하는 것
(C) 특별한 제안을 하는 것
(D) 질문에 대답하는 것

2. 화이트 박스는 어떤 종류의 업체인가?
(A) 건축 회사
(B) 의류 상점
(C) 인터넷 서비스 제공업체
(D) 웹사이트 디자인 회사

3. 청자가 제공받는 것은 무엇인가?
(A) 무료 상담
(B) 무료 배송
(C) 할인된 가격
(D) 고급 디자인

Questions 4-6 refer to the following telephone message.

M: Hi, this is Antonio from Tony's Repair. I'm calling regarding a laptop computer you dropped off last week. I have good news and bad news. The good news is **4** we have found the problem. It was the battery. It needs to be replaced. The bad news is the warranty on your laptop is over, so **5** you have to pay a small fee for the new battery. Here is what we can do for you. We know that you've been using our service for a long time, so if you want us to replace the battery, **6** we will give you a 25% discount on the new battery. Please give us a call and let us know what you want to do.

남: 안녕하세요, 토니 수리점의 안토니오입니다. 저는 고객님이 지난주에 맡긴 노트북 컴퓨터 때문에 전화드렸습니다. 좋은 소식과 안 좋은 소식이 있습니다. 좋은 소식은 **4** 우리가 문제점을 찾았다는 것입니다. 문제는 배터리였습니다. 그것은 교체되어야 합니다. 안 좋은 소식은 고객님의 노트북 보증 기간이 끝났기 때문에, **5** 고객님은 새로운 배터리에 대한 비용을 약간 지불하셔야 한다는 것입니다. 저희가 고객님을 위해 할 수 있는 일은 다음과 같습니다. 고객님이 저희 서비스를 오랫동안 이용해 주신 것을 알고 있기 때문에, 만약 고객님이 배터리 교체를 원하신다면, **6** 저희가 새로운 배터리를 25퍼센트 할인해 드리겠습니다. 전화 주셔서 고객님이 원하시는 사항을 말씀해 주시기 바랍니다.

4. 노트북 컴퓨터의 문제점은 무엇인가?
(A) 일부 부품이 분실됐다.
(B) 배터리가 작동하지 않는다.
(C) 팬이 작동하지 않는다.
(D) 더 많은 메모리가 필요하다.

5. 화자에 따르면, 청자는 무엇을 해야 할 것인가?
(A) 제조사에 전화하기
(B) 부품 비용 지불하기
(C) 새로운 장비 구입하기
(D) 노트북 찾아오기

6. 화자는 무엇을 제안하는가?
(A) 새로운 키보드
(B) 쿠폰
(C) 무료 설치
(D) 할인

Point 02 공공장소 안내 방송

Check-up Test

1. (C) 2. (D) 3. (D) 4. (D) 5. (B) 6. (B)

Questions 1-3 refer to the following announcement.

W: Attention all passengers! **1** East Wind Airlines' flight 457 to Bangkok is now ready for boarding at gate 12. All passengers should proceed to gate 12 with their boarding passes ready. **2** This flight was supposed to leave at 8 A.M. but it was delayed for 40 minutes **3** due to current weather conditions. We apologize for the delay and changing departure time. Again, all passengers on flight 457 to Bangkok should now report to gate 12 for immediate boarding.

여: 모든 승객들에게 알립니다! **1** 이스트 윈드 항공의 방콕행 457 항공편이 지금 12번 게이트에서 탑승 준비가 완료되었습니다. 모든 탑승객들은 탑승권을 준비하시고 12번 게이트로 이동해 주십시오. **2** 이 항공편은 오전 8시에 출발할 예정이었으나, **3** 현재 기상 상태로 인해 40분 동안 지연되었습니다. 지연과 출발 시각 변경에 사과 드립니다. 다시 한 번, 방콕으로 가는 457 항공편의 모든 승객들은 즉각적인 탑승을 위해 지금 12번 게이트로 오실 것을 알립니다.

1. 안내 방송은 어디에서 들을 수 있겠는가?
(A) 기차역에서
(B) 비행기에서
(C) 공항에서
(D) 여행사에서

2. 안내 방송에 따르면, 무엇이 변경되었는가?
(A) 도착 시각
(B) 항공편 번호
(C) 출발 게이트
(D) 출발 시각

3. 무엇 때문에 변경이 불가피했는가?
(A) 기계적인 문제
(B) 수하물 뒤섞임
(C) 이전 항공편의 지연
(D) 기상 상태

Questions 4-6 refer to the following announcement.

W: Attention visitors. **4** The Modern Arts Museum's exhibit rooms will be closing in half an hour. The museum's café and gift store will remain open until 9. **5** If you checked your personal items or clothes when you entered, do not forget to collect them before you leave. **6** Remember that a new exhibit, "19th century paintings," will be opening next week. You can get a free brochure for this exhibit as you're leaving the museum today. Once again, the museum will be closing in half an hour.

여: 방문객님들께 안내드립니다. **4** 현대 미술관의 전시실은 30분 후에 폐관 예정입니다. 미술관의 카페와 기념품점은 9시까지 영업을 할 것입니다. **5** 입장할 때 개인 소지품이나 의류를 맡기셨다면, 나가시기 전에 해당 물품들을 가져가시는 것을 잊지 마시오. **6** 새로운 전시인 "19세기 그림"은 다음 주에 공개될 예정임을 기억해 주시기 바랍니다. 오늘 미술관에서 나가시면서 해당 전시회에 대한 무료 책

자를 받아보실 수 있습니다. 미술관이 30분 후에 폐관할 예정임을 다시 한 번 알려 드립니다.

4. 안내 방송의 주된 목적은 무엇인가?
(A) 고객들에게 특별 세일을 알리는 것
(B) 카페의 일일 특별 메뉴를 설명하는 것
(C) 카페까지 가는 길을 알리는 것
(D) 미술관의 폐관 시간을 알리는 것

5. 화자가 청자들에게 무엇 하기를 상기시키고 있는가?
(A) 기념품 구매하기
(B) 소지품 챙기기
(C) 간식 주문하기
(D) 티켓 준비하기

6. 화자의 말에 따르면, 다음 주에 무슨 일이 있을 예정인가?
(A) 대회가 열릴 예정이다.
(B) 새로운 전시회가 열릴 예정이다.
(C) 개업 할인 행사가 종료될 예정이다.
(D) 보수 공사가 시작될 예정이다.

1. 메시지의 목적은 무엇인가?
(A) 등록 절차를 설명하는 것
(B) 길을 알려 주는 것
(C) 영업시간을 알려 주는 것
(D) 진료 예약에 대한 방침을 설명하는 것

2. 2월에 어떤 일이 일어날 것인가?
(A) 공사가 시작될 것이다.
(B) 주소가 바뀔 것이다.
(C) 추가적인 서비스가 제공될 것이다.
(D) 부서가 이전할 것이다.

3. 왜 청자는 0번을 눌러야 하는가?
(A) 녹음을 반복하기 위해
(B) 메시지를 남기기 위해서
(C) 담당자와 통화하기 위해서
(D) 추가적인 메뉴를 듣기 위해서

Questions 4-6 refer to the following announcement and train ticket.

M: Attention, passengers on board train 109 to Sydney. **4** Due to the heavy snow, we'll need to stop at the next station while the train tracks are cleared. You'll be allowed to get off the train but please do not leave the train station. We apologize for the inconvenience. **5** I hope that our arrival to Sydney won't be delayed more than a half an hour. We'll keep you updated. Meanwhile, to compensate you for the wait, **6** you'll be provided with a free meal voucher. It can be used at any café or restaurant in the station.

남: 시드니행 109 열차에 탑승하신 승객 여러분 주목해 주세요. **4** 폭설 때문에, 열차 선로가 정리되는 동안, 다음 정거장에서 정차해야 할 것입니다. 여러분들은 열차에서 내리셔도 되지만, 기차역을 떠나지 마시기 바랍니다. 불편을 드려 죄송합니다. **5** 시드니 도착 시간이 30분 이상 지연되지 않기를 바라고 있습니다. 새로운 소식은 바로 알려 드리겠습니다. 그동안 여러분들이 기다려 주시는 데 대한 보상으로, **6** 무료 식사권을 드리겠습니다. 이 식사권은 기차역 내의 모든 카페와 식당에서 사용이 가능합니다.

Chapter Test

1. (B)	2. (A)	3. (D)	4. (C)	5. (C)
6. (D)	7. (C)	8. (D)	9. (D)	10. (C)
11. (B)	12. (C)			

Questions 1-3 refer to the following recorded message.

W: **1** You've reached the location and directions information line of Pittsburgh General Hospital. Our main entrance is located on Queens Street, Exit 66 off Bell Highway. However, please be aware that **2** beginning February, Queens Street will be under construction, which may affect your route to the hospital. During the construction, we recommend that all drivers use the south entrance instead of our main entrance on Queens Street. As usual, patients and visitors are able to park in our free parking garage. For additional information about our hospital, **3** please press 0 now to hear a list of menu options.

여: **1** 귀하는 피츠버그 종합병원의 위치 및 길 안내 회선에 전화하셨습니다. 저희의 중앙 출입구는 벨 고속도로 66번 출구로 나오면 있는 퀸스 가에 위치해 있습니다. 그러나 **2** 2월부터는 퀸스 가에 공사가 진행될 것이기 때문에 병원으로 오는 길에 영향을 줄 수도 있다는 것을 알아 두십시오. 공사 동안 운전자들은 퀸스 가 중앙 출입구 대신에 남쪽 출입구를 이용하시길 권합니다. 평상시처럼, 환자와 방문객들은 저희 무료 주차장에 주차하시면 됩니다. 저희 병원에 대한 추가적인 정보를 원하시면 **3** 메뉴 선택 목록을 듣기 위해 지금 0번을 눌러 주세요.

출발 퍼스 도착 시드니
열차 번호: HJ 1052
출발: 오전 10:00
5 도착: 오후 3:00
승강장: A10

4. 화자에 따르면, 문제의 원인은 무엇인가?
(A) 보수
(B) 정전
(C) 악천후
(D) 엔진 고장

5. 시각 자료를 보시오. 화자에 따르면, 어떤 정보가 변경될 것인가?
(A) 퍼스
(B) HJ 1052
(C) 오후 3:00
(D) A10

6. 화자는 무엇을 제공할 예정이라고 말하는가?
(A) 지역 지도
(B) 대체 교통편
(C) 할인권
(D) 식사권

Questions 7-9 refer to the following announcement.

M: **7** Good morning, Green Fresh Market shoppers. Thank you for shopping with us today. **8** We would appreciate if you would fill out our customer survey. For your convenience, there are tables staffed by our customer service representatives. One is in the bakery section, and one is next to the register counter. It won't take much of your time. And your feedback will help us to find out how we can improve our customer service. **9** Those who complete the survey will receive a coupon for your next purchase. Thank you for shopping with us.

남: **7** 안녕하세요, 그린 프레시 마켓 쇼핑객 여러분. 오늘 저희 가게에서 쇼핑해 주셔서 감사합니다. **8** 여러분들께서 저희 고객 설문지를 작성해 주시면 매우 감사하겠습니다. 여러분들의 편의를 위해서, 고객 서비스 상담원이 배치된 테이블이 있습니다. 하나는 제과 코너 쪽에, 하나는 계산대 옆에 있습니다. **시간이 오래 걸리지는 않을 것입니다.** 또한 여러분들의 의견은 저희 고객 서비스 개선 방법 조사에 도움이 될 것입니다. **9** 설문 조사를 완료하시는 고객들은 다음 물건 구매 시 사용할 수 있는 쿠폰을 받으시게 됩니다. 저희 가게에서 쇼핑해 주셔서 감사합니다.

7. 안내 방송은 어디서 나오고 있는가?
(A) 공항에서
(B) 철물점에서
(C) 슈퍼마켓에서
(D) 식당에서

8. 화자는 왜 "시간이 오래 걸리지는 않을 것입니다"라고 말하는가?
(A) 오류를 정정하기 위해서
(B) 제품을 홍보하기 위해서
(C) 변경을 요청하기 위해서
(D) 참여를 장려하기 위해서

9. 청자들은 어떻게 해야 쿠폰을 받을 수 있는가?
(A) 제품을 구매함으로써
(B) 회원 가입을 함으로써
(C) 웹사이트에 방문함으로써
(D) 서류를 작성함으로써

Questions 10-12 refer to the following telephone message and order form.

W: Hi, Donald. **10** It's Melissa from the marketing department at Carla Fashion Company. Yesterday I ordered some pamphlets for our upcoming events. **11** I just noticed that there is a mistake in the number of pamphlets for the conference in Sydney. We'll actually need to add 500 more for the event. If possible, **12** I'll stop by the shop this Friday to pick them up. Thanks.

여: 안녕하세요, 도날드 씨. **10** 칼라 패션 회사의 마케팅 부서에서 근무하는 멜리사입니다. 저는 어제 곧 있을 저희 행사를 위한 팸플릿을 주문했습니다. **11** 시드니에서 열릴 학회를 위한 팸플릿 수에 오류가 있는 것을 방금 발견했습니다. 사실 그 행사에 500개가 추가로 필요합니다. 가능하다면, **12** 이번 주 금요일에 가게에 들러서 그것들을 찾아가겠습니다. 감사합니다.

주문서	
고객: 칼라 패션	
제품: 안내 책자	
500	연수회
11 1,000	학회
2,000	고객 설문
20,000	제품 출시

10. 화자는 어떤 부서에서 근무하고 있겠는가?
(A) 회계
(B) 인사
(C) 마케팅
(D) 디자인

11. 시각 자료를 보시오. 어떤 수량이 수정되어야 하는가?
(A) 500
(B) 1,000
(C) 2,000
(D) 20,000

12. 화자는 이번 주 금요일에 무엇을 할 예정이라고 말하는가?
(A) 연설 진행
(B) 송장 수령
(C) 주문품 픽업
(D) 웹사이트 확인

업무 회의 & 광고

Point 01 회의 발췌

Check-up Test
1. (D) 2. (D) 3. (A) 4. (C) 5. (D) 6. (A)

Questions 1-3 refer to the following excerpt from a meeting.

> M: I would like to inform everyone about the upcoming move to **1 the International Trade Building**. We've chosen that building because it has a **great view** of the Laurens River from our offices. We are using the same moving company that we used when we moved into this building five years ago. Those of you who were here at that time might remember the process. They are going to come and pack all the office furniture and electronic equipment. You need to pack your own stuff. It's a good time to organize all your documents. **2 Please go through all documents** in your departments and throw out materials you don't need. Make sure everything is done by Tuesday night. **3 The movers will be transporting everything on Wednesday.** Let me know if you have any questions.

> 남: 모두에게 곧 있을 1 인터내셔널 트레이드 빌딩으로의 이사에 대해 알려 드립니다. 우리는 그곳 사무실에서 로렌스강의 1 멋진 경관을 볼 수 있기 때문에 그 빌딩을 선택했습니다. 우리는 5년 전 이 빌딩으로 이사를 올 때 이용했던 같은 이사 업체를 이용할 것입니다. 그 당시에 여기에 계셨던 분들은 아마도 그 절차를 기억하실 것입니다. 그들이 와서 모든 사무실 가구와 전자기기들을 포장할 것입니다. 여러분들은 본인 물건들을 꾸려야 합니다. 모든 서류들을 정리하기에 좋은 시간입니다. 2 여러분들의 부서에 있는 모든 서류들을 살펴보고 필요하지 않은 것들은 버려 주세요. 모든 준비는 화요일 밤까지 완료되도록 확실히 해 주십시오. 3 이삿짐 업체에서 수요일에 모든 것을 옮길 예정입니다. 문의 사항이 있으시면 알려 주세요.

1. 화자에 따르면, 인터내셔널 트레이드 빌딩이 제공하는 이점은 무엇인가?
(A) 시내와 더 가깝다.
(B) 사무실이 더 크다.
(C) 임대료가 더 저렴하다.
(D) 경관이 좋다.

2. 직원들은 무엇을 하도록 요청받는가?
(A) 강을 따라 내려가기
(B) 개인 서류들 없애기
(C) 모든 가전제품의 전원 차단하기
(D) 파일들 분류하기

3. 이사는 언제 있을 예정인가?
(A) 수요일

(B) 목요일
(C) 금요일
(D) 토요일

Questions 4-6 refer to the following excerpt from a meeting.

> W: As you all know, **4 Capital Logistics has announced this morning that they are going to release a new management program.** So we are going to have one more program on the market that will compete with our own management software program. For those of you in sales, **5 you need to get in touch with our current customers,** and show them that our software is the best on the market. People in strategic planning have made this report based on the intelligence they have gathered on the new software. **6 Review it thoroughly before you talk to our clients,** and be careful that the information does not leak out.

> 여: 여러분 모두 아시다시피, 4 캐피탈 로지스틱스가 오늘 오전에 새로운 경영 프로그램을 출시할 예정이라고 발표했습니다. 따라서 시장에서 우리의 경영 소프트웨어 프로그램과 경쟁할 또 하나의 프로그램이 생기게 되었습니다. 판매부서의 여러분들은, 5 현 고객들과 접촉해서 우리의 소프트웨어가 시장에서 최고임을 보여 주어야 합니다. 전략 기획팀에서 새로운 소프트웨어에 관하여 그들이 수집한 정보를 토대로 이 보고서를 작성하였습니다. 6 고객들과 이야기하기 전에 그것들을 철저히 검토하시고 정보가 유출되지 않도록 조심하시기 바랍니다.

4. 화자에 따르면, 오늘 오전에 무엇이 발표되었는가?
(A) 새로운 경영진
(B) 두 부서의 합병
(C) 새로운 제품 출시
(D) 특별 광고

5. 청자들은 누구에게 연락하라고 지시받는가?
(A) 경쟁사
(B) 프로그래머
(C) 마케팅 직원
(D) 현재 고객

6. 청자들은 무엇을 검토하도록 요청받는가?
(A) 기밀 보고서
(B) 새로운 가격 목록
(C) 프로그램 이름
(D) 제품 설문

Point 02 광고

Check-up Test
1. (D) 2. (B) 3. (D) 4. (B) 5. (A) 6. (D)

Questions 1-3 refer to the following radio advertisement.

M: 1 Are you thinking about changing your carpet? Have you been looking for the right area rug that will match your home or office? Look no more! Rosedale Flooring has all the answers! We offer hundreds of products to meet all your needs, and we have a huge range of different colors to help you find the exact color you want in 2 our newly expanded showroom. For a limited time only, we are offering 30% off on all products in the store. So come on out to our fabulous showroom in Rosedale Mall. 3 You must hurry because the sale ends this Sunday.

남: 1 카펫 교체를 고려하고 계신가요? 당신의 집이나 사무실에 어울리는 알맞은 깔개를 찾고 계셨나요? 더 이상 찾지 마세요! 로즈데일 플로어링이 모든 정답을 가지고 있습니다! 저희는 여러분의 모든 요구를 충족시키는 수백 가지 제품들을 제공하고, 정확히 당신이 원하는 색상을 찾는 것을 돕기 위해 엄청나게 다양한 여러 색상이 2 새롭게 확장된 저희 전시실에 있습니다. 오직 한정된 기간 동안, 매장 내 모든 제품들을 30% 할인된 가격에 제공하고 있습니다. 그러니 빨리 저희 로즈데일 몰에 있는 멋진 전시실로 오십시오. 3 세일은 이번 주 일요일에 끝나니 서두르세요.

1. 어떤 상품이 광고되고 있는가?
(A) 정원용 꽃
(B) 사무기기
(C) 실내 장식품
(D) 바닥에 까는 것

2. 매장에 어떤 변화가 있었는가?
(A) 새로운 제품이 도착했다.
(B) 전시실이 확장되었다.
(C) 관리자가 교체되었다.
(D) 나무 바닥으로 된 공간이 추가되었다.

3. 언제 세일이 끝날 예정인가?
(A) 목요일에
(B) 금요일에
(C) 토요일에
(D) 일요일에

Questions 4-6 refer to the following advertisement.

W: Vikings Business Supplies is 4 the place for affordable office furniture for businesses of all sizes. We also include a one-day express delivery service if you are in a rush! Our 100% satisfaction policy guarantees that if you are not happy with your product, 5 you can return it and get a refund for the entire cost and no questions will be asked. 6 You can visit our website to modify all of our products to fit your specifications and needs. Visit our showroom on 438 Richmond Street or our website at www.vikingsofficesupplies.com.

여: 바이킹스 비즈니스 서플라이즈는 4 모든 규모의 업체를 위해 알맞은 가격으로 사무용 가구를 제공하는 곳입니다. 저희는 또한 고객님이 급하실 경우 당일 특급 배송 서비스도 제공해 드립니다! 100% 만족 정책은 고객이 제품에 만족하지 않을 시, 5 반품하고 전액 환불을 받으실 수 있도록 보장하며 그 어떤 질문도 하지 않을 것입니다. 6 저희 웹사이트를 방문하셔서 고객님의 사양과 요구에 맞도록 모든 저희 제품을 조정하실 수 있습니다. 리치몬드 거리 438번지에 있는 저희 전시장을 방문하시거나 저희 웹사이트 www.vikingsofficesupplies.com을 방문해 주세요.

4. 어떤 종류의 업체가 광고되고 있는가?
(A) 주택 청소 서비스
(B) 가구 공급업체
(C) 인테리어 디자이너
(D) 웹디자인 회사

5. 광고에 따르면, 고객들은 무엇을 받을 수 있는가?
(A) 전액 환불
(B) 무료 배송
(C) 특별 할인
(D) 선물

6. 청자들은 온라인으로 무엇을 할 수 있는가?
(A) 주문
(B) 주문 상태 확인
(C) 주소 변경
(D) 제품 주문 제작

Chapter Test
1. (D) 2. (A) 3. (C) 4. (B) 5. (D)
6. (A) 7. (B) 8. (C) 9. (A) 10. (C)
11. (A) 12. (C)

Questions 1-3 refer to the following radio advertisement.

W: Fairmont's Summer Clearance Sale is finally here! 3 Starting today until this Saturday, 1 all men's, women's and kids' clothing is on sale. Everything in the clearance section is 40% off. 2 We must make room for new arrivals for fall next week, so we have to get rid of our summer items. Now is your chance to buy your favorite brands at a greatly reduced price. **3** The sale ends this Saturday, so you must hurry before they are all gone!

여: 페어몬트 상점의 여름 재고 정리 세일이 드디어 시작됐습니다! **3** 오늘부터 시작해서 이번 주 토요일까지 **1** 모든 남성복, 여성복, 그리고 아동복을 세일합니다. 재고 정리 구역에 있는 모든 것들은 40% 할인됩니다. **2** 저희는 다음 주 가을 시즌 신상품들을 위한 공간을 마련해야 해서 여름 상품들을 정리해야 합니다. 지금이 당신이 좋아하는 브랜드의 상품들을 엄청나게 할인된 가격으로 구입할 수 있는 기회입니다. **3** 세일이 이번 주 토요일에 끝나니, 여러분들은 물건들이 모두 떨어지기 전에 서두르셔야 합니다!

1. 페어몬트 상점에서는 어떤 종류의 상품들을 판매하는가?
(A) 가구
(B) 청소 도구들
(C) 주방 용품들
(D) 의류

2. 상점은 왜 할인된 가격으로 물건을 팔고 있는가?
(A) 새로운 상품들을 위한 공간을 만들고 있다.
(B) 파산하는 중이다.
(C) 여름 동안 영업을 하지 않을 것이다.
(D) 신규 지점을 축하하고 있다.

3. 판촉 활동은 언제 끝나는가?
(A) 목요일에
(B) 금요일에
(C) 토요일에
(D) 일요일에

Questions 4-6 refer to the following talk.

M: Hi, everyone, I'm glad to see you all for today's meeting. **4** You've all done a great job of selling our Delta brand of camping equipment this year. At this meeting, I want to tell you about **5** the new product line that we are launching in March. In addition to tents, sleeping bags and backpacks, we will also be offering a line of outdoor clothing. It will be your job to sell these products to all the stores on your client lists. But before we talk about sales calls, **6** let's move to the display room and take a look at the new items.

남: 안녕하세요, 여러분. 오늘 회의에서 여러분 모두 뵐 수 있게 되어 기쁩니다. **4** 올해 델타 브랜드의 캠핑 장비를 잘 판매해 주셨습니다. 이번 회의에서는 **5** 3월에 출시하는 신제품 라인에 대해 말씀드리고 싶습니다. 텐트, 침낭, 배낭뿐만 아니라 아웃도어 의류 라인을 선보일 것입니다. 고객 명단에 있는 모든 상점에 이 물품들을 파는 것이 여러분의 일입니다. 영업 상담에 관해 얘기하기 전에 **6** 진열실로 가서 새로운 제품을 보도록 합시다.

4. 누구에게 얘기하고 있는가?
(A) 기술자들
(B) 영업 사원들
(C) 의상 디자이너들
(D) 회사 임원들

5. 3월에 무슨 일이 있을 것인가?
(A) 가격이 인상될 것이다.
(B) 카탈로그가 발송될 것이다.
(C) 새 상점이 문을 열 것이다.
(D) 새 제품이 이용 가능하게 될 것이다.

6. 청자들은 무엇을 할 것인가?
(A) 샘플 제품 보기
(B) 고객 명단 확인
(C) 포장 사양 논의
(D) 진열대 설치

Questions 7-9 refer to the following advertisement.

M: The F6600-D copy and print system looks complicated, but **7** taking the time to learn its functions will make any number of everyday office tasks easier. First, it's fast: **8** it makes copies at a speed of thirty-five pages a minute. It does much more than that. **8** It has scanner and fax functions as well. With this machine you're getting four office tools in one — with the F6600-D copy and print system you'll no longer need to own and maintain a scanner, a fax machine, and a printer. Think about the space in your office that will be freed up. And all this functionality comes for just under two thousand dollars. Don't miss out. **9** The sale ends this weekend.

남: F6600-D 복사 및 인쇄 시스템은 복잡해 보이지만, **7** 시간을 들여 이것의 기능을 익히면 매일의 사무실 업무들이 더 쉬워질 것입니다. 첫째, 이것은 빠릅니다. **8** 분당 35페이지의 속도로 복사합니다. 이것뿐만이 아닙니다. **8** 스캐너와 팩스 기능도 갖추고 있습니다. 이 기계 하나로 네 가지 사무용 기기를 갖추게 되는 것입니다. F6600-D 복사 및 인쇄 시스템 하나면 당신은 더 이상 스캐너, 팩스, 프린터를 보유하고 관리할 필요가 없습니다. 여유가 생길 사무실의 공간을 생각해 보세요. 이 모든 기능이 다 합쳐 2,000달러도 안 됩니다. 놓치지 마세요. **9** 이번 주말에 세일이 끝납니다.

7. 누가 이 광고에 관심을 보이겠는가?
(A) 레스토랑 사장들
(B) 사무 직원들
(C) 컴퓨터 수리점들
(D) 가구점들

8. 화자가 "이것뿐만이 아닙니다"라고 말할 때 의미하는 것은 무엇인가?
(A) 회사가 여러 번 기부를 해 왔다.

(B) 회원권은 더 많은 장점을 가지고 있다.
(C) 제품이 추가 기능을 가지고 있다.
(D) 소프트웨어는 다른 기기와 호환이 가능하다.

9. 이번 주말에 무슨 일이 있을 것인가?
(A) 세일이 끝날 것이다.
(B) 기사가 실릴 것이다.
(C) 광고 캠페인이 시작될 것이다.
(D) 보증이 만료될 것이다.

Questions 10-12 refer to the following excerpt from a meeting and menu.

W: Before we open our restaurant today, I have some important announcements. First, the shipment from our fruit distributor won't arrive until this weekend. So we do not have fresh fruit for dessert this week. Instead **10** we'll offer Wednesday's dessert on Thursday. Please remind our customers about that. Next, **11** we have a new server, Katie Wilson. She will do some training and start serving next week. **12** Her training schedule has been posted in the staff room. If anyone wants to help out with any of the training, just let me know.

여: 오늘 식당 영업을 시작하기 전에, 중요한 공지가 있습니다. 우선, 이번 주말이 되어야 과일 공급업체에서 배송품이 도착할 것 같습니다. 그래서 이번 주에는 디저트용 신선한 과일이 없습니다. 대신에 **10** 우리는 수요일 디저트를 목요일에 제공할 예정입니다. 고객들에게 이 점에 대해서 안내해 주시길 바랍니다. 다음으로 **11** 새로운 서버인 케이티 윌슨 씨가 들어왔습니다. 그녀는 교육을 받고 다음 주부터 서빙을 시작할 예정입니다. **12** 그녀의 교육 일정은 직원실에 게시되어 있습니다. 만약 교육에 도움을 주고 싶은 분은 저에게 알려 주세요.

오늘의 디저트	
- 올가 식당 -	
월요일	초콜릿 케이크
화요일	치즈 케이크
10 수요일	브라우니 쿠키
목요일	신선한 과일 타르트

10. 시각 자료를 보시오. 화자는 이번 주에 어떤 디저트가 두 번 제공될 것이라고 말하는가?
(A) 초콜릿 케이크
(B) 치즈 케이크
(C) 브라우니 쿠키
(D) 신선한 과일 타르트

11. 케이티 윌슨 씨는 누구인가?
(A) 서버
(B) 상담원
(C) 요리사
(D) 업체 대표

12. 화자는 직원실에서 무엇을 볼 수 있다고 말하는가?
(A) 주문서
(B) 특별 메뉴판
(C) 교육 계획
(D) 새로운 유니폼

Chapter 3 설명/연설 & 투어

Point 01 설명/연설

Check-up Test
1. (D) 2. (A) 3. (C) 4. (C) 5. (D) 6. (A)

Questions 1-3 refer to the following talk.

M: **1** Thank you for coming to the architecture photography workshop for beginners. You are going to learn all the basic techniques you need to know about photographing buildings. Today, **2** we are going to visit the Davenport Mansion, the one-hundred-year-old house that was used as a governor's mansion for many years. Once we get there, you'll quickly discover why it's a great place to learn photography. Before we get on the bus, let's check and see that everyone has the right gear. I would assume that most of you have brought your own equipment. If you haven't, we have some cameras, lenses, tripods, etc. that you can rent. **3** I'm going to hand out the papers now. If you are going to rent the equipment, please fill it out and bring it to the front.

남: **1** 초보자를 위한 건축물 사진 촬영 워크숍에 참여해 주셔서 감사합니다. 여러분은 건물을 촬영하는 것과 관련하여 알아야 하는 기본 테크닉을 모두 배우게 될 것입니다. 오늘, **2** 우리는 수년간 주지사의 공관으로 사용되었던 백 년 된 건물인 데이븐포트 맨션을 방문할 예정입니다. 그곳에 가면, 그 건물이 사진을 배우기에 좋은 장소인 이유를 바로 알아차리게 될 것입니다. 버스에 타기 전에, 모두들 적절한 장비를 갖추었는지 점검하도록 하겠습니다. 대부분은 자기 소유의 장비를 가져오셨으리라 생각합니다. 만약 가져오지 않았다면, 여러분이 대여할 수 있는 카메라, 렌즈, 삼각대 등을 저희가 보유하고 있습니다. **3** 이제 제가 서류를 나누어 드리겠습니다. 이 장비들을 대여하시려면, 그것을 작성하셔서 앞으로 가져오시기 바랍니다.

1. 워크숍은 무엇에 대한 것인가?
(A) 장비를 조립하는 것
(B) 집을 스케치하는 것
(C) 부동산을 임대하는 것
(D) 건물의 사진을 찍는 것

2. 청자들은 어디로 갈 예정인가?
(A) 역사적인 주택으로
(B) 부동산 업체로
(C) 미술관으로
(D) 지역 공원으로

3. 화자는 무엇을 배부할 것인가?
(A) 사진 장비
(B) 필기구
(C) 장비 대여 양식
(D) 건물 지도

Questions 4-6 refer to the following talk.

> W: Hi, everyone. **4** Today is the first day of the new employees orientation. The things you will learn over the next three days will be very important for your employment here. **5** You need to attend all sessions in order to use all the equipment in the factory. Safety is our top priority here, and we take it very seriously. **6** At the end of the third day, you will receive a document certifying that you have completed the training successfully. You need to keep it at your workstations at all times, because sometimes you are asked to present it during a safety inspection.
>
> 여: 안녕하십니까, 여러분. **4** 오늘은 신입 사원 오리엔테이션의 첫째 날입니다. 앞으로 사흘 동안 여러분이 배우게 될 것은 이곳에서 근무하는 데 있어서 매우 중요한 것입니다. **5** 공장에 있는 모든 장비를 사용하기 위해서, 여러분은 모든 교육에 참석해야 합니다. 이곳에서는 안전이 우리의 최우선 사항이며, 우리는 그것을 매우 중요하게 여깁니다. **6** 셋째 날 마지막에, 여러분은 교육을 성공적으로 수료했다는 것을 증명하는 서류를 받게 될 것입니다. 안전 검사 기간 동안에 때때로 그것을 제시해야 하기 때문에, 여러분은 그것을 작업 장소에 항상 비치하고 있어야 합니다.

4. 청자들은 누구일 것 같은가?
(A) 시설 방문자
(B) 안전 검사관
(C) 신입 공장 직원
(D) 교육 담당자

5. 청자들은 왜 프로그램을 완수해야 하는가?
(A) 그것이 게시되게 하기 위해
(B) 특별 암호를 받기 위해
(C) 임금 인상을 받기 위해
(D) 기계를 다루기 위해

6. 청자들은 프로그램 마지막에 무엇을 받게 될 것 같은가?
(A) 수료 증명서
(B) 기계 시연
(C) 공장 유니폼
(D) 회사 사무실 견학

Point 02 투어(관광/견학)

Check-up Test
1. (B) 2. (A) 3. (D) 4. (D) 5. (B) 6. (B)

Questions 1-3 refer to the following talk.

> M: **1** Welcome to the Madison Central Art Museum, and **2** thank you for purchasing this audio tour guide of the Lisa Thompson's Modern Sculpture Exhibit. This exhibit is the largest collection of Ms. Thompson's work ever assembled. You can see that each of the sculptures has a number beside it. To listen to the information about a particular piece, just press that number on the keypad of your audio device. **3** If you'd like to listen to these instructions again at any time, just press number 0.
>
> 남: **1** 메디슨 중앙 미술관에 오신 것을 환영합니다. 그리고 **2** 리사 톰슨의 현대 조각 전시회의 이 오디오 투어 가이드를 구입해 주셔서 감사합니다. 이 전시는 지금까지 열렸던 톰슨 씨의 작품 컬렉션 중 가장 큰 규모입니다. 여러분은 각 조각상들 옆에 번호가 있는 것을 볼 수 있을 것입니다. 특정 작품에 대한 정보를 들으시려면, 여러분이 가지고 계신 오디오 장치의 키패드에 해당 번호를 눌러 주십시오. **3** 언제라도 이 설명을 다시 듣길 원하신다면 0번을 눌러 주십시오.

1. 청자들은 어디에 있을 것 같은가?
(A) 사진 스튜디오에
(B) 미술관에
(C) 호텔에
(D) 페인트 공장에

2. 화자는 리사 톰슨 씨에 대해서 무엇이라고 말하는가?
(A) 그녀는 조각가이다.
(B) 그녀는 상을 받은 적이 있다.
(C) 그녀는 사업주이다.
(D) 그녀는 다른 나라 출신이다.

3. 화자에 따르면, 청자들이 다시 듣기를 원한다면 무엇을 해야 하는가?
(A) 요청서 제출하기
(B) 관람 후에 관리자와 연락하기
(C) 고객 서비스 센터 방문하기
(D) 장비의 특정 번호 누르기

Questions 4-6 refer to the following talk.

> W: Hello everyone, and welcome to the Royal History Research Center. My name is Jessie Cohen and **4** I'll be your guide today. Since Royal History Research Center is located in a historic building, I'll begin by telling you about some of the architectural features of the building. Afterwards, we'll step inside to see

some artworks displayed in the building. 5 The building is especially well known for the temporary residence of Henry III who was one of the kings of England. And we'll see many items which the royal family used. And 6 you can stay after the tour if you want, because there will be a photo session available with people wearing traditional costumes in front of the building.

여: 안녕하세요, 여러분, 왕립 역사 연구 센터에 오신 것을 환영합니다. 저는 제시 코헨이고, 4 오늘 여러분의 가이드입니다. 왕립 역사 연구 센터는 역사적인 건물에 위치해 있기 때문에 건물의 건축학적 특징들에 대해 말씀드리는 것으로 시작하겠습니다. 그 다음에 안으로 들어가서 건물 안에 전시되어 있는 예술 작품들을 감상할 것입니다. 5 이 건물은 특히 영국의 왕들 중 한 명이었던 헨리 3세의 임시 거주지였던 것으로 잘 알려져 있습니다. 그리고 우리는 왕실에서 사용했던 여러 물건들을 살펴볼 예정입니다. 그리고 6 건물 앞쪽에서 전통 의복을 입은 사람들과의 사진 촬영 시간이 있기 때문에, 원하신다면 투어를 마친 후에 남아 주세요.

4. 화자는 누구인가?
(A) 식당 주인
(B) 조사관
(C) 박물관 기증자
(D) 여행 가이드

5. 화자에 따르면, 왕립 역사 연구 센터는 무엇으로 잘 알려져 있는가?
(A) 경치가 좋은 위치
(B) 영국 왕의 거주지
(C) 희귀 도서 소장
(D) 계절 메뉴

6. 화자는 건물 앞에서 무엇 하기를 추천하는가?
(A) 기념품점 방문
(B) 사진 촬영
(C) 음식 시식
(D) 벤치에서 휴식

Chapter Test
1. (B)	2. (C)	3. (B)	4. (D)	5. (C)
6. (A)	7. (D)	8. (D)	9. (A)	10. (C)
11. (D)	12. (A)			

Questions 1-3 refer to the following talk.

M: Ladies and gentlemen, 1 welcome to the Johnson Candy factory. As you all know, 2 we're one of the oldest candy factories in the world. And we have been making delicious sweets for over a hundred years. On our tour today, you'll see how candy is made and packaged from start to finish. I'll show you around our entire manufacturing facility. You'll be able to see our employees working on assembly lines. 3 After the tour, you will receive some free packets of samples of our most popular chocolates and candy.

남: 신사 숙녀 여러분, 1 존슨 사탕 공장에 오신 것을 환영합니다. 여러분 모두 알고 계시다시피, 2 저희는 세계에서 가장 오래된 사탕 공장 중의 하나입니다. 그리고 저희는 100년이 넘게 맛있는 사탕들을 만들어 오고 있습니다. 오늘 우리의 투어에서 여러분은 사탕들이 어떻게 만들어지고 포장되는지를 처음부터 끝까지 보시게 될 것입니다. 저는 여러분이 저희 모든 생산 시설들을 둘러보도록 안내해 드릴 것입니다. 여러분은 조립 라인에서 작업하고 있는 저희 직원들을 볼 수 있을 것입니다. 3 투어를 마친 후에, 여러분은 저희의 가장 유명한 초콜릿과 사탕 무료 샘플들을 받으실 것입니다.

1. 공장에서 생산하는 것은 무엇인가?
(A) 가전제품
(B) 사탕
(C) 자동차
(D) 신발

2. 공장의 어떤 점이 특별한가?
(A) 상을 받은 시설이다.
(B) 국내에서 가장 규모가 크다.
(C) 가장 오래된 공장들 중 하나이다.
(D) 얼마 전에 보수되었다.

3. 청자들이 투어 후에 받게 될 것은 무엇인가?
(A) 무료 쿠폰들
(B) 제품 샘플들
(C) 행사 달력
(D) 설문지

Questions 4-6 refer to the following announcement.

W: Good evening, 4 I'm Sophia Alexander, the head librarian of the National University Library. 5/6 I want to welcome you all to the International Culture Center which has generously agreed to host this evening's fund raising concert and reception to benefit the library. The proceeds that we raise tonight will allow us to expand our library collection, hire additional staff, and offer more after-school programs for children. So, please be generous. But now, let's turn to the entertainment events of the evening. It's my pleasure to introduce conductor Perry Davis and the St. Evans Symphony Orchestra.

여: 안녕하세요, 저는 국립 대학 도서관의 4 수석 사서인 소피아 알렉산더입니다. 5/6 오늘 저녁 도서관을 위한 모금 행사 콘서트와 연

회를 주최하는 데 흔쾌히 동의해 준 국제 문화 센터에 오신 여러분 모두 환영합니다. 오늘 밤 모금되는 수익금으로 우리는 도서관의 장서를 확장하고, 추가 직원을 채용하며, 아이들을 위한 더 많은 방과 후 수업 프로그램을 제공할 수 있을 것입니다. 따라서 아낌없이 기부해 주시기 바랍니다. 그러나 지금은 즐거운 저녁 공연을 시작할 차례입니다. 지휘자인 페리 데이비스 씨와 세인트 에반스 교향악단을 소개합니다.

4. 화자는 누구인가?
(A) 라디오 진행자
(B) 학교 교장
(C) 지휘자
(D) 사서

5. 이 담화는 어디에서 들을 수 있을 것 같은가?
(A) 대학교에서
(B) 도서관에서
(C) 콘서트홀에서
(D) 영화관에서

6. 행사의 이유는 무엇인가?
(A) 모금하는 것
(B) 영화를 상영하는 것
(C) 상을 수여하는 것
(D) 예술가에게 경의를 표하는 것

Questions 7-9 refer to the following announcement.

W: Welcome to the 10th Annual Conference on International Game Industry, everyone. We are sorry for the delays in registration. Unfortunately, 7 we are having some problems with our computer network system, and we are unable to process your registrations. In order to help us expedite the check-in process, 8 please have your confirmation letter ready to show us as proof of payment. And because of these technical difficulties, we postponed the first keynote speech until 2 P.M. 9 This way, everyone can check in before the event begins. Thank you for your patience.

여: 제10회 연례 국제 게임 산업 학회에 오신 모든 분들을 환영합니다. 등록이 지연되어 죄송합니다. 유감스럽게도, 7 저희 컴퓨터 네트워크 시스템에 약간의 문제가 있어서 여러분의 등록을 처리할 수 없습니다. 저희가 입장 수속 과정을 더 신속히 처리하도록 돕기 위해, 8 지불 증거로 저희에게 보여 주실 수 있도록 확인서를 준비해 주세요. 그리고 이러한 기술적인 문제 때문에, 첫 번째 기조연설을 오후 2시로 연기했습니다. 9 이렇게 하면 모든 사람이 행사가 시작하기 전에 입장 수속을 할 수 있습니다. 기다려 주셔서 감사합니다.

7. 화자는 어떤 문제를 언급하는가?
(A) 일부 다과들이 아직 준비되지 않았다.
(B) 방에 좌석들이 충분하지 않다.
(C) 일부 연설자들이 도착하지 않았다.
(D) 네트워크 시스템이 제대로 작동하지 않는다.

8. 청자들은 무엇을 제시하라고 요청받는가?
(A) 영수증
(B) 신분증
(C) 작성 완료한 신청서
(D) 확인서

9. 화자는 왜 "첫 번째 기조연설을 오후 2시로 연기했습니다"라고 말하는가?
(A) 참가자들을 안심시키기 위해
(B) 마감일을 연장하기 위해
(C) 행사를 홍보하기 위해
(D) 제안을 수락하기 위해

Questions 10-12 refer to the following talk and chart.

M: Good to see you again, everyone. Did you enjoy your lunch? This afternoon, 10 we're talking about when a customer calls to request an upgrade to their service plan. Look at this visual aid here. It shows all the plans we have. Of these four plans, many customers have the one that includes only custom TV channels. But 11 you should explain that the best deal includes preferred TV channels plus phone. As you already know, 12 we have an incentive policy. If you sell more than five of that plan in one month, you will receive a bonus accordingly.

남: 여러분들을 다시 만나게 되어 기쁩니다. 점심 식사는 맛있게 하셨나요? 오늘 오후에 10 우리는 고객들이 서비스 요금제 업그레이드 요청을 위해 전화를 한 경우에 대해서 이야기를 나누어 볼 것입니다. 이 시각 자료를 봐 주세요. 여기에는 우리가 제공하는 모든 요금제가 있습니다. 이 4개의 서비스 중에서 많은 고객들이 맞춤 TV 채널만 포함된 서비스를 사용하고 있습니다. 하지만 11 여러분들은 최고의 상품이 선호 TV 채널과 전화를 포함한 것임을 설명해 주셔야만 합니다. 여러분이 이미 알고 계시겠지만, 12 우리에게는 인센티브 정책이 있습니다. 한 달에 5회 이상 이 요금제를 판매하시면, 이에 상응하는 보너스를 받으실 수 있을 것입니다.

AT&A 텔레콤 서비스 요금			
베이직	스탠다드	스마트	11 프리미엄
20달러/월	32달러/월	37달러/월	55달러/월
인터넷	인터넷 맞춤 TV	인터넷 맞춤 TV 전화	인터넷 선호 TV 전화

10. 청자들은 누구일 것 같은가?
(A) 웹사이트 개발자
(B) 관리 직원
(C) 콜 센터 직원

(D) 지점장

11. 시각 자료를 보시오. 화자는 어떤 요금제가 최고라고 말하는가?
(A) 베이직
(B) 스탠다드
(C) 스마트
(D) 프리미엄

12. 청자들에게 무엇이 제안되는가?
(A) 보너스
(B) 상품권
(C) 무료 상품
(D) 추가 휴가

(B) 다른 길을 이용하는 것
(C) 좀 더 천천히 운전하는 것
(D) 집에 머물러 있는 것

3. 이 정보는 얼마나 자주 제공되는가?
(A) 매 10분마다
(B) 매 15분마다
(C) 매 30분마다
(D) 매 시간마다

방송 & 인물 소개

Point 01 방송(뉴스/날씨/교통)

Check-up Test
1. (A) 2. (B) 3. (D) 4. (B) 5. (D) 6. (A)

Questions 1-3 refer to the following radio broadcast.

M: This is Arnold Parker with **3** the hourly traffic updates. The big news this morning is **1** traffic throughout the Starkville area is slow because of the ongoing rainstorm, which is expected to continue throughout the day. Due to the storms, some fallen trees are blocking access to the city highway to the Eastern Region. So **2** you should consider using Route 12 instead. **3** The next hourly traffic report will be coming up at 10. For all the latest updates, please stay tuned.

남: **3** 매시간 교통 정보를 전하는 아놀드 파커입니다. 오늘 아침의 주요 뉴스는 **1** 계속되고 있는 폭우 때문에 스타크빌 전역의 차량 통행이 지체되고 있다는 것이며, 이는 하루 종일 계속될 것으로 예상됩니다. 이 폭우로 인해 쓰러진 나무들이 동부 지역으로 가는 도시 고속도로의 진입을 막고 있습니다. 그래서 **2** 대신 12번 도로를 이용하는 것을 고려하셔야 합니다. **3** 다음 매시간 교통 정보는 10시에 찾아옵니다. 최신 정보를 계속 전해드리니 계속 청취해 주시기 바랍니다.

1. 무엇이 교통 정체를 일으키고 있는가?
(A) 폭우
(B) 교통사고
(C) 멈춰진 차량
(D) 공사

2. 청자들은 무엇을 하도록 권고받는가?
(A) 도로 공사를 피해 가는 것

Questions 4-6 refer to the following radio broadcast.

W: And now for today's business news. **4** Kings Food Manufacturing announced yesterday its plan to acquire Green Health Inc. Kings Food Manufacturer was founded 15 years ago as a small regional grocery store in town. However, for the past few years it has rapidly grown. **5** This acquisition will allow Kings Food to take over Green Health's business in organic food all over the nation. **6** A spokesperson for the company said an arrangement was made for all of Green Health employees to continue their jobs with Kings Food Manufacturing.

여: 이제 오늘의 비즈니스 뉴스 시간입니다. **4** 킹스 푸드 제조는 어제 그린 헬스 사를 인수하는 계획을 발표했습니다. 킹스 푸드 제조는 시내의 작은 지역 식품점으로 15년 전에 설립되었습니다. 하지만 지난 몇 년간 빠르게 성장했습니다. **5** 이 합병으로 인해 킹스 푸드가 전국에 걸친 그린 헬스 사의 유기농 식품 사업을 인수하게 됩니다. **6** 회사의 대변인은 모든 그린 헬스 사 직원들은 킹스 푸드 제조에서 계속 일할 수 있도록 협의가 되었다고 말했습니다.

4. 방송은 주로 무엇에 대한 것인가?
(A) 건강 식이요법
(B) 회사 인수
(C) 유기농 식품의 수요 증가
(D) 새로운 지역 사업체의 개업

5. 킹스 푸드 제조는 앞으로 무엇을 할 것인가?
(A) 해외 시장으로 확장
(B) 비즈니스 컨설턴트 고용
(C) 마케팅 비용 축소
(D) 유기농 식품 판매

6. 대변인이 발표한 것은 무엇인가?
(A) 직원들은 일자리를 유지할 것이다.
(B) 급여가 올라갈 것이다.
(C) 회사는 이름을 바꿀 것이다.
(D) 새로운 광고가 방영될 것이다.

Point 02 인물 소개

Check-up Test
1. (D) 2. (C) 3. (A) 4. (A) 5. (D) 6. (C)

Questions 1-3 refer to the following introduction.

W: **1 I am so excited to have Chef Suzuki with us today.** As you all know, he is one of the most popular chefs in the world, and **2 he's going to be the judge of today's cooking competition**. Ever since he was a little kid, he enjoyed cooking. His first teacher was his father, who was a sushi chef. He traveled through most Southeast Asian countries in his 20s. In a recent interview, **3 he said that his traveling has influenced him the most** in his cooking. When you take a look at the menu at his restaurant Little Tokyo, you can tell how much it has influenced him. Please welcome Chef Suzuki.

여: 1 오늘 요리사 스즈키 씨를 모시게 되어 매우 흥분됩니다. 여러분 모두 아시다시피, 그는 세계에서 가장 인기 있는 요리사들 중 한 명이고, 2 오늘 요리 대회의 심사 위원입니다. 그는 어린아이였을 때부터 요리를 즐겨 했습니다. 그의 첫 번째 스승은 초밥 요리사였던 아버지였습니다. 그는 20대에 대부분의 동남아시아 나라들을 여행 했습니다. 최근 인터뷰에서 3 그는 여행이 그의 요리에 가장 큰 영향을 주었다고 말했습니다. 그의 레스토랑인 리틀 도쿄에서 메뉴를 보면, 그것이 그에게 얼마나 많이 영향을 주었는지 알 수 있을 것입니다. 요리사 스즈키 씨를 환영해 주세요.

1. 스즈키 씨의 직업은 무엇인가?
(A) 작가
(B) 여행 가이드
(C) 리포터
(D) 요리사

2. 스즈키 씨는 오늘 무엇을 할 예정인가?
(A) 요리 준비
(B) 시연
(C) 대회 심사
(D) 책 사인

3. 화자에 따르면, 스즈키 씨에게 가장 많이 영향을 준 것은 무엇인가?
(A) 그의 세계 여행
(B) 그의 아버지의 가르침
(C) 그의 프랑스에서의 공부
(D) 그의 특별한 친구들

Questions 4-6 refer to the following talk.

M: **4 It is my pleasure to introduce our speaker of the night, Dr. Robert Lim.** Dr. Lim has been a board member of City Parks Association for five years, and he has been teaching a course at Emerson University in the School of Forestry and Wildlife Sciences. **5 I'm sure you are familiar with his latest book,** *A Guide to Western Trees*, which details how to take care of trees. Tonight, **6 Dr. Lim will share with us some very useful tips on maintaining healthy trees.** Here comes Dr. Lim.

남: 4 오늘 밤의 연사인 로버트 림 박사님을 소개하게 되어 기쁩니다. 림 박사님은 5년 동안 시립 공원 협회의 이사로 활동하고 있으며, 에머슨 대학교의 임학 및 야생식물학 대학에서 강의를 하고 있습니다. 나무를 돌보는 방법을 상세히 알려 주는 5 그분의 최신 저서인 <서부의 나무들 안내>를 잘 알고 계실 것이라고 생각합니다. 오늘 밤, 6 림 박사는 나무를 건강하게 가꾸는 것에 관하여 아주 유용한 팁을 공유해 주실 것입니다. 림 박사님을 소개합니다.

4. 담화의 목적은 무엇인가?
(A) 초청 연사를 소개하는 것
(B) 상을 수여하는 것
(C) 투표로 이사를 뽑는 것
(D) 새로운 공원을 홍보하는 것

5. 화자에 따르면, 림 박사는 최근에 무엇을 하였는가?
(A) 나무를 심었다.
(B) 학교를 졸업했다.
(C) 공원에 갔다.
(D) 책을 출판했다.

6. 림 박사는 무엇에 대해 말할 것인가?
(A) 강의하는 것
(B) 이사가 되는 것
(C) 나무 돌보기
(D) 두 가지 일 하기

Chapter Test
1. (C) 2. (B) 3. (D) 4. (B) 5. (B)
6. (B) 7. (A) 8. (A) 9. (B) 10. (B)
11. (C) 12. (C)

Questions 1-3 refer to the following radio broadcast.

M: This is QWKP, Huntsville's best easy rock radio station. I'm your host, Andy Moore. You are listening to "*Pop Goes the World*." **1 On today's program, we are going to have James Kenmore in the studio.** As you all know, he is the lead vocal of our own Huntsville band "Starz." He not only sings, but **2 he wrote all the songs in their first CD album, "First Starz."** Today, we are going to talk about their concert on Friday at the Huntsville Civic Center. This is their first concert this year, so we are all excited. During the show, 3 we are going to give away ten tickets to Friday night's concert, so stay tuned.

남: 헌츠빌 최고의 이지 록 라디오 방송국인 QWKP입니다. 저는 여러분의 호스트 앤디 무어입니다. 여러분들은 지금 '팝 고즈 더 월드'를 듣고 계십니다. 1 오늘 프로그램에서는 제임스 켄모어를 스튜디오로 모실 예정입니다. 여러분들 모두 아시다시피 그는 우리 헌츠빌의 밴드인 '스타즈'의 리드 보컬입니다. 그는 노래를 할 뿐만 아니라 2 그들의 첫 번째 CD 앨범인 <퍼스트 스타즈>의 모든 노래들을 작곡했습니다. 오늘 우리는 금요일에 헌츠빌 시민 회관에서 열릴 그들의 콘서트에 대해 이야기해 보겠습니다. 이것은 올해 그들의 첫 번째 콘서트라서 우리 모두가 기대를 하고 있습니다. 프로그램이 진행되는 동안 3 저희는 금요일 밤 콘서트 티켓 10장을 선물로 드릴 예정이니, 채널 고정하세요.

1. 담화는 주로 무엇에 관한 것인가?
(A) 이 주의 노래
(B) 새 CD 발매
(C) 지역 밴드
(D) 퀴즈 쇼

2. 화자가 밴드 CD에 대해서 언급한 것은 무엇인가?
(A) 시에 헌정되었다.
(B) 리드 보컬에 의해 작곡된 노래들이 포함되어 있다.
(C) 곧 발매될 예정이다.
(D) 좋은 평가들을 받았다.

3. 라디오 방송국은 청취자들에게 무엇을 제공할 것인가?
(A) 사인이 된 CD
(B) 할인 쿠폰
(C) 무대 뒤 출입증
(D) 콘서트 티켓

Questions 4-6 refer to the following talk.

M: Ladies and gentlemen, 4 it's my pleasure to present this year's best employee award to Penny Marshall. As the vice president of Dexia Group, 5 Ms. Marshall has been an important player in the Asian automobile market. 6 Ten years ago, the Asian automobile market had deteriorated and many car manufacturers withdrew their product lines. Since then, Ms. Marshall has worked closely with local dealers to coordinate many projects to take over the largest share of the Asian market. Many of these projects were very successful and our sales have increased dramatically. Now, let's give a big hand for Ms. Marshall who has worked tirelessly to contribute to our company.

남: 신사 숙녀 여러분, 4 페니 마샬 씨에게 올해의 최우수 직원상을 수여하게 되어 기쁩니다. 덱시아 그룹의 부사장인 5 마샬 씨는 아시아 자동차 시장에서 중요한 역할을 해 왔습니다. 6 10년 전, 아시아 자동차 시장이 악화되었고, 많은 자동차 제조업체들이 생산 라인을 철수했습니다. 그 이후로 마샬 씨는 아시아 시장에서 가장 큰 점유율을 차지하기 위해 현지의 중개인들과 긴밀히 협력하여 여러 프로젝트들을 조정해 왔습니다. 그 프로젝트들 중 많은 것들이 아주 성공적이어서 우리의 매출은 극적으로 증가했습니다. 이제 우리 회사를 위해 지치지 않고 일해 온 마샬 씨에게 큰 박수를 보내 주시기 바랍니다.

4. 연설의 목적은 무엇인가?
(A) 프로젝트를 제안하는 것
(B) 시상하는 것
(C) 관광 명소를 홍보하는 것
(D) 예산을 발표하는 것

5. 마샬 씨는 누구인가?
(A) 시 공무원
(B) 자동차 회사 직원
(C) 건축 회사의 중역
(D) 박물관 큐레이터

6. 화자는 아시아 시장에 관해 무엇이라고 말하는가?
(A) 수요가 증가해 왔다.
(B) 악화되었었다.
(C) 변동을 거듭해 왔다.
(D) 너무 많은 제약이 있다.

Questions 7-9 refer to the following radio broadcast.

W: Welcome back. This is Radio 101 and before Joseph gives us a traffic update, 7 I'd like to tell you about a sandwich place in a neighborhood called 'Enjoy San.' Yesterday, I stopped by and 8 talked to the owner, Jessica Baker about some of the unusual flavors available at the shop, like mint chicken and olive tuna. This June, Jessica Baker traveled throughout Europe and 8 that's where she got the idea to include these unique flavors in her menu. I tried the olive tuna sandwich and I give it a 5-star rating. So, 9 go on over to "Enjoy San" and enjoy some great new tastes.

여: 반갑습니다. 여기는 라디오 101입니다. 조셉이 교통 정보를 전해 드리기 전에 7 제가 '인조이 샌'이라는 동네 샌드위치 가게에 대해 말씀드리려고 합니다. 어제 저는 이 가게에 들러 민트 치킨, 올리브 참치와 같은 8 이 가게에서 맛볼 수 있는 색다른 풍미를 가진 음식들에 대해 주인인 제시카 베이커 씨와 이야기 나눴습니다. 올 6월 제시카 베이커 씨는 유럽 전역을 여행했습니다. 그리고 8 바로 거기서 그녀는 메뉴에 이런 독특한 풍미를 포함시켜야겠다는 아이디어를 얻게 됐다는군요. 저는 올리브 참치 샌드위치를 먹어봤는데 제 점수는 별 다섯 개입니다. 9 여러분도 '인조이 샌'에 가셔서 아주 맛있는 새로운 맛을 즐겨 보세요.

7. 화자는 무엇에 대해 보도하고 있는가?
(A) 지역 업체
(B) 역사적인 명소
(C) 음식 축제
(D) 책 사인회

8. 화자는 왜 "제시카 베이커 씨는 유럽 전역을 여행했습니다"라고 말하는가?
(A) 일부 메뉴의 출처를 설명하기 위해
(B) 관광 명소를 추천하기 위해
(C) 비용에 대한 걱정을 표현하기 위해
(D) 여행사를 홍보하기 위해

9. 화자는 무엇을 권하는가?
(A) 아이스크림 가게를 방문할 것
(B) 새로운 맛의 음식을 먹어볼 것
(C) 다음 보도 내용을 들을 것
(D) 요리 수업을 들을 것

(C) 전문 학회
(D) 모금 행사

11. 화자에 따르면, 청자들은 웹사이트에서 무엇을 할 수 있는가?
(A) 공연 티켓 구매
(B) 업체 명단 확인
(C) 활동 신청
(D) 기부

12. 시각 자료를 보시오. 행사는 어느 요일에 진행될 예정인가?
(A) 목요일
(B) 금요일
(C) 토요일
(D) 일요일

Questions 10-12 refer to the following news report and weather forecast.

W: And now for local news. **10** Swan City's Annual Family Fun Day will be held outside at City Square. Last year's event was successful with over 2,000 people in attendance. There were many things to do with your family on that day. This year, a new activity has been added. It's a Family Dancing Contest. **11** Those who want to participate in the contest need to sign up in advance online. More information is now available on its website. **12** The weather forecast says we can see some sunshine, but it will be mostly cloudy. Please make sure to bring a jacket on the day of the event.

여: 지역 뉴스 시간입니다. **10** 스완 시의 연례 가족의 날이 야외인 시티 스퀘어에서 진행될 예정입니다. 작년 행사는 2,000명 이상이 참가하여 성공적이었습니다. 그날에 가족들과 할 수 있는 행사가 많이 있었습니다. 올해에는 새로운 활동이 추가되었습니다. 그것은 가족 댄스 콘테스트입니다. **11** 콘테스트 참가를 원하시는 분들은 사전에 온라인으로 신청해야 합니다. 더 자세한 정보는 웹사이트에서 확인하실 수 있습니다. **12** 일기 예보에 따르면, 햇살은 볼 수 있지만 대부분 흐릴 것입니다. 행사일에 재킷을 가져오시기 바랍니다.

목요일	금요일	**12** 토요일	일요일
비	흐림	부분적으로 맑음	맑음

10. 이야기되고 있는 행사는 무엇인가?
(A) 음악 콘테스트
(B) 가족 행사

PART 5 & 6

Chapter 1 명사

개념 정리 Check-up Test
A ① 마이크, 손님 ② 톰, 회계사 ③ 광고 회사, 영업 직원
  ④ 대표, 임원진 ⑤ 도움, 사무실
B ①, ②, ④, ⑦, ⑧, ⑫, ⑭, ⑮
C ① 주어 ② 보어 ③ 목적어 ④ 목적어 ⑤ 목적어

Point 01 명사 자리
Check-up Test
1. (B) 2. (A) 3. (A) 4. (B) 5. (B)

1. 명사 자리
우선권은 신규 회원들에게 주어질 것이다.

2. 명사 자리
우리는 신제품 개발을 계획하고 있다.

3. 명사 자리
우리 분석가들이 추천한 내용이 매우 유익하다는 것을 알게 될 것이다.

4. 명사 자리
온라인 구매 확인서는 24시간 내에 이메일로 귀하께 전송될 것입니다.

5. 명사 자리
컨설팅 회사가 특별한 할인 행사를 제공하고 있다.

Point 02 가산 명사 = 셀 수 있는 명사
Check-up Test
1. (B) 2. (A) 3. (B) 4. (C) 5. (A)

1. 가산 명사
친구가 나에게 편지를 썼다.

2. 가산 명사
조립 구역에서 근무하는 사원들은 보호 장비를 착용해야 한다.

3. 가산 명사
해피 푸드 사는 중국에서 가공 식품 판매의 선두 주자가 되었다.

4. 가산 명사
제조업체가 유통업체들로부터 불만을 받은 후에 포장이 다시 디자인되었다.

5. 가산 명사
매년 연말에 부서 관리자가 업무 평가를 진행한 이후에, 급여 인상이 결정된다.

Point 03 불가산 명사 = 셀 수 없는 명사
Check-up Test
1. (A) 2. (B) 3. (A) 4. (A) 5. (C)

1. 불가산 명사
그 회사에 대한 정보를 저에게 주시기 바랍니다.

2. 불가산 명사
아버지는 항상 저에게 유용한 조언을 해주십니다.

3. 불가산 명사
새로운 캠페인에는 총괄 이사의 최종 승인이 필요하다.

4. 불가산 명사
매니저는 장비 추가 구매를 권장했다.

5. 가산 명사
마케팅팀은 아이들이 매일 인터넷을 얼마나 사용하는지 알아보기 위한 조사를 실시했다.

Point 04 명사 앞에 나오는 수량 표현
Check-up Test
1. (A) 2. (A) 3. (A) 4. (B) 5. (B)

1. 가산 명사
많은 졸업자들이 취업 박람회에 참여하고 있다.

2. 수량 형용사
모든 직원들은 회사에서 그들만의 개인 이메일 주소를 받았다.

3. 수량 형용사
그는 그들에게 전화로 많은 정보를 알려 주었다.

4. 관사
호텔 로비에서, 손님은 체크인 후에 포터에게 객실로 짐을 가져다 놓으라고 요청할 수 있다.

5. 수량 형용사
이 교수의 강의에 참석하고 싶은 학생들은 모두 이번 주말까지 등록해야 한다.

Chapter Test
1. (C) 2. (D) 3. (A) 4. (A) 5. (D)
6. (B) 7. (A) 8. (A) 9. (D) 10. (D)

1. 가산 명사
패션 월드 서비스는 10년 넘게 여성복 분야의 선두 업체였다.

2. 명사 자리
연기 감지기 설치를 포함시킬 수 있도록 예산을 조정해 주십시오.

3. 가산 명사
올해 HD 자동차의 수입이 5천만 달러 증가했는데, 이는 작년보다 50퍼센트 증가한 수치이다.

4. 명사 자리
최근 수익성 변화는 신임 사장 때문일 수 있다.

5. 가산 명사
증가된 소비자 관심 덕분에 컴퓨터 소매업자들이 수입 증가를 경험하고 있다.

6. 명사 자리
물건을 받으신 후에, 물품 배달을 확정하기 위해서 저에게 이메일을 보내는 것을 잊지 마세요.

7. 수량 표현
익스플로러 이노베이션은 미국의 많은 주요 도시에 분점을 갖고 있는, 로스앤젤레스에 있는 유명한 과학박물관이다.

8. 명사 자리
사람들이 약에 지나치게 의존하기 때문에 의사들은 사람들에게 수면제 과다 복용을 피할 것을 경고한다.

9. 불가산 명사
첫 번째 강연 이후, 노박 교수의 유익한 발표 덕분에 두 번째 강연의 참석자 수는 거의 세 배가 되었다.

10. 불가산 명사
도쿄와 상하이 두 곳 모두에 있는 법률 사무소는 지역 주민들에게 무료 상담을 제공한다.

Chapter 2 동사의 형태

개념 정리 Check-up Test

A ① arrived ② decide ③ hope, visit
   ④ appointed ⑤ are required

B ① O ② X, taken ③ O ④ X, is ⑤ X, submit

C ① appointing → appointed ② doing → do
   ③ recognizing → recognized ④ does → do
   ⑤ do → does, sold → sell

Point 01 자동사 vs. 타동사

Check-up Test
1. (A)   2. (A)   3. (B)   4. (A)   5. (A)

1. 자동사
국제 학회가 주말 동안 서울에서 개최될 것이다.

2. 자동사
고객들이 콘퍼런스 센터에 도착했을 때, 대표의 환영 연설이 막 끝났다.

3. 자동사
오전 수업을 신청하는 사람들은 시 예술 의회의 후원을 받는 모든 활동에 참가할 수 있다.

4. 타동사
우리 비서인 크리스틴 머레이 씨는 오전 9시부터 오후 6시까지 오는 모든 전화를 받는다.

5. 자동사
우리 디지털 카메라의 판매가 급격하게 떨어져서, 나는 신제품을 제작할 때라고 생각한다.

Point 02 2형식 동사

Check-up Test
1. (A)   2. (B)   3. (A)   4. (B)   5. (C)

1. 형용사 자리
기술 전문가는 데이터 분석을 사용하여 시장 동향이 예측 가능해진다고 주장한다.

2. 동사 어휘
몰디브는 여행자들에게 가장 인기 있는 휴가 장소이다.

3. 형용사 자리
대부분의 인턴들은 처음에는 열의가 넘쳐 보이지만 일단 업무가 자신의 능력을 넘어선다는 것을 깨닫게 되면 쉽게 자신감을 상실한다.

4. 동사 어휘
유벤투스 은행에서 지난 10년간 일한 후에 알레산드로 델 토로는 마침내 지점장이 되었다.

5. 형용사 자리
엑슨 사는 통합된 시스템을 개발해왔기 때문에, 그 회사는 지역적으로나 전국적으로 점점 더 부각되고 있다.

Point 03 4형식 동사와 5형식 동사

Check-up Test
1. (A)   2. (A)   3. (B)   4. (A)   5. (D)

1. 4형식 동사
발레로 에너지는 직원들에게 특별한 복리 후생 혜택을 주기로 결정했다.

2. 형용사 자리

책임자는 즉시 모든 조립 라인을 점검하는 것이 필요하다고 생각한다.

3. 형용사 자리
영업부장은 지난 분기 영업 통계를 보고 놀랐다.

4. 동사 어휘
우리는 수상을 큰 업적으로 여겼다.

5. 동사 어휘
조스티 사는 피츠패트릭 씨에게 영업직을 제안했다.

Point 04 사람 목적어만 취하는 동사

Check-up Test
1. (B) 2. (B) 3. (A) 4. (D) 5. (B)

1. 동사의 형태
고객들은 펙의 법률 사무소가 금요일에 휴일이라서 문을 닫을 것이라는 알림을 받는다.

2. 동사 어휘
당신이 그곳에 도착하면 마누엘 씨의 비서가 마누엘 씨에게 당신이 도착했다고 전할 수 있도록 그녀에게 알려 주세요.

3. 동사 어휘
리버티 투자 클럽은 귀하의 관심에 대해 감사를 드리며 또한 이를 환영합니다. 그리고 부동산 투자에 관련된 다른 분들과 함께 하시도록 초대합니다.

4. 동사 어휘
더글라스 씨는 우리 사건에 적용되는 연방 식약품 및 화장품 법률의 조항에 대해 우리에게 조언을 해주었다.

5. 동사 어휘
노블 씨에게 발표를 준비해야 한다고 꼭 알려 주세요.

Chapter Test
1. (C) 2. (C) 3. (B) 4. (B) 5. (A)
6. (A) 7. (D) 8. (C) 9. (B) 10. (B)

1. 동사 어휘
오늘 회의에 참석하지 못한 사람은 인사과로 연락해야 한다.

2. 동사 어휘
HBOS는 모든 결정 사항과 최근의 변화들을 투자자들에게 알리기 위해 노력하고 있다.

3. 동사 어휘
우리 상사인 슈피겔 씨는 직원들이 4시 이후에 30분간 휴식 시간을 갖도록 허용해준다.

4. 동사 어휘
어떤 사람들은 그들의 마을에 새로운 화학 공장을 건설하는 것에 반대하지만, 많은 사람들은 일자리를 창출하기 때문에 그것에 대해 찬성한다.

5. 동사 자리
무선 기술의 발달 덕분에, 노트북 사용자들은 심지어 도로에 있을 때에도 인터넷을 사용할 수 있다.

6. 동사 어휘
우리 회사는 지난 몇 년에 걸쳐 단골 고객들을 많이 만들었다.

7. 동사 어휘
재고 관리는 지점장의 업무에 포함되어 있다.

8. 동사의 형태
홀리 카페의 아시아 요리는 다양한 채소와 함께 제공된다.

9. 동사 어휘
오늘 아침 프레젠테이션은 고객들이 제약 분야에 투자하는 것을 고려해 보게 했다.

10. 동사 어휘
엔지니어들이 새롭게 개발된 소프트웨어의 오작동을 완벽하고 흠 없이 처리하길 기대하고 있다.

Chapter 3 동사의 수 일치/태/시제

개념 정리 Check-up Test
A ① is doing/능동태 ② will be launched/수동태
　　③ was donated/수동태, is broken/수동태
　　④ are supposed/수동태
　　⑤ has been teaching/능동태
B ① was locked ② was seen ③ are expected
　　④ are given ⑤ was elected
C ① 과거 진행 시제 ② 현재 완료 진행 시제
　　③ 현재 시제 ④ 과거 시제 ⑤ 미래 시제

Point 01 동사의 수 일치

Check-up Test
1. (A) 2. (B) 3. (B) 4. (C) 5. (D)

1. 동사의 수 일치
정보의 일부가 빠져 있다.

2. 동사의 수 일치
드릴 장비를 사용하는 사람은 보안경을 착용해야 한다.

3. 동명사
구직자를 돕는 것은 퀘벡에서 고용률을 올릴 수 있는 가장 좋은 방법이다.

4. 동사의 수 일치
미르 씨는 그의 회사의 새로운 TV 광고를 보고 그것의 품질에 무척 흡족해한다.

5. 동사의 수 일치
각 과정의 자격 요구 조건은 프로그램마다 다양하다.

Point 02 수동태

Check-up Test
1. (A) 2. (A) 3. (A) 4. (A) 5. (D)

1. 동사의 형태
이번 워크숍의 프로그램은 기획자에게 확인을 받아야 한다.

2. 동사의 형태
퀸 씨는 우리 지사를 캘리포니아로 확장할지 미시간으로 확장할지를 여전히 고민하고 있다.

3. 동사의 형태
연구부서의 그랜트 교수는 학생들에게 영감을 주는 강의를 제공하는 것으로 알려져 있다.

4. 동사 어휘
인수에 관한 모든 세부 사항들은 그 보고서에 설명될 것이다.

5. 동사의 형태
토요일에 근무 예정인 한 자원봉사자는 어제 병원으로부터 그의 업무에 관한 편지를 받았다.

Point 03 빈출 수동태 표현

Check-up Test
1. (B) 2. (B) 3. (A) 4. (D) 5. (A)

1. 동사의 형태
수업 시간에 전자 기기를 사용해서는 안 된다.

2. 동사의 형태
판매량은 천억을 초과할 것으로 예상된다.

3. 동사의 형태
공장의 자리에 지원한 지원자들은 적어도 하나의 노동 허가서를 보유할 것이 요구된다.

4. 동사 어휘
전 직원들은 기계를 작동시킬 때 보안경을 착용해야 한다.

5. 동사의 형태
KPMG는 시청자들에게 강한 인상을 남기는 광고를 제작하는 것으로 유명하다.

Point 04 시제 결정 요소

Check-up Test
1. (B) 2. (B) 3. (A) 4. (B) 5. (A)

1. 동사 시제
내년 베이징에서 개최되는 채용 박람회에서 인턴이 채용될 예정이라는 공지가 있다.

2. 동사 시제
하비 씨가 신규 주문을 보낼 때쯤에는 이미 베스트 오피스 서플라이에서는 새로운 가격표를 발표할 것이다.

3. 동사 시제
직원의 인사기록은 허가 없이 배포되어서는 안 된다.

4. 동사 시제
기술부에서 승인을 받자마자, 우리 팀은 프로젝트를 시작했다.

5. 동사 시제
우리 구매부는 매주 금요일마다 사무용품을 주문한다.

Point 05 현재 시제

Check-up Test
1. (A) 2. (B) 3. (A) 4. (C) 5. (B)

1. 동사 시제
일단 넬슨 씨는 다음 달에 홍콩으로 가서, 공장을 둘러본 다음 가격을 협상할 것이다.

2. 부사 어휘
캐미언 차량 정비소는 여름철에 항상 영업시간을 연장한다.

3. 동사 시제
다음 분기 동안, 우리 주주들은 회계부서에서 예상한 순이익 증가를 볼 수 있기를 희망한다.

4. 부사 어휘
대부분 도시의 보도는 대개 폭이 1미터이다.

5. 동사 시제
세미나 자료집이 학회가 시작하기 이틀 전에 모든 참석자들에게 발송될 것이다.

Point 06　과거 vs. 현재 완료

Check-up Test

1. (B)　2. (A)　3. (A)　4. (C)　5. (D)

1. 동사 시제
지난 30년간 그 어느 때보다도 더 많은 소녀와 여성들이 모든 종목의 스포츠에 참여해 오고 있다.

2. 동사 시제
파크 씨는 지난 20년이 넘게 동일한 회사에서 여러 가지 다른 부서에서 근무했다.

3. 동사 시제
이사인 파커 씨는 일 년 내에 회사의 이윤을 20퍼센트까지 상승시키겠다고 벌써 약속했다.

4. 동사 시제
맥대니얼 씨가 로렌 스포츠에 합류한 이후로 3개월이 지났다.

5. 동사 시제
지난 30년 동안 마케팅 업계에서 유명 인사였던 폴 뉴먼 씨가 브렌즈윅 대학교의 초청 강사가 될 것이다.

Chapter Test

1. (D)　2. (B)　3. (B)　4. (A)　5. (B)
6. (A)　7. (C)　8. (C)　9. (C)　10. (D)

1. 동사의 형태
지금까지 대회의 수상자들은 전화와 이메일로 통보를 받았다.

2. 동사의 형태
방문객들은 오전 9시부터 오후 4시 사이에 시립 박물관을 견학해 왔다.

3. 동사의 형태
우리 진료소는 지역 주민들에게 적당한 가격에 우수한 치과 치료를 제공하고 있다.

4. 동사의 형태
도서관 사서는 이달 말까지 어떠한 연체된 책이나 학술지라도 반납되기를 요청했다.

5. 동사의 형태
유능한 관리자는 모든 직원이 최선을 다할 수 있는 근무 환경을 조성한다.

6. 동사 어휘
이 방법을 사용하면서 드러난 문제점은 대부분의 기업주들이 인터넷 마케팅이나 웹의 기초에 대한 토대가 부족했다는 것이다.

7. 동사 어휘
이 유인물들을 교과서 대체물로 여겨서는 안 된다.

8. 동사의 형태
살레르노 씨의 제안과는 달리, 시몬스 씨는 한 명 대신 두 명의 비서를 고용하길 원한다.

9. 동사 시제
헨더슨 엔터프라이즈가 자동차 부서의 구조조정을 할 때 많은 수의 선임 관리자들이 해고되었다.

10. 동사의 형태
제닝 박사의 세미나는 오늘과 내일 오후 101호에서 열릴 예정이다.

Chapter 4　대명사

개념 정리 Check-up Test

A　①, ③, ⑤, ⑦, ⑨, ⑩, ⑫, ⑮
B　① 주격　② 소유격　③ 소유 대명사　④ 소유격
　　⑤ 재귀 대명사
C　① she　② herself　③ them　④ your　⑤ him

Point 01　인칭 대명사의 격

Check-up Test

1. (A)　2. (B)　3. (B)　4. (C)　5. (B)

1. 인칭 대명사 – 주격
우리는 그가 이곳에 없었다는 것을 안다.

2. 인칭 대명사 – 소유격
하스 씨와 그의 팀은 내일 학회에 프레젠테이션 자료를 완성해서 가져오라는 지시를 받았다.

3. 인칭 대명사 – 소유격
우리의 상사는 그녀의 팀을 관리할 것을 요청받았다.

4. 인칭 대명사 – 목적격
그들 그룹의 구성원들은 모두 다 선발되었으나, 포먼 씨가 그들과 함께할지도 모른다.

5. 인칭 대명사 – 소유격
부대표가 내일 우리 사무실에 방문할 예정이오니, 그의 모든 서류들을 준비해 주십시오.

Point 02　재귀 대명사

Check-up Test

1. (B)　2. (B)　3. (B)　4. (C)　5. (D)

1. 재귀 대명사
제인은 이와 같은 사무실에서 그녀가 직접 모든 일을 다 할 수는 없다.

2. 재귀 대명사
뉴턴 박사는 다른 환자들을 상담하느라 너무 바쁘기 때문에 자신이 직접 약속 일정을 잡는 일은 드물다.

3. 재귀 대명사
롱 씨는 그의 보고서를 혼자서 끝내야 했다.

4. 재귀 대명사
그녀의 뛰어난 실적을 통해 로빈 씨는 그녀 스스로 우리 회사의 귀중한 자산임을 증명했다.

5. 재귀 대명사
스텔라 씨는 혼자서 표적 집단 면접을 시작했지만, 이후에 다른 마케팅 담당자들의 도움을 받았다.

Point 03 one, another, other, the other 구분하기

Check-up Test
1. (A) 2. (A) 3. (A) 4. (B) 5. (B)

1. 부정 형용사
선두적인 온라인 쇼핑몰 중 하나인 모나는 온라인 고객들에게 다른 할인 대신에 쿠폰만 제공한다.

2. 부정 대명사
제공된 세 가지의 선택권 중에 두 개는 우리가 이용할 수 없지만, 나머지 하나는 수용 가능하고 우리 예산 내에 있다.

3. 부정 형용사
다른 제품들은 우리가 기대했던 만큼 수익성이 있지 않았다.

4. 부정 대명사
신규 사용자용 설명서에는 한 이메일 계정에서 다른 이메일 계정으로 메일을 복사하는 방법이 나와 있다.

5. 부정 대명사
NJ 운송은 출퇴근하는 사람들에게 가장 경제적인 교통수단이지만, 다른 것들도 효율적이다.

Point 04 those와 one

Check-up Test
1. (A) 2. (B) 3. (A) 4. (D) 5. (C)

1. 지시 대명사
휴가를 떠나려고 계획 중인 사람들은 특별 할인을 한번 볼 필요가 있다.

2. 지시 형용사
당신은 그 보고서들을 정오까지 제출하기로 되어 있습니다.

3. 지시 대명사
주요 대여 대리점의 올해 수익은 작년과 유사하다.

4. 지시 대명사
필립 씨는 최근 관리자로 승진했지만, 그의 직원들은 다른 팀의 직원들보다 더 경험이 있다.

5. 부정 대명사
검사관들은 하나는 더 견고한 반면 다른 하나는 더욱 세련된 디자인을 갖추고 있다고 말한다.

Chapter Test
1. (D) 2. (C) 3. (A) 4. (C) 5. (C)
6. (C) 7. (C) 8. (B) 9. (A) 10. (D)

1. 인칭 대명사 - 주격
모든 항공사들은 티켓 소지자인 당신에게 신분증명서를 제시하기를 요청한다.

2. 인칭 대명사 - 소유 대명사
데브라 씨와 나는 업무 스타일이 비슷하기 때문에, 단기 목표를 달성할 수 있을 것이라고 확신한다.

3. 지시 대명사
가구 사업체들의 올해 매출액은 지난 2년간의 것과 비슷하다.

4. 부정 대명사
킴벌리 식료품 가게는 모든 상인들에게 계약 갱신을 제안했으며, 대부분이 이미 서명을 했다.

5. 인칭 대명사- 소유격
이 경제 전망은 대부분의 회사들이 그들의 인건비를 줄일 것이라고 예측했다.

6. 부정 대명사
우리 가게에서 X-5 레이저 프린터가 매진되었기 때문에, 당신 가게에 물건이 있다면, 즉시 일부를 저희에게 발송해 주십시오.

7. 부분 대명사
출발하기 전에, 역무원들은 반드시 승객들로부터 각각의 티켓들을 수거해야 한다.

8. 재귀 대명사
직원 감사 만찬을 위해 핀레이 씨는 직원들을 위해 뷔페 테이블을 준비하고 다양한 음식들을 맘껏 먹도록 했다.

9. 인칭 대명사 - 주격
세계적으로 유명한 잡지인 <왓슨 파이낸셜>은 가장 유망하다고 여기는 스타트업 기업의 명단을 발표했다.

10. 재귀 대명사
청중들은 토론이 진행되는 동안에 서로 대화를 나누지 않도록 요청받는다.

Chapter 5 형용사

개념 정리 Check-up Test

A ①, ②, ④, ⑥, ⑧, ⑮

B ① technical ② considerate ③ useful
    ④ present ⑤ a variety of, interesting

C ① strategic ② financial ③ These ④ Our
    ⑤ competitive

Point 01 형용사 자리

Check-up Test
1. (B) 2. (A) 3. (A) 4. (A) 5. (D)

1. 형용사 자리
처음 광고비를 지출한 후에 회사는 5일 이내에 빚을 갚았다.

2. 형용사
직원들이 계속 생산적이기만 하다면, 우리는 우리의 월간 목표들을 모두 달성할 수 있을 것이다.

3. 형용사 자리
만약 당신이 성공한 건축가가 될 것을 계획한다면, 당신은 반드시 시각 예술 분야에 폭넓은 지식을 보유해야 한다.

4. 형용사 자리
통신 판매 제품을 구매하실 때는, 스미스 인더스트리 기업 앞으로 모든 수표를 발행하시기 바랍니다.

5. 형용사 자리
알리안츠에서 개인 정보는 엄격히 기밀이 유지되며 직원들의 허가가 있을 시에만 공개될 수 있다.

Point 02 형용사와 부사 구별하기

Check-up Test
1. (A) 2. (B) 3. (A) 4. (A) 5. (B)

1. 형용사 자리
우리는 크고 둥근 검은색 나무 테이블을 사야 한다.

2. 형용사 자리
3개월의 교육 후에, 신입 사원들은 회사 정책에 매우 익숙해졌다.

3. 형용사 자리
브라운 홀세일즈의 직원이 그들 중에 가장 설득력 있었기 때문에 뉴캐슬 사의 사장은 그 회사에서 물품을 받기로 했다.

4. 형용사 자리
호텔 제타에는 이용할 수 있는 방이 없지만 호텔 오메가에는 아직도 방이 좀 있다.

5. 부사 자리
모리토 호텔은 작년에 수리를 진행한 이후로 점점 더 인기 있는 학회 진행 장소가 되고 있다.

Point 03 수량 형용사

Check-up Test
1. (A) 2. (A) 3. (A) 4. (D) 5. (C)

1. 수량 형용사
프레젠테이션이 끝난 후 많은 직원들이 회의실 보수에 찬성표를 던졌다.

2. 수량 형용사
모든 자료집에는 우리 지점들의 목록뿐만 아니라 우리 회사에 대한 소개도 포함되어 있다.

3. 수량 형용사
모든 직원들은 비서에게 그들의 계좌 정보를 제출해야 된다는 것을 다시 한 번 말씀드립니다.

4. 수량 형용사
최근 소비자 보고서는 각각의 고객들은 경제에 대해 확신이 있다는 것을 보여 준다.

5. 수량 형용사
보레스터 프로덕츠 직원들은 누구든 금요일 오후 3시까지 주간 보고서를 제출해야 한다.

Point 04 사람 수식 형용사 vs. 사물 수식 형용사

Check-up Test
1. (B) 2. (B) 3. (B) 4. (A) 5. (B)

1. 형용사 어휘
프레젠테이션에서 보여진 신제품 디자인의 개발 과정은 분명하고 이해하기 쉬웠다.

2. 형용사 어휘
PDSVA는 기밀 서류의 안전한 보관 서비스를 제공한다.

3. 형용사 어휘
우리 경영 간부는 그레이 박사가 새로운 에너지원을 공동으로 개발하기 위해 우리 회사에 합류했다는 것을 듣고 기뻐했다.

4. 형용사 어휘
맛은 그렇게 뛰어나지 않을 수 있지만 타파스의 즐거운 분위기는 타파스를 시내에서 가장 인기 있는 레스토랑 중 하나로 만든다.

5. 형용사 어휘
나는 그가 회의에 참석할 거라고 확신한다.

Chapter Test
1. (A) 2. (A) 3. (A) 4. (A) 5. (D)
6. (B) 7. (C) 8. (C) 9. (B) 10. (D)

1. 형용사 어휘
5년 넘게 ABC 레스토랑에서 종업원으로 일한 사람은 누구든지 관리자 자리에 지원할 자격이 있다.

2. 형용사 자리
다음달부터, 모든 런던 주택가 도로의 제한속도는 시속 60킬로미터로 변경될 예정이다.

3. 형용사 자리
이메일에 계약서를 첨부할 때, 문서 보안을 유지해야 한다.

4. 형용사 어휘
페르디난드 씨가 팀을 조직하는 동안 볼드윈 씨가 고객들과의 연락을 책임졌다.

5. 동사의 형태
근무 시간 후에 적절한 신분증 없이는 누구도 그 건물에 들어갈 수 없어야 하는 것이 필수다.

6. 한정사
개업 의사는 매 2년마다 의사 면허를 갱신해야 한다.

7. 수량 형용사
이 씨는 모든 신입 사원들을 위해서 일련의 워크숍을 진행할 것이다.

8. 형용사 어휘
현재의 생산 속도로 프라임 테크는 이번 여름까지 수요를 맞추기에 충분한 제품을 제조할 것이다.

9. 형용사 자리
축제에서 가장 인상적인 부분은 재즈 콘서트였다.

10. 형용사 자리
케임브리지 박물관 방문객에게는 견학 중에 다른 사람들을 배려하여 사진 촬영을 삼갈 것이 요청된다.

Chapter 6 부사

개념 정리 Check-up Test
A ①, ⑤, ⑧, ⑩, ⑬, ⑮
B ① promptly ② hard ③ only ④ Fortunately
  ⑤ approximately
C ① sharply, 정도 부사 ② usually, 빈도 부사
  ③ Only, 강조 부사 ④ carefully, 방법 부사
  ⑤ lately, 시간 부사

Point 01 부사 자리

Check-up Test
1. (B) 2. (B) 3. (A) 4. (D) 5. (B)

1. 부사 자리
새로운 분류 소프트웨어 덕분에, 모든 온라인 지원서가 쉽게 처리됐다.

2. 부사 자리
교육 관계자들은 토익 시험은 부정 행위를 막기 위해 면밀히 감시될 것이라고 말한다.

3. 부사 자리
허브 향신료는 인도 음식에서 역사적으로 중요한 역할을 해왔다.

4. 부사 자리
K-마트의 많은 고객들은 현지에서 생산된 식품에 기꺼이 돈을 더 지불한다.

5. 부사 자리
박 씨는 ABC 마트에서 점포 주인으로 일을 시작했지만, 그 이후 그는 전국적으로 유명한 사업가가 되었다.

Point 02 특정 시제와 어울리는 부사

Check-up Test
1. (B) 2. (A) 3. (A) 4. (A) 5. (A)

1. 부사 어휘
저희가 최근에 다른 곳으로 이사를 했기 때문에, 위에 명시된 새로운 우편 주소로 연락하십시오.

2. 부사 어휘
디자인팀은 벌써 자동차의 대략적인 스케치를 하기 시작했다.

3. 부사 어휘
우리는 한때 그 모델을 생산했다.

4. 부사 어휘
종이와 카트리지는 주로 모서리 옆에 있는 첫 번째 수납장에 보관된다.

5. 부사 어휘
윌튼 제조사는 곧 서울에 대형 시설을 열 예정입니다.

Point 03 빈출 부사 (1)

Check-up Test
1. (B) 2. (A) 3. (A) 4. (C) 5. (C)

1. 부사 자리
최근에 발표된 보도에 따르면, 경기 침제기 동안 그 나라의 화폐 가치가 급격하게 하락했다.

2. 부사 어휘
전국 대학교 신입생들의 거의 30퍼센트가 최소 하나의 보충 강좌를 신청해야 한다.

3. 부사 어휘
공항은 호텔에서 대략 20킬로미터 떨어져 있다.

4. 부사 어휘
거의 6개월 동안의 보수 공사 후에, 14번 가 기차역은 목요일에 운영을 재개할 것이다.

5. 부사 어휘
뉴스에서 아이슬란드의 지진 피해가 보도된 후 자원봉사자의 수가 급격하게 많아졌다.

Point 04 빈출 부사 (2)

Check-up Test
1. (B) 2. (A) 3. (A) 4. (D) 5. (C)

1. 부사 어휘
지역 회관을 위한 김 씨의 디자인이 우리 부서의 모든 사람들에 의해 높게 평가되었다.

2. 부사 어휘
우리 회사는 직원들에게 좋은 근무 환경을 제공하는 것의 중요성을 아직 깨닫지 못했다.

3. 부사 어휘
그들은 새로운 특허를 얻기 위해 시장에서 가장 좋은 보험에 가입하는 것이 추가 비용을 들일 만한 가치가 있다고 판단했다.

4. 부사 어휘
이사회는 다음 시즌을 위해 새로 개발된 제품을 아직 공개하지 않고 있다.

5. 부사 어휘
영업 관리직들을 위한 새로운 재정적인 인센티브 계획이 일부 직원들에게 매우 유리할 것임이 증명될 것이다.

Chapter Test
1. (C) 2. (D) 3. (B) 4. (A) 5. (B)
6. (C) 7. (C) 8. (D) 9. (B) 10. (A)

1. 부사 어휘
이토 씨가 10년 이상 학업을 미룬 끝에, 결국 경영학 학위를 받았다.

2. 부사 어휘
우리의 직불 카드는 도시에 있는 거의 모든 호텔과 식당에서 사용이 가능합니다.

3. 부사 어휘
저희 웹사이트에서 물건에 대해 더 알아보시려면, 그저 "확인" 버튼을 클릭하세요.

4. 부사 어휘
시내 상인들은 12월 한 달 동안 늦게까지 문을 열기로 합의했다.

5. 부사 어휘
앤더슨 씨는 고용 계약서에 이미 서명을 했으나 복지 혜택에 대해서도 얘기를 해야 한다.

6. 부사 자리
작년에 위 문제로 고생하고 난 후로 로페즈 씨는 건강 검진을 받기 위해 자주 병원에 간다.

7. 부사 어휘
최근 연구는 온라인 보고 시스템이 사무용품 주문 오류를 크게 줄인다는 것을 발견했다.

8. 부사 자리
환불 금액은 영업일 이틀 내로 당신의 계좌로 입금될 것이다.

9. 부사 어휘
그린 씨는 건축학을 공부했지만 지금은 목공 일을 하고 있다.

10. 부사 어휘
내부 커뮤니케이션 시스템의 설치 후에, 직원들은 이제 출장 중에도 그들의 컴퓨터에 있는 파일들을 이용할 수 있게 될 것이다.

Chapter 7 분사

개념 정리 Check-up Test
A ①, ③, ⑤, ⑦, ⑧, ⑩, ⑬, ⑭, ⑮
B ① revised ② broken ③ experienced ④ rising ⑤ interesting
C ① conducting → conducted ② stood → standing ③ activate → activated ④ made → making ⑤ stay → staying

Point 01 분사 자리

Check-up Test
1. (B) 2. (A) 3. (A) 4. (A) 5. (B)

1. 형용사 자리
켄싱턴 사는 제안된 유통 센터를 위한 잠재적 부지를 찾기 위해 지역 자산 관리 회사를 고용했다.

2. 형용사 자리
매년 6월 샌프란시스코의 포도원은 여행자들과 와인 전문가들로 너무 붐비게 된다.

3. 형용사 자리
그 고객은 판매 권유와 발표가 매우 설득력 있다고 생각했다.

4. 형용사 자리
인턴이 완성된 제품을 금요일까지 상사에게 가져갈 것이다.

5. 분사 자리
정책 입안자들은 자연 과학에 중점을 둔 많은 새로운 학교 프로그램을 실행할 계획이다.

Point 02 감정 동사의 분사

Check-up Test
1. (A) 2. (A) 3. (B) 4. (D) 5. (D)

1. 감정 동사의 분사
마케팅팀은 놀라운 회복을 보였다.

2. 감정 동사의 분사
관광 산업의 감소는 지역 경제에 걱정스러운 결과를 가져올 수 있었다.

3. 감정 동사의 분사
이 교육훈련 프로그램에 관심이 있는 직원들은 미리 등록해야 한다.

4. 감정 동사의 분사
그 영화는 매우 인기가 많았지만 대부분 비평가들은 감동을 받지 못했다.

5. 감정 동사의 분사
이사회는 고객 만족을 유지하기 위해 새로운 서비스를 시행하기로 결정했다.

Point 03 현재 분사 vs. 과거 분사

Check-up Test
1. (B) 2. (A) 3. (A) 4. (B) 5. (B)

1. 과거 분사
동봉된 요금 별납 봉투에 대금을 넣어서 9월 20일까지 돌려보내 주시기 바랍니다.

2. 과거 분사
우리 직원 중 한 명이 제안한 역에서 불필요한 요금을 줄이기 위한 아이디어는 잘 수용되었다.

3. 현재 분사
불과 3초 내에, 다른 사람에게 오래 지속되는 인상을 남긴다.

4. 현재 분사
조립 라인에서 직원들을 감독한 그의 경험 때문에, 로페즈 씨는 작업 공정을 감독하도록 임명되었다.

5. 과거 분사
센트럴 트레인은 진행 중인 기차역 보수 공사로 인해 발생되는 불편에 대해 사과드립니다.

Point 04 분사 구문

Check-up Test
1. (B) 2. (A) 3. (A) 4. (A) 5. (C)

1. 과거 분사
오늘 오전 회의에서 논의된 바와 같이, 그들은 6월 29일 금요일 정오에 당신의 사무실에 도착할 것이다.

2. 현재 분사
길을 걷다가 그녀는 친구를 만났다.

3. 과거 분사
도시의 중심에 위치한 관광 안내소는 현대 문화의 지속성과 이해를 증진시키고 있다.

4. 과거 분사
지난 분기의 실망스러운 수익과 비교했을 때 이번 달 수치는 고무적인 경향을 보인다.

5. 현재 분사
새해 안내 책자를 디자인한 후에, 모든 지역 유통업자들에게 보내십시오.

Chapter Test
1. (B) 2. (B) 3. (A) 4. (A) 5. (C)
6. (B) 7. (C) 8. (B) 9. (A) 10. (D)

1. 과거 분사
ASC 출판사에서 곧 나올 아동용 도서는 아일린 쉔 씨가 삽화를 그리고 있다.

2. 과거 분사
당신에게 프랑스에 본사를 두고 있는 유럽 운영 관리자로의 승진을 제안하게 되어 기쁩니다.

3. 과거 분사
인사과는 제임스 씨가 그 일에 가장 적합한 후보자라고 확신한다.

4. 과거 분사
우리는 여기 칼 인더스트리에 새로운 이사가 팀에 합류하게 된 것을 알려 드리게 되어 기쁩니다.

5. 현재 분사
대금을 보내실 때, 송장의 아래 부분이 포함되었는지 확인해 주십시오.

6. 현재 분사
글로리 컨설팅 회사는 신흥 소매업자들에게 경쟁력 있는 사업 전략을 제공함으로써 그들을 돕는다.

7. 과거 분사
이 광고가 나오기 전에 구매된 상품에 대해서는 특별 할인이 적용되지 않는다.

8. 동명사
앤더슨 엔터프라이즈의 경영진들은 국제 서비스에 관한 새로운 지침을 만드는 과정에 있다.

9. 과거 분사
켈로그 경영 대학원은 다음 학기 등록에 관심이 있는 사람들을 위해 5월 1일에 오리엔테이션을 열 예정이다.

10. 현재 분사
대니얼 멀더 씨는 우리의 새로운 영업 그룹 중에서 올해의 가장 유망한 일원으로 선출되었다.

Chapter 8 to부정사/동명사

개념 정리 Check-up Test

A ①, ③, ⑦, ⑮
B ① 명사(보어) ② 부사 ③ 명사(목적어) ④ 형용사
   ⑤ 형용사
C ① be → to be ② been → to be
   ③ sell → to sell ④ leave → to leave
   ⑤ find → finding

Point 01 to부정사 vs. 동명사

Check-up Test
1. (A) 2. (A) 3. (A) 4. (C) 5. (A)

1. to부정사를 목적어로 취하는 동사
우리는 기술적인 문제에 대한 해결책을 찾는 데 실패했다.

2. 동명사를 목적어로 취하는 동사
회의는 수요일 오후이지만, 우리는 조사원들이 수집한 데이터들을 계산하는 것을 아직 끝내지 못했다.

3. 보어 역할을 하는 to부정사
이 워크숍의 목적은 직원들에게 효과적인 시간 관리 요령에 관한 정보를 제공하는 것이다.

4. 목적어를 동반하는 동명사
야간 매니저의 직무는 요청 메모가 있는 모든 고객 기록을 확인하는 것을 포함한다.

5. to부정사를 목적어로 취하는 동사
제이슨 제조사는 경영 활동에 영향을 미치는 부서 간의 의사소통을 향상시키려고 애쓰고 있다.

Point 02 to부정사 vs. 전치사 to

Check-up Test
1. (B) 2. (A) 3. (B) 4. (B) 5. (D)

1. 전치사 to + 동명사
우리 마케팅팀은 새로운 소프트웨어의 출시를 기대하고 있다.

2. to부정사
청결한 사무실을 유지하기 위하여, 시나 씨는 모든 직원들에게 흘리기 쉬운 음식을 가져오지 말라고 조언했다.

3. 전치사 to + 동명사
우리는 적절한 가격을 제공함으로써 고객 기대를 넘어서는 데 최선을 다하고 있다.

4. 전치사 to + 동명사
많은 편집자들에게 이메일은 사무실에 가지 않고 집에서 일을 할 수 있는 것을 의미한다.

5. 전치사 to + 동명사
모든 방문객들은 공장에 들어가기 전에 보호 장비를 착용해야 한다.

Chapter Test
1. (A) 2. (D) 3. (D) 4. (D) 5. (C)
6. (C) 7. (A) 8. (C) 9. (B) 10. (A)

1. to부정사
품질 보증에 관한 자세한 정보 혹은 새로운 제품을 등록하시려면, 고객 서비스 부서로 연락 주십시오.

2. to부정사
글렌윅 유기농 농장과 델마 식품 체인점은 시장 점유율을 높이기 위해 전략적 제휴 관계를 맺었다.

3. to부정사
우노시티 운송 회사는 현지 공급업체들과 좋은 거래를 협상할 수 있다.

4. to부정사
<주간 경제 잡지>에 광고를 싣기 위해서는, 귀하의 신청서와 세부 사항을 ads@weeklyeconomic.com으로 이메일로 보내 주십시오.

5. 동명사
기술 혁신의 효과가 명확하지 않기 때문에 그것을 조사하는 것은 결코 쉽지 않다.

6. 동명사
우리에게 당신의 일정을 미리 알려 주시면 출장 중에 당신이 필요한 것들을 더 잘 준비할 수 있습니다.

7. 동명사
마요르카 마케팅 회사는 주력 매장의 개장을 위한 모든 홍보 행사를 준비할 것이다.

8. 동명사
진로를 결정하는 데 어려움을 겪는 졸업생들에게 도움이 될 수 있는 소책자를 만들 필요가 있다.

9. 동명사
역사를 공부하는 목적은 사회, 경제와 정부의 패턴을 이해하기 위함이다.

10. 동사 어휘
네이시 백화점은 직원들이 특별 휴가를 가질 수 있도록 하기 위해 내일 문을 닫을 것이다.

Chapter 9 접속사

개념 정리 Check-up Test
A ①, ②, ③, ⑥, ⑩, ⑫, ⑭, ⑮
B ① X ② either, or ③ which ④ because
  ⑤ since
C ① That, 명사절 접속사 ② who, 관계 대명사
  ③ as well as, 상관 접속사 ④ Both, and, 상관 접속사
  ⑤ Since, 부사절 접속사

Point 01 접속사 vs. 전치사 vs. 부사

Check-up Test
1. (B)   2. (A)   3. (B)   4. (C)   5. (B)

1. 접속사 자리
유가가 꾸준히 오르고 있음에도 불구하고 여전히 자동차에 대한 수요가 높다.

2. 접속사 자리
질리언 무어가 감독한 새 영화는 흥행을 할 것이라 기대되긴 했지만, 대부분의 비평가들은 그 영화를 혹평했다.

3. 접속사 자리
새로운 규정에 따르면, 모든 근로자들은 압착기가 작동하는 중에는 안전 고글과 장갑을 착용해야 한다.

4. 접속사 자리
직원들은 컴퓨터가 모두 꺼지기 전에는 빌딩을 나서면 안 된다.

5. 접속사 자리
앤절라 앤드류스는 가장 자격을 갖춘 지원자였기 때문에 새 편집장으로 고용되었다.

Point 02 부사절 접속사

Check-up Test
1. (B)   2. (A)   3. (A)   4. (A)   5. (A)

1. 부사절 접속사
회의가 끝나면 회계부서의 직원들이 그들의 보고서들을 제출할 것이다.

2. 부사절 접속사
최근 경제가 상승 추세를 보이기 때문에 전문가들은 올해 말까지 경기가 회복될 것이라고 예상한다.

3. 부사절 접속사
회사가 성장하면서 시장 점유율도 증가하였다.

4. 부사절 접속사
비록 힐먼 씨가 이번 주에 돌아오진 않지만, 그는 거래와 관련된 이메일을 우리에게 보낼 것이다.

5. 동사의 형태
그레이엄 씨가 우리의 요청을 승인하면, 우리는 금요일과 토요일에 더 적은 시간 근무할 수 있을 것이다.

Point 03 명사절 접속사

Check-up Test
1. (B)   2. (B)   3. (A)   4. (D)   5. (D)

1. 명사절 접속사
설문 조사는 대중들의 요구가 지난 몇 달간 증가하고 있다는 것을 보여 준다.

2. 명사절 접속사
김 씨가 여기서 거의 10년 동안 일했다는 것은 그의 헌신을 보여 준다.

3. 명사절 접속사
SSN의 직원들은 누가 새로운 CEO로 선택될지 모른다.

4. 명사절 접속사
이 수업 계획은 '대중 매체와 정부 415'에서 무엇을 배우게 될지 보여 준다.

5. 명사절 접속사
우린 기념 파티를 밀턴 호텔에서 열 것인지 헤리 공원에서 열 것인지 결정하지 못했다.

Point 04 접속사 뒤에 주어가 없다면?

Check-up Test
1. (B) 2. (B) 3. (B) 4. (A) 5. (B)

1. 부사절 접속사
우리 지원 담당 직원과 상담하기 전에 주의 깊게 설명을 읽어 보십시오.

2. 부사절 접속사
판매자와 구매자가 둘 다 서명하기 전까지 그 계약은 합법적이지 않다.

3. 등위 접속사
켈리 가구는 고객들에게 전액 환불 또는 어떤 것이든 선호하는 다른 품목으로 교체를 해 준다.

4. 명사절 접속사
이사회는 오늘 그 계약에 서명할 것인지를 결정할 것이다.

5. 부사절 접속사
대중을 위한 연설을 준비할 때 오디오 시스템이 잘 작동하는지 체크하십시오.

Chapter Test
1. (D) 2. (A) 3. (D) 4. (D) 5. (D)
6. (D) 7. (A) 8. (B) 9. (A) 10. (A)

1. 부사절 접속사
카나 씨는 이제 퇴직했기 때문에, 그의 취미에 집중할 수 있다.

2. 명사절 접속사
룰라 제조사와 같은 회사는 경쟁 업체들이 어떤 제품들을 개발하려는지 알아야 한다.

3. 등위 접속사
나바로 씨가 금요일에 외출할 예정이어서, 그의 비서가 금요일에 회의에 대신 참석할 것이다.

4. 명사절 접속사
그 도서관의 편리한 점은 자동화된 대출 시스템이다.

5. 상관 접속사
회원 신청은 전화와 인터넷 중 하나를 이용해서 할 수 있다.

6. 명사절 접속사
게임 개발 업계의 직원들은 새로운 게임들을 즐기는 사람들에게 그것(게임)이 얼마나 잘 맞는지에 대해서 자주 이야기를 나눈다.

7. 부사절 접속사
로페즈 씨가 발표를 조정할 수 있다면, 출발 날짜는 5월 10일로 변경될 것이다.

8. 부사절 접속사
그 교수는 학생들이 두 개 대신 하나의 에세이를 쓰도록 커리큘럼을 변경하는 것을 고려하는 중이다.

9. 부사절 접속사
엘리자베스는 기사를 쓴 지 5년이 되었지만, 기자로 일한 것은 얼마 되지 않았다.

10. 부사절 접속사
기념품점이 박물관 옆에 위치해 있어서 많은 관광객을 끌어들인다.

Chapter 10 관계사

개념 정리 Check-up Test
A ②, ③, ⑩, ⑫, ⑭
B ① who, 주격 ② which, 목적격 ③ that, 주격
   ④ whose, 소유격 ⑤ whom, 목적격
C ① I know the man who[that] is standing in the lobby.
   ② This is a book for students whose first language is not Korean.
   ③ Edinburgh University Library has rare book collections which[that] are internationally important.

Point 01 관계사의 선택

Check-up Test
1. (B) 2. (A) 3. (A) 4. (D) 5. (C)

1. 주격(사물) 관계 대명사
에너지 보충을 위해 자주 이용되는 스포츠 음료는 운동선수들에게 큰 도움이 된다.

2. 소유격 관계 대명사
도커즈 씨는 보험 분야에 10년이 넘는 경력을 지닌 3명의 지원자들 중 한 명이다.

3. 목적격(사물) 관계 대명사
우리는 그들이 대여한 도서관 책들을 반납해야 할 때가 되면 상기시키기 위해 이메일을 보낼 것이다.

4. 주격(사람) 관계 대명사
고객 서비스 분야에서 일하는 사람들에게 운영 관리에 대한 기본적인 이해는 필수적이다.

5. 주격(사람) 관계 대명사
무료 콘서트 표는 7월 1일 전에 온라인으로 보험을 구매한 사람이면 누구나 이용 가능하다.

Point 02 목적격 관계 대명사

Check-up Test
1. (B) 2. (B) 3. (A) 4. (D) 5. (A)

1. 목적격 관계 대명사
그 회사는 내년에 7명의 신입 사원을 채용하기로 결정했는데, 그들은 모두 여성으로 예상된다.

2. 목적격 관계 대명사
관리자들은 종종 몇 가지 행동 방침 중에서 결정해야 하는데, 그것들 중에서 어떤 것도 전적으로 옳거나 잘못된 것은 없다.

3. 목적격 관계 대명사 생략
나는 그가 최근에 쓴 책을 좋아한다.

4. 목적격 관계 대명사
그 학교는 다양한 배경을 지닌 직원들을 채용하려 노력하지만, 현재 10명의 교사만 있으며, 대부분은 남자이다.

5. 부분 대명사
페스트 주 동물 건강 및 식품 통제소는 판매 기간이 지난 물건들을 홍보하는 것을 금지시켰는데, 그 물건들 중 다수는 원래의 유통 기간이 삭제되어 있었다.

Point 03 관계 부사

Check-up Test
1. (A) 2. (B) 3. (B) 4. (A) 5. (B)

1. 전치사+관계 대명사
내가 지금 언급하고 있는 안내서는 이 회사의 정책들에 관한 것이다.

2. 주격(사물) 관계 대명사
매년 최신 콘셉트 카를 선보이는 그 모터쇼는 만 명이 넘는 참석자들을 끌어 모은다.

3. 관계 부사
여러분들은 역사적인 와키타카 현수교에 있는 번지 점프대로 이동할 것이고, 그곳에서 여러분은 아래 물 쪽으로 50미터 곧바로 떨어지는 짜릿한 낙하를 즐길 수 있습니다.

4. 전치사+관계 대명사
우리 회사가 유통 센터를 건설하길 원했던 땅이 팔렸다.

5. 장소를 나타내는 관계 부사
환영 연회가 진행되고 있는 컨벤션 홀은 공항 근처에 있다.

Point 04 복합 관계사

Check-up Test
1. (B) 2. (A) 3. (A) 4. (D) 5. (A)

1. 복합 관계 부사
퇴근 후 어디를 가든 당신은 시내에서 동료를 만나게 될 것이다.

2. 복합 관계 대명사
자원봉사자들에게는 행사 이후에 남아 있는 판촉물 어느 것이든지 가져가는 것이 허용된다.

3. 관계 대명사
다른 회사에서 6개월 넘게 근무한 신규 직원들은 수습 기간의 단축이나 면제를 신청할 수 있다.

4. 복합 관계 대명사
자세한 정보를 알고 싶으면, 지원자들은 전화로든 이메일로든 그들이 선호하는 어떤 방법으로 문의할 수 있다.

5. 복합 관계 부사
부동산 온라인은 새로운 아파트의 임대가 가능할 때마다 웹사이트를 업데이트한다.

Chapter Test
1. (D) 2. (C) 3. (D) 4. (B) 5. (C)
6. (B) 7. (D) 8. (D) 9. (A) 10. (A)

1. 복합 관계 대명사
모든 상사들은 맡은 일이 무엇이든 간에 그 일에 익숙해져야 하는 신입 직원들을 교육할 책임이 있다.

2. 주격 관계 대명사
우리 경제 전문가가 이번 주에 다루어질 계획에서 문제점을 찾아냈다.

3. 부정 대명사+of+목적격 관계 대명사
10개의 상자를 받았으며, 그중 2개가 운송 중에 예상치 못하게 손상되었다.

4. 주격 관계 대명사
드류 산업은 디트로이트에 공장을 하나 더 건설할 것이고, 이로써 이 회사는 제조 과정을 더 신속하게 할 수 있을 것이다.

5. 소유격 관계 대명사
시티 센터 미술관은 지역 미술가들을 후원하고 있는데, 이 미술가들의 작품은 올여름부터 전시될 것이다.

6. 관계 부사
우리는 현지인들이 치료를 받고 있는 보건소에 가야 할 것이다.

7. 목적격 관계 대명사
3시까지 우체국으로 와서 귀하가 주문한 특별 배송품을 찾아가세요.

8. 주격 관계 대명사
일부 산업에서는 고용 기반을 지역 학교들에 의존하고 있는데, 그들은 취업 박람회를 정기적으로 개최한다.

9. 주격 관계 대명사
올해의 가장 주목할 만한 발견을 한 과학자에게 노벨상이 수여됐다.

10. 목적격 관계 대명사의 생략
당신이 저축하는 총액은 어떤 계획을 선택하느냐에 달려 있다.

Chapter 11 비교/가정법/도치

개념 정리 Check-up Test

A ① sharper, the sharpest ② firmer, the firmest
③ more rapidly, most rapidly
④ more profitable, the most profitable
⑤ more energetically, most energetically

B ① efficient ② efficiently ③ more recently
④ the highest

C ① most ② as ③ the best ④ more

Point 01 비교급

Check-up Test
1. (B) 2. (A) 3. (B) 4. (D) 5. (B)

1. 비교급
증가된 수요 때문에 우리는 작년보다 주문들을 더욱 빨리 배달할 수 있는 방법들을 찾아야 한다.

2. 비교급
오늘날의 변화무쌍한 기업 환경은 과거에 우리가 해야 했던 것보다 더 빠르게 새로운 기량들을 습득할 것을 요구한다.

3. 원급 비교
응급 상황의 경우, 가능한 한 빠르게 건물에서 떠나시기 바랍니다.

4. 비교급
국립 박물관은 매년 10,000명 이상의 방문객들을 끌어모은다.

5. 비교급
디지털 사진술의 발달이 시티스크래이핑 이미징의 실험실이 최신 장비를 갖춰서 유지하는 것을 전보다 더 힘들게 만든다.

Point 02 최상급

Check-up Test
1. (A) 2. (B) 3. (A) 4. (B) 5. (B)

1. 최상급
사우스웨어 인더스트리스는 시중에서 가장 질 좋은 수제 가죽 지갑을 만들어 낸다.

2. 최상급
휴대폰으로 채팅하고 파일을 보내는 것은 10년에 걸쳐 가장 혁신적인 의사소통 수단이라고 여겨질 것이다.

3. 최상급
매니저가 인터뷰한 10명의 후보자들 중에 잼 씨가 가장 자격이 있다.

4. 최상급
우리의 신제품 화장품의 포장 디자인은 지금까지 본 것 중 가장 혁신적이다.

5. 최상급
엔북 XS는 오늘날 상점에서 구매할 수 있는 가장 빠른 노트북이라고 광고되고 있다.

Point 03 가정법

Check-up Test
1. (B) 2. (B) 3. (B) 4. (B) 5. (C)

1. 가정법 과거
우리가 좀 더 재활용을 하기 위한 수고를 아끼지 않는다면, 쓰레기 매립지 수를 줄일 수 있을 것이다.

2. 가정법 과거 완료
만약 회계사가 자격을 잘 갖추었다면, 경영진은 그에게 기밀 파일에 대한 접근 권한을 주었을 것이다.

3. 가정법 과거 완료의 도치
내가 당신의 요청들을 알았더라면, 나는 그것을 처리했을 텐데.

4. 가정법 과거 완료
기차를 일찍 탔더라면, 직장에 늦지 않았을 텐데.

5. 가정법 과거 완료
만약 사무실 관리자가 팩스가 제대로 작동하지 않는다고 들었다면, 그녀는 더 일찍 수리업체에 전화할 수 있었을 것이다.

Point 04 도치

Check-up Test
1. (B) 2. (A) 3. (B) 4. (A) 5. (A)

1. 가정법 도치
클럽의 다른 회원이 당신을 겨냥한 모욕적인 메시지를 게시판에 올린 것을 발견하신다면 저희에게 즉각적으로 알려 주셔야 합니다.

2. 부정어 도치
우리가 트라이테크 사에 투자하자마자 주식 시장이 폭락했다.

3. 보어 도치
당사의 표준 기밀 계약서 한 부를 동봉합니다.

4. 부정어 도치
중국 정부의 정책은 대다수의 외국 회사들에 긍정적이지 않다.

5. 부사(구) 도치
IT업계의 일부 마케팅 담당자만이 최근에서야 인공 지능의 중요성을 인정한다.

Chapter Test
1. (D) 2. (D) 3. (A) 4. (C) 5. (C)
6. (B) 7. (A) 8. (C) 9. (B) 10. (C)

1. 비교급
이번 시즌의 입장권은 우리의 예상보다 더 빠르게 매진되었다.

2. 도치
모든 서류가 준비되면, 건설 허가가 처리되는 데는 오직 2주가 걸릴 것이다.

3. 가정법
고객들로부터 의견을 받지 않았더라면 성공을 거둘 수 없었을 것이다.

4. 비교급
혼자서 단기 주택을 찾는 것은 그가 예상했던 것보다 더욱 어려웠다.

5. 비교급
AECOM 테크놀로지 회사에서 근무하고 있는 누구도 주디스 칼드웰 씨보다 더 열정적으로 직원들의 복지와 근무 환경 개선을 위해 노력하는 사람은 없다.

6. 최상급
매직 소프트가 판매하고 있는 모든 PC 게임들 중에 미스티 아일랜드가 십대들에게 가장 인기가 많은 게임이다.

7. 비교급
지난 분기에 앤더슨 컨설팅 엑스포트는 예상보다 직원들에게 훨씬 더 높은 판매 목표를 설정했다.

8. 비교급
맥그래디스 패스트푸드점은 고객들이 보다 더 쉽게 주문할 수 있도록 하기 위해 셀프서비스식의 키오스크 시스템을 도입했다.

9. 비교급
영업직 면접은 오전 8시 정각에 시작했기 때문에 제임슨 씨는 평소보다 더 일찍 도착해야 했다.

10. 비교급
평균보다 높은 티켓 가격에도 불구하고, 다음 6개월 동안의 새로운 연극의 공연이 모두 매진되었다.

Chapter 12 전치사

Chapter Test
1. (A) 2. (D) 3. (D) 4. (A) 5. (D)
6. (A) 7. (C) 8. (B) 9. (A) 10. (D)

1. 전치사 자리
환불을 받기 위해서는 물품이 구입 후 30일 이내에 반품되어야 한다.

2. 전치사
관리자의 승인이 없이는 실험실 출입이 허가되지 않을 것입니다.

3. 전치사
경쟁력 있는 복리 후생 제도 때문에, 앤더슨 법률 사무소의 직원들은 강한 충성심을 갖고 있습니다.

4. 전치사
저희 빵집은 주말을 제외하고 매일 오전 7시부터 오후 2시까지 문을 엽니다.

5. 전치사
최우수 텔레비전 광고상의 발표는 만찬 시간에 있을 것이다.

6. 전치사
우리 직원 대부분은 25년 근무 후에 연금 전액을 수령할 자격을 갖는다.

7. 전치사
주요 관광 명소와의 근접성 때문에 로얄 호텔은 자주 예약이 꽉 찬다.

8. 전치사
차량의 주차 브레이크를 풀기 위해서는, 발로 페달을 가볍게 누르셔야 합니다.

9. 전치사 자리
어제 오타와에서 진행된 오찬에서 부대표는 이사회에 인사했다.

10. 전치사
우체국을 지나 걸어가면 거리 끝에서 잭 앤 제니스 아이스크림을 볼 수 있을 겁니다.

PART 6

개념 정리 Check-up Test

A ① February, 10 / March 21st ② they also offer
B ① attend ② consultation
C ① Accordingly ② Instead

Point 01 품사를 묻는 문제

Check-up Test

1. (A) 2. (D) 3. (A) 4. (C)

문제 1-4는 다음 편지를 참조하세요.

> 앤더슨 씨께,
>
> 1 저는 지난 두 달 넘게 귀하께서 정산하지 못하는 이유에 대해 설명을 요청하고자 여러 번 연락을 드렸습니다. 2 현재 지불해야 하는 총 금액은 7,000달러입니다. 이 금액에 대한 자세한 내용은 첨부된 파일을 확인하십시오.
>
> 이러한 요청을 무시했기 때문에, 이전에 당사와 유지했던 훌륭한 신용도를 훼손하고 있습니다. 3 게다가 추가 연체금이 발생하고 있습니다.
>
> 4 다음 5일 안에 귀하께서 이 편지에 답변을 주지 않으신다면, 미불 금액을 추심 기관에 의뢰할 수밖에 없습니다.
>
> 그런 극단적인 조치를 취할 수밖에 없음을 유감스럽게 생각합니다. 하지만 오늘 위에 명시된 금액을 지불하시면, 신용 등급을 유지하실 수 있습니다.

Point 02 동사의 시제를 묻는 문제

Check-up Test

1. (C) 2. (B) 3. (B) 4. (D)

문제 1-4는 다음 이메일을 참조하세요.

> 수신: 엘리샤 올슨
> 발신: 도널드 에르난데스
> 날짜: 12월 15일
> 제목: 데스크탑 출판 프로그램
>
> 1 10월 19일에 AG 호텔의 홍보물 제작을 외부 회사에서 회사 내부의 데스크탑 출판 소프트웨어 프로그램으로 전환할 가능성에 대한 조사를 요청하셨습니다. 2 이 요청에 따라, 저는 10월 27일에 제안서를 제출했습니다.
>
> 모든 조사가 계획대로 완료되었음을 알려 드리게 되어 기쁩니다. 3 결론에 이르렀으며 저는 결론에 대한 제안을 첨부된 보고서인 '데스크탑 출판 소프트웨어: 비교 분석'의 마지막 부분에 제시하였습니다.

> 제가 이번 프로젝트를 진행하게 해주셔서 감사합니다. 4 이 프로젝트는 유익했을 뿐 아니라 매우 흥미로웠습니다. 이 프로젝트 관련하여 질문이나 의견이 있으시면, 저는 당신과 기쁘게 의논할 것입니다. 또한 다른 분야의 조사를 할 수 있는 기회가 생긴다면 감사하겠습니다. (050) 555-1254로 전화를 주시거나 dhernandez@kion.com 으로 메일을 보내 주시기 바랍니다.

Point 03 적절한 연결어를 찾는 문제

Check-up Test

1. (B) 2. (A) 3. (C) 4. (C)

문제 1-4는 다음 편지를 참조하세요.

> 소중한 고객님께,
>
> 저희 식당을 이용해 주셔서 감사합니다. 1 지난 5년 동안, 저희는 저희 음식 가격을 처음 개업할 때와 동일하게 유지하려고 노력해왔습니다. 2 안타깝게도, 원재료의 급격한 가격 상승 때문에 7월 1일부터 가격을 4퍼센트 인상해야만 합니다. 저희는 이러한 가격 상승을 막고자 온갖 노력을 다해왔습니다. 3 하지만 음식의 질과 타협하고 싶지는 않습니다. 최고의 재료를 사용하는 것이 여러분들이 식당에 오실 때마다 행복하게 만듭니다. 4 저희 음식이 여전히 큰 가치를 가지고 있다는 것을 여러분들이 알게 될 것이라 믿습니다. 지지해 주셔서 감사드리며, 계속 모실 수 있기를 바랍니다.
>
> 진심을 담아,
>
> 브라운 포터
> 식당 지배인

Point 04 어휘를 묻는 문제

Check-up Test

1. (D) 2. (C) 3. (A) 4. (B)

문제 1-4는 다음 메모를 참조하세요.

> **전 직원에게 알립니다.**
>
> 1 이사회는 회사 복장 규정을 변경하기로 결정했다고 발표했습니다.
>
> 다음 달부터 직원들은 회사명과 로고가 인쇄된 새로운 티셔츠를 입어야 합니다.
>
> 2 직원들은 모두 티셔츠 한 장을 무료로 받게 될 것입니다. 근무 시간에는 이 티셔츠를 착용하셔야 합니다. 3 추가 셔츠는 장당 12달러에 구입할 수 있습니다.
>
> 첨부된 주문서에 원하는 사이즈를 표시하여 주시기 바랍니다. 해당되는 사항이 있으시면, 대금을 동봉해 주세요. 4 모든 주문은 늦어도 4월 15일 목요일까지 구매과 제시 로페즈 씨에게 보내 주셔야 합니다.

Point 05 빈칸에 알맞은 문장을 고르는 문제

Check-up Test
1. (A) 2. (C) 3. (C) 4. (C)

문제 1-4는 다음 편지를 참조하세요.

8월 7일

브라운 씨에게,

1 귀사의 영업직 기회를 논의하기 위해 만나 뵙게 되어 기뻤습니다. 인터뷰가 진행되는 동안 당신의 비전을 듣는 것이 즐거웠습니다. 2 저는 판매원으로 근무한 적이 있기 때문에 제가 그 자리에 완벽한 지원자라고 생각합니다. 또한 저는 영업 자료를 분석하기 위해 귀사에서 사용하는 컴퓨터 프로그램에 대한 광범위한 지식을 갖고 있습니다. 3 특히 저는 데이터엑셀 200으로 작업을 한 경험이 있습니다. 4 마지막으로 저는 귀사에 귀중한 자산이 될 수 있다고 생각합니다.

이 직책에 저를 고려해 주셔서 감사합니다.

진심을 담아,

로저 무어

Chapter Test
1. (D) 2. (C) 3. (B) 4. (B) 5. (B)
6. (A) 7. (A) 8. (B) 9. (B) 10. (C)
11. (D) 12. (A) 13. (D) 14. (B) 15. (B)
16. (D)

문제 1-4는 다음 공지문을 참조하세요.

고객님도 알고 계시겠지만, 회원권이 8월 19일에 만료됩니다. 1 첨부된 양식을 작성해 회원권을 갱신하시고, 맥스 토탈 피트니스에서 제공하는 고객님의 몸을 건강하고 아름답게 만드는 최신 장비와 기계를 계속 사용하세요.

2 중단 없이 서비스가 계속되게 하기 위해서, 자동 청구 프로그램에 등록하실 것을 추천합니다. 3 일단 등록이 되시면, 이후에 고객님이 회원권을 다시 갱신해야 하는 불편을 겪으실 필요가 없습니다.

4 또한 좋은 소식이 있습니다. 5주년을 기념하기 위해, 저희는 새로운 요가 프로그램인 '제나의 버닝 요가' 한 달 체험권을 제공해 드릴 예정입니다. 이 프로그램에 등록하시면, 요가 매트를 무료로 받으실 수 있습니다. 더 많은 정보는 저희 웹사이트 www.maxfitness.com 을 방문해 주세요.

문제 5-8은 다음 이메일을 참조하세요.

쿠마 씨께,

5 지난달에 다녀오신 출장에 대한 경비 보고서를 보내 주셔서 감사합니다. 하지만 경비 보고서를 작성할 때 따라야 하는 몇 가지 정책들을 알려 드리고자 합니다. 우선, 당신이 본인의 경비 보고서에 서명을 하시면, 법적으로 효력이 없는 것으로 간주될 것입니다. 6 대신에 상환이 처리되기 위해서는 관리자가 보고서에 서명을 해야 합니다. 7 또한 전액 상환을 받으시려면, 영수증을 첨부하시길 바랍니다. 이것은 출장 중에 청구한 실제 금액을 증명하는 데 사용됩니다. 8 필요한 부분을 수정하신 후에, 보고서를 다시 제출해 주십시오.

감사합니다.

진심으로,
재스민 레너드

문제 9-12는 다음 기사를 참조하세요.

4월 1일: 9 진스 포 올 휴먼의 청바지와 스커트의 판매가 유럽 지역에서 급증했다. 9 이러한 급격한 판매 증가로 인하여, 9 진스 포 올 휴먼은 올해 말까지 파리와 런던 그리고 로마에 공장과 단독 매장들을 열 예정이다. 10 마드리드 지점은 현재 5개의 상점을 운영하고 있다. 11 또한 이달 말까지 2개의 매장을 추가로 운영할 것으로 예상된다.

9 진스 포 올 휴먼의 창립자이자 수석 디자이너인 마이클 글라스 씨는 말했다. "경쟁이 치열한 유럽 패션 시장에서 우리 브랜드가 이 정도로 성공을 거둘 것이라고 전혀 예상하지 못했습니다. 여전히 꿈같이 느껴집니다. 12 매장과 공장의 추가는 다른 나라에서 주문해 추가의 배송료를 지불해야 하는 고객들의 번거로움을 없애줄 것입니다."

문제 13-16은 다음 편지를 참조하세요.

7월 7일

데릭 코헨 씨
벨빌 웨이 472번지
39530 미시시피 빌록시

코헨 씨에게:

실버 은행을 이용해 주셔서 감사합니다. 고객님께서는 실버 은행과 한스 금융 회사가 보다 나은 서비스를 제공하기 위해 함께하게 됐다는 소식을 최근에 들으셨을 것입니다. 13 7월 1일부로 두 금융 회사는 합병됐습니다. 14 저희는 지금 한-실버 은행이라는 이름으로 운영하고 있습니다. 고객님의 계좌에 당장의 변화는 발생하지 않을 것입니다. 15 하지만 고객님께서는 다양한 상품을 이용하실 수 있게 될 것입니다. 16 저희가 새롭게 제공하는 상품을 중점으로 다루고 있는 동봉 책자를 살펴보시기 바랍니다. 이 상품들에 대해서 더 궁금한 점이 있으시면 가까운 지점을 방문하시거나 저희 홈페이지 (www.HSbank.com)를 방문해 주세요.

계속해서 서비스를 제공할 수 있는 기회를 주셔서 감사드립니다.

진심을 담아,

맥스 버틀러
경영 이사

PART 7

문제 유형

Point 01 주제/목적을 묻는 문제

출제 포인트 정리

수신: 앤디 워싱턴 <awashington@demountservices.com>
발신: 타일러 린든 <tylerlinden@ursulacorp.com>
날짜: 6월 7일
제목: 송장 관련

워싱턴 씨에게,

우르술라 사에서 작업하신 바닥 관리 서비스에 대해 제가 오늘 받은 송장의 오류를 지적하기 위해 이 이메일을 보냅니다. 송장 번호는 551328입니다. 80달러 정도의 금액이 더 부과된 것 같습니다. 15′ × 22′ 구역은 다른 모든 층들과 마찬가지로 29일에 서비스를 받기로 되어 있었는데, 작업자들이 도착했을 때 그 방을 사용 중인 사람들이 있었습니다. 저는 모든 작업자들에게 그 방의 청소 일자를 연기한다고 말해 달라고 보수 직원에게 요청했습니다. 저희가 바로 지불할 수 있도록 5월에 받은 서비스에 대해 수정된 송장을 보내 주시기 바랍니다.

이메일의 목적은 무엇인가?
(A) 청구서의 요금에 대해 이의를 제기하는 것
(B) 카펫 수선을 요청하는 것
(C) 작업팀이 늦게 도착한 것에 항의하는 것
(D) 향후 서비스에 대한 할인을 요청하는 것

Check-up Test

1. ⓐ, (A)   2. (D)

1.

전 직원들에게,

ⓐ 재닛 클래런스가 저희 첼시 지점의 인사부장으로 오게 된 것을 여러분들께 알려 드리고자 합니다. ⓑ 영국 지사로 전근 오기 전에, 클래런스 씨는 2년 동안 KTBM의 아테네 지사에서 인사부 차장으로 근무하였습니다. ⓒ 그녀는 그곳에서 KTBM의 전 지사에서 현재 사용되고 있는 좀 더 효율적인 채용 절차를 개발하고 실행하여, 주목할 만한 업적을 남겼습니다. ⓓ 또한, 그녀는 회사에서 신입 사원의 실무 교육 과정을 간소화할 수 있는 직원 개발 프로그램을 만들어 냈습니다.

(A) 직원을 소개하는 것
(B) 정책 변화를 공지하는 것

문제 2는 다음 이메일을 참조하세요.

발신: 마리아 페트로브스키 <mariapetro@onlineshop.com>
수신: 고객 서비스 직원 <숨은 참조>
제목: 고객 이메일 처리
날짜: 1월 7일

요즘 많은 고객들이 전화를 하기보다는 이메일을 보냅니다. 그래서 우리는 고객의 이메일에 대한 답신 형식을 표준화하려고 합니다. 다음 사항들을 기억해 주시길 바랍니다.

■ 제목을 꼭 쓰십시오. 메시지를 요약하여 여기에 적어야 합니다. 또한 여러분의 고객 서비스 ID 번호도 포함시켜야 합니다. 그렇게 하면 각 사례를 식별하는 데 도움이 될 것입니다.
■ 이메일을 발송하기 전에, 철자에 실수가 없는지 확인하시길 바랍니다.
■ 우리 회사의 로고가 이메일의 상단부에 있어야 합니다. 로고 삽입 방법을 모르신다면 상사에게 물어보십시오.

마리아 페트로브스키
고객 서비스 책임자

2. 이메일의 목적은 무엇인가?
(A) 고객의 주소를 요청하는 것
(B) 직원 이메일 사용법을 묻는 것
(C) 가장 알맞은 고객 서비스 전화를 설명하는 것
(D) 답변에 대한 지침들을 알려 주는 것

Point 02 발신자와 수신자에 관한 정보를 묻는 문제

출제 포인트 정리

수신: 댄 콜
발신: 잉그리드 스틸러
날짜: 6월 2일
제목: 6월 10일 설치

친애하는 콜 박사님께,

며칠 전 회의에서 논의했던 것처럼, 모든 의료 센터는 믿을 만한 전력 공급이 필요합니다. 저희의 태양열 패널 시스템이 보다 우수한 에너지 공급원이 될 수 있을 것이라고 생각합니다. 실제로, 이것이 비용 효율적이고 동시에 친환경적이라는 것을 깨닫게 되실 것입니다. 저희는 근무 외 시간에 이 시스템을 설치할 예정이므로, 어떤 불편도 없을 것이라는 점 또한 말씀드리고 싶습니다.

진심으로,

잉그리드 스틸러
판매 부장

스틸러 씨는 어떤 종류의 업체에서 근무할 것 같은가?
(A) 유지 보수 서비스
(B) 에너지 회사
(C) 의료 인력 알선 회사
(D) 인터넷 서비스 제공업체

Check-up Test
1. ⓑ/ⓒ, (A)   2. (A)

1.

행복한 집
당신을 초대합니다
ⓐ 당신의 가족들이 행복을 누릴 수 있게 하기 위해

ⓑ 당신의 집을 새로 디자인하고, 공간을 넓히고, 좋은 기분을 느낄 수 있게 도와드립니다!
■ ⓒ 모든 방을 최신 스타일로 재단장해 드립니다.
■ 저희 전문가들이 벽지와 카펫과 가구 선정을 도와드립니다.
■ 방당 가격은 500달러밖에 안 되며, 3개 이상은 20퍼센트 할인됩니다.
■ ⓓ 집을 떠나고 싶지 않으세요? 걱정하지 마세요. 저희가 방문합니다.
■ 모든 작업은 '행복한 집'에서 해드립니다. 고객님은 손가락 하나 움직이지 않으셔도 됩니다.

이달의 특혜
전반적인 집 개조를 주문하시면,
신상 벽장 정리함을 무료로 드립니다!

우편 번호 10723, 잭슨빌 털사 로 3273번지, 806-786-9844

(A) 개조 대행사
(B) 부동산

문제 2는 다음 안내문을 참조하세요.

인도네시아로 입국할 때, 성인은 각자 면세로 최대 주류 1리터와 담배 200개비, 시가 50개 또는 잎담배 100그램 중 한 가지를 반입하는 것이 허용됩니다. 카메라, 비디오카메라, 휴대용 라디오, 카세트 녹음기, 쌍안경 및 스포츠 장비들은 출국할 때 가지고 나갈 것이라면 허용됩니다. 그것들을 신고하셔야만 합니다. 화기, 중국 인쇄물 및 약품, 휴대용 무전기 및 무선 전화기는 금지됩니다. 필름, 이미 녹화된 비디오테이프, 그리고 레이저 디스크는 검열 위원회에서 조사를 받아야만 합니다. 출입국시에, 외화나 여행자 수표 이용에 대한 제한은 없습니다. 그러나 5백만 루피아를 넘은 인도네시아 화폐의 반입과 반출은 금지되어 있습니다.

2. 이 공지의 대상은 누구인가?
(A) 여행자
(B) 공무원
(C) 보안요원
(D) 공항 검색원

Point 03 구체적인 정보를 묻는 문제

출제 포인트 정리

2월 24일

콜스태드 노르웨이
고객 서비스 부서

고객 서비스 담당자께,

작년 8월 5일, 저는 Z-501 콜스태드 냉장고를 구매하였습니다. 알고 계시는 것처럼, 그 제품은 일반적으로 1년간 품질 보증이 됩니다.

약 2주 전, 냉장고에서 이상한 소리가 나서, 2월 12일에 기술자를 불렀습니다(송장: 553NM 9). 기술자는 컴프레서에서 결함을 찾아냈고 부품을 교체해야 한다고 말했습니다. 수리는 5일 안에 끝날 것이라고 했지만 10일이나 걸렸습니다. 결과적으로, 약 200달러어치의 음식이 상해버렸습니다. 거기에 덧붙여서, 저는 어제 컴프레서와 인건비에 대한 청구서를 받았습니다.

제가 아는 바로는, 1년간의 보증은 부품과 인건비를 모두 포함합니다. 청구서가 취소되어야 할 뿐만 아니라, 콜스태드 사는 늦어진 수리로 인해 버려진 음식물에 대해서도 책임이 있다고 생각합니다. 이 서신을 받는 대로 연락주시기 바랍니다.

충심으로,
미리암 페커

페커 씨는 언제 냉장고 수리를 요청했는가?
(A) 2월 10일
(B) 2월 12일
(C) 2월 24일
(D) 3월 2일

Check-up Test
1. ⓑ, (B)   2. (C)

1.

채용 박람회
여러분 모두 SIT(세이모어 기술 협회)의
제5회 연례 채용 박람회 워크숍에 참여해 주시기 바랍니다!

올해의 발표와 강연은 아래와 같습니다.

시간	강의	강사
오전 10시 15분 ~ 오전 11시 30분	ⓐ 강의 1: "첫날부터 천천히 경력 쌓기"	라나 애플스 공동 진행자. SIT 경력 개발팀
오전 11시 30분 ~ 오후 12시 30분	ⓑ 강의 2: "완벽한 이력서와 자기소개서 작성"	제이콥 그랜트 공동 진행자. SIT 경력 개발팀
오후 12시 30분 ~ 오후 1시 30분	ⓒ 강의 3: "성공적인 면접의 비결"	필립 누네즈 (초청 강사) 비즈니스 커뮤니케이션 교수, 워터스 경영 대학원
오후 2시 30분 ~ 오후 4시	ⓓ 강의 4: "당신의 자원은 어디에 있는가?"	사브리나 키스 트루먼&바흐 최고 경영자

이전의 워크숍과 같이 올해 채용 박람회도 무료입니다.
강의 3과 강의 4 사이에 간단한 식사가 제공될 예정입니다.

(A) 라나 애플스
(B) 제이콥 그랜트
(C) 필립 누네즈
(D) 사브리나 키스

문제 2는 다음 공지문을 참조하세요.

> 데일리 테크
> 가장 믿을 만한 첨단 기술 소식지
>
> 독자 여러분께,
>
> 오늘, 기분 좋은 발표가 있습니다! 다음 주부터 독자 여러분은 매주 월요일 신문에서 '유레카!'라는 새로운 섹션을 만나게 되실 겁니다. 이 새로운 섹션은 이전에 다른 섹션에서 다뤘던 퍼즐, 첨단 기술 소식, CEO 인터뷰 등 유용한 정보와 함께 신선하고 흥미로운 특집 기사로 채워질 것입니다. 또한, 카를로스 구티에레즈 씨의 인기 테크놀로지 칼럼과 여러분들이 2년 연속 최고의 리뷰어로 선정한 프레더릭 만 씨의 제품 리뷰도 볼 수 있을 것입니다. 아울러 국내 최고 비즈니스 컨설턴트인 마이클 알루신 씨의 새로운 전문가 상담 칼럼도 읽어보시게 될 것입니다.
>
> '유레카!'는 다음 주부터 테크 앤 넷 웹사이트에도 게재됩니다. 유레카온더웹은 온라인으로 여러분의 의견과 지역 소식 그리고 사진을 게시할 수 있는 새로운 독자 이용 온라인 공간을 운영할 것입니다. 다음 주 월요일인 3월 13일에 http://www.dailytech.com/eureka 를 확인해 보시기 바랍니다.

2. 막 새 칼럼을 쓰기 시작한 사람은 누구인가?
(A) 카를로스 구티에레즈
(B) 프레더릭 만
(C) 마이클 알루신
(D) 폴 보렐리

Point 04 미래 상황 또는 요청/당부/제안/방법을 묻는 문제

출제 포인트 정리

> 최우수 영업 사원 시상식
>
> 윙슬라이드 모터의 뛰어난 영업 사원에게 상을 수여하는 오늘 밤 자리에 함께해 주시기 바랍니다. 메건 부흐너 씨를 올해의 최우수 영업 사원으로 발표하게 되어 기쁩니다. 그녀는 가장 높은 판매 기록을 달성하였으며, 그녀의 회사에 대한 전반적인 공헌과 헌신은 높이 평가될 만한 가치가 있습니다.
>
> 12월 7일 일요일
> 안티가 로 115번지 바로크 호텔
>
> 만찬은 오후 6시 30분에 시작되며,
> 시상식은 오후 8시에 시작됩니다.
>
> 명단에 이름을 올리려면, 늦어도 11월 17일까지 마케팅 부장 제나 팍슨 씨에게 jenpaxon@wingslidemotors.com으로 이메일을 보내 주시기 바랍니다. 참석 여부를 확인한 후에, 팍슨 씨가 무료 티켓을 우편으로 보내 드릴 것입니다.

수령인들은 행사에 참석하기 위해 무엇을 해야 하는가?
(A) 12월 7일까지 입장권 구입
(B) 회사의 웹사이트 방문
(C) 호텔 직원에게 연락
(D) 회사 직원에게 이메일 발송

Check-up Test

1. ⓒ, (B)   2. (A)

1.

> ⓐ 올해부터 새로운 전통이 시작되어, 시상식은 5월 8일 다이너스티 호텔에서 열리는 경축 행사에서 메인 이벤트가 될 것입니다. ⓑ 행사에는 다섯 가지의 코스 요리와 경매, 그리고 시상이 포함됩니다. ⓒ 경매에서 나오는 수익금은 새로운 건물을 짓고 젊은이들과 지역 사회를 후원하는 교육 사업 지원금으로 사용될 것입니다. ⓓ 올해 행사에 관한 질문이 있으시다면, 주저하지 마시고 저에게 연락 주십시오.
>
> 협조해 주셔서 감사합니다.

(A) 지역 사업 계획
(B) 지역사회 개선 프로그램

문제 2는 다음 이메일을 참조하세요.

> 수신: 전 직원
> 발신: 줄리안 아마도르
> 제목: 송별회
> 날짜: 8월 2일
>
> 동료들에게,
>
> 모두 알고 계시는 바와 같이, 크리스토퍼 부스 씨가 9월 말에 Km & G사에서 퇴직할 예정입니다. 크리스토퍼 씨는 Km & G에서 약 40년간 근무해 왔습니다. 그는 1976년 마케팅부에서 처음으로 근무를 시작했고, 15년 후에는 영업부로 옮겨서 20년간 근무했습니다. 회사의 부사장으로서의 마지막 5년은, 우리가 앞으로 그를 얼마나 그리워할지를 보여 줍니다.
>
> 우리는 10월 15일 피가로 식당에서 공식적인 송별회를 개최할 예정입니다. 참석할 수 있는 분은 저에게 연락해 주시기 바랍니다. 크리스토퍼 씨의 선물을 준비하는 데 돈을 기부하고자 하시는 분은 판매부의 돈 존슨 씨 또는 수잔 보일즈 씨에게 연락바랍니다.
>
> 줄리안 아마도르

2. 참석을 원하는 직원은 누구에게 연락해야 하는가?
(A) 줄리안 아마도르
(B) 크리스토퍼 부스
(C) 돈 존슨
(D) 수잔 보일즈

Point 05 Not-question 및 추론 문제

출제 포인트 정리

구인

직책: 안내 데스크 보조
근무 시간: 상근

직무 내용: 이 자리는 친절하고 기꺼이 도움을 주려 하며 (D) 전문적인 인상을 주는 사람이면 누구에게나 적합합니다. 안내데스크 보조의 주요 업무는 손님을 맞이하고 등록하는 일과, 결제 정보를 받고 방을 배정하는 일입니다. 또한 담당자는 (A) 일일 영수 일지를 기록하고 은행에 예금해야 할 현금과 수표를 준비해야 할 책임이 있습니다. 이상적인 지원자는 관광 서비스 경영의 기본 과정을 수료한 분이어야 합니다. 지원자는 (C) 영어와 최소 한 개의 아시아 국가 언어를 유창하게 할 수 있어야 합니다. 만약 귀하가 상기 조건을 충족하신다면 귀하의 이력서와 자기소개서를 amandalogan@marshall.com으로 보내주시기 바랍니다. 직책에 대해 로건 씨와 직접 이야기하길 원하시면 린덴 드라이브 가 2200번지에 있는 저희 사무실에 월요일부터 금요일까지 오후 1시에서 6시 사이에 언제든 방문해 주세요. 다만 저희 전화는 고객을 상대하느라 바쁘기 때문에 전화 연락은 피해 주시기 바랍니다.

해당 직책의 자격 요건으로 제시되지 않은 것은 무엇인가?
(A) 금융 거래를 기록하는 방법을 아는 것
(B) 교통편 편성에 대한 전문 지식
(C) 한 개 이상의 언어를 할 수 있는 능력
(D) 사무적인 용모

Check-up Test
1. ⓐ, (B)   2. (D)

1.

8월 12일

친애하는 가족, 친구, 그리고 동료들에게,

가치 있는 일을 도울 수 있는 특별한 기회를 여러분께 알려 드리기 위해 이 편지를 씁니다. 저는 전국 크로스 컨트리 협회에서 후원하며, 9월 10일 토요일에 진행되는 제15회 연례 자선 달리기 행사에 참가할 예정입니다. ⓐ 이 행사를 위한 준비로, 저는 일주일에 서너 번씩 17킬로미터 정도를 달리고 있습니다. ⓑ 전국 크로스 컨트리 협회는 경주자들의 지구력을 위한 훈련은 물론, 안전하고 건강한 운동과 식습관 개선을 돕는 비영리 단체입니다. ⓒ 우리는 금전 및 물품을 기부받아 전 세계적으로 가치 있는 일에 쓰여지도록 보내고 있습니다. ⓓ 저희 지역 지부는 현재 가난한 지역의 아이들을 위한 백신 주사 비용을 지불하기 위한 기금을 모으고 있습니다.

(A) 조깅하는 사람들을 훈련시키는 일
(B) 건강 비디오를 제작하는 일

문제 2는 다음 기사를 참조하세요.

상하이, 5월 19일 — 개발사인 SEKA 게임스의 인기 있는 레이싱 게임 속편인 '레이싱 카'가 오늘 오후 일찍 출시되었다. 기대에 찬 수천 명의 팬들이 게임이 동나기 전에 구입하기 위해 아침 일찍부터 게임 판매점 앞에 줄을 섰다.

SEKA 게임스가 스스로 기획한 광고 전략은 성공적인 것으로 드러났다. 레이싱 카의 출시를 목 빠지게 기다리고 있던 팬들로 이 게임은 금방 인터넷에서 뜨거운 화제가 되었다. 레이싱 카의 새 버전은 지난 버전에 비해 크게 다르지 않지만, 이용자들의 요청에 의해 차량들의 업데이트 버전을 포함시켰다. 대부분의 게임사들은 효과적인 비디오 게임 광고에 초점을 맞추는 외부 회사에 의존하기 때문에 많은 사람들이 레이싱 카가 주목을 받기에는 무리가 있다고 믿었다. 그와 대조적으로 SEKA 게임스는 전문 레이서들을 고용해 TV와 온라인 광고에 등장시킨 자사의 마케팅 팀을 활용했다. 또한 이 유명 인사들 중 몇몇은 게임 유저들과 레이싱 팬들을 끌어들이기 위해 몇몇 상점에서도 모습을 드러냈다.

2. SEKA 게임스에 대해 언급된 것은?
(A) 그들의 본사는 상하이에 위치하고 있다.
(B) 그들은 최근 다른 회사와 합병하였다.
(C) 그들의 제품들은 타 경쟁사들의 제품보다 더 비싸다.
(D) 그들은 고객들의 의견에 주의를 기울인다.

Point 06 동의어 문제

출제 포인트 정리

진저 씨께,

우선 클래식 윈저 아파트 단지를 잘 안내해 주신 데 대해 감사의 말씀을 드립니다. 건물 자체도 놀랍도록 아름다웠고, 시설들은 새 것처럼 보였으며, 무엇보다 저는 그곳의 위치가 특히 마음에 들었습니다. 당신이 추천해 주신 바다가 보이고 별도의 저장 공간이 있는 방을 고려해 보았으나, 저는 대신 발코니가 있는 방으로 결정했습니다. 저는 공원이 내려다보이는 목재로 된 실외 발코니가 있다는 점이 마음에 들었습니다.

스키퍼타운에서 제가 체류하는 기간은 저의 해외 업무 기간에 달려 있다는 점을 고려할 때, 제가 이곳에서 오랜 기간 머물 것 같지 않기 때문에 타이베이에서 제 가구들을 가져오지 않기로 결정했습니다. 8월 14일에 이사할 수 있으면 좋을 것 같습니다. 우리가 시간을 조정하고 나면, 서류 작업을 완료하고 주차 공간을 신청하기 위해 당신 사무실에 들르겠습니다. 또한 보증금을 준비해 가도록 하겠습니다.

존 매든

이메일에서 첫 번째 단락, 다섯 번째 줄에 있는 단어 "overlooks(~을 내려다보다)"와 의미가 가장 가까운 것은
(A) ~에 대하여 잊다
(B) ~의 전망을 제공하다
(C) ~에 대한 변명을 하다
(D) ~의 안을 점검하다

Check-up Test

1. 경우, (A)   2. (D)

1.

> **모든 승객들은 주목하세요!**
>
> 오늘도 저희 역을 이용해 주셔서 감사합니다. 더 나은 서비스를 제공하기 위해, 센트럴 파크 역은 시설 개선 공사에 착수할 것입니다. 이 공사는 7월 10일부터 8월 12일까지 진행될 예정입니다. 이 기간 동안, 일부 승강장은 폐쇄될 예정입니다. 이런 경우, 평상시 그 승강장들에 정차하던 열차들은 다른 곳에서 정차할 것입니다. 승강장에 관해서 역내 안내방송에 귀를 기울여 주시거나 전광판의 일정표를 확인해 주세요. 열차 도착과 출발 시간은 동일하게 유지될 것입니다.
>
> 일부 티켓 자동 발급기와 출구들도 또한 폐쇄될 것입니다. 역내에 위치한 모든 상점과 음식점은 정규 영업시간에 운영이 될 것입니다. 지하철 회보에서 이 보수 공사에 관해서 확인하실 수 있으며, 그것은 매표소에서 이용하실 수 있습니다.
>
> 이 공사가 여러분에게 끼칠 불편에 대해
> 미리 사과의 말씀을 드립니다.
>
> **센트럴 파크 역사 관리소**

(A) 상황
(B) 그릇, 용기

문제 2는 다음 이메일을 참조하세요.

> 수신: 이사벨라 글로리아 <bellegloria@elecmail.com>
> 발신: 클라크 류 <clarkliu@spectrum.com>
> 날짜: 5월 23일
> 제목: 업데이트
>
> 글로리아 씨에게,
>
> 고객님께서 주방과 침실에 갈색과 파랑색을 선택하신 것에 찬성합니다. 하지만, 선택하신 욕실 색상은 조금 우려가 됩니다. 초록색은 고객들 대부분이 장기적으로 만족하지 못하는 대표적인 색상입니다. 다시 한 번 생각해 보시고 저에게 알려 주세요.
>
> #B51 메탈릭 블랙을 제외하고는, 고객님 목록에 있는 다른 모든 색상은 준비할 수 있을 것 같습니다. 매그니피코 사는 최근 그 색상 생산을 중단했습니다. 하지만, 아방 사에서 생산하는 비슷한 색상이 있습니다. 제품 번호는 #B106이며, 한번 보시는 것이 좋을 것 같습니다. 그리고 고객님의 질문에 관하여 답변을 드리자면, 페인트 작업은 6월 5일에 시작할 수 있을 것이며, 이렇게 하면 27일 전까지 고객님의 아파트가 보기 좋게 모양을 갖추도록 작업을 완료할 수 있는 충분한 시간이 있을 것입니다.
>
> 감사합니다,
>
> 클라크 류, 컬러 상담가
> 스펙트럼 인테리어

2. 이메일에서, 두 번째 단락 네 번째 줄에 있는 단어 "shape(모양)"와 가장 유사한 것은?
(A) 패턴(무늬)
(B) 수치
(C) 계획
(D) 상태

Point 07 의도 파악 문제

출제 포인트 정리

> **데이비드 터커** [오후 7:02] :
> 안녕하세요, 테리 씨. 당신이 이미 퇴근을 했다는 것을 알고 있습니다. 하지만 출장을 가기 전에 여쭤봐야 하는 질문이 있습니다.
>
> **테리 스콧** [오후 7:04] :
> 문제없어요. 어떻게 도와드릴까요?
>
> **데이비드 터커** [오후 7:05] :
> 저는 시드니 차량 대여소에 있는데, 직원들이 보험에 대해서 묻고 있습니다. 회사 출장이 처음이기 때문에, 관련 정책에 대해서 전혀 모르겠습니다. 보험을 구매해야 할까요?
>
> **테리 스콧** [오후 7:08] :
> 당연하죠, 차량 대여 전에 보험이 필요합니다.

오후 7시 4분에 스콧 씨가 "It's not a problem(문제없어요)"이라고 썼을 때 의미하는 것은 무엇인가?
(A) 그는 회사 정책에 관한 정보를 쉽게 얻을 수 있다.
(B) 그는 사무실로 돌아갈 것이다.
(C) 그는 터커 씨의 질문에 기꺼이 답변할 것이다.
(D) 그는 터커 씨에게 보험에 가입하지 말라고 조언한다.

Check-up Test

1. ⓓ, (B)   2. (C)

1.

> **보니 웰스** [오전 10:03]
> 노엘 씨, ⓐ 인터뷰에 늦어서 죄송합니다. 저는 아직 가고 있어요. 그곳에 20분 후에 도착할 것 같아요.
>
> **노엘 스탠리** [오전 10:05]
> 괜찮습니다. 우선 저 혼자 ⓑ 엠마 존슨 씨를 인터뷰할 수 있습니다.
>
> **보니 웰스** [오전 10:06]
> 감사합니다. 그녀는 ⓒ 다른 인쇄 회사에서 근무한 경력이 있는 지원자입니다.
>
> **노엘 스탠리** [오전 10:07]
> 네, 단지 주문을 따라가기 위해 누군가를 채용해야 할 만큼 ⓓ 우리 회사가 많이 성장했다는 게 믿어지지 않네요.
>
> **보니 웰스** [오전 10:08]
> 맞아요! 곧 만나요!

오전 10시 8분에, 웰스 씨가 "I know(맞아요)"라고 썼을 때 의미하는 것은 무엇인가?

(A) 그녀는 이전에 스탠리 씨를 만난 적이 있다.
(B) 그녀도 역시 회사의 성장이 놀랍다.

문제 2는 다음 온라인 채팅 대화를 참조하세요.

> **제인 무어 [오전 9:45]**
> 안녕하세요. 제 물건의 도착 여부를 아시는 분이 계신가요? 크리스틴 기업에서 물건을 보냈습니다. 그것은 제품 샘플입니다.
>
> **재스민 잭슨 [오전 9:45]**
> 이곳 접수처에는 물건이 없습니다. 2층에 있는 우편실을 확인해 보는 것은 어떨까요?
>
> **오스카 에반스 [오전 9:46]**
> 제인 씨, 이곳에 크리스틴 기업에서 보낸 물건이 있지만, 이름이 적혀 있지 않습니다.
>
> **제인 무어 [오전 9:46]**
> 그게 제 것인 것 같습니다. 다시 한 번 운송 라벨을 확인해 주실 수 있나요?
>
> **오스카 에반스 [오전 9:47]**
> 죄송합니다. 당신의 이름이 적혀 있네요. 너무 작았어요.
>
> **제인 무어 [오전 9:48]**
> 감사합니다. 당신의 사무실로 내려가겠습니다.

2. 오전 9시 47분에, 에반스 씨가 "Sorry(죄송합니다)"라고 말할 때 의미하는 것은 무엇이겠는가?
(A) 그는 이미 물건을 발송했다.
(B) 그는 무어 씨가 이름 철자를 불러주기를 원한다.
(C) 그는 라벨을 읽다가 실수했다.
(D) 그는 고객과의 회의에 늦었다.

Point 08 문장 위치 찾기 문제

출제 포인트 정리

> **급여 산정 기간 및 근무 시간 기록표 정책**
>
> 이번 달 15일에 만료되는 급여 산정 기간에 해당하는 모든 수표는 다음 달 22일까지 우송될 것입니다. -[1]- 이번 달 23일에 만료되는 급여 산정 기간에 해당하는 수표는 다음 달 30일에 우송될 것입니다.
> -[2]- 이런 경우 수표는 전날 발급될 것입니다. 모든 정규직 직원들은 급여 산정 기간 만료에 앞서 은행 자동 이체 등록을 하시기 바랍니다. -[3]-
>
> **근무 시간 기록표**
> 모든 근무 시간 기록표에 대해 다음 마감일이 설정되었습니다.
> 월 단위 급여 지급 - 해당 월의 마지막 근무일
> 격주 단위 급여 지급 - 13일 및 30일
>
> **중요!**
> 마감 시간까지 근무 시간 기록표를 제출하지 않거나 은행 자동 이체를 등록하지 않은 모든 직원에게는 지급이 연기될 것입니다. -[4]-
> 이 정책에는 예외가 없을 것입니다.

[1], [2], [3], [4]로 표시된 위치 중 다음 문장이 들어가기에 가장 적절한 곳은?

"휴일 또는 긴 주말 동안에 만료되는 급여 산정 기간에 대해서는 예외가 있습니다."

(A) [1]
(B) [2]
(C) [3]
(D) [4]

Check-up Test
1. ⓐ, (B)   2. (C)

1.

> 관계자 분께,
>
> 몇 달 후에, 저는 국제 섬유 산업 회의에 참석하기 위해 중국으로 떠날 것이며, 상하이에서 며칠간 머물 곳이 필요합니다. 두어 달 전에 제 동료 한 명이 귀하의 호텔에서 머물렀는데, 저에게 이 호텔을 적극적으로 추천하였습니다. -[1]- 최근에 귀하의 호텔 웹사이트에 접속하려고 할 때 호텔 시설의 일부를 보수하고 있다는 메시지를 보게 되었습니다. 다행스럽게도, 여행 잡지에서 이 이메일 주소를 우연히 보았습니다.
>
> 호텔의 객실 요금과 현재 이용 가능한 객실에 대한 정보를 저에게 제공해 주실 수 있으신지요? 저는 5월 10일부터 5월 13일까지 상하이에 있을 계획이기에 이 기간 동안 머무를 싱글 룸이 하나 필요합니다. -[2]-
>
> 미리 감사의 말씀을 드립니다. 답변 기다리고 있겠습니다.
>
> 진심을 담아,
> 아니타 올슨

"ⓐ 게다가, ⓓ 출장객들을 위한 ⓒ 특별 패키지가 제공되는지를 ⓑ 알려주셨으면 합니다."
(A) [1]
(B) [2]

문제 2는 다음 편지를 참조하세요.

> 코치 씨께,
>
> 11일에 고객님께서 보내 주신 편지 잘 읽었습니다. Eco-100T의 생산이 올해 초에 종료되었습니다. -[1]- 하지만 고객님께서 물건을 저희에게 보내 주신다면 저희는 여전히 기기를 수리해 드릴 수 있습니다. 저희는 알 수 없는 손상이나 제품 분실에 대해서는 책임지지 않기 때문에 반드시 물건을 상자 안에 안전하고 단단하게 넣어 주세요. -[2]- 저희가 고객님의 식품 가공기를 받고난 후, 물건의 상태를 점검한 후에 저희 기술자들 중 한 명이 수리 사양에 대해 논의하기 위해 전화를 드릴 것입니다. 수리받기를 원하신다면 수리비를 지불하셔야 할 것입니다. -[3]- 저희는 비용을 받자마자 수리를 진행할 것입니다. 대부분의 경우 결함이 생긴 물건 수리는 보통 이틀에서 사흘 정도 소요되므로 열흘 안에 Eco-100T를 돌려받을 수 있을 것입니다. -[4]- 다른 문의할 점이 있으시면 301) 225-2599로 저희 고객 지원팀이나 기술 지원팀 직원에게 전화해 주십시오.

진심으로,

나이크 블레이크
서비스 및 보증 담당 직원

2. [1], [2], [3], [4]로 표시된 위치 중 다음 문장이 들어가기에 가장 적절한 곳은?
"비용은 수표나 신용카드로 결제하실 수 있습니다."
(A) [1]
(B) [2]
(C) [3]
(D) [4]

Chapter Test

1. (C)   2. (D)   3. (A)   4. (D)   5. (D)
6. (C)   7. (A)   8. (C)   9. (D)   10. (B)
11. (D) 12. (C) 13. (B)

문제 1-3은 다음 편지를 참조하세요.

FR 캐논
런던 시, 스프링 가든즈 8번지
우편 번호 SW1A 2BN

5월 12일

앨리 보웬
런던 시, 석세스 플레이스 24번지
우편 번호 NW1 4SA

보웬 씨께,

고객님께서 보증서에 의거하여 수리를 위해 저희에게 반송하신 2 (C) MP3 플레이어를 동봉하였습니다. 1/2 (A) 고객님께서는 (첨부된) 보증서 조항을 위반하셨기 때문에 수리를 진행할 수 없었습니다.

내부 배터리 교체를 위해 권한 없는 자가 플레이어를 분해했다는 사실을 저희 쪽 기술자가 알아냈습니다. 사고로 인한 파손이나 일상적 사용에 의한 마모, 제조상의 결함은 보증서에 의해 보상되지만, '자격이 있는 제조업체나 공식 인증 센터가 아닌 자에 의한 제품 변경이나 교체에 의한 손상'은 보상하지 않습니다. 이러한 조사 2 (B) 결과에 관한 자세한 보고 사항 또한 첨부하였습니다.

25달러의 고정 요금으로 수리를 받을 수 있는 3 가까운 저희 수리 매장으로 귀하의 플레이어를 가져가시기를 권해 드립니다.

양해해 주셔서 감사드리며, FR 캐논 MP3 플레이어를 선택해 주셔서 감사드립니다.

진심을 담아,

에반 윌리엄스
서비스 부장
동봉물 있음

---

1. 편지의 주요 목적은 무엇인가?
(A) 수리 견적서를 보내는 것
(B) 고객의 최근 구매에 대해 감사하는 것
(C) 요구 사항이 처리되지 않은 이유를 설명하는 것
(D) MP3 플레이어에 관한 정보를 요청하는 것

2. 편지에 포함되지 않은 것은 무엇인가?
(A) 보증서
(B) 결과 보고서
(C) MP3 플레이어
(D) 환불금

3. 보웬 씨에게 어떻게 하라고 조언하는가?
(A) 지역 수리 매장 방문
(B) 새로운 모델 구매
(C) 보증 연장 신청
(D) FR 캐논 상담원에게 연락

문제 4-5는 다음 온라인 대화를 참조하세요.

마리 모건 [오후 1시 31분]
안녕하세요, 누네즈 씨. 무엇을 도와드릴까요?

랄프 누네즈 [오후 1시 33분]
5 안녕하세요, 앨리스 사무용품 주문 건의 배송 확인 이메일을 막 받았는데, 아직 도착하지 않았어요.

마리 모건 [오후 1시 34분]
죄송합니다. 주문 번호를 말씀해 주실 수 있나요?

랄프 누네즈 [오후 1시 36분]
잠시만이요. NA-1009-5218입니다.

마리 모건 [오후 1시 41분]
감사합니다. 4 굿포인트는 단골 고객이군요. 거래해 주셔서 감사합니다. 5 저희 기록에 따르면, 이메일이 잘못 전달된 것 같습니다. 주문하신 물품은 오늘 오후에 출고될 예정이니, 수요일에 받으실 것입니다.

랄프 누네즈 [오후 1시 45분]
그래서 그랬군요. 그 물품이 이렇게 일찍 도착한다는 것에 놀랐습니다. 도와주셔서 감사합니다.

---

4. 굿포인트에 관하여 언급된 것은 무엇인가?
(A) 고객 정책을 변경했다.
(B) 배달 회사이다.
(C) 모건 씨를 채용했다.
(D) 이전에 앨리스 사에서 주문을 한 적이 있다.

5. 오후 1시 45분에, 누네즈 씨가 "That explains it(그래서 그랬군요)"라고 쓸 때 의미하는 것은 무엇이겠는가?
(A) 그는 이메일을 확인하지 못했다.
(B) 그는 주문 번호를 기억하지 못한다.
(C) 그는 주문이 변경된 것을 알게 되었다.
(D) 그는 물건을 받지 못한 이유를 확인했다.

문제 6-9는 다음 광고를 참조하세요.

> **6** 귀하를 이번 주 금요일, 토요일, 일요일(9월 23, 24, 25일)에 열리는 클로버랜드 아파트 개장식에 모시오니, 도시의 최고 주거 단지들 가운데 한 곳을 둘러보십시오.
>
> 금요일에는 오후 5시부터 7시 30분까지, 그리고 토요일과 일요일에는 오전 9시부터 오후 4시까지 안내원이 함께 하는 단지 투어가 있을 예정입니다. 또한, 토요일 오전 11시부터 오후 2시까지는 다과와 라이브 밴드, 경품 추첨이 있는 축하 행사가 있을 것입니다.
>
> 그러니 방문하셔서 딥 크릭 호수가 보이는 언덕의 정상에 위치한 아름다운 아파트 단지 주변을 거닐며 좋은 시간을 가져 보세요. 소풍을 즐길 수 있는 호수로 가는 **8 (A)** 산책로가 여러 개 있으며, **7** 바로 호수 가장자리에는 클럽하우스가 있습니다. 단지는 너무 조용해서 마치 시골에 와 있는 것 같은 느낌을 받으실 수 있지만, 기차로 몇 정거장만 가시면 몽고메리의 시내에서 쇼핑을 하거나 박물관을 가는 등 도시적인 삶을 즐기실 수 있습니다.
>
> 침실이 2-4개인 아파트 중에서 고르실 수 있습니다. 모든 아파트에는 최고의 가전제품을 갖춘 **8 (B)** 널찍한 고급 부엌이 포함되어 있습니다. 바닥은 모두 단단한 목재로 만들어졌으며 창고는 선택 사항입니다. 외식을 하고 싶으시다면 **8 (D)** 클로버랜드 단지 내에 있는 마틴스에서 고급 식사를 즐기실 수도 있습니다. 마틴스는 연중무휴로 24시간 영업합니다.
>
> 귀하는 1년이나 2년 동안 이 아름다운 아파트를 임대하실 수도 있습니다. **9** 9월 30일 전에 임대를 하시면 250달러를 상으로 받으실 수 있습니다!
>
> 클로버랜드에 관심이 있으시고 더 많은 정보를 원하신다면 저희 웹사이트 www.cloverland.org를 방문해 주십시오.

6. 무엇을 광고하고 있는가?
(A) 도시 공원의 확장
(B) 미술관 투어
(C) 신규 아파트 단지
(D) 주방용품 가게

7. 세 번째 단락, 세 번째 줄에 있는 단어 "right(바로)"와 가장 유사한 것은?
(A) 바로
(B) 바르게
(C) ~ 안에
(D) 지체하지 않고

8. 클로버랜드의 특징으로 열거된 것이 아닌 것은?
(A) 산책 장소
(B) 넓은 부엌
(C) 수영장
(D) 식당

9. 9월 30일 이전에 계약을 하는 사람에게는 무엇이 제공되는가?
(A) 마틴스 식사 할인권
(B) 야유회 초대
(C) 박물관 입장권
(D) 현금 보상

문제 10-13은 다음 이메일을 참조하세요.

> 발신: 애나 림
> 수신: 벤 월리스
> 제목: 피터즈버그에 관한 정보
> 날짜: 6월 16일
>
> 월리스 씨께
>
> **10** 뉴먼의 태양 에너지 학회에 참석하시는 모든 분들을 위해 저희는 피터즈버그에서 방문해 보실 만한 곳들의 리스트를 만들었습니다. 아래는 방문해 보실 것을 추천해 드리는 장소입니다. -[1]-
>
> • 피터즈버그의 중심부에 있는 동상 옆에 아직도 역사적인 건물들이 서 있는 작은 도로가 있습니다. -[2]- **13** 이 술집은 200년의 전통이 있는 곳이며, 이국적인 맛의 음식을 판매합니다. 그곳에서는 이 지역에서 가장 맛있는 핫도그와 햄버거를 판매한다는 것을 잊지 마십시오.
>
> • 날씨가 좋다면, 에드윈 그린즈 공원에 반드시 가보셔야 합니다. **11** 호텔에서 잠깐 버스를 타기만 하면 됩니다. 이 큰 공원에서 저녁에 축제나 카니발과 같은 신나는 행사가 열리니, 피터즈버그에 있는 동안 이것들을 놓치지 마십시오. -[3]-
>
> • 오렌지 해변에 들러서 산책로를 걸어 보십시오. 산책로를 따라 독특한 물건들을 판매하는 많은 상점들이 있으니, 쇼핑을 하실 수도 있습니다.
>
> **12** 피터즈버그에 대해서 더 알기를 원한다면, 저희 여행 정보센터가 귀하께서 머무시는 오픈 밸리 호텔에서 아주 가까운 곳에 있으니 시간이 나시면 언제든지 들러 주십시오. -[4]-
>
> 감사합니다.
>
> 애나 림
> 지역 홍보 담당자

10. 이메일은 왜 작성되었는가?
(A) 회의 안건을 업데이트하기 위하여
(B) 현지 명소를 알려 주기 위하여
(C) 회의 장소까지의 가는 방법을 알려 주기 위하여
(D) 행사 취소를 발표하기 위하여

11. 에드윈 그린즈 공원에 대해 무엇이 언급되고 있는가?
(A) 쇼핑센터이다.
(B) 버스 정거장이다.
(C) 비 오는 날에는 문을 닫는다.
(D) 호텔에서 가깝다.

12. 월리스 씨는 피터즈버그에 관한 추가 정보를 얻으려면 무엇을 해야 하는가?
(A) 연회 참가
(B) 상사에게 연락
(C) 관광 안내소 방문
(D) 가이드가 있는 여행 상품 구매

13. [1], [2], [3], [4]로 표시된 위치 중 다음 문장이 들어가기에 가장 적절한 곳은?
"이 오래된 건물들 중, 브라운 적스라고 불리는 오래된 술집이 하나 있습니다."

(A) [1]
(B) [2]
(C) [3]
(D) [4]

3. 이메일 수신자들은 왜 상사와 연락하라는 조언을 받는가?
(A) 바스케즈 씨의 발표에 의견을 제공하기 위해
(B) 라이츠 씨와 회의를 잡기 위해
(C) 정책 변화에 대해 더 알기 위해
(D) 직원 안내서를 한 부 받기 위해

 지문 유형

Point 01 이메일 및 편지(E-mail & Letter)

Check-up Test
1. (B) 2. (D) 3. (C)

문제 1-3은 다음 이메일을 참조하세요.

> 수신: 영업부 전 직원
> 발신: 니나 바스케즈 <ninavasquez@tnbcompany.com>
> 날짜: 4월 17일 수요일
> 제목: 직원 안내서
> 첨부: 중요 업데이트
>
> 직원들에게
>
> 1 T&B사 직원 안내서가 수정되었습니다. 수정된 정보는 직원 홈페이지에 게시되어 있습니다. 모든 정보를 확인하시려면, '직원 안내'를 클릭하세요. 또한 이 이메일에 해당 문서 파일을 첨부하였습니다. 1 시간을 내어 그 파일을 검토하시고, 최근에 변경된 사항들이 포함되어 있으니 강조 표시된 부분에 초점을 맞추실 것을 모든 직원들께 조언드립니다.
>
> 2 다음 주 금요일 회의에서, 저와 인사부의 라이츠 씨가 영업부에 영향을 줄 수 있는 모든 정책 변화에 대해 설명해 드릴 것입니다. 저희가 그 사항들을 상세히 설명한 후에, 여러분은 변화와 관련하여 질문을 하실 수 있으실 것입니다. 3 수정된 정책에 대해 더 알고 싶은 분은 직원 안내서를 가져가서, 본인의 상사와 이야기해 보실 것을 권합니다.
>
> 감사합니다,
>
> 니나 바스케즈
> 판매부장

1. 이메일의 목적은 무엇인가?
(A) 새로운 인사부장을 소개하는 것
(B) 직원들에게 업데이트된 규정을 알리는 것
(C) 직원들에게 중요한 문서를 복사하라고 요청하는 것
(D) 새롭게 디자인된 웹사이트에 대한 의견을 듣는 것

2. 이메일에 따르면, 다음 주에 어떤 일이 발생할 예정인가?
(A) 웹사이트에 있는 정보가 수정될 것이다.
(B) 새로운 광고 캠페인이 시작될 것이다.
(C) 환영회가 본사에서 열릴 것이다.
(D) 영업부 직원들이 회의에 참석할 것이다.

Point 02 공지 및 메모(Notice & Memo)

Check-up Test
1. (B) 2. (B) 3. (C)

문제 1-3은 다음 정보를 참조하세요.

> **뮤직 인사이드**
> **원고 제출 안내**
>
> <월간 뮤직 인사이드>에서 출간용 미청탁 원고를 받습니다. 1 저희의 스타일과 선호 사항에 부합할 수 있도록 여러분 모두 최신 호의 내용을 숙지할 것을 조언해 드립니다. 귀하의 원고는 이전에 다른 출판물에 사용된 적이 없으셔야 합니다. 원고는 모두 500에서 1,700자 사이로 작성되어야 하고, 행간은 한 줄씩 떨어 주셔야 합니다. 자필 원고는 심사 대상에서 제외된다는 점에 유의하여 주십시오.
>
> 원고는 전자 우편이나 보통 우편으로 보내실 수 있습니다. 2 선호하시는 연락 수단에 대한 정보를 포함하셨는지 반드시 확인해 주십시오. 어떠한 이유로든, 원고를 돌려받길 원하신다면, 원고를 보내실 때 우편 요금이 지불된 반송용 봉투를 동봉해 주셔야만 합니다. 저희는 보통 제출물에 대해 원고 수령 후 4주에서 6주 안에 응답을 드립니다. 아래 제시된 주소로 원고를 보내 주세요.
>
> 미국, 우편번호 47011
> 미시간 주 디트로이트 시
> 카렌턴 가 1557번지
> 월간 뮤직 인사이드
> 편집장 피터 라이언
> 이메일: peteryan@mgmonthly.com
>
> 3 원고가 채택된 분에게는 원고의 길이에 따라 400에서 1,000달러 사이의 원고료를 지불해 드릴 것입니다. 원고료는 원고가 채택된 5일 후에 당신의 계좌로 송금됩니다.

1. 정보에서 저자의 원고가 게재되는 데 도움이 될 것이라고 제안한 것은 무엇인가?
(A) 아이디어에 대한 사전 승인 받기
(B) 가장 최근에 발행된 잡지 읽기
(C) 제안된 월간 주제에 대해 쓰기
(D) 짧은 기사 쓰기

2. <월간 뮤직 인사이드>에 제출하는 모든 원고에 포함되어야 하는 것은 무엇인가?
(A) 이전 출판물을 명시한 자기소개서
(B) 선호하는 연락 방법에 대한 세부 정보
(C) 우편 요금이 지불된 반송용 봉투
(D) 원고 사본 두 부

3. 출판용으로 채택된 원고들에 대해 언급된 것은?

(A) 이전에 출판이 되었을 수도 있다.
(B) 1,500자 미만이어야 한다.
(C) 원고 길이에 따라 원고료가 지급된다.
(D) 그것들은 다음 호에 게재될 것이다.

Point 03 문자 메시지 및 온라인 채팅 (Text Message & Online chatting)

Check-up Test
1. (A)   2. (D)   3. (B)

문제 1-3은 다음 전자 게시판을 참조하세요.

> **해롤드 모리슨** [오전 10:00]
> 안녕하세요. 우리의 새로운 유니폼이 막 도착했어요. 1 여러분들의 유니폼을 가져가시면서, 어떻게 생각하시는지 말해 주세요.
>
> **조앤 누네즈** [오전 10:55]
> 와우, 스카프 대신 브로치가 있네요. 스카프는 쉽게 흘러내려서 승객을 모실 때 방해가 되었거든요.
>
> **마리 케네디** [오전 11:13]
> 좋아요. 하지만 밝은 회색 블라우스는 거의 흰색처럼 보여요. 2 흰색은 쉽게 더러워지잖아요. 몇 년 전에 그것들 때문에 문제가 있었거든요. 기억하는 사람 있어요?
>
> **태미 로스** [오전 11:20]
> 저는 블라우스에 달린 멋진 칼라와 검은색 금속 단추가 마음에 드네요. 우리 회사 이미지하고 잘 맞아요.
>
> **조앤 누네즈** [오후 12:00]
> 저는 블라우스의 색이 좋다고 생각해요. 우리 현재 유니폼 색보다 더 나아요.
>
> **길버트 첸** [오후 12:20]
> 3 저는 주머니가 달린 게 좋아요. 승객들을 모실 때 매우 유용할 거예요.

1. 모리슨 씨는 왜 메시지를 보냈는가?
(A) 의견을 묻기 위해
(B) 문제점을 보고하기 위해
(C) 변경된 일정을 알리기 위해
(D) 정책 변경 사항을 확인하기 위해

2. 오전 11시 13분에 케네디 씨가 "Does anyone remember that(기억하는 사람 있어요)"라고 적을 때 의미하는 것은 무엇이겠는가?
(A) 그녀는 기내에서 근무하는 것을 선호한다.
(B) 그녀는 하얀색을 좋아한다.
(C) 그녀는 브로치가 더 낫다는 것에 동의한다.
(D) 그녀는 색깔이 문제가 될 것이라고 생각한다.

3. 첸 씨는 새로운 유니폼에 대해서 어떻게 생각하는가?
(A) 유니폼의 색상을 좋아한다.
(B) 유니폼에 추가된 것을 좋아한다.
(C) 유니폼이 너무 얇다고 생각한다.
(D) 그는 유니폼이 유행하는 스타일이라는 점이 마음에 든다.

Point 04 광고(Advertisement)

Check-up Test
1. (B)   2. (C)

문제 1-2는 다음 광고를 참조하세요.

> **히스 로지**
> 만족을 주는 품질
>
> 1 히스 로지는 분주한 뉴타운의 상업 지역 중심부에 위치해 있습니다. 10년 넘게 저희는 고객들에게 유동적인 회의 및 연회 장소, 세탁 서비스, 그리고 주요 공항 셔틀 서비스를 포함한 비할 데 없는 비즈니스 서비스를 제공해 왔습니다.
>
> 모든 고객들을 위해 저희는 다음과 같은 편의 시설들을 완전 무료로 제공합니다.
>
> • 2 (A)와이파이 인터넷 연결
> • 2 (D)256개의 케이블 TV 채널
> • 24시간 룸서비스(아침 식사 포함)
> • 구두 닦기 서비스
> • 피트니스 시설 이용
> • 2 (B)신문이나 잡지 배달
>
> 히스 로지는 시내 및 주요 관광지와 단지 몇 블록 떨어진 곳에 있습니다. 뉴타운에서 즐겁게 지내실 수 있음을 보장합니다.
>
> 우편번호 61930
> 일리노이 주, 뉴타운 시
> 페전트 가 4890번지
>
> 연락 번호: (601) 0099-9911
> www.heathlodge.com

1. 이 광고는 어디에서 찾아볼 수 있을 것 같은가?
(A) 식당 안내서에서
(B) 비즈니스 잡지에서
(C) 박물관 책자에서
(D) 예술 관련 출판물에서

2. 무료 서비스로 언급되지 않은 것은 무엇인가?
(A) 인터넷 접속
(B) 신문 배달
(C) 공항 교통편
(D) TV 프로그램

Point 05 양식(Form)

Check-up Test
1. (B)   2. (C)   3. (A)

문제 1-3은 다음 양식을 참조하세요.

**파이낸셜 타임즈
정기 구독 신청서**

<파이낸셜 타임즈>는 세계 금융 시장에 대한 가장 풍부하고 새로운 정보를 제공해 드립니다. 3. <파이낸셜 타임즈>는 수백만 명이 구독하는 명성이 높은 비즈니스 잡지이며, 귀하가 고객의 투자 자산에 대해 보다 정확한 판단을 할 수 있도록 도와드릴 것입니다.

1 매주, 수상 경력이 있는 이 잡지는 금융과 경제계의 전문가들이 작성한 기사와 칼럼을 특집으로 다룹니다. <파이낸셜 타임즈>는 항상 새로운 관련 소식들을 계속 알려 드릴 것입니다. 전화하셔서 <파이낸셜 타임즈>를 오늘 받으세요!

다음 중 하나를 선택하세요.
_____ <파이낸셜 타임즈> 2년 계약 (96회분)
420.00달러 - 가판대 가격의 50% 할인
_____ 2 <파이낸셜 타임즈> 1년 계약 (48회분)
240.00달러 - 가판대 가격의 40% 할인
___√___ <파이낸셜 타임즈> 6개월 (24회분)
150.00달러 - 가판대 가격의 30% 할인

지불 방법:
(√) 현금, ( ) 수표, ( ) 신용카드: _____

이 름: 3 그레고리 스틸
주 소: 우편번호 60603, 일리노이 주 시카고 시, 빌라 가 340번지

귀하의 첫 번째 잡지는 도착하는 데 3주에서 4주 정도 걸립니다.

1. 얼마나 자주 <파이낸셜 타임즈>가 발행되는가?
(A) 매일
(B) 매주
(C) 매달
(D) 매년

2. 1년 정기 구독료는 얼마인가?
(A) 48달러
(B) 150달러
(C) 240달러
(D) 420달러

3. 그레고리 스틸 씨에 대해서 암시된 것은 무엇인가?
(A) 시카고에 있는 재정 자문가이다.
(B) <시카고 선>을 정기 구독하고 있다.
(C) 볼프강 앤 브라더스에서 3주간 근무했다.
(D) <파이낸셜 타임즈>에 칼럼을 쓰고 있다.

Point 06 기사(Article)

Check-up Test
1. (B)   2. (D)   3. (B)

문제 1-3은 다음 기사를 참조하세요.

진정한 스페인을 맛보자

쇼핑객들이 '스페인'이라는 단어를 들으면 가장 먼저 떠올리는 것은 바르셀로나일 것입니다. 그러나 잠깐! 1 바르셀로나에서 멀지 않은 곳에서 당신은 스페인 최고의 쇼핑 지역을 찾을 수 있습니다. 2 바르셀로나 동쪽으로 차로 15분만 가면 아마도 가이드북에서 언급된 적 없는 도시인 타라고나에 도달할 수 있을 것입니다. 이 소도시에는 도자기, 보석, 모자, 그리고 목각 장식품과 같은 전통적인 지역 예술품들을 판매하는 상점이 30곳 이상 있습니다.

"타라고나는 전형적인 관광지는 아닙니다. 이곳의 상점들은 주로 지역 예술가들의 작품을 팔고 있죠"라고 에스파나 보석점의 주인 후아나 게이츠는 말합니다. "여기에서 팔리는 물품들은 대부분 수작업으로 만든 것이어서 관광객들이 좋아하는 것 같습니다. 저는 이것이 타라고나를 스페인의 다른 도시와 구별되게 만드는 것이라고 생각합니다. 이것은 예술가들과 지역 업체 모두에게 정말 좋은 일입니다."

3 (D) 매년 5월, 타라고나 거리에서 5일간 비바 마나나 축제가 열린다는 것은 말할 것도 없습니다. 축제가 열리는 동안 3 (C) 예술가들은 거리를 따라 부스를 설치하여 공예품들을 파는데, 이국적인 스페인 음식과 음악이 곁들여집니다. 3 (A) 이 축제는 매년 인기를 더해가고 있어서 이 축제 기간에 타라고나에 방문하시려면 미리 계획을 짜두는 것이 현명합니다. 타라고나 지역 여관은 두 달 전에 미리 예약해야 합니다. 아니면 바르셀로나에는 호텔이 많이 있으니까 그곳으로 예약할 수 있습니다.

1. 이 기사는 주로 무엇에 관한 것인가?
(A) 어떤 도시의 역사
(B) 어떤 도시에서의 쇼핑 기회
(C) 어느 지역 예술가의 작품들
(D) 관광객들을 위한 숙박 업소

2. 기사에 따르면, 타라고나에 대해 사실인 것은 무엇인가?
(A) 멋진 여관과 호텔들로 유명하다.
(B) 기차로 갈 수 있다.
(C) 멋진 경치로 유명하다.
(D) 바르셀로나 인근에 있다.

3. 비바 마나나 축제에 대해 언급되지 않은 것은 무엇인가?
(A) 점점 인기가 상승하고 있다.
(B) 일반에 무료로 제공된다.
(C) 음악 공연을 특징으로 한다.
(D) 매년 열린다.

Chapter Test

1. (B)	2. (B)	3. (C)	4. (C)	5. (B)
6. (A)	7. (B)	8. (C)	9. (B)	10. (D)
11. (B)	12. (D)	13. (C)	14. (C)	15. (D)
16. (D)	17. (B)	18. (D)	19. (C)	

문제 1-3은 다음 안건을 참조하세요.

라이어슨 미술관 중역 회의
여름 회의 안건, 8월 11일

장소: 라이어슨 호텔, 회의실 A
1 점심: 오후 12시 – 1시 라이어슨 호텔 선셋 식당

시간	발표자	주제
오후 1시 – 1시 30분	데이비드 런던, 최고 재무 책임자	예산 현황
오후 1시 30분 – 2시	2 네이트 메르카도, 마케팅 부장	반년간의 방문객 수
오후 2시 – 2시 30분	노라 브라운, 전시회 관리자	다가오는 전시회 소개
오후 2시 30분 – 3시	레이시 노턴, 교육 프로그램 관리자	3 학생 교육 활동 프로그램의 확대 제안
오후 3시 – 3시 15분	이안 페이즐리, 미술관 관장	내년 이사회 회장 후보자 지명

1. 회의에 대해서 언급된 것은 무엇인가?
(A) 새로운 의장이 회의를 주관할 것이다.
(B) 회의 참석자들에게 식사가 제공될 것이다.
(C) 미술관 회의실에서 회의가 열릴 것이다.
(D) 미술관 직원들은 모두 회의에 참석할 수 있다.

2. 누가 미술관 방문객 수에 대해 보고할 것인가?
(A) 데이비드 런던
(B) 네이트 메르카도
(C) 노라 브라운
(D) 이안 페이즐리

3. 미술관에 대해서 추측할 수 있는 것은?
(A) 올해 들어 지금까지 수입이 지출을 초과했다.
(B) 새로운 전시회를 위한 추가 자금을 찾고 있다.
(C) 학생들을 위한 교육 프로그램을 제공한다.
(D) 관장이 가까운 시일 내에 사직할 것이다.

문제 4-6은 다음 광고지를 참조하세요.

앤 아버의 아시아 비즈니스 그룹이
지역 사회 행사에 당신을 초대합니다.

성장 전망: 앤 아버 근교의 아시아계 미국인 사업 활성화

4 토론 위원단:

바카니 맨달루 박사
미시간 중부 비즈니스 협회 이사

디아오 챈 씨
아시아 비즈니스 그룹 회장
다이너스티 주식회사 소유자
앤 아버의 아시아 비즈니스 그룹의 창립 멤버

6 **마코토 타나카 박사**
미시간주 입실란티 소재 미시간 주립 대학 경영 심리학 교수
<오늘날 미국의 중소기업>의 저자

이 지역 사회 행사는 중서부 지역의 모든 아시아계 사람들에게 경영

전략의 기본 원칙들을 소개합니다. 창업을 준비하는 방법에 관해 배우며, 당신에게 적합한 유형의 사업을 찾는 데 도움을 받을 수 있는 좋은 기회가 될 것입니다. 토론 위원들은 이러한 귀중한 정보들을 당신과 기꺼이 공유하고자 할 것입니다.

날짜: 11월 2일 금요일
시간: 오후 5시 30분에서 8시 30분까지
비용: 25달러 (앤 아버에 거주하는 학생은 10달러)
5 장소: 모셔 조던 홀
48104 미시간 주 앤 아버
게디스 거리 1316

이 행사에 참가를 원하시는 모든 분들에게 저녁이 무료로 제공될 것입니다. 등록은 734-657-8617로 저희에게 전화 주시거나, www.abocommunity.com을 방문해 주시기 바랍니다.

4. 어떤 행사가 홍보되고 있는가?
(A) 책 사인회
(B) 제품 시연
(C) 공개 토론회
(D) 학술 강연회

5. 행사는 어디에서 열릴 것인가?
(A) 아시아계 비즈니스 그룹에서
(B) 모셔 조던 홀에서
(C) 미시간 중부 비즈니스 협회에서
(D) 미시간 주립 대학에서

6. 타나카 박사에 대해 언급된 것은 무엇인가?
(A) 미시간에 있는 대학에서 경영학을 가르친다.
(B) 아시아 역사에 대하여 연설할 계획이다.
(C) 미시간에서 작은 업체를 소유하고 있다.
(D) 아시아 비즈니스 그룹의 일원이다.

문제 7-10은 다음 광고를 참조하세요.

월드 잡 서치

고용주용
7 월드 잡 서치(WJS)는 고위 임원직 충원을 전문으로 하는 온라인 기반 채용 웹사이트입니다. 8 (B) 저희의 특별히 훈련을 받은 상담원들이 저희 고객사들을 위해 고학력의 자질과 경력을 갖춘 지원자들을 찾습니다. 상담원들은 목록에서 적합한 사람을 찾기 위해 3만 건이 넘는 이력서들을 분석합니다. 그리고 지원자들의 더 상세한 프로필을 만들기 위해 사전 인터뷰를 진행합니다. 그 후에 고용주들은 8 (A)/(D) 어떤 지원자들이 그들 회사에 가장 적합한 인재로 9 간주되는지에 대한 추가 추천서가 첨부된 지원자 프로필 목록을 받게 됩니다.

구직자용
7 월드 잡 서치(WJS)는 구직자들에게 전도유망한 직업 리스트를 제공하고 이러한 기업과 연결시켜 드립니다. 10 WJS의 유료 회원이 되시면, 저희 온라인 검색 엔진에 접속하여 35개국 이상에 있는 검증받은 채용 정보를 볼 수 있습니다. 저희는 최소 10만 달러 이상의 연봉을 제공하는 회사들의 채용 정보를 매일 업데이트하고 있습니다. 또한 회원들에게는 저희만의 독자적인 비즈니스 월간 잡지인, <월드 비즈니스 타임즈>를 매달 보내 드립니다. 이 잡지에는 다른 비즈

니스 잡지들에서 거의 찾아보기 힘든 희귀한 정보들이 들어 있습니다. 언제든지 www.wjsjobs.com에서 회원이 되실 수 있습니다.

7. WJS의 목표는 무엇인가?
(A) 고위 임원직 구직자들의 이력서 개선을 돕는 것
(B) 최고 고용주들과 실력을 갖춘 구직자들을 연결시켜 주는 것
(C) 회사가 생산성을 높이도록 돕는 것
(D) 임원급 직원들을 새로운 산업 분야에서 일할 수 있도록 교육시키는 것

8. 광고에 따르면, 고객사에게 제공되는 것이 아닌 것은 무엇인가?
(A) 구직자 리스트
(B) 함께 일할 수 있는 전문가
(C) 3만 건의 이력서를 직접 볼 수 있는 권한
(D) 고용 대상으로 고려해야 하는 사람에 관한 제안

9. 첫 번째 단락 일곱 번째 줄에 있는 단어 "regarded(간주되는)"와 의미가 가장 유사한 것은?
(A) 보다
(B) 간주하다
(C) 관련있다
(D) 걱정하다

10. WJS를 이용하는 구직자들에 관해 언급된 것은 무엇인가?
(A) 여러 개의 언어를 말한다.
(B) 대학교에서 가르친 적이 있다.
(C) 연봉 10만 달러까지 벌기를 원한다.
(D) 유료 회원에 가입할 수 있다.

문제 11-13은 다음 편지를 참조하세요.

NS 오피스 디포

4월 24일
스콧 테일러
구매부
H&K 제작사

테일러 씨께

11 이번 달에 H&K 제작사에서 주문하신 사무용품들을 동봉하였습니다.

주문하신 내역은 다음과 같습니다.
- 회사 로고가 있는 인쇄용지 25상자
- 회사 로고가 있는 5x7 사이즈 봉투 300장
- 회사 로고가 있는 3링 바인더 25개

12 주문량은 3월에 체결한 계약서에 근거하였습니다. 고객님께서는 올해 말까지 위에 명시된 품목을 동일한 수량으로 매달 25일에 받으시게 됩니다. 내년에 저희와 재계약하시기를 원하신다면 12월에 저희에게 알려 주십시오.

다음 주문 물품은 5월 25일까지 배달될 것입니다. 품목이나 수량을 변경하시길 원하신다면 저희 고객 센터로 (425) 518-5723으로 전화 주시길 바랍니다. 13 고객님께서 주문량을 늘리시면 저희가 특별 할인을 제공할 것임을 알려드립니다. 매달 14일에 주문이 되면 변경이나 환불은 불가능합니다.

이용해 주셔서 감사합니다.

충심으로,
매튜 A. 위어

11. 이 편지의 목적은 무엇인가?
(A) 주문 대금 지불 요청
(B) 배달 물품 확인
(C) 고객과의 계약 조건 변경
(D) 새로운 회사 로고 디자인 제안

12. H&K 제작사의 4월 주문과 관련하여 언급된 것은?
(A) 인쇄 문제로 인해 늦게 도착했다.
(B) 테일러 씨는 3월에 주문을 하여 할인을 받았다.
(C) 테일러 씨가 전화상으로 추가 주문한 물품까지도 포함되어 있다.
(D) 주문 물품의 양이 이전 달과 다르지 않다.

13. 편지에 따르면, NS 오피스 디포가 제공하는 것은 무엇인가?
(A) 사용하지 않은 반송품에 대한 환불
(B) 매달 14일까지 테일러 씨의 다음 주문품 배달
(C) 주문량이 더 많아진 품목에 대한 할인
(D) 연말이 되면 테일러 씨와 회사 간의 자동적인 계약 연장

문제 14-15는 다음 기사를 참조하세요.

정시 비행 증가

15 6월 17일 – 14 지난주 항공 교통부에서 발표한 보고서에 따르면, 미국의 모든 항공사들이 5월에 정시 비행 기록 최고치를 기록했다. 15 미국의 6개 대형 항공사에 관한 연구는 이 항공사들의 정시 도착률이 4월 86%에서 증가해 지난달에는 90%에 달했다는 것을 보여 준다. 이 연구는 또한 지난해 정시 도착률 최고치는 10월에 83%였고 지난해 정시 도착률 전체 평균은 78%였음을 보여 준다.

14. 이 기사는 무엇에 관한 것인가?
(A) 정부 정책
(B) 공항 계약서
(C) 항공사 관련 연구
(D) 여행 계획

15. 항공사들의 5월 정시 도착률은 얼마였는가?
(A) 78%
(B) 83%
(C) 86%
(D) 90%

문제 16-19는 다음 기사를 참조하세요.

세계 비즈니스 보도
카이저 철강회사

16, 17 매사추세츠 주 보스턴의 중심에 본사를 두고 있는 카이저 철강회사는 전 세계적으로 많은 고객을 가진 국제적으로 잘 알려진 철강 공급업체 중의 하나이다. 주된 공급품은 판금이며 전 세계 곳곳의 철도 건설을 위해 사용된다. 카이저 철강회사는 철강 제조업체인 델린저 앤 브라더스의 지분 35%를 소유하고 있다. 18 인도의 뭄바

PART 7_Chapter 2 지문 유형 **085**

이에 위치한 델린저 앤 브라더스는 아시아 시장에 초점을 두고 있다.

내구성이 가장 강한 철강 제품을 개발하기 위한 노력으로, 19 카이저 철강회사는 프랑스, 칸의 르 블랑 철강과 철과 티타늄 재료를 혼합하기 위한 방법을 공동으로 개발하고 있다. 두 제조업체의 프로젝트 연구원들은 칸에 위치한 새로 지은 연구소에 모여 있다.

16 카이저 철강회사는 직원 5,000명을 두고 있으며, 12개 국가에서 약 300개의 공장을 운영하고 있다. 현사장인 케빈 스파이크스 씨는 15년 이상 카이저 철강회사를 이끌어 오고 있다.

16. 기사의 목적은 무엇인가?
(A) 건축 자재에 대해 비평하는 것
(B) 기업 대표의 임명을 발표하는 것
(C) 기업의 분기별 소득을 요약하는 것
(D) 기업의 국제적 활동을 설명하는 것

17. 카이저 철강회사의 본사는 어디에 있는가?
(A) 칸에
(B) 보스턴에
(C) 뭄바이에
(D) 시카고에

18. 델린저 앤 브라더스 사에 대해 언급된 것은 무엇인가?
(A) 새로운 회사이다.
(B) 직원이 대략 5,000명이다.
(C) 연구 센터이다.
(D) 지역 공급업체이다.

19. 기사에 따르면, 르 블랑과 카이저는 어떤 관계인가?
(A) 르 블랑은 카이저의 판금을 재활용한다.
(B) 카이저가 르 블랑을 소유하고 있다.
(C) 르 블랑과 카이저는 프로젝트 파트너이다.
(D) 르 블랑과 카이저는 합병할 계획이다.

클래식 BLT 7.5달러
(신선한 양상추와 토마토를 곁들인 얇게 썬 베이컨)

클래식 이탈리안 8.5달러
(이탈리안 소스를 곁들인 살라미, 체다 치즈, 그리고 올리브)

칠면조 딜라이트 8.5달러
(머스타드를 곁들인 칠면조 고기 흰살과 채소)

수프림 발디오스 10달러
(타르타르소스를 곁들인 새우, 게살, 그리고 참치)

푸른 완두콩 2달러

후식
오늘의 파이 4.5달러
아이스크림 선디 2.5달러

음료
오렌지 레모네이드 1.5달러
아이스티 2달러

뉴저지 주, 팰리세이즈 파크 시, 브로드 가 240번지, 골든 이글 다이너 — 도시에 있는 많은 샌드위치 가게들 중에서 골든 이글 다이너는 가장 최근에 생긴 가게입니다. 이 식당은 높은 질의 음식을 제공하는 동시에 메뉴 중에서 가장 비싼 것이 10달러로 비교적 저렴한 가격을 책정하는 식당 중 하나로 여겨지고 있습니다.

사이드 디시는 아주 특별하지는 않지만 실제로 다른 평범한 샌드위치 가게들 것보다 나아 보입니다. 그것은 바로 샌드위치가 골든 이글 다이너에서 가장 높은 평가를 받을 만하다는 말입니다. 샌드위치들은 모두 오븐에서 갓 구워진 빵을 사용하여 만들어지고 고기는 신중히 조절된 온도에서 조리됩니다. 그곳의 샌드위치 중에서 살라미 샌드위치는 반드시 먹어봐야 하는 것입니다. 얇게 썬 살라미는 치즈 및 올리브와 완벽하게 어울린다는 것을 알 수 있습니다. 게다가 달콤하고 새콤한 이탈리안 소스는 이미 완벽한 이 샌드위치의 맛에 즐거움을 더해줍니다.

결론적으로 저는 모두에게 다음에 점심을 먹으러 나가실 때 골든 이글 다이너에서 먹어볼 것을 권합니다. 파이를 주문할 예정이라면 반드시 최소한 두 개를 주문하세요.

후기 작성자는 어떤 메뉴가 특별히 좋다고 언급하는가?
(A) 클래식 BLT
(B) 클래식 이탈리안
(C) 칠면조 딜라이트
(D) 수프림 발디오스

Chapter 3 다중 지문 유형

Point 01 이중 지문(Double Passages) 연계 문제

출제 포인트 정리

골든 이글 다이너

점심 메뉴
월요일 – 목요일
오전 11시 – 오후 4시

샌드위치
골든 이글 오리지널 6달러
앤디스 스타일 7달러
(양파를 곁들인 체다 치즈)

사이드 디시
새콤한 피클 1.5달러
양배추 샐러드 2달러
어린 당근 2달러

Check-up Test
1. (D)   2. (C)   3. (A)   4. (B)   5. (C)

문제 1-5는 다음 이메일들을 참조하시오.

발신 : 데이비드 앨런 <davallen@marketingtoday.com>
수신 : 첸 샤오 후이 <chenxh@marketingtoday.com>
날짜 : 4월 21일
제목 : 마케팅 세미나 일정

안녕하세요, 샤오 후이 씨,

1 저는 7월에 열리는 마케팅 세미나의 일정 초안을 보내 드렸습니다.

귀하를 비롯한 다른 위원들이 그것을 검토해 주시면 감사하겠습니다. 3 저는 이 세미나를 위해 준비를 하고 있는 홍콩에 있는 모든 분들에게 감사드립니다. 로얄 팰리스 호텔을 예약해 주신 것에 대해서도 진심으로 감사드립니다.

데이비드

첫째 날	오전 10:30 오후 12:00 오후 2:00	3층 다이아몬드 홀에서 기조연설과 소개 호텔 스카이라크 테라스 식당에서 야외 점심 식사 3층 세미나실 3-9호에서 그룹 회의
둘째 날	오전 10:00 오후 12:15 오후 2:30	3층 세미나실 3-9호에서 그룹 회의 2 2층 호텔 스토브 식당에서 점심 식사 3층 세미나실 3-9호에서 그룹 회의
셋째 날	오전 10:30 오후 12:00 오후 3:00	3층 킨제이 홀 C와 D에서 발표 리허설 4 호텔 시크릿 가든에서 야외 점심 식사 3층 다이아몬드 홀에서 그룹 발표

발신 : 첸 샤오 후이 <chenxh@marketingtoday.com>
수신 : 데이비드 앨런 <davallen@marketingtoday.com>
날짜 : 7월 9일
제목 : 세미나 기간 동안의 날씨

데이비드 씨에게,

저희에게 약간의 문제가 있습니다. 5 기상청 웹사이트에 가서 세미나 기간 동안의 일기 예보를 확인해 보았습니다. 아래에 보시는 바와 같이, 날씨가 문제가 될 수도 있습니다. 4 마지막 이틀의 점심 장소를 서로 바꾸라고 호텔 측에 말하는 것이 최선이라고 생각합니다. 7월 13일이 되어야 일정표를 인쇄할 예정이니 다행입니다.

그럼 좋은 하루 되세요.
샤오 후이

홍콩 일기 예보		
5 7월 15일 화요일 32℃ 맑음	7월 16일 수요일 31℃ 맑고, 바람 약간	7월 17일 목요일 27℃ 흐리고, 소나기 가능성 85%

1. 첫 번째 이메일에서 세미나 일정에 대해서 알 수 있는 것은 무엇인가?
(A) 홍콩에 있는 위원회에서 만들었다.
(B) 작년의 세미나 일정과 비슷하다.
(C) 참석자에게 보내졌다
(D) 여전히 진행 중이다.

2. 호텔 3층에 위치해 있는 시설이 아닌 것은 무엇인가?
(A) 킨제이 홀
(B) 다이아몬드 홀
(C) 스토브 식당
(D) 세미나실 7호

3. 첸 씨에 대해 언급된 것은?
(A) 세미나 준비를 돕고 있다.
(B) 기조연설을 할 것이다.
(C) 홍콩에 있는 일기 예보관과 대화를 나누었다.
(D) 로얄 팰리스 호텔에서 일한다.

4. 첸 씨는 수요일에 어느 곳에서 점심이 제공되어야 한다고 제안하는가?
(A) 다이아몬드 홀에서
(B) 시크릿 가든에서
(C) 스토브 식당에서
(D) 스카이라크 식당에서

5. 회의는 언제 시작하기로 되어 있는가?
(A) 7월 9일
(B) 7월 13일
(C) 7월 15일
(D) 7월 16일

Point 02 삼중 지문(Triple Passages) 연계 문제

출제 포인트 정리

수신 제이드 솔로몬 <info@solomonestate.com>
발신 릴라 루페 <llupe@vivamail.com>
날짜 7월 5일
제목 주택 임대

솔로몬 씨께,

제 친구가 당신께 연락해 보라고 했습니다. 남편과 저는 다음 달부터 임대할 집을 찾을 예정입니다. 1 저희는 적어도 침실 3개와 정원을 가꿀 수 있는 마당 하나가 있으면 좋겠는데 그것이 저희가 가장 좋아하는 취미입니다. 저희 둘 다 시내에서 근무하기 때문에, 1 15분을 넘지 않는 한, 시내까지 운전해서 가는 것은 개의치 않습니다. 2 마지막으로 저희는 최소 1년 동안 거기서 거주하길 원합니다.

다음 주부터 괜찮은 집을 보러 다닐 수 있다면 정말 좋겠네요. 근무 시간 동안 02-542-1213으로 언제든지 전화하시면 저와 연락이 가능합니다만, 제가 집(02-679-1213)에 있는 저녁 시간에 전화 주시면 확실히 통화할 수 있으리라 생각합니다. 가능한 한 빨리 이 일에 대해 얘기를 나눌 수 있기를 바랍니다.

진심으로,

릴라 루페

레이 시티의 임대 주택
제이드 솔로몬이 소개하는 부동산

카네기 코트 99번지 ----------- 주당 270달러
7층에서 내려다보이는 아름다운 해안 전망과 도시 중심에 위치한, 중간 크기의 침실 3개, 욕실 1개가 딸린 콘도미니엄. 주차 공간 이용이 용이하고, 도보 거리에 버스 정류소가 있음.

스튜어트 거리 27번지 ----------- 주당 340달러
베란다, 침실 3개, 욕실 2개, 차고 1개로 구성된 단층집. 시내까지 차로 약 20분 거리. 최대 1년 임대 가능.

챔버레인 가 790번지 ----------- 주당 370달러
큰 침실 5개, 욕실 3개. 교외의 조용한 환경으로 둘러싸여 있음. 열차로 25분이면 시내에 갈 수 있음. 넓은 차고 1개. 최대 2년 임대 가능.

샌드빌 파크웨이 33번지 ---------- 주당 370달러
해변 근처 교외에 위치한, 현대식 1 침실 4개, 욕실 2개, 울타리로 둘러싸인 1 마당과 자동차 한 대가 들어가는 차고가 있는 집. 1 자동차로 10분이면 시내에 도착. 임대 기간 협상 가능.

솔로몬 앤 어소시에이트
59016 레이 시티, 몬트클레어 드라이브웨이 2200번지
567 321 2146
www.solomonestate.com
이상적인 보금자리를 선택하기 위한 최고의 선택!

수신 릴라 루페 <llupe@vivamail.com>
발신 제이드 솔로몬 <info@solomonestate.com>
날짜 7월 8일
답신 주택 임대

루페 씨에게,

임대 주택 문의 이메일을 보내 주셔서 감사합니다. 저는 10년 넘게 이 근방에 위치한 주거지를 맡아 일을 진행해 왔습니다. 요청하신 대로, 저는 모든 건물들을 확인했고 당신의 요구 사항에 적합한 곳을 찾아냈습니다.

하지만, 2 마지막에 언급하신 요구 사항에 관해서는 그 집의 소유주와 우선 논의해 봐야 합니다. 가능한 한 빨리 이 문제에 대해 당신께 알려 드리겠습니다.

그 집에 대해 궁금한 것이 있다면, 언제든지 제 휴대전화 760-5424-1909로 연락 주십시오. 이에 대해 가능한 한 빨리 이야기를 나누기를 바랍니다.

진심을 담아,

제이드 솔로몬

---

1. 광고에 있는 어느 집이 루페 씨의 요구에 가장 맞겠는가?
(A) 카네기 코트 99번지
(B) 스튜어트 거리 27번지
(C) 챔버레인 가 790번지
(D) 샌드빌 파크웨이 33번지

2. 솔로몬은 부동산 주인과 무엇에 대해서 이야기해야 하는가?
(A) 임대 기간
(B) 임대료
(C) 차고 개조
(D) 할부 가능성

Check-up Test
1. (C)   2. (A)   3. (B)   4. (D)   5. (A)

문제 1-5는 다음 일정과 이메일들을 참조하세요.

[초안 - 7월 7일]

크롬웰 페이퍼 사

2 오전 7:30 - 오전 8:30 아침 식사 및 대표 시작 연설
오전 8:30 - 오전 10:30 워크숍 1: 용지 공급에 대한 현 추세 분석
1 오전 10:30 - 오후 12:30 워크숍 2: 크롬웰 제품의 개괄
오후 12:30 - 오후 1:30 점심 식사
4 오후 1:30 - 오후 3:30 워크숍 3: 제안서 작성 기초 배우기
오후 3:30 - 오후 4:00 휴식
4 오후 4:00 - 오후 6:00 워크숍 4: 발표하기

발신 부엘라 쿠퍼 <buela@cromwellpp.com>
수신 칼리 드 레옹; 라이언 매카시; 타니아 페레이라; 제인 S 야마시로
날짜 7월 10일
제목 워크숍 일정

모든 분들께,

곧 있을 신입 영업 사원 교육 프로그램에 몇 가지 변경 사항이 있음을 알리고자 이렇게 메일을 드립니다. 먼저, 2 제임슨 씨는 오전 8시 30분까지 회의에 참석할 예정이기 때문에, 유감스럽게도 아침 식사 시간의 시작 연설을 하실 수가 없을 듯합니다. 저희는 제임슨 씨를 대신할 연설자를 찾기보다는 아침 식사를 신입 사원들이 서로 자기소개를 할 수 있는 오리엔테이션으로 3 바꾸기로 결정했습니다.

위에서 언급한 변경 사항에 외에도, 이번 교육 프로그램의 감독관인 램지 씨의 일정이 맞지 않는 관계로, 4 저희는 마지막 두 개의 워크숍 일정을 서로 바꾸기로 결정했습니다. 애석하게도, 저 또한 이번 교육 프로그램에 참석할 수가 없습니다.

라이언 씨, 변경된 일정을 업데이트하고 배포할 뿐만 아니라 참석자 모두에게 이 정보를 분명하게 전달해 주시기를 부탁드립니다. 이후에 제게 확인 연락을 주세요.

부엘라 쿠퍼

발신 라이언 매카시 <rmaccarthy@cromwellpp.com>
수신 부엘라 쿠퍼 <buela@cromwellpp.com>
날짜 5 7월 11일
답장 워크숍 일정

쿠퍼 씨께,

변경된 사항을 알려줘서 고맙습니다. 5 어제 회의가 매우 생산적이었던 것으로 들립니다. 저도 참석하고 싶었지만 막판에 시애틀로의 출장 때문에 어찌할 수가 없었습니다.

당신이 요청하신 대로 변경된 일정을 우리 회사 사이트에 업데이트 하였지만 제게 신입 영업 사원들의 명단이 없기 때문에 모두에게 당신의 메시지를 보내지 못하였습니다. 그래서 저는 아침에 당신에게 몇 차례 전화를 하였습니다. 당신의 비서가 오늘 당신이 사무실에 없다고 이야기해 주었습니다. 이 이메일을 받는 대로 저에게 전화주세요.

라이언 매카시

---

1. 오전 10시 30분에서 오후 12시 30분까지 영업 사원들은 무엇을 할 것인가?
(A) 영업 교육 담당자와의 만남
(B) 자기소개
(C) 회사 제품 학습

(D) 생산 시설 견학

2. 크롬웰 페이퍼 사의 대표는 누구인가?
(A) 제임슨 씨
(B) 매카시 씨
(C) 쿠퍼 씨
(D) 램지 씨

3. 첫 번째 이메일에서, 첫 번째 단락, 네 번째 줄의 단어 "turn(바꾸다)"과 의미가 가장 가까운 것은?
(A) 교대하다
(B) 바꾸다
(C) 가져오다
(D) 고려하다

4. 첫 번째 이메일에 따르면, 참가자들은 언제 제안서 작성에 대해서 배울 것인가?
(A) 오전 7:30 – 오전 8:30
(B) 오전 8:30 – 오전 10:30
(C) 오후 1:30 – 오후 3:30
(D) 오후 4:00 – 오후 6:00

5. 매카시 씨에 대해 제시된 것은 무엇인가?
(A) 7월 10일에 모임에 참석하지 못했다.
(B) 워크숍 참석을 고민하고 있다.
(C) 워크숍 중 한 개를 이끌 것이다.
(D) 쿠퍼 씨에게 전화할 것이다.

Chapter Test
1. (D) 2. (C) 3. (B) 4. (A) 5. (B)
6. (C) 7. (D) 8. (D) 9. (C) 10. (C)

문제 1-5는 이메일과 설문지를 참조하시오.

발신: 로널드 스티븐스 <ronstevens@elitehuntinghotels.com>
수신: 댄 이노산토 <dinosanto@flipmail.com>
날짜: 1월 3일
제목: 엘리트 헌팅 호텔 투숙

확인 번호: 20700650050532
3 VIP 회원 번호: 100382MWL

이노산토 씨께,

1 엘리트 헌팅 호텔을 선택해 주셔서 감사합니다! 호텔 예약에 관한 세부 사항들은 아래에 명시되어 있습니다. 예약을 변경해야 할 경우 reservations@elitehuntinghotels.com으로 이메일을 보내 주시길 바랍니다. 보증금을 환불받기 위해서는 최소 일주일 전에 취소를 해 주셔야 합니다.

호텔 위치: 우편번호 89014, 뉴욕 주 피닉스 시, 후버 가 2005번지
객실: 12층, 더블 베드 2개
2 체크인: 1월 17일 토요일 오후 3시 이후
체크아웃: 1월 19일 월요일 오전 11시까지
객실의 인원 수: 2
객실 요금 회원가: 1박당 199달러

티켓 주문, 관광 예약, 교통편 같은 서비스를 위해서는 services@elitehuntinghotels.com으로 프런트데스크에 연락해 주십시오.

호텔에 머무르시는 동안 즐거우셨기를 바랍니다!
앞으로 고객님께 더 나은 서비스를 제공하기 위하여,
잠시 설문지를 작성해 주시면 감사하겠습니다.

1. 엘리트 헌팅 호텔을 어떻게 알게 되었나요?
TV _____ 잡지 ✓ 여행사 _____ 인터넷 _____ 기타 _____

2. 여행의 목적은 무엇인가요? 휴가

4 3. 코지 스카이에서 식사를 해보셨나요? 그러시다면 음식은 어떠셨나요?
우수함 _____ 좋음 _____ 보통 ✓ 불만족 _____

5 4. 객실 서비스의 질은 어떠셨나요?
우수함 ✓ 좋음 _____ 보통 _____ 불만족 _____

5. 이름과 이메일 주소 (선택) 댄 이노산토 dinosanto@flipmail.com

귀하께서 VIP 회원이 아니라면 오늘 가입하세요!
3 모든 VIP 회원들은 객실 예약 시에 15% 할인을 받으실 수 있으며, VIP 회원에게만 드리는 혜택을 받으실 수 있습니다. 더 많은 정보는, 818-9909-1255로 전화를 주시거나 저희 웹사이트 www.elitehuntinghotels.com을 방문해 주세요.

1. 이메일의 목적은 무엇인가?
(A) 여행 보상 프로그램을 홍보하는 것
(B) 호텔 투숙객에게 더 큰 객실을 제공하는 것
(C) 설문지 참여를 요구하는 것
(D) 숙박 예약을 확인하는 것

2. 이노산토 씨는 언제 엘리트 헌팅 호텔에 도착했을 것 같은가?
(A) 1월 3일
(B) 1월 10일
(C) 1월 17일
(D) 1월 19일

3. 이노산토 씨에 대해 언급된 것은 무엇인가?
(A) 영화 티켓을 주문했다.
(B) 할인된 숙박료를 지불했다.
(C) 여행사 서비스를 이용했다.
(D) 출발일을 변경했다.

4. 엘리트 헌팅 호텔에 대해 언급된 것은 무엇인가?
(A) 식당이 있다.
(B) 1월에 개장했다.
(C) 고객들이 주로 출장객이다.
(D) 라디오에서 광고한다.

5. 설문지에서 이노산토 씨에 대해 알 수 있는 것은 무엇인가?
(A) 그는 안내원으로부터 유용한 정보를 얻었다.
(B) 그는 객실의 청결도에 매우 만족했다.
(C) 무료 인터넷 서비스에 대해 감사해했다.
(D) 그는 뉴욕에 자주 오는 방문객이다.

문제 6-10는 다음 소책자, 이메일과 정보를 참조하세요.

페퍼시티 가든

6 페퍼시티 가든은 전 세계 방문객들에게 20년 이상 가장 인기 있는 명소 중의 하나입니다. 그리고 올해에는 이 근사한 곳을 사랑할 수밖에 없는 이유가 더 있습니다! 이번 여름에, 페퍼시티 가든에서는 나무 심기 축제, 수목원 견학과 도슨 숲을 둘러보는 가이드 투어와 같은 새로운 이벤트가 제공될 예정입니다. 9 토요일 저녁에는 콘서트가 개최될 예정입니다. 작년과 동일하게, 장미 투어에서는 가장 이국적인 장미들을 보시게 될 것입니다. 7월부터, 저희는 실내 정원 가꾸기에 관심이 있는 사람들을 위한 수업을 열 것입니다. 저희의 경험이 풍부한 강사들이 꽃과 먹을 수 있는 채소를 어떻게 재배하는지 여러분께 보여 드릴 것입니다.

절기별 개장 시간 (6월 21일 - 10월 8일)
월요일 - 화요일: 오전 8시 - 저녁 7시
수요일 - 금요일: 오전 8시 - 저녁 10시
9 토요일: 오전 8시 - 저녁 8시
일요일: 오전 8시 - 저녁 6시

7 토요일 콘서트는 예약이 필요합니다.
저희 웹사이트 www.peppercitygardens.com을 방문해 주세요.

수신: 이사벨 다코타
발신: 에드윈 위건
날짜: 7월 22일
제목: 페퍼시티 가든 여행

9 지난 토요일 가족과 함께 페퍼시티 가든에서 너무나 즐거운 시간을 보냈습니다. 추가 요금 없이, 저희 가족은 정원에서 완벽한 하루를 보냈습니다. 저에게 안내 책자를 보여 주셔서 너무 감사드립니다.

날씨는 환상적이었답니다. 10 제가 장미 투어를 하고 있는 동안에, 줄리아와 아이들은 나무 심기 축제에 참가했습니다. 꽃들은 아름다웠으며, 8 저희의 가이드는 아주 해박한 사람이었습니다. 의심의 여지없이, 그것이 그날 제가 가장 좋았던 부분이었습니다. 당신의 추천은 분명히 따를 만한 가치가 있었습니다. 제가 사는 근처에 이렇게 멋진 곳이 있었다는 것을 생각도 못했습니다. 9/10 밤에는 재즈 콘서트가 열리기 때문에, 저희는 가든이 문을 닫을 때까지 머물러 있었습니다. 이번 여행에 당신과 함께 하지 못한 점이 아쉽습니다. 다음에, 우리와 꼭 함께 가도록 해요.

페퍼시티 가든을 소개해 주셔서 다시 한 번 감사드립니다.

진심으로,
에드윈 위건

페퍼시티 가든
가족 입장권 가격

티켓 종류		스탠다드	실버	10 골드	프리미엄
입장료		O	O	O	O
활동	나무 심기	X	O	O	X
	장미 정원 (가이드 투어)	X	X	O	O
	견학	X	X	X	O
	가정 원예 수업	X	X	X	O
	음악 콘서트	O	O	O	O

6. 소책자의 목적은 무엇인가?
(A) 학회 일정을 업데이트하는 것
(B) 자선 단체에 기부를 요청하는 것
(C) 관광 명소에 대한 정보를 제공하는 것
(D) 꽃집을 홍보하는 것

7. 저녁 콘서트에 관하여 언급된 내용은 무엇인가?
(A) 티켓이 할인된 가격에 제공된다.
(B) 나무 심기 축제와 동시에 시작된다.
(C) 일주일 내내 열린다.
(D) 온라인으로 예약을 할 수 있다.

8. 이메일에 따르면, 위건 씨는 페퍼시티 가든에서 무엇을 하였는가?
(A) 기업이 후원하는 행사에 갔다.
(B) 수업에 참석했다.
(C) 숲 속을 산책했다.
(D) 가이드 투어를 했다.

9. 위건 씨는 언제 페퍼시티 가든을 떠났는가?
(A) 저녁 6시에
(B) 저녁 7시에
(C) 저녁 8시에
(D) 저녁 10시에

10. 에드윈 위건 씨는 어떤 입장권을 구매했을 것 같은가?
(A) 스탠다드
(B) 실버
(C) 골드
(D) 프리미엄

ACTUAL TEST

PART 1
1. (D) 2. (C) 3. (C) 4. (D) 5. (C) 6. (B)

PART 2
7. (A) 8. (B) 9. (B) 10. (A) 11. (B) 12. (C)
13. (B) 14. (C) 15. (B) 16. (B) 17. (A) 18. (C)
19. (B) 20. (A) 21. (C) 22. (A) 23. (B) 24. (A)
25. (C) 26. (B) 27. (C) 28. (C) 29. (B) 30. (B)
31. (C)

PART 3
32. (A) 33. (D) 34. (D) 35. (C) 36. (A) 37. (C)
38. (A) 39. (D) 40. (B) 41. (A) 42. (B) 43. (A)
44. (A) 45. (C) 46. (B) 47. (A) 48. (C) 49. (B)
50. (A) 51. (B) 52. (D) 53. (D) 54. (B) 55. (C)
56. (A) 57. (D) 58. (B) 59. (A) 60. (B) 61. (D)
62. (B) 63. (A) 64. (C) 65. (B) 66. (C) 67. (B)
68. (C) 69. (C) 70. (B)

PART 4
71. (B) 72. (C) 73. (B) 74. (D) 75. (C) 76. (D)
77. (B) 78. (A) 79. (C) 80. (B) 81. (A) 82. (C)
83. (C) 84. (D) 85. (B) 86. (C) 87. (B) 88. (C)
89. (B) 90. (C) 91. (A) 92. (D) 93. (D) 94. (B)
95. (C) 96. (C) 97. (B) 98. (B) 99. (B) 100. (B)

PART 5
101. (B) 102. (C) 103. (C) 104. (A) 105. (C)
106. (D) 107. (B) 108. (D) 109. (B) 110. (A)
111. (D) 112. (A) 113. (D) 114. (C) 115. (C)
116. (D) 117. (C) 118. (C) 119. (B) 120. (D)
121. (B) 122. (C) 123. (D) 124. (B) 125. (A)
126. (B) 127. (D) 128. (B) 129. (A) 130. (B)

PART 6
131. (D) 132. (C) 133. (B) 134. (D) 135. (D)
136. (D) 137. (B) 138. (A) 139. (A) 140. (D)
141. (C) 142. (B) 143. (C) 144. (D) 145. (B)
146. (A)

PART 7
147. (B) 148. (C) 149. (D) 150. (A) 151. (A)
152. (D) 153. (C) 154. (B) 155. (A) 156. (C)
157. (C) 158. (C) 159. (D) 160. (B) 161. (B)
162. (D) 163. (C) 164. (D) 165. (C) 166. (A)
167. (B) 168. (C) 169. (B) 170. (C) 171. (B)
172. (A) 173. (C) 174. (A) 175. (A) 176. (B)
177. (C) 178. (D) 179. (D) 180. (D) 181. (D)
182. (B) 183. (B) 184. (C) 185. (B) 186. (B)
187. (C) 188. (A) 189. (D) 190. (B) 191. (B)
192. (D) 193. (C) 194. (B) 195. (A) 196. (C)
197. (D) 198. (A) 199. (B) 200. (D)

PART 1

1.
(A) A man is opening a door.
(B) A man is putting on a hat.
(C) A man is talking to a neighbor.
(D) A man is watering plants.
(A) 남자가 문을 열고 있다.
(B) 남자가 모자를 착용하는 중이다.
(C) 남자가 이웃과 이야기하고 있다.
(D) 남자가 화초에 물을 주고 있다.

2.
(A) A woman is adjusting a scarf.
(B) A woman is cleaning a store.
(C) A woman is reaching for an item.
(D) Boxes are being stacked on a cart.
(A) 여자가 스카프를 고쳐 매고 있다.
(B) 여자가 가게를 청소하고 있다.
(C) 여자가 물건에 손을 뻗고 있다.
(D) 박스들을 카트에 쌓고 있다.

3.
(A) Some people are packing their instruments.
(B) Some people are performing outdoors.
(C) A person is using a camera.
(D) A man is pulling a curtain.
(A) 사람들이 악기를 싸고 있다.
(B) 사람들이 야외에서 공연을 하고 있다.
(C) 한 사람이 카메라를 사용하고 있다.
(D) 한 남자가 커튼을 치고 있다.

4.
(A) One of the men is glancing at his wrist watch.
(B) A monitor is being turned on.
(C) A man is using a tool to examine a patient.
(D) They're seated across from each other.
(A) 남자들 중 한 명이 손목시계를 힐끗 보고 있다.
(B) 모니터가 켜지고 있는 중이다.
(C) 남자가 환자를 진찰하기 위해 도구를 이용하고 있다.
(D) 사람들이 마주보고 앉아 있다.

5.
(A) Some documents are being put away.
(B) Coffee is being poured into a cup.
(C) A laptop has been placed on the desk.
(D) Some people are standing behind a desk.

(A) 서류들이 치워지고 있다.
(B) 커피가 컵에 부어지고 있다.
(C) 노트북이 책상에 놓여 있다.
(D) 사람들이 책상 뒤에 서 있다.

6.
(A) A cushion is positioned on the table.
(B) A light fixture is suspended on the ceiling.
(C) A tile floor is being polished.
(D) Some pictures are displayed on the rack.

(A) 쿠션이 테이블 위에 놓여 있다.
(B) 조명이 천장에 매달려 있다.
(C) 타일 바닥을 닦고 있다.
(D) 그림들이 선반에 전시되어 있다.

PART 2

7. Who is going to give the speech?
(A) Ms. Suzuki.
(B) In March.
(C) At the museum.

누가 그 연설을 할 예정인가요?
(A) 스즈키 씨요.
(B) 3월에요.
(C) 박물관에서요.

8. When is the meeting room closed?
(A) I can't open it.
(B) At 6 o'clock.
(C) It's close to my office.

회의실은 언제 문을 닫나요?
(A) 저는 그것을 열 수 없어요.
(B) 6시에요.
(C) 그곳은 제 사무실과 가까워요.

9. Where can I find Mr. Lester's room?
(A) Sure, no problem.
(B) Down the hall.
(C) Tomorrow, I believe.

레스터 씨의 방을 어디에서 찾을 수 있을까요?
(A) 물론이죠, 문제없어요.
(B) 복도를 따라가면 있어요.
(C) 내일이라고 생각해요.

10. Would you like me to refill your drink?
(A) No, thank you.
(B) I filled out the form.
(C) John referred you.

음료를 다시 채워드릴까요?
(A) 아니요, 감사합니다.
(B) 저는 그 서식을 작성했어요.
(C) 존이 당신에게 알아보라고 했어요.

11. Why did you call the technician?
(A) Mr. Adams will.
(B) Because the printer is broken.
(C) At 10:30.

왜 기술자에게 전화했나요?
(A) 애덤스 씨가 할 거예요.
(B) 왜냐하면 프린터가 고장 났거든요.
(C) 10시 30분에요.

12. Weren't you there on Tuesday?
(A) It's on Thursday.
(B) They're not here.
(C) No, I was out.

화요일에 거기 있지 않았나요?
(A) 그것은 목요일이에요.
(B) 그들은 여기에 없어요.
(C) 아니요, 저는 나가 있었어요.

13. Mr. Kingston is going to visit today.
(A) About this time yesterday.
(B) Isn't he on a trip?
(C) Yes, I've been there.

킹스턴 씨는 오늘 방문할 예정입니다.
(A) 어제 이 시간 무렵에요.
(B) 그는 여행 중이지 않나요?
(C) 네, 저는 거기 가봤어요.

14. Where did you buy those pants?
(A) I have some pens in the bag.
(B) I'll do it by Friday.
(C) I bought them at a mall.

그 바지 어디에서 샀어요?
(A) 저는 가방에 펜이 몇 자루 있어요.
(B) 금요일까지 하겠습니다.
(C) 쇼핑몰에서 샀어요.

15. How can I get to the nearest bus stop?
(A) It usually stops here.
(B) Turn right on Lawrence Road.
(C) Maybe close to September.

가장 가까운 버스 정류장에 어떻게 가죠?
(A) 그것은 보통 여기 서요.
(B) 로렌스 로에서 우측으로 도세요.
(C) 아마 9월쯤에요.

16. Why were you late for work?
(A) No, it's later today.
(B) I couldn't find my keys.

(C) It was working fine.
회사에 왜 지각했나요?
(A) 아니요, 오늘 이따가요.
(B) 제 열쇠를 찾을 수가 없었어요.
(C) 그것은 잘 작동하고 있었어요.

17. What are you going to bring to the Christmas party?
(A) I won't be attending.
(B) Yes, it was a great party.
(C) I ate a lot already.
크리스마스 파티에 무엇을 가지고 올 예정인가요?
(A) 저는 참석하지 않을 거예요.
(B) 네, 그것은 굉장한 파티였어요.
(C) 저는 이미 많이 먹었어요.

18. Should we begin the presentation or wait a little longer?
(A) I brought two presents.
(B) It was not that long.
(C) We have a lot to do, so let's start.
프레젠테이션을 시작할까요, 아니면 좀 더 기다릴까요?
(A) 저는 선물을 두 개 가져왔어요.
(B) 그렇게 길지 않았어요.
(C) 우린 해야 할 일이 많아요, 그러니 시작합시다.

19. When is the commercial scheduled to air?
(A) The flight has been cancelled.
(B) It will start in June.
(C) There will be special guests.
그 광고는 언제 방송될 예정이죠?
(A) 그 항공편은 취소되었습니다.
(B) 6월에 시작될 거예요.
(C) 특별 손님들이 올 예정입니다.

20. Who is the vice president of this firm?
(A) You will meet him this morning.
(B) Brian is going to call.
(C) I have confirmed the date.
이 회사의 부사장은 누구인가요?
(A) 오늘 아침에 그분을 만나게 될 거예요.
(B) 브라이언 씨가 전화할 거예요.
(C) 제가 그 날짜를 확인했어요.

21. Why don't we take a subway to the gallery?
(A) You can have some.
(B) It's not this way.
(C) It might be faster.
미술관까지 지하철을 타고 가는 게 어때요?
(A) 당신이 몇 개 가져도 돼요.
(B) 그것은 이쪽이 아니에요.
(C) 그게 아마 더 빠르겠네요.

22. What's the bi-weekly magazine called?
(A) I read it on the weekend.
(B) She called Mary several times.
(C) The title is on the front page.
그 격주로 발행되는 잡지 이름이 뭐죠?
(A) 저는 그것을 주말에 읽었어요.
(B) 그녀는 메리에게 수차례 전화했어요.
(C) 앞 페이지에 제목이 있어요.

23. Don't you want to attend the annual banquet?
(A) No, there is not a bank here.
(B) I'm looking forward to it.
(C) Yes, it was very good.
연례 연회에 참석하실 생각 없으신가요?
(A) 아니요, 여기에는 은행이 없어요.
(B) 저는 그것을 고대하고 있어요.
(C) 네, 그것은 매우 좋았어요.

24. I really enjoyed the seminar.
(A) I'm sorry I missed it.
(B) The speaker is going to be Dr. Horton.
(C) It's the semi-final.
그 세미나는 정말 즐거웠어요.
(A) 유감이지만 전 못 갔어요.
(B) 연설자는 호튼 박사가 될 거예요.
(C) 그것은 준결승전이에요.

25. Can you come to work an hour early on Friday?
(A) I usually walk to the office.
(B) They are closed.
(C) I should be able to do that.
금요일에 한 시간 일찍 출근할 수 있나요?
(A) 저는 보통 사무실에 걸어서 가요.
(B) 그들은 문을 닫았어요.
(C) 그렇게 할 수 있을 것 같아요.

26. Isn't your laptop computer broken?
(A) I will put it in the bottom drawer.
(B) Yes, but it's finally working again.
(C) I'm going to the lab.
당신의 노트북 컴퓨터 고장 나지 않았나요?
(A) 제일 아래 서랍에 넣어 둘게요.
(B) 네, 하지만 마침내 다시 작동하고 있어요.
(C) 저는 실험실에 갈 거예요.

27. Mr. Hamilton's letter hasn't arrived yet, has it?
(A) No, he hasn't.
(B) It's filed at the reception desk.
(C) Do you want some?
해밀턴 씨의 편지는 아직 도착하지 않았죠, 그렇죠?
(A) 아니요, 그는 하지 않았어요.
(B) 그것은 프런트 데스크에 보관되어 있어요.
(C) 좀 드릴까요?

28. Are you new here or have you lived here for a while?
(A) I'm going to leave soon.
(B) I can wait a little longer.
(C) I moved here two years ago.

여기 새로 오셨나요, 아니면 한동안 거주하셨나요?
(A) 저는 곧 떠날 거예요.
(B) 저는 좀 더 기다릴 수 있어요.
(C) 저는 2년 전에 이곳으로 이사를 왔어요.

29. Could I get a copy of the bus schedule?
(A) The bus to New York.
(B) They're available at the ticket counter.
(C) Your coffee is ready.

버스 시간표를 한 장 얻을 수 있을까요?
(A) 뉴욕행 버스요.
(B) 매표창구에서 받으실 수 있습니다.
(C) 당신 커피가 준비됐어요.

30. How did you avoid the traffic jam on Glen Avenue this afternoon?
(A) He is a great trainer.
(B) I took a different route.
(C) That's terrific news.

오늘 오후에 글렌 가의 교통 체증을 어떻게 피하셨나요?
(A) 그는 유능한 트레이너입니다.
(B) 저는 다른 길을 이용했어요.
(C) 그것 참 좋은 소식이네요.

31. Did you post the notice about the new project for next week?
(A) The game was postponed.
(B) To purchase a new projector.
(C) I thought Nancy was going to do it.

다음 주에 하는 새 프로젝트에 대한 공지를 게시하셨나요?
(A) 그 경기는 연기되었어요.
(B) 새 프로젝터를 구입하기 위해서요.
(C) 저는 낸시 씨가 할 거라고 생각했어요.

PART 3

Questions 32-34 refer to the following conversation.

W: **32** Have you heard about the packaging Ms. Parker wanted for the new perfume samples?

M: No, I haven't heard about that yet.

W: She decided that the samples should be boxed individually.

M: How many boxes do we have to order and when do we need them by?

W: Well, **33** the cosmetics will be officially launched on August 1st, so all the samples will have to be ready by then.

M: OK, **34** I'll call our supplier and ask them to send us boxes for the sample bottles.

여: 파커 씨가 원한 새로운 향수 샘플의 **32** 포장에 대해 들었나요?
남: 아니요, 저는 아직 그것에 대해 들은 바가 없어요.
여: 그녀는 샘플들을 따로따로 상자에 넣기로 했어요.
남: 상자를 몇 개나 주문해야 하고 언제까지 필요할까요?
여: 글쎄요, **33** 그 화장품들은 공식적으로 8월 1일에 출시될 거라서 그때까지 샘플들을 모두 준비해야 할 거예요.
남: 알겠어요. **34** 제가 공급사에 연락해서 샘플 병들을 넣을 상자들을 보내 달라고 요청할게요.

32. 화자들은 무엇에 관해 상의하고 있는가?
(A) 샘플 포장
(B) 해외여행 일정
(C) 신제품 가격
(D) 지역 신문 광고

33. 8월에 어떤 일이 일어나는가?
(A) 제품 이름이 선택될 것이다.
(B) 일련의 회의들이 열릴 것이다.
(C) 마케팅 부장이 은퇴할 것이다.
(D) 제품이 공식적으로 출시될 것이다.

34. 남자는 무엇을 할 것인가?
(A) 예산 세우기
(B) 회의 일정 변경하기
(C) 디자인 승인하기
(D) 주문하기

Questions 35-37 refer to the following conversation.

M: Julian, **35** it looks like we are getting close to the art gallery. We probably should start looking for a place to park.

W: **35** I'm really looking forward to the art exhibit. I've wanted to see it ever since **36** I read about it in the *Daily News* last week.

M: Well, I guess the publicity from that newspaper article has paid off. It looks like there is a big crowd. Actually, I don't see any available parking space on this street at all.

W: **37** I think there is a car park around the corner. Why don't we try parking there? It would just be a short walk to the gallery from there.

남: 줄리안 씨, **35** 미술관에 가까이 온 것 같아요. 슬슬 주차할 공간을 찾아야 할 거예요.

여: 35 전 이 미술 전시회를 정말로 기다렸어요. 지난주에 36 <데일리 뉴스>에서 그것에 대해 읽었을 때부터 보고 싶었어요.

남: 그 신문 기사의 홍보가 성공한 것 같아요. 사람들이 엄청나게 온 것 같네요. 이 거리에는 주차할 데가 정말 한 군데도 보이지 않네요.

여: 37 모퉁이 근처에 주차장이 있는 것 같아요. 그쪽에 주차하는 게 어때요? 거기서 미술관까지 잠깐 걸으면 돼요.

35. 화자들은 어느 행사에 참가할 계획인가?
(A) 음악 연주회
(B) 회사 야유회
(C) 미술 전시회
(D) 출판 세미나

36. 여자는 그 행사에 대해 어떻게 알게 되었는가?
(A) 그녀는 신문 기사를 읽었다.
(B) 그녀의 친구가 그 행사에 관해 이야기했다.
(C) 그녀는 TV 광고를 보았다.
(D) 그녀는 직장에서 안내 책자를 얻었다.

37. 여자는 무엇을 제안하는가?
(A) 도움 요청하기
(B) 지도 참고하기
(C) 주차장에 주차하기
(D) 미술관 근처를 걷기

Questions 38-40 refer to the following conversation.

W: Hello, this is Linda Wilson 39 in the editorial department. 38 I'm calling because I haven't received my check for the last pay period.

M: 39 Linda Wilson in the editorial department? Let me see. We sent the paycheck by mail last Friday to your home address. You should've received it by now.

W: But it hasn't arrived yet. What should I do? I've already been waiting a week.

M: Well, when there is a delay like this, 40 we can stop payments on the original check and issue a new one. You could pick it up in the payroll department later today.

여: 안녕하세요, 저는 39 편집부의 린다 윌슨입니다. 38 지난 급여 지급 기간에 수표를 받지 못해서 전화드렸습니다.

남: 39 편집부의 린다 윌슨이요? 한번 봅시다. 지난 금요일에 집 주소로 급여 지급 수표를 보냈습니다. 지금쯤 받으셨어야 하는데요.

여: 그러나 아직 도착하지 않았습니다. 제가 어떻게 해야 하죠? 이미 일주일째 기다리고 있는 거예요.

남: 음, 이렇게 지연될 경우에는 40 우리는 원래 수표에 대한 지급을 정지시키고 새 수표를 발행해 드릴 수 있어요. 오늘 중으로 급여 지급부로 오셔서 수표를 찾아가세요.

38. 여자는 무엇에 대하여 전화하고 있는가?
(A) 분실된 급여 지급용 수표
(B) 표
(C) 주문품의 배달
(D) 신문 기사

39. 여자는 어떤 부서에서 근무하는가?
(A) 인사부
(B) 회계부
(C) 고객 서비스부
(D) 편집부

40. 남자는 무엇을 하겠다고 하는가?
(A) 호텔의 퇴실 수속
(B) 다른 수표 발행
(C) 우체국으로 가기
(D) 예약

Questions 41-43 refer to the following conversation.

M: Good evening, I would like a table for three. 41 Are you still serving dinner?

W: I'm sorry we are closing in a few minutes. We close at ten. 42 Why don't you try the restaurant across the street? It's open until eleven.

M: Well, it looks like they have quite a crowd over there. I might do that. Do you close at ten every day? What are your weekend hours like?

W: We have the same hours on the weekend. 43 We are open from 9 A.M. to 10 P.M. every day.

M: Thanks, I'll come back later this weekend.

남: 안녕하세요. 세 사람이 앉을 테이블을 원합니다. 41 아직 저녁 식사가 가능한가요?

여: 죄송하지만 몇 분 후에 문을 닫을 거예요. 저희는 10시에 문을 닫습니다. 42 길 건너에 있는 식당에 가 보시는 게 어떨까요? 그곳은 11시까지 영업합니다.

남: 음, 그곳엔 사람이 꽤 많이 있는 것 같네요. 그렇게 해야겠어요. 매일 10시에 문을 닫나요? 주말 영업시간은 어때요?

여: 주말에도 영업시간은 동일해요. 43 매일 오전 9시부터 저녁 10시까지 영업합니다.

남: 감사합니다. 이번 주말에 다시 올게요.

41. 대화는 어디에서 이루어지고 있는가?
(A) 식당에서
(B) 가구점에서
(C) 박물관에서
(D) 보석 상점에서

42. 여자는 무엇을 제안하는가?
(A) 휴식을 취하는 것
(B) 다른 식당으로 가는 것

(C) 오늘 늦게 다시 오는 것
(D) 우선 예약을 하는 것

43. 여자가 본인의 식당에 대해 말하는 것은 무엇인가?
(A) 매일 9시에 문을 연다.
(B) 11시 정각에 문을 닫는다.
(C) 단골손님이 많다.
(D) 저녁 특선 요리가 있다.

Questions 44-46 refer to the following conversation.

M: Do you know **44 Julie, the new hire?** Well, she submitted her sales report yesterday.
W: How was it? Is it good?
M: I just finished analyzing it. It looks good.
W: **45** I think Julie should do a presentation for our department about her report.
M: She's never done that before. Uh… **45 I could present the report.**
W: No, it will be a good chance for a new employee to learn more. **46 I'll organize a meeting** with the Sales Department next week.

남: **44** 신입 사원인 줄리 아세요? 음, 그녀가 어제 매출 보고서를 제출했어요.
여: 어땠어요? 괜찮나요?
남: 제가 방금 그것의 분석을 끝냈어요. 괜찮아 보이네요.
여: **45** 저는 줄리가 우리 부서를 대표하여 그녀의 보고서에 대해서 발표해야 한다고 생각해요.
남: 그녀는 전에 그걸 해본 적이 없어요. 음… **45** 제가 그 보고서를 설명할 수 있을 거예요.
여: 아니에요. 그건 신입 사원이 더 많이 배울 수 있는 좋은 기회가 될 거예요. 제가 다음 주에 영업부와의 **46** 회의를 준비할게요.

44. 줄리는 누구일 것 같은가?
(A) 신입 사원
(B) 기자
(C) 고객
(D) 접수원

45. 남자는 왜 "그녀는 전에 그걸 해본 적이 없어요"라고 말하는가?
(A) 오해를 바로잡기 위해
(B) 칭찬하기 위해
(C) 걱정을 표하기 위해
(D) 도움을 더 요청하기 위해

46. 여자는 무엇을 할 것이라고 말하는가?
(A) 보고서 수정
(B) 회의 일정 잡기
(C) 인터뷰 진행
(D) 홍보 준비

Questions 47-49 refer to the following conversation with three speakers.

W1: **47** Jamie, do you know if those color printers have arrived yet? I think you ordered them a month ago. Have you received anything from the distributor?
W2: Yes, I just got an e-mail this morning saying that the printers are on their way.
M: Hmm, they should be here by Wednesday. I heard that **48** the model we ordered is selling so fast that the manufacturer couldn't keep up with demand.
W1: I'm not surprised to hear that. I know it has received a lot of good reviews and the price is reasonable.
W2: Actually, there is usually a $10 shipping fee, but **49** the distributor said they won't charge us for shipping because of the delay.

여: **47** 제이미 씨, 그 컬러 프린터들이 도착했는지 아시나요? 한 달 전에 당신이 주문한 것 같은데요. 배급업자에게서 연락받은 것 있나요?
여2: 네, 오늘 아침에 그 프린터들이 배송 중이라는 이메일을 받았어요.
남: 흠, 수요일까지 여기에 도착해야 해요. **48** 우리가 주문한 그 모델이 아주 잘 팔려서 제조사가 수요를 맞추지 못했다고 들었어요.
여1: 놀랄 일도 아니네요. 그 프린터는 평이 아주 좋고 가격도 합리적이에요.
여2: 사실, 보통 10달러의 배송 요금이 있지만 지연됐기 때문에 **49** 배급업자들이 배송비를 청구하지 않겠다고 했어요.

47. 제이미는 최근에 무엇을 했는가?
(A) 사무기기를 주문했다.
(B) 콘퍼런스에 참가했다.
(C) 제품 디자인을 개발했다.
(D) 노트북 컴퓨터를 구입했다.

48. 남자는 제품에 대해 무엇이라고 말하는가?
(A) 최근에 다시 디자인되었다.
(B) 더 이상 구할 수 없다.
(C) 판매가 매우 잘되고 있다.
(D) 제조 비용이 상승하였다.

49. 공급업체가 제안한 것은 무엇인가?
(A) 업그레이드된 모델
(B) 무료 배송
(C) 보증 기간 연장
(D) 차후 주문 건에 대한 할인

Questions 50-52 refer to the following conversation.

W: George, **50** I need to talk to you about the exhibition for new local artists. **51** Maybe after your interview?

M: My interview was canceled.

W: OK. So, I just looked over your plans.

M: What did you think of them?

W: I liked the plans overall. But I'm concerned that we do not have enough in our budget. **52** You'll need to go and talk to the manager about this and see what we can do.

여: 조지, **50** 저는 새로운 지역 예술가들을 위한 전시회에 관해서 당신과 얘기를 해야 해요. **51** 아마도 인터뷰 이후에 괜찮죠?

남: 인터뷰는 취소됐어요.

여: 알겠습니다. 그럼 제가 방금 당신의 계획안을 살펴봤는데요.

남: 어떻게 생각하세요?

여: 전반적으로 그 계획안은 좋습니다. 그렇지만 우리가 충분한 예산이 없는 게 걱정되네요. 이것에 대해서 **52** 상사에게 가서 이야기하고 우리가 무엇을 할 수 있는지 알아봐야 합니다.

50. 화자들은 어느 업체에서 일할 것 같은가?

(A) 미술관
(B) 건축 사무실
(C) 여행사
(D) 의류 회사

51. 남자는 왜 "인터뷰는 취소됐어요"라고 말하는가?

(A) 초대를 거절하기 위해
(B) 그가 시간이 있다는 것을 알려 주기 위해
(C) 일정 변경에 대해 걱정을 표현하기 위해
(D) 예상치 않은 문제를 논의하기 위해

52. 여자는 남자에게 무엇을 하라고 말하는가?

(A) 지역 예술가에게 연락
(B) 상품권 배부
(C) 모금 행사 준비
(D) 상사와의 회의

Questions 53-55 refer to the following conversation with three speakers.

M1: Hi, Vera, **53** how are your preparations coming for the new employee training next week? I know this is your first time running the session, so I thought you might have some questions.

W: Oh, thanks for checking. In fact, I am just wondering if we have any more copies of **54** the handbook with our safety guidelines. I want to make sure everyone gets a written copy.

M1: We have plenty of those handbooks. Richard can help you with that. **54** Richard, could you bring some handbooks to Vera?

M2: **54** Sure, I'll go get some for you, Vera.

M1: Is there anything else you'd like help with?

W: Well, if you have time, **55** would you all be willing to attend part of the session to give me some feedback? I'd really appreciate any suggestions to improve my future presentations.

남1: 안녕하세요. 베라 씨, **53** 다음 주에 있을 신입 사원 교육 준비는 잘 되어 가나요? 당신은 이번에 처음 교육을 진행하는 것이니까 궁금한 것이 있을 것 같은데요.

여: 아, 확인해 줘서 고마워요. 사실 **54** 우리의 안전 수칙이 포함된 안내서가 더 있는지 알고 싶어요. 저는 모두가 책자를 받게 하고 싶어요.

남1: 안내서는 많아요. 리처드 씨가 그 부분은 도와줄 수 있어요. **54** 리처드 씨, 안내서를 베라 씨에게 가져다줄 수 있나요?

남2: **54** 물론이죠, 제가 몇 개 가져올게요. 베라 씨.

남1: 도움을 받고 싶은 다른 부분은 없으세요?

여: 음, 시간 있으시면 **55** 모두 교육에 일부 참석하셔서 피드백을 좀 주실 수 있으세요? 이후의 제 발표를 향상시킬 어떠한 의견이라도 감사히 받을게요.

53. 여자는 무엇을 준비하고 있는가?

(A) 출장을 계획하는 것
(B) 연회에 참가하는 것
(C) 인터뷰를 하는 것
(D) 교육을 진행하는 것

54. 리처드는 여자에게 무엇을 가져다줄 것인가?

(A) 보호 장비
(B) 안전 지침서
(C) 프로젝터
(D) 사무용품

55. 여자는 남자들에게 무엇을 하라고 말하는가?

(A) 제안을 하는 것
(B) 주문을 하는 것
(C) 피드백을 주는 것
(D) 조사를 수행하는 것

Questions 56-58 refer to the following conversation.

M: Hi, Joanna. **56/57** I'm calling about refreshments for the International Fashion Industry Seminar on Friday next week. You asked me to check with you by the end of this week to confirm the order.

W: Yes. As we discussed last time, we'll have 20 participants on Friday and we will be needing coffee, tea, juice, and muffins in the morning. And sandwiches and soft drinks for lunch.

M: Right, I'll go ahead then and get the order ready. That will be 950 dollars total for both breakfast and lunch.

W: Oh, I forgot. 58 Could you add some fruits to the breakfast?

남: 안녕하세요, 조애나 씨. 56/57 다음 주 금요일에 국제 패션 산업 세미나에서 쓸 다과 관련해서 전화드립니다. 주문 확인을 위해 이번 주말까지 당신에게 확인하라고 하셔서요.

여: 네. 지난번에 우리가 얘기했듯이 금요일에 20명이 참석할 것이고 아침에 커피와 차, 주스, 머핀이 필요합니다. 그리고 점심으로 샌드위치와 청량음료가 필요하고요.

남: 알겠습니다. 그럼 주문하신 대로 준비되도록 진행하겠습니다. 아침과 점심 둘 다 해서 총 950달러가 될 겁니다.

여: 아, 깜빡했네요. 58 아침에 과일을 추가해 주시겠어요?

---

56. 남자는 누구일 것 같은가?
(A) 출장 요리업자
(B) 회계사
(C) 은행원
(D) 해외 영업 담당자

57. 세미나는 언제 열릴 것인가?
(A) 이번 주 월요일
(B) 다음 주 월요일
(C) 이번 주 목요일
(D) 다음 주 금요일

58. 조애나는 어떤 변경을 요청하는가?
(A) 회의실
(B) 추가 음식
(C) 회의 안건
(D) 초청 연사

Questions 59-61 refer to the following conversation.

M: You will have to make some changes to the front page of tomorrow's morning edition. 59 I just confirmed that James Miller, president of JK Group, is retiring. He's planning to announce it at the JK headquarters on Main Street this afternoon.

W: Oh, this will be big news. Mr. Miller has been dedicated to the community as well as his company. 60 The charitable program he led had a big impact on our society.

M: That's why I'd like you to be at the JK headquarters. I've already asked our photographer to be there, but 61 I'd like you to interview Mr. Miller. And be sure to ask him what he plans to do after his retirement.

남: 내일 아침 신문의 1면을 좀 변경해야 할 것 같아요. 59 JK 그룹의 사장인 제임스 밀러 씨가 은퇴를 한다는 것을 방금 확인했어요. 그는 오늘 오후에 메인 가에 있는 JK 본사에서 그것에 대해 발표할 것이라고 하네요.

여: 오, 큰 뉴스거리가 되겠네요. 밀러 씨는 그의 회사뿐만 아니라 지역 사회에 많은 헌신을 해왔습니다. 60 그가 이끌어왔던 자선 프로그램은 우리 사회에 큰 영향을 끼쳤습니다.

남: 그래서 당신이 JK 본사에 갔으면 좋겠어요. 저는 이미 사진사에게 그곳으로 가 달라고 요청했지만, 61 당신이 밀러 씨와 인터뷰를 해 주길 바랍니다. 그리고 그가 은퇴 후에 무엇을 할 계획인지 꼭 물어보세요.

---

59. 화자들은 무엇에 대해 이야기하고 있는가?
(A) 사장의 은퇴
(B) 새로운 부사장의 고용
(C) 다가오는 회사의 이벤트
(D) 지역 사회 설문 조사 결과

60. 제임스 밀러는 지역 사회를 위해 무엇을 했는가?
(A) 도심 지역에 새로운 활력을 주었다.
(B) 자선 프로그램을 시작했다.
(C) 지역 학교에서 봉사를 했다.
(D) 정부 지출을 축소했다.

61. 남자는 여자에게 무엇을 하라고 요청하는가?
(A) 미래의 프로젝트에 대한 아이디어 제안
(B) 제임스 밀러의 사진 찾기
(C) 기사 편집
(D) 인터뷰 진행

Questions 62-64 refer to the following conversation and hotel directory.

M: 62 Thank you for staying with us at the Muraz Hotel. Here is your room key. Do you have any questions about our facilities?

W: Well, I'm attending the Leeds International Financial Forum. I'm not sure where the conference hall is.

M: You can see it on this pamphlet. It shows what is located on each floor.

W: Thanks. And, 63 is there some place in the hotel where I can use the Internet with my laptop?

M: Sure, 64 we do have a business lounge. You can also use some office equipment such as a printer.

W: Great. 64 I'll head up there and check my e-mail.

남: 62 무라즈 호텔을 이용해 주셔서 감사합니다. 여기 당신의 객실 열쇠입니다. 우리 시설에 관해 질문이 있으신가요?

여: 음, 저는 리즈 국제 금융 포럼에 참가할 거예요. 회의장이 어디에 있는지 잘 모르겠습니다.

남: 이 소책자를 보시면 됩니다. 소책자에 각층에 무엇이 있는지 나와 있습니다.
여: 감사합니다. 그리고 63 호텔에 제 노트북으로 인터넷을 이용할 수 있는 곳이 있나요?
남: 물론이죠. 64 비즈니스 라운지가 있습니다. 프린터와 같은 사무용 기기도 사용하실 수 있습니다.
여: 좋네요. 64 거기로 가서 제 이메일을 확인해야겠어요.

무라즈 호텔	
5-7층	객실
4층	피트니스 센터
64 3층	비즈니스 라운지
2층	회의장
1층	식당

62. 남자는 누구일 것 같은가?
(A) 초청 연사
(B) 호텔 직원
(C) 식당 매니저
(D) 행사 주최자

63. 여자는 무엇에 관하여 묻는가?
(A) 인터넷 접속
(B) 수리점
(C) 세탁 서비스
(D) 지역 명소

64. 시각 자료를 보시오. 여자는 다음에 몇 층으로 갈 것인가?
(A) 1층
(B) 2층
(C) 3층
(D) 4층

Questions 65-67 refer to the following conversation and chart.

M: Have you seen the design Jennifer created? I think it's perfect for 65 our bakery.
W: She showed me a picture of it yesterday. It'll look great on our employee uniforms.
M: Anyway, have you found a printing store for our uniforms?
W: I have a list of printing stores here. Most won't print fewer than 30 uniforms. But there's one place that doesn't require so many to be ordered at once.
M: Great, we can go with that one. 66 We only need 10 now.
W: OK, I'll order them right away.

M: Just make sure that we'll get them before 67 our bakery's grand opening on June 15.

남: 제니퍼가 만든 디자인을 봤어요? 그건 65 우리 빵집에 완벽하다고 생각해요.
여: 그녀가 어제 사진을 보여 줬어요. 우리 직원 유니폼에 정말 잘 어울릴 거예요.
남: 어쨌든, 우리 유니폼을 위한 인쇄소를 찾았나요?
여: 여기 인쇄소 목록이 있습니다. 대부분 30개 미만의 유니폼은 인쇄하지 않으려고 해요. 그렇지만 한 번에 그렇게 많이 주문할 필요가 없는 곳이 한 곳 있습니다.
남: 좋아요, 그곳에서 하면 되겠어요. 66 우리는 지금 10개만 필요하니까요.
여: 알겠습니다, 바로 주문할게요.
남: 67 6월 15일에 있는 우리 빵집 개업 전에 받아야 한다는 것만 잊지 마세요.

회사	최소 주문	유니폼당 가격
지니 인쇄	40	5.8달러
에반	30	6.0달러
66 미키	10	6.2달러
제인 인쇄	50	5.6달러

65. 화자들은 어디에서 일할 것 같은가?
(A) 디자인 회사에서
(B) 빵집에서
(C) 식당에서
(D) 옷 가게에서

66. 시각 자료를 보시오. 화자들은 어느 회사를 선택할 것 같은가?
(A) 지니 인쇄
(B) 에반
(C) 미키
(D) 제인 인쇄

67. 남자는 6월 15일에 무슨 일이 있을 거라고 말하는가?
(A) 일부 가구가 배달될 것이다.
(B) 새로운 업체가 개업할 것이다.
(C) 시상식이 열릴 것이다.
(D) 할인이 끝날 것이다.

Questions 68-70 refer to the following conversation and map.

W: Thank you for calling Annie's Laundry Service. How can I help you?
M: Hi, Annie. It's Sean. I'm on Queens Avenue across from City Hall now. 68 I've almost finished returning the clothes, but 69 this last one doesn't have an address on it.

W: Hmm, no address? Check the name tag, Sean.

M: Okay, it's Julie Page.

W: Hmm, let me see. That is supposed to be returned to her office, Grand Tower.

M: I see. **70 On Perry's Street, next to the Subway station.** Thanks.

여: 애니 세탁 서비스에 전화 주셔서 감사합니다. 어떻게 도와드릴까요?

남: 안녕하세요, 애니 씨. 저는 션이에요. 저는 지금 시청 맞은편 퀸즈 가에 있어요. **68** 저는 옷을 거의 다 가져다주었는데 **69** 이 마지막 한 개가 주소가 없어요.

여: 음, 주소가 없어요? 이름표를 확인해 보세요, 션.

남: 알겠습니다, 줄리 페이지네요.

여: 음, 어디 봅시다. 그건 그녀의 사무실인 그랜드 타워로 보내주기로 되어 있네요.

남: 알겠습니다. **70** 페리 가에서 지하철역 옆에 있는 거군요. 감사합니다.

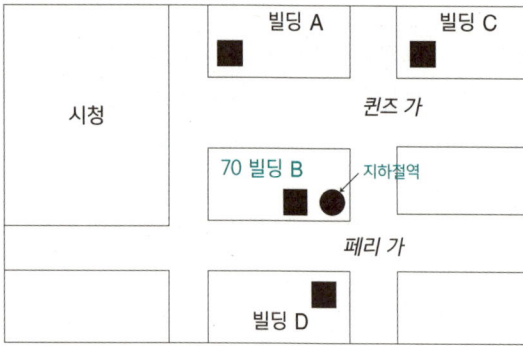

68. 남자는 누구일 것 같은가?
(A) 자산 관리자
(B) 공무원
(C) 배달원
(D) 우편 배달원

69. 남자는 어떤 문제가 있다고 말하는가?
(A) 잘못된 곳에 배달되었다.
(B) 도로에 사고가 발생했다.
(C) 일부 정보가 누락되었다.
(D) 물품이 손상되었다.

70. 시각 자료를 보시오. 남자는 다음에 어디로 갈 것인가?
(A) 빌딩 A로
(B) 빌딩 B로
(C) 빌딩 C로
(D) 빌딩 D로

PART 4
Questions 71-73 refer to the following radio broadcast.

M: Do you have any plans for this weekend? If you don't, **71 why don't you come out and join GXPW radio at the grand opening of the Henderson Art Center this Saturday?** The new art center is located beside Henderson Community Park. We will be there all day hosting lots of games and mini concerts. **72 The local comedian Mike Rogers** will be performing at 7 P.M. Mike's show is a ticketed event, and you can purchase tickets at the door. We have the best seats available, and **73 we'll be giving out these tickets for free to the first five callers.** The number is 478-0582. Call right now!

남: 이번 주말에 어떤 계획이 있으신가요? 없으시다면 **71** 이번 주 토요일에 오셔서 헨더슨 아트 센터의 개관식에서 진행되는 GXPW 라디오 방송에 함께하시는 게 어떤가요? 새로 개관하는 아트 센터는 헨더슨 지역 공원 옆에 위치해 있습니다. 저희는 그곳에서 많은 게임과 작은 콘서트들을 하루 종일 주최할 것입니다. **72** 이 지역의 코미디언인 마이크 로저스 씨가 오후 7시에 공연을 할 것입니다. 마이크 씨의 공연은 유료 행사이며, 티켓은 입구에서 구입할 수 있습니다. 저희는 제일 좋은 좌석들을 보유하고 있으며 **73** 이 입장권을 먼저 전화 주시는 다섯 분께 무료로 드리도록 하겠습니다. 전화번호는 478-0582입니다. 지금 전화 주세요!

71. 어떤 종류의 행사가 개최될 예정인가?
(A) 시상식
(B) 개관식
(C) 기념일 축하 행사
(D) 스포츠 행사

72. 마이크 로저스 씨는 누구인가?
(A) 라디오 방송국 직원
(B) 화가
(C) 코미디언
(D) 가수

73. 청취자들은 왜 라디오 방송국에 전화해야 하는가?
(A) 자원봉사를 신청하기 위해
(B) 티켓을 받기 위해
(C) 예술품을 구입하기 위해
(D) 안내 책자를 요청하기 위해

Questions 74-76 refer to the following telephone message.

W: Hi, **74 my name is Becky Derrick from Leon Law Associates. 75 I called last week, and made a reservation at your restaurant for four people.** I've asked for a private room, and chose menu B. I'm calling because I just found out that one of our guests is a vegetarian. So **76** I have to make some adjustments to the menu selection. Since I'm just across the street from you, **76** I can come over this afternoon, and discuss the changes. Please let me know if three o'clock is okay for you.

여: 안녕하세요. **74** 저는 리언 법률 협회의 베키 데릴입니다. **75** 저는 귀하의 레스토랑에 지난주에 전화를 해서 4명의 자리를 예약했습니다. 저는 개인실을 요청했고 메뉴 B를 선택했습니다. 제가 전화를 드린 이유는 저희 손님들 중에 한 명이 채식주의자라는 것을 알았기 때문입니다. 그래서 **76** 메뉴 선택을 좀 변경해야 합니다. 제가 귀하의 식당 맞은편에서 근무하고 있기 때문에 **76** 오늘 오후에 들러서 변경 사항에 대해 논의할 수 있습니다. 3시가 어떠신지 알려 주시길 바랍니다.

74. 화자는 어디에서 근무할 것 같은가?
(A) 회계 사무소에서
(B) 광고 대행사에서
(C) 식당에서
(D) 법률 사무소에서

75. 화자는 지난주에 무엇을 했는가?
(A) 디너파티를 개최했다.
(B) 학회에 참가했다.
(C) 예약을 했다.
(D) 휴가를 갔다.

76. 화자가 "제가 귀하의 식당 맞은편에서 근무하고 있습니다"라고 말할 때 의미하는 것은 무엇인가?
(A) 주문한 제품은 곧 배달될 것이다.
(B) 그녀는 청자를 놀라게 하길 원한다.
(C) 그녀는 도움을 줄 수 있다.
(D) 그녀는 청자가 있는 장소에 쉽게 방문할 수 있다.

Questions 77-79 refer to the following advertisement.

W: Do you run a business? **77** Have you always wanted to have good software to manage all your products? I have good news for you. The new TSN inventory software is your answer! **78** It will solve all of your inventory problems by allowing you to customize the program to meet your needs. By choosing specific features for your business, you will spend less time managing your inventory. **79** The monthly business magazine *Business World* gave it five stars and highly recommended it. You can read all about it in the April issue.

여: 사업체를 운영하고 계신가요? 그리고 **77** 모든 제품을 관리할 수 있는 좋은 소프트웨어를 항상 원하셨나요? 저에게 좋은 소식이 있습니다. 새롭게 출시된 TSN 재고 관리 소프트웨어가 그 해답입니다! **78** 고객의 필요에 따라 프로그램을 맞출 수 있기에 재고 관리에 따르는 문제를 모두 해결할 수 있습니다. 귀하의 사업에 맞는 특정 기능을 선택함으로써 재고 관리를 하는 시간을 훨씬 더 줄일 수 있습니다. **79** 월간 경제 잡지인 <비즈니스 월드>는 별 5개의 최고 점수를 주며 적극적으로 추천했습니다. 4월호에서 이것과 관련된 모든 것을 읽을 수 있습니다.

77. 어떤 제품이 광고되고 있는가?
(A) 금융 잡지
(B) 소프트웨어 프로그램
(C) 기록 장치
(D) 보안 카메라

78. 화자는 제품에 대해 어떤 점을 강조하는가?
(A) 맞춤이 가능하다.
(B) 저렴하다.
(C) 사용하기 쉽다.
(D) 크기가 작다.

79. 청자들은 어떻게 더 많은 정보를 얻을 수 있는가?
(A) 안내 책자를 요청하여
(B) 수신자 부담 전화번호로 전화하여
(C) 잡지 기사를 읽어서
(D) 이메일을 보내서

Questions 80-82 refer to the following telephone message.

M: Hello, Ms. Waterfall. This is Gary Carlton from Pine Ridge Furniture. I've called to let you know that the bed you ordered has arrived this morning. **80/81** I would like to confirm the delivery date you wanted, Wednesday, August 24th. **81** Our delivery team will be there between 1 P.M. and 5 P.M. Our men will assemble your bed and pick up the old one. If you have any questions about the product, you can ask them. **82** If that time does not work for you, please call me at 572-5823. Have a nice day.

남: 안녕하세요, 워터폴 씨. 저는 파인 리지 가구점의 게리 칼턴입니다. 고객님께서 주문하신 침대가 오늘 아침에 도착했다는 것을 알려드리기 위해 전화를 드렸습니다. **80/81** 고객님이 원하신 배달일이 8월 24일 수요일이 맞는지 확인하고 싶습니다. **81** 배송팀이 오후 1시에서 5시 사이에 갈 것입니다. 저희 직원이 침대를 조립하고, 기존 침대를 수거해 갈 것입니다. 제품에 대해 질문이 있으시면 그들에게 문의하시면 됩니다. **82** 만약 그 시간이 안 되신다면, 572-5823으로 전화 주시길 바랍니다. 좋은 하루 보내십시오.

80. 전화를 건 목적은 무엇인가?
(A) 제품을 소개하는 것
(B) 배달 날짜를 확인하는 것
(C) 포장에 대한 정보를 주는 것
(D) 시간을 변경하는 것

81. 화자에 따르면, 수요일에 무슨 일이 있을 것인가?
(A) 주문한 제품이 배송될 것이다.
(B) 프로젝트가 완성될 것이다.
(C) 기계가 수리될 것이다.
(D) 제품이 출시될 것이다.

82. 청자는 무엇을 요구받는가?
(A) 제품의 사진을 찍기
(B) 가게에 방문하기
(C) 필요하면 일정 조정을 위해 전화하기
(D) 운전사에게 지불하기

Questions 83-85 refer to the following talk.

M: Ladies and gentlemen, I would like to welcome all of you to the annual APX Agency company dinner. As you all know, 83 this event is held to show how much we appreciate all your hard work. The management is well aware that without your dedication, 84 APX could not have become the leader in the graphic design industry. So thank you. At this time, 85 I must especially thank those who worked on the sign for the city project. Most of you know that we didn't charge for that. 85 It was our gift to the city. However, the sign was so beautiful that it received a lot of publicity. Great job, people!

남: 신사 숙녀 여러분, 연례 APX 에이전시 회사 만찬에 오신 모든 분들을 환영합니다. 여러분 모두 아시다시피, 83 이 행사는 여러분들의 노고에 감사를 표하기 위한 자리입니다. 여러분들의 헌신 없이는 84 APX가 그래픽 디자인 산업의 선두 주자가 될 수 없었을 것이라는 사실을 경영진들은 잘 알고 있습니다. 그래서 감사합니다. 이 시점에서 85 저는 특히 시 프로젝트를 위해 표지판을 작업하신 분들에게 감사드려야 하겠습니다. 그것에 대한 비용을 청구하지 않았다는 것을 여러분들 대부분이 알고 계실 것입니다. 85 그것은 시에게 주는 선물이었습니다. 하지만 그 표지판은 매우 아름다워서 언론의 많은 관심을 받았습니다. 잘해 주셨습니다!

83. 행사의 목적은 무엇인가?
(A) 새로운 변화들을 알리는 것
(B) 신제품을 홍보하는 것
(C) 직원들을 인정하는 것
(D) 건물을 봉헌하는 것

84. 화자는 어디서 일할 것 같은가?
(A) 시청에서
(B) 마케팅 회사에서
(C) 레스토랑 체인점에서
(D) 그래픽 디자인 회사에서

85. 화자가 "그것에 대한 비용을 청구하지 않았다"라고 말할 때 의미하는 것은 무엇인가?
(A) 그는 계약서 갱신을 원했다.
(B) 그는 청구서에 실수를 저질렀다.
(C) 표지판은 기부되었다.
(D) 가격을 낮추었다.

Questions 86-88 refer to the following announcement.

W: Good morning, passengers. 86 This is an announcement for East Asian Airlines Flight 757 to Hong Kong. 87 Unfortunately, this flight is overbooked. If you're available to take a later flight, please come to our customer service center. 88 All volunteers willing to give up their seats on this flight will receive a voucher for a discounted ticket for your next trip. Please see our service representative if you are interested. Thank you for your understanding.

여: 승객 여러분들, 안녕하세요. 86 홍콩행 이스트 아시안 항공사 757편에 대한 안내 말씀을 드리겠습니다. 87 안타깝게도, 이 항공편은 초과 예약되었습니다. 다음 항공편을 이용하셔도 되신다면, 고객 서비스 센터로 와 주십시오. 88 이 항공편의 좌석을 포기할 의사가 있으신 자원자들에게는 다음 여행 시에 사용하실 수 있는 할인권을 제공해 드릴 예정입니다. 관심이 있으시다면, 저희 고객 서비스 직원에게 알려 주십시오. 양해해 주셔서 감사합니다.

86. 이 안내 방송은 어디에서 나오고 있는가?
(A) 기차역에서
(B) 공장에서
(C) 공항에서
(D) 극장에서

87. 화자는 무엇이 문제라고 이야기하는가?
(A) 기상 상태가 좋지 않다.
(B) 좌석이 초과 예약되었다.
(C) 일부 장비가 손상을 입었다.
(D) 직원이 부족하다.

88. 화자는 무엇을 제공하는가?
(A) 샘플 제품
(B) 렌트카
(C) 할인권
(D) 무료 회원권

Questions 89-91 refer to the following introduction.

M: Welcome to Ford House. My name is James Moore and I'll be leading your tour today. I'm happy to introduce to you 89 one of the most famous writers of all time, Kevin Ford. You will learn about his personal life and philosophy behind his works today. This was his house. He both lived and worked here. 90 During the tour, you will see the bed he slept in, the desk where he wrote his books, and many pictures as well. After we tour the building, we will go over to the auditorium next door. We will show you a short movie about the author. 91 Let's start with the living room.

남: 포드 하우스에 오신 것을 환영합니다. 제 이름은 제임스 무어이고, 오늘 여러분의 견학을 진행할 것입니다. 89 역사상 가장 유명한 작가들 중 한 명인 케빈 포드를 소개해 드리게 되어 기쁩니다. 여러분들은 오늘 그의 작품들 뒤에 숨은 그의 개인적인 삶과 철학에 대해 배우게 될 것입니다. 이곳은 그의 집이었습니다. 그는 여기에서 거주하며 작품을 썼습니다. 90 견학이 진행되는 동안 여러분들은 그가 잠을 잤던 침대, 그가 책을 썼던 책상, 그리고 많은 사진들도 볼 것입니다. 건물을 둘러본 후에 우리는 옆 건물에 있는 강당으로 넘어갈 것입니다. 여러분들에게 이 작가에 대한 짧은 영화를 보여 드릴 예정입니다. 91 그럼 거실부터 시작합시다.

89. 케빈 포드는 누구인가?
(A) 화가
(B) 작가
(C) 정치가
(D) 사업가

90. 화자에 따르면, 견학 동안에 무엇을 볼 것인가?
(A) 짧은 역사 영화
(B) 희귀 도서
(C) 가구
(D) 조각품

91. 청자들은 다음에 무엇을 할 예정인가?
(A) 거실 보기
(B) 공원 방문하기
(C) 도서 구매하기
(D) 점심 먹으러 가기

Questions 92-94 refer to the following excerpt from a meeting.

W: 92 I have an important announcement to make regarding the upcoming move to a new building. I know all of us are very excited about it. As you know, we've been scheduled to move on Friday, but the moving company called this afternoon and told us that they had a cancellation. 93 They are offering a discount if we move on Thursday instead. We can save a lot of money, 93 so I would like to take advantage of it. So I have to ask you a big favor. Make sure that you have packed everything before you leave the office on Wednesday. 94 Since we are moving on Thursday, we are all going to take Thursday off while the movers work. I appreciate your cooperation.

여: 92 곧 있을 새 빌딩으로의 이사와 관련해 중요한 공지가 있습니다. 저는 우리 모두가 이에 관해 매우 들떠 있다는 것을 알고 있습니다. 여러분들도 아시다시피 우리는 금요일에 이사하기로 예정되어 있었는데, 오늘 오후에 이삿짐센터에서 전화를 해서, 취소 건이 생겼다고 알려왔습니다. 93 그들은 우리가 대신 목요일에 이사하면 할인을 제공할 것입니다. 우리는 많은 돈을 아낄 수 있으므로, 93 저는 이것을 기회로 활용하고 싶습니다. 그래서 여러분들에게 큰 부탁을 해야 합니다. 수요일에 사무실을 떠나기 전에 반드시 모든 짐들을 싸 놓으시기 바랍니다. 94 우리는 목요일에 이사하기 때문에, 물건을 나르는 사람들이 일하는 동안 목요일 근무를 쉴 예정입니다. 여러분의 협조에 감사드립니다.

92. 화자는 주로 무엇에 대해서 이야기하고 있는가?
(A) 낡은 기계들 교체하기
(B) 새로운 장비 설치하기
(C) 사무실 이사하기
(D) 벽에 페인트칠하기

93. 화자는 왜 "우리는 많은 돈을 아낄 수 있습니다"라고 말하는가?
(A) 도움을 요청하기 위해
(B) 제안을 거절하기 위해
(C) 오해를 바로잡기 위해
(D) 일정이 변경된 이유를 설명하기 위해

94. 청자들은 목요일에 무엇을 해야 하는가?
(A) 모든 소지품 싸기
(B) 하루 쉬기
(C) 한 시간 일찍 도착하기
(D) 박스 풀기

Questions 95-97 refer to the following excerpt from a meeting and graph.

M: Good morning, thanks for attending our monthly staff meeting. Today, first of all, I'd like to discuss our progress in developing our new portable photo printer. 95 We received market research results from our advertising agency. So please take a look at the results. Regarding its speed, it had 10 points. Hmm... we won't be able to change the design at this step. But look at this other feature. 96 It has only 6 points so that's what I want you to work on. I know you've been busy these days. But 97 I'd like you to suggest some ideas by this weekend. We'll have a meeting on this issue again next Monday.

남: 안녕하세요, 월간 직원회의에 참석해 주셔서 감사합니다. 오늘은 우선 새로운 휴대용 포토 프린터의 개발 진행 상황에 대해서 논의하고 싶습니다. 95 우리는 광고 대행사로부터 시장 조사 결과를 받았습니다. 그러니 이 결과를 확인해 주세요. 속도에 대해서는 10점을 받았습니다. 음… 저희는 지금 단계에서는 디자인을 변경할 수는 없을 것입니다. 하지만 다른 항목을 보십시오. 96 이 항목은 6점밖에 받지 못했기 때문에, 여러분이 이 부분을 작업해 주시면 좋겠

습니다. 여러분들이 요즘 바쁜 것을 알고 있습니다. 그럼에도 **97** 이번 주말까지 여러 아이디어를 제안해 주셨으면 합니다. 이 문제와 관련해서 다음 주 월요일에 다시 회의가 있을 예정입니다.

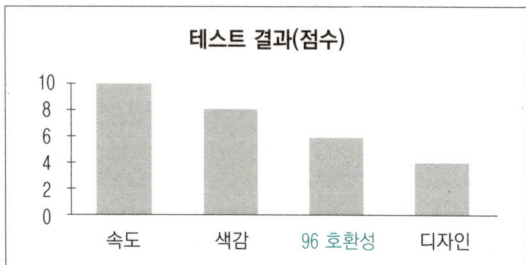

95. 화자는 피드백을 어디에서 얻었다고 이야기하는가?
(A) 관리자 회의
(B) 업계 잡지
(C) 광고 회사
(D) 직원들

96. 시각 자료를 보시오. 청자들은 어떤 항목에 대해 작업할 것인가?
(A) 속도
(B) 색감
(C) 호환성
(D) 디자인

97. 청자들은 이번 주말까지 무엇을 하기를 요청받는가?
(A) 상사와 상담하기
(B) 제안하기
(C) 보고서 업데이트하기
(D) 다른 판매 회사 찾기

Questions 98-100 refer to the following instructions and floor plan.

W: Okay, listen up, everyone. Next week, one of our summer concert series "One Summer Night" will be here at the Golden Bridge Hall. As you know, **98** I'm very excited that all tickets have already sold out. And one more thing, **99** the renovations for the gate closest to the stage are complete. That will allow our customers to use all four doors. And finally, our new brochures will arrive tomorrow. So **100** please have them ready for customers to pick up at each of the doors on that night.

여: 모두들, 잘 들어 주시길 바랍니다. 다음 주에, 여름 콘서트 시리즈 중 하나인 '어느 여름날의 밤에'가 이곳 골든 브릿지 홀에서 진행될 예정입니다. 아시다시피, **98** 입장권이 전부 매진되어 매우 기쁩니다. 그리고 한 가지 더 말씀드리자면, **99** 무대와 가장 가까운 문의 보수 공사가 마무리되었습니다. 이것으로 고객들이 4개의 문을 모두 사용하실 수 있습니다. 그리고 마지막으로, 우리의 새 책자가 내일 도착할 예정입니다. 그러니 **100** 그날 밤에 각각의 문에서 고객들이 가져갈 수 있도록 준비해 주십시오.

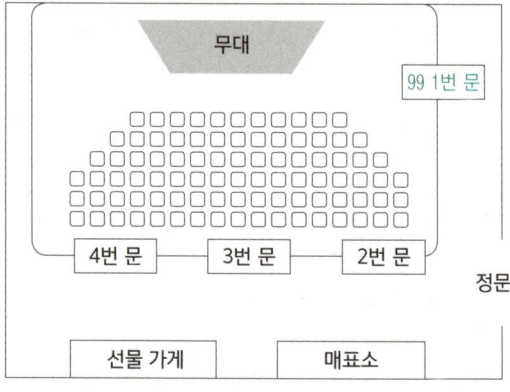

98. 화자에 따르면, 행사와 관련해 무엇이 언급되었는가?
(A) 현지 밴드가 공연할 것이다.
(B) 입장권은 더 이상 구매가 불가능하다.
(C) 라이브로 방송될 것이다.
(D) 시리즈 중 마지막이 될 것이다.

99. 시각 자료를 보시오. 콘서트 홀 중 어느 부분이 최근에 보수되었는가?
(A) 정문
(B) 1번 문
(C) 2번 문
(D) 4번 문

100. 화자는 청자들에게 무엇을 하라고 알려 주는가?
(A) 일정을 업데이트할 것
(B) 자료를 내놓는 것
(C) 유니폼을 착용할 것
(D) 가는 방향을 알려줄 것

PART 5

101. 인칭 대명사
첸 씨는 다음 주에 세인트 베리 서점에서 인턴쉽을 마칠 것이다.

102. 동사 어휘
늦게 제출한 교육 수업 신청서는 받아들여지지 않을 것이다.

103. 형용사 자리
귀하가 작성한 임대 계약서를 관련 서류와 함께 6월 1일까지 우편으로 보내야 합니다.

104. 명사 자리
그 프로젝트는 남부 지역 개발에 중요한 기여를 했다.

105. 형용사 어휘
만약 귀하의 송장이 잘못되었다면, 우리에게 가능한 한 빨리 연락주세요.

106. 동사 시제
로페즈 씨는 지난주에 도시 재개발 프로젝트에 관해 건축가와 상담했다.

107. 전치사
우리의 연례 연회는 대개 12월의 금요일 밤에 개최된다.

108. 명사 자리
앨런 씨가 휴가로 자리를 비우는 동안 브라운 씨가 공사 현장 감독자로 임명되었다.

109. 명사 어휘
컴퓨터 시스템을 업그레이드하기 전에 작업 관련 파일을 저장하는 것은 사용자의 책임이다.

110. 형용사 자리
모든 영업 담당자들은 고객들과 미팅이 있지 않는 한 편안한 복장을 입어도 될 것이다.

111. 부사절 접속사
그 매니저는 국내외 시장에 동일하게 경험이 있기 때문에 회사의 중요한 자산이 되었다.

112. 동사의 형태
아시아 공장의 관리자들은 새로 출시된 컴퓨터의 생산량을 50%까지 증가시키라는 지시를 받았다.

113. 전치사
GT 사는 자사의 최신 자동차 V-3000을 대규모의 온라인 판촉 캠페인을 통하여 홍보할 것이다.

114. 형용사 어휘
직원 안내서는 고객의 불만을 처리할 수 있는 다양한 방법에 대한 절차를 설명한다.

115. 부사 자리
서울에서 서북쪽으로 한 시간 거리에 위치한 우리의 본사는 차나 버스로 접근이 용이하다.

116. 전치사 자리
모든 재정 전문가들은 짧은 마감 기한에도 제시간에 분석 보고서를 제출할 것을 요청받는다.

117. 명사 어휘
세라 투자사 직원들은 재직을 증명하는 것을 보여 주면 근처 상점에서 할인을 받을 수 있다.

118. 부사 어휘
톰 식당 체인에서 10년간 근무한 끝에 릴리안은 마침내 최우수 직원 상을 받았다.

119. 부사 자리
아시아 은행은 최근의 인수에 관한 귀사의 협조에 깊은 감사를 드립니다.

120. 동사 어휘
질 스콧 씨는 자동 급여 시스템에 관한 다음 교육 세미나 일정을 10월 10일로 잡았다.

121. 분사
양 씨는 그의 엄청난 성공 덕분에 승진되었다.

122. 관계 대명사
스타 여행사는 출장을 자주 다니는 사업가들에게 특별 할인을 제공한다.

123. 대명사
주말에 초과 근무를 하는 것이 가능한 사람은 누구나 상사에게 이메일을 보내야 한다.

124. 부사 어휘
예상치 못한 지연 때문에, 우리는 연구 부서에 이번 주 후반으로 회의를 연기시키도록 요청했다.

125. 접속사 자리
그들이 내일 회의에서 결과를 발표할 계획이든 아니든 간에 광고에 관한 설문지는 오늘 내로 제출해야 한다.

126. 부사 어휘
우리는 제시간에 도착했지만 사람이 너무 많아서 앉기 위해 거의 한 시간을 기다려야 했다.

127. 동사 시제
컴퓨터를 다시 시작했는데도, 계속해서 제대로 작동하지 않으면, 서비스 직원에게 연락하세요.

128. 비교급
줄리 식당의 메뉴는 아멜 식당보다 더 다양한 신선한 음식을 포함한다.

129. 명사 어휘
우리의 전국에 걸친 소매점은 고객들에게 최상의 서비스를 제공할 것이다.

130. 동사 어휘
JBL 광고사에서 근무하는 박 씨는 고객과의 의사소통 능력이 뛰어나다.

PART 6

문제 131-134는 다음 이메일을 참조하세요.

수신: 재닛 밀러
발신: 국제 건설 협회
날짜: 5월 6일
제목: 회원으로 가입해 주셔서 감사합니다
첨부: 가이드북

밀러 씨에게,

국제 건설 협회에 가입하기로 결정해 주셔서 감사합니다. **131** 저희 기관은 다양한 프로그램과 서비스를 통해 전 세계 건설인 사회의 건강과 안전을 지원합니다.

132 저희의 주요 임무는 업계에 높은 안전 기준을 주장하여 건설 환경을 개선시키는 것입니다. 저희는 또한 신입 및 경력 건설 현장 근무자들을 위해 전문적으로 개발된 자료를 제공하고 있습니다. **133** 그것들은 안전 규정 및 법규에 대한 최신 정보를 다루고 있습니다.

134 첨부된 파일은 저희 협회 회원들이 받고 있는 혜택을 자세히 설명하고 있습니다. 저희는 당신께서 보다 안전하고, 보다 나은 건설 전문가가 되는 데 일조할 수 있기를 고대합니다.

국제 건설 협회

문제 135-138는 다음 기사를 참조하세요.

런던(8월 10일) - 135 중국의 유명 의류 제조업체인 친 첸 의류는 곧 유럽에 자사의 의류를 출시할 것이다. EU 의류 뉴스와의 인터뷰에 따르면, 이 회사의 대표인 로버트 첸 씨는 자사의 최신 스포츠웨어와 액세서리의 첫 번째 선적물이 몇 주 후에 중국에서 출발할 것이라고 이야기했다. 136 그것들은 빠르면 9월에는 유럽 소비자들이 이용할 수 있게 될 것이다. 137 첸 씨는 친 첸의 사업 이동이 유럽에서 스포츠웨어에 대한 수요가 증가한 덕분으로 보았다. 138 "점점 더 많은 유럽 사람들이 캐주얼한 옷을 입는 것이 최근 트렌드이고, 우리 회사가 바로 이것을 제공할 것입니다."

문제 139-142는 다음 정보를 참조하세요.

제4회 연례 폭스 타운 도서 박람회

제4회 연례 폭스 타운 도서 박람회가 3월 20일 월요일에 시작됩니다. 139 이 행사는 3월 26일 일요일까지 계속됩니다. 100명이 넘는 유명 작가와 유명 인사가 초대되었습니다. 140 낭독, 저자 사인회와 패널 토론회가 예정되어 있고, 약 3,000명이 참석할 것으로 예상됩니다.

141 행사는 베스트셀러 소설가 타마라 프랜시스 씨와 칼 컬쳐 출판사의 대표 멜빈 딘 씨가 출판 산업의 최근 경향을 주제로 한 기조 토론으로 월요일 오전 10시에 시작될 것입니다. 142 두 발표자 모두 폭스 타운 출신입니다. 행사와 출연 작가를 모두 기재한 목록을 포함한 박람회 세부 사항은 폭스 타운 도서 박람회 웹사이트(www.foxtownbookfair.com)를 참고하세요.

문제 143-146은 다음 편지를 참조하세요.

에버그린 가게를 이용하시는 고객님께,

에버그린 가게의 단골 고객 혜택 프로그램 가입에 관심을 가져 주셔서 감사합니다. 143 이 프로그램의 회원이 되시면 고객님은 많은 흥미로운 혜택을 즐기실 수 있을 것입니다. 144 회원 등록을 하시면 고객님은 세일에 관한 정보를 미리 알 수 있고, 매장 내 비공개 행사에 대한 특별 출입증을 받으실 수 있습니다.

프로그램 가입은 쉽습니다. 145 동봉된 신청서를 지역 매장으로 가져오세요. 그러면 매장에 있는 저희 고객 서비스 직원이 고객님의 신청서를 처리하여, 회원 카드를 발급해 드릴 것입니다.

146 회원 카드로 처음 물건을 구매하시고 4주 이내에, 적립하신 포인트를 상세히 보여 주는 월간 내역서와 자격을 획득하신 혜택 보증서를 받아보실 수 있습니다. 회원 가입은 무료이며 언제든지 취소하실 수 있습니다. 오늘 에버그린 가게에 오셔서 혜택을 받으시기 바랍니다!

진심을 담아,

앤 도일 올림
고객 서비스 부장
동봉물 있음

PART 7

문제 147-148은 다음 기사를 참조하세요.

147 매출 증가: 레드라인 자동차

미시간 디트로이트, 3월 5일 - 레드라인 자동차는 자동차 제품군의 연간 판매액을 발표했다. 보고서에 따르면 작년과 비교해서 올해의 판매량이 4.5% 증가했다. 이 증가분은 업계 전문가들이 예상했던 비율인 2.2%의 거의 두 배 이상이다. 하지만 4년 전만 해도 7.0%씩 꾸준히 증가했던 회사에게는 여전히 충분히 높지 않다. 148 회사 임원들은 여전히 긍정적이다. 그들은 레드라인 자동차가 앞으로 4년 동안 자동차 생산량을 늘릴 준비를 하고 있다고 발표하면서 자신감을 나타냈다.

147. 기사의 목적은 무엇인가?
(A) 새로운 자동차를 광고하는 것
(B) 매출 증가를 보도하는 것
(C) 시장의 새로운 트렌드를 설명하는 것
(D) 디트로이트에 공장이 설립될 예정이라는 소식을 알리는 것

148. 회사의 임원들에 대해 언급된 것은 무엇인가?
(A) 증가 규모에 실망했다.
(B) 보고서의 정확성에 대해 자신이 있다.
(C) 4년 동안 더 많은 자동차를 만들기를 원한다.
(D) 공장을 다른 나라로 이전할 계획을 하고 있다.

문제 149-150은 다음 양식을 참조하세요.

피들러 회사 보안 센터

4월 3일, 주차장 입구에 새로운 보안 게이트가 설치될 예정입니다. 주차장에 차를 주차하시는 분들은 보안 센터에 연락을 하셔서 출입 허가증을 받으셔야 합니다. 출입 허가증은 한 곳의 주차 구역 출입만 허용합니다. 150 만약 다른 장소에도 주차를 하고 싶으시다면, 관리자의 허가를 받으셔야 합니다.

149 주차 허가증을 요청하기 위해서 아래의 정보를 작성하셔서 이 양식을 4월 1일까지 보안 센터로 제출해 주십시오. 문제가 있으면, 내선 번호 30으로 자비에르 리마 씨에게 연락하셔서 도움을 받으세요.

여기를 잘라서 아래 부분을 제출해 주세요.

직원 정보

이름: 149/150 크리스티 파나마		사원 번호: 3462
부서: 기술부	사무실: 207	주차 구역: 2A
추가적인 주차 구역이 필요한가? Yes No		주차 구역: 3C

차량 정보

150 승인 허가자: 루이스 코스타		날짜: 3월 28일
브랜드: 웍스웨건	모델명: 걸프	색상: 검은색
자동차 번호판: LZC53U		

149. 파나마 씨는 왜 이 양식을 제출할 것인가?
(A) 신분 확인 명찰을 요청하기 위해
(B) 연구 세미나를 신청하기 위해
(C) 그녀의 직원 정보를 정정하기 위해

(D) 주차장 출입 허가를 받기 위해

150. 코스타 씨에 대해 언급된 것은 무엇인가?
(A) 파나마 씨의 매니저이다.
(B) 가끔 사무실로 운전을 해서 출근한다.
(C) 주차 구역을 한 개 이상 이용한다.
(D) 보안 센터에서 근무한다.

문제 151-152는 다음 광고를 참조하세요.

KH Headhunter.com

대형 다국적 기업에서 고위 관리직에 관심이 있는 지원자를 찾고 있습니다. 이 회사는 152 (A) 뛰어난 의사소통 능력과 팀 통솔력을 지닌 동기 부여가 된, 독립적이며, 매우 유능한 인물을 찾고 있습니다.

151 그 직위는 회사의 고급 제품 및 서비스의 대중 이미지를 책임지고 그에 대해 보고하기 위해 이사회와 직접 상대해야 합니다. 그 직위는 중요 제휴업체와 주요 단골 고객과의 관계를 개발하고 유지하는 것과 더불어 제품 출시를 감독하는 역할을 포함합니다.

지원을 희망하는 분들은 152 (B) 경영학 석사 학위를 소지해야 하며 152 (C) 대형 IT 기업에서 최소 10년 이상 근무한 경력이 있어야 합니다.

관심이 있으시면, 이력서와 경력을 잘 드러내는 자기소개서를 jklopez@khheadhunter.com으로 보내 주시기 바랍니다.

---

151. 합격한 지원자는 누구에게 보고를 할 것인가?
(A) 회사 임원들
(B) 주요 고객들
(C) 새로운 소비자들
(D) 제품 관리자

152. 지원자들에게 요구되는 사항이 아닌 것은?
(A) 뛰어난 화술
(B) 고급 비즈니스 교육
(C) 기술 분야의 경력
(D) 회사 제품에 대한 지식

문제 153-154는 다음 문자 메시지를 참조하세요.

더스틴 파커 [오전 11:15]
오늘 회의를 위해 식사 10인분을 주문했는데, 여기 8개밖에 없네요.

앤 양 [오전 11:16]
정말요? 주문한 것을 모두 확인했다고 생각했는데요. 죄송합니다. 지금 식당에 전화를 걸고 그곳으로 바로 갈게요.

더스틴 파커 [오전 11:28]
153 회의는 대략 30분 후에 끝날 것 같아요. 얼마나 더 걸려요?

앤 양 [오전 11:29]
153 대략 20분요. 음식을 만들어 놓지 않았어요. 하지만 곧 끝나요.

더스틴 파커 [오전 11:30]
154 브라이언 씨가 지금 우리의 신규 냉장고를 위한 마케팅 계획에 대해 발표하고 있어요. 이것이 발표의 마지막입니다.

앤 양 [오전 11:31]
네, 그의 발표가 끝나기 전에 그곳에 도착할 거예요.

더스틴 파커 [오전 11:32]
좋네요. 그때 뵙겠습니다.

---

153. 오전 11시 29분에, 양 씨가 "They're just about done though(하지만 곧 끝나요)"라고 썼을 때 의미하는 것은 무엇인가?
(A) 점심 식사 시간이 늦어질 것이다.
(B) 회의는 거의 끝났다.
(C) 식사 대부분이 사라졌다.
(D) 주문이 곧 준비될 것이다.

154. 파커 씨에 관해 사실일 것 같은 것은 무엇인가?
(A) 회의를 주도하고 있다.
(B) 전자회사에서 근무한다.
(C) 고객들을 위해 선물을 주문했다.
(D) 자신의 점심 식사를 가져오는 것을 잊어버렸다.

문제 155-157은 정보지를 참조하세요.

홀리 세인필드
비정기 전시회: 홀리 세인필드의 필생의 작품
10월 15일 – 12월 7일
1층과 2층 갤러리

155 보헤미안 문화 박물관은 이번 가을에 20세기의 존경받는 사진작가이자 작가인 '홀리 세인필드의 필생의 작품'을 포함한 전시회를 개최합니다. –[1]–. 이 전시회는 세인필드 씨의 삶의 배경을 집중 조명하고, 그녀의 경력이 어떻게 발전되었는지 보여줄 것입니다. 그녀의 어린 시절과 현재의 삶을 묘사하는 사진과 일기가 전시될 예정입니다. –[2]–. 이번 전시회에서는 그녀가 과거에 살았던 캘리포니아에 있는 집과 남 캘리포니아의 중심부에 위치한 현재의 집에서 우수한 작품들을 모았습니다. 157 그녀의 글과 사진 모음은 갤러리의 1층과 2층에서 전시될 것입니다. –[3]–.

이 경이로운 전시회는 사전 예약이 필수적입니다. 티켓은 9월 2일부터 판매될 것이고, 보헤미안 문화 박물관의 웹사이트인 www.bohemianmuseum.com을 방문해야만 구입이 가능합니다. –[4]–. 156 모든 티켓 구매자는 티켓에 인쇄된 날짜와 시간에만 전시회 관람이 가능합니다. 전시회와 관련해서 더 많은 정보를 원하신다면, (764) 188-1888번으로 보헤미안 문화 박물관에 전화하시기 바랍니다.

---

155. 이 정보지의 목적은 무엇인가?
(A) 다가오는 행사에 대해 알리는 것
(B) 새 박물관의 개관을 알리는 것
(C) 최근에 발표된 연극을 광고하는 것
(D) 새로 개봉된 영화를 홍보하는 것

156. 티켓에 대해 언급된 것은 무엇인가?
(A) 10월 15일 전에는 구매가 불가능하다.
(B) 온라인으로는 구매할 수 없다.
(C) 특정한 날에 사용되어야 한다.
(D) 언제든지 취소가 가능할 것이다.

157. [1], [2], [3], [4]로 표시된 위치 중 다음 문장이 들어가기에 가장 적절한 곳은 어디인가?
"게다가, 지하에서 홀리 세인필드 씨의 짧은 다큐멘터리가 상영될 예정입니다."
(A) [1]
(B) [2]
(C) [3]
(D) [4]

문제 158-160은 다음 정보를 참조하세요.

이너 선 극장
158 근무 일정 방침

주의: 이 방침들은 변경될 가능성이 있습니다. 변경 사항이 있을 경우, 전 직원들에게 사전에 알려드리게 됩니다.

정규 직원
정규 직원들은 일주일에 40시간을 근무해야 합니다. 정규 직원들의 일반적인 근무 일정은 주중 하루 9시간이지만, 주말 근무에 맞춰 조정될 수도 있습니다. 정규 직원들은 한 주에 근무 시간이 40시간을 초과할 경우에 추가 수당을 받을 것입니다. 정규 직원들은 급여의 5%에 해당하는 주택 보조금을 받을 수 있는 자격이 됩니다. 한 시간의 점심시간이 모든 정규 직원들에게 제공됩니다.

시간제 직원
40시간보다 적게 근무하는 사람들은 시간제 직원으로 간주됩니다. 매니저와 근무 일정을 조정할 수 있습니다. 일반적으로, 시간제 직원들은 근무 계약서에 명시된 근로 시간을 초과해서는 안 됩니다. 159 그러나 관리자의 승인에 따라, 시간제 직원들도 특정 프로젝트 업무에 대해 초과 근무를 했을 때 초과 근무 수당을 받을 수 있습니다. 시간제 직원들은 급여의 3%에 해당하는 주택 보조금을 받을 수 있는 자격이 됩니다. 한 시간의 점심시간이 시간제 직원들에게도 제공됩니다.

임시 직원
소수의 임시 직원들이 종종 필요합니다. 160 이러한 유형의 직원들은 계약 협상에서 그들의 근무 일정이 결정됩니다. 정규 직원 및 시간제 직원과는 다르게, 임시 직원들은 주택 보조금 수령 대상에서 제외됩니다. 또한 추가 근무 수당을 요청할 수 있는 자격도 없습니다. 이너 선 극장의 다른 직원들처럼, 한 시간의 점심시간이 모든 임시 직원들에게도 제공됩니다.

---

158. 정보가 작성된 이유는 무엇인가?
(A) 신입 직원들이 고용되었음을 알리기 위해
(B) 변경된 회의 날짜를 알리기 위해
(C) 근무 시간과 복지 혜택에 관한 규정을 설명하기 위해
(D) 집을 구할 때 필요한 정보를 제공하기 위해

159. 시간제 직원에 대하여 언급된 것은 무엇인가?
(A) 정규 직원들이 받는 것과 동일한 주택 보조금을 받는다.
(B) 근무 일정에 재택근무가 포함된다.
(C) 특별한 프로젝트 업무를 위해서만 고용된다.
(D) 관리자의 승인에 따라 초과 근무를 할 수 있다.

160. 임시 직원들은 무엇을 협상할 수 있는가?
(A) 주택 보조금의 액수
(B) 그들이 받게 되는 일정 유형
(C) 그들이 받을 초과 근무 수당 액수
(D) 그들의 점심 휴식 시간 길이

문제 161-163은 다음 광고를 참조하세요.

개점 축하

시로코 아울렛
1503 그랜드 스테이트 복합 건물 (제나 보석 및 액세서리 옆)
07301, 뉴저지, 테너플라이

50달러 이상 구매하시면 폴라로이드 카메라가 무료
162 (그랜드 스테이트 복합 건물에서만)

161 특별 할인:
속옷과 양말 20% 할인
신발(스포츠용품만) 25% 할인
패션 액세서리 35% 할인

8월 1일부터 8월 30일까지 제공
영업시간: 오전 9시부터 오후 9시까지

단지 연 50달러로 모든 구매에 10%의 추가 할인 혜택을 드리는 회원 카드를 신청하여 받으세요.
162 그랜드 스테이트 복합 건물 또는 파인 힐 플라자에서 카드를 신청하세요.
또한 온라인으로 회원 카드를 받으실 수도 있습니다!

저희 홈페이지를 방문하세요.(www.sciroccooutlets.com)
163 이번 주 동안만, 저희 홈페이지에서 목걸이를 구매하시면 50%의 할인 혜택을 받으실 수 있습니다!

---

161. 시로코 아울렛은 아마 어떤 종류의 상품을 전문적으로 다루고 있는가?
(A) 전자 제품
(B) 의류
(C) 책
(D) 가구

162. 시로코 아울렛에 관해서 언급되는 것은?
(A) 특별 할인은 1주일 동안 지속될 것이다.
(B) 8월 1일에는 저녁 10시까지 영업을 할 것이다.
(C) 판매원들이 고도의 훈련을 받았다.
(D) 두 곳 이상의 매장이 있다.

163. 고객들이 온라인으로 구매하면 할인을 받을 수 있는 것은 어떤 상품인가?
(A) 회원 카드
(B) 카메라
(C) 목걸이
(D) 신발

문제 164-167은 다음 이메일을 참조하세요.

발신: 레이첼 카터, 공원 관리자 <rcarter@kalamazoo.com>
수신: 165 보리스 베커 <bbecker@kalamazoo.com>, 알렉스 김 <alexkim@kalamazoo.com>
제목: 6월 16일 계획
날짜: 6월 7일

이번 주에, 네 개의 도보 여행 그룹들이 칼라마주에서 종일 하이킹 활동에 참여할 예정입니다. **164/165** 여러분은 그들이 일요일 아침에 도착했을 때 이 그룹들과 만날 것이고, 그들에게 산 주변 시설에 대해 소개할 것입니다. 네 개의 그룹 중 두 그룹은 야영지에서 하룻밤을 머무를 것이기 때문에, 여러분은 그들에게 산불, 식량 보관, 바른 쓰레기 처리와 같은 사안에 대한 정책과 규칙에 대해 빠짐없이 설명해 주셔야 합니다. 마지막으로, **166** 모든 그룹들이 도보 여행을 시작하기 위해 방문자 센터에서 떠나기 전에 그들 모두가 새로워진 우리 웹사이트의 최신 소식들을 확인하게 해야 합니다.

우리 기술지원팀 덕분에, 누구에게나 공원 웹사이트 탐색이 용이합니다. 만약 아직 웹사이트를 방문하지 않았다면, 방문하여 새로운 배치, 특히 등산객들이 유용하다고 생각할 만한 부분에 대해 숙지하세요. 이것들 중 일부에는 지역 일기 예보, 우리의 새로운 여행 계획, 그리고 출력 서비스의 링크가 포함되어 있습니다. 이 기능들은 등산객들이 그들의 체력 수준과 그들이 등산에 투자하기 원하는 총 시간에 기초하여 그들만의 등산 지도를 제작하는 데 도움을 드릴 수 있습니다. **167** 그리고 이 지도들은 출력 가능하고, 등산객들이 등산로를 지나는 동안 가이드 역할을 할 수 있습니다. 지도를 출력하는 것은 무료이나, 공원 시설물들을 좋은 상태로 유지하기 위해서 기부는 환영한다고 언급해 주세요.

164. 이메일의 목적은 무엇인가?
(A) 새로운 등산로를 공지하는 것
(B) 방문객 안내소로 가는 길을 알려 주는 것
(C) 지역 일기 예보를 알려 주는 것
(D) 공원 직원들에게 지침을 제공하는 것

165. 보리스 베커 씨와 알렉스 김 씨는 일요일 아침에 무엇을 할 것 같은가?
(A) 공원 관리자와 만남
(B) 야영지 예약
(C) 방문객들에게 정책에 관한 정보 제공
(D) 공원 등산로에서 등산객 안내

166. 모든 등산객들이 어디에서 만나기로 예정되어 있는가?
(A) 방문자 센터에서
(B) 식품 보관 지역에서
(C) 기술 지원 사무소에서
(D) 야영지에서

167. 이메일에 따르면, 등산객들은 자신들이 사용할 용도로 무엇을 출력할 수 있는가?
(A) 모임 일정
(B) 등산로 지도
(C) 공원 규율
(D) 산장 예약권

문제 168-171은 다음 온라인 채팅 대화를 참조하세요.

앨런 고메즈 [오전 09:15]
안녕하세요, 여러분. **169** 이번 주 목요일에 함께 모였으면 합니다. 여러분들 모두 아시다시피, 저희 매출이 감소해 왔습니다. 우리는 새로운 계획을 모색할 필요가 있습니다.

트레이시 헤인즈 [오전 09:16]
네, 맞습니다.

앨런 고메즈 [오전 09:17]
168/169 사무용품에 대한 수요가 감소하고 있습니다. 그래서 더 많은 제품을 포함하도록 하워드의 카탈로그를 확장하는 것이 하나의 해결책이 될 수 있다고 생각합니다.

조나단 그레이엄 [오전 09:18]
청소 제품이요. 모든 기업체들은 사무실에 그것들이 필요합니다.

칼라 로메로 [오전 09:19]
좋은 생각입니다. 휴게실에서 사용하는 커피메이커와 전자레인지와 같은 가전제품을 살펴보는 것도 좋을 것 같습니다.

트레이시 헤인즈 [오전 09:20]
동의합니다. 우리들은 사무용 가구도 판매할 수 있습니다.

앨런 고메즈 [오전 09:22]
모두 좋은 생각입니다. **170/171** 목요일 회의에서, 여러분들 각자 자신의 생각들을 발표해 주셨으면 합니다. 그리고 발표에는 공급 회사와 가격을 포함해 주세요. 임원들에게 제안서를 제출하기 위해서는 해당 정보가 반드시 필요합니다.

칼라 로메로 [오전 09:22]
170 알겠습니다.

앨런 고메즈 [오전 09:24]
질문 있으신가요? 오늘 오후에 지침을 이메일로 보내 드리겠습니다.

168. 하워드는 현재 어떤 종류의 제품을 판매하는가?
(A) 청소용품
(B) 사무용 가구
(C) 사무용품
(D) 부엌용품

169. 오전 9시 15분에, 고메즈 씨가 "We need to come up with some new directions(우리는 새로운 계획을 모색할 필요가 있습니다)"라고 썼을 때 의미하는 것은 무엇인가?
(A) 회의는 다른 장소에서 진행되어야 한다.
(B) 회사는 더 다양한 상품들을 판매해야 한다.
(C) 회의는 더 많은 주제에 초점을 맞춰야 한다.
(D) 회사는 사무실을 이전해야 한다.

170. 로메로 씨는 다음에 무엇을 할 것 같은가?
(A) 가전제품 구매
(B) 동료들에게 이메일 발송
(C) 조사
(D) 예산 보고서 준비

171. 고메즈 씨는 임원들에게 무엇을 제공할 예정인가?
(A) 최근 매출 보고서
(B) 비용 관련 정보
(C) 사무 공간 변경 계획
(D) 신입 직원 채용 추천서

문제 172-175는 다음 이메일을 참조하세요.

날짜: 12월 20일 목요일
수신: 지미 레이너 <jimraynor@stcpractice.co.uk>
발신: 샘 듀란 <samduran@stcpractice.co.uk>
제목: 휴가

안녕하세요, 지미 씨,

172/175 다음 주에 휴가에서 돌아올 때까지 일주일 동안 저의 업무를 담당해 주시기로 한 것에 대해 감사드립니다. -[1]-.

173 우선, 아시다시피 우리 사무실 바로 밖에 팩스가 있습니다. 174 매일 오전과 오후에 팩스에서 모든 서류들을 가져오실 부탁드립니다. 서류들을 즉시 나누어 주어야 하는 것을 잊지 마십시오. 또한 공동 경영자들을 위해 일정을 잡고 확인해 주는 것도 제 업무 중 하나입니다. 다음 주 그들의 일정이 이미 잡혀 있습니다만, 만약에 대비해서, 제가 그들의 일정표를 당신의 책상 위에 올려놓았습니다.

-[2]-. 혹시 모르고 계실 경우를 대비해, 수요일 오전 10시 30분에 101호실에서 사례 검토 회의가 있습니다. 회의를 하는 동안 노트 필기를 한 후, 타이핑을 해서 점심 식사 전에 부서의 모든 사람들에게 이메일로 보내 주시길 바랍니다. -[3]-.

마지막으로, 금요일 오후까지는 우리의 고객들에게 모두 송장을 보내 주셔야 합니다. 도움이 필요하시다면 저나 새라 씨에게 연락해 주십시오. -[4]-.

도와주셔서 감사합니다!

진심을 담아,

샘 듀란
행정 담당 비서

172. 이메일의 목적은 무엇인가?
(A) 지시 사항을 전달하는 것
(B) 신입 직원의 업무를 설명하는 것
(C) 공식적으로 휴가를 요청하는 것
(D) 회의 안건을 마무리하는 것

173. 레이너 씨와 듀란 씨에 대해 암시된 것은 무엇인가?
(A) 비슷한 시기에 채용되었다.
(B) 다른 날에 일한다.
(C) 사무실 공간을 함께 쓴다.
(D) 직접 만난 적이 없다.

174. 이메일에 따르면, 듀란 씨가 매일 수행하는 업무는 무엇인가?
(A) 팩스 문서 나누어 주기
(B) 고객에게 청구서 발송하기
(C) 회의에서 노트 필기하기
(D) 휴일 일정 잡기

175. [1], [2], [3], [4]로 표시된 위치 중 다음 문장이 들어가기에 가장 적절한 곳은 어디인가?
"당신께서 처리해야 할 업무들에 대한 세부 사항을 알려 드리겠습니다."
(A) [1]
(B) [2]
(C) [3]
(D) [4]

문제 176-180은 다음 회람과 이메일을 참조하세요.

돌턴 테크놀로지

발신: 인사부 디노 하디
수신: 행정실 게일 메드나
날짜: 2월 6일
제목: 신입 직원 오리엔테이션

176 아시다시피 곧 있을 신입 직원 오리엔테이션을 위한 물품을 준비해야 할 때입니다. 당신은 우리의 단골 공급업체로부터 아래에 명시된 대부분의 물품들을 받으실 수 있습니다. 하지만, 179 오피스 맥스는 우리 회사의 로고가 새겨진 플래너를 이번에는 177 공급할 수 없다고 알려 왔음을 명심하시기 바랍니다.

2월 23일에 시작하는 오리엔테이션 전에 세미나실 준비가 완료되기 위해서 모든 물품들은 늦어도 2월 20일까지 도착해야만 합니다. 주문을 하고나면 저에게 연락을 해서 언제 주문했는지 확인해 주시고, 예상 배송일자를 알려 주세요.

귀하의 도움에 대해 감사드립니다.

물품 목록

노트	200개
10개입 펜	220개
바인더 클립	222박스
179 돌턴 로고가 새겨진 플래너	290개

발신: gmedna@daltontechnology.com
수신: alopez@daltontechnology.com
날짜: 2월 7일 13:20
제목: 곧 있을 오리엔테이션 물품 주문
첨부: 오리엔테이션용 물품

로페즈 씨께,

디노 하디 씨가 신입 직원 오리엔테이션에 사용할 물품들을 주문하고 있습니다. 첨부된 것은 그의 구입 주문서입니다. 저는 이미 오피스 맥스에서 이전에 승인받은 물품들을 주문했습니다. 178 가급적 빨리 그가 요청한 주문 제작되는 물품들의 구매를 승인해 주시길 바랍니다. 179 이 물품들은 리처 오피스 서플라이 사에서 주문할 예정입니다. 일단 당신께서 이 거래를 승인해 주시면, 180 저는 구매부서의 제니퍼 코헨 씨께 이 주문의 처리를 요청할 것입니다. 하디 씨는 저에게 늦어도 2월 20일까지 모든 물품이 필요하다고 말했습니다.

진심으로,

게일 메드나

176. 회람은 왜 쓰였는가?
(A) 새로운 판매 회사의 정보를 제공하기 위해
(B) 행사를 위한 물품들을 요청하기 위해
(C) 일련의 행사들을 설명하기 위해
(D) 로고 디자인에 대한 변경을 제안하기 위해

177. 회람에서, 첫 번째 단락 네 번째 줄의 "available(구할 수 있는)"과 의미가 가까운 것은 무엇인가?
(A) 사용되는
(B) 이야기되는
(C) 구매되는
(D) 예약되는

178. 이메일의 목적은 무엇인가?
(A) 세미나실을 예약하는 것
(B) 최근 주문을 확인하는 것
(C) 직책에 누군가를 추천하는 것
(D) 구입에 대한 승인을 요청하는 것

179. 리처 오피스 서플라이 사에서 구매될 것은 무엇인가?
(A) 노트 패드
(B) 펜 묶음
(C) 바인더 클립
(D) 플래너

180. 제니퍼 코헨 씨에 대해 언급된 것은 무엇인가?
(A) 행사 기획을 담당하고 있다.
(B) 주문을 승인했다.
(C) 오피스 맥스와 이미 연락을 한 적이 있다.
(D) 구매부서에서 근무하고 있다.

문제 181-185는 다음의 광고와 목록을 참조하세요.

"스타 여행사" 투어를 즐기세요

181 "스타 여행사" 투어는 여러분에게 시드니, 캔버라 그리고 멜번 근교의 역사적인 지역에서 다양한 지역 음식을 제공합니다. 182/184 (A) 각 지역에서 그 지역만의 특별한 음식을 시식하시게 되며, 경험 많은 우리 가이드가 여러분이 방문하는 각 지역의 역사와 문화에 대한 정보를 이야기해 드립니다.

남부 도시 (시드니)

이 투어는 음식 투어입니다. 첫 번째 장소에서는 에피타이저를 먹게 됩니다. 183 두 번째 장소에서는 샘플 음식으로 구성된 점심을 제공받고 시드니 출생이며 수상 경력이 있는 요리사이자 주인인 게일 코헨 씨를 만나게 됩니다. 다음 식당들에서 여러분은 그 식당에서 가장 맛있는 음식을 맛보게 될 것입니다. 그리고 디저트는 마지막 방문지에서 제공됩니다.

시간: 오후 12시 ~ 오후 3시 매주 월요일부터 금요일까지
(토요일과 일요일은 이용 불가)

184 (B) 포함 내역: 모든 음식과 생수 그리고 지역 지도와 투어 중에 방문한 모든 식당과 가게들에 대한 자세한 내용을 담고 있는 책자

비용: 1인당 60달러

다른 투어에 대한 정보를 더 원하시면
050-854-5289로 전화 주시거나 저희 웹사이트
www.startravelworld.com을 방문해 주시기 바랍니다.

남부 도시 식당
여러분들은 아래의 나열된 순서대로 식당들을 방문하게 됩니다.

1. 휴고스 프렌치
그랜드 가 145번지에 위치
프랑스 남부 요리 전문

183 2. 스페이드
이스트 가 107번지에 위치
184 (D) 점심시간에는 유럽식 요리와 라이브 음악이 나옵니다.

예약 필수

3. 오타루 스시
퀸즈 가 1004번지에 위치
일본의 최고를 보여 주는 요리

4. 조이스 스위티
킹스 파크 가 356번지에 위치
전통적이고 이국적인 달콤한 맛
185 목요일에는 영업을 하지 않습니다.

오코네일스 초콜릿 카페
킹스 파크 가 380번지에 위치
즉석에서 만드는 프랑스식 초콜릿
185 조이스 스위티가 문을 닫을 때 대신 방문하는 곳입니다.

---

181. 광고문에서 스타 여행사 투어에 대해서 언급된 것은 무엇인가?
(A) 단체 할인을 제공한다.
(B) 시드니에 위치해 있다.
(C) 온라인 예약을 제공한다.
(D) 여러 도시들에서 투어를 제공한다.

182. 가이드에 관하여 언급된 것은 무엇인가?
(A) 식당에서 채용했다.
(B) 역사에 관한 정보를 제공한다.
(C) 2개 이상의 언어를 구사한다.
(D) 관광부에서 상을 받았다.

183. 투어 참가자들은 코헨 씨를 어디에서 만날 것인가?
(A) 휴고스 프렌치에서
(B) 스페이드에서
(C) 오타루 스시에서
(D) 조이스 스위티에서

184. 남부 도시 투어에 포함되어 있지 않은 것은?
(A) 역사적인 정보
(B) 인근의 지도
(C) 향후 여행의 할인 쿠폰
(D) 음악 공연

185. 투어 참가자들은 무슨 요일에 오코네일스 초콜릿 카페를 방문할 것인가?
(A) 수요일
(B) 목요일
(C) 금요일
(D) 토요일

문제 186-190은 다음의 광고와 이메일들을 참조하세요.

---

186 캔자스 시티에 있는 브라운스톤 홀은 어떤 행사에도 완벽한 분위기를 제공합니다. 브라운스톤은 회의, 연회, 또는 야외 파티 등 대부분의 단체를 수용할 수 있을 만큼 충분히 큽니다. 자체 음식점을 통하여, 저희는 고객들에게 출장 연회 서비스를 제공할 수도 있습니다. 저희에게는 여러분들에게 최상의 만족을 안겨드리기 위해 여러분들을 도와드릴 잘 훈련된 직원들이 있습니다.

브라운스톤의 예약이 매우 빠르게 마감되기 때문에, 중요한 행사를 계획 중이라면, 최소 3주 전에 미리 연락을 부탁드립니다. 예약을 위해 rico@brownstone.com로 이메일을 보내주시고, 아래 정보들도 알려 주시기 바랍니다.

▶ 이름, 조직, 연락처
▶ 행사의 유형
▶ 행사 날짜와 시간
▶ 초대 손님 수
▶ 연락 가능한 시간

187 (B) 브라운스톤 홀의 회원들은 결코 전액을 지불할 필요가 없다는 것을 기억하세요!
저희 회원이 되고 싶으시면, 저희 웹사이트 www.brownstonehall.net로 방문해 주세요. 187 (A)/(D) 교육 기관이나 비영리단체들에게도 할인된 가격이 적용됩니다.

수신: 도널드 리코 <rico@brownstone.com>
발신: 마이클 히달고 <MichHidalgo@colemanart.com>
제목: 객실 예약
날짜: 8월 15일

리코 씨께,

안녕하세요, 제 이름은 마이클 히달고이고, 콜먼 아트센터의 이벤트 관리자입니다. 188/189 저희는 9월 17일 저녁 7시에 연례 연회를 위해 귀사의 시설 중 하나를 빌리려고 생각 중입니다.

예약하기 전, 저는 그날에 이용 가능한 공간들을 간단히 둘러보고 싶습니다. 또한 연회에서 외부 출장 뷔페 서비스를 이용하는 것이 가능한지 알고 싶습니다. 연락하기에 편한 시간은 모든 평일 저녁 5시에서 8시 사이입니다. 제 전화번호는 417-888-7878입니다.

미리 감사드립니다.

진심으로,

마이클 히달고

수신: 마이클 히달고 <MichHidalgo@colemanart.com>
발신: 도널드 리코 <rico@brownstone.com>
답장: 객실 예약
날짜: 8월 16일

히달고 씨께,

귀하께서 진행하시는 행사를 위해 저희 시설과 출장 뷔페 서비스에 관해 문의를 해 주셔서 감사합니다. 189 안타깝게도, 요청하신 날에는 그 주 내내 보수 공사가 진행될 예정입니다. 190 원하신다면, 시외에 위치한 다른 회의장을 추천해 드릴 수 있습니다. 귀하의 아트센터에서 15분 소요될 것입니다. 해당 장소에 관심이 있으시다면, 미리 그쪽으로 연락을 할 수 있게 알려 주십시오. 불편을 드려 죄송합니다.

진심으로,

도널드 리코

---

186. 광고문에서 홍보하는 것은 무엇인가?
(A) 새로 생긴 음식점
(B) 임대 시설
(C) 비즈니스 회의
(D) 미술 전시회

187. 어떤 그룹이 할인 적용을 받지 못하는가?
(A) 비영리 단체
(B) 브라운스톤 홀의 회원
(C) 브라운스톤 홀 직원의 친척
(D) 교육 기관

188. 어떤 유형의 행사를 히달고 씨가 계획하고 있는가?
(A) 회사 만찬
(B) 사내 연수
(C) 시상식
(D) 연례 학회

189. 9월 17일에 브라운스톤 홀에서 무슨 일이 일어날 것 같은가?
(A) 연회가 개최될 것이다.
(B) 예술 전시회가 무료로 제공될 것이다.
(C) 특가 판매가 종료될 것이다.
(D) 공사가 진행될 것이다.

190. 리코 씨는 히달고 씨에게 무엇 하기를 조언하는가?
(A) 날짜 이동
(B) 장소 변경
(C) 행사 세부 사항 전달
(D) 추가 객실 임대

문제 191-195는 다음의 이메일들과 이벤트 일정표를 참조하세요.

수신: 에드워드 마이어스 <edmyers@qwayne.com>
발신: 재닛 찰스 <jcharles@qwayne.com>
날짜: 2월 17일
제목: 일정표 초안
첨부 파일: 행사 일정표 초안

안녕하세요, 에드워드 씨,

191 3월과 4월의 일정표 초안 작성을 막 완료했습니다. 이 이메일에 일정표를 첨부했으며, 저희 웹사이트 행사란에 게시할 예정입니다. 192 하지만, 4월 28일 행사 장소가 아직 확정된 것이 아니라는 점에 주의 부탁드리며, 이는 일정이 변동될 수 있다는 것을 의미합니다. 질문이 있으시거나 일정의 변경을 원하신다면 저에게 알려 주세요.

진심을 담아,

재닛

Q웨인 기업 협회
3-4월 행사
193 모든 행사는 파크 리조트 호텔에서 열립니다.

3월 14일: 오전 11시 - 오후 3시	**195 4월 16일**: 오전 11시 30분 - 오후 12시 45분
행사: 사업 전략 과정	**행사**: 인맥 형성 오찬 (뷔페)
장소: 1층 대강당	**장소**: 해산물 가든
비용: 현장 등록 50달러	**비용**: 사전 등록 20달러 또는 현장 등록 30달러
주의: 사전 등록 가능 (40달러)	

3월 20일: 오전 9시 - 오후 3시 **행사**: 국제 직업 박람회 **장소**: 조던 연회장 **비용**: 30달러 **주의**: 사전 등록만 가능	**주의**: 200명만 참석 가능 사전 등록 권장 **192 4월 28일**: 오후 5시 - 오후 7시 30분 **행사**: 부동산 투자 세미나 **장소**: 1층 대강당 **비용**: 40달러 **주의**: 사전 등록 불가능

수신: 재닛 찰스 <jcharles@qwayne.com>
발신: 에드워드 마이어스 <edmyers@qwayne.com>
날짜: 3월 3일
제목: 회의 관련 새로운 소식

재닛 씨께,

이미 알고 계시듯이, 매달 1일에 행사 위원회 회의를 개최합니다. 가장 최근 회의는 이틀 전 오전 11시부터 12시까지 진행되었습니다.

몇 가지 추가된 정보들을 알려 드리겠습니다. **194 저희는 인맥 형성 오찬을 연장하기로 결정해서 이제 오후 1시에 행사가 종료될 것입니다.** 시작 시간은 동일합니다. 이것들은 최종 변경 사항이므로 웹사이트도 변경해 주시길 바랍니다. **195 그런데 혹시 괜찮으시다면 4월 16일 행사 때 접수처에서 업무를 좀 해 주실 수 있으시겠습니까?**

감사합니다.

에드워드

---

191. 찰스 씨는 왜 이메일을 작성하였는가?
(A) 안건에 대해 피드백을 받기 위해
(B) 일정표 초안을 제공하기 위해
(C) 정책 변경 사항을 알리기 위해
(D) 보고서를 수정하기 위해

192. 어느 행사가 변경될 수 있는가?
(A) 사업 전략 과정
(B) 국제 직업 박람회
(C) 인맥 형성 오찬
(D) 부동산 투자 세미나

193. Q웨인 기업 협회에서 제공하는 행사에 관하여 언급된 것은 무엇인가?
(A) 온라인 예약이 필요하다.
(B) 한 달에 한 번만 진행된다.
(C) 동일한 호텔에서 진행될 것이다.
(D) 협회 회원들에게만 제공된다.

194. 두 번째 이메일에 따르면, 인맥 형성 행사에 관하여 사실인 것은 무엇인가?
(A) 그 행사의 장소는 변경되었다.
(B) 그 행사의 시간이 연장될 것이다.
(C) 그 행사는 취소되었다.
(D) 그 행사는 더 많은 광고가 필요하다.

195. 마이어스 씨가 찰스 씨에게 요구하는 것은 무엇인가?
(A) 인맥 형성 오찬에서 일하기
(B) 행사 진행하기
(C) 초청 연사와 조사 결과 공유하기
(D) 초청 연사 추천하기

문제 196-200은 다음의 이메일들과 일정표를 참조하세요.

발신: 비니 페르마 <vfermat@secadvisor.com>
수신: 메리 비터 <maryvitter@secadvisor.com>
제목: 홈즈 앤 자렛 회사
날짜: 9월 7일 화요일 오후 4시 15분

안녕하세요. 메리 씨.

197/198 9월 15일 수요일 오후 3시부터 5시까지 홈즈 앤 자렛 회사 (H&J) 담당자들과의 회의 일정을 지금 막 잡았어요. 196 우리는 이 기회를 진지하게 여겨서 우리의 보안 서비스의 강점을 국내의 선두 건설 회사 중 하나에 적절히 소개해야 합니다. H&J와의 첫 번째 회의를 어떻게 준비할지에 대해 아침에 이야기할 것입니다.

198 저는 안토니오 씨에게 메트로 시티행 열차 일정을 확인해 달라고 부탁했고, 당신의 사무실로 한 장을 팩스로 보내라고 했어요. 질문이 있습니다. 9월 15일에 이곳 잉글우드 사무실에 올 것인가요? 만약 그렇다면 안토니오에게 잉글우드에서 메트로 시티로 가는 열차표 두 장을 예약해 달라고 부탁할 것입니다. 만약 아니라면, 안토니오에게 연락해서 브론선에서 출발하는 표가 있는지 확인해 달라고 하세요.

H&J는 오후 2시 30분에 메트로 시티 역에서 우리를 태워갈 택시를 준비해 줄 것입니다. **200 그들은 또한 오후 6시에서 8시까지 메트로 시티에 위치한 하바나 딜라이트라는 레스토랑에서 몇몇 H&J 직원들과의 정찬에 우리를 초대했습니다.** 식당은 역에서 15분 거리에 있으므로 우리는 오후 8시 15분 즈음 잉글우드로 돌아가는 열차를 탈 수 있을 것이라고 생각합니다.

비니

레일 커넥트

일정 정보, 9월-10월
스카치타운-메이턴 라인

열차 번호	**198** **1922(WD)**	1023 (WE)	7849 (HD)	2007 (EX)
잉글우드	오전 11:18	오전 11:21	오전 11:37	오후 1:41
브론선	오전 11:59	오후 12:02	–	–
크리스탈 레이크	오후 12:42	오후 12:45	–	–
호스빌	오후 1:23	오후 1:26	오후 12:53	–
메트로 시티	오후 2:15	오후 2:18	–	–
샌 마리노	오후 2:47	오후 2:50	오후 1:26	오후 3:18

EX – 급행 서비스는 어디에도 정차하지 않습니다.
WE – 주말에만 운행합니다.
198 WD – 월요일에서 금요일까지만 운행합니다.
HD – 휴일 일정 ; 모든 역에 정차하지는 않습니다. 9월 12일과 10월 3일에 운행됩니다.

열차의 자동 응답 전화 서비스는 24시간 열차 정보를 제공합니다. 002-3355로 전화하세요.

열차 표
신용카드로 구입하시려면:
역 입구에 있는 매표소나 199 (D) 웹사이트 www.railconnect.com/tickets에 접속해 표를 구입하여 출력할 수 있습니다.

현금으로 구입하시려면:
199 (A)/(C) 대합실 근처의 렉싱턴 가판대, 매표소, 혹은 탑승하여 구입할 수 있습니다. 탑승하여 표를 구입하시면 5달러의 추가 요금이 있다는 것을 유념하세요.

발신: 메리 비터 <maryvitter@secadvisor.com>
수신: 비니 페르마 <vfermat@secadvisor.com>
답장: 홈즈 앤 자렛 회사
날짜: 9월 8일 수요일 오전 11시

안녕하세요, 비니 씨

홈즈 앤 자렛 회사와의 회의에 관한 당신의 이메일을 받았습니다. 하지만 저는 9월 15일에 브론슨에 있을 예정입니다. 200 제안하신 대로, 오늘 아침에 여러 번 안토니오 씨에게 전화를 하여 표를 예약하려고 했지만 그는 받지 않았습니다. 저는 지금 고객과의 회의에 들어가야 하니, 그에게 연락하여 티켓 구매가 가능한지 확인하여 그가 표를 구할 수 있는지 알려 주시겠어요? 신경 써 주셔서 감사합니다.

진심을 담아,

메리

---

196. 페르마 씨는 어떤 종류의 기업에서 근무하고 있는가?
(A) 여행사
(B) 건설 회사
(C) 보안 회사
(D) 식당 체인점

197. 홈즈 앤 자렛에 대해 언급된 것은?
(A) 그 기업의 사무실은 가장 가까운 기차역에서 30분 거리에 위치해 있다.
(B) 그 기업은 시큐리티 어드바이저와 수년간 협력 업체였다.
(C) 그 기업의 최근 프로젝트는 하바나 딜라이트를 위한 새로운 건물을 건설하는 것이다.
(D) 그 기업은 선두적인 건설 회사 중 하나이다.

198. 회의에 참석하기 위해 페르마 씨는 어느 열차를 탈 것 같은가?
(A) 열차 번호 1922
(B) 열차 번호 1023
(C) 열차 번호 7849
(D) 열차 번호 2007

199. 일정표에 따르면, 열차 표를 구입할 수 있는 방법으로 언급되지 않은 것은?
(A) 열차에 승차하여 돈을 지불
(B) 철도 자동 전화 시스템을 이용
(C) 렉싱턴 가판대로 가는 것
(D) 레일 커넥트의 홈페이지를 방문

200. 비터 씨에 관하여 암시된 것은 무엇인가?
(A) 페르마 씨와 함께 기차에 탑승할 것이다.
(B) 메트로 시티에서 진행되는 회의에 참석할 수 없다.
(C) 스스로 이미 티켓을 예약했다.
(D) 9월 15일 H&J 직원과 저녁 식사를 할 것이다.

Memo

Memo

Memo

Memo

Memo

토익 목표 점수로 가는 지름길

영단기 토익
다이렉트 700+

LC+RC 한 달 완성

> **LC와 RC를 한 권에!** 토익 700+ **한 달 완성 프로젝트**
> 토익 왕초보도 쉽게 공부할 수 있는 **6단계 학습** 구성
> 토익이 만만해지는 **출제 포인트 완벽 정리**
> 누구보다 친절한 **해설 PDF 무료 제공**

파트별 교재

| 영단기 2기적 토익 LC | 영단기 2기적 토익 PART 5&6 | 영단기 2기적 토익 PART 7 | 영단기 토익 PART 7 유형별 공식 40 |

실전모의고사

| 영단기 신토익 LC+RC 빈출모의고사 | 영단기 토익 실전 1000제 1 LC | 영단기 토익 실전 1000제 1 RC | 영단기 토익 실전 1000제 2 LC | 영단기 토익 실전 1000제 2 RC |

영단기 오픽 & 토익스피킹 교재

| 영단기 OPIc | 영단기 OPIc 실전모의고사 | 영단기 토익스피킹 | 20시간에 끝내는 토익 스피킹 Lv. 6-7 | 영단기 토익스피킹 실전모의고사 |

영단기 지텔프 교재

| 정재현 지텔프 Level 2 | 지텔프 기출문제 Level 2 | 지텔프 독해 유형별 기출문제 Level 2 | 지텔프 문법 유형별 기출문제 Level 2 |

누적 수강생 수 756만*,
수강후기 31만*으로 검증된 강의력.
10년째 영단기를 꾸준히 찾는 이유!
* 영단기 수강생 설문조사 결과 영단기 찾는 이유 1위 강사진 54% (2020년 10월 27~31일)
* 영단기 사이트 내 수강후기 누적건수 314,439개 (2020년 11월 23일 기준)

영단기만의
압도적 강사진

그동안 경험할 수 없던 차원이 다른 강의력!
지금 영단기에서 경험해보세요!